Personnel and
human resources
administration

The Irwin Series in Management and the Behavioral Sciences

L. L. CUMMINGS AND E. KIRBY WARREN   *Consulting Editors*
JOHN F. MEE   *Advisory Editor*

Personnel and human resources administration

LEON C. MEGGINSON
Professor of Management
Louisiana State University

1977
Third edition

RICHARD D. IRWIN, INC.   Homewood, Illinois   60430
Irwin-Dorsey Limited   Georgetown, Ontario   L7G 4B3

Previous editions were published under the title:
Personnel: A Behavioral Approach to Administration.

© RICHARD D. IRWIN, INC., 1967, 1972, and 1977

All rights reserved. No part of this publication may be reproduced, stored in a retrieval system, or transmitted, in any form or by any means, electronic, mechanical, photocopying, recording, or otherwise, without the prior written permission of the publisher.

Third Edition

First Printing, February 1977

ISBN 0-256-01909-6
Library of Congress Catalog Card No. 76–28888
Printed in the United States of America

*To
William A. Megginson,
who provided me with my pride in the past;
and to
Tom and Gayle, John and Nancy,
Bill and Jay,
who are my hope for the future.*

Preface

Recent events have made conventional personnel practices and programs obsolete. That is why this edition has been completely rewritten. While retaining the broad overall flavor of previous editions, this one stresses the technical aspects of personnel and human resources administration with special emphasis on the effectiveness of the programs, procedures, and methods used.

This third edition is professionally oriented, with special attention given to the role of the personnel executive performing the personnel function in an ongoing organization. In addition to the historical, philosophical, and theoretical material included in the first and second editions, this edition also stresses the technical, analytical, legal, and pragmatic approaches to performing the personnel job itself.

The text emphasizes the performance of the personnel function in nonbusiness organizations as well as business firms; it deals with the performance of employees in white-collar and professional occupations as well as blue-collar and service activities. Considerable emphasis is given to equal employment opportunities for women, minorities, older workers, the handicapped, and veterans. The "American" aspects of personnel and human resources administration are deemphasized and the more "universal" aspects are highlighted.

The presentation of the material is based upon a firm foundation of research findings, particularly the results of empirical research as reported in the scholarly and professional journals. These findings cover the latest treatment of the more important subjects such as the provision of equal employment opportunities and other legal requirements, unionization of public employees, personal and career development, current motivational approaches, and personnel research. The theoretical and analytical concepts are presented in the text, while the practical aspects are presented as illustrations in the body of the text itself and in the case problems at the end of each part. In addition, selected cases at the end of the text serve to integrate the theoretical and practical material into a unified whole.

Because of the expansion of courses in organizational behavior, along with the appearance of outstanding texts in the field, this aspect of personnel administration is minimized in this edition. Conversely, the legal aspects are emphasized along with the technical and practical matters. The material is complete, yet is not too detailed and repetitious. It is organized so that the text is broken up with subheadings to make reading and learning easier.

The subject is presented from an eclectic point of view, rather than adhering strictly to one viewpoint. Schematic presentations are used at the beginning of each part to show how the material is integrated. Each chapter begins with an outline of what is to be learned; there are flow diagrams relating the material to the overall personnel function; and each chapter ends with the material being applied to the actual performance of the personnel function. Then, each part is tied together with true cases from real organizations.

The material is designed to help the reader to: (1) develop an awareness of the universality of the personnel function and its importance to organizations; (2) become familiar with the processes of effectively planning for, recruiting, selecting, developing, utilizing, and maintaining an organization's human resources from the point of view of the entire organization; and (3) keep current with the newer views and progressive steps leading toward improved employer-employee relationships.

The text attempts a broad and straightforward presentation of the subject matter. Its organization serves two purposes: (1) it can be used as an undergraduate text where the emphasis is on the text material proper, and (2) it can also serve as a very handy graduate text by making use of the extensive reference lists and suggestions for further study at the end of each chapter and the footnotes in the body of the text. These will serve to guide the graduate student in his or her readings in the area of personnel and human resources administration. It is hoped that both purposes are well met.

ACKNOWLEDGMENTS

So many people are involved in producing a book that it is impossible to acknowledge the contribution of each one. The contributions of some, however, are so great that they must be mentioned.

I am greatly indebted to Raymond V. Lesikar, Chairman, Department of Management, for his encouragement and understanding.

Invaluable assistance in the form of critical evaluations and suggestions was provided by F. Marion Fletcher, Edmond Gray, O. Jeff Harris, Eugene McCann, and Jerry Wallin of Louisiana State University; Kae H. Chung, Wichita State University; Rosemary Pledger, the University of Houston at Clear Lake City; Thomas J. Gardner, the City University of New York; Gerald L. Rose, the University of Iowa; Thomas F. Urban, Texas A & M University; Virginia S. Hill, the University of Southern Mississippi; Richard J. Fleming, Ball State University; Chester R. Smith and Thomas B. Maertens, Clemson University; Wayne L. McNaughton, the University of California; M. Michael LeBoeuf, the University of New Orleans; C. Ray Gullett, Texas Eastern University; Richard E. Dutton and Jay T. Knippen, the University of South Florida; Archie B. Carroll, the University of Georgia; William Vroman, Tennessee Technological University; Ronald D. Johnson, Northeast Louisiana University; Minnie C. Miles, the University of Alabama; Edgar T. Busch, Memphis State University; Donald Bolon, Ohio University; J. Mark Miller,

West Georgia College; William P. Anthony, Florida State University; Dalton E. McFarland and W. Jack Duncan, the University of Alabama at Birmingham; Thomas W. Zimmerer, Florida Atlantic University; Lyle R. Trueblood, the University of Tulsa; D. W. Belcher, San Diego State University; L. E. Baldwin, the University of West Florida; William L. Gragg, North Carolina State University; Erwin L. Malone, Bloomfield College; R. E. Thompson, New Jersey Institute of Technology; and Roger D. Roderick, Boise State University.

So very many graduate students have contributed to this book, directly and indirectly, that it would be impossible to mention all of them. However, specific recommendations for improving this edition were made by Karen K. Arnold, Christel Capdeville, Alev M. Efendioglu, Kamal Fatehi, Irene Gardemal, and Janice Glab of L.S.U.; Linda Calvert, the University of Houston at Clear Lake City; L. L. Mazzaroppi, Farleigh Dickinson University; Ali R. Parsinia, Iran; Besim Baykal, Turkey; A. D. Sharplin, Monroe; and Bobby Wooten, Lamar University.

Louis Champagne, John Furr, André J. Mulé, and Norman Wardell contributed of their knowledge as practicing personnel executives in order to keep the material reality oriented.

Lakshmanan Krishnamurthi provided invaluable research and editorial assistance for this edition, as did Kae Chung for the first edition and Roy P. Patin, Jr. for the second edition. Bill Megginson read the manuscript and made many helpful, practical suggestions for its improvement.

To Jo Anne Martin, who unselfishly gave of her time and effort to translate my longhand and dictation into the typed manuscript, goes my undying appreciation.

While all made definite contributions toward improving this edition of the text, any limitations or shortcomings in the book are mine.

Finally, my family—especially my children—paid the price for this book to be written.

January 1977   LEON C. MEGGINSON

Contents

part one
Why study personnel administration

1 The role of personnel and human resources in organizations   2

Increasing importance of human resources. Increasing knowledge of employee behavior. Implications and applications for personnel executives.

2 The growing importance of personnel and human resources administration   16

Definition of personnel and human resources administration. The improving role of the personnel function. What functions do personnel executives perform? Responsibility for performing the personnel function. Personnel administrators need a new type authority. Implications and applications for personnel executives.

Cases for further study, 39

part two
The context of personnel administration

3 The historical context   45

Early happenings. Personnel administration in the American colonies. The Civil War and its aftermath. World War I and its aftermath. The "Roaring Twenties." The "Great Depression" and its aftermath. World War II and its aftermath. The "Fabulous Fifties." The period of activism. The growing economic independence of employees. Implications and applications for personnel executives.

4 The institutional context   65

Growing governmental involvement. Areas of involvement. Personnel functions involved. How to cope with this increasing involvement.

xiv Contents

    5 The sociocultural context   86

        The sociocultural environment. The educational environment. The technological environment. The changing work environment. Implications and applications for personnel executives.

    6 Trends in U.S. and other labor forces   114

        Factors affecting changes in the labor force. Estimated demand for workers. Anticipated supply of available employees, 1985. Meeting the needs of special groups. Applications and implications for personnel executives.

Cases for further study, 140

part three
Recruiting and selecting personnel

    7 Personnel and human resource planning   147

        Growing importance of personnel-human resource planning. Objectives of personnel planning. Functions involved in human resource planning. Different stages of human resource planning. Steps in personnel-human resource planning. A new approach to personnel-human resource planning. Personnel planning in other economies. Evaluating effectiveness of personnel-human resource planning. Implications and applications for personnel executives.

    8 Recruiting personnel   172

        Developing sources of potential employees. Methods used in recruiting. Some special considerations in college recruiting. Effects of public policy on recruiting. Evaluating the effectiveness of recruiting activities. Implications and applications.

    9 The selection procedure   191

        Developing an effective selection procedure. First stage: Establishing selection policies. Second stage: Identifying and choosing selection criteria. Third stage: Gathering information about potential employees. Fourth stage: Evaluating information and assessing applicant. Fifth stage: Making the decision to accept or reject applicant. Sixth stage: Communicating the decision. Implications and applications for personnel executives.

    10 Evaluating information and assessing applicants   218

        Requirements for effective use of selection techniques. Evaluating biographical inventories. Evaluating test results. Using the interview to evaluate applicants. Implications and applications for personnel executives.

11 Selecting supervisory and executive talent   245

Shortage of managerial personnel. Some special aspects of managerial planning. How to identify managerial talent. Specialized techniques for identifying and selecting executives. Implications and applications for personnel executives.

Cases for further study, 265

part four
Maximizing personnel potential

12 Personnel development strategies   273

Establishing development objectives. Assigning responsibility for development. Assessing development needs. Designing development programs. Conducting developmental programs. Evaluating effectiveness of development programs. Implications and applications for personnel executives.

13 Executive development   296

Objectives of executive development. Establishing parameters to executive development. Determining developmental needs. Methods used in developing executives. Appraising and evaluating executive development. Groups requiring special attention. Implications and applications for personnel executives.

14 Career planning and development   323

Using performance appraisals for developmental purposes. Using counseling in career planning and development. Providing progression within the organization. Using "management by objectives" in career development. Groups needing special attention. Implications and applications for personnel executives.

15 Maximizing personnel potential   347

Enhancing an individual's self-perception. How leadership style affects employee growth. How motivation can affect employee growth. Implications and applications for personnel executives.

Cases for further study, 369

part five
Effects of reward and penalty systems on personnel effectiveness

16 Determining overall compensation policies   379

Functions of compensation. Factors affecting an organization's compensation policies and practices. Implications and applications for personnel executives.

17 Using compensation to provide equity   396

Establishing compensation policies. Types of wage differentials. Determining job rate differentials. Determining individual rates of pay. Special problems of managerial remuneration. Implications and applications for personnel executives.

18 Using compensation to reward performance   419

The underlying theory. Using incentive wages to reward performance. Using profit-sharing plans as stimulants to productivity. Using merit wage increases as stimulants to productivity. Using bonus plans as stimulants to productivity. Using companywide productivity sharing systems. Implications and applications for personnel executives.

19 Using employee benefits to reward loyal service   444

Background. Objectives of benefit programs. What are employee benefits? Extent of employee benefits. Legally required benefits. Voluntary programs. Implications and applications for personnel executives.

20 Using discipline as a penalty system   466

Current concepts of discipline. How discipline is achieved under the judicial due process. Authority for administering discipline. Discipline in nonbusiness organizations. Implications and applications.

Cases for further study, 484

part six
Effects of industrial relations on personnel administration

21 How industrial relations affect personnel administration   493

Laws providing the industrial-relations framework. What are union objectives? How do unions achieve their objectives? Some changing union tactics. Membership in unions and employee associations. Implications and applications for personnel executives.

22 Improving industrial relations in the individual organization   514

     A model for predicting the degree of conflict. Recognizing the union. Negotiating the agreement. Living with the agreement. Implications and applications.

Cases for further study, 540

part seven
Maintaining the work force

23 Handling difficult people problems   549

     Role of counseling. Areas requiring counseling. Implications and applications for personnel executives.

24 Maintaining health and safety   562

     Why occupational health and safety are so important. Maintaining occupational health. Maintaining safety. What can be done to improve safety. Occupational Safety and Health Act. Implications and applications for personnel executives.

25 Coping with the future   582

     Expected modifications of the environment. Expected changes in personnel functions. Qualifications needed in future personnel executives. What is needed to perform the personnel function successfully. Quo vadis, personnel executive?

Cases for further study, 600

part eight
Integrating cases   605

Case index   625

Name index   627

Index   635

part one

Why study personnel administration

1. The role of personnel and human resources in organizations
2. The growing importance of personnel and human resources administration

Cases:
 I-1. The Pepper Bush
 I-2. OK! Who's Passing the Buck?

Introduction

"Take away all our factories, our trades, our avenues of transportation, and our money," said Andrew Carnegie, "but leave me our organization, and in four years, I will have reestablished myself." This statement illustrates the truth that the most important aspect of administration is selecting, developing, and motivating people.

The ultimate objective of most institutions is the efficient production of goods or the effective performance of services for their clients—while also providing for their employees' personal satisfaction. These objectives can best be achieved through the efficient use of the organization's human resources, along with its financial and physical assets. However, all these factors of production need to be integrated into a productive personnel system.

It is within this system's concept that we look at the importance of human resources and their management. At the heart of this system are people, for they provide the productive capacities to utilize the other resources, as shown in Chapter 1.

The possibilities for the greatest achievements and improvements are to be found in *effectively* managing personnel and human resources. The successful performance of this function by *all executives* is the foundation of any well-managed organization. This is the central thought of Chapter 2.

Chapter 1

The role of personnel and human resources in organizations

Increasing importance of human resources
   Some problems involving human resource utilization
   The role of human resources in economic and organizational development

Increasing knowledge of employee behavior
   Early contributions to knowledge
   Toward a more rational approach
   The "Hawthorne experiments" and their aftermath
   Contributions of the behavioral scientists

Implications and applications for personnel executives

1
The role of personnel and human resources in organizations

Princes and lords are but the breath of kings. An honest man's the noblest work of God.
ROBERT BURNS, *The Cotter's Saturday Night*

Try not to become a man of success but rather try to become a man of value.
ALBERT EINSTEIN

A small firm used several craftsmen to do plumbing, heating, and wiring of both residential and commercial construction. The demand for its services increased rapidly, but it could not keep up because of the shortage of personnel. After unsuccessfully trying to recruit trained personnel, it started its own training program. This also did not work, for the available personnel preferred the easier work, better benefits, and greater security of the larger industrial and governmental institutions in the area. The firm finally abandoned its service activities and became a supplier of equipment and supplies.

This true situation explains the vital role played by personnel in today's organizations. It also illustrates one of the basic laws of economics, the law of supply and demand.

A study of economics leads to at least three conclusions, namely:

1. Human wants are insatiable, while the means of satisfying them are limited;

2. The economic factors of production are land, capital, labor, and entrepreneurship. The first three are often referred to in management literature as physical, financial, and human resources; while the last is often called management and/or organization; and

3. The productive use of these scarce resources results from a series of allocative decisions. The goals of an individual determine how his* resources will be used, whether those resources are skills, money, or machinery. (1)

As is true of the other resources, capable human resources are scarce.

---

* The common words "his," "he," "him," "man," or others used in a similar way in this text are intended to refer to persons of *either* sex and are not used to denote persons of a particular sex.

It should be obvious that an adequate supply of physical and financial resources does not alone ensure the economic development of an organization. Instead, it is the entrepreneurial spirit and executive initiative which discover and utilize those resources, as well as an adequate supply of human resources in the form of well-educated, developed, and motivated personnel. Yet, without people, the other inanimate resources would be worthless.

This chapter will try to show that relationship. First, the increasing value of human resources will be explained. Then it will be shown how our increasing knowledge of human behavior can enhance the effectiveness of personnel.

INCREASING IMPORTANCE OF HUMAN RESOURCES

Although there is no clearly stated and adequate definition of the term *human resources,* it can be thought of as the *total knowledge, skills, creative abilities, talents, and aptitudes of an organization's work force, as well as the value, attitudes, and beliefs of the individuals involved.* It is the sum total of the inherent abilities, acquired knowledge, and skills represented by the talents and aptitudes of the employed persons.

The quantity and quality of human resources are functions of the number of productive individuals, their inherent abilities, and the extent to which those abilities are modified through environmental factors such as education, training, and development. Those productive factors are realized in the abilities of employees to produce within the limitations imposed by existing organizations, technologies, and other resources. They also manifest themselves in the individuals' abilities to generate new ideas, develop new and improved capital goods, and otherwise modify the available physical and financial resources in order to achieve greater productivity and human satisfaction.

Unfortunately these resources are often wasted through underemployment; obsolescence of skills; lack of work opportunities for the older and younger workers, minority groups, and women; poor personnel practices; and the difficulties of adjusting to change. Also, an organization rarely "buys" employees' productivity in the sense that they are paid in direct proportion to what they produce; instead, it buys their time for the period they are on the job and hopes that productivity will result. Thus, as human resources account for such a large proportion of economic output, there are tremendous possibilities for increasing productivity through the intelligent development of employee abilities in the industrial, commercial, governmental, and service complexes of our economic systems.

That's what this book is all about!

Some problems involving human resource utilization

Any study of the methods to be used in increasing the productive abilities of an organization presents two problems. First, how can it enlarge the quantity and improve the quality of its pool of productive personnel? Second, how can it utilize those capabilities most efficiently in order to achieve the desired level of production of goods and services and provide the optimum personal satisfaction to the members of the organization? These questions are basic to any discussion of personnel administration and will be analyzed throughout this book. However, underlying all the presentations is the assumption that the *primary objective of any institution is to utilize its human resources to the optimum extent feasible in order to achieve predetermined goals.*

The role of human resources in economic and organizational development

Economic and management literature has often neglected to emphasize the importance of the human function in organizations. First, there has been a lack of knowledge about human behavior, as well as about the contribution it has made to organizational development. Second, as will be seen in the next chapter, the responsibility for performing the personnel function has often been delegated to lower levels of management, where the emphasis is upon machines, facilities, programs, and procedures, and their effective use as a means of achieving effective operations. Finally, human resources have been neglected because of the loss of individual dignity and creativity through developments such as mechanization, automation, and the growth of large and complex organizations. (2)

Role in economic development. Only in the last 30 years have economists become interested in the importance of human resources as a form of capital. (3) Yet the building of modern nations results from the development of people and the organization of human capacities. While capital, natural resources, foreign aid, and international aid play important roles in such economic growth, none of these factors is more important than an efficient pool of well-educated, well-trained, and highly developed personnel.

The United States has approximately 5 percent of the world's population and 7 percent of the total land area; yet, it produces about one-half of the world's wealth and receives about 40 percent of the total annual income. This feat can only be accomplished through combining the efforts of around 90 million employed people, including 10 million managers, with the natural resources and technology, even though 98 percent of the energy used flows from mechanical and chemical sources. (4)

A similar conclusion can be reached concerning Canada, for its abundant natural resources went unexploited until it was settled by a group of hardworking, economically motivated individuals. (5)

Finally, research by David C. McClelland has shown that managers and executives in countries with the highest economic development scored considerably higher on desire-for-achievement tests than did executives in the less developed economies. (6)

Role in organizational development. Nearly a century has elapsed since Frederick W. Taylor began the research which resulted in the "scientific management" movement. While most of the intellectual activities involved in observing, analyzing, and understanding human behavior since then have attempted to develop theories, principles, or concepts explaining the role of people in organizations, the results can be summarized in the statement that the *effectiveness of an organization is determined by the caliber of its human resources.* One research study confirmed this conclusion by estimating that it would cost a firm from two to ten times its annual payroll just to bring the organization back to its present level of performance if all persons except the president were to leave. (7)

Need for a creative environment. If the performance of human resources is to be effectively enhanced, personnel executives need to realize that each employee has a certain amount of creative potential. They should, therefore, develop a working environment within the organization which will encourage personal growth and development as well as creative thinking, for it has been estimated that we apply only about 10 to 20 percent of our mental powers to the job. (8)

In most healthy organizations, realizing that individuals need a sense of equilibrium and growth which is derived from participating in creative organizational activities, management sets norms of performance that induce employees to achieve their own satisfaction, as well as achieving goals.

From this discussion, it can be concluded that the *primary function of the professional managers—either public or private—is to work with people, not with things.*

Need for interaction of resources. A word of caution, however, is needed at this point. While human resources are quite important, it must be remembered that productivity results from the *interaction* of human resources with physical factors and technology in an organized setting.

It is an error to compare the performance of machines and workers, for they are not comparable; rather, they are complementary to each other. Machines serve as tools and as production systems, while people work best on jobs with optimum difficulty. If a job is too easy, they become bored; if it is too difficult, they become fatigued, discouraged, and frustrated to the point of quitting. The use of machines as productive tools tends to make a difficult job easier, and an impossible job possible.

Machines are needed to produce goods. Human resources are becoming less important in the direct production of goods. Capital, in the form of technology, mechanization, and automation, has become the primary productive factor in that area as machines can often produce better, faster, and cheaper. Yet, using unmanned machines as complete productive systems poses a difficult problem. To the extent that production is predictable and controllable—and when consistent performance is required—the machine system is probably preferable to manual operations.

People are needed for flexibility and creativity. Yet, such systems tend to be inflexible. So, if flexibility is desired, or if the job is critical, manual operations or human support for the machine is essential, for most management problems involve one simple, frustrating element, namely, the unpredictability of events. So, until machines are more nearly perfected than at present, wherever an intricate step must be performed, or a vital decision must be made and acted upon, some member of the human race will still be needed and used.

> A news item tells of a company in Los Angeles that installed a computer to do its accounting activities and financial analyses. When there was a severe breakdown of the computer, the firm had to hire 11 people to do the work. The headlines read: "Computer Has 'Nervous Breakdown'/Replaced by 11 People."

People are still important and wanted! Paradoxically, while many skills are becoming obsolete, the demand for people to do creative and responsible work is increasing. Because a relatively small group of scientific, technical, professional, and managerial personnel is bringing about the increased productivity through their creative abilities, there will be a shift in the use of human resources from producing goods to performing services.

"Well, I guess the old company picnic has changed over the years, eh fellas? Fellas?"

Source: *Morning Advocate*, November 24, 1975, p. 13A; © 1975 by NEA, Inc. Reprinted by permission of NEA.

Limitations to the development of human resources. Although it is desirable for an organization to utilize its human resources effectively, there are certain constraints and limitations which should be mentioned. If there is an overabundance of employees or if they are incapable or inadequately trained, the effectiveness of the organization will probably suffer. However, if the primary objective of an institution is to provide social services, then this becomes an ethical question rather than one of economic analysis.

INCREASING KNOWLEDGE OF EMPLOYEE BEHAVIOR

The improved role of personnel administration has largely resulted from an expanding knowledge of employee behavior. This increased understanding has come from many sources, but it is largely the result of expanded research by the behavioral scientists and of adaptation and synthesis by management scholars. However, the earlier theorists and practitioners laid the groundwork for their research and conclusions.

Early contributions to knowledge

The early philosophers were greatly concerned with human behavior and provided us with many currently accepted ethical value judgments. Also, the teachings of the great religious leaders can form the basis of effective personnel administration.

Machiavelli. Machiavelli, a Florentine public servant, anticipated Fiedler's *contingency theory of leadership* (9) when he said in *The Prince* that a ruler or leader can make people respect him but he can not make them love him; therefore, he should do that over which he has control and make them respect him. (10) This truth underlies the presently popular *contingency theory of management*.

Robert Owen. Probably the first concerted study of employee behavior resulted from the "Industrial Revolution." A new economic system, (11) and the invention of numerous machines to improve manufacture, led to the "factory system" with its mass-production processes. These changes resulted in an increased supply of material goods, but they also resulted in extensive adverse changes in the conditions of employment. Despite the general malpractices, one man arose to make a great contribution to modern personnel administration.

Robert Owen, a British businessman, reformer, and humanitarian, believed that the physical, social, and economic environments influence the physical, mental, and psychological development of workers. Therefore, in order to increase productivity, it was necessary to improve the position of employees by removing them from the adverse environment or changing that environment by providing more satisfactory living and working conditions.

Owen implemented this philosophy by organizing model villages next to his cotton mills in Scotland; introducing such unheard-of facilities as shower baths and toilets into the factories, which were cleaned and painted and in which windows were installed for light and ventilation; organizing day schools for the children and night schools for the workers; and raising the minimum age for employing children to 11 years, and shortening their work day to 10 hours. Later he abolished child labor entirely.

Toward a more rational approach

Around the beginning of this century, other significant contributions were made to the knowledge of human behavior.

Taylor and his colleagues. Frederick W. Taylor began conducting experiments which resulted in his principles of "scientific management." These included:

1. Determining the science of each job.
2. Selecting the right person for the job.
3. Training the person to perform the job in a scientific manner.
4. Compensating the person with a financial incentive.
5. Separating the managerial from the nonmanagerial functions. (12)

Taylor believed that workers were sources of "untapped energy" ready to do good work if properly trained and fairly treated. He argued that workers should be induced to join his "mental revolution" by their supervisors who, in turn, had to abandon their right of instant dismissal and to substitute "just cause" as a standard for separation from the job. This management philosophy became the first barrier to the common-law right of the employer to fire anyone for any—or no—cause.

Other knowledge developed by Taylor and his colleagues—Carl Barth, Henry Gantt, Harrington Emerson, Frank and Lillian Gilbreth, and others—included:

1. Using the scientific approach to evaluate work and select and train employees; and
2. The concepts of division of labor, systems and methods analysis, and many others.

The results of this new knowledge was a reduction of the personalized employer-employee relationship, the internalization of rules and regulations, and the segregation of decision making in the managerial group. All these served to decrease the significance and initiative of individual employees. This criticism does not apply to Taylor himself, for he viewed the new method as a complete mental revolution on the part of the workers and management. Later, however, especially during the 1920s, the "efficiency experts," "systematizers," and other practitioners of the new methods used their form without understanding their substance; they emphasized the techniques without understanding the philosophy behind them. This misapplication of the principles of "scientific management" resulted in many abuses and misuses of the basic concepts.

Henri Fayol. Henri Fayol, a French industrialist, combined the practical wisdom resulting from 50 years' experience in the steel industry with his powers of observation and a simplified writing style to summarize the essence of management "principles" which could and should be applied to all forms of human organizations and which could be taught as a separate discipline. (13)

Other early contributors. Many other practitioners and scholars contributed to the increasing knowledge of human behavior. Wilhelm Wundt established a behavioral laboratory in Leipzig in 1879. The Simon-Binet tests of mental abilities were published in France in 1905. James M. Cattell, Walter D. Scott, and Hugo Munsterberg actively sought ways of applying psychology to employee behavior, especially through developing employment tests. The latter published the first book specifically dealing with management behavior. (14) Lilliam Gilbreth followed his example the same year by publishing *The Psychology of Management.* (15) The first personnel book was published by Ordway Tead and Henry Metcalf in 1920. (16)

The "Hawthorne experiments" and their aftermath

It is usually accepted that the behavioral approach to personnel administration started with the productivity studies at the Western Electric Hawthorne plant.

Beginning in 1924, a series of experiments was conducted to determine the effects of changes in the physical environment upon productivity. The results were inconclusive, so a new series of experiments was conducted by Elton Mayo, Fritz Roethlisberger, and others from Harvard University from 1928 to 1932. (17) These studies emphasized the human organization of industry, the factory as a social system, and the importance of communications and morale. The researchers concluded that a sense of participation, being selected for the experiments, and being a member of the team were more important stimulants to their productivity than economic self-interest, lighting, rest periods, and other physical factors.

The investigators also concluded that organizations were in reality composed of individual social systems. This finding has been verified and expanded by subsequent research to include the *systems concept of organization and management.*

Other contributors who added to the expanding knowledge were Oliver Sheldon, a British manager who pleaded for developing a philosophy of management (18); Mary Parker Follett, a social worker who called management a profession and who said that a leader's style resulted from the interplay of the leader, the followers, and the situation (19); and Chester Barnard, a telephone executive, who explained the informal organization. (20)

Contributions of the behavioral scientists

Although there is no general agreement as to what the behavioral science disciplines are, an acceptable definition of a *behavioral science* is *a body of systemized knowledge concerning how humans behave, the relationship between that behavior and the total environment, and why people behave as they do.* (21)

The use of the behavioral sciences in organizations is not altogether new. As industry grew and expanded during World War I, the fields of *industrial psychology* and *sociology* were used extensively, as they were also used in World War II. However, the integration of findings of cultural anthropologists into administration is relatively new. *Cultural anthropology* is primarily the study of people, what they are, and what has made them what they are. It studies people's heredity and previous cultural environment in order to explain their present behavior.

The research findings of this group have made people aware of themselves and their environment, which has aided individual managers in adjusting to changes in their own situation while understanding the effects of their cultural heritage upon their behavior—as well as that of their subordinates.

Although it is an overgeneralization, it can be stated that the main contribution of the behavioral sciences has been the development of a frame of reference to be used by personnel administrators in understanding, predicting, and influencing employee behavior. This analytical, rational, and reasoning method of thinking should help you to become a better personnel administrator.

> A manufacturing company of 2,000 employees in northeastern Ohio found in 1972 that absenteeism was 4.4 percent for whites and 7.1 percent for blacks, and the turnover rate was 7 percent and 30 percent, respectively. A behavioral study was made of the attitudes of the two groups in order to determine the factors causing this differential. Only pay, external conditions (defined as all the environmental factors outside of the factory), supervision, and recognition were found to be significantly different.
>
> While the company did pay better wages than most industries in its area, the blacks lived near a rubber plant which paid the highest wages in the entire area. Thus, the manufacturing firm's wages were relatively lower and did not meet the black employees' expectations. Yet, the critical external factor was discovered to be *transportation,* as the black employees lived in an area nine miles from the plant. "No ride" and "car trouble" were given as the most prevalent reasons for absenteeism.
>
> Also, the blacks perceived that they were not treated as well as their white counterparts, even though they were treated "fairly." (22)

IMPLICATIONS AND APPLICATIONS FOR PERSONNEL EXECUTIVES

The primary purpose of this chapter has been to put the importance of human resources into proper perspective as a basis for performing the personnel function. Specifically it has shown the importance of human resources, including some constraints upon their development, and traced the development of our knowledge of human behavior.

An attempt was made to establish a framework within which an intelligent analysis of the performance of the personnel function can be undertaken. From the pertinent research findings presented, and based upon the assumption that organizations wish to utilize human resources effectively in order to reach predetermined goals, the following hypotheses explaining the cause and effect relationships between the utilization of human resources and productivity of an organization—and the derived employee satisfactions—are suggested.

1. *An organization's performance and resulting productivity are directly proportional to the quantity and quality of its human resources.*

   In 1970, a firm which had sold in large volume to the military during the Vietnam War found itself with excess capacity and personnel. To economize, it drastically reduced its work force, including many skilled and experienced craftsmen and technicians. When the recession was over in early 1972, its demand increased rapidly, but it had to turn down orders as it could not find personnel to replace those it had terminated, as they had taken other jobs.

2. *While employee performance must be evaluated in economic terms of efficiency and effectiveness, it can be best achieved through recognizing and enhancing the human dignity of each employee.*

   Seven maids worked in a large nursing home. Two of them—Mary and Jane—did much better work than the others. When the others did sloppy work, the supervisor sent Mary and Jane to correct it. The work of the others deteriorated, as did the attitudes of the two good workers.

   The "personnel officer" suggested definite areas be assigned to each maid. This was done, and each one was held responsible for her work meeting standard. Performance increased greatly.

3. *The quantity and quality of human resources can be effectively increased through education, training, and personal development.*

   The personnel manager of a large hospital was informed of an opening in an executive development program and asked if she would like to send one of her upper-level managers to it. Her answer was, "Yes, we like to invest in our people." She considered the expenses of the entire operation as "contributions to the 'bottom line,' as they make money for the hospital."

It can be concluded that management exerts strong influence upon the use of technology and the natural resources through the use of knowledge, skills, attitudes, motivations, and methodology of people and the existing culture. The executive's job, therefore, is to bring the physical, financial, and human resources into a harmonious relationship with technology which will contribute to the betterment of the members of the organization.

DISCUSSION QUESTIONS

1. What is the basic assumption underlying any discussion of the importance of human resources? Do you think it is a valid assumption to make in studying the importance of human resources to an organization?
2. Why is the development of personnel important in the utilization of human resources? What are the implications for personnel administration?
3. Discuss the constraints upon human resource development.
4. Discuss the contributions of the behavioral scientists to the study of personnel.
5. Discuss each of the hypotheses and show whether they are valid or not.

REFERENCES AND SUGGESTIONS FOR FURTHER STUDY

1. See any basic economic text for further discussion of these two truisms. I used T. J. Hailstones and M. J. Brennan, *Economics,* 2d ed. (Cincinnati, Ohio: South-Western Publishing Co., 1975), pp. 4, 38–50.
2. Harold J. Leavitt developed this proposition very well in "Unhuman Organizations," *Harvard Business Review,* vol. 40, no. 4 (July–August 1962), pp. 90–98.
3. At that time, John Kenneth Galbraith entered the controversy over the relative value of machines versus personnel. He stated that a well-educated and well-trained work force was not only an economic resource, but was a nation's greatest form of capital. John Kenneth Galbraith, "Men and Capital," *Saturday Evening Post* (March 5, 1960), p. 32.

    In his 1960 presidential address to the American Economic Association, Theodore W. Schultz chided economists for not treating human resources explicitly as a form of capital and as the product of investment whereby production is achieved. He emphasized that this capital has been in part a deliberate investment that has grown in Western societies at a faster rate than conventional (nonhuman) capital and that its growth may well be the most distinctive feature of those economic systems. Theodore W. Schultz, "Investment in Human Capital," *American Economic Review,* vol. 51, no. 1 (March 1961), p. 1.

    Eli Ginzberg, in a study for the "Conservation of Human Resources" project, supported the conclusion of Schultz that the human resources should be thought of as capital. He found that the human resources were the key to all economic development. Eli Ginzberg, "Man and His Work," *California Management Review,* vol. 5, no. 2 (Winter 1962), p. 21.
4. This conclusion is based upon the findings of John F. Mee, "Science and Management," *Advanced Management Journal,* vol. 29, no. 4 (October 1964), pp. 34–35, although the figures have been updated.

    There are several indications that our vaunted productivity may be declining. Congress has created a new agency to cope with the worrisome problem of lagging productivity in U.S. industry. It has established a National Center for Productivity and Quality of Working Life as an independent agency in the executive branch to replace the ineffectual National Commission on Productivity and Work Quality created in 1970 to monitor productivity gains and losses. See *Business Week* (September 1, 1975), p. 67.

5. It has been concluded that England was successful in settling the New World because colonization "being a branch of business enterprise, . . . could not flourish without a fortunate combination of authority and self-government; the one, guaranteeing order and cooperation; the other, individual initiative necessary to cope with strange and protean circumstance." See Charles A. Beard and Mary B. Beard, *The Rise of American Civilization,* new ed. (New York: Macmillan Co., 1934), pp. 15–16.
6. David C. McClelland, "Business Drive and National Achievement," *Harvard Business Review,* vol. 40, no. 4 (July–August 1962), pp. 99–112.
7. See R. L. Kert and W. C. Pyle, "Human Resource Accounting II," *Financial Analyst Journal,* vol. 27, no. 1 (January–February 1971), pp. 75–84, for more details.
8. The first estimate was made by Margaret Mead, "A Look at Human Capacities," reprinted from *The Lamp* (Summer 1963); while the second was reported by Paul W. Athan, "Developing Reliable Human Resources," *Personnel Journal,* vol. 43, no. 4 (April 1964), pp. 185–88.
9. See Fred E. Fiedler, *A Theory of Leadership Effectiveness* (New York: McGraw-Hill Book Co., 1967), for an explanation of this theory.
10. Count Carlo Sforza, *The Living Thoughts of Machiavelli* (New York: Fawcett World Library, 1958). It was originally published in 1532.
11. This new economic system was proposed by a moral philosopher at Glasgow University, Adam Smith, in *An Inquiry into the Nature and Causes of the Wealth of Nations,* 1776. He said there were natural laws, such as the law of supply and demand which would regulate economic relationships to the benefit of society.
12. Frederick W. Taylor, *Principles and Methods of Scientific Management* (New York: Harper & Bros., 1911).
13. Henri Fayol, *General and Industrial Management* (London: Sir Isaac Pitmann & Sons, Ltd., 1949), p. 33. The French version was first published in 1916.
14. Hugo Munsterberg, *Psychology and Industrial Efficiency* (Boston: Houghton Mifflin Co., 1913).
15. Lillian Gilbreth, *The Psychology of Management,* 1913.
16. Ordway Tead and H. C. Metcalf, *Personnel Administration, Its Principles and Practice* (New York: McGraw-Hill Book Co., 1920).
17. See J. F. Roethlisberger and W. J. Dickson, *Management and the Worker* (Cambridge, Mass.: Harvard University Press, 1939), for a description of these experiments. The studies have been criticized for their assumptions, methodology, and conclusions. See Daniel Wren, *Evolution of Management Thought* (New York: Ronald Press, 1972), pp. 370–89, for these criticisms.
18. Oliver Sheldon, *The Philosophy of Management* (London: Sir Isaac Pitmann & Sons, Ltd., 1939).
19. Mary Parker Follett, *Freedom and Co-ordination* (London: Management Publications Trust, Ltd., 1949), pp. 47–60; and L. Urwick, ed., *The Golden Book of Management* (London: Newman Neame, Ltd., for the International Committee of Scientific Management (CIOS, 1956), p. 133. Notice how her thoughts span the gap between those of Machiavelli and Fiedler.

20. Chester I. Barnard, *The Functions of the Executive* (Cambridge, Mass.: Harvard university Press, 1938).
21. For an enlightening discussion of the behavioral sciences, see Charles A. Myers, "Behavioral Sciences for Personnel Managers," *Harvard Business Review,* vol. 44, no. 4 (July–August 1966), pp. 154–62.
22. Stephen S. McIntosh, "Social Scientist Meets Industrial Practitioner," *Personnel Journal,* vol. 53, no. 1 (January 1974), pp. 38–44.

Chapter 2

The growing importance of personnel and human resources administration

Definition of personnel and human resources administration

The improving role of the personnel function
  Previous low status
  Now, a position of high status

What functions do personnel executives perform?
  Recruiting and selecting personnel
  Maximizing employee potential
  Maintaining reward and penalty systems
  Strategies for dealing with employee associations
  Maintaining the work force
  Performing specific creative activities

Responsibility for performing the personnel function
  Need for a clear understanding of areas of responsibility
  Need for a coordinated approach

Personnel administrators need a new type authority
  Staff authority
  Functional authority

Implications and applications for personnel executives

2
The growing importance of personnel and human resources administration

Personnel is by no means a one-man function or a one-man department. Your production and your personnel problems are one and the same problem. You cannot solve one without the other.

GLENN GARDINER

Every program involving people is actually a line responsibility—but that does not mean that the personnel man should simply turn the problem over to the line and leave them to figure it out.

JAMES D. PERLEY

In 1971, General Motors separated the industrial relations activities from all the other personnel activities. Dr. Stephen H. Fuller, former professor at the Harvard Business School, was made "vice president of human resources" and assigned the responsibility for performing all of the personnel activities except dealing with industrial relations.

This action by this giant corporation is indicative of the growing importance of personnel and human resources administration. Many other institutions are also elevating the personnel function to a high level in the organizational structure. Increasingly the chief executive officer (CEO) is saying, "Check it out with personnel first," before instituting a new program, locating a new facility, or doing anything involving human resources.

The purpose of this chapter is to develop these thoughts, which will then provide you with a frame of reference to study the rest of the material in this text. Specifically the material will:

1. Provide a working definition of personnel and human resources administration;
2. Explore further the improving role of personnel;
3. Identify and explain the specific functions included under the overall designation, "personnel function," and show how they are achieved;
4. Specify the areas of authority and responsibilities involved in performing the personnel function; and
5. Explain the new type authority being used by personnel executives.

DEFINITION OF PERSONNEL AND HUMAN RESOURCES ADMINISTRATION

There is really no short definition of the term which is satisfactory, but a working definition of personnel and human resources administration is: *the performance of all managerial functions involved in planning for, recruiting and selecting, developing, utilizing, rewarding, and maximizing the potential of the human resources of an organization.*

This definition includes developing a sense of values and a way of thinking and then applying them to one's dealings with other people in an organization. The definition assumes a deliberate choice between maximizing individual performance and maximizing personal job satisfaction, if the two are incapable of being achieved concurrently.

Based upon this philosophy, all managerial personnel in organizations, either private or public, profit or nonprofit, large or small, must be considered to be performing the personnel function.

While the term should probably be used in this more inclusive sense, in this text it refers to the *performance of the personnel function by personnel executives in the personnel department.* That is the only way a coherent, integrated, but inclusive presentation can be made without excessive overlapping with other disciplines such as organization theory and behavior.

The theories and practices discussed in this book apply also to all types of organizations, including governments, schools, churches, hospitals, and others.

> A church with around 5,000 members, a budget of over $800,000, and a staff of over 20 full-time professional, clerical, food service, and maintenance personnel, as well as about the same number of part-time employees, has a full-time, professional business administrator. Among her other duties is the performance of the personnel function. While she is directly supervised by the pastor, the objectives, policies, procedures, and other personnel matters are set by the personnel committee, composed of men and women of the church. The day-to-day personnel activities are handled by the administrator on an informal basis.

THE IMPROVING ROLE OF THE PERSONNEL FUNCTION

In order to understand the improving role of the personnel function, it would help to review briefly what it has been in the past. The recent problems facing personnel administrators and their departments have primarily resulted from a perceived low status.

Previous low status

The perceived low status of personnel resulted from at least four causes, namely, (*a*) disrespect for the function and those performing it—deservedly or not; (*b*) low position in the organization; (*c*) a lack of expertise in performing the function; and (*d*) a poor "self-image" by personnel managers.

Low status in the eyes of others. Personnel managers have been viewed as contributing little to the essential functioning of the organization. While other administrators were focusing on the difficult problems of financing, pollution control, and construction of complex production facilities, personnel managers were often perceived as performing necessary, but not very challenging, assignments involving routine plans, programs, procedures, and detailed activities such as "keeping the union out," handling employment details, doing wage and salary surveys, and handling employee welfare programs.

This lack of involvement on the part of personnel people in the key issues led to frustrations on their part, as well as on the part of top executives. Consequently, personnel managers were caught in a dilemma—namely, whether the personnel function was essentially a welfare or administrative function or one which was capable of contributing effectively to the organization. (1) Also, the personnel function was placed at a low level in the organizational structure, and untrained people who weren't needed elsewhere were assigned to perform the function. The results were low status and prestige for the personnel manager—and his department. (2)

The irony of it all is that often top management of an organization will assign the personnel function a low status but then indirectly give it credit for the success of the organization. (3)

Low position in the organizational structure. Another problem with the personnel function has been its low level in the organizational structure. The wrong organization structure can discourage line managers from seeking help from the personnel department. If several personnel executives must be contacted to solve a single problem, it does inhibit people from going to them for help. We now know that the size and reporting level of personnel departments are not as important to their effectiveness as the role assigned to them, their own internal organization, and the caliber of their staffs. (4)

Inadequate expertise. Now it is time to mention another quite prevalent problem, namely, the inadequate expertise of some of those performing the function. All too frequently, top management has assigned a mediocre line manager to perform the personnel function. (5) Sometimes it was to "kick him upstairs" or to "reward him for good performance elsewhere."

When unsuccessful operating managers are made personnel managers, they cannot command the needed respect of other line managers. Also, research shows that some personnel people have too often shown little knowledge of, or interest in, broader organizational concerns. (6)

Poor "self-image". It is difficult to say what is "cause" and what is "effect" as far as the personnel administrators' poor "self-image" is concerned. Yet, we do know that they have been frustrated for they have tended to perceive themselves as filling low-level positions and being treated inferior to other managers. Therefore, they have agreed with the image other managers had of them, namely, that they performed a predominantly static role. (7)

The personnel administrators' self-perception has also been influenced by their need to make independent decisions, while serving as advisors to line managers. (8) In fact, they have often selected and developed those line managers as their subordinates.

Consequences of these deficiencies. These weaknesses of many personnel departments make them especially vulnerable during times of budget cutting. While labor costs are direct and visible, most benefits derived from effective personnel administration are indirect and often intangible. For example, the relationship between improved profits and the costs of undertaking a comprehensive job enrichment effort is difficult to see at best. Because of this difficulty, the personnel department is one of the first areas to be trimmed in hard times and one of the last to be increased in an economic upswing. Such management actions are particularly shortsighted, for while human resources account for between 40 and 70 percent of the total costs in most businesses, personnel staff costs usually range between 1 and 2 percent of the total payroll. (9) This leverage suggests that productivity increases resulting from more effective and relevant personnel action programs can have a significant impact upon revenue and profits.

Another consequence of these deficiencies is the difficulty of getting the more qualified people to enter the field. (10)

Now, a position of high status

All this is now changing! The personnel function—and its performance—is being viewed as a complex system, with each part being interrelated, interdependent, and interacting. Top management knows that in order to meet changing needs, personnel policies and organization must be developed on a total systems basis. Figure 2–1 shows this concept of personnel as part of a total system.

FIGURE 2–1
The place of personnel in a total system's context

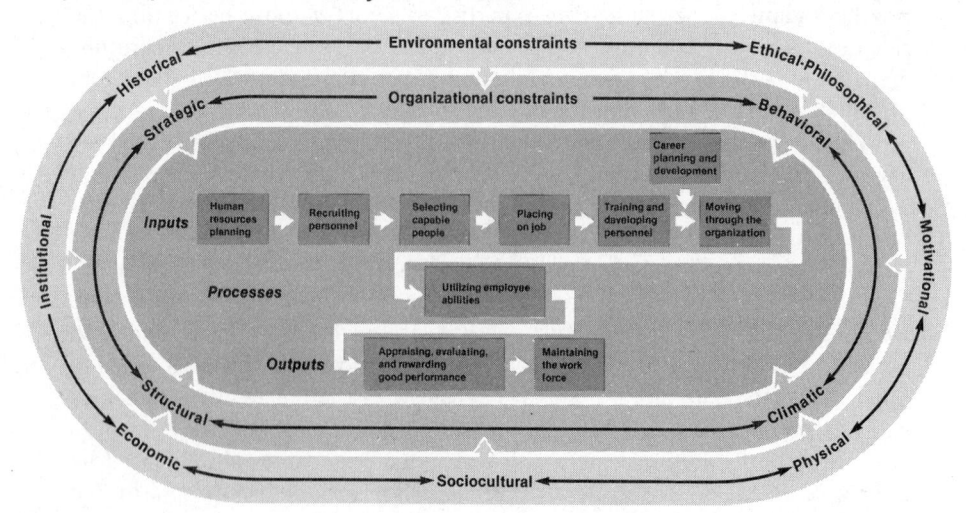

There is now a greater realization of the need for "human resource experts," just as there has long been a recognition of need for experts in other management areas.

Some consequences of the change. Because of the impact of the behavioral sciences or other pressures, personnel departments have moved increasingly in recent years into such complex and sophisticated areas as assessment centers, executive career planning and development, organization development (OD), selection research, and job enrichment. As a result, the problem of managing the personnel function has been compounded. Indeed it can be said that the sophistication of personnel programs is increasing arithmetically, while the complexity of choosing the best ones and managing them is increasing geometrically.

For the improved personnel departments to make more meaningful contributions to their organizations, there must be knowledgeable, competent, and committed personnel specialists, an appreciation by top managers of how to utilize the personnel departments more effectively, and informed personnel executives who are alert to what is desired of them by others in the organization.

Pressures on top management both from within and from outside the organization are forcing high-level executives to reconsider not only the nature of the services the personnel function ought to provide, but also the role of personnel in the organization. When top managers are willing to accept their own responsibility for the quality of life in the organization, they will make sure their personnel directors and staff are able people to whom the freedom necessary for their expanded role can be delegated. (11)

Managing human resources in a period of change. One conclusion which should become evident from the previous discussion is that many of the existing techniques used by personnel executives operate more smoothly in stable, predictable situations. However, when conditions of change occur—as is now happening—those procedures tend to become limitations to adapting to change. This requires new techniques to be introduced which can operate during these periods of change.

There now seems to be a growing awareness among professional personnel administrators that the function is moving beyond the personnel technology of recordkeeping, controlling merit increases, filling out forms for the government, coordinating training conferences, and other traditional and classical activities and moving into the broader area of overall human resource management. Yet, human resource management is not simply a new label to be attached to the traditional and compartmentalized personnel department; it is a new and exacting role. It places personnel executives in challenging situations where they can participate in decisions directly affecting the success or failure of their organizations. To the "new breed" of personnel administrators, this is the opportunity to strengthen the influence and impact of their departments and get them into the "mainstream of the administrative process" where they belong.

The new personnel director of an operating division of American Telephone & Telegraph Company was appointed to the job with new and expanded responsibilities. He was told to "select and develop people who can run this company in order to assure our retirement pay."

Yet, the true value of this new human resource management lies in its ability to respond effectively to performance objectives and developmental opportunities. This assures that the right people with the required mix of knowledge and skills will be in the right place, at the right time, and at the right cost to achieve organizational objectives.

Harry Levinson predicted this change some time ago when he said each personnel executive must reestablish one's credentials by becoming an "internal organizational consultant in the behavioral sciences." (12) He viewed the new personnel specialists as general practitioners in the psychological, sociological, and anthropological processes in work organizations who tend to concentrate on diagnosis and define problems of people at work and who help their organizations to avoid or eliminate potential difficulties and people problems.

It can now be concluded that personnel administrators are beginning to play a central role in the management drama in the more progressive organizations. The proper role of personnel managers has grown from soft, naive concepts of human relations to hard, sophisticated concepts of organizational growth and planned change.

Playing the new role. There are several surveys indicating that both organizations and their personnel executives are not only aware of, but are conforming to, this new role. The National Industrial Conference Board (NICB) found that while service activities take most of the personnel department's time in 246 large corporations (largely manufacturing) *planning for change is their most important role.* (See Table 2–1 for details.)

The survey also found that 138 of the 249 personnel units (55 percent) were headed by a vice president; and the heads of 161 of the units reported to the president or the chairman of the board. (13)

The Bureau of National Affairs (BNA) found in another study of manufac-

TABLE 2–1
The roles played by personnel units in 236 large corporations

Role	Considered to be the most important	The role taking the most time
Advise and counsel top management in initiating and recommending changes	148	53
Service to the line and other staff groups	78	174
Control and policy of directives and policies	10	9

Source: Allen R. Janger, *Personnel Administration: Changing Scope and Organization* (New York: National Industrial Conference Board, Studies in Personnel Policies, No. 203, 1966), p. 16.

TABLE 2–2
Titles of top personnel and industrial relations administrators

	Percent of administrators with each title		
Title	All companies	Larger companies	Smaller companies
Personnel director	28	26	33
Industrial relations director	16	17	13
Personnel manager	11	10	13
Employee relations director	9	9	10
Vice president	19	26	7
Other	16	12	23

Source: Bureau of National Affairs, *The Personnel Department* (Washington, D.C.: Personnel Policies Forum, Survey No. 92, November 1970), p. 6.

turing, nonmanufacturing, and nonprofit organizations that 19 percent of the personnel administrators were vice presidents and 65 percent of the executives reported directly to the president of the organization. (See Table 2–2 for details.)

The improving role is also reflected in the position description shown in Figure 2–2.

WHAT FUNCTIONS DO PERSONNEL EXECUTIVES PERFORM?

There is no agreement among scholars as to what personnel functions should be performed by personnel executives. However, three separate surveys provide some insights from which some generalizations can be made.

The NICB study found the following functions to be considered as "most important": (14)

Function	Percentage of executives considering it "most important"
Management development, personnel planning and/or organization planning	97
Labor relations	87
Compensation and benefits	64
Recruitment and employment	63

The BNA study found that of 39 representative functions, eight of ten personnel and industrial relations departments had *full responsibility* for recruiting, wage surveys, military and other leaves of absence, group insurance, health and medical services, counseling, union relations, personnel recordkeeping, and personnel research; while two-thirds of them also *participated independently* in planning general personnel policies, selection, induction and orientation, educational and scholarship programs, job evaluation, vacations and holidays, recreation and social, and service and performance awards. (15)

Table 2–3 summarizes a later study which shows the differences between

FIGURE 2-2

POSITION DESCRIPTION

JOB TITLE... Director of employee relations ... DATE ... July 8, 1969 ....

DEPARTMENT ... Employee relations ...... REVIEWED BY ....

BASIC FUNCTION

To plan and formulate for the approval of the president personnel and labor relation policies, practices, and programs. Provide direction and assistance in a staff capacity to the various departments and executives in carrying out the personnel and labor relation responsibilities.

REPORTS TO: President
SUPERVISES: Personnel manager, employee benefit manager, employee activity coordinator

---

DUTIES AND RESPONSIBILITIES:

1. Direct the execution of the company's approved personnel and labor relation policies and program.
2. Provide general supervision for the companywide activities of personnel administration, medical services, wage and salary administration, supervisory training, management development, safety, insurance benefits, and labor relations.
3. To advise and assist department heads and supervisors in the interpretation and application of personnel and labor relation policies and programs.
4. Analyze the effect of various personnel and labor relation policies and practices. Recommend any changes in or additions to such policies and practices.
5. To formulate and direct execution of company's labor relation policies and programs.
6. Be spokesman for company in negotiating labor agreements and handling grievances and arbitration.
7. To advise and assist the various departments in the interpretation and application of the labor relation policies and programs, labor agreements, and labor legislation.
8. Analyze the effect of various labor relation policies and practices, and recommend changes or additions to such policies and practices.
9. To consult with department heads and executives on a day-to-day administration of union contracts, and to supply data to department heads of unorganized departments.
10. To maintain communications with international and local union officials for the exchange of information.
11. To keep general council of company informed on all pending labor matters.

Source: Bureau of National Affairs, *The Personnel Department* (Washington, D.C.: Personnel Policies Forum, Survey No. 92, November 1970), p. 18.

TABLE 2–3. Functions and activities of the personnel administration department desired by executives and line managers (percentages)

	Activities										
	Policy		Advice		Service		Control		None		Rank	
Functions	E	M	E	M	E	M	E	M	E	M	E	M
Collective bargaining	30	44	30	29	22	35	11	25	44	25	26	26
Civil rights	56	60	52	60	22	38	30	36	4	2	12	6
Complaints and grievances	37	51	68	69	52	51	26	27	4	0	9	5
Counseling	37	40	37	69	48	55	19	27	4	0	23	9
Discipline	41	49	57	71	33	27	4	29	11	6	24	15
Employee communications	37	44	52	51	59	60	19	27	7	2	11	14
Fringe benefits	52	71	44	44	67	66	56	44	0	2	1	1
Health and safety	41	60	52	56	44	58	22	40	7	2	10	2
Hiring decisions	30	44	59	69	30	47	30	33	4	6	16	7
Incentive programs	41	31	44	40	30	24	33	18	19	20	20	28
Job descriptions	48	42	30	54	48	38	63	31	0	9	5	21
Job design	15	25	37	38	19	24	19	15	19	24	27	29
Layoffs and discharges	48	42	41	66	37	35	22	29	11	6	21	17
Organizational planning	22	27	55	64	19	31	19	11	7	11	15	25
Orientation of new employees	59	58	37	44	63	62	48	38	0	2	3	3
Pay raises	37	58	56	62	33	31	22	40	0	10	19	10
Performance appraisal	52	46	56	58	22	24	30	42	0	7	13	19
Personnel planning	41	33	56	66	33	40	21	25	7	9	18	22
Personnel research	41	55	26	33	59	47	26	36	4	2	17	18
Personnel surveys	56	67	26	26	56	53	33	42	4	2	8	12
Promotions	37	42	67	62	7	25	11	31	7	9	25	23
Public relations	22	44	37	29	19	40	7	26	30	16	28	24
Recruiting	59	69	37	31	59	44	44	44	4	0	4	11
Selection	41	71	52	55	41	31	37	29	0	0	7	13
Selection testing	48	60	41	29	56	51	56	33	0	2	2	16
Setting wages and salaries	41	62	56	58	30	38	30	42	0	2	14	4
Training	48	47	59	49	37	57	33	40	7	6	6	8
Transfers	44	44	56	55	19	36	26	31	0	6	22	20
Union contract administration	30	40	15	27	22	33	11	16	44	24	29	27
Average responses	41.0	49.6	43.9	50.8	37.6	40.9	28.0	31.3				

Executives (E) = 27; Line Managers (M) = 55

Source: H. C. White and R. E. Boynton, "Role of Personnel: A Management View," *Arizona Business*, vol. 21, no. 8 (October 1974), p. 19. Data based on results of questionnaire administered under the direction of the authors. By permission of publisher: Bureau of Business and Economic Research, College of Business Administration, Arizona State University.

the desires of executives who supervised the activities of the personnel administrators in their firms and the wishes of the managers in the same firms who did not supervise, nor were supervised by, the personnel manager.

The table shows that the *executives who supervised personnel administrators* wanted them to: (*a*) give them advice and counsel, 44 percent; (*b*) do policy initiation and formulation, 41 percent; (*c*) provide service, 38 percent; and (*d*) exercise control by monitoring the performance of established personnel policies, procedures, and practices, 28 percent. The executives were *quite willing* for the personnel officers to perform the functions of: (*a*) fringe benefits, (*b*) selection and training, (*c*) orienting new employees, (*d*) recruiting, and (*e*) job descriptions. They were *less willing* to let the personnel people do: (*a*) union contract administration, (*b*) public relations, (*c*) job design, (*d*) collective bargaining, and (*e*) promotions.

The *line managers* ranked the activities in the same order, namely, advice, 51 percent; policy, 50 percent; service, 41 percent; and control, 31 percent. There was a divergence, though, on the willingness to have the personnel administrators perform the personnel function. Their *willingness was ranked* as follows: (*a*) fringe benefits, (*b*) health and safety, (*c*) orientation of new employees, (*d*) setting wages and salaries, and (*e*) handling complaints and grievances. They were *less willing* to let the personnel specialists handle: (*a*) job design, (*b*) incentive programs, (*c*) union contract administration, (*d*) collective bargaining; and (*e*) organizational planning.

It is interesting to note that on the average, for all of the functions and activities, *the line managers were willing to accept more involvement by the personnel department than did the executives supervising the personnel specialists.*

For purposes of this book, the personnel functions are grouped under the headings:

1. Recruiting and selecting personnel;
2. Maximizing employee potential;
3. Maintaining reward and penalty systems;
4. Strategies for dealing with employee associations; and
5. Maintaining the work force.

Recruiting and selecting personnel

Personnel executives are usually given authority over the personnel-human resource planning, recruiting, and selection functions. In this capacity, they have the direct responsibility for determining job and work requirements and setting other qualitative and quantitative personnel requirements. They must also recruit, select, and maintain an adequately trained work force, including providing management succession in organizations.

Maximizing employee potential

Probably the most universal and basic personnel and human resource activity involves educating, training, and developing employees. Special emphasis is currently being placed upon career planning and development, especially management development.

Maintaining reward and penalty systems

The compensation function is quite significant as a reward system. It involves developing a wage and salary plan which is externally competitive and internally consistent. Provision is usually made for sharing productivity gains with employees. In addition, discipline must occasionally be resorted to as a form of negative reward.

LOUIE By **HARRY HANAN**

Courtesy Harry Hanan, News Syndicate Co., Inc.

Strategies for dealing with employee associations

One of the growing realities of organizational life is that employees have a *dual allegiance*. There is a loyalty to the institution, to be sure, but also there is often a superior allegiance to the associations to which employees belong. These associations include the more traditional labor unions, as well as the newer groups such as professional associations. These associations are having a great effect upon employee abilities, attitudes, and productivity. One of the important functions of personnel executives of the future will be establishing —and maintaining—cooperative relationships with these associations.

Maintaining the work force

This function is quite important, for the increasingly complex environment demands more effective efforts to make employees more productive than has been necessary in the past. Some of the complexities are caused by human resistance to change and the consequent need for overcoming this resistance. The entry of minority groups into the work force also demands a higher form of executive guidance. From the personnel point of view, this function involves establishing the environment for productivity, serving as a counselor to difficult and troubled employees when required, maintaining health and safety, administering employee benefits, and preparing employees for retirement.

Performing specific creative activities

With their new and higher status, personnel executives—with the CEO's support—are developing and refining their expertise in:

1. Conducting attitude surveys and other communications programs;
2. Studying the effectiveness of changing work hours and work life-styles;
3. Redesigning jobs;
4. Planning and developing employee careers;
5. Developing organizational changes and modifications; and
6. Doing similar creative activities. (16)

RESPONSIBILITY FOR PERFORMING THE PERSONNEL FUNCTION

Personnel executives cannot be fully effective unless they know what activities they are to manage, who is to assist them, to whom they report, and who reports to them. They need to know within what limits they may operate, over what activities they have authority, and to what degree they will be held accountable for performing those activities.

One of the recurring dilemmas in studying management is the placement of responsibility for managing human resources. While tacitly agreeing with Lawrence Appley that "Management is personnel administration" (17) and that performing this function is the responsibility of *all* managerial personnel, I think we must also remember that it is the job of personnel executives to see that this is done well, rather than do it themselves. Thus, there are certain clearly defined areas of obligation and accountability. (18)

The pressures of an increased sense of professionalism by personnel executives seems to be generating a desire on their part to occupy more completely the traditional personnel field. These findings also suggest that the traditional line-staff organization does not necessarily create conflict since there is growing agreement as to the appropriate relationship between the personnel and line executives. (19)

Need for a clear understanding of areas of responsibility

One assumption underlying the material in this book is that *there is a definite and positive correlation between the effective utilization of its human resources and an organization's efficiency.* This efficiency can best be achieved through adopting the systems concept of interrelated and interacting responsibility for managing people at work. Yet, there are distinct groups which are assumed to share this responsibility in a typical organization.

In essence, *top management* sets objectives and does planning and organizing; *middle management* controls the operating procedures connected with primary objectives and carries out the policies of top management; *first-line supervisors* interpret the policies to the employees, adjust grievances, influence attitudes, direct work, and, in turn, interpret the employees' interests upward to higher management. The *staff specialist* assists all of them by providing expert advice and guidelines.

Line management. Line managers cannot delegate their responsibility for the personnel administration function by appointing staff and functional executives to be responsible for it, for accountability ultimately resides with the line organization. The data in Table 2-3 indicate that if line managers are given policy guidelines concerning the various personnel functions, and have the opportunity to obtain additional advice and guidance from the personnel department in carrying out these functions, in most cases they would probably prefer to perform many of the functions themselves. With support of policy and advice, they have indicated that they would even accept some increased control and measurement of their personnel administration related performance.

Top management. The CEO, who is ultimately accountable for the success or failure of an organization, cannot abdicate the obligation to see that these policies are established, communicated to the lower levels of the organization, and adhered to by the involved individuals.

Yet, historically, personnel administration has been neglected by top management in comparison with the time, effort, and money devoted to other aspects of organizational operations. Now, however, this responsibility to establish and disseminate the overall objectives and policies that guide the other managers in performing this function is being more effectively carried out. What has not been recognized, though, is that except for being "fair yet firm" and other pleasant characterizations, *top management frequently does not know precisely what it wants done in the personnel field.* Top management does, however, know what it does not want. It does not want costly turnover, a class action EEOC suit, or the loss of its most promising personnel.

Middle management. As the responsibility for implementing the delegated functions through day-to-day direction and supervision resides with all line managers in the organization regardless of their level in the hierarchy, middle management is obligated to assist top management in performing its duties through: receiving the programs and policies from above, interpreting and disseminating them to subordinates for compliance and implementation, and serving as an upward communicator to make the needs of subordinates known and understood by top management.

First-line supervisors. These are probably the most important individuals in achieving the objective of effective human resources management. They direct, supervise, control, and otherwise manage the activities of the individuals within their jurisdiction. It cannot be overemphasized, therefore, that the obligation for actually performing the routine, day-to-day aspects of the personnel function resides with, and upon, the first-line supervisors.

As individual employees have little or no opportunity to see other higher-level managers, their only contact is usually through their supervisors. Consequently, the immediate supervisor represents "management" to the employees, for the actions, attitudes, and methods used in performing the managerial duties are interpreted as being those of the organization.

> The manager of a large department with 65 employees and four supervisors had to replace one of the supervisors who was retiring. On Friday afternoon he offered the job to the individual he considered most capable and asked her to think about it over the weekend. When the new supervisor came in on Monday, she said: "I used to think of us in the department as 'we,' versus the supervisors, who were 'them.' Now, I'm one of 'them' and I must change my way of thinking."

Responsibility of the personnel administrator. It has been shown that the personnel administrator's role is increasing in importance. Therefore, the personnel function should be placed in a higher and influential position in the organization and have the aggressive backing of top management. The personnel executive could then be held directly accountable by the CEO for developing policies and procedures to permit the human resources to function in such a manner that the organizational needs and goals will be adequately met.

Need for a coordinated approach

The previous discussion emphasizes that an *integrated personnel system* is needed, for the personnel function is interrelated and interacts with all other functions. Therefore, the personnel function cannot be separated from the other organizational activities, nor can any manager abdicate the responsibility for performing the function.

Finally, one reason for the mass confusion over the organizational responsibility for the personnel function is a confusion of titles. While all managers manage personnel, designations such as "personnel superintendent," "personnel officer," "personnel director," "personnel manager," "personnel administrator," "personnel specialist," "personnel officer," and "personnel executive" are usually reserved for the manager assigned the specific responsibilities for managing the total personnel function. Terms such as "manager of industrial relations" and "manager of employee relations" appear to split the duties of labor relations from the other aspects of personnel administration. However, personnel departments, regardless of how they are defined, are now assuming increased responsibilities for the personnel functions discussed in this chapter.

PERSONNEL ADMINISTRATORS NEED A NEW TYPE AUTHORITY

A great weakness formerly found in performing the personnel function was that personnel executives had only staff authority to advise their superiors, without any line authority to assure compliance with their recommendations.

Now, they are being given a new and stronger type of authority, namely, *functional authority.*

Staff authority

Theoretically, staff authority is the right to give advice, counsel, and guidance to one's immediate superior and to make recommendations for implementing them. Either the superior or the staff specialist may take the initiative in establishing communication between them. If the superior feels a need for counsel, the subordinate is asked for it; if the subordinate feels that the higher executive needs advice pertaining to personnel activities, it is offered. The superior then uses line authority to carry out the recommendations. This relationship is shown in Figure 2–3.

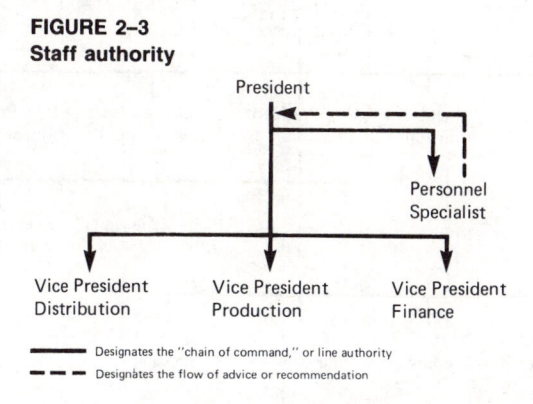

**FIGURE 2–3
Staff authority**

```
                        President
                        ↑┌─────────┐
                        │         ↓
                        │     Personnel
                        │     Specialist
        ┌───────────────┼───────────────┐
        ↓               ↓               ↓
   Vice President  Vice President  Vice President
    Distribution    Production       Finance
```

──── Designates the "chain of command," or line authority
– – – Designates the flow of advice or recommendation

This theoretical arrangement rarely works in actual practice. Instead, there is usually bypassing of lines of authority, which often results in conflict between line authority—resulting from one's position—and staff advice—resulting from specialized competence. Organizations can no longer rely on achieving their objectives solely through the traditional vertical channels of authority. These are now changing in the direction of a more diffused relationship, based upon the use of functional authority.

Functional authority

The functional concept, which was developed by Taylor and accepted by his followers, lost out in general appeal relative to the line-staff concept advanced by Emerson. Now, Taylor's ideas are emerging as one of the three most important forms of authority. It is felt that in the forseeable future it might become the dominant form in personnel relations.

Functional authority is the *right given to staff specialists to command compliance with methods, procedures, policies, and timing of one unique function of the organization, such as accounting, personnel, research, or others requiring specialized knowledge.* The responsible executives have authority over *how* and *when* that function will be performed, regardless of where it is performed in the organization. They have authority to tell the operating managers and others not under their command how that activity will be performed and when it will be performed in their organizations. A workable definition of this new concept—as far as personnel is concerned—is *authority delegated to personnel managers which is to be exercised over a personnel function that is a part of the duties of other executives who are normally not subordinate to them.* Figure 2–4 shows this relationship.

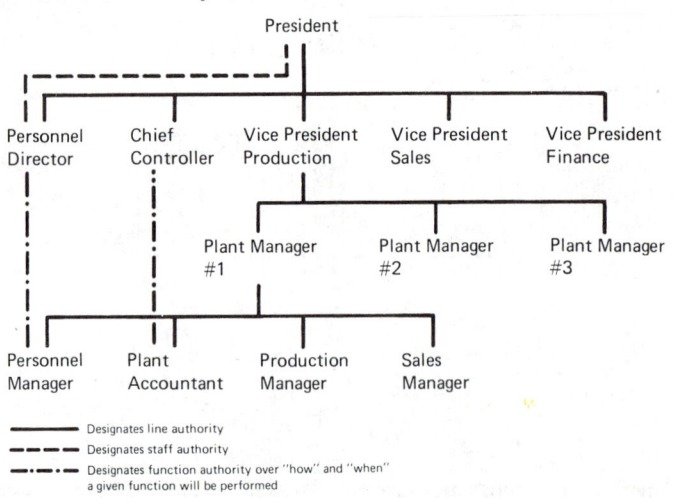

FIGURE 2–4
Functional authority

```
                                  President
        ┌─────────────────────────────┼──────────────────┬──────────────────┐
   Personnel      Chief         Vice President    Vice President    Vice President
   Director     Controller        Production           Sales            Finance
                                      │                  │                │
                              ┌───────┴──────┐           │                │
                          Plant Manager  Plant Manager            Plant Manager
                              #1             #2                        #3
        ┌────────────┬─────────────┬──────────────┐
   Personnel       Plant        Production       Sales
   Manager      Accountant      Manager         Manager
```

─────── Designates line authority
─ ─ ─ ─ Designates staff authority
─·─·─·─ Designates function authority over "how" and "when" a given function will be performed

The major criticism of this system is that it apparently violates the unity-of-command principle enunciated by Fayol, which states that every activity must have a manager with complete overall authority and responsibility for its achievement. Therefore, the functional concept creates the problem of reconciling the "full authority" of line managers with the "functional authority" of the specialists.

And yet there is no real violation of the unity-of-command principle. In addition to having authority over policy decisions and procedural questions, the holders of functional authority frequently have authority over other matters. In actual life there are many superiors for everyone. This is true in the home, school, society, and the business enterprise, for there are many people who tell us what to do. Also, there is no place for absolute authority in our culture today. Authority is limited by law, custom, company policy, labor unions, and mores.

The "personnel manager" of a department store with over 400 employees and $1 million sales reports directly to the two owners of the firm. In addition to handling all aspects of recruiting and selecting, training and developing, compensating, and maintaining the work force, he also helps the owners with organizational planning and development. He issues policy statements on matters such as: attendance; bypassing lines of authority; and locating, planning the construction of, and setting up the organizational structure for, a new branch store. He promotes people to managerial positions and even discharges personnel for violating certain rules.

IMPLICATIONS AND APPLICATION FOR PERSONNEL EXECUTIVES

In too many institutions, the personnel function has been held in low repute, had a bad self-image, and consequently fell short of achieving its potential contribution to the organization.

Now, largely as a result of competitive pressures and environmental factors, all this is changing—for the better! Chief executive officers (CEOs) are increasingly saying, "Check this with personnel before you move on it." The expertise and specialized knowledge of personnel executives now permits them to exercise greater authority over the personnel function wherever it is performed in the organization. The function is also looked upon as an integral part of all administrative and managerial activities, including setting objectives and motivating employees to achieve them.

The following hypotheses were developed.

1. *The performance of the personnel function varies according to the type and size of the organization.*
2. *Personnel relationships in small groups, especially in service-type institutions, tend to be spontaneous and flexible.* Figure 2–5 illustrates a *typical* personnel department in a small manufacturing firm.

> A nursing home with around 70–75 professional and nonprofessional employees has assigned the personnel function to the assistant administrator, who also carries the title "personnel manager." She does the human resource planning, recruiting (including putting ads in the papers and contacting employment

FIGURE 2–5
Organizational chart for the personnel department of a manufacturing corporation of 300 employees

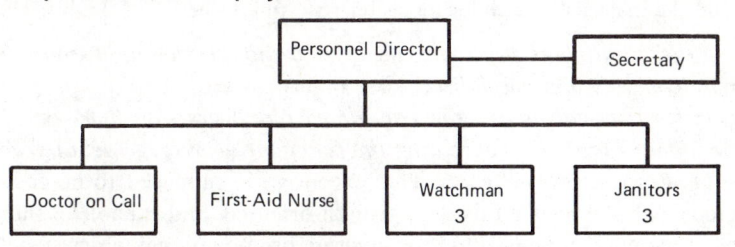

```
                    ┌──────────────────┐      ┌───────────┐
                    │ Personnel Director│──────│ Secretary │
                    └──────────────────┘      └───────────┘
                             │
      ┌──────────────┬───────┴───────┬──────────────┐
┌──────────────┐ ┌──────────────┐ ┌──────────┐ ┌──────────┐
│ Doctor on Call│ │First-Aid Nurse│ │ Watchman │ │ Janitors │
│              │ │              │ │    3     │ │    3     │
└──────────────┘ └──────────────┘ └──────────┘ └──────────┘
```

Source: Bureau of National Affairs, *The Personnel Department* (Washington, D.C.: Personnel Policies Forum, Survey No. 92, November 1970), p. 17.

agencies), interviewing, hiring, orientation and placement, handling of complaints, and other activities. The paper work involving payroll, reports to governmental agencies, and other clerical details is handled by a computer service.

3. *With increasing organizational size and increasing numbers of employees, and where the operations must meet cost effectiveness criteria, the management of human resources tends to become more difficult and to require well-defined objectives, policies, procedures, rules, regulations, and other devices for securing orderly behavior.* Therefore, the problem for personnel administrators becomes one of achieving the advantages of size without reducing managerial and nonmanagerial productive capacities and satisfactions. A typical personnel department in a medium-sized nonmanufacturing firm is shown in Figure 2–6.

FIGURE 2–6
Organizational chart of the employee relations department of a nonmanufacturing corporation of 1,000 employees.

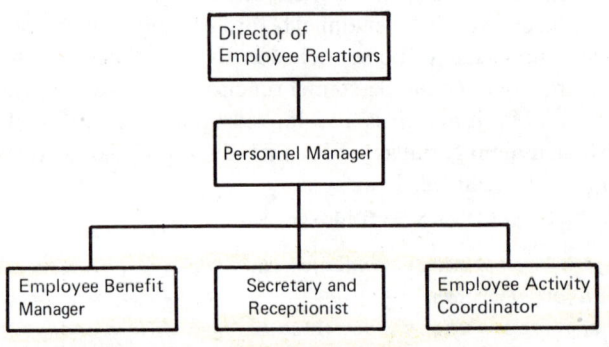

```
              Director of
              Employee Relations
                     |
              Personnel Manager
                     |
         ┌───────────┼───────────┐
   Employee Benefit  Secretary and  Employee Activity
   Manager           Receptionist   Coordinator
```

Source: Bureau of National Affairs, *The Personnel Department* (Washington, D.C.: Personnel Policies Forum, Survey No. 92, November 1970), p. 17.

In a hospital with over 345 beds and 1,150 employees, the "personnel administrator" reports directly to the administrator, but she is "advised" by a public committee composed of the personnel manager of a local manufacturer, a professor of personnel management, an insurance agent, the owner of a small marketing establishment, and a physician. She is responsible for setting objectives, establishing personnel programs, and handling the technical aspects of the personnel function. In turn, she has a training director, an employment director, and the manager of a childcare center reporting to her.

4. *In larger multiplant operations, the organizational structure becomes much more complex and specialized.* (See Figure 2–7.)
5. *Even staff specialists are now considered managers with line—or at least functional—authority, executing the functions of management in order to achieve organizational goals.* This executive is supposed to be cost-conscious, achievement-motivated, growth-oriented, and capable of integrating personnel policies into the overall organizational objectives, as a group's success comes primarily through the efforts of its people.

FIGURE 2-7
Multiplant manufacturing corporation (35,000–40,000 employees)

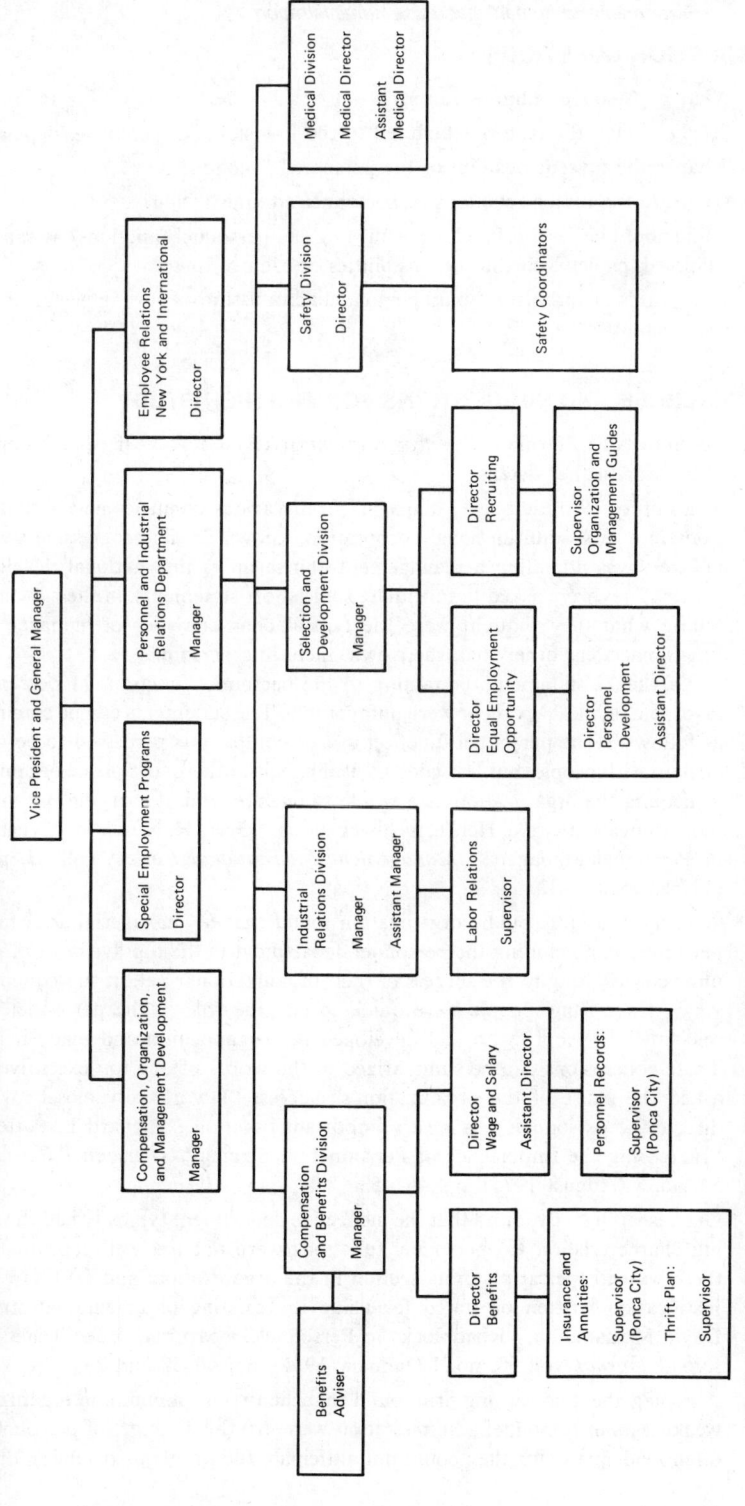

Source: Bureau of National Affairs, *The Personnel Department* (Washington, D.C.: Personnel Policies Forum, Survey No. 92, November 1970), p. 24.

DISCUSSION QUESTIONS

1. What is personnel administration?
2. Briefly discuss the factors which led to the low status of personnel departments.
3. What is the present position of the personnel function?
4. What are the major functions of personnel administration?
5. Who should be responsible for performing the personnel functions? What are the relationships between the responsibilities of each of them?
6. What kinds of authority should personnel administrators have in performing their responsibilities?

REFERENCES AND SUGGESTIONS FOR FURTHER STUDY

1. See Stanley M. Herman, *The People Specialists* (New York: Alfred A. Knopf, Inc., 1968), for further details.
2. A group of 19 middle-level managers from various countries and various functions in a large multinational corporation, known for its progressive personnel policies, was attending a management course at its international development center. They were asked to formulate some short statements, in their own words, telling what they thought were the typical characteristics of managers in six functional areas other than their own, including personnel.

   Of the 72 statements pertaining to the personnel function, 71 percent were favorable, while 29 percent were unfavorable. The statements can be summarized as follows: "The personnel function in this company is perceived to be good at dealing with people, but less good at dealing with other parts of the organization, at helping the organization as a whole to change, and at carrying out anything more than a static role. Hence, its lower status." Geert H. Hofstede, "Frustrations of Personnel Managers," *Management International Review,* vol. 13, no. 4–5 (1973), pp. 127–32.
3. A study of a large public organization found that 61 managerial and staff-level personnel *not* including the personnel department in the top five most important units contributing to the success of their organizations. Yet, in subsequent interviews, these same people were quick to cite the role of the personnel unit in selecting the people who had developed the organization and made it unique. These conclusions can be summarized in the words of one top executive, when asked the cause of the organization's success: "I work very closely with the director of personnel; it is a very important function." Richard L. Pattenaude, "Increasing the Importance of Personnel: A Strategy," *Personnel Journal,* vol. 54, no. 8 (August 1975), pp. 451–53.
4. One research study found that the ineffective department typically had the following characteristics: (*a*) personnel functions were not too well coordinated; (*b*) there was no speical planning section in the organization; and (*c*) there was no justification written or stated for using the existing organizational structure. David McLaughlin, "Roadblocks to Personnel Department Effectiveness," *Personnel Journal,* vol. 50, no. 1 (January 1971), pp. 46–50 and 79.
5. A management consulting firm found that the two most common organizational weaknesses in personnel administration were: (*a*) the directors of personnel were often inadequate, for they could not anticipate the problems troubling the com-

pany or they underestimated the possible effects of the problems; and (*b*) there were frequent cases where personnel managers did recognize the problems but received little or no support from above and had no authority to do anything about the difficulties. In almost every case where these weaknesses existed, it was concluded that the presidents did not understand or did not accept their own accountability for personnel administration. "Who's Responsible for Personnel Policy?" *Iron Age,* vol. 201, no. 2 (January 11, 1968), p. 21 ff.

6. See Fred K. Foulkes, "The Expanding Role of the Personnel Function," *Harvard Business Review,* vol. 53, no. 2 (March–April 1975), pp. 71–84, for the results of these studies. This article is one of the best written recently on the improving role of personnel. You are strongly urged to read it!

7. This conclusion was verified by a group of 17 personnel managers of the previously mentioned multinational company. (See note 2 above.) They were asked their views concerning their *personnel department's objectives,* in general, and their *own personal job objectives.* Both types of objectives were divided into *creative* contributions and *operational* contributions to the organization. Creative contributions dealt with building the organizational system, policy making, setting and changing the rules. Operational contributions dealt with fulfilling one's role in the organizational system and operating according to the rules that had been set.

   The results of the study showed that these personnel managers saw themselves as operating in *departments* that mostly succeed in their operational contributions to the organization (keeping the organizational machine running and operating according to the rules that were set) but mostly failing in their creative contributions. The *personnel managers themselves,* however, experience more personal failures in their operational contributions and more personal successes in their creative contributions.

8. See Harrison Trice and George Ritzer, "The Personnel Manager and His Self-Image," *Personnel Administration,* vol. 53, no. 1 (January–February 1972), pp. 46–50, for an interesting discussion of this dilemma.

9. See Logan M. Cheek, "Cost Effectiveness Comes to the Personnel Function," *Harvard Business Review,* vol. 51, no. 3 (May–June 1973), p. 97, for further details.

10. Fred Foulkes has pointed out that fewer than 150 of the Harvard Business School's 39,000 graduates are in either industrial relations or personnel. (See note 6 above). Many of them feel that the personnel field is "low status" and "bad news." Also, few employers recruit Harvard MBAs for personnel jobs, as too many employers think that if you are interested in personnel work you do not need an MBA.

    Of the people sent to Harvard's Advanced Management Program in recent years, only 37 of the last 1,500 (with six from government, four from the oil industry, and two from a single company) have been from the personnel or industrial relations areas.

11. For example, in a large U.S. financial services company, a relatively young person, inexperienced in personnel work but with a capacity to learn rapidly, was asked to head the function. In the words of a top official of the organization, the person selected "is one of the three guys who might become president of this company, and we wanted to try him out and give him some experience in personnel for two or three years." (See note 6 above).

12. See Harry Levinson, *The Exceptional Executive: A Psychological Conception* (Cambridge, Mass.: Harvard University Press, 1968), pp. 228–229, for more information.
13. Allen R. Janger, *Personnel Administration: Changing Scope and Organization* (New York: National Industrial Conference Board, Studies in Personnel Policies, No. 203, 1966), pp. 14–15.
14. Ibid., p. 21.
15. Bureau of National Affairs, *The Personnel Department* (Washington, D.C.: Personnel Policies Forum, Survey No. 92, November 1970), p. 2.
16. Some specific types of information being developed by higher status personnel administrators are: (*a*) statements of total personnel requirements over a given period; (*b*) assessments of current personnel inventories; (*c*) definitions of critical variances existing between personnel requirements and inventory; (*d*) identification of alternatives for eliminating unneeded personnel and obtaining needed personnel; (*e*) projections of personnel costs; and (*f*) recommendations concerning organizational plans. Robert R. Guthrie, "Personnel's Emerging Role," *Personnel Journal,* vol. 53, no. 9 (September 1974), pp. 657–61 and 666.
17. Lawrence A. Appley, "Management Is Personnel Administration," *Personnel,* vol. 46, no. 2 (March–April 1969), pp. 8–15.
18. The responsibility for performing the personnel function is dependent somewhat on the organizational structure, and, as modern organizations become more complex, the personnel activities cross traditional lines of authority and responsibility in order to coordinate these activities successfully. As the *project approach* is becoming more popular; it is important that future personnel managers take a look at what will happen to the responsibility of the personnel management function in the future. C. Ray Gullett, "Personnel Management in the Project Organization," *Personnel Administration/Public Personnel Review,* vol. 1, no. 3 (November–December 1972), pp. 17–22.
19. A study of 71 organizations provides some empirical insights into this line-staff conflict and indicates a partial answer. The personnel administrators spent approximately 90 percent of their time on activities such as supervising subordinates, planning department activities, and gathering and providing information, with only 10 percent of their time left for exercising control over the personnel actions of other management officials.

    There was general agreement in the perception of the role of top-level personnel administrators, and the perceived conflict between them and line managers was low. There was general agreement that personnel executives should have a stronger role in organizational decision making. Yet the personnel managers' desire was far stronger than the line managers', thus indicating that there may be potential conflict in this area. James A. Belasco and Joseph A. Alutto, "Line-Staff Conflicts: Some Empirical Insights," *Academy of Management Journal,* vol. 12, no. 4 (December 1969) pp. 469–77.

CASES FOR FURTHER STUDY

I-1. The Pepper Bush*

Sherman Kent,† an electrical engineer and a graduate of one of the foremost universities in the Southwest, determined that his future lay in operating a restaurant. This idea evolved by accident over a period of time when Sherman did the cooking for hunting and fishing trips with friends. He used jalapeno pepper liberally to flavor the food and combined it with cheese to form a spread to enhance the flavor of meat.

His hunting and fishing companions suggested that he should market his product. As the discussions became more serious, they agreed to back him financially if he would establish and manage a restaurant specializing in hamburgers with the special recipe jalapeno cheese sauce. Thus, the Pepper Bush was born.

Sherman opened the small restaurant in a suburban community of approximately 15,000 near a large metropolitan area in the spring of 1973. While he was the operating partner, two other partners helped finance the business by securing a small loan from a local bank. He secured a building with a seating capacity of 50 and equipped it to serve the usual line of short-order food services. Though he specialized in hamburgers with the special jalapeno and cheese sauce, he also served the usual line of hamburgers, french fries, beverages, and so forth. His principal competition was franchise food operations such as MacDonald's and Burger King.

By the summer of 1975, business had increased to an expected gross of $125,000 and Sherman was thinking of expanding. Financing could be secured from the bank, and a newer and larger site could be found in the vicinity of the present restaurant.

The personnel policies of the Pepper Bush could be described as highly unstructured. When Sherman opened the restaurant, he hired a cook, three waitresses, and a dishwasher by running ads in the local papers. He did much of the cooking himself and performed all of the management functions. In 1975, his employees consisted of two cooks, five full-time waitresses, two part-time waitresses, and three dishwashers.

One of the cooks, Alvin Marsh, also served as assistant manager. Alvin was

---

* Prepared by William V. Rice and Robert McGlashan, University of Houston at Clear Lake City.

† The names of most organizations and persons mentioned in the cases in this book are fictitious, although the organizations, persons, and situations are real.

39

one of the first employees hired and had been with Sherman throughout the two-and-a-half-year existence of the Pepper Bush. He served as manager in Sherman's absence and for the previous six months had been actively involved with Sherman in hiring new employees. When a vacancy occurred, one of the employees would bring a friend to Sherman to be interviewed, or Sherman would run an ad in the local paper.

The interview was relatively brief, no formal application was required, and the applicant was either hired on the spot or told immediately that he would not be hired. Turnover of employees had been remarkably small. Two of the waitresses had been at the Pepper Bush since it opened. Sherman stated that the low turnover rate was due to the fact that he took a personal interest in each of his employees and took into account individual differences. For example, he did not require any uniform dress. Most of the waitresses wore jeans and a blouse, and the male help could wear their hair as long as they desired. He also allowed a "very flexible schedule of work," with the various classes of employees working out their own substitutions, as long as each category is covered during the appropriate hours.

Sherman had no formal job descriptions and his training consisted of on-the-job training. For example, all waitresses were expected to be able to work the cash register, wait tables, clean the tables, and, if on the last shift, clean up for the night. But, if the waitresses were too busy, the cook might also work the cash register or clean the tables. All employees were expected to do whatever needed doing.

The proposed expansion would complicate Sherman's personnel problems. The "personal touch," the paternalistic attitude which Sherman had taken toward his employees, (the average age of the 10 full-time employees was 21), was a luxury he could afford. But, if he expanded, and he expected to at least double the number of employees within the next six months, would he need a more formalized organizational structure? Sherman and Alvin also discussed the overall personnel problems.

Questions

1. Should Sherman and Alvin continue the present unstructured informal personnel policy if they did not expand?
2. How would the proposed expansion impact on this policy?

I-2. OK! Who's Passing the Buck?*

Executive vice president: "Good morning, gentlemen. As you know, the purpose of this staff meeting is to get on top of some of our *supervision and management* problems. You've all had time to look into the situation insofar as your respective

---

* R. C. Burkholder, "As You Were Saying—OK! Who's Passing the Buck?" *Personnel Journal,* vol. 51, no. 11 (November 1972), pp. 846–47. "Reprinted with permission," *Personnel Journal,* copyright November 1972.

divisions are concerned, so you should be prepared to discuss the problems and recommendations for resolving them. Let it all hang out, as they say, and tell it like it is! Joe?"

Manufacturing: "Well, we're still having problems with *orientation.* Personnel is doing a pretty fair job of orienting new employees to the company, but our new people are not being oriented to the manufacturing division. I think personnel should develop, schedule, and conduct orientation sessions designed specifically to and for manufacturing employees."

Transportation: "I agree with Joe. We need a similar program for transportation personnel."

Treasurer: "Me too."

Budget: "Same here."

Industrial relations: "Why not have personnel assume responsibility for orienting all new employees to all units at all levels of the company organization?"

Engineering: "We'll buy that."

Marketing: "We're not on top of the *employee suggestion and awards program.* Marketing hasn't received an employee suggestion or presented an award since 1965! We think personnel should come up with some meaningful direction and guidance to encourage more use of the program."

Research and development: "It seems to me that personnel isn't fully involved in the area of *disciplinary actions.* We have three potential and two active cases in R&D now and personnel hasn't made a move to step in and take over. We think they should be more aggressive in matters of this kind."

Engineering: "Our *safety and accident prevention* program is a complete flop! Perhaps if personnel prepared a detailed safety plan for each of our divisions . . ."

Planning: "And conducted safety meetings, at least weekly, for all personnel . . ."

Engineering: ". . . we could improve our accident record."

Manufacturing: "I wonder if personnel couldn't do a better job of *employee counseling.* Our employees are continually complaining about the lack of counseling, and our supervisors and foremen simply don't have the time to do it. I believe personnel should assume full responsibility for all employee counseling."

Purchasing: "Something has to be done about *job descriptions!* I'm not exaggerating when I say that at least 80 percent of our employees in purchasing are operating under outdated or inaccurate job descriptions. I'd like to suggest that personnel schedule some time to review, analyze, and update each and every employee's job description as soon as possible."

Treasurer: "Our biggest problem has to do with *performance standards and evaluation.* Personnel hasn't established performance standards or evaluated the performance of our employees since I don't know when. Don't you think they should provide this service at least once a year?"

Public relations: "I think one of our major problems lies in the area of *directing and coordinating* our efforts and activities. The old left hand and right hand, you know. We'd like to see personnel look into the situation—across the board—and come up with some proposals for our people to work with."

Budget: "I agree with PR, but our people simply don't or won't *communicate*—internally *or* externally—and I think personnel should do something about it."

Transportation: "How do you fellows feel about *delegation?* Some of our people in transportation delegate too much; others don't delegate at all. I'd like to make a recommendation that personnel see to it that our employees delegate properly and effectively."

Legal: "I don't know if this is a matter of recruitment, orientation, or training, but I think personnel will have to do something about the fact that too many of our people lack the necessary education, background, experience, or inclination to make good and valid decisions. *Decision making* is . . ."

Marketing: "Speaking of *training,* our people are being overtrained. Train, train, train! I'm always approving the attendance of marketing personnel at some kind of training session or other! Why can't personnel establish quotas . . . or something?"

Planning: "Our people aren't getting enough training, and I think employee morale, along with work performance, is suffering as a result. We think personnel should see to it that planning people are included in more in-and out-company training sessions."

Industrial relations: "We're getting plenty of training, but it's not always the right kind . . . or the wrong people got it . . . or it wasn't needed in the first place . . . or . . ."

Engineering: "I agree with industrial relations."

Purchasing: "What did he say?"

Research and Development: "I don't know, but doesn't personnel have the responsibility for determining who needs what training and how, when, and where to get it?"

Manufacturing: "I'd like to suggest that personnel develop a company program which will provide all employees with the scientific, technical, administrative, and clerical training they need—no more, no less."

Executive vice president: "You getting all this, Harvey?"

Personnel: "Yes sir. I'll put my staff on it first thing in the morning."

Questions

1. What does the case show about the overexpectations other managers sometimes have of the personnel officer and staff?
2. If you were the personnel officer, how would you begin ("first thing in the morning") to implement the suggestions made?
3. What order of priorities would you set up?
4. What assistance would you request from the line managers?

part two

The context of personnel administration

3. The historical context
4. The institutional context
5. The sociocultural context
6. Trends in U.S. and other labor forces

Cases:
    II–1. Average Company, Inc.
    II–2. Division of Labor
    II–3. The New Work Force

Introduction

When he was president of Bell & Howell, Senator Charles Percy said, "The principal function of personnel management is to anticipate change." That conclusion is especially appropriate now, for changes are occurring very rapidly in the environment in which the personnel function is performed. If you are to be successful as a personnel executive, you must anticipate and be prepared to cope with those changes.

Personnel executives exert considerable influence over the behavior of the members of an organization. In order to do this most effectively, they must be able to *predict* human behavior; this necessitates an *understanding* of the *cause-effect relationships between environment and behavior.* Therefore, an understanding of changes in environmental factors affecting behavior is essential for effective personnel administration. This understanding should be increased if the following hypotheses are valid:

1. *The total environment has a direct influence upon job performance, but the effect may be* either *positive* or *negative.*
2. *The work environment is influenced by the combined effects of the physical, technological, political, economic, cultural, social, and spiritual surroundings.*

FIGURE II-1
The environmental context of personnel

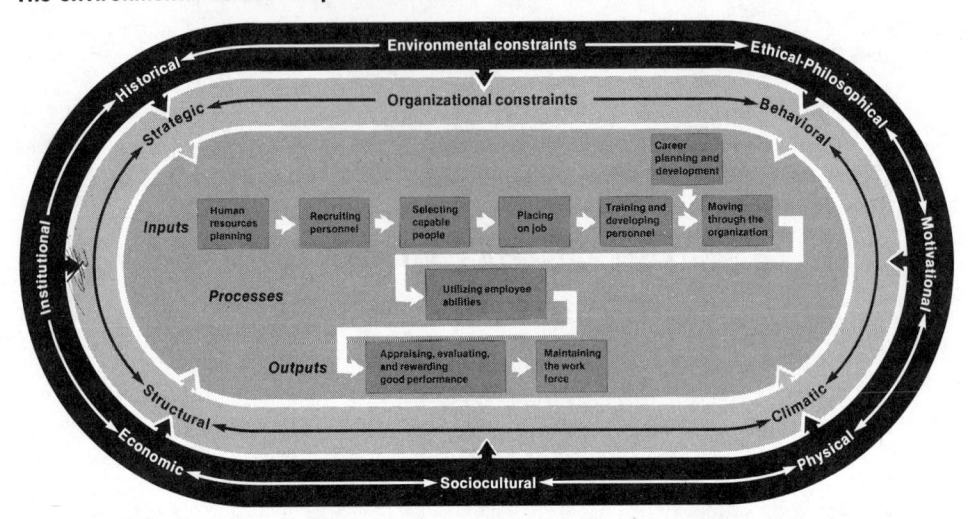

3. *Today's economic environment is vastly different from yesterday's; that into which you will enter as managers will be increasingly more different and difficult; and that environment is now being shaped and its parameters established by the events you now see occurring.*

It is important to study the personnel function in historical perspective in order to understand and appreciate the present and, hopefully, to anticipate the future. This is done in Chapter 3.

The results of increasing government involvement in personnel administration, including the effects of industrial relations, are explored in Chapter 4.

In order to gain a true perspective of the part played by the total environment on the performance of the personnel function, it is essential to understand and appreciate the importance and the implications of the sociocultural environment and its significance to the management of people. This is presented in Chapter 5.

Studying the environment also includes studying trends in the overall labor market. Some of these changes are explored and analyzed in detail in Chapter 6.

Chapter 3

The historical context

Early happenings
  Slavery
  Serfdom
  The guild system
  The "Industrial Revolution"

Personnel administration in the American colonies
  Effects on personnel administration
  Relevance to you

The Civil War and its aftermath
  Effects on personnel administration
  Relevance to you

World War I and its aftermath
  Effects on personnel administration
  Relevance to you

The "Roaring Twenties"
  Effects on personnel administration
  Relevance to you

The "Great Depression" and its aftermath
  Effects on personnel administration
  Relevance to you

World War II and its aftermath
  Effects on personnel administration
  Relevance to you

The "Fabulous Fifties"
  Effects on personnel administration
  Relevance to you

The period of activism
  Movements during the period
  Relevance to you

The growing economic independence of employees
  New type employees
  Effects upon manager's use of authority and financial incentives

Implications and applications for personnel executives

3

The historical context

The dogmas of the quiet past are inadequate to the stormy present.
ABRAHAM LINCOLN

Those who cannot remember the past are condemned to repeat it.
SANTAYANA

On a pedestal in front of the U.S. Supreme Court is a quotation from Shakespeare which says, "What is past is prologue." This statement emphasizes the truth that the future performance of the personnel function can be made more effective by studying its historical context. A review of the evolutionary background of the present personnel philosophies, principles, policies, and practices will help personnel administrators understand why they have developed as they have. And, an understanding of what happened in the past should enable them to recognize evolving patterns in personnel administration—which could in turn assist them to avoid repeating past mistakes.

EARLY HAPPENINGS

Although the field of personnel administration as a discipline of study is relatively young, the precepts upon which its current theory is based had their origins deep in history, for there is relatively little that is new. (1) For example, the minimum wage rate and incentive wage plans were included in the Babylonian Code of Hammurabi around 1800 B.C. The Chinese, as early as 1650 B.C., had originated the principle of division of labor (specialization), and they understood labor turnover even in 400 B.C. The span of management and related concepts of organization were well understood by Moses around 1250 B.C. and the Chaldeans had incentive wage plans around 400 B.C. Ancient men with their stone axes, adzes, and other flint tools may not have understood the principle of transfer of skill from humans to the machine, but they were, nevertheless, applying the principle, and this separated them from lower creatures.

While personnel administration as we now know it did not exist prior to the "Industrial Revolution," there were several distinct types of relationships involving employers and their subordinates during the previous period. These relationships are colloquially designated as "slavery," "serfdom," and the "guild system."

Slavery

Slavery, as an economic institution and an organized system of employment, proved ineffective and gradually declined. As slaves were primarily stimulated by a desire to avoid punishment rather than a wish to achieve, they had little interest or initiative in their work. Also, as slaves began to perform an increasing proportion of the manual and clerical activities, work itself came to be considered repugnant and degrading, and free men were reluctant to work—and their civilizations declined.

Serfdom

The serfs' income largely depended upon their initiative, energy, and ambition, thus providing some positive incentive which increased the serfs' productivity and reduced the need for supervision. With the emergence of manufacturing and commercial industries as dominant economic forces, serfdom declined in importance and had largely disappeared before the end of the Middle Ages. (2)

The guild system

The development of crude manufacturing brought laborers from their homes, where they were self-sufficient, to cities. This movement led to the guild system. Within the guild itself there were clear-cut differences between the master craftsmen, the journeymen, and the apprentices. The *masters* were the owners of the shops and employed the traveling *journeymen,* who in turn were applying their learning in order to become more skilled. The *apprentices* were young learners who usually worked for their board, lodging, and a small allowance. During the initial stages of the system, all three classes of workers were a closely knit social group, because their success depended upon their working together. *This was the early beginnings of personnel management, as the system involved selecting, training, developing, rewarding, and maintaining workers.* Wage and salary administration and collective bargaining over wages and working conditions were in evidence under this system.

The "Industrial Revolution"

Although the forces of economic and social change operate with relentless persistence, the changes are often so slow that they are not perceived by us until they are made obvious by some crisis. Inevitably the old economic, social, and political systems yielded to the new. So, there emerged the events, organizations, institutions, energy supply, and inventions that we call the "Industrial Revolution."

The changes were precipitated in manufacturing by a new economic doctrine and by the invention and utilization of new tools, processes, and machines. (3) The economic doctrine was based upon the French concept of *laissez-faire, laissez-passer,* (4) which was the forerunner of the free enterprise system. Adam Smith, in trying to explain the effects of the system, said there were natural laws, such as the law of supply and demand, which should regulate economic relationships to the benefit of society. (5)

There was a great price to pay for the many benefits received. Workers were crowded into a work environment that consisted of great concentrations of people among many machines in small, dingy, dirty factories. (6) Working and living conditions were unsanitary and fostered the spread of disease. Many psychological problems resulted from excessively long working hours, monotony, fatigue, noise, strain, and the ever-present danger of accidents.

The gap between the owners and the employees widened, with the result that it was impractical to maintain the personal relationship that had existed before. Mechanization made the work so simple that it became practical to employ women and children, and they began to replace men. Many social and economic injustices were perpetrated in the name of economic freedom.

The events of this period had several effects which are still relevant to a study of personnel administration, including: (*a*) the place of work has changed from the home to a central work area; (*b*) the method of production changed from manual to machine operations, because of the transfer of skills from the workers to the machines; (*c*) the migration from rural areas to urban areas started, with the consequent concentration of industry in selected places; and (*d*) the separation of owners and managers from close relationships with their employees began.

PERSONNEL ADMINISTRATION IN THE AMERICAN COLONIES

Many of the forces of early colonial life have exerted an important influence upon the modern United States. This generalization applies not only to the economic aspects of life, but also to the cultural, social, religious, and political areas. It can be said that the most dominant force shaping the work environment at that time was the cultural heritage of the colonists, (7) and this force has continued to have a strong influence on the American culture.

In essence, the economic history of the United States has been an account of technological progress. The "Industrial Revolution" did not occur in the American colonies at the same time it did in Europe; at that time, the colonies were in a stage of agricultural development and primitive industrialism.

Effects on personnel administration

As land was plentiful and was available to anyone with the initiative and energy to clear and use it, economic growth was stimulated. Capital was scarce, but *labor was the scarcest of the productive factors.* As is true in such economic situations, the scarcest factor of production carried the highest economic price, and labor was considered more valuable than either land or capital. The emerging industrialism which replaced agriculture as the dominant occupation demanded increasing quantities of labor, including wage earners, indentured workers, and slaves.

Industrial development was slow in the colonies, but beginning with the Revolutionary War—and especially after the War of 1812—there was an increasing emphasis upon industrial development rather than agriculture. As capital began to accumulate and as the organization for development of the industrial system grew, there was an increased need for labor. This need was met by an expanding population, which resulted from a high birthrate and from increased immigration.

This large increase in the labor supply had an adverse effect upon the economic and social system. (8) With the population increase came problems such as increased pauperism and unemployment. Slums developed; and real wages and the standard of living of the workers were steadily pushed downward. In fact, the two decades preceding the Civil War constitute one of the most discouraging periods that the American wage earner has ever experienced.

Relevance to you

The central lesson of the early colonial period was centered around a recognition of the importance of human resources. With labor being the scarcest of the economic factors of production, workers were in a preeminent position which they have largely retained until this time in the United States. The owners emphasized investment in land and capital in order to enhance and conserve the output of labor.

THE CIVIL WAR AND ITS AFTERMATH

From 1861 to 1865, many changes occurred that have unalterably affected our lives, both private and working. First, the war established the fact that this country would have a strong, centralized government; business firms and labor organizations would be correspondingly large and powerful.

Effects on personnel administration

The period between the Civil War and World War I saw a great increase in all aspects of the American economy. There was a rapid expansion to the West, with a consequent growth in population, transportation, and new industries such as mining, ranching, and communications. Also, commercial and industrial activities, which eventually made this country the world's greatest industrial power, began to emerge.

The corporate form of organization began to displace the proprietor and/or partnership type of ownership. This led to a further widening of the gap between the workers and owners, with a consequent increase in the importance of the personnel function. However, because business consolidation and concentration led to such domination of the economic environment, Congress passed the Sherman Antitrust Act in 1890 to limit the monopolistic power of management. It is still the basic law regulating management activities.

Although labor organizations had been active since the beginning of the new republic, they did not have a successful growth until much later. The story of unionism during the period was a story of short-lived associations of craftsmen with which employers dealt grudgingly or not at all.

The Knights of Labor was organized in 1869, but it did not long survive. In 1881, the American Federation of Labor (AFL) was organized; in 1886, it was reorganized and was the predominant labor organization until 1955, when it merged with the Congress of Industrial Organizations (CIO). By 1913, labor had achieved such a position of prominence that it was granted its own separate place in the President's cabinet, the Labor Department. The following year, the Clayton Act provided labor unions with exemption from prosecution as conspiracies in restraint of trade, although the courts did not always interpret it that way. (9)

During this time, another element entered the business arena. Frederick W. Taylor began conducting experiments which culminated in his principles of "scientific management." (10) These principles included determining the science of each job, selecting the right man, training him to perform the job in a scientific manner, compensating him with a financial incentive, and separating the managerial from the nonmanagerial functions. These are still the precepts upon which the effective utilization of human resources is based.

Relevance to you

There were two primary consequences of this period which are relevant to the study of personnel management. They were: (*a*) industrial production replaced agriculture as the predominant employer of people, and we became an industrial nation; and (*b*) "big" organizations replaced "small" ones, resulting in a strong central government, in the corporate form of business organization, and in strong national labor unions.

WORLD WAR I AND ITS AFTERMATH

As the social, political, and economic systems of the world have become more complex, they have also become more interdependent, so that disruptions in any of these systems in any major country is felt by all. Consequently, when the peace and tranquility of Europe came to a crashing halt in August 1914 with the commencement of World War I, the repercussions were felt in this country as well as in others.

Effects on personnel administration

The long-run consequences of the war environment upon the personnel management function cannot be overemphasized. This was truly *the beginning of modern personnel administration.* Prior to that time, the changes had been evolutionary and time was permitted to adapt and adjust to them, but the effects of war-related activities were drastic, as well as immediate.

The first significant effect of the war was an increase in the demand for labor which far exceeded the available supply. The resulting shortage was accentuated by a decline in the flow of immigrants, the return of thousands of Europeans to their homelands to serve in their armies, and the entry of over 4 million persons into the military. This labor shortage greatly strengthened the position of the workers and the unions that represented them. Part of the increased demand was met by the million or more women who at that time entered the industrial labor force. (11)

Labor's improved position was reflected in a doubling of union membership from 1914 to 1920, or from 7 percent to 12 percent of the labor force. Another indication of the union's growing acceptance and importance was the appointment of labor leaders to most of the boards and committees being established to pursue the war effort.

The government insisted that *personnel departments* be installed in plants manufacturing war supplies. (12) This requirement gave a great boost to improving the entire personnel management discipline. But probably the greatest influence upon the employment function was the establishment of the Committee on Classification of Personnel in the U.S. Army. It operated upon the basic assumption that human resources are not solely a function of numbers, but also of appropriate skills. Therefore, personnel specifications were established, based upon an analysis and definition of duties and responsibilities and setting physical, intellectual, educational, and technical requirements; and then testing, interviewing, and rating systems were set up for proper selection.

Labor turnover and mobility became significant factors. For the first time, large numbers of employees were uprooted from their jobs and homes and shown new jobs and living opportunities. For many of them, it was their first time to enjoy the freedom of choosing where they would work—and most of them enjoyed it. Labor stability has never been the same since! Later the popularity of the automobile, which was made possible by Henry Ford's use of the assembly-line technique and interchangeable parts, added to this mobility.

Finally, the abnormal labor demand-supply relationship enhanced the relative position of individual employees in their relationship to management and organizations. The basis of the later "human relations" movement was set, for both management and labor had begun to realize that individual workers were really important.

Relevance to you

Some of the specific consequences which are still influencing the performance of the personnel function were: (*a*) the increased role of labor—especially unions—in government activities; (*b*) a mobility of labor, including the migration from rural to urban areas (Except for the reverse migration during the

1930s, this movement has continued until today.); (c) the movement of females into the work force; (d) a blending of the lessons of the "Industrial Revolution" imported from Europe with the uniquely American "scientific management" movement to set the foundation for the tremendous productive capacity of World War II; and (e) a changing life-style, especially the "romance" between the people and the automobile!

THE "ROARING TWENTIES"

Although there was a short-lived recession in 1920 and 1921, the decade following the war was considered to be a period of "perpetual prosperity." Total production increased over twice as fast as the population, productivity per employee increased by the same amount, prices remained relatively stable, the cost of production declined, and "real wages" increased.

Effects upon personnel administration

As indicated previously, the employee-employer relationship had already begun to improve as a result of the critical labor shortage resulting from the war and the extensive labor problems during and following the conflict. Employers, adopting a more enlightened and constructive program which has been called "welfare capitalism," emphasized the *mutual goals* of labor and management, with corresponding *mutual responsibilities* for achieving them. Employee-management cooperation was used for the purposes of increasing production, achieving efficiency, eliminating waste, adjusting grievances, and improving the material and social well-being of workers. While new personnel policies and the new approach to human administration were adopted by the more enlightened employers, it should not be assumed that all the managers followed this approach. Many of them remained the "hard-nosed manager."

Relevance to you

The relevance of this period to future personnel administrators can really be summarized by the term "industrial democracy." Specifically it involved: (a) a decline in strong, dynamic, personal business leadership and an emphasis upon "group leadership"; (b) the movement toward worker representation, resulting in the union movement of the 1930s and the collective bargaining activities of employee associations in the 1960s; and (c) the beginning of the "human relations movement."

THE "GREAT DEPRESSION" AND ITS AFTERMATH

The period of "perpetual prosperity" ended on October 29, 1929, when stock prices abruptly declined approximately 40 points to usher in the "Great Depression." (13) Although the Hoover administration did all it could to stem the tide, the inexorable economic forces from within—but more especially those from outside—the country were too great and too far advanced not to run their course.

Effects on personnel administration

In 1933, a new administration headed by Franklin D. Roosevelt came to power and immediately began to pass laws affecting the personnel management function. For example, the *National Labor Relations Act* (1935) made collective bargaining compulsory on the part of the employer (and also the individual employee), doomed the so-called company unions, and significantly increased union membership. The *Social Security Act* (1935) provided for unemployment insurance, "old-age pensions," and disability and death benefits. The *Fair Labor Standards Act* of 1938 (Wages and Hours Law) regulated the minimum wage and the maximum hours for workers of firms engaged in interstate commerce.

However, probably the most significant event of the period was the Supreme Court's decision in *National Labor Relations Board* v. *Jones and Laughlin Steel Corporation* (1937) that the National Labor Relations Act was constitutional. Thus, manufacturing within a state was included in the "interstate commerce clause" of the Constitution. With this new interpretation, Congress was in a position to become even more involved in personnel management activities.

In spite of the laws, union activities, and other efforts, unemployment was still a problem. Although the number of unemployed persons declined from 13 million (25 percent of the total labor force) in 1933, to 9 million (17 percent of the labor force) in 1939, the unemployment problem was not solved until World War II started in Europe.

Relevance to you

Of all the historical periods, this one probably had the greatest influence on the performance of the personnel function. Some of the specific influences were: (*a*) a craving for personal and job security, which in turn led to a decline in individualism and an acceptance of collective action; (*b*) a shift from unilateral personnel management, with its authoritarian methods, to a bilateral relationship with management speaking for business and the unions speaking for the workers—with the government serving as the arbiter; (*c*) emphasis on employee's "right" to jobs versus the owner's right to property; and (*d*) an abnormally low birthrate, which led to the shortage of the supply of workers in the 1950s and 1960s, with the consequent emphasis upon newer management philosophies and styles.

WORLD WAR II AND ITS AFTERMATH

During World War II, the position of employees was again strengthened by the scarcity of capable workers to supply the war production needs. The siphoning off of 15 million men and women, many already employed by industry, into the armed forces left a labor shortage which was most difficult to fill. Complicating this problem was the fact that many of the jobs associated with the war effort were in highly technical fields, such as optics, electronics, and aeronautics.

Effects on personnel administration

To accomplish the task of filling these jobs—in many instances with workers entering industry for the first time—and motivating employees to greater productivity, several old and new disciplines—including, among others, industrial psychology, industrial sociology, cultural anthropology, and operations research—were extensively used. These efforts to study and channel human behavior toward increased productivity and greater employee satisfaction have greatly enhanced the knowledge of, and practice of, personnel management.

"Fringe benefits." Although wages and prices were legally controlled, the measures were not entirely successful. While the attempt to "freeze" wages at the prevailing levels for each skill was relatively successful, the law of supply and demand was still at work. One of the methods used to avoid the effects of this law—and thus attract badly needed employees—was to increase the use of *fringe benefits.* (14) As employers could not use variable wage rates as a method of attracting workers, they offered such inducements as paid meals, transportation, clothing, housing, insurance premiums, retirement programs, and so forth; and paid time off from work for various reasons, sick leave, holidays, and vacations.

Union security. Another major consequence of the war was the emphasis upon *union security.* The National War Labor Board interpreted Section 7(a) of the *Wagner Act* (which gave the workers the *right* to engage in union activities) to mean that such activities were *mandatory* on the part of all employees. (15)

Technological advances. Two technological developments of the period have had a great effect upon the personnel function. First, there was the successful development of the *electronic computer,* which aided us in acquiring and using knowledge. Not only did the computer change the way of doing work, but it also changed organizational structures, the type of employees needed, and the method of attracting employees. The second factor, *nuclear energy,* made it feasible to obtain energy from matter itself and freed us from relying solely upon fossil fuels as our primary source of energy.

Governmental actions. Among the significant governmental actions which had a lasting effect upon personnel administration was the creation of the Personnel Procedures Section in the War Department, the National War Labor Board to handle labor disputes, the Psychological Research Unit in the Air Corps, and the Training Within Industry (TWI) program in the War Manpower Commission.

Prior experience with major wars showed that after the armistice the decline in demand for labor from curtailed war activities and the increased supply of labor caused by returning military personnel resulted in lower employment and income. In order to minimize the effects of this interaction after World War II, Congress passed the *Servicemen's Readjustment Act of 1944*, which provided free training and educational opportunities, as well as low-interest loans for houses and business properties. This increase in the *quantity and quality* of knowledge made it possible for us to develop and expand the aerospace industry following the launching of "Sputnik I" in 1957.

The *Employment Act of 1946* made it the duty of the federal government to do all in its power to achieve maximum production, employment, and purchasing power. It redirected the emphasis from productivity to "full employment," which became the primary objective of economic policy. (16) Some of the abuses of the system today can be traced to this act.

Because of the unparalleled expansion of industry and jobs, coupled with relatively effective wage and price controls during World War II, and as a consequence of the emphasis on savings during the period, there was a ready fund of over $136 billions which provided the pent-up "effective demand" which led to the relatively uninterrupted sustained economic boom lasting until 1957. (17)

The *Marshall Plan,* which helped Europe rebuild itself, while expanding markets for our products and technology, also led to an emphasis upon international management and increased the demand for employees.

Sociocultural changes. Another significant development was the increased education of females between 1940 and 1950. This set the stage for the increasing economic independence of this group, plus the increasing participation rate in the work force.

No discussion of this period would be complete without a discussion of the increased birthrate during World War II and the "baby boom" beginning in 1946. (18) At about the same time, Dr. Spock was writing his "baby book" which emphasized the importance of giving children what they want so that they will not feel rejected. It is felt that the large number of unplanned children—plus the changed parental philosophies—and the relative affluence and sense of euphoria of the parents molded the attitudes of the young people which resulted in the "idealism" and "militancy" culminating in the events of the late 1960s. This, in turn, led to the "new generation" of workers in today's economic arena. (19)

New industries. In turn, these factors led to entirely new industries or the expansion of old ones. Residential construction moved from that of single units to mass production, as exhibited by Levitt in his "Levitt Towns." Television began to supplant movies and radio as a means of entertainment—and a source of employment. Air conditioning, synthetic fibers, frozen food and drinks, prepackaged foods, "miracle drugs," miniaturization, electronics, and other industries increased the demand for—and the requirements of—employees with higher-level skills and knowledge.

Relevance to you

The relevant aspects of this period to a future personnel manager are numerous and complex. Some of the more important consequences were: (*a*) new technology and education have caused—and resulted from—new industries requiring new and higher-level occupations; (*b*) emphasis upon "full employment," with the government increasingly being the "employer of last resort"; (*c*) union security, resulting in many employees being coerced into joining unions; and (*d*) emphasis upon employee benefits.

THE FABULOUS FIFTIES

After the "Korean Conflict," which in reality was an extension of World War II, there began a quiet period of "peace and prosperity" which was unparalleled in recent history.

Effects on personnel administration

Some of the factors leading to growth during this period were the interstate highway system, which led to the tremendous production of automobiles, and the leisure industry; new construction techniques which led to an expansion of housing, especially apartments; the "great American dream," which said that if one obtained an education, especially a college degree, one's future was assured; the aerospace industry, following Sputnik I, which led to the outflow of resources for expansion of the scientific and technical knowledge and the introduction of whole new industries; education, especially of blacks; and the declining birthrate, beginning in 1957.

Relevance to you

While it is difficult to isolate the influences of this period on personnel, two consequences do stand out. First, there was the shift from industrial production to service industries. Second, there was the generation of "unwarranted expectations" on the part of young people, blacks, and females, and their belief that utopia had arrived! This led to the shock, disillusionment, agitation, upheavals, and convulsions of the 1960s and early 1970s.

THE PERIOD OF ACTIVISM

The period from 1961 to the present can largely be characterized as one of "activism." There were several streams of activity, or "movements," running through this period.

Movements during the period

Equal employment opportunities. The first movement was the "civil rights" theme, or equal employment opportunities for minorities and poverty groups. While the movement began in 1954 with a mandate for equality in education and progressed in 1955–56 to demands for equality in public accommodations, this study is primarily interested in efforts to achieve equal economic opportunities. These activities—starting with Executive Order 10925 in 1961—have involved three stages. First, attempts were made to increase the employment of minorities. The second stage involved attempts to improve employability through increased education, training, and development. Providing upward mobility through promotions, transfers, and upgrading, as well as cross-industrial mobility, is now occurring in the third stage.

The "Women's Liberation" movement, which began with Title VII of the Civil Rights Act of 1964, has greatly enhanced the position of females in all aspects of economic activity, especially in hiring, training, and promotion to managerial positions.

Later, affirmative action programs were also required for older and handicapped workers and for veterans.

Unionization of public, professional, and farm personnel. A second movement was the emphasis upon unionizing government, professional, and farm employees. This trend began with the issuance of Executive Order 10988 in 1962. It was followed by executive orders and state and federal legislation leading to this fastest growing area of union activities.

Technological development. The "race to the moon," started by Kennedy in 1961 and achieved under Nixon in 1969, greatly expanded employment opportunities, especially in the higher-level jobs. It also spun off whole new industries resulting from the space technology.

Help for poverty groups. The "war on poverty," begun by Johnson in 1965, has resulted in the ability of many individuals and families to be able to survive without being included in the work force. This in turn enhanced employment in jobs related to public and private welfare activities, as well as resulting in "effective demand" by individuals in this group for goods and services. This then increased the demand for other workers.

Youth movement. The "teenage culture" developed during this time. The "younger generation" placed emphasis upon: (*a*) the "rights" and "privileges" of the group; (*b*) the purchasing power of the group, which opened up mass markets for new products and services; and (*c*) the rebellion against the "older generation, (20) the "establishment," and "prevalent life-styles. (21)

Social responsibility. Finally, the growth of "advocacy groups" in the areas of ecology, safety, consumerism, and employment of minority groups has vitally affected the performance of the personnel function, for it has led to the emphasis upon "social responsibility" by private business.

Relevance to you

The relevance of recent changes for the performance of the personnel function were admirably explained in a recent article. (22) Our old institutions based upon individualism, sanctity of property rights, competition, limited government interference, and scientific specialization and fragmentation are becoming "unmoored." Newer institutional forms are taking their place, based upon the newer premises that:

1. Individual fulfillment occurs through participation in an organic social process;
2. Rights of membership in organizations are overshadowing property rights;
3. The need to satisfy consumer desires is replacing competition as a means for controlling the uses of property;
4. The role of government is inevitably expanding; and
5. If we are to experience reality, we must perceive of entire systems, not just parts.

THE GROWING ECONOMIC INDEPENDENCE OF EMPLOYEES

Anyone reviewing the history of personnel administration should conclude that the status of workers and the roles and relationships in which they have been involved have undergone, and continue to undergo, great change. In essence, employees have risen from a position of servitude to one of status; and, in the developed countries, they have risen from a position of status to one of virtual economic freedom—with great social, economic, and political power.

Management can no longer assume that present or potential employees are completely dependent upon a given employer—or even *any* employer—for survival. While they may depend upon the organization for satisfying certain needs, management is also dependent upon them for achieving organizational goals. (It is assumed that the individuals will also achieve their own goals in the process.) In current cultural, economic, legal, and political environments, new assumptions are having to be made concerning the basic nature, beliefs, and motivation of employees.

New type employees

In order to make this distinction clearer, the different types of workers should be discussed. For lack of a better term, the term "older employees" is used to refer to those accepting the older concepts of organizational theory such as hierarchical structure; working for future rewards—as well as for current ones; belief in hard work, commitment, thrift, and frugality, as a way of life; and the use of efficiency and effectiveness as management criteria. (23)

Characteristics of newer employees. The term "newer employees" is used to refer to those who believe in working but who do not center their whole life-style around the work environment. Many of these individuals have little interest in belonging to a formal organization but prefer to relate to an individual, even if it is their supervisor, rather than to the organization as a whole. If not satisfied with their present working conditions, they tend to quit and move elsewhere in hopes of finding what they are seeking. In general, the newer workers feel there is really no compelling need to work, but they do it to satisfy their higher needs for creativity, achievement, prestige, self-expression, and "to do their own thing." (24) This group wants impartiality but not impersonality, and *they want rewards now rather than working for years toward a distant goal.*

Different motivators. Another aspect of the growing independence of employees is the changing concept of the *economic man,* which assumes that people behave in a rational, analytical manner and respond to economic factors such as wages, costs, prices, and profits. Although economic incentives were at one time considered to be the prime motivators, it is now realized that factors such as personal dignity, security, recognition, creative and challenging work, responsibility, achievement, and participation are also important motivators. Therefore, the problem is *not* a question of whether employees desire the economic benefits *or* the nonmonetary benefits, but that they demand both in order to accommodate an otherwise unpleasant existence in the economic and/or organizational environments.

Importance of the individual. Behavior in a social and/or economic system must ultimately be evaluated in relation to the behavior of its individual members. Choices in our productive system tend to be the choices of individuals, which place them in a preferential position as the most important unit in our economic systems. Individuals are generally free to make their own decisions concerning their welfare and productivity. Whether that productivity be high or low—depending upon their willingness or reluctance to perform—the right to make the decisions are their own.

Because of the economic rights gained by employees, they have achieved many of the same prerogatives that owners, professionals, and managers had in earlier times—such as retirement benefits, insurance programs, and time off with pay.

Effects upon manager's use of authority and financial incentives

It can be inferred from the above analysis that workers are currently in a preeminent position and are not necessarily dependent upon one employer for their material survival. In fact, with the various social programs available, they are no longer even dependent upon a job for survival. It follows that management must rely more on persuasion and positive motivation and less on economic coercion.

Empirical evidence on *labor turnover* tends to confirm this relationship. For example, during the depressed economic period from 1957 through 1964, the *layoff rate* in the U.S. was consistently higher than the *quit rate,* as employees tended not to leave their jobs voluntarily. However, beginning in 1965—when the effects of the new social legislation began to be felt and the Vietnam War increased the demand for labor—and going through 1969, the *quit rate* was considerably higher than the *layoff rate.* (25)

As the changes in our economics have lessened our dependency upon work

FIGURE 3–1
Relationship between employees' economic independence and management's use of authority and financial incentives

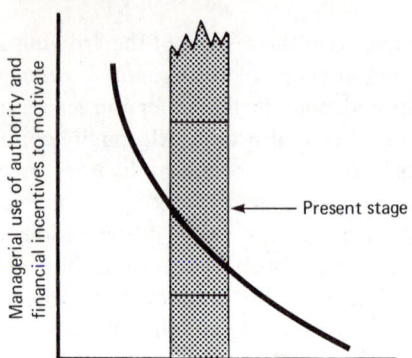

Managerial use of authority and financial incentives to motivate (y-axis)

← Present stage

Employee's economic independency (x-axis)

as a means of survival and as employees have tended to become more economically independent, management's exercise of traditional authority and financial rewards to motivate them has declined, and new methods have become necessary. Figure 3–1 illustrates this relationship, particularly as it pertains to the present. It can be seen that as the employees' economic independency increases, the managerial use of authority decreases. It is estimated that we in the United States are presently in the stage shown.

To the extent that this new status induces the workers to be more productive —and thereby benefit themselves, their employers, and their nations—it is desirable. If, instead, workers use their new independence to avoid increasing their productivity, then the upgrading of their place has been in vain.

IMPLICATIONS AND APPLICATIONS FOR PERSONNEL EXECUTIVES

The personnel function is performed in organized settings in the present time. However, the performance of that function is affected by the historical context formed by the backgrounds of those concerned. If personnel managers understand the historical background of the economy in which they operate, they should be able to perform the function more effectively and efficiently.

With increased knowledge of their own and their subordinates' cultural heritage, personnel managers should have a better understanding of the overall environment affecting their attitudes, decisions, and actions. Also, employee actions and reactions are better understood and are, therefore, more predictable when viewed in historical perspective. With an increase in their knowledge, understanding, and ability to predict the behavior of personnel, personnel administrators should be better able to influence and control that behavior. (This will be discussed further in the next chapter.)

These changes, which tend to set the stage upon which management performs the personnel function, come into focus in the environments in which personnel executives operate. These environments will be discussed in the following chapters.

These influences—as well as the historical one—force personnel managers to ask a crucial question, namely, "With so many radical changes taking place each year, and, as the rate of change will accelerate, how will organizations survive in the decade ahead?" The only feasible answer is to attract and motivate people who are as flexible as the events of the times and who are not locked into a particular discipline or a set way of thinking about a problem. What is needed are employees—managerial and nonmanagerial—who look at change as a creative, thought-provoking, dynamic way of life.

DISCUSSION QUESTIONS

1. Just how important is a knowledge of the historical context in studying a subject of this nature? Explain your answer.
2. What effects of the occurrences from 1929–41 do you see in your present environment? Explain.
3. What effects of World War II do you see in personnel management practices of today? Explain.
4. What are some of the social, economic, and political changes you see occurring in the next decade?
5. Do you agree with the statement that "it is no longer assumed that 'profit maximization' is the primary goal of a manager"? Explain.
6. Take any *one* of the movements during the "period of activism" and explain what has happened to the movement since 1975.
7. Do you agree that our *old* institutions have become "unmoored"? Explain.
8. Are employees as economically independent as indicated? Explain.

REFERENCES AND SUGGESTIONS FOR FURTHER STUDY

1. This presentation is based upon the African-European-American stream of history and is based upon the Judeo-Christian philosophy and religious beliefs. For an excellent discussion of the development of the divergent trends in the course of history that resulted in the Asian and European cultures and societies, see James T. Shotwell, *The Long Way to Freedom* (New York: Bobbs-Merrill Co., Inc., 1960), pp. 43–55.
2. However, as late as 1861, 20 million serfs were still found in Russia. See W. Bowden, M. Karpovich, and A. P. Usher, *An Economic History of Europe since 1750.* (New York: American Book Co., 1937), p. 600, for a fascinating study of this subject.
3. Although the inventions that are usually attributed to this period were associated with the cotton and woolen industries, there were numerous other ones in diverse fields of endeavor. Ibid., pp. 110–26.

4. Alfred Marshall, *Principles of Economics,* 8th ed. (New York: Macmillan Co., 1948), p. 757. The term meant that a person should be permitted to make what he wanted to and to go where he pleased.
5. Adam Smith, *An Inquiry into the Nature and Causes of the Wealth of Nations,* 1776.
6. Many of these "factories" were deserted monastaries or similar buildings.
7. It is recognized that the "American culture" is based upon the "melting pot" concept and is a blending of heterogenous cultures from every part of the known world. However, the early mainstream of this cultural heritage can be traced back to Anglo-Saxon England. In turn, the English heritage can be traced back to the "Hallstatt culture," which developed in Austria around 800 B.C. and then "spread northward to the British Isles." See A. L. Kroeber, *Anthropology,* rev. ed. (New York: Harcourt, Brace & World, Inc., 1948), p. 731. According to Dr. William Haag, professor of anthropology, in a lecture at Louisiana State University, December 17, 1963, the main differentiating element of this culture was the "fealty to the clan, or tribe, rather than the hero worship that was characteristic of the Mediterranean cultures." This trait led to the concept of the "strong man," or the superindividualistic leader which has been characteristic of the countries of the Mediterranean area. During the last century the nature of the culture has changed greatly. Now the Mediterranean, African, and Oriental cultures have become dominant factors in determining the economic, political, and social environment.
8. "Separated from the native Americans by culture, language, and religion, immigrants tended to form homogeneous communities within the cities, close to the factories." Eugene V. Schneider, *Industrial Sociology* (New York: McGraw-Hill Book Co., 1957), p. 63.
9. The rationale for the change was the concept that a person's labor was a human right, not a commodity. It is interesting to note that this concept is diametrically opposed to that of Karl Marx, who emphasized that the value of a product was the value of the labor embodied in it, and, therefore, the value of labor tended to equal the value of goods. See *Das Kapital,* vols. I (1867), and III (1894).
10. Frederick W. Taylor, *Principles of Scientific Management* (New York: Harper & Bros., 1911).
11. They never left it! By 1920, women accounted for 20.6 percent of the labor force, and this figure has risen markedly since. See Chester A. Morgan, *Labor Economics* (Homewood, Ill.: Dorsey Press, 1962), p. 23.
12. Cyril C. Ling, *The Management of Personnel Relations* (Homewood, Ill.: Richard D. Irwin, Inc., 1965), p. 323. The following discussion is heavily indebted to this source.
13. The Consumer Price Index fell 24 percent between 1929 and 1933, while average weekly wages fell 33 percent; total employment fell 18 percent—nonfarm employment fell 23 percent—and unemployment rose from 3.2 to 24.9 percent; industrial production dropped 36 percent; and corporate profits almost ceased to exist—dropping 95 percent; while the Dow Jones industrial average went from 381 to 41—a drop of 90 percent. "The Outlook," *Wall Street Journal* (November 25, 1974), p. 1.

If you would like to better understand this period, and its continued effect upon you, read William Manchester, *The Glory and the Dream* (Boston: Little, Brown and Co., 1974), vol. I, chap. 1, "The Cruelest Year."

14. Harold W. Davey, *Contemporary Collective Bargaining* (New York: Prentice-Hall, Inc., 1951), p. 190: "The primary motivation at that time was to soften the rigidities of the wage stabilization program by granting various concessions at the fringe." Many of the companies were operating on a "cost-plus" contract, whereby profits were based upon a fixed percentage of the total cost of production. As the company received a certain percentage of the cost as its profit, any increase in total cost increased the amount of profit. Therefore, the introduction of these "fringes" increased profits by increasing the total cost of the product. Needless to say, when the war was over and these contracts were terminated, many of the companies tried to go back to the original concepts of efficient and effective operations but were unable to do so because of union pressure.

15. The union shop, whereby new employees were required to join the union within 30 days and old employees had to maintain their union membership as a condition of employment, was quite prevalent. Later the closed shop, whereby the company could only hire and retain in its employ union members, was extensively used. It was banned in most industries by the Labor-Management Relations Act of 1947.

16. See Neil H. Jacoby, *Can Prosperity Be Sustained?* (New York: Henry Holt and Co., 1956), pp. 17–29, for an excellent analysis of the law and its possible consequences.

17. See Manchester, *The Glory and the Dream,* chap. 13, "The Fraying Flags of Triumph," for further elaboration of this point.

18. It has been estimated that by the mid-1960s there were between 20 and 30 million *more* people than had been forecast and planned for earlier. Manchester, *The Glory and the Dream,* p. 525.

19. One of the most perceptive insights into this situations was provided by Ian H. Wilson, in charge of General Electric's Business Environment Research and Forecasting unit, in an interview in *MBA,* vol. 9, no. 10 (November 1975), pp. 42–46, entitled "Does GE Really Plan Better?" He emphasized that breaking out of old modes of thinking is very difficult, for we have difficulty in making personal changes to new modes of thinking. Changed beliefs, changed policies, and changed strategies emerge slowly.

    Probably the best hope for social change lies in the predominance of the younger generation, "the fantastic numbers in the 25–34 age group that are coming upon us." They were brought up in a climate of changing trends and attitudes, and they are comfortable operating in this mode. They understand this type of world much better than the older generation, whose main conditioning was in the Depression, the war, and postwar periods, and this postwar period has finally ended. The 1947–73 period had a lot of continuity to it in terms of population and economic growth, affluence, the declining cost of energy, and relatively stable inflation. But every one of those dimensions has now changed. The next 25 years are going to be substantially different. Future analysis will probably show that the period of 1973–75 marked a watershed economically, as 1965–70 or 1967–71 marked a watershed socially. The break point is not sharp, but now all the major dynamics and attitudes that characterized the postwar period have finally changed. We're now into something new.

20. Senate Majority Leader, Mike Mansfield, once observed, "In my younger days I used to blame the older generation for the trouble they got us into. Now here I am in the older generation, and trouble is still with us."

21. In his play, *Promenade, All,* David V. Robison provides us with a glimpse of eight decades of American life by focusing on six generations of one family, whose business, button manufacturing, changes through time just as the people do, evolving from buttons to zippers to cosmetics and electronics.

    It illustrates the truth that while culture and customs change, people are enduringly and eternally very human; while "people" remain the same, individuals continue to be uniquely different. Fathers and sons may yearn for college, or business success, or more experience with the mysterious sex, but seldom do the expectations and aspirations of one generation coincide with the hopes of the next. The "generation gap" is not just a product of the shoddy workmanship of today's mechanized society; parents of long ago endured roughly similar exasperations, for each generation has its own attitudes, goals, and foibles. No matter how one generation progresses or changes decade after decade, husbands and wives, parents and children love and fight with one another. That is how they grow.

22. James H. Carrington, "The Personnel Executive and Social Responsibility," *Personnel Journal,* vol. 49, no. 6 (June 1970), pp. 504–7; and L. L. L. Golden, "Profit Alone Is Not Enough," *Saturday Review,* vol. 53, no. 33 (August 8, 1970), p. 55 ff.

23. George Cabot Lodge, "Business and the Changing Society," *Harvard Business Review,* vol. 52, no. 2 (March–April 1974), pp. 59–72.

24. For more information about this subject, see Charles Denova and William K. McClelland, "The Psychedelicacies Involved in the 'Now' Employee versus Management," *Supervision,* vol. 32, no. 5 (May 1970), pp. 3–5. They named the older employees "Managementdom" and the newer ones "Nowdom."

25. Rates were computed from various issues of *Monthly Labor Review.*

Chapter 4

The institutional context

Growing governmental involvement
  Causes of the change
  Directions of the change

Areas of involvement
  Jurisdictional areas
  Type of organization involved
  Type of legal action
  Communications requirements

Personnel functions involved
  Recruiting and selecting personnel
  Employee development programs
  Compensation and hours of work
  Health and safety
  Employee protection, security, and benefits
  Employee relations

How to cope with this increasing involvement
  Learn all about the laws
  Challenge undesirable laws
  Become involved in the political system
  Find a better legal-political environment
  Ignore the law and hope it "goes away"
  Live with it

4
The institutional context

The highest and best form of efficiency is the spontaneous cooperation of a free people.
WOODROW WILSON

Wayne State University was charged with pension bias against women in 1973. It went to court to find out which federal pension rules it should follow for its female employees. The EEOC insists women and men should draw *equal pension benefits* upon retirement; but the Labor Department says employers need only *equalize contributions* to pension funds, not benefits. As women outlive men, insurers charge employers more to give them equal benefits.

The college feared making greater pension contributions to women to equalize their benefits would violate federal equal-pay laws. It asked a three-judge federal panel to resolve the interagency dispute, which Washington officials had tried for months to end.

This case exemplifies the difficulty personnel executives have in conforming to the institutional context in which they operate. The legal-political and industrial relations environments impose boundaries within which personnel and human resources administration is performed. Because organizations did not take the measures needed to protect employees, governments stepped in. (1)

GROWING GOVERNMENTAL INVOLVEMENT

It is very difficult to select the most important aspects of this extensive and complex environment. Yet, to cover all of them would only confuse you—and fill the rest of this book. Instead, an overview of the factors will be provided in this chapter, then more details will be found in later chapters as the personnel functions are discussed. As their influence provides the institutional context of personnel, they are discussed early in the book so you can refer back to them as you study the subject further.

While it is obviously impossible in today's complex socioeconomic systems to return to an "unfettered capitalistic free-enterprise system," it might be time to at least slow the movement in the other direction. (2)

Causes of the change

One of the prime causes of the modification in the role of business and government is the increasingly complex world in which the personnel function is performed. Organizations are much more diverse and complex, as we now operate in interdependent economic, social, and political systems. (3) Also, organizational activities are more complicated, as there is mass production, distribution, transportation, education, communication, and consumption.

Most people now view government as a tremendous operation in partnership with labor, management, and individuals. With the rapid increase in research and development expenditures, decisions affecting economic growth now heavily fall upon organizations (4) and the government. (5)

Directions of the change

In an effort to attain employment equality, the government has used "plans for progress," "compliance reviews," "affirmative action programs," and "quotas." The word "quotas" is often not used in discussing the concept, but synonyms such as "goals" and "timetables" are used.

These efforts to place more minority group members and women in better positions raise the question about how these groups can be helped without doing an injustice to those who can not be blamed for past unfairness. This is the dilemma which has personnel executives cornered and from which they are seeking a way out.

In order to understand the problem better, let us look at it another way. Figure 4–1, which shows a social solidarity and legal emphasis continuum, is a useful way of explaining how this has occurred—and how the executives may resolve the dilemma.

The stage of *extreme segregation and exclusion* where the discrimination and prejudice of dominant group members lead to the creation and exclusion of one or more minorities is shown at the top. This was the situation in the United States prior to World War II, as reflected in certain statutes in force throughout the country at that time. This was a period of *laissez-faire* in personnel work.

The next stage is one of *fair employment practices and antidiscrimination,* as reflected in some of the federal executive orders during World War II and the enactment of state antidiscrimination legislation in a few states such as New York. Segregation on the job started to be broken up, and there was a high amount of stress on law which would oppose discrimination. The personnel manager felt pressure in a relatively small way to change the way organizations were managed, but the law was still *against something,* namely, discrimination, and focused upon complaints of people who were discriminated against. The third stage, compliance, was the method emphasized in policing fair employment practices in respect to government contractors during the 1950s. The emphasis was less on the law than upon the responsibility of a contractor to adhere to the letter of the legal contract with the federal government. Compliance in this sense was not so much *anti-* as *pro- something.* Personnel managers who worked for a contractor necessarily took action to conform with fair employment practices.

**FIGURE 4–1
Social solidarity and legal emphasis continuum**

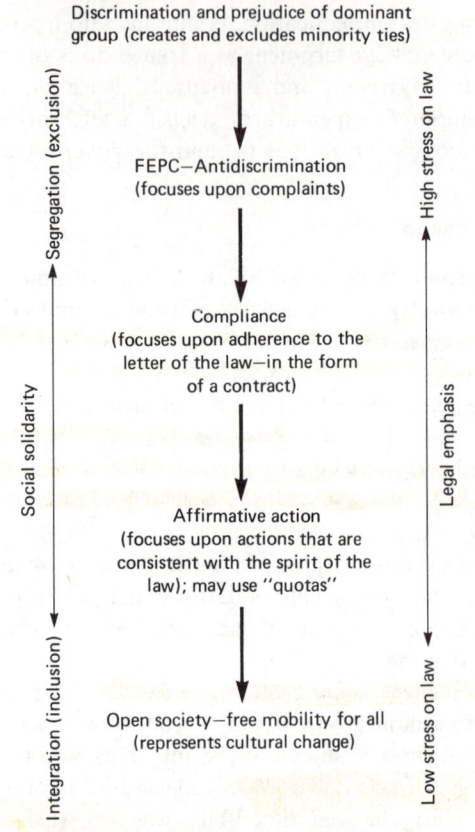

Discrimination and prejudice of dominant group (creates and excludes minority ties)

↓

FEPC—Antidiscrimination
(focuses upon complaints)

↓

Compliance
(focuses upon adherence to the letter of the law—in the form of a contract)

↓

Affirmative action
(focuses upon actions that are consistent with the spirit of the law); may use "quotas"

↓

Open society—free mobility for all
(represents cultural change)

Left axis: Social solidarity — Segregation (exclusion) ↔ Integration (inclusion)
Right axis: Legal emphasis — High stress on law ↔ Low stress on law

Source: Thomas H. Patten, Jr., "Personnel Management in the 1970s: The End of *Laissez-Faire,*" *Human Resource Management,* vol. 12, no. 3 (Fall 1973), p. 11.

The *affirmative action* stage was ushered in with the passage of the *Civil Rights Act of 1964* and a series of executive orders during the 1960s. Under affirmative action, personnel managers are asked not only to make sure that fair employment practices existed, but also to go several steps further and plan what could be positively done to place or promote minority group members in nontraditional and better positions. "With the advent of quotas, the rising militancy of women, and the revolution of rising expectations among minorities, EEO has become an awesome concept for the personnel manager." (6)

Stage five shows an *open society* where there is free mobility for all. This is probably the stage which today's personnel executives wish was presently at hand. That day is probably so far off, however, that the time between now and then is going to be difficult and cause many personnel people to despair for the duration of their careers.

AREAS OF INVOLVEMENT

Making the personnel executive's job more difficult is the fact that the legal-political environment involves *different*—and often conflicting—jurisdictional areas, namely, the federal government, state, and local governments. Also, different *types of organizations* operate under differing rules and regulations—some of which are also in conflict. Another source of possible difficulty and confusion is the *types of legal involvement*, namely, executive orders issued by the President, legislation passed by Congress, decisions made by administrative agencies, and court decisions. Finally, the *logistical problem* of publicizing the laws and receiving reports from the managers poses a difficult problem.

Jurisdictional areas

The Tenth Amendment to the U.S. Constitution reserves to the individual states the powers not specifically granted to the federal government. Operating under this amendment, the individual states have enacted laws and developed their own body of legal and political constraints upon the performance of the personnel function.

The Constitution explicitly grants Congress the right to pass laws affecting the "general welfare" and "interstate commerce." Frequently these federal constraints come into conflict with state laws—and vice versa. Then the courts have to determine who has the proper jurisdiction.

Expanding role of federal government. The concept of "interstate commerce" limited the involvement of the federal government in personnel activities until recently. Yet, in *National Labor Relations Board* v. *Jones and Laughlin Steel Corporation* (1937), when the primary issue was whether manufacturing within a state was included within the interstate commerce clause of the Constitution, the court decided that it was. Therefore, Congress was in a position to become more involved in the employer-employee relationship, which it is now doing.

How jurisdictional conflict arises. In general, governmental involvement in personnel has tended to operate as follows: (*a*) a state will pass legislation involving a given personnel practice or policy; (*b*) other states follow the example of the lead state until the legislation becomes generally acceptable; (*c*) either before or after the previous step, the chief executive of the state or federal government will issue an order pertaining to that practice within the executive branch of government itself, and for government contractors; (*d*) Congress will then pass a law applying the previous restrictions or benefits to firms engaged in interstate commerce; (*e*) administrative bodies make decisions as to how to apply this law; and finally (*f*) the courts interpret the constitutionality of the law.

Conflict between federal and state laws. It can be readily seen that this pattern has a built-in tendency for conflict. For example, most states passed laws restricting females from working certain hours or lifting certain weights. Then Congress passed *Title VII of the Civil Rights Act* which said employment practices cannot be based upon sex. The courts must decide which takes priority. (7)

Conflict between federal laws. Conflicts also arise between laws and regulations of the same jurisdiction. For example, there is a conflict between the *Occupational Safety and Health Act (OSHA)* (1970), which requires separate restrooms for males and females, and *Title VII*, which says there cannot be separate restrooms based on sex.

Probably more difficult will be the task of the courts in deciding between the right of minorities under *Title VII* and the seniority rights of employees with union-management agreements under the *National Labor Relations Act (NLRA)* (1935). This conflict was triggered when the Labor Department ordered a sweeping overhaul of employment policies of the nation's largest private telephone company, AT&T, and struck down a long-standing seniority system at the Bethlehem Steel Corporation plant at Sparrow's Point, Maryland. (8) Now, the controversy is raging with seniority apparently winning over race and sex. (9) Layoff according to seniority is as firm a policy for many nonunion firms as it is for unionized ones, and most employers believe that the EEOC will lose this one in the courts. For most unions, this attempt to replace seniority with minority rights is a declaration of war, for seniority is one of the *most* basic union beliefs.

Type of organization involved

The activities you are in, the number of employees you have, and your clients tend to determine your legal-political environment. For example, *all employers engaged in interstate commerce* are subject to OSHA requirements; such employers with 15 or more employees are covered by Title VII; but employers of 25 or more employees are the only ones covered by the *Age Discrimination in Employment Act of 1967.*

Government contractors and subcontractors, or contractors under federally assisted construction contracts, are covered by *Executive Order 11246,* issued in 1965, as amended by *Executive Order 11375* in 1967.

State and local governments are subject to the *Equal Employment Opportunity Act of 1972.*

Other organizations may be covered by state and local laws, federal laws, or no law at all. For example, only in 1975 did the State of California pass the *Agricultural Labor Relations Act* involving farm employers.

Type of legal action

The type of legal action involved also varies. Legislation is a law issued by Congress or a local governing body, which is passed by representatives in a regularly scheduled session of the legislative body. Executive orders are issued by the chief executive—namely, the President of the United States or a governor of a state. While it carries the same weight as legislation, it is not passed by a group of legislators, but is signed by the executive. Sometimes these actions come into conflict. For example, the *Labor-Management Relations Act (1947)*, commonly called the *Taft-Hartley Act, exempts employees of government* from its protection; yet, *Executive Order 10988*, issued by President Kennedy in 1962, as amended, *gives government employees the right to join and participate in union activities.*

In addition to these two types of involvement, decisions of *administrative agencies* also have the force of law. After the rules and regulations are promulgated in the *Federal Register*, they then have the effect of law. Next, they are published in the *Code of Federal Regulations*. Then various government agencies begin enforcing the regulation.

Finally, *court decisions* also have the effect of law. For example, Congress specifically included in Title VII a provision that tests could be used for selection purposes as long *as they were not intended or used to discriminate.* Yet, in *Griggs* v. *Duke Power Company*, 3FEP Cases 175 (1971), the U.S. Supreme Court not only prohibited tests which excluded blacks, but also employment selection practices that "are fair in form, but discriminatory in operation." This, then, is the "law of the land"—discrimination is defined in terms of consequences rather than motive; effect rather than purpose.

Communications requirements

In addition to the legal aspects of government involvement, there is also a communications aspect. Almost all the laws require notification of coverage to employees, which is usually done by means of posters on bulletin boards, letters, memos, and direct oral communication. These all involve time, effort, and expense.

> A speaker at a personnel management conference had finished speaking on government involvement in personnel. Someone asked the question, "What is the most important thing I should do in order to comply with the regulations you mentioned?" The answer, half-facetious and half-serious, was, "Get a LARGE bulletin board!"

Another aspect that many personnel managers consider burdensome is the requirement for sending reports to the regulatory agencies. For example, *Title VII* requires the completion of an "Employee Information Report" Form 100 (EEO–1). (See Figure 4–2.) According to many personnel managers, this is the most unpleasant aspect of government involvement. (10)

PERSONNEL FUNCTIONS INVOLVED

Although almost all areas of personnel are involved with government rules and regulations, the ones most affecting the personnel manager's decision making are: recruitment and selection; training and development; compensa-

72 Personnel and human resources administration

FIGURE 4-2
EEO Form 1

Section D — EMPLOYMENT DATA

Employment at this establishment--Report all permanent, temporary, or part-time employees including apprentices and on-the-job trainees unless specifically excluded as set forth in the instructions. Enter the appropriate figures on all lines and in all columns. Blank spaces will be considered as zeros.

In columns 1, 2, and 3, include ALL employees in the establishment including those in minority groups.

Job Categories (See Appendix (5) for definitions)	Total Employees Including Minorities (1)	Total Male Including Minorities (2)	Total Female Including Minorities (3)	Negro (4)	Oriental (5)	American Indian (6)	Spanish Surnamed American (7)	Negro (8)	Oriental (9)	American Indian (10)	Spanish Surnamed American (11)
Officials and managers	119	35	84	5				9			
Professionals	228	16	212					3	1		2
Technicians	255	35	220	5				107			
Sales workers											
Office and clerical	209	19	190	1				50			
Craftsmen (Skilled)	29	26	3	1			2	3			
Operatives (Semi-skilled)	26	11	15	6				15			
Laborers (Unskilled)	6	6		6							
Service workers	379	98	281	79				225			
TOTAL →	1,251	246	1,005	103			2	412	1		2
Total employment reported in previous EEO-1 report	1,198	241	957	102			3	394	4		3

(The trainees below should also be included in the figures for the appropriate occupational categories above)

| Formal On-the-job trainees | White collar | | | | | | | | | | |
| | Production | | | | | | | | | | |

* In Alaska include Eskimos and Aleuts with American Indians

1. NOTE: On consolidated report, skip questions 2-5 and Section E.
2. How was information as to race or ethnic group in Section D obtained?
   1. ☒ Visual Survey   3. ☐ Other — Specify ....
   2. ☐ Employment Record
3. Dates of payroll period used — 4/25/76 — 5/8/76

4. Pay period of last report submitted to this establishment
   4/27/75 — 5/10/75
5. Does this establishment employ apprentices?
   This year? 1 ☐ Yes 2 ☒ No
   Last year? 1 ☐ Yes 2 ☒ No

Section E — ESTABLISHMENT INFORMATION

1. Is the location of the establishment the same as that reported last year?
   1 ☒ Yes 2 ☐ No 3 ☐ Did not report last year 4 ☐ Reported on combined basis

2. Is the major business activity at this establishment the same as that reported last year?
   1 ☒ Yes 2 ☐ No 3 ☐ No report last year 4 ☐ Reported on combined basis

OFFICE USE ONLY

3. What is the major activity of this establishment? (Be specific. i.e., manufacturing steel castings, retail grocer, wholesale plumbing supplies, title insurance, etc. Include the specific type of product or type of service provided, as well as the principal business or industrial activity.

General Hospital

Section F — REMARKS

Use this item to give any identification data appearing on last report which differs from that given above, explain major changes in composition or reporting units, and other pertinent information.

Section G — CERTIFICATION (See instructions G)

Check one
1. ☐ All reports are accurate and were prepared in accordance with the instructions (check on consolidated only)
2. ☒ This report is accurate and was prepared in accordance with the instructions.

Name of Certifying Official	Title **President**	Signature	Date 5/26/75
Name of person to contact regarding this report (Type or print)	Address (Number and street)		
Title	City and State	ZIP code	Telephone Area Code / Number / Extension

All reports and information obtained from individual reports will be kept confidential as required by Section 709 (e) of Title VII.
WILLFULLY FALSE STATEMENTS ON THIS REPORT ARE PUNISHABLE BY LAW, U.S. CODE, TITLE 18, SECTION 1001

tion and hours of work; health and safety; employee protection, security, and benefits; personal rights of employees; and employee relations.

Recruiting and selecting personnel

There are several federal laws and regulations affecting the recruitment and selection of minorities—including blacks, Spanish surnamed Americans, Orientals, American Indians, and others; females; older workers; veterans; the handicapped; and children. Probably the best way of presenting this is to show which regulations apply to which demographic group and to what types of organization.

Minorities and women. For those *firms engaged in interstate commerce,* the basic law is *Title VII of the Civil Rights Act of 1964,* as amended by the *Equal Employment Opportunity Act of 1972.* It applies to employers with 15 or more employees. (11)

The law is enforced by the Equal Employment Opportunity Commission (EEOC), as shown in Figure 4–3. It is composed of five members appointed

---

FIGURE 4–3
Agencies that enforce equal employment opportunity laws

Equal Employment Opportunity Commission

Handles complaints of bias against women, blacks, religious groups, other minorities. Can file suits against employers with 15 or more employees and against labor unions with more than 15 members after efforts at conciliation.

Office of Federal Contract Compliance Programs

Located in the Labor Department, this office monitors job policies of companies holding federal contracts or subcontracts valued at more than $10,000. Contractors are required to take "affirmative action" to end—or prevent—job discrimination and other civil rights violations.

Employment Standards Division

This unit, located in the Labor Department, is responsible for setting employment standards, including programs dealing with job discrimination against older workers.

United States Civil Service Commission

Reviews employment policies of federal agencies to attack discrimination in government jobs. Consults with state and local governments to establish and improve merit hiring systems.

Civil Rights Division of Justice Department

Files lawsuits against either private employers or labor unions charged with engaging in a "pattern or practice of discrimination." Also, can bring individual or "pattern" suits against state and local governments for job discrimination against women, minorities, religious groups, or the elderly.

by the President and approved by the Senate. The commission's responsibility is to assure that everyone will be considered for hiring on the basis of their ability and qualifications, without regard to race, color, religion, sex, or national origin.

The commission has two basic responsibilities. First, it investigates complaints of discrimination and, if it finds they are justified, seeks a full remedy by the process of conciliation or through the courts. Second, it promotes programs of voluntary compliance to put the idea of equal employment opportunity into actual operation. Under Title VII, the commission is concerned with discrimination by four major groups—employers, public and private employment agencies, labor organizations, and joint labor-management apprenticeship programs.

Title VII makes it unlawful: (*a*) for any *employer* to discriminate in hiring or firing; wages, terms, conditions or privileges of employment; classifying, assigning or promoting employees or extending or assigning use of facilities; and training, retraining or apprenticeships; (*b*) for any *employer or employment agency* to print, publish, circulate or cause the printing, publishing, circulation of advertisements or any other statement or announcement relating to employment expressing any specification, limitations or preferences based on race, color, religion, sex, or national origin; or to discriminate in receiving applications or classifying or referring for employment; (*c*) for any *labor organization* to exclude or expel from membership, discriminate against any individual; limit, segregate, or classify membership, refer to or fail to refer for employment on the basis of race, color, religion, sex, or national origin; or to cause or attempt to cause an employer to discriminate.

For organizations with federal contracts. For organizations with contracts or subcontracts with the federal government and for contractors under a federally assisted construction contract, the basic regulation is *Executive Order 11246,* which requires equal employment opportunities for all persons. (12) *Executive Order 11375* amended it to prohibit explicitly discrimination based upon sex.

Enforcement. While the overall responsibility for enforcing these orders is in the hands of the Labor Department's Office of Federal Contract Compliance Programs (OFCCP) (see the Secretary's Order No. Four for details), the primary and specific responsibility for enforcement rests with each of the contracting and compliance agencies. (13)

The contractor will include the same provisions in every subcontract or purchase order issued so that such provisions are binding on each subcontractor or vendor.

Some selected enforcement agencies. Some of the enforcing agencies and their activities are discussed below.

> On July 1, 1975, the Defense Department quietly notified its procurement offices that General Motors Corporation—which sold $300 million worth of goods and services to the Pentagon in fiscal 1974—was not in compliance with

the executive order and was not to be awarded the next contract on which it was a low bidder. (14)

The *United States Employment Service* (*USES*) was used by three Presidents to implement minority legislation until 1972. The result was that while total nonfarm employment was rising "about 10 percent" the employment service's "placement shrank 30 percent" and "the number of placements of disadvantaged workers also fell." (15) Since 1972, the service has been primarily performing its more traditional role of lining up skilled workers for employers.

In 1971, the *Labor Department's* Bureau of Apprenticeship and Training put new rules into force requiring more participation of minority groups in apprenticeship programs.

The *Agriculture Department,* accused of reviewing only 4 percent of the 21,000 firms it is supposed to check, is under pressure from civil rights advocates to increase hiring and promotions by government contractors. (16)

Affirmative action programs. In addition to the general requirements, AAPs must be established in an effort to recruit minorities and women. Their provisions include: (*a*) signing up with the state employment service; (*b*) limitations on questions which may be asked on employment applications; (*c*) goals and timetables determining the available percentages of minorities and women in local labor force must be established; and (*d*) testing must be avoided unless it has been shown to be free of bias and is validated to correlate directly with job performance.

Some of the special problems involving sex discrimination are: (*a*) What are bona fide occupational qualifications (BFOQ): (*b*) is maternity equivalent to other illnesses for hospitalization insurance purposes; and (*c*) is maternity a "disability" or "sickness" for purposes of wage continuation plans?

For state and local governments. The *Equal Employment Opportunity Act of 1972,* which amended Title VII, covers employees of state and local governments.

Older workers. During the 1960s, the effect of the wartime and post-World War II "baby boom" began to be felt in the job market. Consequently, there was a general decline in hiring of workers 40 years old and over. Congress passed the *Age Discrimination in Employment Act* to prevent discrimination against individuals between the ages of 40 and 65. (17) The enforcing agency is the Employment Standards Division, U.S. Department of Labor.

Veterans. The *Vietnam Era Veterans' Readjustment Assistance Act of 1972* provides for job counseling, training, and placement service for veterans. In addition, it required organizations with federal contracts of $10,000 or more to have AAPs for hiring disabled and Vietnam veterans.

Handicapped. The *Rehabilitation Act of 1973* requires federal contractors with contracts in excess of $2,500 to take affirmative action to hire the handicapped. Also it prohibits discrimination against anyone because of any physical or mental handicap.

Employee development programs

There are many state and federal programs which cooperate with organizations in training and developing present and future employees. Some of the more popular ones are:

1. The *National Apprenticeship Act of 1937*, which sets forth policies and standards for apprenticeship programs;
2. The *Comprehensive Employment and Training Act of 1973 (CETA)*, which replaced many categorical programs including the Manpower Development and Training Act of 1962, provides federal assistance in training unemployed and underemployed workers, particularly youths with or without previous work experience; and
3. JOBS (Jobs Opportunities in the Business Sector) Program, which encouraged businessmen to submit proposals for contracts for on-the-job training for the disadvantaged, hard-core unemployed.

Compensation and hours of work

Compensation. The basic federal law setting minimum wages and overtime at the rate of 1½ times the regular rate of pay for over 40 hours is the *Fair Labor Standards Act of 1938*, as amended.

The *Equal Pay Act of 1963* was amended in 1972 to cover not only hourly rated female personnel, but also around 15 million executive, administrative, and professional employees and outside salespeople. It requires employers to pay females the same as they do males for performing the same work. (18)

The *Public Construction Act of 1931 (Davis-Bacon Act)* says that construction firms with public contracts may pay "the prevailing wage" rate—as determined by the Secretary of Labor—to their workers. Also, all hours over eight worked in one day—as well as over 40 in one week—must be paid at 1½ times the regular rate. The *Public Contracts Act of 1936 (Walsh-Healey Act)* requires similar provisions for other government contracts. The *Service Contract Act of 1965* requires firms providing services on a contract basis *to the government to pay minimum* wages and provide certain benefits.

Around 4 to 5 million of the new group brought under the act's coverage in 1972 were women. Among jobs newly covered are professor, engineer, chemist, buyer, programmer, writer, and editor.

Hours of work. The *Fair Labor Standards Act* limits minors aged 14 to 16 to working only three hours per day when school is in session and only eight hours per day at other times. The law has special provisions for employment of full-time students at rates lower than minimum wages.

Most states have laws pertaining to the hours of work for children, but most of the state laws dealing with hours for females have been decreed by the courts to be in conflict with Title VII.

Holidays. Federal law requires that the federal government designate Monday to be the day for celebrating Washington's birthday, Memorial Day, Labor Day, and Columbus Day.

Health and safety

State laws and administrative procedures have traditionally set health and safety standards and provided for enforcement by on-site inspection.

Occupational Safety and Health Act. The federal *Occupational Safety and Health Act of 1970 (OSHA)* assumed much of this authority and responsibility. (19)

The law covers *every* employer in interstate commerce but specifically excludes federal, state, and local government employees and employees covered by other federal safety and health laws—such as the *Atomic Energy Act of 1954* and the *Federal Coal Mine Health and Safety Act*. It brought under its "umbrella" other laws going back to 1937.

It is enforced by the Occupational Safety and Health Administrator, U.S. Department of Labor, and the Occupational Safety and Health Review Board.

Worker's compensation laws. All states now have workers' compensation laws.* Under these provisions there is a scale of benefits workers will receive for specific losses—such as an arm—and a percentage of salary they will receive for injuries, as well as coverage of medical care and rehabilitation training. The key factor is that the cost of such coverage to each firm varies with its safety record. This provides an incentive to encourage safety. (20)

Employee protection, security, and benefits

Several of the oldest federal laws provide for employee protection, security, and benefits, along with some that were passed recently.

Social Security Act. The *Social Security Act of 1935* provided for a federal old-age and survivor's insurance program, along with a federal-state system of unemployment insurance. It also provided for assistance to the needy aged, needy and dependent children, and the needy blind. While the original act provided for only old-age insurance and unemployment insurance, survivor's insurance was added in 1939 providing monthly life insurance payments to the widow and dependent children of a deceased worker. In 1956, disability insurance was added. In 1966, health insurance benefits—commonly known as "medicare"—and other benefits for retired employees were added.

The pension and death and disability provisions of the act—as amended —apply to those engaged in interstate commerce, and—on an elected basis— state and local governments, religious organizations, and others. The unemployment compensation provisions apply to business firms only.

As the requirements are so complicated—and controversial—they will be discussed in Chapter 23 rather than here.

Employee Retirement Income Security Act. Another federal law aimed at protecting employees' rights and pension programs, which is having tremendous impact on personnel work, is the *Employee Retirement Income Security Act of 1974 (Pension Reform Law)*, which requires all private retirement programs to meet federally required standards. While a firm is not required

---

* These were formerly referred to as "workmen's compensation laws."

to have a plan, if it does, the plan must be financially sound and easily understood by the plan participants. (21) Also, firms with plans that cover 100 or more employees must submit detailed descriptions of the plans and annual reports to the Department of Labor. This also applies to other employee welfare benefit plans.

Employee relations

The basic federal labor law of the land is the *National Labor Relations Act, 1935* (*NLRA,* also referred to as the *Wagner Act*), as amended by the *Labor-Management Relations Act, 1947* (*LMRA,* also referred to as the *Taft-Hartley Act*), the *Labor-Management Reporting and Disclosure Act, 1959* (*LMRDA,* also referred to as the *Landrum-Griffin Act*), and other amendments.

While it is difficult to condense the NLRA into a few statements, it can be said that it essentially did three things: (*a*) permitted workers to form or join unions of their own choosing without fear of prosecution from the antitrust laws; (*b*) substantially limited the rights and discretion of management by having working conditions determined *bilaterally at the bargaining table* rather than *unilaterally at the place of occurrence;* and (*c*) established machinery in the form of the National Labor Relations Board (NLRB) to administer the law.

Rights of employees. Employees have essentially five rights under this act, namely, the right to:

1. Self-organization;
2. Form, join, or assist labor organizations of their choosing;
3. Bargain collectively through those representatives;
4. Engage in concerted activities needed for mutual aid or protection;
5. Refrain from, as well as engage in, such concerted activities, except where there is a valid union shop agreement. (The LMRA included Section 14(b), which gave states the right to pass laws prohibiting the union shop. These laws take priority over the federal law.)

Restrictions on management's rights. There are some specific activities forbidden to management which tend to restrict its rights. Those specific restrictions were designated "unfair labor practices" and include the following:

1. Interfering with, restraining, or coercing employees in exercising their rights under Section 7;
2. Dominating or interfering with the formation or administration of unions or contributing financial or other support to them;
3. Discriminating in regard to hire or tenure of employment or any term or condition of employment to encourage or discourage membership in any labor organization;
4. Discharging or otherwise discriminating against employees for filing charges or testifying in the administration of this act; and

5. Refusing to bargain collectively with the representatives designated by the majority of the employees in the appropriate bargaining unit.

While management had restrictions placed on some of its rights, it was granted certain others. Among those, are the right to:

1. Refuse to bargain with supervisory personnel;
2. Freedom of speech as long as there was no threat of reprisal or force, or any promise of benefit, during a representation election; and
3. Seek a representation when the union claimed it represented the employees, even if the union did not desire one.

Restrictions on union's rights. Certain limitations were placed on the rights of unions in the form of "unfair labor practices," which include:

1. Coercing employees into participating in union activities, or restraining them from doing so freely;
2. Forcing employers to discriminate against employees in violation of act. (The LMRA prohibited unions from forcing management to discharge an employee for nonunion activities if management "had reason to believe" that the union had been guilty of discrimination in excluding the worker from union membership, except through refusing to pay uniformly required and nonexcessive initiation fees and dues);
3. Refusing to bargain in good faith;
4. Featherbedding; and
5. Engaging in, or causing employees of any employer to engage in, a strike or labor boycott where the purpose is to force management into illegal or undesirable acts.

Administration of the law. The judicial powers of the act are vested in a five-person National Labor Relations Board (NLRB), while its administrative duties are handled by the general counsel. The primary responsibilities of the NLRB are to:

1. Set up the procedures for elections to determine the employees' choice of a bargaining agent;
2. To determine if a majority of the workers do want a union to represent them; and
3. Investigate and prosecute complaints of unfair labor practices under the law.

The representation elections, as well as the investigation of unfair labor practices, are held under the supervision of the general counsel; while the judicial decisions involving unfair labor practices are made by the board in Washington.

Effects upon personnel management. At first, managers did not believe the Supreme Court would uphold the legality of the act as it involved manufacturing, and, in the earlier *Knight case,* the Court had said that Congress could not pass laws affecting manufacturing within a state. Many businessmen accepted the law and learned to live with it; others took a "wait-and-see" attitude; but others actively fought it. There followed one of the truly bloody periods in the history of union-management relations, particularly in the automobile and steel industries. Yet, when the act was upheld by the Supreme Court in *NLRB* v. *Jones and Laughlin Steel Company,* the unions gained much prestige, strength, and power. Union membership increased from about 3 million in 1932 to around 9 million in 1939.

HOW TO COPE WITH THIS INCREASING INVOLVEMENT

As this is the legal-political framework within which you must operate as a personnel manager, how do you cope with it? There are several things you can do, such as:

1. Learn as much as you can about the laws;
2. Challenge detrimental or harmful laws;
3. Become involved in the legal-political system;
4. Find a better legal environment—if possible;
5. Ignore the law, and hope it "goes away"; and
6. Learn "to live with it."

Learn all about the laws

The first suggestion for coping is through knowledge, for in knowledge there is strength. Learn as much as you can about the laws, their applications to you and your business, what is required for you to be in compliance, and to what extent the law might even be to your advantage. For example, many companies wanted to "clean up the environment" and reduce pollution, but it was economically not feasible because if one firm spent the money necessary to achieve the results—and others did not—it might "price itself out of the market." However, with the passage of the *Clean Air Act of 1970* and other environmental acts, *all* members of an industry had to comply. Therefore, most firms could afford to do what they had wanted to do before, for everyone now had to do it.

The many federal assistance acts can also work to your advantage. Some companies prefer to have a union—even with the union shop clause—so that discipline can be shifted from it to the union.

Challenge undesirable laws

A second approach is to challenge any law or regulation that you think is detrimental or harmful to you or your employees. Admittedly this is a costly procedure and probably will require your trade or professional association, or a group of individuals, to pool their resources to challenge the laws.

Become involved in the political system

A third method—and one which is now feasible and appropriate—is to become *involved in the legal-political system*. The new Campaign Practices Law permits organizations to set up political action committees (PACs) which will tend to lessen the competitive advantage now held by unions. A group of 50 people can form such a committee, voluntarily solicit and donate funds, and use those funds the same way COPE and other union political action committees do. By this means, you can legally donate money, time, and effort to people of your choice who will influence the laws and their interpretations the way you want them to be influenced. A variation of this procedure is to become involved in the election process and help to get people who will be favorable to your point of view appointed to the administrative bodies that administer the laws.

Find a better legal-political environment

A fourth possibility is to locate where there is a favorable legal-political climate. Many states have passed laws favorable to business in order to attract industry. Examples are the Balancing Agriculture with Industry (BAWI), whereby public funds are used to build facilities and tax inducements are given to attract industry. As payroll costs are such an important item to most organizations, you might seek states that have worker's compensation, unemployment insurance, and related laws that are not "antibusiness."

A variation of this method is to move to a state that has a "right-to-work" law, so that you will not have as many—or at least the same—"problems" with unions.

Ignore the law and hope it "goes away"

Fifth, while it is not recommended, another possibility is to ignore a law you consider to be unconstitutional, unwarranted, or unjustified. Many businessmen did this in the mid-1930s, assuming that the National Labor Relations Act would be declared unconstitutional. Later, when it was declared valid, they adhered to it.

To repeat, this method is not being advocated, but it is always a possibility if an individual or firm so desires.

Live with it

Finally, you may decide that it is advisable to learn "to live with" the situation. Therefore, you will do what is necessary to be in compliance with the environment.

DISCUSSION QUESTIONS

1. How would you describe the effects of the institutional context on performance of the personnel function?
2. Do you perceive the government involvement as "desirable" or not? Explain.
3. Do you envision the complexity of this environment to increase, decrease, or remain about the same? Explain.
4. Evaluate the suggestions for coping with the increasingly complex environment.

REFERENCES AND SUGGESTIONS FOR FURTHER STUDY

1. For example, when worker's compensation was first proposed in state legislatures around the turn of the century, it was hotly contested by businessmen, for it violated the "master-servant doctrine," whereby the employee assumed—and thereby accepted—the dangers associated with the job as a necessary condition of employment. The validity of such laws was in doubt until *Jeffrey Manufacturing Co.* v. *Blagg,* 235 U.S. 571 (1915).
2. See James T. Shotwell, *The Long Way to Freedom* (New York: Bobbs-Merrill Co., Inc., 1960), for an excellent discussion of what happens when the role of government becomes "oppressive."
3. According to Carter Henderson, co-director of the Princeton Center for Alternative Futures, a new computer model, developed at MIT, will analyze the interplay of some 2,000 variables in examining major social and economic pressures now confronting the United States, "Surprises and Survivors," *Bell Telephone Magazine,* vol. 54, no. 5 (September–October 1975), p. 25.
4. It has been asserted that "the main business is business." Yet some policies may be more socially desirable and acceptable than others. Responsibility has now shifted from the owners and workers to the organization itself. See Charles E. Griffin, "The Locus of Social Responsibility in the Large Corporation," *Michigan Business Review,* vol. 23, no. 2 (March 1971), pp. 5–10.
5. For example, around 60 percent of all scientific research and development in the United States has been financed and/or performed by the federal government, and many of the benefits of this new knowledge are shared with industry. Thus, the government has helped to accelerate technological development, which, in turn, has led to a further abandonment of the free-enterprise concept. If you would like further information or examples, see Dan H. Fenn, Jr., ed., *Managing America's Growth Explosion* (New York: McGraw-Hill Book Co., 1961), pp. 211–13.
6. See Thomas H. Patten, Jr., "Personnel Management in the 1970s: The End of Laissez Faire," *Human Resource Management,* vol. 12, no. 3 (Fall 1973), pp. 7–19, for more about this thought and what personnel managers might do about it.
7. See Ethel Bert Walsh, "Sex Discrimination and the Impact of Title VII," *Labor Law Journal,* vol. 25, No no. 3, (March 1974), pp. 150–54, for a discussion of some of the things which new or old employers should keep in mind as far as sex discrimination is concerned. These include laws which limit the number of hours women can work or set any limits on lifting and carrying of heavy objects of weights by women, as these laws have been outlawed by Title VII. These old laws did not consider each woman on her own merits, but stereotyped every

woman as being frail and weak. The courts have shown that the key element which they are looking for is that each law take the individual employee into account and not allow for any general group characteristic to be applied without regard for the individual. The old laws are in direct violation of the due process clause of the Fourteenth Amendment.

8. See "The Fight against Bias in Seniority," *Business Week* (February 10, 1973), pp. 56–58, for a discussion of these two cases.

9. A suit by black workers alleged Continental Can Company and United Steel Workers of America, Local 2369, violated Title VII by using seniority as the sole criterion for laying off workers at its Harvey, Louisiana, plant. The U.S. District Court in New Orleans ruled in favor of the minorities. "Last Hired, First Fired Takes It on the Chin," *Business Week* (March 19, 1974), p. 166.

The Fifth U.S. Circuit Court of Appeals ruled in favor of seniority. "Trends in Labor," *U.S. News & World Report* (July 28, 1975), p. 70.

Jersey Central Power & Light was bound by an International Brotherhood of Electrical Workers contract that protected seniority and a 1974 EEOC conciliation agreement pledging to increase its percentages of minority and women workers. The firm had to lay off employees. It used seniority. The U.S. District Court in Newark ordered it to favor minorities.

The U.S. Court of Appeals in Philadelphia declined to replace seniority with minority employment, for "Congress had not mandated such a sweeping remedy and only Congress could do so." See "Seniority Squeezed Out Minorities in Layoffs," *Business Week* (May 5, 1975), pp. 66–67.

One possible solution to this dilemma is "inverse seniority" whereby the most senior person is permitted to elect temporary layoff instead of the junior employee who may be more adversely affected. See R. T. Lund, D. C. Bumstead, and S. Friedman, "Inverse Seniority: Timely Answer to the Layoff Dilemma," *Harvard Business Review,* vol. 53, no. 5 (September–October, 1975) pp. 65–72, for estimated requirements, cost factors, and benefits involved in adopting such a system.

10. An Exxon official spelled this problem out quite clearly at a National Petroleum Refiners Association conference in Houston, according to the *Oil & Gas Journal.* The company "saw the handwriting on the wall and early in 1974 started keeping track of the personnel and cost associated with its reporting load."

The score thus far: 409 reports filed to 45 different federal agencies, excluding tax reports at three governmental levels. Of these, 55, or 13 percent, were introduced in the past year and a half. The cost to Exxon is the equivalent of 112 employees, at a cost of more than $3.5 million a year. "Truly, Mountains of Paperwork," *Baton Rouge Sunday Advocate* (November 30, 1975), p. 2B.

11. The key sentence reads: "It shall be an unlawful employment practice for an employer (1) to fail or refuse to hire or to discharge any individual or otherwise to discriminate against any individual with respect to . . . compensation, terms, conditions, or privileges of employment, because of such individual's race, color, religion, sex, or national origin; or (2) to limit, segregate, or classify . . . employees in any way which would deprive or tend to deprive any individual of employment opportunities or otherwise adversely affect his status as an employee because of such individual's race, color, religion, sex, or national origin."

12. This order was merely the latest in a series of executive orders going back to

Roosevelt's issuance of Executive Order 8802 in 1941. Its immediate predecessor was Executive Order 10925, issued in 1961.

13. In general, it states that government contractors will not "discriminate against any employee or applicant for employment because of race, color, religion, sex, or national origin. The contractor will take affirmative action to ensure that applicants are employed—and that employees are treated during employment —without regard to their race, color, religion, sex, or national origin."

14. "GM Confirms Cut-off of Federal Jobs over Antibias Plan," *Wall Street Journal*, July 22, 1975, p. 10.

15. More information can be obtained by reading B. E. Calme, "U.S. Employment Service Switching Focus from Minorities to Supplying Skilled Labor," *Wall Street Journal* (March 12, 1973), p. 16.

16. See J. C. Hyatt, "Toothless Tiger? All Sides Criticize Law Barring Job Bias by Federal Contractors," *Wall Street Journal* (November 11, 1975), p. 1.

17. The key phrase of the act is: "It shall be unlawful for an employer (1) to fail or refuse to hire or to discharge any individual or otherwise discriminate against any individual with respect to his compensation, terms, conditions, or privileges of employment, because of such individual's age; (2) to limit, segregate, or classify . . . employees in any way which would deprive or tend to deprive any individual of employment opportunities or otherwise adversely affect . . . the status as an employee, because of such individual's age, or (3) to reduce the wage rate of any employee in order to comply with this act."

18. The key sentence is: "No employer having employees subject to any provisions of this section shall discriminate, within any establishment in which such employees are employed, between employees on the basis of sex by paying wages to employees in such establishment at a rate less than the rate at which he pays wages to employees of the opposite sex in such establishments for equal work on jobs the performance of which requires equal skill, effort, and responsibility and which are performed under similar working conditions. . . . "

19. The declared purpose and policy of the law is that all employers engaged in a business affecting commerce who have employees have the general duty to furnish each of the employees a place of employment free from recognized hazards causing, or likely to cause, death or serious physical harm. Employers have the specific duty of complying with safety and health standards promulgated under the act, and all employers also have the duty to comply with those standards, rules, and regulations which are applicable to their own actions and conduct.

20. As many employers are often reluctant to hire the handicapped because they fear an increase in worker's compensation insurance costs, some states have passed "second injury fund" laws. These set up a state agency to reimburse employers or their insurance carriers for part of the worker's compensation costs when a handicapped employee is injured on the job.

21. This act has for the first time legally required clarity in communication of on-the-job benefits to employees. It places the responsibility for clear, concise communication of benefit plans squarely on the shoulders of management. Management must take nothing for granted in assuring a shared understanding of plan intent and detail. Wise managers will "read the handwriting on the wall" and begin as soon as possible to evaluate the effectiveness of current practices in order

to do whatever is needed to comply. A positive spin-off of that action will be that the employees will gain a better understanding of exactly what the organization is doing for them.

If the Secretary of Labor decides that management's description of its benefit and pension plan is not "adequate," a fine can be levied. If the inadequacy is "willful," imprisonment for the plan's administrator can result. In addition, if a plan's participants or beneficiaries feel that anything about the plan has been kept from them, they may sue for relief and can be awarded court costs and attorney's fees. The court may also impose fines of $100 per day for proven violations.

See Rudolph Kagerer, "Do Employees Understand Your Benefits Program?" *The Personnel Administrator,* vol. 20, no. 6 (October 1975), pp. 29–31.

Chapter 5

The sociocultural context

The sociocultural environment
   Cultural variables
   Effects of cultural differences on personnel and human resources administration

The educational environment
   Relationship between knowledge and performance
   Increasing education level of employees in the United States
   Effects upon personnel administration

The technological environment
   Consequences of technological development
   Effects upon personnel administration

The changing work environment
   Definitions
   Roles played by work
   Changing perceptions of work
   What workers want from their jobs
   Job dissatisfaction and efforts to overcome it
   Effects upon personnel administration

Implications and applications for personnel executives

5
The sociocultural context

*So our virtues lie in the
Interpretation of the time.*
SHAKESPEARE

*If a man does not keep pace with his companions,
Perhaps it is because he hears a different drummer.
Let him step to the music which he hears,
However measured or far away.*
HENRY DAVID THOREAU

The era in which we are now living has been variously designated as a "cyberculture," the "postindustrial age," and the "postindustrial society." The basis of these conclusions is the fact that many economic systems are now able to produce a sufficient supply of goods for expected consumption with more people required to distribute those goods and provide business and personal services than is required to produce the goods themselves. This has been true in the United States for over a decade.

Personnel managers are now expected to do more than just cope with the accelerating changes occasioned by this different kind of economy; they need to plan and control those changes and attempt to guide their managerial and nonmanagerial personnel away from harmful or detrimental modifications of existing behavioral patterns and into more desirable ones. (1)

The sociocultural context is very difficult to discuss—as well as to cope with—as it is so all-inclusive, yet so ill-defined and indistinct.

A nation's cultural system is composed of three horizontal layers, namely, the technological stratum on the bottom, the social layer imposed upon that, and a philosophical level on top. (2) As a cultural system is a total system, changes in any of the levels will have an effect upon the others, such as:

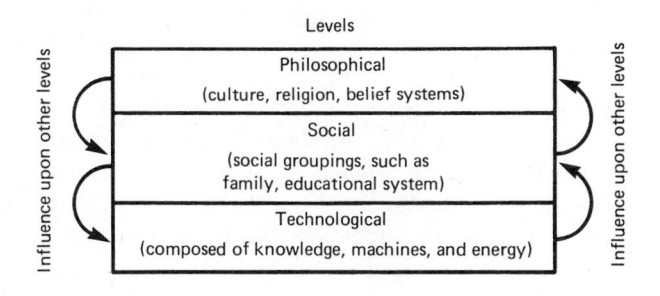

	Levels	
Influence upon other levels	Philosophical (culture, religion, belief systems)	Influence upon other levels
	Social (social groupings, such as family, educational system)	
	Technological (composed of knowledge, machines, and energy)	

87

Yet, the technological stratum, which is the basic and primary one, largely influences the change in the other two levels. For example, the technological development of television has had a great influence upon our social habits, as well as family relationships. In turn, it has had profound influences upon our philosophical beliefs and ethical value judgments. Air conditioning, another technological development, has also changed our social habits, modified the buildings in which we live and work, and influenced our life-styles. It can be concluded that TV brought us indoors and air conditioning keeps us there, thus altering our social systems.

The same relationship is true in organizations. New machines and processes lead to new social groupings and interpersonal relationships. Conversely, the philosophical level can also influence the other levels. For example, our ethical value systems and spiritual beliefs will determine whether a given technological advance will be utilized.

While it is impractical to cover all aspects of the environment that are relevant to a study of personnel administration, the ones which have the greatest relevancy will be discussed in relative detail. These include the sociocultural, educational, and technological environments and their relationships to the overall work environment.

THE SOCIOCULTURAL ENVIRONMENT

The management discipline is founded upon some generally accepted concepts, as you have probably learned in other courses. Yet, in carrying out these principles, managerial practices, and philosophies in different cultures (either between countries or between varying cultures in your own country or state), there are factors which have a modifying effect. For example, although the principle of efficiency is applicable in all cultures, different environments determine how the principle will be applied.

Cultural variables

Since culture involves the knowledge, beliefs, art, morals, laws, customs, language, attitudes, values, norms, and any other capacities and habits required by individuals as members of society, (3) people who are born and develop in a given cultural system will have a different behavioral pattern from those who grow up in another one.

This assumption does not deny the fact that every individual is born with a different physical makeup and mental capacity. Instead, it is claimed that an individual's hereditary differences are modified by the same cultural influences as are the capacities of other members of the same group.

Effect of family background on values. It has long been realized that a person's family background has an important influence in shaping one's value judgments. However, recent research has determined more precisely the relationship between certain factors in the individual's family background and one's work values. (4)

It was found that if a boy grows up in a materialistic atmosphere, he will view work as a means of obtaining economic and material returns from a given job. If he is the product of a cultured atmosphere and grows up in a cohesive family group, he is likely to consider work important for the chance it gives him to make social and cultural contributions. The cultural element also determines the future employee's heuristic and creative abilities. Thus, if he is exposed to artistic, literary, and scientific activities early in life, he will welcome the chance to be creative in his work assignments. Finally, the family's position on, and movement up, the social ladder will affect his desire for achievement and prestige. (However, the last relationship has not been conclusively proven through research.)

Later research at the University of Texas corroborated this result. It indicates that "Texas youth are and have been assimilating parental value systems into their own to a greater extent than the public generally assumes." (5)

Among the research findings was one which showed that the impact of the

BERRY'S WORLD

"This is AWFUL! Junior's living in a hippie commune and it says he's from an upper-middle-class family instead of an UPPER-CLASS family!"

© 1970 by NEA, Inc. Reprinted by permission of NEA.

family, especially the parents, was quite deep and extensive. The mother was cited by 83 percent of respondents as the major source of influence, and the father was second with an 80 percent rating. The other top 10 sources of influence were spouse, fiance, or steady; friends; books; dating; professor in one's own department; job; event of national importance; and roommate. Also identified as powerful sources of influence were students' peers.

Another research study has shown that individuals with wealthy parents will choose occupations involving greater monetary risks. As a result, individuals from wealthier families receive, on the average, higher incomes. (6)

Also, these values tend to remain with us through our adult lives and into our old age. (7)

Relationship between home organization and job involvement. There are indications that there is a complementary relationship between the goals employees set for their family and those they set for themselves in their organizational framework. There are two divergent relationships as far as the home organization and the work organization are concerned. In general, the more job-involved people are, the more they tend to structure their family relationships along the line of the organizational relationships. Employees who fail to obtain job satisfaction and ego involvement in their work tend to have more interest in domestic activities. (8)

A growing managerial elite? Although we pride ourselves in this country upon the selection of managerial leaders up "through the ranks," a group of British researchers found that the recruitment of the American business "elite" since 1801 has been remarkably stable. The managers in that category were found to originate in a highly favorable social and economic environment. These researchers concluded that only between 8 and 20 percent of those individuals came from "working-class" families. (9)

These findings were corroborated by a later study of the social and cultural backgrounds of about 1,000 of the top officers of the 600 largest nonfinancial corporations in the United States. Yet, this phenomenon seems to be changing. In 1900, 8 percent of the executives were sons of "employees," as opposed to 70 percent who were sons of "businessmen," and 22 percent had fathers who were "professional." In 1964, 29 percent were sons of "employees," 49 percent had fathers who were "businessmen," and 22 percent came from "professional families." Yet it was found upon analysis that of the 29 percent whose fathers were "employees," only 9 percent were sons of "skilled," "semiskilled," and "unskilled" labor. (10)

Apparently a similar elitism exists among top academic and government administrators. (11)

Effects of cultural differences on personnel and human resources administration

The knowledge of management principles is not automatically transferable into effectiveness unless personnel administrators develop their own managerial philosophies and practices which can be applied to, and accepted in, people from different cultural backgrounds. In fact, one of the biggest failures of managers moving from one culture to another has been their unfamiliarity with, and general disregard for, the customs, laws, and conditions in the new culture. Empirical evidence indicates a high degree of correlation between our understanding of the cultural variables in another society and our ability to adjust successfully to that culture. (12)

Problems of cross-cultural movement. Since culture is also defined as cultivated behavior acquired through social learning, it is assumed that *personnel engaged in cross-cultural operations can assimilate another culture through the social learning process.* If we cannot learn to adjust to another society, the cultural differences, or cross-cultural conflict, may interfere with our performance. When individuals with a given "cultural set" are confronted with a different cultural set, they may be accepted or rejected by the people in another society during the process of adjustment. In turn, the individuals might accept or reject them. Although the cross-cultural conflict is inevitable in the process of adjustment, it can be eliminated, or at least minimized, in time through the learning procedure.

Management principles and functions are assumed to be universal and are the same, regardless of where they are performed. Thus, personnel administration is personnel administration whether you are in Toledo or Toronto, New York or New Orleans, Memphis or Mexico City. However, differences do exist in performing the personnel functions and in applying the principles to given situations, depending upon the cultural backgrounds of the personnel involved. Differential cultural backgrounds, managerial resources and skills, managerial philosophies, and business environments may cause variations in the personnel manager's performance of the personnel activities. The problem is to be able to determine those concepts which can be transferred with effectiveness to other cultures.

Problems of managing personnel from varying cultures. Herein lies a dilemma for future personnel executives, namely, dealing with employees from diverse cultural backgrounds. While our personalities are unique—even in our own culture—this difference is compounded when we are exposed to people with different cultural heritages and personalities. Thus, people's cultural attitudes are important in determining their effectiveness as personnel managers when managing people from another culture or with a different heritage. This truth is very important when minority groups, who tend to have an entirely different life-style, are involved.

Contemporary human resource management gives much credence to "future time orientation," "contingency theory," and "expectancy theory," all of which hypothesize that the future will hold a certain increasing probability for advancement or high level of reward available for superior performance. Yet, for poor people and "ghetto dwellers," those theories don't seem to work, at least not in the short run. The poor either cannot gain jobs or cannot keep them as they have been behaviorally oriented to think of the present. While almost all employment is based on the long-range future, the poor or ghetto resident looks only to the short run. Consequently, if employment is available, it may only be taken advantage of until some short-run problem is solved. An example may be taking employment to pay for a new wardrobe or color television. Because organizations must be managed with regard to long-run criteria maximization, constant rehiring and training of employees is impractical.

Therefore, the poor or minority individuals must be selected, developed, utilized, and rewarded differently, for their values often differ from the manager's. (13)

THE EDUCATIONAL ENVIRONMENT

Leonardo da Vinci—sculptor, painter, engineer, musician, architect, and scientist—was the towering example of the Renaissance scholar who believed in broadening the intellectual scope of higher education. Yet, it is doubtful that we will ever see another da Vinci simply because, during the 500 years since the Renaissance, knowledge has become so abundant and complex that one human being can amass and store only a small fraction of it. This statement indicates one of the great problems beginning to face personnel administrators, namely, how to deal with a more highly educated work force.

Relationship between knowledge and performance

It is now recognized that skills and knowledge can easily become obsolete in the same way as machines, technology, and other factors. They must constantly be kept up-to-date if the individual organization, or nation, is to survive. It has been estimated that in the future about 20 to 25 percent of an engineer's time must be spent in educational experiences on the job or on the organization's time. (14) Another estimate is that graduate engineers must spend 10 percent of their time each year extending their knowledge *just to keep up with current graduates;* and 20 percent, if they want to remain of equal value to their employer and society. (15) While these generalizations apply to any nation or culture, their application to the United States will be given as an example.

Increasing education level of employees in the United States

The total U.S. population is considerably more educated than it has ever been. The same is true of all occupations and the civilian labor force.

From 1964 to 1974. As seen in Table 5–1, the number of *persons in the labor force* who had completed four years of high school or more increased by 22.7 million between 1964 and 1974. Around 70 percent of the almost 90 million persons in the civilian labor force had completed four years of high school, and about 15 percent had finished four years of college.

TABLE 5–1
Increase in labor force and its educational level (in 000s)

	1964	1974	1964–74 Change
Total labor force	69,926	89,633	+19,707
Less than 4 years of high school	30,599	27,580	− 3,019
Elementary: 8 or less	17,183	11,397	− 5,786
High school: 1–3 years	13,416	16,183	+ 2,767
4 years of high school or more	39,327	62,053	+22,726
High school: 4 years	24,123	35,132	+11,009
College: 1–3 years	7,385	13,493	+ 6,108
4 years or more	7,819	13,428	+ 5,609

Source: Beverly J. McEaddy, "Educational Attainment of Workers, March 1974," *Monthly Labor Review*, vol. 98, no. 2 (February 1975), p. 64.

Both whites and blacks gained in median educational attainment over the decade. The proportion of the white labor force with at least a high school diploma increased from 59 percent to 70 percent, while the proportion of blacks rose from 35 percent to 54 percent.

In 1990. The labor force will probably have an even higher educational background in 1990. The heavy influx of relatively well-educated younger workers into the labor force, which will occur at approximately the same time that many less-educated, older workers will be leaving the labor force, promises a major change in the educational level of workers. (See Figure 5–1 for details.)

Effects upon personnel administration

There are several consequences of these changes. First, the increased knowledge has *raised the productivity of employees and, consequently, enhanced their earning capacity.* (16) Second, this knowledge has tended to limit employment opportunities of the unskilled and the uneducated and led to their becoming unemployable or unpromotable.

Another result of this increased education has been *mobility* and *high turnover.* In a nationwide study of over 30,000 college graduates, it was found that within three years more than half of the men and four-fifths of the women had left their first employer. (17) Although the degree of satisfaction or dissatisfaction with the working environment has a significant relation to turnover, the much discussed conflict between the developing "social values" of the students and their actual work experiences did not seem to materialize. Three years after graduation, the reported reasons for turnover tended to be for the more materialistic ones of money and advancement and less for the social values.

Personnel managers may face a problem of *employee alienation and frustration* which is being built into much of Western society. We have long sold our

FIGURE 5–1
Percent of civilian labor force with at least four years of high school and at least four years of college, by age, 1970–72 actual and 1990 projected

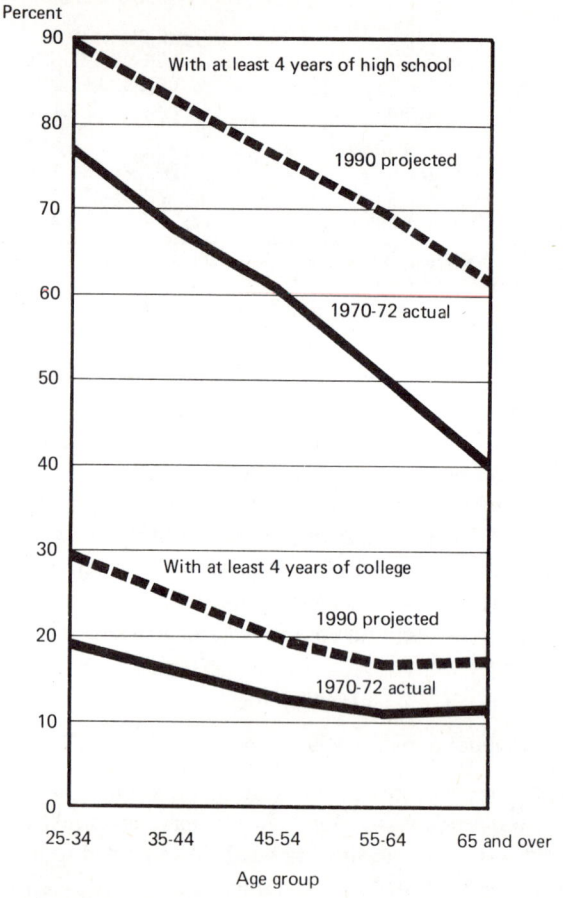

Source: *Bulletin to Management* (Washington, D.C.: Bureau of National Affairs, March 21, 1974), p. 6.

youth on education as the best route to increased status, power, and income. But increasing numbers of college-trained youth are now bumping into the reality that pyramids narrow at the top. It has been estimated that perhaps 2.5 million college graduates will be competing for blue-collar and lower-level white-collar jobs during the next decade.

In the late 1960s in the United States, two basic demographic lines crossed: More people in the adult labor force now have at least one year of college than there are higher-level jobs to absorb them. (18)

	1960	1970
Percent of adult labor force with one or more years of college	19	27
Percent of total employment represented by managerial, administrative, technical, and professional jobs	20	22

THE TECHNOLOGICAL ENVIRONMENT

Technological development continues to proliferate! The last two decades have been marked by technological explosions in many fields, especially in new fields such as *ecology* and the *environment*. Consequently, the personnel administrators' responsibilities are further complicated, for they must try to maintain a balance between the need for effective performance—which can be achieved only with large-scale production—and the need to relieve human tensions resulting from the magnitude of the present changes.

Consequences of technological development

Historically it is difficult to dispute the premise that technological development creates jobs. However, there is now a new problem facing personnel managers. The two stages in mechanization which followed the "Industrial Revolution" included the ones in which (*a*) employees' skills and productivity were enhanced, and (*b*) labor was partially displaced by capital. Now, a third stage appears to be emerging in which machines will be capable of almost entirely replacing people, and completely automatic operations will be used in producing goods and services. Automation is, therefore, construed by some personnel executives as a new problem which should be dealt with as such. However, I believe that automation is only accelerating mechanization and, as such, is only a continuation of a process begun centuries ago. Yet, there have been both favorable and adverse consequences.

Favorable consequences. Some of the more favorable results of technological development are: (*a*) increased productivity, (*b*) increased employment, and (*c*) general upgrading of jobs.

Increased productivity. There is little argument that technological development has increased production, cut costs, improved service, generated new products, and enhanced quality. For example, in the industrialized countries, productivity has averaged an increase of around 4 percent per year in the United States to around 15 percent in Japan during the last 25 years. From 1958 to 1969, output per worker-hour in the major household appliance industry, one of the most technically-oriented in the United States, increased 5.8 percent per year as compared with 4 percent for all manufacturing. (19)

While it is generally accepted that technological improvements underlie high living standards, (20) fear of their consequences is also present—not only among employees, but also among entrepreneurs, for these changes can easily force marginal, high-labor-cost firms out of business.

Increased employment. Actual unemployment as a result of automation is relatively uncommon. For example, despite the rapid movement toward office mechanization, there is little evidence that any substantial number of workers have been thrown out of jobs; the trend has been in the opposite direction. It appears that the volume of paper continues to grow more rapidly than the decrease in jobs caused by the computer revolution.

> The Stanford Research Institute studied the reasons why two banks, two electronics manufacturers, and three warehouses automated and reviewed the consequences of these actions. It was found that some workers were transferred within the same company and some retired, *but no one was laid off.* (21)

Upgrading of jobs. In general, there will be a decrease in the number of unskilled, routinized jobs, for employees will be used more effectively (*a*) through using machines to do more of the boring and tedious work, and (*b*) by having customers do much of the service for themselves, as is true in quick service food franchises. (22) Employees will be able to do more interesting and creative work, with a resultant upgrading of their jobs.

> *The Dictionary of Occupational Titles* listed around 17,000 job definitions when it was first published in 1939. Since then, it has added over 12,000 new job definitions, mostly in connection with new technologies such as computers and space vehicles.

At the 50th Anniversary Symposium of the Hawthorne Studies held at Oak Brook, Illinois, November 11–13, 1974, Paul Lawrence emphasized that the basic characteristics of jobs have changed in the last 50 years, largely as a result of "new techniques." (23) As shown in Figure 5–2, the result has been a shift *from* jobs whose content dealt with "certainty" *to* ones with "uncertainty."

At the same time, human capacities to handle job uncertainty has increased significantly, as shown in Figure 5–3.

The result of these shifts is a "gap" between job content and the human

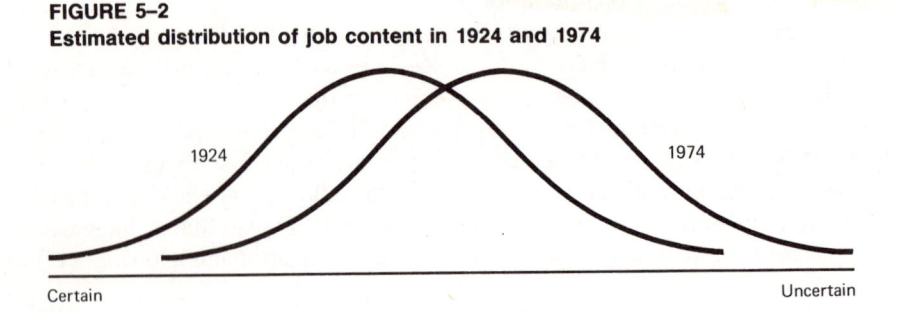

FIGURE 5–2
Estimated distribution of job content in 1924 and 1974

Certain   Uncertain

FIGURE 5–3
Estimated distribution of human capacity to handle job uncertainty in 1924 and 1974

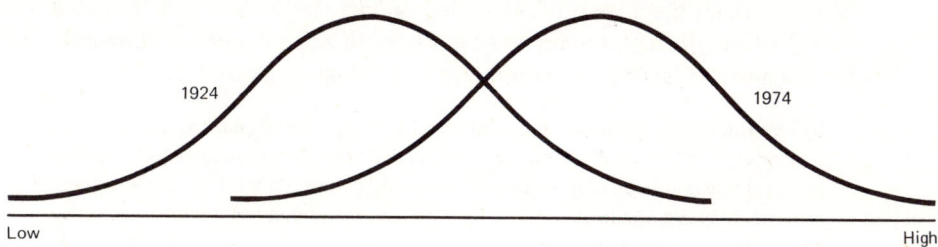

1924   1974

Low   High

capacity to perform the jobs. Figure 5–4 provides a visual estimate of the magnitude of personnel management's problem of matching people and jobs and using personnel more effectively.

Unfavorable consequences. Among the unfavorable results of technological development are job displacement and disturbed group relationships.

Job displacement. Many employees who might otherwise have been used to perform the technically advanced activities or related jobs have not been physically, mentally, educationally, emotionally, or temperamentally capable of adapting to these new skills, duties, and responsibilities.

Around 8.5 million people were unemployed in the United States in 1975, while lack of personnel was hampering economic expansion. Nearly a half million jobs went unfilled. (24) An analysis of the unemployed showed a partial cause. Few were skilled; the jobs "paid too little"; employers were reluctant to hire laid-off workers; it was hard to match up persons, jobs, and places; and employees were not in such financial difficulties that they would willingly lower their ambitions.

Disturbed group relationships. Automation *tends* to disrupt the many informal interpersonal relationships found in all organizations. The interactions between employees on the same level, as well as between superior and subordinates, tend to decline. Also, there is less social interaction among workers when several small machines, each with a worker, is replaced by one or two large machines with a control room with a single operator.

FIGURE 5–4
Estimated fit of job content and human capacity in 1974

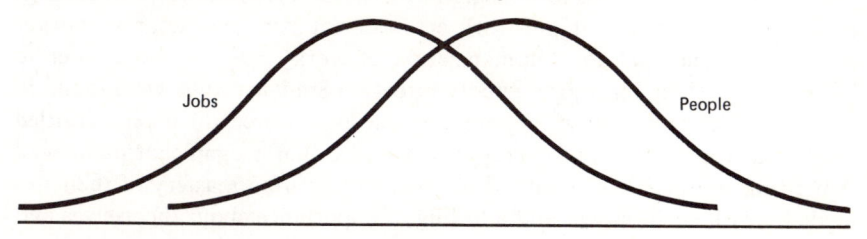

Jobs   People

Effects upon personnel administration

How one views the advent of technological changes is largely determined by the *perceived effects* of it upon one's position. In general, personnel managers have tended to favor automation and technological development.

> The Industrial Relations Association of Chicago found that the status of the personnel manager was thought to be enhanced through automation, with better data being available on employees, selecting and training of personnel being given high priority, organizational planning activities being increased with centralized information and processing centers, and greater utilization of personnel. (25)

Personnel managers must adjust to this new environment, just as they have been forced to adapt to changes in other physical and social environments of the past. The essential problem facing personnel executives of the future is how to increase their knowledge of human behavior and how to utilize this information to develop organizationally to keep pace with the rapidly developing technology.

Some specific ways in which technological development will influence the performance of the personnel function are:

1. Increased use of functional authority, because of the concentration of authority near the top of the organization;
2. Improved personnel selection strategies, as the newer technologies will require more intelligence, education, judgment, and skills in creativity;
3. Newer personnel development strategies, as professional and managerial obsolescence will be an increased threat;
4. Improved reward and punishment systems, for higher-level employees will tend to become frustrated when part of the individuality and creativity of their work is eliminated;
5. Different strategies for dealing with employee associations, because of the changing nature of work which reduces group solidarity, erodes union power, and reduces the effectiveness of strikes; and
6. More need to prepare employees for retirement.

THE CHANGING WORK ENVIRONMENT

The sagging productivity rate in the United States and its worldwide ramifications seem to be related to changes in the work surroundings. The findings of one study suggest that the work environment is a key factor in worker productivity and that the "humanization of work" may be the answer to increasing our long-term productivity rate. (26) Similar results were found in a Health, Education, and Welfare Special Task Force document entitled "Work in America." (27) This report concluded that a significant number of Americans are dissatisfied with their lives and desire a mastery of their immediate work environment and a feeling of importance about themselves and their work.

These, and related conclusions, led the U.S. Senate to pass the *Worker Alienation Research and Technical Assistance Act of 1972,* which provided for research into solutions for this growing problem in our country.

Employee alienation results from many complex and interrelated causes. Some of these are rooted in the sociocultural environment; some, in the organizational environment; and some, in ourselves. Alienation results in manifestations of employee resentment such as absenteeism, wildcat strikes, and inferior quality products, and this behavior effects not only operating expenses, but the entire organization pays a higher price for such negative attitudes and their consequences.

> A two-year survey of 1,300 workers at ten industrial plants turned up a "significant statistical relationship" between job dissatisfaction and psychologically induced ailments. Workers describing themselves as unhappy with work more often showed real cases of headaches, fatigue, colds, and other common ailments. (28)

Definitions

As usual, we need to define our terms for the discussion to be meaningful.

Work. Work is the activity in which we exert physical and mental strength in order to do something useful for some form of gain, usually—but not always—monetary reward. Sustained physical or mental effort to overcome obstacles results in the achievement of some desired objective. In essence, *work* is a *productive activity, involving physical or mental exertion, which is scheduled on a routine basis, and is usually paid for.*

Occupation. An *occupation* is the *overall activity in which we engage and is usually the principal productive activity of our life.* The term involves the very nature of the activities being performed, their level in an organization, the importance of the results, and the skills, aptitudes, abilities, knowledge, education, and training necessary for their performance.

Job. A *job* refers to *a specific role or function in a given organization, usually involving a specific set of tasks, duties, functions, and responsibilities.* A problem for personnel managers is the fact that a job is usually composed of both mandatory and discretionary factors. (29) The *mandatory*, or prescribed, content refers to those things which *all* workers who hold that job must do in order to avoid a charge of negligence or insubordination; that is, it is the minimum required of an applicant for one to be hired. The *discretionary* part is composed of the decisions and activities that *any* employee is authorized to make if one chooses. This is the part which can be expanded to make the job more meaningful to the firm and to the individual. Rewards are usually based upon this part.

Roles played by work

Work provides us with an opportunity to *play the part of provider for our families* and to be useful and productive members of society. It is the means by which we achieve our objectives in life, whatever those objectives may be. If the tasks demanded of us are compatible with our abilities, values, attitudes, considerations of status, and patterns of interaction with other people, we tend to play the role successfully. In playing the role, we adapt ourselves to our socioeconomic system.

> A recent study found that garbage collectors don't feel bad about their low-status jobs. While they are often aware their jobs are held in low repute, they don't let that mar their own self-esteem. The workers seemed to focus mainly on "their extra-occupational statuses," rather than defining themselves in terms of their careers.
>
> Black collectors had an easier time coping with the image problem, because the community is "more likely to evaluate black men in terms of realistic possibilities." Whites, on the other hand, had to battle individually against some neighborhood scorn. Having a separate sanitation workers union, as in Detroit, helped bolster self-esteem.
>
> The study showed that most collectors liked their work and didn't want it "humanized." (30)

Many studies have shown that employed people will not voluntarily give up their work role, because of its ability to relate them to a meaningful environment. For example, it was found in a sample of 401 employed persons that 80 percent of them would continue to work even if they inherited enough money to live comfortably for the rest of their lives. (31)

Along the same line of reasoning, studies by Professor Eli Ginzberg, director of the Conservation of Human Resources Project at Columbia University, have shown that work regulates the life of individuals who are the operating units in our economy. (32) He concluded that individuals must have an opportunity for expressing themselves through their work and that this is the best way for relating themselves to reality and to the world around them.

In 1956, Robert Dubin made a study of industrial workers to determine if their work was their central life interest. He concluded 24 percent were job-oriented and 76 percent were nonjob-oriented, and "work" was not their central life interest. (33) Instead, the workers preferred human associations, and the preferred areas of behavior were outside their employment.

A later researcher applied the same methodology to a group of 331 first- through third-level supervisors employed by six Michigan manufacturing firms. Contrary to Dubin's results, John Maurer discovered that the lower- and middle-level supervisor's central life interests were 54 percent job-oriented and 46 percent nonjob-oriented. (34) However, the results were lower than Dubin's test of professional nurses, who were 79 percent job-oriented and 21 percent nonjob-oriented. Also the researcher found no significant correlation to indicate age as a factor for central life interest determination.

A study of a large group of blue- and white-collar civil service employees in an isolated setting found work to be more important in providing satisfaction than church, educational, recreational, and/or leisure activities. (35)

It can be concluded from these and other studies that the meaning of work to individuals is related to the type work they do and to their level in the organization. It can be generalized that work tends to be the central life interest of managers and supervisors, skilled workers, and scientific, technical, and professional personnel; it is less important to lower-skilled workers, and to those with narrow, specialized jobs.

Changing perceptions of work

Work has declined in importance in the minds of many employees, though it is still the central life interest of some. While there have been four ways of viewing the importance of work in our lives, essentially there are only two. First, work was considered to have intrinsic value, and through its performance we receive pleasure and a sense of self-fulfillment; second, while work is not satisfaction-yielding within itself, it is a means of obtaining satisfaction elsewhere. Yet, there have been several variations of these two.

Work has intrinsic value. During earlier periods, work was considered to be satisfaction-yielding—within itself.

After the "Industrial Revolution," the intrinsic value of work tended to be diminished, and it became less desirable. Human energy was replaced by machine energy, and mechanized and industrialized cities replaced small rural communities. Specialization, mechanization, and standardization of jobs deprived workers of much of the creativity and personality of previous work.

There are indications that young people are now returning to the acceptance of this view of work. The booming "do-it-yourself" market may be a function of economics, but it could also be a search for the intangible sense of satisfaction that accompanies making something for yourself.

Work has moral value. The Puritanic theory of work is based upon the belief that work has moral and spiritual value, and through working, one expresses one's knowledge and love of God, man, and self. (36) It is the method by which people attain the ultimate objectives in life. By working hard, they obtain the life to which they want to become accustomed, a life of comfort, leisure, and a nourishing family experience.

This concept was quite prevalent until World War II. Apparently it is still held by many middle-class professional and managerial workers in Western societies. To them, work gives purpose, challenge, and responsibility to life. (37)

Today younger workers tend to reject this ethic. They think it is socially unnecessary, it has been used to exploit workers, its religious premises are dubious, and its practical effects unhappy.

Work and leisure should be balanced. This perception of work is based upon the apparent tendency of work to become separate from other aspects of life; it is just a way of providing funds to buy leisure time. (38) This emphasis upon leisure and the pursuit of pleasure may be the prototype of the future economic system.

Having discovered leisure in a setting which is at last practical, people will probably never again view work with the same intensity they felt when it was essential for survival. Although this feeling is not new—Aristotle said, "The end of labor is to gain leisure,"—at least the newer employees consider leisure and pleasure as of equal value to work. As evidence of this, the annual hours of work have decreased from around 3,750 to 1,800 in the last century and the workweek has changed at the rate of three hours per decade since 1900.

In summary, people are less dependent upon one job, one employer, and work itself as a means of survival and satisfaction. As welfare programs and other means of survival have proliferated, it is no longer true that if we "do not work," we "do not eat."

Work is necessary to satisfy human needs. This view contends that people work to satisfy the craving which is most pressing on them at a given moment of time. To the extent these needs can be satisfied by working on a given job, with a given organization, they are the concern of the personnel administrator.

There is no one generally accepted classification of human motives. Probably the best distinction is that which differentiates between the *physiological motives* stemming directly from the physical needs of the organism, the satisfaction of which is essential to the survival or physical well-being of us individuals, including respiration, hunger, thirst, elimination, pain avoidance, mating, and so on; and *secondary, learned, social, or psychogenic motives,* which are those not directly related to the physical needs.

What workers want from their jobs

In general, workers usually want to *know they are doing a good job,* not just to impress the boss, but to satisfy their own obligation to themselves, their families, and their friends. This involves the satisfaction of measuring up to their abilities. They also want enough *money* to provide them with the basic necessities of life and *job security* to continue receiving those benefits.

From a practical point of view, these conclusions seem valid. As seen in Tables 5–2 and 5–3, employees want an interesting and challenging job—as well as advancement and recognition. But income and security seem to be increasingly important to them.

TABLE 5–2
A. What college students seek from a job

	1973 Percent	Rank	1970 (71) Percent	Rank
Challenge of job	77	(1)	64	(1)
Ability to express yourself	68	(2)	56	(2)
Money	61	(3)	36	(3)
Job security	58	(4)	33	(5)
Chance to get ahead	51	(5)	35	(4)
Prestige of job	28	(6)	15	(6)

B. What blue-collar workers seek from a job

	1973 Percent	Rank
Interesting work	66	1
Good pay	65	2
See results of your work	60	3
A chance to use your mind	58	4
Develop skills/abilities	57	5
Participation in decision	56	6
Recognition for good work	52	7

Source: Daniel Yankelovich, "Youth Attitude toward Work," *Business and Society Review*, no. 11 (Autumn 1974), pp. 46–47. Reprinted from *Business and Society Review*, No. 11 Autumn 1974. Copyright 1974, Warren, Gorham, and Lamont, Inc., 210 South Street, Boston, Mass. All rights reserved.

TABLE 5–3
Supervisory motivational responses to question: "Why I wanted to become a supervisor?"

	Major motivational responses	Total number responses	Percent of the total number responses	Percent of supervisors who listed this response
1.	More money	60	25	92
2.	Advancement	38	15	58
3.	A challenge	31	12	48
4.	Enjoy leadership	26	10	40
5.	Self-improvement	23	9	35
6.	More value to the company	18	7	28
7.	Enjoy working with people	17	7	26
8.	Job diversification	15	6	23
9.	Provide better living for my family	12	5	19
10.	Status and/or prestige	10	4	15
	Total	250	100%	—

Source: Paul W. Cummings, "Operation: Supervisor," *Personnel Journal* (August 1975), p. 449. "Reprinted with permission." *Personnel Journal*, copyright August 1975.

Job dissatisfaction and efforts to overcome it

There is much difference of opinion—and even controversy—over the extent and causes of job dissatisfaction and how to overcome it. Job satisfaction does not result merely from the job, the individual, or the environment; a combination of all these factors is necessary. As a result, almost everyone studying the question reaches different conclusions. Part of the problem is that there are so many factors determining whether workers will be satisfied or not, and these are not always covered in research studies. Some of the factors are age, sex, race, education, occupation, place of employment, type of organization, geographic location, religious beliefs, and the "social system."

Extent of job dissatisfaction. It has become increasingly evident during recent years that the degree of job satisfaction and dissatisfaction appear to be universal. In a national comparison of job satisfaction by occupations, the *percentage of satisfied workers* in the six most highly industrialized countries was essentially the same—approximately 80 percent. (39) While some studies find satisfaction to be lower, most find it to be higher. (40)

The findings of seven respected studies done from 1958 to 1973 *tend* to indicate that:

1. Whites are *more satisfied* than blacks,
2. Older workers are *more satisfied* than younger ones,
3. Men are *more satisfied* than women,
4. Workers in high status jobs are *more satisfied* than those in lower status ones;
5. Employees who are more professional are *more satisfied* than those who are not, and
6. Workers with a high school education are *less satisfied* than those with less or with more schooling.

The extent of *satisfaction* seems to have reached a *low point* with the Lordstown strike of 1972. (41) Now, there is much evidence that either there was not that much dissatisfaction or workers have found ways to cope with—and even accept—the situation. The answer probably lies in the middle—there are some boring jobs (see Figure 5–5), but there are many which are not. The effective personnel manager can probably match people and jobs to overcome the problem.

Efforts to overcome job dissatisfaction. If it is true that performance is a function of abilities × motivation × expectancy, $P = f(A \times M)E$, then the ways to increase job satisfaction include:

1. Match employee abilities and job requirements through job redesign and selective employment;
2. Use the newer motivational techniques; and
3. Have employee expectations be more realistic.

Job redesign. Performance is improved when employees are doing work which has meaning, worth, dignity, and status, as well as challenging their abilities and keeping them busy. (42) Some of the more popular efforts now being made by personnel managers to redesign jobs to make them more meaningful are:

1. Job enlargement and enrichment programs,
2. Work module job rotation systems,
3. Work improvement suggestion systems,
4. Shorter workweek, and
5. Flexible working hours.

Newer motivational techniques. In addition to trying to upgrade the jobs and employee abilities, personnel managers are training and encouraging line

FIGURE 5-5

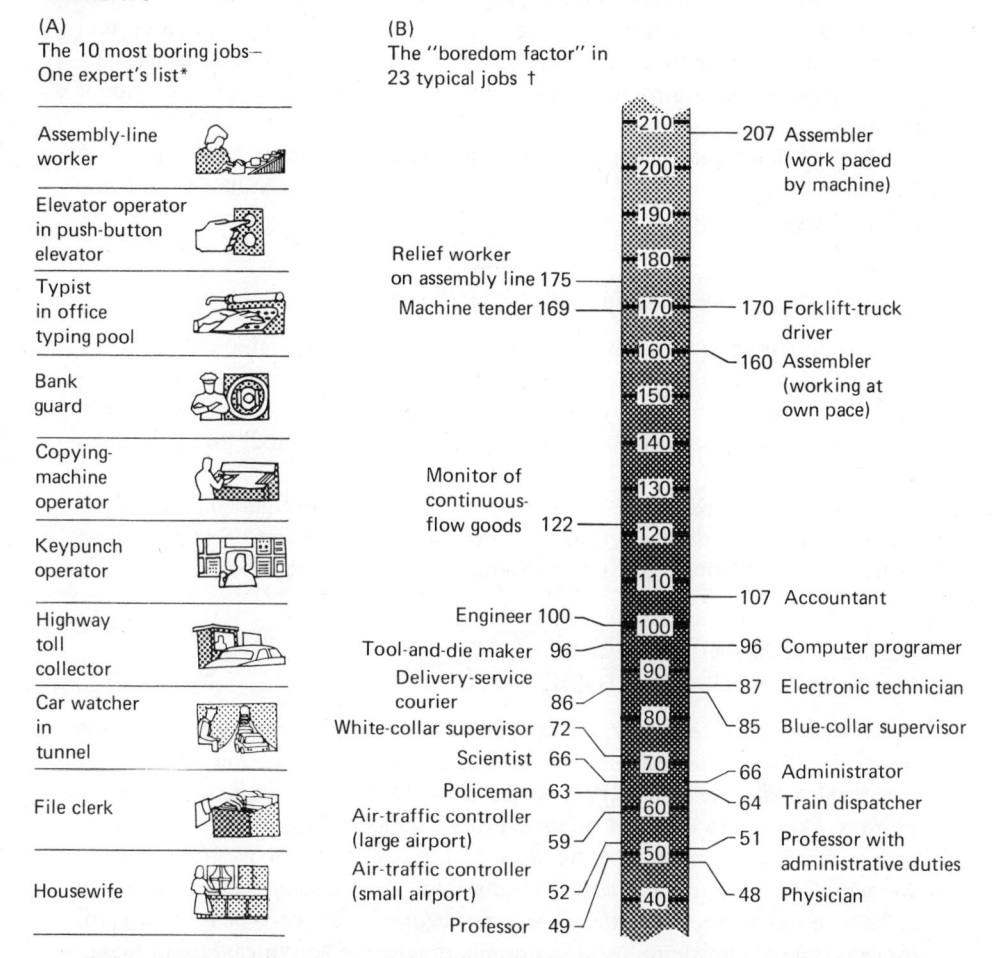

(A) The 10 most boring jobs— One expert's list*

Assembly-line worker
Elevator operator in push-button elevator
Typist in office typing pool
Bank guard
Copying-machine operator
Keypunch operator
Highway toll collector
Car watcher in tunnel
File clerk
Housewife

(B) The "boredom factor" in 23 typical jobs †

Score	Job
207	Assembler (work paced by machine)
175	Relief worker on assembly line
170	Forklift-truck driver
169	Machine tender
160	Assembler (working at own pace)
122	Monitor of continuous-flow goods
107	Accountant
100	Engineer
96	Tool-and-die maker
96	Computer programer
87	Electronic technician
86	Delivery-service courier
85	Blue-collar supervisor
72	White-collar supervisor
66	Scientist
66	Administrator
64	Train dispatcher
63	Policeman
59	Air-traffic controller (large airport)
52	Air-traffic controller (small airport)
51	Professor with administrative duties
49	Professor
48	Physician

* Which day-to-day tasks involve the most drudgery, the least payoff in satisfaction? Personnel consultant Roy Walters, head of a New Jersey management firm, provides the above list of ten. Jobs are given at random, not necessarily in order of boredom.

† Based on interviews with 2,010 workers performing 23 different jobs, the Institute for Social Research at the University of Michigan drew up "boredom factors" for each occupation—with 100 the average and the higher the rating, the more boring the job.

Source: "Reprinted from 'U.S. News & World Report.'" "Those 'Boring' Jobs—Not All That Dull," *U.S. News & World Report* (December 1, 1975), pp. 64–65. "Copyright 1975 U.S. News & World Report, Inc."

managers to use more appropriate motivation. Some of the more popular of these—which will be discussed in Chapter 15—are:

1. Operant-reinforcement analysis, including organizational behavior modification (OBM);
2. Expectancy models;
3. Equity models; and
4. Goal theory.

Realigning expectations. During the last decade, many of the newer employees developed "unwarranted expectations" of what they were to do and the rewards they were to receive, as far as work and their jobs were concerned. When those expectations were not achieved, dissatisfaction and alienation resulted.

More realistic recruiting, selection, and reward systems have tended to correct this deficiency. Yet, personnel managers must continue to aid line management in this move.

Effects upon personnel administration

Although it has been shown that while work is not essential to the economic survival of individuals, it is necessary to assure the continued existence of organizations and nations. Also, the performance of some meaningful work, whether for compensation or not, is essential for our mental and emotional well-being.

As a consequence of these generalizations, personnel managers must improve their day-to-day selection, training, and development of employees in order to have a better "fit" between employees and their jobs.

IMPLICATIONS AND APPLICATIONS FOR PERSONNEL ADMINISTRATORS

The environmental factors discussed indicate that personnel administration must plan for technologically-oriented production systems and service-type organizations in the future. Prior to 1870, we were an agricultural nation, as more workers were engaged in agriculture and extractive industries than all others. From then until 1966, we were an industrial nation, as more workers were producing manufactured products than were engaged in farming and extractive industries. Since then, we have become a service-type economy, for more people are now employed in nonmanufacturing activities than in manufacturing, construction, transportation, agriculture, and communication endeavors. This trend is expected to continue—or even accelerate—during the next one-third century.

These changes will require a different type personnel executive in the future, for there must be a more "humanistic" approach to performing the personnel function.

The traditional personnel management approach must be changed, and increased emphasis should be given to the full utilization of employees' talents and training, their status, and their opportunities for developing their professional careers. Authority, discipline, and financial rewards will play less of a role, while achievement, recognition, responsibility, creative and challenging work, and related factors will serve as stimulants to improve performance. The intrinsic value of work will be more significant than the extrinsic value to be obtained from materialistic rewards.

The following hypotheses can be developed from the material in this chapter:

1. *Personnel administrators' effectiveness depends upon their ability to adjust and adapt to the cultural environment in which they operate and perform the personnel functions, provided their technical proficiency and managerial philosophy remain the same.* This will necessitate a study of cultural differences wherever personnel managers operate and perform the personnel function. It will also require that students studying personnel administration understand this relationship if they are to perform the function successfully in the years to come when the work force will be composed of increasingly diverse cultural variations.
2. *There is a direct and proportional (although delayed) relationship between a nation's measurable expenditure for knowledge and its productivity and prosperity; an organization's productivity and performance are directly proportional to the amount spent to acquire knowledge;* and *our material level of well-being is a function of the time, effort, and energy expended in enhancing our knowledge—everything else remaining the same.* (43) It follows from these hypotheses that personnel executives in organizations should try to enhance the knowledge of employees so that their performance will increase and our material well-being will be enhanced.
3. Technological development is based upon the fact that *even though workers may be temporarily displaced, the reductions in cost resulting from such advances in knowledge, energy resources, and mechanization will open mass markets for the products involved and result in reabsorption of the displaced persons;* and *the machines which displace labor in one industry must be produced by labor in another industry.*
4. *Job satisfaction varies directly and proportionately with the extent to which the needs of the individual worker which can be satisfied in a job situation are actually satisfied.* Therefore, workers whose personal needs are satisfied on the job are more likely to remain on the job as productive employees than those whose needs are not satisfied in the work situation.
5. *The greater the intrinsic value of work being performed, the more satisfying it is to the individual performing it.* Thus, the greater is its value and meaning to an employee.
6. *The greater the satisfaction-yielding characteristics of a specific job, the less need there is for external motivation;* conversely, *the less satisfaction-yielding the job, the greater the need for external motivation and the greater the chances for disrupted working relationships.*
7. *The greater the status attributed to work, an occupation, or a specific job, the more satisfaction-yielding it becomes to the performer.*

DISCUSSION QUESTIONS

1. Take each of the environmental factors discussed in this chapter and show the following: (*a*) How will each one of them affect a personnel administrator ten years

from now? Twenty years from now? (*b*) How would you suggest preparing to cope with each of them? (*c*) Show the relationship(s) between each of them.
2. What are the pressures for accelerating technological development, and what are the forces resisting it, from the economic viewpoint?
3. Does technological development really have an adverse effect on employment? Why or why not? What are the real problems of employment as far as it is concerned?
4. How does the mechanization of work affect the intrinsic value of work and job satisfaction?
5. Do you view job satisfaction as declining or increasing? Explain.
6. What suggestions have you for improving job satisfaction?
7. Evaluate some of the present efforts to overcome job dissatisfaction!

REFERENCES AND SUGGESTIONS FOR FURTHER STUDY

1. A research study showed that personnel executives were conscious of these forces of change, both internal and external, such as changing economic patterns, technological changes, expanding markets, and increasingly complex laws and regulations. However, the most significant finding was that executives in both large and small firms agreed that these changes were taking place gradually in an evolutionary process rather than drastically in a revolutionary manner. See Edward A. Johnson, "The Nature and Direction of Changes in Personnel Management," *Personnel Journal*, vol. 48, no. 4 (April 1969), pp. 275–81, for other details.
2. This conclusion and the resulting diagram are based upon (but modified from) the findings in Leslie A. White, *The Science of Culture: A Study of Man and Civilization* (New York: Farrar, Straus and Co., Inc., 1949), p. 392.
3. E. B. Tylor, *Primitive Culture: Researches into the Development of Mythology, Philosophy, Religion, Language, Art, and Custom*, 3d ed. (London: John Murray, 1891), p. 1; and A. L. Kroeber, *Anthropology*, new ed. (New York: Harcourt, Brace & World, Inc., 1948), pp. 7–8.
4. John F. Kinnane and Martin W. Pable, "Family Background and Work Value Orientation," *Journal of Counseling Psychology*, vol. 9, no. 4 (Winter 1962), pp. 320–25.
5. "Significant Collegiate Sources of Influence" (Austin, Tex.: Office of Vice President of Student Affairs, University of Texas, 1968). The study covered 831 seniors who were graduated from the university in May 1968, when the Vietnamese war was at its pinnacle. An extensive questionnaire was sent to all 2,355 graduates, with 35 percent responding.
6. Allen G. King, "Occupational Choice, Risk Aversion, and Wealth," *Industrial and Labor Relations*, vol. 27, no. 4 (July 1974), pp. 586–97.
7. If you are contented when you are 30, you will feel the same way when you reach 70. That's the conclusion of the Institute for Human Development in San Francisco, whose researchers interviewed a group of 142 men and women in 1928–29 and then reinterviewed them in 1968–69. Reported in *Parade* (September 14, 1975), p. 7.

8. Robert Rapoport and Rhona Rapoport, "Work and Family in Contemporary Society," *American Sociological Review,* vol. 30, no. 3 (June 1965), pp. 381–94.
9. R. Bendix and F. L. Howton, "Social Mobility and the American Business Elite," *British Journal of Sociology,* vol. 4, no. 4 (December 1957), pp. 357–69.
10. *The Big Business Executive* (New York: *Scientific American,* 1965). This study was conducted by Market Statistics, Inc., in collaboration with Dr. Mabel Newcomer, under the sponsorship of *Scientific American.*
11. Michael R. Ferrari, "The Origins and Careers of American Business, Government, and Academic Elites," *California Management Review,* vol. 12, no. 4 (Summer 1970), pp. 26–32.
12. This conclusion is based upon a 13-year research involving in-depth interviews with over 250 managers in around 55 countries. For further details, see Leon C. Megginson, "The Cultural Aspects of, and Problems Associated with, the Transfer of Management Style, Skills, and Know-How," *Proceedings of the Thirty-Fourth Annual Meeting of the Academy of Management, 1974.*
13. For information to help you understand the effects of demographic variables upon value systems, see V. S. Flowers et al., *Managerial Values for Working* (New York: AMACOM, an AMA Survey Report, 1975).
14. Willis M. Tate, president, Southern Methodist University, "Things Aren't Like They Used to Be," *Proceedings of the 26th Conference of the University Personnel and Management Conference,* University of Texas, 1964, p. 35.
15. "The Rising Crisis in Skills: More Jobs Than Skills," *Steel* (September 7, 1964), p. 41.
16. The annual survey of educational attainment found the following relationships between education and earnings:

Median dollar earnings of year-round full-time workers 18 and older, by education and sex, March 1973

Sex and occupation	Total	Elementary, 8 years or less	1 to 3 years of high school	4 years of high school	1 to 3 years of college	4 years or more of college
Men						
Total..............	$10,201	$7,577	$ 8,946	$10,073	$10,960	$14,662
White collar..........	12,132	8,795	10,019	10,734	11,923	15,041
Professional and technical	13,206	8,800	10,850	11,959	11,819	14,440
Managers and administrators, except farm	13,000	9,614	10,316	11,954	13,365	17,271
Clerical and sales...	10,230	8,145	9,587	9,825	10,475	12,864
Blue collar..........	9,386	8,099	9,075	9,970	10,061	10,768
Service..............	7,802	6,241	6,957	8,735	9,545	10,750
Farmers and farm laborers	5,212	4,098	4,708	6,156	7,643	8,750

Median dollar earnings of year-round full-time workers 18 and older, by education and sex, March 1973—Continued

Sex and occupation	Total	Elementary, 8 years or less	1 to 3 years of high school	4 years of high school	1 to 3 years of college	4 years or more of college
Women						
Total................	$5,970	$4,303	$5,037	$5,769	$6,465	$ 8,925
White collar..........	6,664	5,102	5,692	6,071	6,649	8,997
Professional and technical	8,725	5,500	6,306	7,819	8,146	9,232
Managers and administrators, except farm..........	7,063	6,000	5,781	6,581	7,906	10,350
Clerical and sales...	5,899	4,871	5,611	5,876	6,097	6,934
Blue collar...........	5,070	4,486	5,105	5,386	5,469	5,833
Service..............	3,308	3,758	4,039	4,551	5,429	6,278
Farmers and farm laborers	2,861	3,350	2,667	1,250	750	5,750

17. Harold Mayfield, "People at Work," *Personnel,* vol. 47, no. 3 (May–June 1970), pp. 4–7.

18. For a discussion of the implications of this trend, along with some efforts to study and meet this problem, see "The Quality of Working Life," *Ford Foundation Letter* (New York: Ford Foundation, September 1, 1975), p. 3.

    See also, Peter F. Drucker, "Managing the Knowledge Worker," *Wall Street Journal* (November 7, 1975), p. 10.

    It has even been said that "it's absolutely absurd that in this country today there should be seven million people going to college. There are not seven million people who want to go to college, or who want to read Plato or Aristotle or Montesquieu. And there's no reason why they should. But we've developed this idea about degrees and about learning, and we have failed to see that there aren't enough jobs for those who learn certain things." Leo Rosten, on the CBS News Special, *Conversations with Eric Sevareid,* August 24. © 1975 CBS, Inc.

19. H. E. Henneberger and H. F. Gale, "Productivity in the Major Household Appliance Industry," *Monthly Labor Review,* vol. 93, no. 9 (September 1970), pp. 39–42.

20. It should be pointed out that technological development and the material scale of living are also functions of a society's value system. For example, in a country where the people have a materialistic set of values, there will be greater material development—everything else being equal—than in a country with predominately nonmaterialistic values. However, this question is beyond the scope of this book.

21. See *Management Decisions to Automate,* U.S. Department of Labor, Manpower/Automation Research Monograph, No. 3 (1965), p. 7, for these and other results of automating.

22. For a fascinating discussion of this trend and its effects on personnel management, see "America's Eating-Out Splurge," *Business Week* (October 27, 1975), pp. 43–46.
23. Paul R. Lawrence, "Individual Differences in the World of Work," in E. L. Cass and F. G. Zimmer, eds., *Man and Work in Society* (New York: Van Nostrand Reinhold Co., 1975), pp. 19–29.
24. Ralph E. Winter, "Over 400,000 Jobs Go Begging in an Era of 8.5 Million Jobless," *Wall Street Journal,* vol. LV, no. 112 (June 10, 1975), p. 1. Earlier it had been estimated that the figure for unfilled jobs was nearer a million. "A Million Jobs Go Begging," *Business Week* (March 17, 1975), pp. 44–46.
25. Julius Rezler, "Automation and the Personnel Manager," *Advanced Management Journal,* vol. 32 (January 1967), pp. 76–81.
26. For these and other findings, see Michael A. Fryer and Thomas W. Zimmer, "The Work Environment: Key to Greater Productivity?" *Personnel Administrator,* vol. 20, no. 1 (January 1975), pp. 38–42.
27. *Work in America* (Cambridge, Mass.: MIT Press, 1973).
28. This study was done by Joseph Weintraub, a Babson College professor. See *Wall Street Journal* (December 2, 1975), p. 1, for further details and specific examples.
29. This distinction was first made by Wilfred Brown, "What Is Work?" *Harvard Business Review,* vol. 40, no. 5 (September–October 1962), pp. 128–29.
30. This study was done by Edward Walsh, University of Michigan. He worked with sanitation workers in Detroit and Ann Arbor, Michigan, and in Minneapolis. See *Wall Street Journal* (September 9, 1975), p. 1, for details.
31. This research was done, and reported on, by Nancy B. Morse and Robert S. Weiss, "The Function and Meaning of Work on the Job," *American Sociological Review,* vol. 20, no. 2 (April 1955), pp. 191–98.

    I have duplicated their research with first-line supervisors (mostly Southern while males) since 1965. The answers have varied from a high of 96 percent in 1966 to a low of 65 percent in 1974. The figure for white females has varied from 100 percent to 76 percent. The results for black males tend to be slightly lower than white males almost every time.

    Morse and Weiss found that the older the worker, the greater the tendency to keep on working. In the mid-1960s, my research showed the same thing. The results changed during the mid-1970s. Now those born since 1945 tend to want

    Percent who would:

	Go on working	Quit work	Not sure
Men	76	20	4
Women	67	31	2
Whites	74	23	3
Nonwhites	69	30	1
Earn under $10,000	66	29	5
Earn over $15,000	85	12	2
Age 18–24	90	8	2
Age 40–59	67	31	2
Age 60 or more	52	33	14

    Source: *Parade* (June 3, 1973), p. 15.

to keep on working more than other groups; those born before 1933 are next; and those born between 1933 and 1945 have the least desire to keep working.

With one or two variations, similar results were found in a study by Thomas C. Sorensen. See "Do Americans Like Their Jobs?" *Parade* (June 3, 1973), pp. 15–16.

32. Eli Ginzberg, "Man and His Work," *California Management Review,* vol. 5, no. 2 (Winter 1962), pp. 21–28.
33. Robert Dubin, "Industrial Workers' Worlds: A Study of the Central Life Interests of Industrial Workers," *Social Problems,* vol. 3, no. 3 (January 1956), pp. 131–42.
34. John K. Maurer, "Work as a 'Central Life Interest' of Industrial Supervisors," *Academy of Management Journal,* vol. 11, no. 3 (September 1968), pp. 329–39.
35. Frank Friedlander, "Importance of Work versus Nonwork among Socially and Occupationally Stratified Groups," *Journal of Applied Psychology,* vol. 50, no. 6 (December 1966), pp. 437–41.
36. For a beautiful expression of this belief, see the discourse on "Work" in Kahlil Gibran, *The Prophet* (New York: Alfred A. Knopf, Inc., 1948), pp. 30–34.
37. There is some indication this concept may be held by others. A poll of several thousand employees of Burlington Northern Railroad in 19 states turned up some surprising conclusions. Workers with "a favorable attitude" toward the union also had a favorable attitude toward the boss. The attitude "bears no relationship whatever to the militance of the union or the generosity of the employer" in pay and working conditions. The survey found "strong negative feelings" toward the company and the unions among "underworked," nonproductive or "extravagantly overpaid" employees. Most favorable feelings came from employees whose jobs demand physical effort, mental pressure, or responsibility. Managers and rank-and-filers agreed that "we should have a larger work force but fewer managers and supervisors."

    Employees worried about the future of the railroad industry but not about being fired, laid off, or losing seniority. See *Wall Street Journal* (July 15, 1975), p. 1, and *U.S. News & World Report* (September 8, 1975), p. 50, for details.
38. Paul Lawrence in "Individual Differences in the World of Work," *Man and Work in Society,* reached a similar conclusion at the 50th Anniversary Symposium of the Hawthorne studies. He reported on research done by Arthur Turner and himself with blue-collar workers and said they *reluctantly* concluded that "some workers—by no means all—have been nurtured in urban subcultures that have deeply conditioned them to see work as a simple exchange of time and minimal energy for fair pay and decent conditions. They do not expect to live on the job, only off the job."

    See also, "Blue-Collar Blues?" *Newsweek,* vol. 83, no. 17 (April 29, 1974), p. 90, for similar conclusions from a six-year study at a General Motors plant in Baltimore.
39. Alex Inkeles, "Industrial Man: The Relation of Status to Experience, Perception, and Value," *American Journal of Sociology,* vol. 56, no. 1 (July 1960), p. 6.
40. While the surveys tend to be different in approach and subjects, the following results are offered for your further study: (*a*) Of 2,159 female employees of an electronics firm, only 21 percent were *dissatisfied.* Ray Wild, "Job Needs, Job Satisfaction, and Job Behavior of Women Manual Workers," *Journal of Applied*

Psychology, vol. 54, no. 2 (March 1970), pp. 157–62; (*b*) Of a representative sample of adult Americans, 91 percent of men and 84 percent of women *like their jobs.* Sorensen, "Do Americans Like Their Jobs?" *Parade,* pp. 15–16 (*c*) Irving Kristol found in his studies that "85 percent of American workers answered in the affirmative when asked if they were satisfied with their jobs." Reported in Richard Denzler, "People and Productivity: Do They Still Equal Pay and Profits?" *Personnel Journal,* vol. 53, no. 1 (January 1974), p. 59; and (*d*) In eight Gallup polls of men workers, aged 21–65, from 1963 to 1973, the percent of *"satisfied"* varied from a *low* of 86 percent in 1971 to a *high* of 92 percent in 1966 and 1969.

41. For discussions of the causes and consequences of this landmark strike, see: (*a*) "GM Zeroes in on Employee Discontent," *Business Week* (May 12, 1973), pp. 140–44; (*b*) "Blue-Collar Blues," *Newsweek,* p. 90; (*c*) Hak C. Lee and John J. Grix, "Communication: An Alternative to Job Enrichment," *Personnel Administrator,* vol. 20, no. 6 (October 1975), pp. 20–23.

42. See any basic management text for a discussion of these ideas. In addition, you might want to read: Paul Dickson, "Humanizing the Work Place," and Robert Skole, "Brave New World," *MBA,* vol. 9, no. 3 (March 1975), pp. 31–36, and 39–42, for a discussion of efforts to make work more meaningful. Also, Fred K. Foulkes, "The Expanding Role of the Personnel Function," *Harvard Business Review,* vol. 53, no. 2 (March–April 1975), pp. 71–84.

43. Fritz Machlup, *The Production and Distribution of Knowledge in the United States* (Princeton, N.J.: Princeton University Press, 1962).

Chapter 6

Trends in U.S. and other labor forces

Factors affecting changes in the labor force
    Factors in the general environment
    Factors in the economic environment

Estimated demand for workers
    Demand by industries
    Demand by occupations
    Trends in other countries

Anticipated supply of available employees, 1985
    An increasing supply of potential employees
    Labor force in other countries

Meeting the needs of special groups
    Young people
    Women
    Minorities
    Vietnam era veterans
    Older workers

Applications and implications for personnel executives

6
Trends in U.S. and other labor forces

One-half of today's high school seniors will work in jobs that are not now in existence.
   A corporate recruiter speaking to a high school science teachers convention in 1964.

During 1975, the percentage of U.S. service stations which are partially or wholly self-service increased from around 8.5 to 16.5.

The computer system in the United States now employs 2.2 million people to operate and service around 185,000 computers.

Buried in the government's report of employment for January 1976 was the statement: "The labor force has grown by 1.5 million over the past year, with adult women accounting for 1.1 million of this increase." This fact dramatizes the massive movement of women from the home to the labor market.

These three vignettes illustrate some of the trends occurring in today's labor force, namely, a movement to service industries, employing technical and professional personnel, with an increasing proportion of women employees. The purpose of this chapter is to give you a background, or context, in which to understand the changes taking place in the labor market in the United States and other industrial countries affecting the performance of the personnel function. It should serve as a basis for understanding the macro environment in which a firm does its personnel and human resources planning. The information should help the personnel executive to match the supply of available skills, aptitudes, and abilities found in the supply of workers with the demand, from an industrial and occupational point of view, for their services.

FACTORS AFFECTING CHANGES IN THE LABOR FORCE

During the time that Frederick W. Taylor was developing his principles of scientific management, there were twice as many blue-collar workers as white-collar workers. There were few women employees and relatively few nonwhite workers, outside of agriculture. The managers of business concerns were engaged in the production of goods and services in shops, factories, and service enterprises. Governmental activities were minimal, and there were few public employees.

All this has now changed! Consequently, it is necessary to develop a new framework for studying the available labor force in the U.S. and other countries. This new concept is based upon the premise that the trends mentioned in earlier chapters have drastically and dramatically changed the composition of the work force during the last 75 years. (1)

Factors in the general environment

As the factors in the general environment affecting personnel administration were discussed in detail in previous chapters, they will not be discussed here. Suffice to say that the increasing awareness of the importance of human resources; the shift from the agricultural and extractive industries and manufacturing to service activities; the replacement of manual labor and unskilled jobs with those requiring skill, scientific knowledge, technological acumen, and professional training; the impact of the legal-political system; the increased formal education of employees; rapid technological development; and a shift from the "work ethic" to the "leisure-pleasure" concept will continue to influence the demand for, and supply of, employees.

Factors in the economic environment

There are innumerable economic factors affecting the demand for, and the supply of, workers. However, the most important ones from our point of view are the type of economy, changes in productivity, unemployment, and general economic conditions.

Type of economy. The type of economy will affect the number and type of workers in the labor force in many ways. Therefore, whether the developed economies continue the long-term trend toward becoming *service-type* economies, with the use of greater consumer and public services, or whether they revert to *goods-producing* economies will greatly affect their labor forces. Probably they will continue to become even more service-oriented.

The developing economies will probably continue moving from agricultural and extractive industries toward industrialization and manufacturing.

Changes in productivity. Changes in productivity, both overall and in each industry sector, have an important effect on employment shifts. It can be hypothesized that *as productivity increases, employment will increase slower than increases in demand for goods and services;* but, *with relatively fixed demand, lower productivity rates lead to greater employment.*

> During the last century, the average annual rate of productivity in manufacturing was around 1.45 percent, while that of construction was about 0.5 percent. The lower productivity in construction is estimated to have created around 250,000 jobs during the period—but lost about $650 million per year in housing production.

Several secular forces have affected past changes. First, the average annual rate of increase of 3.1 percent in output per worker-hour in the private sector from the mid-1930s to the mid-1960s, as shown in Figure 6-1, resulted from a major shift of workers from the low-productivity agricultural sector to the high-productivity industrial sector. This trend is about over.

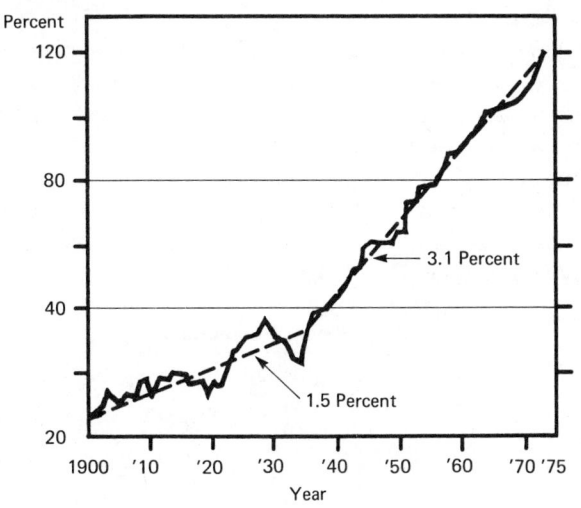

FIGURE 6-1
Output per worker-hour, total private economy (1967 = 100)

Source: *1973 Historical Chart Book,* Federal Reserve System.

Second, the demographic composition of the work force has been changing during the recent past. The size of the labor force grew rapidly as the "baby boom" generation entered it. Also, more women and minorities entered the job market for the first time. As new employees *tend to be less productive* than the average experienced workers, these changes tended to slow the rate of productivity increases.

As the smaller "baby bust" generation (born since 1957) enters the work force, and as the supply of inexpensive energy and raw materials declines, output per worker-hour will probably decline. Another factor restricting increases is the prevailing belief that just maybe productivity is not desirable. A poll conducted for the National Commission on Productivity found 59 percent of those polled (including 46 percent of executives) believe that for productivity to increase, machines will replace people and workers will lose their jobs; 67 percent (47 percent of executives) agree that companies benefit at the expense of workers; and 59 percent (46 percent of executives) believe that people have to work harder to increase productivity. (2) Therefore, it may be difficult to continue to increase output—from a public policy point of view.

Productivity in the private sector is expected to increase at about 3.2 percent per year until 1980 and then decline to around 2.8 percent. While it is predicted that productivity in all sectors—except government enterprises—is expected to decline from 1980 to 1986, the increases will still be high in agriculture, communication, public utilities, and transportation. The smallest increases should be in construction and mining.

Changes in unemployment rate. The unemployment rate has a considerable effect on selection and development strategies. In general, the lower the unemployment rate, the more difficult it is to obtain capable, "efficient" workers—and vice versa.

The Employment Act of 1946 set "maximum" employment as the goal of federal policy. While Congress did not define full employment, it became accepted by economists—in and out of government—as 4 percent. Future projections were made on the basis of either a "3-percent" or a "5-percent" unemployment rate. (3) In fact, the rate stayed between 3 and 6 percent from 1962 to 1974. Now it seems to be clustering around 8 percent in the United States and is also high in other countries, according to the Organization for Economic Cooperation and Development (OECD). In 1975, the rates were: (4)

Percentage of work force unemployed	
United States	8.4
Canada	7.2
Britain	4.7
West Germany	4.5
France	4.0
Italy	3.4
Japan	1.7

Structural changes in our economy during the last decade have made it less capable of generating full employment at stable prices, in spite of public programs designed to do just that.

One cause of the dilemma is the change in the composition of the work force. The economy has failed to absorb the "secondary" workers—teenagers, women, and minorities into the labor-short industries (transportation and public utilities, finance and service industries, and manufacturing) and occupations (managers and administrators, professional and technical, and craft and kindred workers). (5)

In a recession, these "secondary" workers tend to be the first terminated; in recovery, they are the last rehired. As the economy expands and new jobs are created, employers compete for the "primary" workers—who tend to be the better educated, skilled, and experienced white adult men. But, as this group becomes a smaller proportion of the total work force, the employers hire the other workers.

This trend does provide a great opportunity to upgrade the labor force. Competitive pressures force employers to do extensive training and upgrading of these and other employees. These developmental activities tend to improve the quality of the labor force and raise the economy's long-range growth potential.

> Unemployment is not only an economic problem for personnel managers and the unemployed. The latter also pay a high personal price. A Berlin psychiatrist found that a person's life expectancy can be reduced up to five years after job-seeking for over a year. (6)

General economic conditions. While the general economic conditions in a country have a tremendous impact on selection and development strategies, a discussion of them will be left in the economics texts, for the subject is beyond the scope of this text. Suffice it to say that a personnel manager's job would be easier if economic factors did not operate the way they do. If only the supply of qualified workers would parallel increases and decreases in the demand for their services and if unemployment rates and productivity would correlate positively with changes in the business cycle, it would be relatively simple to perform the personnel function. But, if that were to happen, some employer would get the bright idea that personnel managers were not needed!

ESTIMATED DEMAND FOR WORKERS

Demand for workers can be estimated either by industries or by occupations. The two figures will differ, for the former is forecast by *number of jobs,* regardless of who holds them—including multiple job holders—while the latter is an estimate of the number of people needed. According to the *1975 Manpower Report of the President,* the total number of jobs should increase to about 102 million by 1980 and 108 million by 1985. The number of persons needed—*by occupation*—should approximate 96 million in 1980 and 102 million by 1985.

Demand by industries

The demand for labor is increasing faster in public employment than in the private sector, as can be seen from Figure 6-2. The former is currently growing at an annual rate of about 2.1 percent, which should increase to around 2.3 from 1980-1985. (7) However, total employment in the private sector should reach about 85 million by 1980, and 89 million by 1985, as opposed to 17 and 19 million for government. Yet, 18 percent of the jobs in 1985 will probably be in government and 82 in the private sector.

Demand in service-producing industries, 1985. One of the most dramatic changes in employment in recent years has been the shift to service-producing industries. Shortly after the turn of the century, only 3 in every 10 workers were in service industries; by 1960, the weight had shifted to just over 6 in every 10 in service industries; and in 1972, the proportion had grown to just under 7 in every 10. By 1985, over 7 in every 10 workers—or over 76 million

FIGURE 6-2
Percentage distribution of total employment (counting jobs rather than workers) for selected years and projected 1980 and 1985

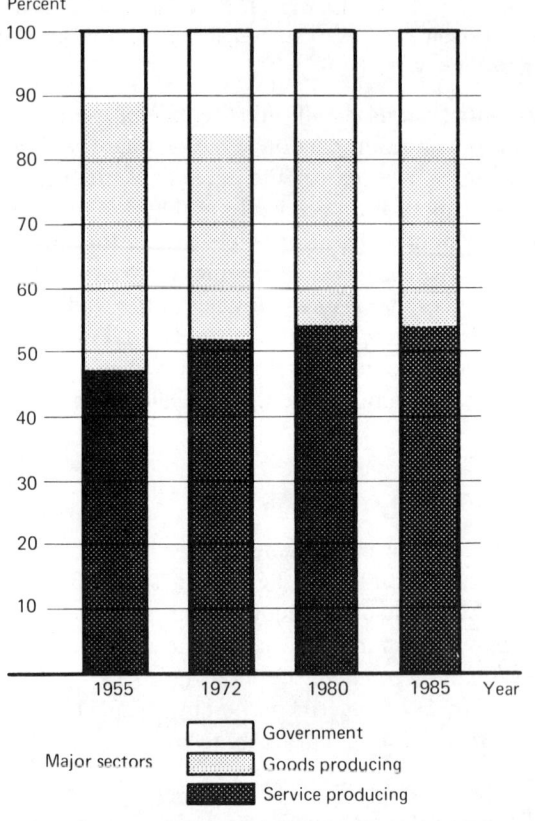

[Bar chart showing percentage distribution across 1955, 1972, 1980, and 1985, with Major sectors: Government, Goods producing, Service producing]

Note: Government includes all federal and state and local civilian employees. Goods producing includes agriculture, mining, construction, and manufacturing. Service producing includes transportation, communications, public utilities, trade, finance, insurance, real estate, and other services.
Source: *Monthly Labor Review,* vol. 96, no. 12 (December 1973), p. 40.

—are projected to be in the service industries. An increase of 18.5 million—or 32 percent—is expected in these industries.

Services. In the service industries (excluding private household), employment will grow at a faster rate than total employment. These industries will increase their share of total jobs from about 20 percent to about 22 percent by 1985, and *they will be the largest single source of jobs.* Employment will rise to 24 million by 1985, up from 17 million.

Employment growth is expected in all the major service industries, but growth in business services is expected to be particularly rapid.

Wholesale and retail trade. At present, wholesale and retail trade is the largest of the service industries. It permeates the entire economic system in a network of wholesale and retail establishments. Trade employment changes are expected to parallel those of the whole economy, with trade's relative share —around 21 percent—of total employment remaining about the same in 1985. Employment in wholesale trade will increase rapidly, especially in automotive equipment and in machinery and supply.

Retail trade employment will expand most rapidly in general merchandise stores and eating and drinking establishments. However, technological developments such as vending machines, other self-service gadgets, and electronic computers for inventory control and billing will tend to limit employment growth.

Government. Recently employment has grown faster in government than in any other sector in the economy. From 1960 to 1972, such employment grew at over twice the rate for total employment. Employment is projected to rise more slowly for the next decade, reaching 18.8 million by 1985. Employment among federal government workers will rise moderately, but state and local employment will probably expand rapidly, except in educational services.

Finance, insurance, and real estate. Employment in these industries is expected to increase much faster than total employment through the next decade but still will account for only about 6 percent of total employment by 1985. Employment, however, will rise to about 6 million.

Transportation, communications, and public utilities. Employment in this group of industries is expected to increase to over 5 million by 1985. Despite this small employment gain, its share of total employment will decline from about 5.5 percent to 5 percent.

Public utilities and communications are highly productive service industries. Hence, even though the services provided by these industries are expected to expand significantly, employment will increase only moderately to 1985 and their proportion of total employment will decline—slightly.

Demand in goods-producing industries, 1985. Although the total output of goods is expected to continue to rise to unprecedented levels during the next decade, the goods-producing industries include the only major industries in which employment is expected to decline—mining and agriculture. Only construction is expected to show a quickened pace of employment growth. The modest rise in employment of 3.5 million—or 13 percent—for the goods-producing industries, in the face of an overall healthy increase in output, reflects their rising productivity.

The goods-producing industries are expected to employ around 31 million people by 1985. However, their share of total employment will drop to about 30 percent.

Manufacturing. Manufacturing is expected to decline from the largest to the *second largest single source of jobs in the economy, second only to services.* Personnel requirements in manufacturing, however, are expected to increase at a slower pace than they are currently experiencing, chiefly because the recent increases in employment in industries heavily oriented toward defense are not expected to continue at the same pace in the 1980s. Employment, however, should rise to over 23 million by 1985, or 22 percent of total jobs.

Personnel requirements, in general, will continue to increase faster in durable goods manufacturing than in nondurable goods industries. As in the past, changes in employment in individual manufacturing industries are expected to vary widely, depending on the impact of technology as well as shifts in demand. The increasing application of technological innovations such as

Reprinted by permission of NEA.

numerically controlled machines, new metal-processing methods, machinery improvements, improved materials handling (including layout), new and improved raw materials and products, instrumentation and automatic controls, and electronic computers, will continue to limit employment growth in these industries.

Contract construction. The construction industry may benefit from an application of existing technology that would increase the output per worker-hour. However, this depends on the outcome of the competition between union and nonunion contractors and what happens in the mortgage market. Prefabricated panels and shells for houses show promise of more widespread use.

The industry is expected to grow at a slightly slower rate than it has for the last decade. Additional demand will come from an expansion in state and local government needs, particularly for transportation construction and from expanding investment in industrial plants. Employment should rise to slightly over 5 million by 1985.

Agriculture. Increased productivity and a continuing concentration of employment on large farms should result in a decline in agricultural employment to around 2 million by 1985. The agricultural share of total employment will probably decline to about 2 percent by 1985. However, this could change if we continue to supply overseas markets as we have been doing for the last few years.

Mining. Employment in mining has been declining for many years, primarily because of high gains in productivity. Mining is expected to have the lowest rate of increase in output among all nonfarm industries. Employment growth will be limited by the increasing use of new and improved labor-saving devices and techniques, such as continous mining machinery systems and more efficient exploration and recovery techniques in crude oil and natural gas extraction. Employment should be around 632,000 by 1985.

The results of these changes can be seen in Figure 6–3.

FIGURE 6–3
Total employment, by industries, as a percentage of total employment by selected years, 1960, 1972, 1980, and 1985

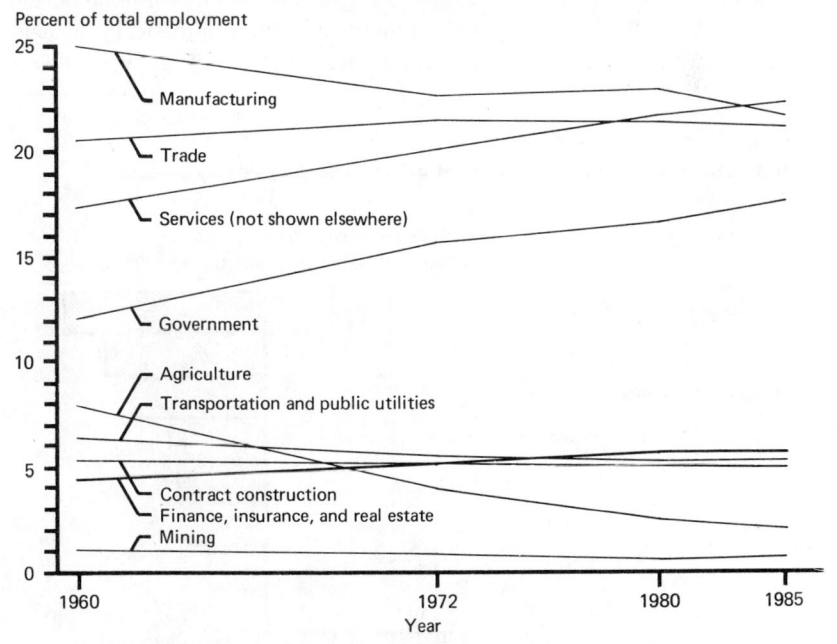

Source: Computed from *Manpower Report of the President, 1975*, p. 314, Table E–10.

Demand by occupations

As just shown, changes in demand for labor by industries during the next decade will have a strong influence on which occupations will grow and which will contract as each industry in the economy requires a specific mix of occupations. Thus, as industries react to changes and adjust to their environments and to each other, the relative importance of specific occupations should also change. For example, occupations in the health-care field will increase rapidly; while those in the educational field will grow more slowly than in previous decades; others—such as mining jobs—will continue their *relative* decline; and service in private households will decline absolutely.

Total employment should reach 95.8 million by 1980 and 101.5 in all occupational groupings, or a 24-percent increase from 1972. The average annual rate of increase for 1972–80 will be greater (3.5 percent) than from 1980–85 (2.5 percent), as the slowdown in the rate of growth of the economy—partially from a reduction in per capita supplies of energy—has its effect.

Increasing demand for white-collar employees. The fastest growing occupational group for over three-quarters of a century has been the white-collar employees. (See Figure 6–4.) This group, which surpassed employment in blue-collar occupations for the first time in 1956, will continue to expand and will account for about 53 percent of all employed workers by 1985. Employment in those occupations will approximate 53.7 million, or 37 percent more than in 1972.

Clerical. Clerical workers, the largest single category in white-collar employment, will be affected by the rapid technological developments in the fields of computers, office equipment, and communication devices, as well as slow-

FIGURE 6–4
Through the mid-1980s employment growth will vary widely among occupations

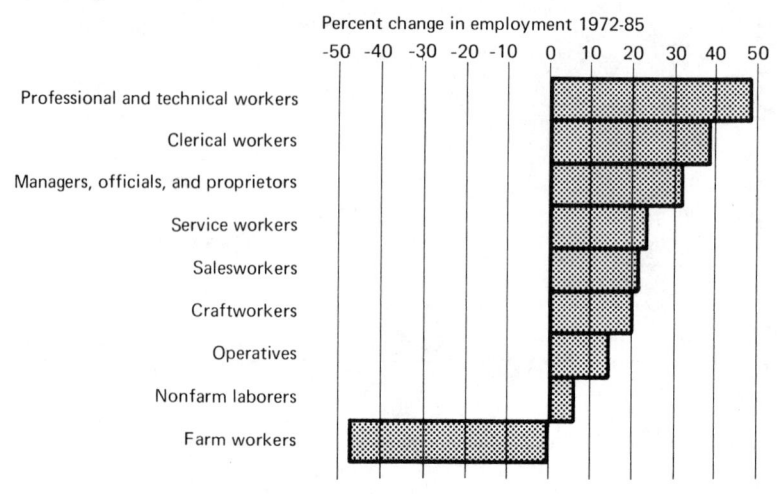

Occupation	Percent change in employment 1972-85
Professional and technical workers	~50
Clerical workers	~45
Managers, officials, and proprietors	~30
Service workers	~25
Salesworkers	~20
Craftworkers	~20
Operatives	~10
Nonfarm laborers	~5
Farm workers	~-40

Source: "Tomorrow's Jobs," *Manpower* (September 1974), p. 22.

downs in the rate of growth in trade and manufacturing during the planning period. These developments should limit employment growth for certain types of clerical workers. Clerical employment should increase its share of total employment to just over 19 percent by 1985 when there will probably be around 19.7 million employed persons in that occupational grouping.

Professional, technical, and kindred. In recent decades, employment growth in these occupations has been greater than that in all other major occupational groups. Requirements for these occupations will probably continue to lead other categories until 1985. Employment in this occupational group should reach about 17.0 million, or just under 17 percent of total employment.

The increasing demand for goods and services and the increasing concentration of the population in metropolitan areas—which will create new demands for professional and technical personnel to work in environmental protection, health care, and mass transportation systems—will cause the increase in demand. Efforts to conserve natural resources—while developing industry—and the quest for scientific and technical knowledge will also create new requirements for professional workers.

Managers, officials, and proprietors. Employment in this group should reach around 10.5 million in the next decade. Its share of total employment will probably continue to about 10 percent by 1980.

Changes in the scale and type of business organization will have divergent effects upon the various segments of this occupational group. The net result of these opposing trends will probably be a slower increase in employment in the manager-proprietor group as a whole, while the demand for salaried managers and officials is expected to grow rapidly with the increasing dependence of both business and government on trained management specialists.

Sales. The projected increase in trade should continue the demand for sales personnel at about the same rate—but at a slightly slower rate of increase than is expected in total employment. Longer store hours and expansion into suburbs should increase demand, but self-service, check-out counters, and vending machines should decrease it. Employment is expected to rise to 6.5 million, or 6 percent of total employment.

Less importance of blue-collar occupations. Blue-collar occupations, a slow-growing occupational group, will probably account for slightly over 32 percent of the work force by 1985, down from 33 percent in 1972. Employment, however, should rise to about 32.8 million. This would represent a 15-percent increase in employment. The actual number employed will depend partially upon training activities, as many occupations within the group, particularly in the skilled craft and foreman category, require years of specialized training.

Operators and semiskilled workers. Employment of these individuals increased sharply as industry shifted to mass-production processes. Now that these processes are well-established, further technological advances are likely to slow employment growth in these occupations during the next ten years. Employment is projected to rise to 15.3 million by 1985.

This group's share of total employment will decline to about 15 percent.

Craftsmen, foremen, and kindred workers. The number employed in this highly skilled group is expected to expand more slowly during the decade than employment, reaching about 13 million. The share of total employment will probably remain stable at around 13 percent. The distribution of the skills needed varies drastically by industry. Manufacturing employs a greater number of skilled workers than any other industry. In construction, however, these workers are a much higher proportion of employees than in any other industry group — one out of every two compared with one in five in manufacturing and transportation and fewer than one in ten in other industries.

Nonfarm laborers. Employment for these laborers is expected to increase only slightly to around 4.5 million despite the rapid employment rise anticipated in manufacturing and construction, the primary employers of laborers. Increased demand is expected to be offset by rising output per worker resulting from the continuing substitution of mechanical equipment for manual labor. Its share of total employment, however, should decline from 5 percent to 4 percent.

A stable demand for service occupations. Demand in the service occupations will continue to expand during the planning period at about the same rate as for all occupations, or about 22 percent. Yet, employment should increase to around 13.4 million. Private household employment will probably decrease by 26 percent, or from 1.4 million persons to 1.1 million. The fastest growing groups should be in health service, welfare service aides, school monitors, and child care — except in the home. Educational services will also grow rapidly as will state and local government jobs.

This occupational group encompasses a wide variety of jobs and a wide range of skill requirements such as FBI agents, policemen, teachers, medical technicians, beauty operators, and janitors. Changing life-styles, such as more leisure time and greater disposable incomes, underlie the increased demand in this grouping.

Declining demand for farm workers. The number of these workers will probably decline by about one-half, or from 3 million to 1.6 million in 1985. This occupational group's share of total employment will also fall from 4 percent to 2 percent in the same period. Continuing earlier trends, decreasing requirements for farm workers will be related to improvements in farm technology and better fertilizers, seeds, feed, and pesticides—if their use is permitted. Also, improved mechanical harvesters for fruits and vegetables should decrease the need for seasonal workers.

Changes in net demand by occupational groupings. These projections of occupational requirements indicate that the total openings arising from occupational growth and replacement needs will be about 61 million between 1972 and 1985. There will be some openings in all the groupings. This means that about 4.6 million jobs will need to be filled every year throughout the period.

Replacement needs will be the most significant source of demand in each of the major occupational areas—white-collar, blue-collar, service, and farm.

These needs will account for about 41 million job openings. The need to replace workers who leave the labor force—primarily because of retirement—will account for around two in every three job openings during the period. Occupational growth will account for the remaining jobs. Replacement needs are likely to exceed the overall needs in those occupations that have a large proportion of older workers who have relatively few years of working life remaining.

Growth needs will reflect industry changes, as well as technological changes during the decade. These, in turn, will largely determine which occupations will grow and which will contract. These needs will cause a demand for about 20 million employees.

Result of these trends. In general, the result of these long-run trends and occupational employment should be as follows:

1. A steady and persistent increase in the proportion of people employed in white-collar occupations;
2. A relatively stable proportion of service workers;
3. A slight decrease in the percent of employment held by blue-collar workers; and
4. A decline in the number and proportion of farm workers.

These changes are shown in Figure 6–5.

FIGURE 6–5
Total employment, by occupations, as a percentage of total employment by selected years, 1972, 1980, and 1985

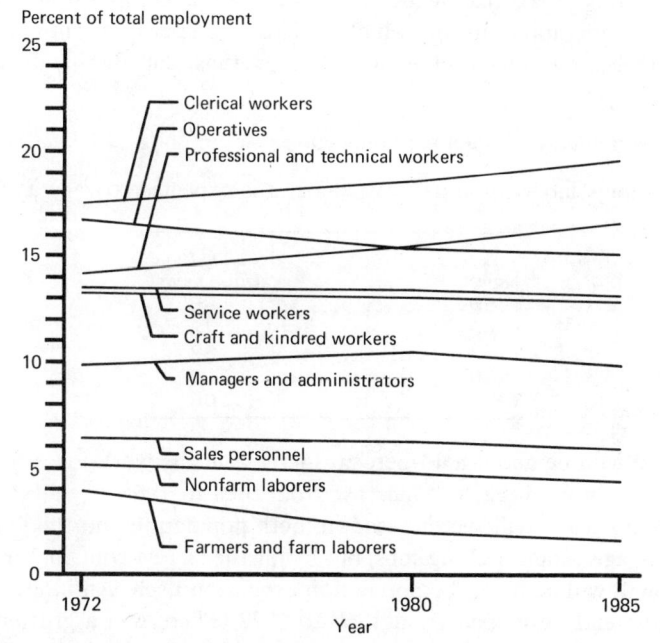

Source: Computed from *Manpower Report of the President, 1975*, p. 314, Table E–9.

Trends in other countries

There are several groups in Great Britain which are now doing studies to forecast needs by industries and occupations. For example, the National Economic Development Council, in estimating total personnel requirements for 17 industries, reached the conclusion that shortages of certain kinds of skilled labor were a threat to the country's economic growth. (8) Yet, during the recent recession, many of the industrial training boards, established under the 1964 Industrial Training Act, "drastically reduced" their intake of school dropouts for training as craftsmen and technicians, as well as their recruitment of student engineers and graduates. (9) In 1974, the House of Commons set up a new personnel services commission to do industrial intelligence and employee forecasting studies.

There has been a rapid increase in the demand for scientists and technologist recruits during the 1960s and 1970s. Also, occupational changes have occurred in industry, especially the engineering industry, resulting in increased needs for managers; administrative, clerical, and office staff; supervisors and foremen; and technicians and draughtsmen; and declining needs for craftsmen and all other employees.

ANTICIPATED SUPPLY OF AVAILABLE EMPLOYEES, 1985

Perceptive personnel managers also need to anticipate the supply of available personnel, as well as the competition from other firms and industries for those potential employees. In the coming decade, there will continue to be the "normal" shifts in the size of the labor force and its composition. Yet, there are some demographic groups which will require special attention, namely, youth, females, minorities, older workers, veterans, and the handicapped.

An increasing supply of potential employees

The nation's labor force has varied—and is expected to vary as follows:

Year	Labor force (in millions)
1950	65
1960	72
1972	89
1980	102
1985	108

There should be about a 14-percent increase in the work force from 1972 to 1980, but only a 6-percent increase from then to 1985.

The next decade will see increases in both population and the proportion of working age people seeking jobs, but by far the largest contributor to labor force growth will be from the population expansion itself. An interesting and significant trend developed from 1960 to 1972. There was a greater growth in the total work force than there was in the working age population. Currently the work force is growing faster (about 1.7 percent per year) than the population (about 1.2), and this trend is expected to continue through at least 1985. Around 60.8 percent of the population is expected to participate in the work force by 1980 and 61.3 percent by 1985—up from 59.2 in 1960 and 60.2 in 1972. Yet, there is a paradox, for while the overall participation rate is increasing that of the men is falling, while that of the women is increasing rapidly. Leaving aside any sociological implications of this movement, it does mean that women will increase as a proportion of the work force, and men will decline.

The number of people in the 35 to 54 and 55 and over age groups has not increased as rapidly as the 20–34 group. Therefore, they have declined—and will continue to decline for the next few years—as a proportion of the total work force. Yet, these are the groups from which most middle and upper levels of executives come. The 45–54 year group actually declined in number—and is expected to continue to decline until 1985. The "prime working age" group —35 to 44—has increased quite rapidly and will continue to do so during the planning period. (See Figure 6–6 for a graphic presentation of these changes.)

FIGURE 6–6
Average annual rates of change in population and labor force, 1960–72 and 1972–85

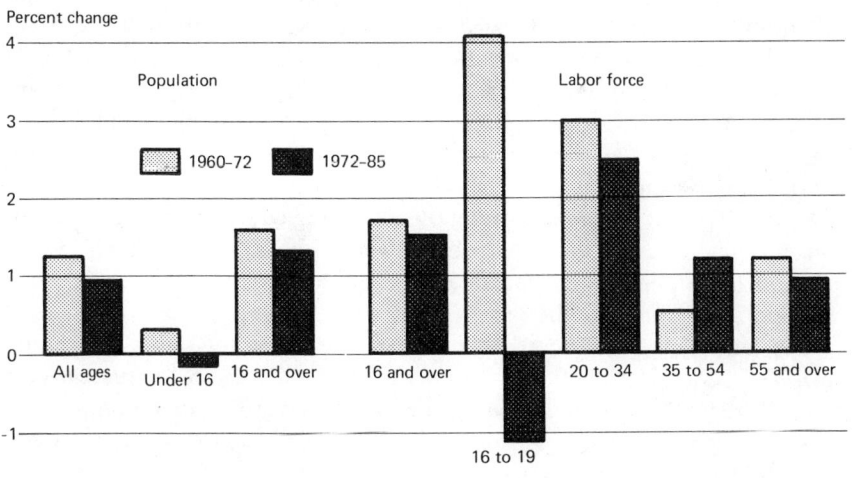

Source: "The United States Economy in 1985: Population and Labor Force Projections," *Monthly Labor Review*, vol. 96, no. 12 (December 1973), p. 12.

Another implication of these data is that human resource programs and policies must be designed to meet the special needs of the new entrants into the work force, especially those entering the managerial ranks for the first time.

Labor force in other countries

While the U.S. labor force is large, that of other countries is also large. As Table 6–1 shows, Japan has the second largest labor force; Germany, the third;

TABLE 6–1
Labor force in selected nations, for selected years (in millions)

Year	United States	Japan	Germany	Great Britain	France	Italy	Canada	Australia	Sweden
1970	82.7	50.7	26.2	24.5	21.0	19.1	8.3	5.4	3.9
1972	86.5	51.1	26.3	24.5	21.4	18.8	8.8	5.6	3.9
1974	91.0	52.1	26.2	24.7	22.0	19.1	9.6	5.9	4.0

Source: *Hardbook of Labor Statistics 1975*, Ref. Ed. (Washington, D.C.: U.S. Government Printing Office, 1975).

Great Britain, the fourth; France, the fifth; Italy, the sixth; and Canada, the seventh; followed by Australia and Sweden.

MEETING THE NEEDS OF SPECIAL GROUPS

It is not sufficient to study the trends in the supply of the total work force. Instead, as was shown in Chapters 3 and 4, there are groups with special needs or problems which must be planned for. These include youth; women; minorities, including black and Spanish-speaking workers; older workers; the handicapped; and the Vietnam era veterans.

Young people

Until World War II, the male work force was relatively young. People went to work younger, had little education, had short life expectancies, and were employed until they were physically unable to work. Since then, life expectancies have increased. The average age of the labor force also increased, at least until 1965, when it started declining. It will continue to go down through 1980 and then go up slightly.

Several cultural factors, including the increasing educational level and general affluence, affect the average age of the work force. As today's youth remain in school longer, enter the labor force later, live longer, and retire earlier, they have more years outside the labor force.

Our labor force has now begun to feel the effects of the wartime and post-World War II baby boom. From 1960 to 1972, the 16- to 19-year-olds flooded the work force, followed by the 20–34 age group. (See Figure 6–6). This trend is now changing. From 1972 to 1985, the 20–34 year group will show the largest increase.

By 1985, 51 percent of the supply of employees should be between 25 and 44 years of age. Those 25 and under will be only 17 percent of the total. The primary result of the large number of youth entering the labor force has been unemployment, as their unemployment rate has also been higher and the disparity is getting greater.

The unemployment rate among youth is higher than for others for several reasons. First, there is disillusionment with their pay, job, or working conditions. Second, these employees hold the less skilled jobs, which tend to be unstable. Third, their lack of education and training hampers them. The unemployment rate among high school and college dropouts tends to be one and one-half times greater than that of their fellow youth. Fourth, a research study indicated that the minimum wage might be causing this, although it was difficult to disentangle such effects from numerous other influences. (10) At least, the attitude of employers was that if there were a substantial differential between youth and adult rates they would increase the employment of youth. In spite of these facts, 55 percent of the 16–24 year olds were working in 1974.

Research has shown that young workers have a difficult time making the transition from life in school to life in industry. (11) First, the increased responsibility and more mature treatment pose problems. Second, their sense of values is different from that of their elders. Since the young have more alternative job opportunities, they fear downgrading, reprimand, and dismissal less than older employees. It was also found that young workers make the transition better when working with an older worker than with a fellow junior employee. However, the young people are now an integral part of the work force, including management, and this is causing many changes. (12)

These young people have a more idealistic approach to living, are not as committed to an organization, do not accept authority without question, and believe in a sharing of responsibility. These qualities will lead to a different approach to management and motivation.

Women

While women have been a significant part of the American labor force for over a century, their roles have been changing during recent decades. Their number, percentage of the total labor force, participation rate, and percent of working wives with schoolage children have increased as follows:

Year	Number (in millions)*	Percent of labor force*	Participation rate (in percent)†	Labor force participation rate of working wives* with school age children‡
1950	18.4	30	34	28
1955	20.5	32		
1960	23.2	33	38	39
1965	26.2	35		
1970	31.5	38	43	49
1973			45	
1974	35.8	39		51
1980			46	
1985			47	

* The number of "working wives" increased 205 percent from 1947 to 1975, while "working husbands" increased only 27 percent. See U.S. Working Women: A Chartbook (Washington, D.C.: U.S. Government Printing Office, 1975), Chart 2.

† Manpower Report of the President, 1975 (Washington, D.C.: U.S. Government Printing Office, 1975), p. 57.

‡ Wall Street Journal (February 2, 1976), p. 1.

Changing worklife pattern. There has been a drastic shift in the women's worklife pattern. A larger proportion is working at each age; a smaller proportion is leaving the labor force during the prime childbearing age; and more are coming in during the middle-age period. Also, a larger proportion of wives and mothers are working.

This trend is evident in both the United States and Canada. In 1970, 40 percent of married women were in the work force in the United States, while 36 percent of them were in the Canadian work force in 1971. The greatest participation occurred in the 45–54 age in the United States and 35–44 group in Canada. Over half of this group in both countries had university degrees and were in the work force. (13)

There is also a side effect of the employment of working mothers—and fathers—namely, the development of day-care centers for preschool children on the institution's premises. This movement has led to reduced absenteeism, turnover, and complaints and grievances, as well as producing "peace of mind" which leads to improved work performance.

Changing educational pattern. Not only are the more recent female labor force entrants younger but also better educated, since a much larger proportion have attended college than was true in earlier years. From 1900 to 1970, the proportion of college and university degrees earned by women increased from 17 to 40 percent; of master's degrees, from 19 to 40 percent; and of doctorates, from 6 to 13 percent. (14)

Changing occupational patterns. As shown in Figure 6–7, there has been a 20-percent increase in the number of women employed in service work in

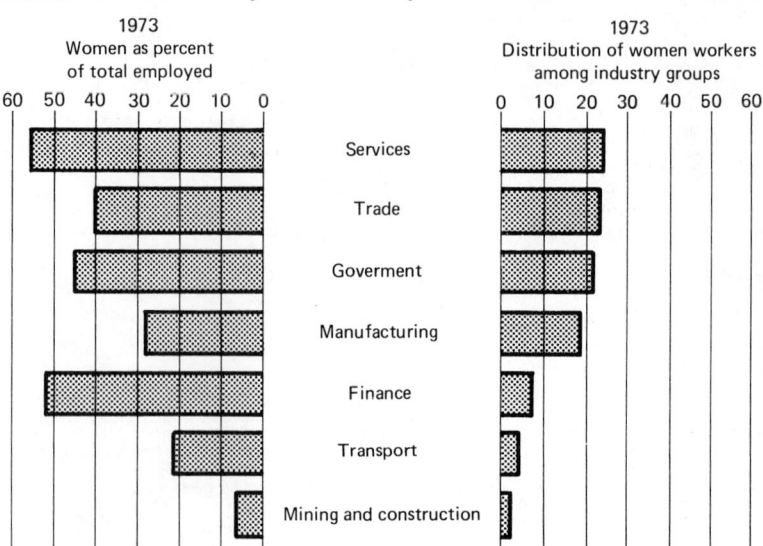

FIGURE 6–7
Women continue to find jobs more easily in some industries than in others

Source: *Manpower Report of the President, 1975* (Washington, D.C.: U.S. Government Printing Office, 1975), p. 61.

the last 15 years, and a 25-percent increase in women employed as professional and technical workers—particularly in teaching and health occupations. There has been a decrease in private household work and a slight decrease in sales and operation. However, more women are still concentrated in the "feminine" stereotyped jobs, working as secretaries and typists, retail clerks, bookkeepers, teachers, and waitresses.

This too is changing. From 1969 to 1973, the percent of all women at Stanford University majoring in biology, chemistry, and physics increased 15 to 30, and 20 percent of its undergraduate women were studying premed. Also, the percent of freshmen women studying engineering increased from 1.2 in 1972 to 7.6 in 1975.

A similar trend is occurring in the skilled trades. From 1960 to 1970 there was an 80-percent increase in women working in the skilled trades. The increase was twice that of women in all fields and eight times the rate of increase for men in skilled trades. (15)

Also, as shown in Figure 6–7, there is an industry concentration, with women being concentrated in services, finance, government, and trade. They represent a majority of the employees in services and finance.

Women have tended to have higher unemployment rates than men. This difference was most often attributed to women's more intermittent labor force participation and, hence, their more frequent status as reentrants into the labor force. While their commitment to work is definitely increasing—and for many may be just as strong as men's—much of their unemployment is still attributable to reentry into the labor market.

It has been held traditionally that turnover (especially the quit rate) and absenteeism among women were so high that men should be hired if stability were needed. Now, research shows that these are dropping for females, not only when compared to their earlier rates, but also when compared with male levels.

> The female quit rate at General Motors decreased from 5.3 percent in 1972 to 4.7 percent in 1973; the male's percentage increased from 1.9 to 2.3.
>
> The turnover percentage for women dropped from 19.6 in 1971 to 11.5 in 1974; that of men, from 7 to 5.1. (16)

Several conclusions can be reached concerning the future status of women in the labor force. Their number and participation rates will increase. Their share of jobs will also increase, particularly in technical and professional, managerial, and service (except household) occupations.

Female occupational distribution results—to a considerable degree—from influences that start in childhood. Role differentiation in early life later affects educational and occupational choices, hours and location of work, and other factors which destine women to lower-level positions in lower-paying industries. If this occupational distribution is to be altered, not only the legal prohibition of discrimination but also some fundamental changes in attitudes must occur within the home, the school, and the workplace. (17)

Trends in other labor markets. Similar trends are occurring in other labor markets. Of all the 94 million women living in the nine nations of the European Economic Community, more than one-third are employed. The specific percentages are:

Denmark	41
Great Britain	37
France	37
West Germany	37
Belgium	34
Italy	28
Luxembourg	26
Ireland	26
Netherlands	25

When women in the normal working ages of 15–64 are considered in selected countries of Europe, Asia, and North America, the percentage of "working women" becomes: (18)

Russia	82	Finland	62	Switzerland	51	Belgium	40
East Germany	80	Sweden	59	Austria	50	Norway	39
Bulgaria	74	Czechoslovakia	59	United States	49	Italy	29
Hungary	73	Denmark	58	West Germany	49	Portugal	25
Romania	73	Japan	56	Australia	45		
Poland	63	England	52	Canada	41		

Minorities

Public policy has long been to prevent discrimination in the employment of minorities. However, the policy has been truly implemented only during the last decade. As shown in Chapter 3, the legislative, executive, and judicial branches of the federal government, as well as most state and local governing bodies, now require equal employment opportunities for these groups.

Also, business groups such as the National Alliance of Businessmen (NAB) set out to create jobs for the "hard-core unemployed." Its "Job Opportunities in the Business Sector" (JOBS) program was designed to create a half-million such jobs between 1968 and 1971. Many private firms also attempted to help these groups. The personnel function was largely reoriented to try to include these individuals in personnel manpower planning.

Blacks. Blacks have made considerable progress during the past decade in their efforts to move upward on the ladder of occupational status. Although they are still overrepresented—relative to whites—in the blue-collar and service occupations and underrepresented in the white-collar ranks, the disparity has been significantly reduced since 1964.

Their employment increased 31 percent during the decade, and their share of jobs rose slightly. The participation rate of black women increased from 48.5 to 49.1 percent; that of the black men decreased from 80.0 to 73.3. (19)

The proportion of black men in the more desirable, highly paid job categories has shown slight but steady progress. No less than one out of five blacks worked in white-collar occupations in 1964; ten years later, however, about one in three blacks had white-collar jobs. Substantial gains were made within the professional, managerial, and sales ranks, but the greatest gains were in the clerical field, with almost a doubling of their share of the market.

Within the blue-collar group, where the proportion of blacks remained relatively stable from 1964 to 1974, there was also significant upward progress, as substantial numbers of them left the ranks of the unskilled and entered the operative and craft trades. There was also a significant reduction in the proportion of blacks in service occupations, particularly private household, where the number employed was cut in half.

The proportion of all male employees who are black doubled in accounting, engineering, medicine, and drafting.

While blacks obviously have a higher unemployment rate than whites, one study showed that variables other than race or color might be the cause. It was shown that the excess black unemployment might be attributable to differences in educational attainment; academic achievement; age; legal constraints; and their occupational, industrial, and regional distributions in the labor force. (20)

Spanish-speaking workers. Workers of Hispanic origin represent roughly 5 percent of the U.S. population, making them our second largest minority group. While professional and white-collar workers—and even prosperous businessmen—are numbered among the Spanish-speaking, far too many are poorly paid laborers.

Spanish-speaking Americans tend to be severely disadvantaged compared with the dominant Anglo population. While their status is roughly equal to blacks in income, occupational status, and unemployment, in education they are far worse off.

As shown in Table 6–2, the occupational distribution of the 3.6 million employed persons of Hispanic origin is similar to that of blacks in that they are concentrated in occupations characterized by high unemployment rates.

The higher unemployment rates of workers of Hispanic origin can also be attributed to the significantly greater proportion of young workers in the Hispanic labor force; lower average levels of educational attainment, sometimes compounded by language problems; and greater relative concentrations in the West, where unemployment tends to be high.

Lack of English facility and other cultural differences—including a partially self-imposed ethnic isolation common to earlier generations of immigrants—leave many Spanish-surnamed people outside the mainstream of economic opportunity.

Their precarious economic position is underscored by the nature of the jobs they hold. Over half of them are in unskilled and low-paid blue-collar, service, and farm jobs. Only 32 percent of Spanish-surnamed people hold white-collar jobs, compared with 51 percent for all Americans.

TABLE 6–2
Employment of white, black, and Spanish-speaking Americans, by occupation group, 1974 [percent distribution]

Occupation group	Total	White	Black*	Spanish-speaking
Total: Number (thousands)	85,936	76,620	8,112	3,609
Percent	100.0	100.0	100.0	100.0
White-collar workers	48.6	50.6	28.9	31.5
Professional and technical	14.4	14.8	8.8	7.0
Managers and administrators, except farm	10.4	11.2	3.4	5.7
Sales workers	6.3	6.8	1.9	3.9
Clerical workers	17.5	17.8	14.8	15.3
Blue-collar workers	34.7	33.9	42.1	47.6
Craft and kindred	13.4	13.8	9.5	12.4
Operatives	16.2	15.5	23.2	26.2
Nonfarm laborers	5.1	4.6	9.4	8.5
Service workers	13.2	12.0	26.3	16.5
Farm workers	3.5	3.6	2.8	4.5

* Data refer to Negro workers only.
Note: Detail may not add to totals because of rounding.
Source: *Manpower Report of the President, 1975* (Washington, D.C.: U.S. Government Printing Office, 1975), p. 35.

Vietnam era veterans

As shown in Chapter 3, many programs were designed to help veterans returning from Vietnam. Apparently they worked, at least for the older vets.

The average unemployment rate for Vietnam era veterans aged 20 to 34 was 6.4 in the last quarter of 1974, while unemployment among nonveterans of the same age group was generally higher—7.5 percent. The rapidly changing age composition of the veteran group has been an important factor in the decline of their unemployment rate below that of the nonveteran group. As most Vietnam era veterans were separated from the armed forces several years ago, they have now entered age groups with generally lower unemployment rates. Consequently, the proportion of veterans in the 20-to-24-year age group, where the jobless rate is relatively high, is now much smaller.

Older workers

For a number of years it was popular to reject those over 40 years old for employment. This practice now violates the *Age Discrimination in Employment Act of 1967.*

Generally, the arguments for not hiring older workers are physical deterioration, expense of fringe benefits, the problem of tenure, and lack of ability.

Contrary to these arguments, experience has shown that it is advantageous to hire people over 40 years of age for several reasons. These include: greater experience and better judgment in decision making; more objectivity about personal goals and abilities, as older workers have already satisfied many of their needs for salary and status and are able to concentrate more on job responsibilities; increased social intelligence and the ability to understand and influence others; decreased risk, as the older person's potentialities can be more easily determined from their performance record; reduced training time, as their previous experience is easily transferable, especially into management positions; and proven value, as the older workers have proven their abilities.

It is felt that institutions are arbitrarily hurting their competitive position through this restriction on their hiring practices. (21)

APPLICATIONS AND IMPLICATIONS FOR PERSONNEL EXECUTIVES

The material in this and previous chapters has established the following premises. First, business and other organizations requiring personnel executives will tend to increase in size and complexity. Second, as technology tends to lead to increase employee productivity, the proportion of people working to support others probably will decline. Thus, there will be a two-class society, those gainfully employed and those unemployed or engaged in "make-work" endeavors. Those working will have a superiority complex, tempered with a sense of bitterness that they are supporting those who do not work; those who are unable to work will have a sense of resentfulness because they are unnecessary and unwanted, but this will be tempered with a superiority complex since they can survive without working. Third, human resources will assume an even greater significance as a factor of production—at least for those gainfully employed. Fourth, while the economic necessity of working will decline, the intrinsic, heuristic, creative, ego-satisfying, and self-fulfillment necessity of working will increase. The work values of the younger employees will tend to be oriented toward the intrinsic, heuristic, and creative aspects, while the older and more knowledgeable employees will be more inclined toward the opportunities for advancement and achievement found in work.

The trends discussed in this part have caused the industrial and occupational employment mixture to change. This "mix" will continue to change and change rather drastically. Thus, personnel executives are faced with new kinds of employees and must adapt their managerial philosophies and practices to these new realities of life.

The information in this part—especially the trends explored in this chapter—should serve as a background perspective and provide guidelines to aid the personnel executive in performing the personnel function more effectively.

Specifically the relationships between the future demand for workers by industry and occupation and the expected, potential supply of employees by demographic, educational, and occupational characteristics should aid one in doing personnel-human resource planning.

Finally, it can be hypothesized that *the lower the unemployment rate, the less the use of selection criteria, the lower the productivity of employees, the greater the need for development, and the higher the unit-labor costs.*

DISCUSSION QUESTIONS

1. What general environmental factors have affected the performance of the personnel function?
2. What changes in our work environment have brought about the changes in the composition of the work force?
3. What groups are most adversely affected by increases in unemployment? Why? Discuss.
4. If you are a college student, what should you do to prepare for your future career in the light of current changing composition and characteristics of the work force?
5. White-collar workers have displaced blue-collar workers as the largest occupational grouping. Discuss.
6. Women constitute an increasing proportion of the labor force. Discuss the implications of this trend.
7. Discuss the implications of the changes in the composition of the work force for personnel executives of the future.
8. There is currently a trend away from employment in goods-producing industries and to service-producing industries. What are some of the possible consequences of this trend?

REFERENCES AND SUGGESTIONS FOR FURTHER STUDY

1. At the turn of the century, ours was a rural agricultural society; it is now an urban service economy. See Paul G. Craig, "Socioeconomic Change and Managing Tomorrow's Work Force," *Personnel Journal,* vol. 48, no. 8 (August 1970), pp. 628–32, for some of the cultural problems.
2. "Productivity Still Has a Bad Name," *Business Week* (January 6, 1973), p. 28.
3. For illustrations of this tendency, see "The U.S. Economy in 1980; A Preview of BLS Projections," *Monthly Labor Review,* vol. 93, no. 4 (April 1970), p. 3 ff.
4. "The Global Impact of Rising Unemployment," *Business Week* (September 1, 1975), p. 46.
5. *Manpower Report of the President, 1975* (Washington, D.C.: U.S. Government Printing Office, 1975), p. 27.
6. *Parade* (October 5, 1975), p. 6.
7. "The United States Economy in 1985: Projections of GNP and Employment," *Monthly Labor Review,* vol. 96, no. 12 (December 1973), p. 29.
8. *The Growth of the Economy* (National Economic Development Council, HMSO, 1964).
9. M. Venning, "Manpower Studies for Industrial Sectors," *Long-Range Planning,* vol. 7, no. 3 (June 1974), pp. 27–33.
10. Thomas W. Gavett, "Youth Unemployment and Minimum Wages," *Monthly Labor Review,* vol. 93, no. 3 (March 1970), pp. 3–12.
11. W. Lean, "Work Problems of Young Factory Employees," *Personnel Practice Bulletin,* vol. 16, no. 2 (June 1960), pp. 26–30.
12. See Judson Gooding, "The Accelerated Generation Moves into Management," *Fortune,* vol. 83, no. 3 (March 1971), p. 101 ff., for an excellent article about the newer type managers.

13. "Labor Force Participation of Married Women," *Statistical Bulletin* (New York: Metropolitan Life Insurance Co., December 1975), p. 9.
14. Rudolph C. Blitz, "Women in the Professions, 1870–1970," *Monthly Labor Review,* vol. 97, no. 5 (May 1974), p. 38.
15. Janice Hedges and Stephen Bemis, "Sex Stereotyping: Its Decline in Skilled Trades," *Monthly Labor Review,* vol. 97, no. 5 (May 1974), pp. 14–21.
16. Mike Tharp, "Improved Image: Women in Work Force Post Better Records for Stability in Jobs," *Wall Street Journal* (November 20, 1974), p. 1.
17. This seems to be occurring very rapidly.

    In the *home,* several things are happening. First, the young women are leaving home to live alone or with a friend just as the young men have been doing for some time. Second, their age at marriage has increased from 20 to 21 since 1950. Third, their fertility rate has dropped "primarily from the intention to have fewer children rather than from postponement of intended births," especially since the mid-1960s. While there was no appreciable change from 1967 to 1974 in the average number of births to women in the 35–39 age group, there was a 17-percent reduction among those aged 30–34, a 26–percent reduction among those aged 25–29, and a 33-percent decrease among those at ages 20–24.

    See "Trends in Expected Family Size in the U.S.," *Statistical Bulletin* (New York: Metropolitan Life Insurance Co., January 1975), pp. 8–11, for further details.

    In *school,* there is also a change taking place. According to the latest annual survey conducted by the University of California at Los Angeles and the American Council of Education, only 28 percent of freshmen entering American colleges and universities in 1975 thought married women should "confine themselves to home and family." Only five years earlier, 48 percent had thought that was women's role in society and did not favor job equality for both sexes. See Barbara J. Katz, "A Freshman Portrait," *National Observer* (January 24, 1976), p. 5.

    At *work,* the recurring negative theme of the "domineering female leader who engenders dissatisfaction among subordinates," is also changing. In research done at a large midwestern university, 100 subjects were formed into 24 teams or firms which competed in one of several oligopolistic market places during an eight-week period. The results *did not* support the view that female leaders with a "high need for dominance" adversely affect follower satisfaction. In fact, male follower groups were happier with these females than with "low need for dominance" female leaders. The results also showed that females with a high need for dominance were better able to handle team interaction—or at least were perceived as being better at it—than were low need for dominance females. See Kathryn Bartol, "Male versus Female Leaders: The Effect of Leader Need for Dominance on Follower Satisfaction," *Academy of Management Journal,* vol. 17, no. 2 (June 1974), pp. 225–33, for further details.
18. Computed from various International Labour Organization reports.
19. *The Social and Economic Status of the Black Population in the U.S., 1974* (Washington, D.C.: U.S. Government Printing Office, 1975), p. 60.
20. Curtis L. Gilbray, "Investment in Human Capital and Black-White Unemployment," *Monthly Labor Review,* vol. 98, no. 7 (July 1975), pp. 13–21.
21. Harold L. Sheppard, "The Potential Role of Behavioral Science in the Solution of the 'Older Worker Problem,'" *American Behavioral Scientist,* vol. 14, no. 1 (September–October 1970), pp. 71–80.

CASES FOR FURTHER STUDY

II-1. Average Company, Inc.

Ted Harper was the plant personnel manager of the Average Company's manufacturing plant, which was located in a medium-sized, highly unionized Southern city. When the plant was established several years ago, management realized that the black population in the area was quite numerous, but the adults were largely uneducated. For this reason, management carefully evaluated all jobs to be filled and set aside approximately 25 percent for black applicants, feeling that they should make an effort to furnish employment to a cross-section of the local population. Standards were set quite high for white employees, but black employees were only required to be able to read and write.

This decision appeared to be a good one for about 20 years. Race relations were excellent, and good performance was obtained from all employees. Outside influences, however, began slowly to create a strain on these relations which more or less came to a head during labor negotiations five years ago. At that time, the greatest problem was to get an agreement with the union which the union committee could sell to their membership concerning equal employment opportunities. There was pressure on the company from the EEOC to comply with the *Civil Rights Act of 1964,* and pressure on the union negotiating committee from its national leadership, caused by their fear of loss of certification over the issue.

Agreement was finally reached that black employees who could meet the same qualifications that had always been applied to white employees would be moved into the progression line formerly open only to white employees. This decision was accepted by the white employees in the bargaining unit; however, they made it clear that they objected to anything more than equal opportunity for the others.

After the contract was signed, the standard tests were given to all blacks who wished to try to qualify for movement into the formerly white progression line. Tests that were administered were identical to the tests previously given to all white employees who had been hired into this group.

Results were very disappointing as no black employee actually qualified. Mr. Harper and the operating managers in the plant were disturbed by this situation. In order to demonstrate that they were acting in good faith, they actually reduced the standards to some degree in order to move three of the blacks into the white group. They justified this action on the basis that the employees concerned were old employees about whom they had a great deal of knowledge and were certain that they could perform at least some of the jobs in this area. They decided, however, that standards would not be lowered for new applicants.

Although the transfers which they made were accepted by members of the white group and work proceeded without incident, some members of the minority group were still not satisfied that they had been given adequate consideration and filed a complaint with the EEOC. They charged that the company had discriminated against them because they were blacks and that they were not able to progress for this reason.

Questions

1. What does this case illustrate about the attitude of some managers as far as minority employment is concerned?
2. What would you do now if you were the personnel manager?

II-2. Division of Labor

Part of the home study assignments for a university executive development program was to read and write a critique on four books between each yearly session. The following comments were received from the personnel manager of an industrial firm. He had read H. F. Merrill, *Classics in Management,* which included a treatise written by Charles Babbage in 1832 entitled *Economy of Machinery and Manufacturers.*

> The division of labor that was true in Charles Babbage's time has drifted into real labor union difficulties today. Although it was true that more production could be maintained with workers doing only one phase of a complicated manufacturing process, automation has now taken over most of these hand-operated jobs. The jobs that are left do not lend themselves to individual crafts or specialists. In the modern automated plant, practically the only hand jobs left are maintenance, and, in most cases, the man whose responsibility it is to fix things needs to be a jack-of-all-trades. Automation will turn history back to the handyman, or else maintenance will be contracted out to service people.
>
> For example, a recent cost study was taken in our plant on cleaning the burner on a 50-gallon hot water heater. The heater originally cost $250. After unionized employees belonging to seven different crafts (operator, insulator, pipe fitter, instrument man, sheet metal worker, electrician, and carpenter) had worked for over eight hours the job was not complete. At that time, the total labor cost was $270. The shop steward informed the maintenance foreman that the craftsmen would have to work overtime to insure hot water in the change house because it was in the contract.
>
> A local plumber quoted a firm price of $15 to clean and adjust the burner.
>
> If the company allowed the plumber to do the job, the workers would go on strike.

Questions

1. What is your evaluation of the sentence, "Automation will turn history back to the handyman, or else maintenance will be contracted out to service people."?
2. Evaluate this problem from the point of view of: (*a*) management; (*b*) a union leader; and (*c*) an employee.
3. How would you attempt to resolve the dilemma faced by management?

II-3. The New Work Force

Tom Jackson, personnel officer in one of Trappy Oil Company's refineries, sat reviewing his just completed meeting with Bob Jay, who had recently been promoted to the position of department head.

Bob had received an M.S. degree in chemical engineering from one of the state colleges seven years earlier. Since joining Trappy, he had progressed rapidly in the plant and had successfully performed jobs of increasing responsibilities. In his new position, his primary responsibility involved the operation, maintenance, and safety for a number of the processing units of the plant. There were about 15 other engineers, around 155 unit operators and mechanical craftsmen, and 15 first-line supervisors in the department.

Bob had been in his new job less than a week when Bill Lockey, first-line supervisor of one of the units, came in to see him about a "personnel" problem. The supervisor, who was obviously upset, told Bob that he was fed up with the people that the company was hiring for him to run his part of the plant. Bill angrily stated that, "If the company gives me one more college graduate to do our job, I can't guarantee the safety and operation of my unit. That damn Jones you gave me last week failed to check the meters last night, and we have run all day making off-spec product. We're lucky to be here today."

Bob was surprised. As he had not worked closely with Bill before he did not know exactly what weight to place on his comments in view of the nature of the outburst. He asked Bill to write up the incident for him, and he would review it and decide what action should be taken about it. Bill agreed and stormed out of Bob's office.

Bob had scheduled conferences with each of his first-line supervisors to discuss their feelings about the "new work force." He received widely varying opinions on the worth of the new group, ranging from, "They are lazy and never had to work a day in their life," to, "They have done things in better ways than we have done them before." Bob had talked to a number of his fellow department heads about the new workers and had also received from them quite varied opinions on the effectiveness of the "new work force."

Bob did not have the responsibility for selecting potential new employees, as this task was done by the personnel officer. However, in his new position, he would be responsible for actually selecting any new employees he might need from a list of "qualified" applicants furnished by the personnel department. So he decided to call the personnel officer to discuss the firm's hiring policies.

Tom Jackson had told Bob that in the last few years the company had undertaken a fairly intensive hiring plan in the plant. This was due to the large number of operators and mechanical craftsmen that were retiring. During World War II, Trappy had greatly expanded its work force—as had all the other refineries. Following the war, there were some layoffs, but most of the employees hired during the war were retained as a matter of company policy. The "overstaffing," resulting from that policy—plus automation in the industry—resulted in a 25- to 30-year period during which employees who quit, were fired, or retired were not replaced.

"Now" said the personnel officer, "this group of employees is reaching the age where they can take early retirement. Many new people are having to be hired and trained in a short period of time."

Bob also learned from the personnel officer that about 65 percent of the firm's process and mechanical employees had been replaced during the last four years—primarily because of retirements. However, nearly a third of the new employees who had two years experience had quit or been fired. The most surprising statistic was that the average education level of the new employees was about three years of college. Many of them had degrees, primarily in education, the social sciences, and biological sciences. The statistics also showed that the pay of the blue-collar workers in the refinery was significantly higher than the pay in the professional fields of most of the graduates.

Questions

1. How do you explain the trends in the refinery?
2. What does it explain about the historical development of personnel management?
3. What does it show about the new work environment?
4. What does it show about the effects of technological development?
5. What would you do now if you were the personnel officer?

part three

Recruiting and selecting personnel

7. Personnel and human resource planning
8. Recruiting personnel
9. The selection procedure
10. Evaluating information and assessing applicants
11. Selecting supervisory and executive talent

Cases:
   III–1.   Companywide Seniority
   III–2.   Outside Help
   III–3.   Selection: In Theory and in Practice
   III–4.   To Do or Not to Do?

Introduction

Most economic and social goals are achieved through cooperative work groups composed of numerous individuals with different objectives, capabilities, and motivations. The main function of personnel executives is to recruit and select the needed human resources in the right quantities and qualities; maximize their potential through training, developing, and moving them into positions where they can operate most productively; utilize their abilities; appraise, evaluate, and reward their performance; and maintain them until they leave the organization, as shown in Figure III–1.

Through the process of *personnel and human resource planning,* an organization's specific personnel requirements needed to reach objectives are determined. This phase of employment is primarily quantitative, as it involves estimates that are computed from sales forecasts, employment and training records, labor turnover records, and other sources of date. Chapter 7 discusses this aspect of personnel selection strategies.

Recruitment involves the effort expended to develop supply sources and to

FIGURE III–1
A system's approach to recruiting and selecting personnel

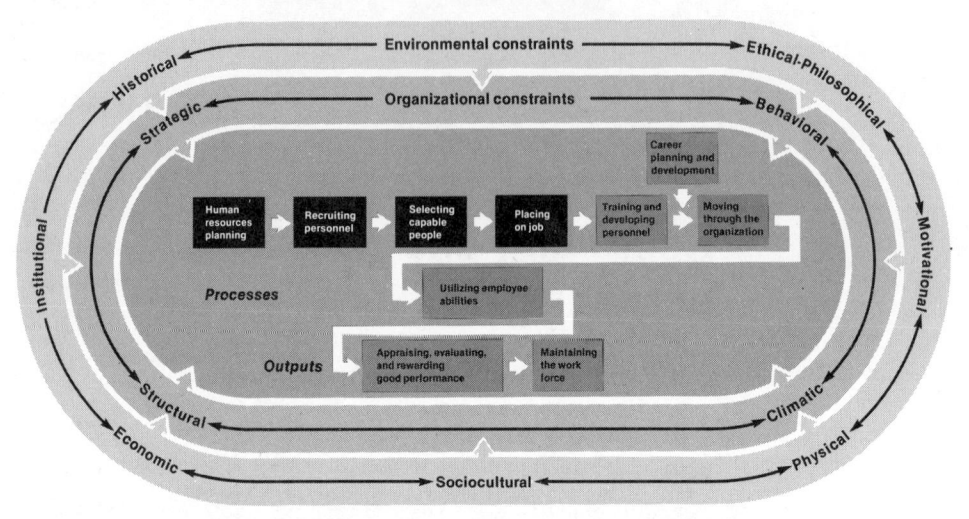

attract, either through advertising, employee referrals, or personal visitation, applicants with the potential characteristics to fill the available jobs, as shown in Chapter 8.

The next step, *selecting* the needed employees and *placing* them on the job, is discussed in Chapter 9. In essence, the available applicants are evaluated, and the persons whose personal qualifications most nearly approximate the specific job requirements are chosen for the positions which need filling.

Chapter 10 deals with *evaluating the data obtained* in the information gathering phase of selection. It specifically analyzes biographical inventories, testing, and interviewing as selection instruments.

Some special problems associated with *providing supervisory and executive talent* are discussed in Chapter 11.

Chapter 7

Personnel and human resources planning

Growing importance of personnel-human resource planning

Objectives of personnel planning

Functions involved in human resource planning
　Designing and redesigning jobs
　Determining job requirements

Different stages of human resource planning

Steps in personnel-human resource planning
　Organizational objectives and plans
　*Determining **overall** human resource requirements*
　Inventory of present human resources
　*Determining **net** new human resource requirements*
　Action programs for filling needs
　Affirmative action program

A new approach to personnel-human resource planning
　Components of the system
　What the system does
　Useful in complying with EEOC and OFCCP guidelines

Personnel planning in other economies

Evaluating effectiveness of personnel-human resource planning
　Some new evaluative techniques

Implications and applications for personnel executives

7
Personnel and human resource planning

The best laid schemes o' mice and men gang aft a-gley.
ROBERT BURNS

No amount of sophistication is going to allay the fact that all your knowledge is about the past and all your decisions are about the future.
IAN H. WILSON

During the spring of 1958, recruiters from a large multiplant firm were on campus interviewing but making no job offers. At the same time, the local plant was laying off graduates hired during the preceding three years. The students were so upset at this obvious inconsistency that even today the firm has a "bad name," and students are reluctant to interview with it.

This is an extreme example of the lack of meaningful planning for personnel needs. Yet, the interest in this aspect of the personnel function by researchers, writers, and teachers is not matched by equal performance by many practicing personnel managers. (1)

The following letter recently received from the personnel director of a chemical plant illustrates this problem.

> There is an obvious failure on the part of many organizations to reevaluate their employment needs periodically. They fail to take into consideration operational improvements made in many of the areas requiring personnel. Many executives are surprised to discover this during a strike situation where they operate their plants with only supervisory personnel. Frequently they find that although they are fewer in number than their normal work force, they actually improve production rates.

The purpose of this chapter is to help you to understand the need for planning for personnel needs and to learn how to do it.

For purposes of this text, *personnel-human resource planning is an integrated approach to performing the planning aspects of the personnel function in order to have a sufficient supply of adequately developed and motivated people to perform the duties and tasks required to meet organizational objectives and satisfy the individual needs and goals of organizational members.*

Figure 7–1 shows the place of planning in a selection system.

FIGURE 7-1
Place of personnel-human resource planning in a selection system

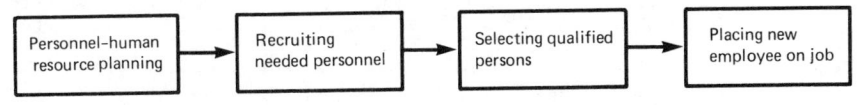

Personnel-human resource planning → Recruiting needed personnel → Selecting qualified persons → Placing new employee on job

GROWING IMPORTANCE OF PERSONNEL-HUMAN RESOURCE PLANNING

If we use the available literature on micro personnel planning as an indication of the quality of theory and practice in the field, the results are quite mixed. (2) However, two conclusions can be reached. First, personnel and human resource planning has been extensively discussed but has not been implemented to the same extent. Second, it is now emerging as one of the more important functions of personnel.

One of the reasons for this lack of implementation is the term has many different meanings. It may apply only to particular types of personnel skills —usually managerial—or it may refer only to forecasting activities—rather than to a full range of planning functions.*

Personnel planning is now becoming more popular—and necessary—as organizations try to cope with the increasingly complex sociocultural, legal-political, and economic environments. Personnel executives can't run away from this complexity; nor can they recapture the conditions of the past. Therefore, they must enlarge their knowledge through research and accelerate their planning activities. In fact, scores of organizations have already set up new, formalized planning systems; others are sure to follow their lead.

> Several companies, such as IBM, Zerox, Exxon, First National City Bank, and General Electric, have set up refined, companywide personnel planning systems. (3)

---

* There is much confusion over which term to use to refer to this overall personnel function. "Manpower" was a very popular term during World War II but passed out of widespread usage after 1945. It reappeared about 1960 and once again became quite popular. Sometimes the word "manpower" is used to refer to "labor," when labor is understood to mean one of the factors of production included in the basic framework of analysis used by economists. In this very broad sense, manpower can be understood to mean generically "personnel" or "employees" in a given organization, whether hourly or salaried, managerial or nonmanagerial, and is, thus, its "work force." Or manpower can be equated with the national labor force. Finally, manpower can be considered tantamount to "human capital" or used as a synonym for "human resources." "Manpower planning," "personnel planning," "employment planning," and other similar terms have been used to refer to the planning aspect of the personnel function. Yet, each of these convey a limited or distorted impression.

Considering the present direction of theoretical and practical thinking, the term "personnel and human resource planning" seems to have the best "fit." However, it and the other terms will be used interchangeably in this chapter for variety's sake.

OBJECTIVES OF PERSONNEL PLANNING

Organizations cannot rely upon finding talented people from outside sources just when they need them. Instead, planning and searching for qualified talent must be done on a continuous basis. Systematic steps must be taken in order to assure that a reservoir of talent is available when needed. Consequently, the objectives of personnel planning are to:

1. Relate human resource needs to the overall activities of an organization;
2. Make long-range estimations of specific—as well as general—needs; and
3. Maximize the return on investment in human resources. Only the last will be discussed at this time.

A relatively new concept in personnel planning is *human resource accounting* which treats employees as capital assets in much the same way that plant and equipment are presently treated. This new system emphasizes that employees are unique entities, requiring individualized consideration. In essence, it attempts through an accounting model to: (*a*) measure the cost of the human resources; (*b*) determine what it would cost to replace the resources; and (*c*) estimate what their value would be based upon their potential earning ability. (4)

If employees were viewed as a capital asset, several changes would probably occur in the management of the resource. Higher management would insist upon the personnel executives recruiting and selecting the best people; more emphasis would be placed upon the completion of human development programs; greater devotion would be given to an individual's developmental activities; and time and consideration would be given to matching employees with jobs in order to ensure that they were placed in challenging positions which would effectively utilize their capabilities.

This form of accounting could provide management with an additional indicator of employees' potential growth before advancement is made in their positions. This system would focus attention on the employees as a *valuable investment* which enhances earning power rather than as an operating expense which acts to drain the organization's financial resources.

FUNCTIONS INVOLVED IN HUMAN RESOURCE PLANNING

Although employee planning, as formerly done, was primarily involved with personnel recruitment, selection, and placement, present trends in human resource planning are to involve *all* of the personnel functions. It is used in designing and redesigning jobs; determining job requirements; recruiting and selecting; maximizing employee potential; utilizing, rewarding, and maintaining the work force—as well as dealing with unions and employee associations. Only the first two will be discussed at this point.

Designing and redesigning jobs

In *job design,* an effort is made to consider both the technical and sociopsychological aspects of the job. *Job redesign* attempts to make the work more meaningful and to help employees perceive that their jobs are important and have dignity, worth, and status. Some forms of job redesign are job enlargement and enrichment, work improvement suggestion systems, behavior modification, shorter work week, and flexible working hours (flextime).

Determining job requirements

Regardless of whether the job is newly designed or redesigned—or has been performed the same way for some time—there are two procedures involved in determining job specifications. First, there is the process of determining the *qualitative aspects* involved, including personal characteristics required of any employee to perform a particular job, such as training time, aptitudes, temperaments, interests, physical capacities, and adjusting to working conditions.

Second, the *quantitative aspects* must be ascertained, including the volume of work to be done and the number of people needed to do it.

Determining qualitative job aspects. Job analysis is the process used to determine the qualitative aspects of job specifications. Although this term is sometimes used synonymously with the term "motion study," there is a distinction between them. *Motion studies* try to improve the methods and techniques of performing the job and include work simplification and elimination. *Job analysis* determines the duties, responsibilities, working conditions, and interrelationships between the particular job as it exists and the other jobs with which it is associated. Thus, *job analysis* can be defined as *the process of gathering pertinent information and determining the component elements of a job by observation and study.*

Job analysis records details concerning training, skills, required efforts, qualifications, abilities, experiences, responsibilities, and so forth, which are needed for the job. In essence, it evaluates the qualitative demands of a job and is the procedure used when a job is studied for any of the following purposes: recruitment and placement of employees; classification and evaluation of present employees; establishment of performance standards; and job evaluation.

How information is used. The first result of a job analysis is a *job description* which is a simple, concisely written statement explaining the contents, essential requirements of a job, and a summary of the duties to be performed. When the factors are explained in detail and the importance and meaning of each subfactor and its degree of importance in rating a specific job are included, and when it contains statements of mental, physical, and other demands required of a person to perform the job successfully, it is called a *job specification.*

This form of job specification, when it gives the personal requirements for fulfilling the job satisfactorily, serves many purposes. It provides the criteria for recruiting and selecting needed employees, determining personal efficiency, training new employees, training and developing existing personnel, achieving work simplification, carrying out salary administration, achieving better performance rating, and granting promotions and transfers.

Used to comply with equal employment guidelines. In order to comply with equal employment guidelines and as part of their affirmative action programs, some firms have described job requirements and specifications in a prepared form to help employees learn something about the many jobs available in the company. The supervisor or the personnel department representative has these sheets and will give an employee the sheet for any job title the person might be interested in. The purpose of these *Job Brief and Qualifications* sheets, as they are called, is to provide an "overview" of a given job and to outline the factors considered in evaluating a person for that job. The sheets usually list the official job and the location in which the job is performed. (For an example, see footnote 5.)

Used to develop behavioral job descriptions. The personnel executive is primarily concerned with the behavioral aspects of job performance, for the person must fit the job for the greatest success. Consequently, the usual job descriptions are of limited value. Current efforts are being made to develop procedures to generate useful behavioral job descriptions which are criterion-related and which have content validity. Under this procedure, personnel specialists can generate behavioral information about various jobs. Specifically these descriptions could:

1. Describe job objectives in the form of "terminal" behaviors;
2. List specific tasks required for desired performance;
3. Differentiate between *routine* and *critical* task performance;
4. List alternative methods of performing job tasks;
5. Specify the criteria used to determine if terminal behaviors have been evident and if the job has been successfully performed;
6. Specify *favorable* and *unfavorable* conditions for obtaining objectives;
7. Specify characteristics of known job incumbent which would change the terminal behavior objective and/or performance criteria; and
8. List the worker's qualifications, education, and/or experience levels required. (6)

Estimating quantitative requirements. When using job specifications for recruiting personnel, the next step is to determine the number of people to be hired in each of the skill categories. In making this quantitative analysis, the personnel executive should consider the business cycle, the stage of development of the individual and the organization, the rate of turnover, as well as many other factors.

First, the *number of employees* needed in each existing and expected job classification is determined by time studies or MTM (7) for the next planning period (e.g., the next year, 5 years, or 30). Next, an *inventory of existing personnel is made* to see what vacancies are expected to occur. *Promotions, transfers, and other internal adjustments are* then *predicted.* Next, *labor turnover,* including retirements, deaths, discharges, disability, quits, and others, *is estimated.* From these analyses, *the number of persons to be recruited is estimated.*

An example will suffice to explain this step.

> The Bell System economists have forecast that by the year 2000, there will be 265 million telephones in the United States and the Bell System will be handling about 800 billion calls a year, including 14 times as many long-distance messages as are now handled. Bell System employment will increase by another half million persons as a result of these changes. (8)

DIFFERENT STAGES OF HUMAN RESOURCE PLANNING

The human resource planning process can be simple or complex, involve a unit or an entire organization, cover a short or long period of time, can be done manually or by machines, and can use models or be descriptive. Also, various organizations use differing practices and levels of sophistication in their planning. These vary with the circumstances of the organizations, including the number of employees; the stage of development of the organization; the technologies involved; and the economic, social, political environment, as well as the abilities and experiences of the executives involved.

According to a leading authority in this area, there are four stages representing successive levels of complexity in forecasting, programming, gathering information, and evaluating personnel planning. They are: (9)

Stage I. Representing a rudimentary, basic approach, might be in a small organization or an entrepreneurial organization in the early stages of growth.

Stage II. Representing a short-range planning cycle and a sensitive but paternalistic management approach, indicates an effort by an organization to supplement its informal, personal management style with more formal, objective tools. Many organizations, particularly those with 3,000 to 10,000 employees, are in this stage.

Stage III. Is used by many major business organizations where the focus is on improved career management. It represents "state-of-the-art" practices involving the use of computer capabilities and coordinated activities aimed at satisfying both short- and long-range needs.

Stage IV. Representing the ultimate in human resource planning practices, may require tools that may be "on the drawing boards," as practices are innovative and experimental. This stage may be viewed as futuristic at this time, even though the techniques are widely discussed in the literature and are the subject of management research.

The more effective planning programs use models to provide a framework to show the relationship between the relevant items of information. The model should be general enough to ensure that the variables included can be reviewed by each subunit to determine which are important and which have no impact and yet be specific enough to be meaningful. It should be a guide to what happens in an organization, but it cannot be used as an exact description of what happens. This must be done by each personnel executive in specific instances in each organization.

STEPS IN PERSONNEL-HUMAN RESOURCE PLANNING

The system proposed in this text is the six-step system shown in Figure 7–2. (10) As shown, it operates at multiple levels. First, objectives and plans are established at the overall organizational level and then distributed to subunits at lower organizational levels. Next, information from all the subunits are summarized and submitted up the line to the top of the organization.

Organizational objectives and plans

The first step in human resource planning is to evaluate organizational objectives and plans, for they and planning are interdependent at all organizational levels. The primary use of personnel planning and programming is to provide the organization with the people needed to perform the activities that will achieve organizational goals. Therefore, the objectives and plans at all levels of the organization provide the basis for determining gross personnel requirements.

Frequently organizational objectives and plans can be considered as a constant for planning purposes. In other situations, particularly in economic organizations, human resources are now being considered as an investment

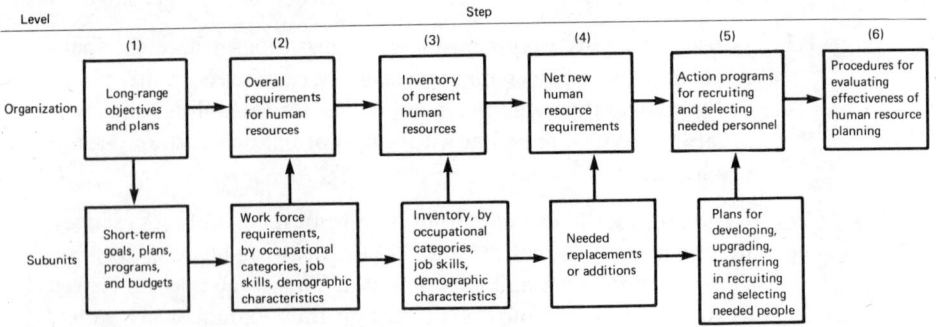

FIGURE 7–2
Human resource planning system

Level	(1)	(2)	(3)	(4)	(5)	(6)
Organization	Long-range objectives and plans	Overall requirements for human resources	Inventory of present human resources	Net new human resource requirements	Action programs for recruiting and selecting needed personnel	Procedures for evaluating effectiveness of human resource planning
Subunits	Short-term goals, plans, programs, and budgets	Work force requirements, by occupational categories, job skills, demographic characteristics	Inventory, by occupational categories, job skills, demographic characteristics	Needed replacements or additions	Plans for developing, upgrading, transferring in recruiting and selecting needed people	

alternative subject to benefit, cost, allocation, and control considerations given to other resources. As efficiency and effectiveness are important in terms of effective utilization of human resources in order to obtain an optimum return on invested capital, knowledge of organizational plans and participation in the planning process are important.

The objectives of private firms may be *both economic and social,* as shown in Chapter 3. While trying to maximize profits, increase share of market, and produce a better product at a lower price, the firm may try to hire minorities and females, clean up the environment, improve safety, and otherwise act socially responsive. Yet, participation in such programs tends to divert physical, financial, and human resources from the primary economic mission.

Determining *overall* human resource requirements

An integral step in any human resource planning system is predicting the need for—and the availability of—people with the "right" characteristics to perform present and future jobs. Therefore, the organization's *overall personnel requirements*—in terms of occupational specialties, job skills, and demographic characteristics—should be predicted. In multiunit organizations, this starts with the individual units and progresses to the organizational level. See Figure 7–3 for a model used at the departmental level in one division of a major corporation, which can serve as a guide in determining unit requirements.

The key to an effective forecasting procedure is to begin with cause and effect relationships. In other words, there is a need to know what factors determine the supply and demand for people. Second, as many factors are beyond the control of the organization, management cannot plan the changes in those variables. However, a forecast can still be made by anticipating possible changes in these uncontrollable factors and projecting their possible impact on the organization's personnel needs.

Inventory of present human resources

The next step is to take an inventory of present personnel to find out the organization's ability to satisfy its needs from within. This may be done very simply or more elaborately. For effective planning, you do need to know essentially the same thing here as in the predicted requirements, namely, the number of people with the required occupational specialties, job skills, and demographic qualifications. Included in the inventory are the present duties of your people, as well as the skills they possess—as indicated by their educational attainments, past work experiences, and participation in training and development programs.

Such an inventory enables a matching of the skills in the organization against overall personnel requirements. It is uneconomic to recruit, hire, and train new people when the needed skills are already on hand. Often, internal adjustments can be made at minimal cost. A personnel inventory is also helpful

FIGURE 7–3
Model of departmental personnel forecasting system

Inventory of present work force
1. Age.
2. Job title.
3. Level of experience.
4. Evaluation of employee potential.

Expected growth of departmental work
(taken from one- and five-year plans
as approved by top management)
1. Number of new projects.
2. Size and responsibility of new projects.
3. Expansion of present projects.
4. Technical developments in other departments.
5. Technical developments outside the company.
6. Developments in professional education (universities).

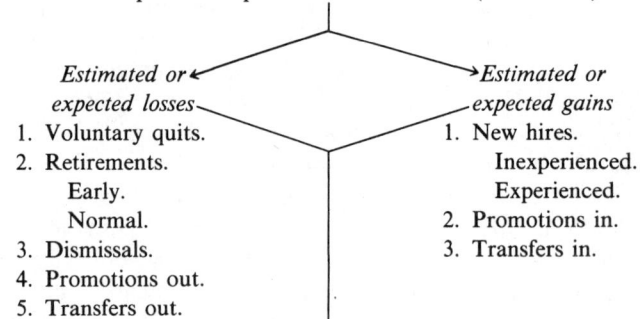

Estimated or expected losses	*Estimated or expected gains*
1. Voluntary quits.	1. New hires.
2. Retirements.	Inexperienced.
Early.	Experienced.
Normal.	2. Promotions in.
3. Dismissals.	3. Transfers in.
4. Promotions out.	
5. Transfers out.	
6. Layoffs.	
7. Death.	

Projected departmental work force
(estimates compared to
past experience)
1. One-year projection.
2. Five-year projection.

*Revision of five-year projection
on basis of yearly projection
results*

Source: Richard P. Peterson, "The Growing Role of Manpower Forecasting Organizations," *MSU Business Topics,* vol. 17, no. 3 (Summer 1969), p. 10.

in total organizational planning, as it provokes inputs concerning the capability of the organization to undertake new programs and for estimating the cost of acquiring additional human resource capabilities.

While expensive computerized personnel data systems are useful for sophisticated employee planning, most organizations cannot afford these systems, nor do they need them. Any system which provides the needed data will suffice. Yet, a computerized personnel information retrieval system should be investigated from a cost-benefit analysis, as potential applications are vast in terms of personnel research and employee planning and control. Once the basic data bank is developed for analysis and planning, its use can be expanded as new programs are developed. (11)

The more progressive organizations, using Stage III planning, have some form of manning table, such a the "Personnel Planning Replacement Chart" shown in Figure 7-4. Each position on the chart is coded according to the incumbent's present performance readiness for promotion.

Determining *net* new human resource requirements

The difference between overall requirements and the personnel inventory becomes the *net new human resource requirements* to be filled by recruitment and hiring. This becomes the personnel objective for the planning period and is the basis for action programs to effect changes in the capability of the organization. While net requirements are the difference between overall requirements and the personnel inventory, other factors such as the timing of personnel needs, age and experience variations, sex and race, and planning lead time may also influence net requirements.

Figure 7-5 illustrates a simplified model, which is supported by three other models for determining "internal supply," "external supply," and "demand," which can be used for determining the net demand for management personnel. (12)

Action programs for filling needs

Human resource programming includes the design and implementation of action programs to assure that the organization's personnel needs are met during the period. These programs emphasize the acquisition and development of human resource skills and involve *all* the personnel functions, including strategies for selecting, developing, utilizing, rewarding, and maintaining personnel.

Changes in personnel programs may take the form of expansion, adjustment, contraction, or a combination of these.

A point of departure in programming is an analysis of present personnel capabilities to see if some needs can be met through internal adjustment, such as promotions, transfers, or upgrading.

Action programs during periods of contraction are very difficult, especially

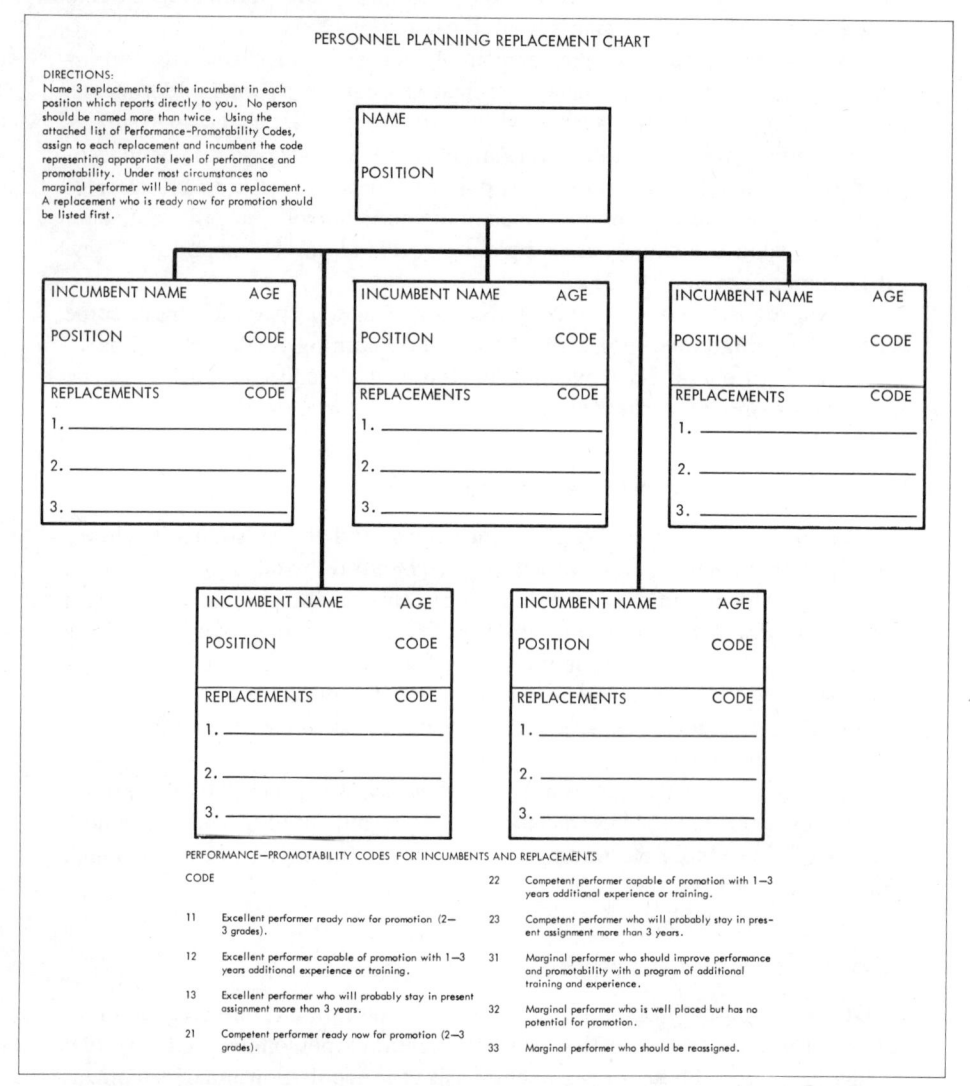

FIGURE 7-4
Personnel Planning Replacement Chart

```
                          PERSONNEL PLANNING REPLACEMENT CHART

DIRECTIONS:
Name 3 replacements for the incumbent in each
position which reports directly to you. No person    ┌─────────────────────┐
should be named more than twice. Using the           │ NAME                │
attached list of Performance-Promotability Codes,    │                     │
assign to each replacement and incumbent the code    │ POSITION            │
representing appropriate level of performance and    └─────────────────────┘
promotability. Under most circumstances no
marginal performer will be named as a replacement.
A replacement who is ready now for promotion should
be listed first.
```

INCUMBENT NAME AGE	INCUMBENT NAME AGE	INCUMBENT NAME AGE
POSITION CODE	POSITION CODE	POSITION CODE
REPLACEMENTS CODE	REPLACEMENTS CODE	REPLACEMENTS CODE
1.	1.	1.
2.	2.	2.
3.	3.	3.

INCUMBENT NAME AGE	INCUMBENT NAME AGE
POSITION CODE	POSITION CODE
REPLACEMENTS CODE	REPLACEMENTS CODE
1.	1.
2.	2.
3.	3.

PERFORMANCE–PROMOTABILITY CODES FOR INCUMBENTS AND REPLACEMENTS

CODE		CODE	
11	Excellent performer ready now for promotion (2–3 grades).	22	Competent performer capable of promotion with 1–3 years additional experience or training.
12	Excellent performer capable of promotion with 1–3 years additional experience or training.	23	Competent performer who will probably stay in present assignment more than 3 years.
13	Excellent performer who will probably stay in present assignment more than 3 years.	31	Marginal performer who should improve performance and promotability with a program of additional training and experience.
21	Competent performer ready now for promotion (2–3 grades).	32	Marginal performer who is well placed but has no potential for promotion.
		33	Marginal performer who should be reassigned.

Source: Vincent R. Ceriello and Leonard Linden, "Management Resource Program," *Journal of Systems Management*, vol. 24, no. 12 (December 1973), pp. 9–10.

for the many "plateaued executives." These managers, who were hired during periods of expansion or replacement, may have reached middle—or even upper—ranks and expect to progress further with the firm's expansion. Yet, when there is a period of recession, there is no place for these individuals to go—except out.

Another vulnerable group are people hired for special programs. What do

FIGURE 7-5
Variables and their relationships to the net demand for management personnel

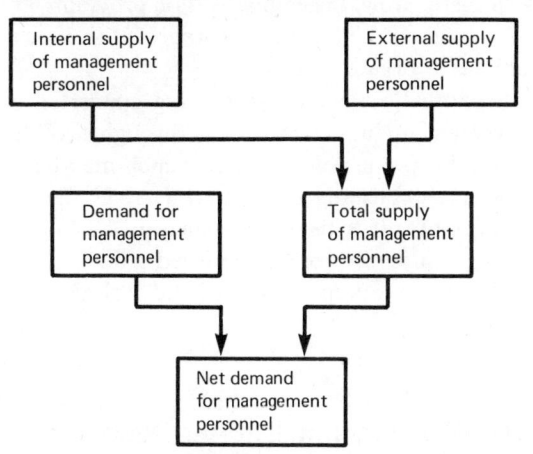

```
┌─────────────────┐              ┌─────────────────┐
│ Internal supply │              │ External supply │
│ of management  │              │ of management  │
│ personnel      │              │ personnel      │
└────────┬────────┘              └────────┬────────┘
         │                                │
         │     ┌─────────────────┐       │
         │     │ Demand for      │       │
         └────▶│ management     │  ┌────▶│
               │ personnel      │  │
               └────────┬────────┘  │
                        │   ┌───────┴──────────┐
                        │   │ Total supply     │
                        │   │ of management   │
                        │   │ personnel       │
                        │   └────────┬─────────┘
                        │            │
                        ▼            ▼
                   ┌──────────────────┐
                   │ Net demand       │
                   │ for management   │
                   │ personnel        │
                   └──────────────────┘
```

Source: N. S. Deckard and K. W. Lessey, "A Model for Understanding Management Manpower: Forecasting and Planning," *Personnel Journal*, vol. 54, no. 3 (March 1975), p. 169. Reprinted by permission from *Personnel Journal*, copyright March 1975.

you do with them when the job or program is over? (13) Allowing turnover and attrition to absorb such individuals is desirable, and temporary layoffs are preferable to permanent layoffs and later rehiring. "Efficiency" and "fairness" should be balanced.

Education, training, and development are other major action programs for meeting the organization's skill requirements.

As will be seen in the balance of this part, as well as in Part IV, government decreed programs—such as affirmative action programs—are increasingly being used in this step.

Affirmative action program

An integral part of any action program for implementing personnel-human resource planning is an affirmative action program (AAP) to provide equal opportunities for employment and advancement to all groups. As shown in Chapter 4, employing institutions are required by law not only to insure that no individual is discriminated against with respect to employment and advancement, but they must try to correct injustices caused by past discrimination. This has been interpreted to mean that organizations must *take positive action to seek out, recruit, select, develop, move, reward, and maintain* individuals who were formerly deprived because of race, color, religion, sex, nation of origin, age, and physical condition.

Earlier, equal employment opportunity efforts were directed only toward recruiting and training such employees. However, times change; people's aspirations, expectations, and perceptions change; and social and personnel customs change with them. Now, the emphasis is on providing greater opportunities for qualified women and minorities to progress to better paying and more prestigious positions in organizations.

In general, these AAPs include: (*a*) making concerted efforts to recruit minorities and women, including recruiting through the State Employment Service; (*b*) placing limitations on questions which may be asked in employment applications; (*c*) establishing goals and timetables, including determining available percentages of minorities and women in the local labor force; and (*d*) avoiding testing, unless it meets established guidelines.

As these AAPs are quite long, involved, and technical, they will only be mentioned here.

A NEW APPROACH TO PERSONNEL-HUMAN RESOURCE PLANNING

Many private and public institutions today have two things in common. They have numerous minority employees, as well as many highly educated and skilled workers with an appreciation of their worth as valuable resources in the organization and a high regard for themselves as individuals. In that context, hiring, placement, training, and counseling processes have to be based on a technology of job and worker analysis that regards workers as "whole persons," capable of growth and self-determination, not as mere cogs to be fitted into some predetermined personnel system.

Traditional job analysis, job descriptions, and job specifications did not achieve this objective. What is needed by the groups mentioned are job descriptions which address themselves to the *task or tasks to be accomplished, to the task-individual interface, and to task (and people) relationships.* Thus, a multiperspective job description is needed which puts the task at the focal point, which is concerned with personal content as well as job content, and which sees individual job relationships in terms of task accomplishment and the accomplishment of organizational objectives. In this framework, the job can best be perceived as part of an active system which relates to, rather than isolates, the job holder. (14)

Functional job analysis (FJA) sometimes referred to as "task analysis," claims to do just that. (15) Its fundamental concepts were developed about 25 years ago by Sidney A. Fine of the U.S. Employment Service in the course of research that was carried on in developing the third edition of the *U.S. Directory of Occupational Titles.* This work was undertaken to improve job placement and counseling for workers registering for employment at local employment service offices. Since 1965, FJA has been applied to bring the disadvantaged and minorities, who had been excluded from the mainstream, into the labor force.

Components of the system

Figure 7–6 represents the basic components of the system. The *worker* component involves those factors which typically result from an analysis of the qualifications required of an individual to perform the job successfully, namely, the worker's capacities (physical, mental, and so forth), experience, education, and training.

The *work organization* component refers to an analysis of the organization and includes such factors as the organization's purpose, goals, resources, constraints and objectives, and the way it is structured to achieve them.

The *work* component results from an analysis of the "task," or job to be

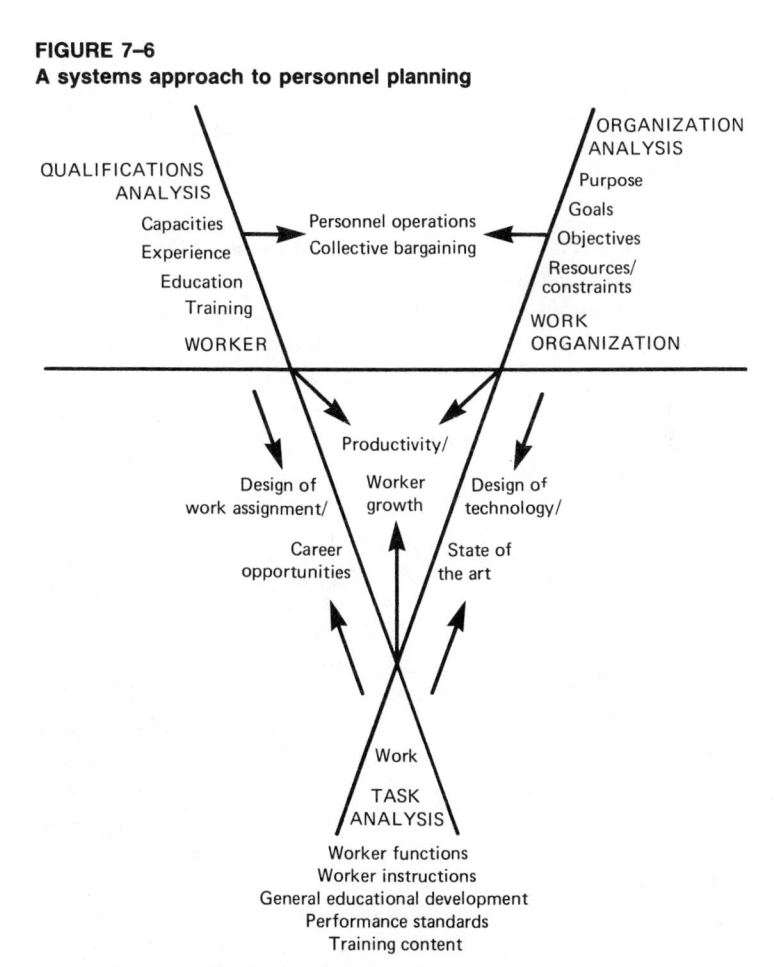

FIGURE 7–6
A systems approach to personnel planning

QUALIFICATIONS ANALYSIS
Capacities
Experience
Education
Training
WORKER

Personnel operations
Collective bargaining

ORGANIZATION ANALYSIS
Purpose
Goals
Objectives
Resources/constraints
WORK ORGANIZATION

Design of work assignment/
Productivity/Worker growth
Design of technology/
Career opportunities
State of the art

Work
TASK ANALYSIS
Worker functions
Worker instructions
General educational development
Performance standards
Training content

Source: Sidney Fine, "Functional Job Analysis: An Approach to a Technology for Manpower Planning," *Personnel Journal*, vol. 53, no. 11 (November 1974), p. 814. Reprinted with permission of *Personnel Journal*, copyright November 1974.

done. It describes what actually is being done and includes performance standards, general educational development needed to perform the job, specific training required, and the nature of the instructions to carry out particular tasks.

Under this systems approach to human resource planning, the interaction and interdependence of the basic components of the personnel system—work, worker, and work organization—means that personnel executives must consider the impact of a given action on all three components in order to stay in control of everyday problems. It also shows why many personnel-human resource problems do not seem to have any "solutions."

What the system does

Functional job analysis is an effective form of work analysis increasingly being used to design jobs and organize career ladders to give workers opportunities within work systems to achieve growth in their abilities and in their incomes. It is also being used to determine the relative and optimal numbers or workers with the necessary kinds of skills needed to achieve a work organization's objectives.

It has helped establish the realization that requirements for the work system cannot depend on educational achievements, for education has a more basic purpose than qualifying people for work. Training, which does prepare people for work, should be based upon the specific needs of a given individual, in a specific work organization, performing a definite task, in accordance with specific instructions and performance standards.

It is also being used to establish lines of mobility across related occupations, such as those requiring engineering or secretarial work, or occupations concerned with mental health, rehabilitation, and education.

Useful in complying with EEOC and OFCCP guidelines

EEOC and OFCCP guidelines stress the need for a valid job analysis as part of the validation procedure required to ensure compliance with the guidelines on recruiting, selection (especially testing), training and development, and promotion. FJA is admirably suited to this purpose because it *focuses on what the workers must know and what they must be able to do;* on the aptitudes and general educational development that they must have in order to benefit from training; and on the length of time required of the average worker to be vocationally prepared for the job. By being both specific and quantitative, this type of analysis helps to eliminate personal biases, hunches, and unsupported traditions from selection decisions, and to point the way toward procedures that are most likely to make optimal use of the individual's abilities, and to assure success on the job.

In summary, FJA is a valuable tool to help ensure the effectiveness of both preemployment screening and promotional procedures, for it allows managers to make those procedures as job-related as possible. Also, by providing an analysis of performance standards, it helps managers to evaluate performance and to counsel their employees on their development and career progress.

The training content portion of the analysis is useful to those who are responsible for conducting both classroom and on-the-job training, for it provides a clear understanding of what employees must know and what they must be able to do in order to progress from one job to another.

PERSONNEL PLANNING IN OTHER ECONOMIES

While many individual organizations in other economies do some type of personnel planning, the realization that market forces alone cannot be relied upon to provide suitable supplies of qualified people at the proper time and place has led many governments to do personnel planning at the national level. (16)

The prime objective of that planning has been to provide data for those planning educational and training programs. However, the purpose varies by country.

In Canada, the projections underlie policies for promoting occupational mobility, career counseling, immigration, and training, (17) primarily by the Economic Council of Canada. Multiple regression techniques have been applied to establish relationships between employee requirements and such factors as earnings, unemployment, hours worked, and population structure. The statistical data available seems to be superior.

The educational aspect of planning has also been dominant in Sweden, where forecasts are expressed in educational categories, as well as industrial and occupational groupings. The long-, medium-, and short-term planning periods also tend to interlock to provide both long-range guidance and, yet, be of use for reeducation and retraining measures. The simple extrapolation approach tends to be used.

In the Netherlands, long-term forecasts are used as a basis of investing in education and training programs. Their plans, which also tend to interlock in time periods, tend to be based upon multiple regression techniques and econometric models, which generate valid data.

The United Kingdom uses a variety of techniques with emphasis on multiple regression, especially for employment statistics. (18) Planning, along with laws such as the *Industrial Training Act* and the *Redundancy Payments Act*, has helped redeploy workers between industries and firms and raise the skill level of the labor force.

Planning tends to be highly centralized in France, (19) where the emphasis is on short-term economic forecasting and planning. The global method of overall planning is extensively used.

EVALUATING EFFECTIVENESS OF PERSONNEL-HUMAN RESOURCE PLANNING

The techniques usually used to evaluate the effectiveness of personnel-human resource planning tend to be simple, subjective, and traditional. In most organizations, the various human resource activities are subject only to personal review by the personnel executive. When problems become obvious, special studies, attitude surveys, or other analyses are often conducted to help management determine the best course of remedial action.

Some new evaluative techniques

However, newer, more rigorous tools and procedures of analysis are now beginning to be used. Some of these include analyzing:

1. *Quantitative data,* including rates and levels of participation in programs, movement of talent, turnover, and absenteeism—and their causes;
2. *Employee attitudes,* based on periodic employee attitude surveys or other forms or organizational climate audit;
3. *Direct expenditures* for such programs as recruitment, training and development, or training of disadvantaged employees;
4. *The breakeven point/payback period* for new hires;
5. *Productivity changes,* the impact of incentive compensation on productivity, and other factors affecting productivity;
6. *Recruitment results,* such as optimal sources of recruits, recruitment practices, and cost of recruiting versus developing talent available internally; and
7. *The economics* of layoff and retention of good talent during periods of staff reductions. (20)

In 1971, Xerox Corporation developed a technique applying the systems approach and program management concepts as part of its long-range personnel-human resource planning strategy. This program evaluation technique of cost effectiveness is now also being used to develop operating budget proposals for selected personnel units throughout the country.

While the details of the program are too voluminous and detailed for this book, the key elements of the procedure are:

1. Define and describe each personnel program—whether proposed or ongoing—in a discrete package;
2. Separate for special treatment those programs that are legally required;
3. Evaluate all programs on the basis of: (*a*) "state of the art," (*b*) ease of implementation, (*c*) net economic benefits, and (*d*) economic risks of not acting; and
4. Rank all programs and allocate and deploy staff resources accordingly.

An example of how the systems operate is shown in Figure 7–7.

IMPLICATIONS AND APPLICATIONS FOR PERSONNEL EXECUTIVES

Personnel-human resource planning is a process for translating overall organizational objectives, plans, and programs into specific performance.

FIGURE 7-7
Xerox's program evaluation form

1. Define and describe the program.	PROGRAM NAME: Service Force Job Enrichment Program			Program No. 16
	DESCRIPTION (objectives, target population, implementation schedule):			
	To extend the job enrichment program for the service force — as piloted in Spring Falls, Avon Hills, and Maplewood branches — to all branches between 1972 and 1976.			
2. Identify and segregate legally required efforts.	Is program legally required?	[ ] Yes	[X] No	
3. Evaluate feasibility: (a) State-of-the-art implications.	STATE OF THE ART	[X] High	[ ] Medium	[ ] Low
(b) Ease of implementation.	EASE OF IMPLEMENTATION	[ ] High	[ ] Medium	[X] Low
(c) Net economic benefits...	ECONOMIC BENEFITS	[X] High	[ ] Medium	[ ] Low

	Potential revenue impact	Probability of occurrence	Probable gross benefit (cost)
Identifiable benefits:			
Reduction in service force turnover of 1 point.	$ 450,000	.2	$ 90,000
Extension of 1.2 point reduction in absenteeism, as demonstrated in pilot project.	$ 2,132,500	.8	$ 1,706,000
Extension of 5% increase in service force productivity, as demonstrated in initial efforts.	$85,500,000	.1	$ 8,550,000
Total benefits	$88,082,500	.12	$10,346,000
Tangible costs to Xerox of acting: Group personnel staff time to develop program, and line management time to implement program in all branches.	($ 472,950)	.9	$ 425,655
Total costs	($ 472,950)	.9	$ 425,655
Probable net benefits (cost)			$ 9,920,345

...and intangibles.

Intangible benefits

Increased morale in service force, with improved customer service and satisfaction.

"Contagious effect" of job enrichment to other groups, e.g., sales and clericals.

Improved service manager development with concurrent sharpening of their motivational skills. As an extreme example, one manager at Avon Hills increased his team's productivity 70%.

(d) Economic risks.

ECONOMIC RISKS	[X] High	[ ] Medium	[ ] Low

Possible consequences of not acting:
Continued escalation of service costs as a percent of revenue.

ASSUMPTIONS AND OTHER CONSIDERATIONS:

Cost estimates assume 4.4 man years of group staff time, .26 man years of branch manager time, and 15.8 man years of service manager time to implement program in a population of 1,053 service managers.

Benefit estimates assume elimination of 3 days absenteeism per month for each of 1,053 service teams, favorable productivity, and that turnover experience in pilot branches can be cascaded to all branches.

Source: Logan M. Cheek, "Cost Effectiveness Comes to the Personnel Function," *Harvard Business Review*, vol. 51, no. 3 (May–June 1973), pp. 99, 103, 104. Copyright ©1973 by the President and Fellows of Harvard College; all rights reserved.

The present lack of personnel planning apparently results from some fault of the personnel executives or inadequate concern by top management, not from inadequate technology. (21) The "state of the art" in planning is such that any level of sophistication is feasible—if the organization is philosophically willing, and financially able, to use it.

While human resource planning has been infrequently, or inadequately, used in the past, several factors are currently leading to a renewed interest in it. Federal contract compliance, including standards for hiring females, minorities, older and handicapped workers, and veterans, has been a real and significant contributor to this trend. Also, the shortage of experienced and capable executives, the expense involved in hiring and maintaining employees, the cost of ineffective utilization of personnel, the growth of knowledgeable workers—and the technologically-related obsolescence of present personnel—and the emphasis on human resource accounting have accelerated the move to introduce, or reactivate, planning. Yet, the methods being used still vary from elementary "guesswork" as to short-range demand and supply to highly sophisticated systems, using computer-based data banks to meet current needs, and/or plans for a long-range matching of supply and demand for expected occupational categories and job skills.

> At Owens-Corning Fiberglass, employee planning is highly individualized. In a program set up under a new Human Resources Department, the total career of each salaried employee is followed from hiring to retirement. A computerized data bank of each employee's skills, education, experience, and other information is used as a basis for career planning, guidance, and appraisals. Each person's skills are analyzed and matched to the firm's needs. (22)

Ironically, everything else being equal, the organizations that need human resource planning most are those in which it is most difficult to do.

First, the more rapidly expanding groups need it more than those with a stable work force or one which is expanding gradually and predictably.

Second, organizations with a high proportion of the more expensive, scientific, technical, professional, and managerial personnel should do more and better planning than those with considerable nonmanagerial workers.

Third, technologically-oriented organizations need planning more than those using existing knowledge in order to match an inadequate supply of capable personnel with escalating demand.

Fourth, the more responsive an organization is to its total environment, the greater is the need for planning, especially that using more sophisticated techniques and longer time frames.

> Because of expanding technology in performing open-heart surgery and the development of related equipment to care for the patients, a progressive hospital planned and opened a Coronary Care Unit (CCU). A sufficient supply of qualified personnel to staff it was not available. After "borrowing" from the limited supply of personnel in the Intensive Care Unit (ICU), there was only enough

people to use one-quarter of the equipped beds when it opened. Even after one year, only one-half the beds was being used.

Fifth, *organizations covered by government regulations* must—in order to be in compliance—do human resource planning in almost all areas of personnel activities.

> A national chemical company, with several hundred products grouped into "about a dozen" lines produced at six plants, tripled its personnel department's training staff and brought in consultants to comply with EEOC and OFCCP regulations. They took three years to do "functional job analysis" for all nonexempt personnel. The results, used for recruiting, selecting, developing, and rewarding personnel, have been accepted as valid.

Sixth, as shown in the previous case, *the more diversified the products produced, or services provided, the greater the need for planning.*

Finally, while it may be obvious, it should be stated that *the larger the organization, the greater is the need for*—and the financial and personnel ability to do—*longer-range and more sophisticated planning.*

There is little agreement as to where the human resource planning function should be located organizationally, except that the personnel executives cannot do it alone; an integrated approach is more effective. (23)

If there is no personnel planning system, how do you begin one? Probably the best way to start is by inventorying existing personnel and expertise to see what shortages currently exist. This should provide a base from which to start doing more advance planning.

As the success of human resource planning is its ability to identify—and correct—imbalances in supply and demand, that is what you should try to do next. If your system indicates a shortage of personnel in a specific area, you can increase overall recruitment; recruit additional minorities, women, or handicapped workers; institute or increase training and development programs; provide transfer or promotion opportunities; lower selection standards; use more overtime; use contracted services; or restructure the organization. However, if your system indicates a surplus in certain areas, you can encourage early retirements; plan orderly discharges or layoffs; upgrade your people for other assignments; trasfer people; or restructure the organization.

There is no "rule-of-thumb" as to what you should do, but the system which "fits" you and your organization is the one you should use.

DISCUSSION QUESTIONS

1. If personnel-human resource planning is so important, why is it not done more extensively and better?
2. Evaluate the use of human resource accounting. (*a*) What do you see as its greatest potential? (*b*) What are its possible limitations?
3. Earlier the term, "personnel planning," was usually used to refer only to determining job specifications and the number of employees to be hired. Either defend that

position, or defend the present trend toward a more extensive and inclusive concept used in this text.
4. Are there changes you would suggest in the planning procedure advocated in this text? Explain.
5. What further suggestions can you make for evaluating the effectiveness of planning?
6. Define and explain how job analysis is performed.

REFERENCES AND SUGGESTIONS FOR FURTHER STUDY

1. Frank H. Cassell has presented one of the best descriptions of this problem in "Manpower Planning: State of the Art at the Micro Level," *MSU Business Topics,* vol. 21, no. 4 (Autumn 1973), pp. 13–20, especially pp. 18–19.

   J. B. Bartlett also found a difference between theory and practice in Great Britain. See "Problems in Manpower Planning," *Personnel Management,* vol. 5, no. 2 (February 1973), pp. 30–31 and 42.

2. In the past few decades, many organizations have put into use a wide range of programs and practices aimed at improving the utilization of their human resources. The thousand largest business and industrial organizations in the world spend over $10 billion each year in human resource management activities, excluding the value of time spent by individuals away from work performing training, development, interviewing, performance planning and review, and other activities. See James W. Walker, "Evaluating the Practical Effectiveness of Human Resource Planning Applications," *Human Resource Management,* vol. 13, no. 1 (Spring 1974), pp. 19–27, for further details and suggestions.

3. See Jon Healey, "Big Push in Manpower Planning," *Dunn's Business Review,* vol. 104, no. 5 (November 1974), p. 103, for discussions of these and other organizations with well-developed planning programs.

4. Probably the best comprehensive treatment of this subject is Eric G. Flamholtz, *Human Resource Accounting* (Encino, Calif.: Dickenson Publishing Co., 1974), especially Chapter 9.

5. One example of a *job brief and qualifications is:*

Job title:	Refinery Mechanic.
Department:	Plant.
Wage scale:	Plant scale 9.
Location:	In all the company's refineries.

   Other information provided includes: (*a*) general duties or a description of some of the major activities of the job, including a brief idea of the type work performed; (*b*) specific requirements for the job, such as hours to be worked, vehicle driving requirements, license requirements, and so forth; (*c*) basic qualifications, including job-related requirements which will be reviewed and evaluated when an individual is being considered for the job. These basic qualifications may include physical requirements, prior experience, previous work record, and so forth; and (*d*) a general statement relating to the education, training, or development that may be required for the job.

6. See Craig E. Schneier, "Content Validity: The Necessity of a Behavioral Job Description," *Personnel Administrator,* vol. 21, no. 2 (February 1976), pp. 38–44. Reprinted with the permission of *The Personnel Administration;* copyright 1976, The American Society for Personnel Administration.

An example of how this kind of job description could work is shown below:

Comparison of ambiguous and terminal behavior job objectives

Ambiguous job objectives	Terminal behavior job objectives
1. To demonstrate satisfactory ability on the job and perform at required standards.	1. To operate the press such that a minimum of 120 pieces are produced correctly each hour, with no more than 1 incorrect (defective) piece produced in any hour.
2. To develop a positive attitude toward the work and to be dependable.	2. To give evidence of willingness to perform the job by not being absent from work except for those reasons and on those days specified by the union agreement; and by being at the proper work place when the shift bell sounds.
3. To be able to communicate effectively with subordinates.	3. To notify each division head of all changes in the budget by written memo to each no later than one day after notification of such change reaches your desk.

---

7. MTM, which means methods-time-measurement, is one of many methods of arriving at synthetic time standards. These predetermined time systems, or "time studies without a stopwatch," developed as a result of studies and research conducted by several famous people. Frederick W. Taylor created interest in time study operations and set down time study stopwatch rules which are still in use today. Frank B. and Lillian M. Gilbreth generated much interest in motion study of operations and established "therbligs," the first scientific classification of motion. Another contributor was H. L. Gantt, whose emphasis on the human factors led to a closer study of job difficulties, the use of standards, and the importance of leadership. Finally, Harrington Emerson helped by introducing concepts of modern management processes such as his "First Principle"—that people work most effectively when they have clearly defined goals.

   For more details, see Clifford Sellie, "The History of Predetermined Motion Times," *Industrial Management,* vol. 16, no. 1 (January 1974), pp. 12–15.

8. Address by H. I. Romnes, chairman of the board, American Telephone and Telegraph Company, to the Pioneer General Assembly, Cleveland, Ohio, September 22, 1970.

9. James W. Walker, "Evaluating the Practical Effectiveness of Human Resource Planning Applications," *Human Resource Management,* vol. 13, no. 1 (Spring 1974), pp. 21, 22, and 25.

10. This system is adopted from: Elmer H. Burack, *Strategies for Manpower Planning and Programming* (Morristown, N.J.: General Learning Corp., 1972); Bruce P. Coleman, "An Integrated System for Manpower Planning," *Business Horizons*, vol. 13, no. 5 (October 1970), pp. 89–95; Robert R. Guthrie, "Personnel's Emerging Role," *Personnel Journal*, vol. 53, no. 9 (September 1974), pp. 657–61; Eric Vetter, "How to Forecast Your Manpower Needs," *Nation's Business*, vol. 52, no. 2 (February 1964), pp. 102–10; and James W. Walker, "Forecasting Manpower Needs," *Harvard Business Review*, vol. 47, no. 2 (March–April 1969), pp. 152–64.

11. See T. J. O'Neil and M. Nath, "Computer Aided Manpower Planning Using On-Line Terminals," *Industrial Management*, vol. 15, no. 3 (March 1973), pp. 1–6, for useful information on this subject.

12. If you are interested in the entire procedure, read N. S. Deckard and K. W. Lissey, "A Model for Understanding Management Manpower: Forecasting and Planning," *Personnel Journal*, vol. 54, no. 3 (March 1975), pp. 169–75.

13. See Donald Sweet, "Something New in Personnel—Out-Placement," *Personnel Journal*, vol. 50, no. 7 (July 1971), pp. 559–64, for an analysis of this problem.

14. See Hollister Spencer, "Task Definition and Exposition: The Catalyst in the Matching Process," *Personnel Journal*, vol. 53, no. 6 (June 1974), pp. 428–34, for an intriguing discussion of the inadequacies of conventional job descriptions and an effort to make them more meaningful to new job seekers.

15. This presentation is based upon Sidney A. Fine, "Fundamental Job Analysis: An Approach to a Technology for Manpower Planning," *Personnel Journal*, vol. 53, no. 11 (November 1974), pp. 813–18; the W. E. Upjohn Institute for Employment Research, *Workshop Manual* (1969); and the description of a chemical firm's program, based upon three years' empirical research on how to satisfy OFCCP requirements.

16. This discussion drew heavily on the article by D. J. Walsh and M. E. Polding, "Manpower Planning," *Personnel Management*, vol. 3, no. 8 (August 1971), pp. 30–32.

17. Mark Blaug, Maurice Preston, and Adrian Ziderman, *The Utilization of Educated Manpower in Industry* (Toronto, Canada: University of Toronto Press, 1967).

18. Felix Paukert, "Technological Change and the Level of Employment in Western Europe," *British Journal of Industrial Relations*, vol. 6, no. 2 (July 1968), pp. 139–55.

19. "Employment Forecasting and Manpower Policy in France," *International Labour Review*, vol. 79, no. 2 (February 1959), pp. 189–203.

20. See Walker, "Evaluating the Practical Effectiveness of Human Resource Planning Applications," *Human Resource Management*, pp. 19–27; and Logan M. Cheek, "Cost Effectiveness Comes to the Personnel Function," *Harvard Business Review*, vol. 51, no. 3 (May–June 1973), pp. 96–105, for an excellent discussion of how the introduction of systematic project evaluation into the personnel department helps increase productivity.

21. Research done for the American Society for Personnel Administration by a group at Indiana University reached a similar conclusion. See Albert N. Navas *et al.*, *Managerial Manpower Forecasting and Planning* (Berea, O.: American Society for Personnel Administration, 1965), for elaboration.

22. Explained in Healey, "Big Push in Manpower Planning," *Dunn's Business Review*, p. 106.
23. Edwin Geisler found that the most common practice is for personnel departments to have the day-to-day responsibility for such planning when it is a separate function. See *Manpower Planning: An Emerging Staff Function* (New York: American Management Assn., Management Bulletin No. 101, 1967), for details.

Chapter 8

Recruiting personnel

Developing sources of potential employees
    Theoretical source of personnel
    Internal sources
    External sources

Methods used in recruiting
    Use of advertising
    Employee referrals
    Consultants
    Scouting
    Electronic assistance in recruiting
    Which method to use

Some special considerations in college recruiting
    Why it is used
    What recruiters look for
    What affects recruiter's success
    What influences applicant's job choice
    Some special approaches used
    Evaluating the effectiveness of college recruiting

Effects of public policy on recruiting
    How public policy affects recruiting
    Compliance experience

Evaluating the effectiveness of recruiting activities

Implications and applications

8
Recruiting personnel

Here lies a man who knew how to enlist in his service better men than himself.

ANDREW CARNEGIE'S EPITAPH

A pathologist, operating a medical testing laboratory near a university, employed around 30 medical technologists. There was a chronic national shortage of technologists which also affected the local laboratory.

As his demand was rising faster than the supply of well-trained technologists, he worked with a local hospital and the university to develop a degree program for technologists. In addition, he had a policy of hiring wives of college students if they were available. As these tended to leave after three or four years to follow their husbands, he had a continually improving caliber of personnel from the university and the incoming wives.

This is admittedly a novel way of recruiting needed personnel, but it shows what innovation and creativity can do. That is what is discussed in this chapter.

Recruitment is the term applied to that phase of personnel management which is concerned with reaching out and attracting a supply of people from which to select qualified candidates for job vacancies. An effort is thus made to attract potential employees with the necessary characteristics and in the proper quantities for the jobs available.

The material in this chapter will be concerned with developing such a system, as shown in Figure 8–1.

DEVELOPING SOURCES OF POTENTIAL EMPLOYEES

After performing personnel planning, the personnel executive must determine what supply sources and methods will be used to search for needed personnel. Effective selection is achieved only through the use of the widest possible range of places from which employees can be obtained.

Theoretical source of personnel

Theoretically the ultimate source of all personnel is some educational institution. As such institutions provide our basic education and generalized training—at various levels—they form the reservoir from which all employees

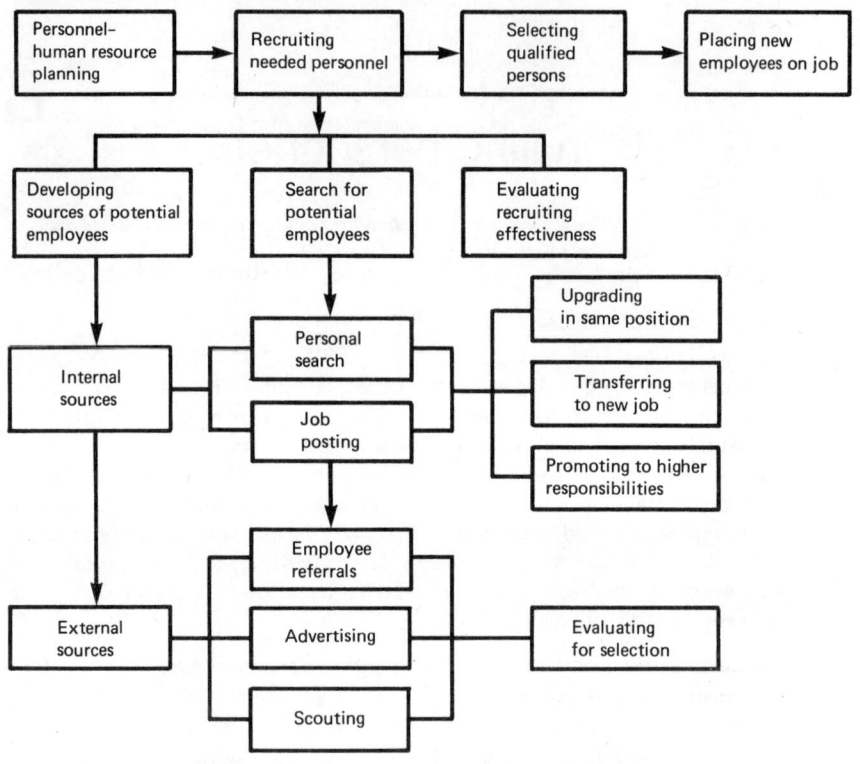

FIGURE 8–1
Place of recruitment in a selection system

eventually are obtained, even if the actual selection is from some other intermediate source. (It is assumed that some of the applicants may not have completed their work at an educational institution but may have dropped out of it.) This relationship between recruitment and educational background can best be understood by seeing how employees progress through an organization.

Figure 8–2 shows the theoretical flow of personnel through a hypothetical organization. It will be noticed that the employees enter the system at the lower part of their occupational grouping, work in a certain job for a period of time, are promoted to supervisory or managerial positions, or leave for any of many reasons. The figure also shows that it is erroneous to think of all the employees entering the firm at the same organizational level. The unskilled, semiskilled, and skilled employees tend to enter at lower wage levels and job classifications than do the clerical; sales; and professional, technical, and scientific employees. Also, each group tends to enter the organization at a successively higher level than does the previous group. As all jobs are not of equal importance to the institution and as all employees are not equally capable, well trained, and well developed, they do not start from the same competitive position. The professional, technical, and scientific employees have a better chance for advancement through the promotional channels than do the other employees, although there are exceptions. In general, there is a tendency for operative employees to progress to the level of supervisor, or even middle management; for clerical and sales personnel to become supervisors and middle-level managers, and even progress into top management; and for professional, technical, and scientific employees to move through the supervisory ranks into the middle and top levels of management, including the chief executive officer's position.

FIGURE 8–2
Theoretical flow of personnel through a hypothetical organization

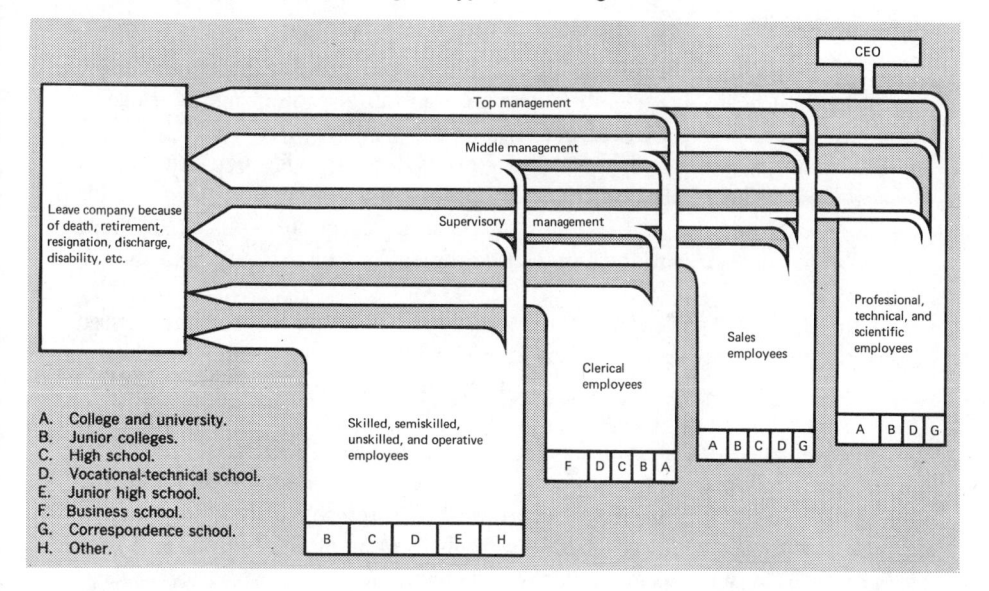

A. College and university.
B. Junior colleges.
C. High school.
D. Vocational-technical school.
E. Junior high school.
F. Business school.
G. Correspondence school.
H. Other.

Internal sources

Although the theoretical source of all personnel is some educational institution, the immediate source of applicants for given jobs is either by movement from within the organization or by recruitment from outside. The majority of positions are filled from internal sources.

There are three methods for obtaining employees internally, namely, through *upgrading* the employee currently holding the position; *transferring* an employee from a less desirable or rewarding job elsewhere in the organization; or *promoting* someone from a lower-level position. These will be discussed in detail in Chapter 14.

A growing practice in achieving internal selection is job posting, whereby available positions are announced and all eligible employees can "bid" on them.

The federal government has now become a strong advocate of this method of filling higher positions. Research shows that the OFCCP has accepted—and even demanded—that posting is one way of achieving equal promotional opportunities. Also, the EEOC has become an advocate of posting procedures. (1) While posting is not required, it is one of the factors looked for when there is a complaint of discrimination. In the absence of this procedure, the organization must demonstrate that its procedure isn't discriminatory. In fact, there are indications that its absence may be illegal in the total context of the selection system.

External sources

Ultimately all job openings must be filled from outside the organization. As individual positions are filled through upgrading, promoting, or transferring employees, those vacated positions must be filled externally.

A growing organization must also go outside to provide personnel for at least its lowest level jobs. But there are other valid reasons for going outside for high-level personnel. Inevitably there needs to be an infusion of "new blood" into an organization to prevent "inbreeding," conformity, and stagnation.

A more valid justification for external hiring is found in problems caused by technological development. Because new skills may be needed in a hurry, it is sometimes necessary to go outside to find individuals with the required education, training, and experience.

When internal promotion policy is followed too rigidly, there are inevitable mistakes in filling higher job requirements. As it is practically impossible to anticipate the skills that will be needed in the future, it is also difficult to hire a person with the required abilities who will enter at the bottom and then progress all the way up through the organization.

The specific sources used to recruit new personnel will depend upon the jobs to be filled, as well as other factors.

Sources used to fill blue-collar positions. Some of the regular sources used are former employees, unsolicited applications, unions, employment agencies, temporary help, and immigrants. Several of these sources merit further comment.

Former employees. Most organizations maintain a roster of former employees which provides a potential source of trained employees. If the worker voluntarily left for a valid reason, is in good standing, and is seeking reemployment—or can be encouraged to return—this source might be used. However, it tends to be static as the chances are good that the former employee has failed to grow or maintain competence.

Unsolicited applications. During periods of normal economic activity, unsolicited inquiries concerning possible employment are received through the mail or at the employment office. Such applications warrant attention if the person's qualifications appear to meet your requirements. However, this source requires greater use of the selection procedure than applicants from other sources, as there has been no preselection or screening.

Studies of a large group of private employers done by the National Industrial Conference Board (NICB) found this source used extensively by banks (100 percent), utilities (97 percent), manufacturing firms (90 percent), and insurance firms (91 percent). Also, it is used more extensively for white-collar employees. (2)

Unions. In some geographic areas and in certain industries, companies rely heavily upon unions as a source of employees. This is particularly true in skilled trades where the union has assumed considerable responsibility for apprenticeship training programs.

This source is used extensively in the construction and shipping industries where it is convenient for the employer and specifically permitted by labor laws. It is also used by many small firms who cannot maintain a personnel staff, yet have variable demand and high turnover. Some examples are transportation, contract maintenance, clothing, and food service.

Private employment agencies. These agencies are increasingly being used as a source of personnel. Some of these agencies are now specializing in only one type of personnel—operations, clerical, managerial, and so forth. Also, they are highly regulated in many states. (3)

In general, a properly qualified agency is in an excellent position to aid in recruitment as it knows the market, the skills available, the skills sought by the employer, and the situations concerning particular employees. Since they have done much of the preliminary screening, their recommendations are valuable. Under this arrangement, a fee is paid—usually by the applicant. (4)

They are not used too extensively for blue-collar jobs. One researcher found that only 19 percent of their placements in Iowa were in blue-collar positions. The NICB study found only 23 percent of manufacturers using this source (5) for blue-collar workers.

Public employment agencies. Another source of recruitment assistance is the employment service operated by the states in cooperation with the U.S. Department of Labor's Employment and Training Administration [through the U.S. Employment Service (USES)]. They are important sources of unskilled and semiskilled workers, particularly for production and service jobs. Now, they are moving more into the clerical, technical, and professional areas.

Effective use of this agency requires that the employer give definite job specifications to the agency and that the agency do more preliminary screening and culling of potential employees. This agency is quite important as a result of public policies affecting recruitment, selection, and training and development of minority groups.

Temporary help. Many companies are now using an alternative source of supply in the form of part-time workers. This source takes two forms. First, people who wish to work less than full time—such as retired persons, students, and workers with time to spare—may be called upon during rush periods.*

Second, leased personnel can be used to do jobs requiring less than full time or during rush periods. Under this arrangement, the company obtains from some outside concern employees who are specialized in performing a given service. This method is particularly useful in clerical and maintenance operations for which an employee with a given specialty can be hired by the hour or day, as the situation dictates. Also, it is quite prevalent in the janitorial field where office buildings (and even some manufacturing plants) use the personnel of a janitorial service organization on a fee basis. The benefits to the company are reduced hiring and salary expenses, minimized turnover, less recordkeeping, lower fringe benefits cost, and better use of highly paid employees. However, before this method can be used, the company must decide whether the problem of what to do with workers displaced by leasing can be satisfactorily solved, whether proper skills are available in the right quality and quantity, and whether the union contract permits it.

> A New York temporary replacement service sought women with "rough, red, dry hand problems" on behalf of an ad agency. The hint of possible TV fame "really played into a lot of people's fantasies," for more than 200 women signed up for auditions. One caller asked: "Do you need a mother and a daughter?"

Others. Some other sources are *vocational-technical schools, manufacturer's training schools, competing firms, veterans,* and *immigrants.*

Sources used in filling white-collar positions. Most of the previous sources can be satisfactorily used in recruiting white-collar employees. For example, it was found in the NICB studies that 65 percent of manufacturing firms used the *public employment services* to attract white-collar workers. Yet, only 7 percent of those using the service thought it was the best source of such workers. Conversely, while 77 percent of the employers used *private agencies* for white-collar employees, 67 percent also thought they were the best source for this type employee.

White-collar workers are also obtained from *business colleges; schools and colleges; correspondence schools; professional, fraternal, and religious organizations;* and *competing firms.* While there is an ethical question involved, the last source is particularly useful for recruiting sales personnel.

A unique approach is used by one firm in selecting its sales personnel. It hires college dropouts, for its experience has shown that these individuals, if carefully selected, make good productive sales personnel with management potential. Such young people generate a lot of enthusiasm at being given a second opportunity to achieve success. (6)

Sources used in recruiting scientists, engineers, and technical personnel. It was found by 131 selected companies that the best methods of recruiting scientists, engineers, and technical personnel are *employee-referral programs, newspaper advertising,* and *specialized employment agencies.* (7) Of the firms

---

* As full-time employees tend to resent being replaced by part-time people, the best time to begin using such a source is when normal attrition occurs.

questioned, 49 percent said that referrals by employees gave excellent results, while 29 percent said ads in newspapers and the use of consultants and executive recruiters gave equally effective results.

Educational institutions are also used extensively for these people. In fact, colleges and universities tend to be the primary—and most effective—source, as we will see later in the chapter. Recruiters prefer this source as it is cheaper than private employment agencies. (8)

Sources used in recruiting managerial personnel. As there are so many factors and variables involved in recruiting these persons, the sources will be discussed in a later chapter, along with an analysis of selection methodology.

METHODS USED IN RECRUITING

Methods of recruiting new employees vary with each organization and recruiter. However, they usually include advertising in various media, employee referrals, consultants, and college recruiting.

Use of advertising

Display and want ads in a newspaper are the most common—and least expensive—forms of recruiting employees. However, there are other media employed, such as trade journals, professional journals, radio, billboards, television, and recordings at special events, such as professional meetings and conventions.

As advertising is so important, we should see what makes it effective—or ineffective. According to one research study, most advertisements are more concerned with the *quantity of replies* than with the *quality of applicants*. (9) The most effective advertising copy for college graduates and for highly qualified personnel—such as experienced engineers, programmers, scientific and technical personnel, and similar types of workers—was found to be geared to their educational level, (10) with the copy being specific as to the placement and conditions of employment for the applicants, as well as opportunities available to them.

Employee referrals

As present employees know the requirements of jobs to be filled and the personal requirements needed of people to fill them, they can assist in recruitment by suggesting potential employees. Research has shown that the suggestions and comments of current employees can be a major factor in determining who is best suited for a particular job.

For example, in a study of the Chicago labor market, it was found that the most widely used channels of recruitment were informal and that *employee referrals* were the most popular method. Of the employers interviewed, 85 percent favored this method. (11)

Similar results were found in a study of three insurance companies. The results indicated that referrals tended to be more successful than the average worker. The quality of the referrals, however, depends upon the morale of the employees, the accuracy of information, and the closeness of the intermediary friend. (12) Occasionally, when there is a great shortage of skilled personnel, a firm will offer a "bonus" to its employees to stimulate their extra effort.

> A hospital was short 75 nurses. It offered a $200 cash bonus to anyone recommending a qualified nurse who was not employed by a competing hospital. The first $100 is paid when the nurse accepts employment; the second is paid at the end of the new employee's third month on the payroll.

This system does have one drawback, namely, the possibility of the formation of cliques and informal work groups, particularly where relatives are involved. Also, if the jobs are of a fiduciary nature, there is the danger of collusion among friends and relatives.

Consultants

Consultants are also used for recruiting, but their talents are ordinarily utilized in the search for scientific, technical, professional, and managerial personnel. However, for all skills that are becoming increasingly scarce, the consultants will be used as recruiters of potential employees.

Scouting

A group of potential employees that deserve special attention is that composed of college graduates. The question is not whether to hire them or not, because with the present state of technology, an organization must employ them for certain positions in order to survive, especially for the more technical jobs. Because of the importance of this method, a complete section will be devoted to it.

Electronic assistance in recruiting

The mechanized world of automation is invading the recruitment field. Electronic data processing now aids the recruiter in hastening the flow of information and in securing data hitherto unobtainable.

There are three ways the computer can assist personnel executives. It can help determine which job characteristics go with which personal preferences to find the best "fit"; it can be hooked up to a telephone network to help private employment agencies locate the person with the desired qualifications; and it can assign daily jobs when several variables are involved. The more progressive organizations are now installing computerized data bases.

Various types of computerized personnel data systems are now becoming popular. While each one varies in detail, in general they attempt to allow the

"I'm Fred Johnson from Personnel, Miss Forbes, and I just had to see if you were all your punch cards said you were."

Saturday Review, February 1, 1964.

user to perform selected recruitment-related functions, such as identifying the "ideal" candidate (if any); considering the marginal (yet acceptable) ones; determining the area/extent of candidates' inadequacies; and forcing the use of logical criteria demanding quantification. Rejected candidates can be counseled in terms of their specific deficiencies, and the personnel in entire departments can be ranked in terms of how well they meet the desired level of skill or education. (13)

Which method to use

An area needing considerable research is which recruiting method to use. While many studies conclude that the relative cost of each method, economic conditions, type industry, and jobs to be filled should be considered, more usable answers are needed.

SOME SPECIAL CONSIDERATIONS IN COLLEGE RECRUITING

College recruiting is a frequently used technique for recruiting scientific, technical, professional, and managerial occupations. In fact, it is thought of as a unique "labor market." It is now the major source of these personnel.

Why it is used

This method is not universally popular, for there are many criticisms of the effectiveness of its use by recruiters. (14) Yet, in one study, most personnel executives viewed this as the most effective method for obtaining this type personnel, and 51 percent hired more college graduates through this method than from all other sources. (15)

This method is used for two main reasons, namely, (*a*) campuses are the best source of higher-level personnel; and (*b*) it is difficult to evaluate an applicant any way other than through a personal interview, and, as it is so expensive to have all applicants visit the firm, it is cheaper and more effective for the recruiter to go to the campus.

What recruiters look for

There are at least three aspects of this question, namely, educational level, demographic qualities, and attributes.

Educational level. The primary emphasis is still on the bachelor's degree for most sales, scientific, and technical positions and for many professional positions, such as for accountants, economists, engineers, and positions in statistics and finance. For managerial positions, the emphasis is shifting to MBAs—especially those with a technical undergraduate degree.

Demographic qualities. While the 225 firms surveyed for the 1976 *Endicott Report* (16) expected to hire 9 percent more bachelor's degree graduates and 11 percent more master's degree candidates, they expected to recruit 45 percent more women (22 percent of all college hires) and 45 percent more blacks (13 percent of all hires). (17)

Attributes sought. There is little agreement concerning what recruiters seek in college graduates. However, a survey of personnel managers in New York and Hawaii found a strong and consistent preference toward graduates who were (*a*) people-oriented, (*b*) business-oriented, and (*c*) quantitatively-oriented. (18) The survey also found that few graduates were meeting the executives' expectations. Only one out of 132 found 80 percent or more of the graduates meeting expectations.

What affects recruiter's success

It has been shown from empirical evidence that the personality and ability of the person who does the recruiting, as well as the methods used and the surroundings in which the recruiting takes place, has an effect upon the quality of those selected and whether they stay with the firm. (19)

These conclusions were verified in a study of 112 first and second year MBAs at Cornell, where the impact of perceived recruitment interviewer traits, behaviors, and attitudes on job candidate interview evaluations and subjective probabilities of accepting a job were studied. (20) The best interviewers were perceived as having more interest and concern, seeing the candidates' strengths and weaknesses, being younger and more successful, and giving the better probability of a higher starting salary. The candidates gave higher probabilities of accepting the job offers from the organization represented by the better interviewers.

What influences applicant's job choice

Today's college students have been found to consider the following factors in job selection: potential for advancement, appealing job, the kind of people they meet in the organization, (21) as well as salary and security.

Similar results were found in a research study of what 500 Florida State University students valued in a prospective job. (22) Given a list of 20 variables concerning a prospective job, they were asked to list them in order of their relative importance. The top factors were "advancement possibilities," "doing work I like," "security and sense of a future," and "starting salary."

Graduate students tend to have slightly different criteria for selecting a job. A survey of 59 male and 20 female MBA students at Wharton School asked students to rank in order from "most preferred" to "least preferred" a series of 27 hypothetical career profiles. While opportunity for advancement was first, salary was second, which could be a result of the prevailing economic conditions. (23)

A study of Columbia's Graduate School of Business found that aggressive interviewing by the student, grades, and outside activities were positively correlated with success. Also, 54 percent of the students had prepared for the interviews by studying the firm's literature and had spent money for clothes for the interview. (24)

Some special approaches used

Some companies are beginning to use the group approach to recruiting college graduates. Instead of inviting prospects to visit the company plant individually, they invite a number of persons to come at one time. This not only saves the time and effort of the firm's officials, but also permits the company to give more prospective employees the red carpet treatment. The acceptance rate resulting from the use of this technique increased from 33.3 to 50 percent. (25)

A method of recruiting that has found favor in some areas is the *Coop Program*. Using this method, an organization can contact a university participating in this program and, through the assigned faculty member, arrange to employ students on a prearranged scheduled basis. In this way, it has an opportunity to observe the prospective employees in on-the-job activities, and, in turn, the students have the opportunity to observe their chosen fields of work as they actually exist. Upon graduation, the organization and the student could arrive at a mutually satisfactory agreement of employment if desired.

Other approaches are *career weekend, summer internships,* and *closed circuit TV.*

Evaluating the effectiveness of college recruiting

If the objective of college recruiting is to deliver a number of well-qualified, college-trained employees who are capable of fulfilling specific job requirements and of developing beyond the jobs for which they are initially hired, then its effectiveness must be measured by how well it does that. One technique is to use the quantitative approach, applying the principles of management by objectives.

Another approach is to use any of the more common ratios, such as:

1. $\dfrac{\text{Number of invitations to visit the organization}}{\text{Number of campus interviews}}$

2. $\dfrac{\text{Number of invitations accepted}}{\text{Number of invitations to visit the organization}}$

3. $\dfrac{\text{Number of job offers}}{\text{Number of visits made to the organization}}$

4. $\dfrac{\text{Number of job acceptances}}{\text{Number of job offers}}$

EFFECTS OF PUBLIC POLICY ON RECRUITING

One of the basic hypotheses of this book is that *personnel administration is an integrated system, and anything affecting one function affects the others.* That relationship also holds true for recruiting. Therefore, in discussing the effects of public policy on it, we must accept the fact that other functions are also affected.

How public policy affects recruiting

Most of the recruitment and selection policies of a few years ago are now obsolete. As many personnel executives believed that compliance would result in increased expenses, decreased productivity, lowered morale and employment standards, and a general decrease in control over their personnel resources, they failed to see that it could actually provide the impetus for developing improved personnel systems that had positive implications. These executives generally recognized that one of their prime responsibilities was maximizing the utilization, conservation, and development of assets, including human assets. However, it is an unfortunate fact of life that only when an organization is being threatened in this area does that responsibility get the attention it should have had all along.

Compliance experience

What progress has been made in complying with public policy? Apparently considerable progress has been made with all groups.

Women. Research has shown that the three primary arguments against equal employment—men's and women's *work,* their *traits,* and their *nonwage* costs—are not verified by the data. (26)

In order to have a job qualified for one particular sex, there must be a "bona fide occupational qualification" (BFOQ), which means that *only* a member of one sex can perform the job. There can also be no group characteristics arbitrarily applied to any and every member of the group, for each person shall be treated as a separate entity. Also, there is a new trend to take sex designations out of job titles. The Census Bureau has reclassified over 50 jobs by removing the suffix "men" in the title and replacing it with "workers" or "operator."

However, the real big push against sex discrimination was the AT&T consent decree. In 1970, the EEOC brought charges before the Federal Communications Commission—which was hearing a Bell System interstate rate case—that the system's hiring and promotion practices were discriminatory. After two years of testimony and negotiations, an agreement was reached on January 18, 1973, between AT&T, the EEOC, and the Department of Labor. Under the firm's AAP, women college graduates hired between July 2, 1965 (the effective date of the *Civil Rights Act*), and 1971 would be sent to assessment centers to be assessed as possible managers and, if found qualified, to receive back pay from the time they became eligible for the management position. Those women and minorities holding craft jobs were to receive salary adjustments. The net result was that while total employment increased only 15 percent, black employment increased 44 percent and Spanish-surnamed employment, 93 percent; about 7,000 women were put in jobs formerly held by men; and 4,000 men took jobs usually held by women. (27)

Minorities. It is now known that employers do not have to agree overtly among themselves in order to discriminate against a minority group. Rather, they may just profess beliefs that convince them that minorities are less productive and aspire to different occupational levels and then channel them into "appropriate" jobs; still, the employers act discriminatorily. (28) A similar practice led to one of the most significant cases involving minorities—the Detroit Edison case.

The suit charged the company with using "word-of-mouth" hiring and seniority practices that effectively perpetuated the existing white labor force. The company and unions denied all allegations, but, as blacks or other minorities held a very small percent of the more desirable, highly skilled, and higher paying jobs, whereas they comprised 44 percent of the population of the city of Detroit, the court ordered Edison in 1973 to pay $4 million and Local 223 was fined $250,000 in punitive damages. The implications of the court decision are many and varied, for personnel practices are being modified in the areas of recruiting, hiring, discipline, discharge, transfer, promotion, and training. (29)

Older workers. The "sleeper" in the entire field of equal opportunity law could be the *Age Discrimination in Employment Act.*

This law seemed innocuous until the middle of 1974, when Standard Oil of California signed a consent decree in a federal court, and the cost was in the neighborhood of $2 million. It was alleged that the employer wanted to save labor costs by clearing out the ranks of older, more experienced, and, therefore, higher paid employees. Some of the employees who had been dismissed were not ordered reinstated, for they were tested and found unable to perform their jobs properly. Yet, they still had to be paid back wages because they were not fired on the basis of their inabilities to do the jobs, but because of their ages.

Another aspect of this law is that help-wanted ads can no longer ask for a "recent college grad," or for a "girl."

Disabled workers. Recently the Labor Department has been enforcing Section 503 of the *Vocational Rehabilitation Act of 1973*. It is now requiring firms with government contracts of at least $2,500 to design AAPs for hiring the handicapped. Enforcement is now "picking up steam."

EVALUATING THE EFFECTIVENESS OF RECRUITING ACTIVITIES

Recruitment is quite costly, so considerable saving can be achieved if its efficiency is enhanced. Those costs include the actual expenses of the procedure, as well as the time of the executives involved. Then the costs of orientation and training must be added to those. The estimates of the total cost of recruiting one person varies from $78 to $134 for chain store retailing, $250 to $1,000 for an engineer, or a technical or clerical worker, to $2,000 to $5,000 for a salesman or administrator. (30) While the actual figure depends upon the type and number of personnel sought, as well as the degree of sophistication of the recruitment program, a usable figure is $2,500 to $3,500.

There is no specific model to be used in evaluating recruitment effectiveness. However, the program evaluation described in the previous chapter (see Figure 7–8), is useful for this purpose as well.

IMPLICATIONS AND APPLICATIONS

Although each manager has the residual obligation for achieving effective recruitment of personnel, the more successful firms have a central placement of responsibility for the function. Specifically there should be one person at the top level of all organizations who is charged with this duty. This is usually the personnel executive, who is responsible for coordinating all recruiting strategies and activities.

In small organizations the task of recruiting is usually undertaken by the firm's owner, by some member of management, or by an agent outside the organization.

But whether the institution is small or large, as the recruitment operation cannot be performed adequately by any one individual, the person fulfilling this obligation usually enlists the support of others. Assistance may be provided by the employees, the union, employment agencies, and consultants.

Small organizations particularly must recruit outstanding people who are versatile, flexible, and expert in their field. They should hire the person to do a job, and, if that is not done, the person must be replaced with someone who can do it, for they cannot afford "to carry" unproductive employees. In recruiting, these firms should emphasize the benefits of the variety of experiences, the opportunity to make an early contribution, and opportunity for quick advancement.

As with the other aspects of personnel and human resource management, recruiting is undergoing tremendous changes. Increasingly public policy will determine recruiting practices and the supply sources used, rather than organizational needs and policies. Yet, in the long run, this may prove to be more beneficial if it forces a more effective personnel system.

There are essentially two places from which personnel can be obtained, namely, from within or without the organization. Selection from within acts as a motivational factor for employees. Yet, as individual positions are filled from internal sources, positions will be vacated which must be filled externally. And if any job requires skills or qualifications which cannot be secured from within, the institution must go outside to find them. It is often desirable to infuse "new blood" into an organization to prevent "inbreeding," conformity, and stagnation. However, employees from outside are sometimes undesirable themselves; they may be inexperienced, likely to change their jobs easily (if they are seeking employment for the first time), unacceptable to their former employers, or marginal workers who have characteristics that cause them to be unproductive employees.

Several hypotheses can be developed from research findings applicable to recruiting personnel. They are:

1. *The greater the number and variety of sources of supply, the greater the chance of finding the individuals(s) most qualified for the jobs;*
2. *The greater the amount of data obtained and studied from the greatest number of potential employers, the greater the career progress, the longer the tenure on the initial job, and the greater the degree of job satisfaction of new college recruits;* and
3. *A downward mobility is occurring, whereby large numbers of young people are likely to obtain less schooling and potentially lower occupational status than their parents, except for females and minorities.*

DISCUSSION QUESTIONS

1. What are some of the methods used in recruiting?
2. Give the advantages and disadvantages of using employee referrals.
3. Do you view public policy as having a greater or lesser effect upon recruiting than was true in 1970?
4. Evaluate the advantages and disadvantages of using EDP for recruiting.
5. Discuss the theoretical flow of personnel in an organization and its implications for the personnel selection function.
6. Discuss three methods of securing employees internally, giving the advantages and disadvantages of each method.
7. Discuss the importance of using external sources of employee supply.

8. Discuss the various external supply sources of employees, giving the advantages and disadvantages of each.
9. What are some practical sources of supply for a firm of between 5,000–10,000 employees which needs (*a*) an engineer, (*b*) a lathe operator, (*c*) a secretary; and (*d*) a manager? What are the advantages and disadvantages of each?

REFERENCES AND SUGGESTIONS FOR FURTHER STUDY

1. See Robert M. Fulmer and William E. Fulmer, "Providing Equal Opportunity for Promotion," *Personnel Journal,* vol. 53, no. 7 (July 1974), pp. 491–97.
2. National Industrial Conference Board (NICB), *Personnel Practices in Factory and Office: Manufacturing* (New York: Studies in Personnel Policy, No. 194, 1974); and *Office Personnel Practices: Nonmanufacturing* (New York: Studies in Personnel Policy, No. 197, 1975).
3. For example, Louisiana passed a law in 1975 requiring private employment agencies to offer their clients a 90-day "no fault" guarantee. The act requires the agency to charge the applicants no more than 20 percent of the normal fee if their employment is ended "for any reason" in less than 90 days.
4. See Max S. Wortman, Jr., "The Role of the Private Employment Agency in a Growing Economy," in Wortman, ed., *Creative Personnel Management* (Boston: Allyn and Bacon, 1967), pp. 118–20, for further details.
5. See Jack W. Skeels, "Perspectives on Private Employment Agencies," *Industrial Relations,* vol. 8, no. 2 (February 1969), pp. 151–61, for clarifying details.
6. "Why This Company Hires—and Trains College Dropouts," *Business Management* (May 1964), pp. 56–58, 94.
7. "How They Recruit Scientists and Engineers," *Business Management,* vol. 26, no. 1 (April 1964), p. 28
8. However, these recruiters also feel that many college students may not have an adequate contribution to make to their organizations. See Terry L. Dennis and David P. Gustafson, "College Campuses versus Employment Agencies as Sources of Manpower," *Personnel Journal,* vol. 52, no. 8 (August 1973), pp. 720–24, for further discussion of the relative merit of the two sources.
9. William A. Douglas, "Job Recruiting Ads: Why Do They Get Stepchild Treatment?" *Printers Ink,* vol. 270, no. 11 (March 11, 1960), p. 90.

    Some outstanding individuals who were recruited through ads are: Tom May, president, Lockheed Georgia Company and vice president, Lockheed Aircraft Corporation; Harlow Curtice, former president of General Motors; former Michigan Governor George Romney; former U.S. Secretary of Commerce Luther Hodges; the late Walt Disney; and Marion Sadler, former president of American Airlines.
10. Apparently the ads should also be designed to leave a favorable impression on both sexes when trying to eliminate "sex stereotyping" from certain job ads. A research study showed men preferred the "both sexes" treatment in ads for former "male" jobs but not for former "female" jobs. The women perceived no difference in their treatment. See Nancy S. Darsey, "The Effect of Sex and Personality Traits on the Perception of Occupational Role Portrayal in Job Recruitment Advertisements," Ph.D. dissertation, Louisiana State University, 1975.

11. Joseph C. Ullman, "Employee Referrals: Prime Tool for Recruiting Workers," *Personnel,* vol. 43, no. 3 (May–June 1966), pp. 30–35.
12. Raymond E. Hill, "New Look at Employee Referrals as a Recruitment Channel," *Personnel Journal,* vol. 49, no. 2 (February 1970), pp. 144–48.
13. See Carlton W. Dukes, "EDP: Personnel File Searching: A Variable Parameter Approach," *Personnel,* vol. 49, no. 4 (July–August 1972), pp. 20–26, for an explanation of a system which meets these requirements.
14. For a discussion of some of these criticisms, see F. Kenneth Dempsey, Jr., "College Recruiting—A Reassessment," *Personnel Journal,* vol. 49, no. 9 (September 1970), pp. 746–49.
15. See Dennis and Gustafson, "College Campuses versus Employment Agencies," *Personnel Journal,* pp. 720–24, for the results of the study, as well as a correlation between acceptance of the method with sources used by the personnel executives.
16. *Trends in Employment of College and University Graduates in Business and Industry* is issued annually by Dr. Frank S. Endicott—placement director emeritus —of Northwestern University.
17. This is difficult to do, for blacks represent only about 2 percent of total enrollment in business schools, according to "The Frantic Competition for Black MBAs," *Business Week* (July 6, 1974), pp. 58–62.
18. The details of the research can be found in Alfred G. Edge and Ronald Greenwood, "How Personnel Managers Rank the Importance of Various Educational Factors in Business Administration Graduates," *Marquette Business Review,* vol. 17, no. 3 (Fall 1973), pp. 113–19. However, the findings were summarized into the following matrix.

A matrix of areas of knowledge, skills and attributes/traits

Levels	Areas of knowledge (*in order of importance*)	Skills (*in order of importance*)	Attributes/ traits (*in order of importance*)
People-oriented (level 1)	Basic skills of management Human relations	Communicate Plan, develop, organize and coordinate Work with and use skills of people Analyze data, propose solutions and make decisions	External personality factors: Tactful, skills in human relations Dynamic, self-starter, leader Motivated
Business oriented (level 2)	Economics Accounting Finance Marketing	Analyze accounting data Analyze financial data	Internal personality factors: Honest, ethical Conscientious, hardworking
Quantitatively-oriented (level 3)	Statistics and quantitative methods	Apply quantitative techniques Utilize a computer	Self-confidence Imaginative Patience, determination

19. Geoffrey Lindenauer, "Does Your Company Repel Job Applicants?" *Business Management,* vol. 33, No. 5 (February 1968), pp. 21–24.
20. C. P. Alderfer and C. G. McCord, "Personal and Situational Factors in the Recruitment Interview," *Journal of Applied Psychology,* vol. 54, no. 4 (August 1970), pp. 377–85.
21. Sang M. Lee, "Job Selection by College Graduates," *Personnel Journal,* vol. 49, no. 5 (May 1970), pp. 392–95.
22. W. Bruce Weale and Odies Ferrell, "Are Recruiters Listening?" *Personnel Journal,* vol. 45, no. 4 (April 1966), p. 216.
23. Robert Addleman, Christopher Carstensen, and Richard Steiner, Jr., "The Lengthening Reach for Opportunity," *MBA* (May 1975), p. 54.
24. Henry Luk, "Interviewing: A Statistical Look at Columbia. '74," *MBA* (November 1974), pp. 43–45.
25. F. J. Skahill, "The Group Approach to College Recruiting," *Personnel,* vol. 40, no. 1 (January–February 1963), pp. 53–58.
26. See Dwight P. Flanders and Peggy E. Anderson, "Sex Discrimination in Employment: Theory and Practice," *Industrial and Labor Relations Review,* vol. 26, no. 3 (April 1973), pp. 938–55, for this and other research results.
27. See Ethel B. Walsh, "Sex Discrimination and the Impact of Title VII," *Labor Law Journal,* vol. 25, no. 3 (March 1974), pp. 150–54, for further details, and an excellent analysis of how the civil rights law is operating.
28. See P. Gurin, "Recent Developments in Equal Employment Opportunity—Psychological Dimensions of Minorities Work Force Participation," *Sloan Management Review,* vol. 15, no. 3 (Spring 1974), pp. 47–48, for further details.
29. See Beverly K. Schaffer, and Sherman F. Dallas, "Racial Bias: The Detroit Edison Case," *Labor Law Journal,* vol. 25, no. 9 (September 1974) pp. 570–77, for further details.
30. Jerry Levine, "Labor Turnover," *Personnel Administration,* vol. 33, no. 6 (November–December 1970), pp. 32–36; Richard B. Peterson, "The Growing Role of Manpower Forecasting in Organizations," *MSU Business Topics,* vol. 17, no. 3 (Summer 1969), pp. 7–14.

Chapter 9

The selection procedure

Developing an effective selection procedure

First stage: Establishing selection policies
    Purpose(s) of selection?
    *Screening out **or** selecting in?*
    *Fitting people to jobs **or** fitting jobs to people?*
    Using same or differentiated procedure?

Second stage: Identifying and choosing selection criteria
    Identifying criteria of successful performance
    Identifying predictors of success
    Determining selection criteria

Third stage: Gathering information about potential employees
    Authorization to hire
    Initial contact with potential employee
    Preliminary interview
    Biographical inventory
    Testing
    In-depth interview
    Verifying background information
    Medical examination

Fourth stage: Evaluating information and assessing applicant

Fifth Stage: Making the decision to accept or reject applicant
    How is decision made?
    Who makes the decision?

Sixth stage: Communicating the decision

Implications and applications for personnel executives

9
The selection procedure

Ability and necessity dwell near each other.
PYTHAGORAS

Progress comes from the intelligent use of experience.
ELBERT HUBBARD

The childhood shows the man, as morning shows the day.
MILTON

Sam Able applied for a job on a forestry crew and was told to report for an interview. Sam, following instructions, climbed through knee-deep snow to keep the 8 A.M. appointment—at the top of a 1,600-foot mountain.

Woody Green, the state forester who arranged the interview said he had 200 applicants for the job and decided the climb would be a good test of motivation and stamina. Able was the first applicant to show up. He got the job!

This case illustrates the use of a performance-based selection criterion which got results. It illustrates the importance of selection in choosing the "right" person for the "right" job. It is not an overstatement to say that personnel selection largely determines the future of an organization, for it provides not only the people to perform current jobs, but also a "pool" of available personnel from which promotions develop the institution's future leadership position.

An overview of an effective selection procedure is given in this chapter; an in-depth analysis of three selection instruments—evaluating biographical data, tests, and interviews—is made in the next chapter; Chapter 11 discusses some problems in the selection of supervisory and executive personnel. Figure 9–1 shows how the selection procedure is related to the other phases of selection.

DEVELOPING AN EFFECTIVE SELECTION PROCEDURE

Although selection is usually thought of in terms of steps or stages, it is in reality a part of the entire personnel function and must be considered so. It is a continuation of the logical sequence beginning with *personnel-human resources planning,* which determines jobs to be filled and their requirements; progressing to *recruitment,* which attracts a group of potential employees from which those capable of performing the job will be selected; and is modified by *determining valid criteria* of successful performance of the jobs to be filled and *searching for valid predictors* of success in those jobs—using those criteria

FIGURE 9–1
How the selection procedure fits into the other procedures

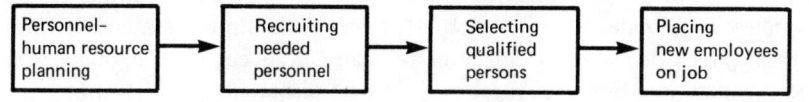

Personnel–human resource planning → Recruiting needed personnel → Selecting qualified persons → Placing new employees on job

—and personal qualities—considered to be effective. It is followed by the development, utilization, rewarding, and maintenance functions of personnel administration.

In the more effective selection procedures, there are several stages, each with several steps. The procedure suggested in this text is shown and explained in Figure 9–2.

Although this is considered to be a "model" procedure, it must be modified to conform to managerial—and organizational—philosophy, public policy, union requirements, and environmental conditions affecting the demand for, and supply of, potential employees.

FIGURE 9–2
A proposed model for effective personnel selection

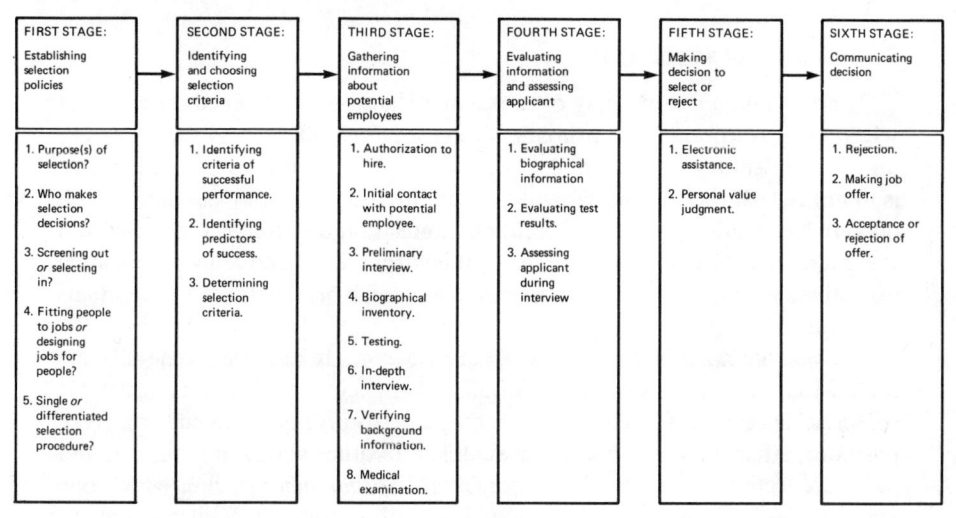

FIRST STAGE: Establishing selection policies	SECOND STAGE: Identifying and choosing selection criteria	THIRD STAGE: Gathering information about potential employees	FOURTH STAGE: Evaluating information and assessing applicant	FIFTH STAGE: Making decision to select or reject	SIXTH STAGE: Communicating decision
1. Purpose(s) of selection? 2. Who makes selection decisions? 3. Screening out *or* selecting in? 4. Fitting people to jobs *or* designing jobs for people? 5. Single *or* differentiated selection procedure?	1. Identifying criteria of successful performance. 2. Identifying predictors of success. 3. Determining selection criteria.	1. Authorization to hire. 2. Initial contact with potential employee. 3. Preliminary interview. 4. Biographical inventory. 5. Testing. 6. In-depth interview. 7. Verifying background information. 8. Medical examination.	1. Evaluating biographical information 2. Evaluating test results. 3. Assessing applicant during interview	1. Electronic assistance. 2. Personal value judgment.	1. Rejection. 2. Making job offer. 3. Acceptance or rejection of offer.

FIRST STAGE: ESTABLISHING SELECTION POLICIES

The performance of the selection function is based upon the assumption that it is possible to find potential employees with the proper combination of personal characteristics required for the successful performance of given jobs. A second assumption is that sufficient valid information can be obtained about the applicants in order to make a valid employment decision. Although these assumptions are not entirely accurate, at least they are valid approximations that will have to suffice until a more "scientific" approach is found. Therefore, selection involves matching the candidate's personal qualifications with the specified requirements of the job. However, this simple statement implies several policy decisions which must be made at successively higher levels of the organization. Some of these will now be discussed.

Purpose(s) of selection?

One of the first policy decisions that must be made is deciding the purpose(s) of selection. Most selection—especially in periods of "depressed" economic conditions—and even in "normal" periods—is for a specific person to perform a given job, with the selection decision being made on the basis of a job requisition stating the qualifications sought in the person to be selected.

Yet, in expansion periods when workers are scarce or where there is high— and predictable—turnover, the personnel department may hire people and "hoard" them until they are needed.

Finally, when there are outstanding applicants available or when a given occupation or job classification is in short supply, individuals may be hired on the expectation of fitting them into the organization—somewhere.

Screening out *or* selecting in?

There is much controversy over whether the selection procedure is one of selection *or* rejection. The primary reason for this difficulty is that the very nature of selection is predictive. (1) As the objective of personnel programs is to utilize best the specific capabilities and interests of employees and as each of them has a unique pattern of abilities, interests, and attitudes resulting from the interaction of inherited qualities and environmental influences, personnel executives must use the predictive techniques which best match the individuals with jobs.

Successive hurdles approach: Screening out. It has been generally accepted that with the evaluation techniques at their disposal, it is easier for personnel specialists to determine whether a person *is not* qualified for a given position, rather than whether one *is* qualified. In other words, it is simpler and more accurate to forecast which individual *will not succeed* than which one *will.* Success is a function of factors such as ability, training, volition, motivation, and drive; and the absence of these qualities is more obvious than their presence. The entire selection process, then, is designed to remove from further consideration the individuals with the factors for failure built into their background and leave the ones with apparent potential for success in the "pool" from which the specific employee is finally chosen. Therefore, selection basically involves detecting the undesirable—or less desirable—candidates for a position and removing them from further consideration. This elimination process is continued for the remaining candidates, with additional applicants being rejected during each succeeding stage of selection.

FIGURE 9–3
The employment procedure constructed as hurdles to be cleared before an individual is selected as an employee

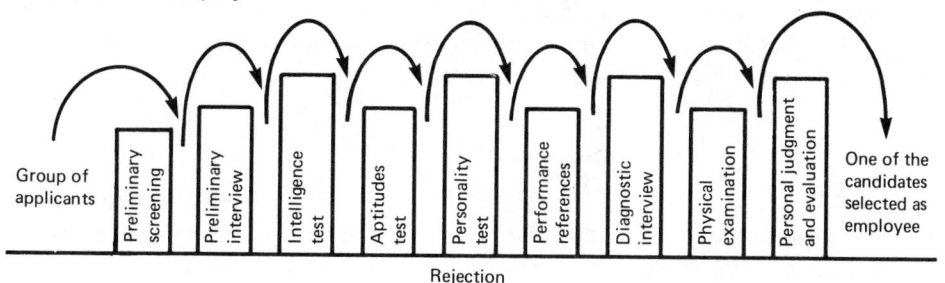

[Diagram: Group of applicants → Preliminary screening → Preliminary interview → Intelligence test → Aptitudes test → Personality test → Performance references → Diagnostic interview → Physical examination → Personal judgment and evaluation → One of the candidates selected as employee. Rejection shown below.]

The selection procedure may thus be construed as a series of hurdles that the prospective candidates must successfully clear in order to get the job (see Figure 9–3). It is readily perceived that the hurdles will be of different heights and in differing sequences, depending upon the organization, the job, and the philosophy of the selecting management. For example, in one case the mental ability test may be given more weight than other factors, making this hurdle higher. In other instances, performance references may be of greater consequence, in which case that hurdle would be higher.

Multiple-correlation approach: Selecting in. The objective of any selection program is essentially the same, namely, to choose those people from among the available candidates who are most likely to succeed on the job. This requires an effort to maximize the probability that the person(s) selected will contribute significantly to the attainment of the organizational goals. Therefore, the selection procedure should be designed so that it will, in fact, identify those individuals with the greatest chances of success.

In order to do this successfully, there should be an identification of statistical relationships between some predictor(s) of success and criteria of success. As there is rarely one personal characteristic which *alone predicts success,* it follows that selection should not be based upon one "hurdle." Instead, the selection decision should be based upon several predictors of success, considered in combination with each other.

An approach which has been less used, but which is now becoming increasingly popular, is based upon the multiple-correlation theory. It assumes that a deficiency in one selection criterion can be compensated for by competence in others. This approach is particularly feasible and desirable in jobs that are either complex or which depend upon the interaction of various abilities for successful performance. (2)

Which approach to use? Obviously, for some routine jobs requiring uniformity of performance on the part of several persons, the former approach may be preferable. Also, some people are manifestly unsuited for certain jobs. Therefore, in the interest of saving the applicants' time and energy—as well as the organization's—the former approach may be more efficient. Finally, if there are only one or two applicants for each position available, the simpler approach may be more desirable.

In other instances, the more complex approach should increase the chances of selecting the persons with the greatest chances of success.

Fitting people to jobs *or* fitting jobs to people?

Whether the selection procedure is viewed as a selection or rejection process, most selection decisions ultimately involve *matching* the personal qualifications of prospective employees with the requirements of the jobs for which they are being considered.

Need for compatibility between employee and job. Research has consistently shown that there is a direct and positive correlation between job performance and measurable employee qualifications, even though there are still many unknown variables affecting standards of performance. (3) Other studies have indicated a positive relationship between employee attitudes and productivity, when the characteristics of both the workers and the jobs are taken into consideration and are satisfactorily matched. (4)

Redesigning the job or reprogramming the person? It can be seen from these and other research findings that the matching procedure begins with, and is predicated upon, an evaluation of an employee's assets and liabilities. The results of this evaluation are then measured against the job standards of the position to be filled. However, it cannot be assumed that these standards are fixed, for they vary as the job and its surrounding environment vary and must constantly be reviewed and updated. Consequently, a policy decision must be made as to whether to fit people to existing jobs or to restructure the jobs to fit the people.

First, it can be generalized that for routine jobs, or where several people need to work together on the same job, it is probably preferable to find people whose qualifications match the job itself. Second, fitting jobs to people, or restructuring the jobs to fit the individuals, is nothing new. During World War II, many male jobs were restructured to be performed by females. An example of this was "Rosie the Riveter," or the inexperienced females who learned to do formerly all male jobs. Today this practice is increasingly being used as a basis of attracting more capable people and satisfying public policy. (For an example, see the AT&T agreement in the previous chapter.) Finally, a malpractice to be avoided is placing people in jobs that demand less ability than they have. This leads to employee frustration, dissatisfaction, and friction.

The set of qualifications which an applicant possesses must be considered in relation to the level of the job to be performed because there are relatively few individuals who can perform successfully in several echelons of an organization. This conclusion is based upon the assumption that each of us has a unique set of qualities which permits us to operate in one or more jobs, or at one or more levels, but not necessarily at all levels. It has been tacitly assumed that the more capable employees should not do work that less capable people could do. However, there is now a theory that the "proper use" of employees' capabilities requires a balance between peak demands and normal use; that is, there should be some routine tasks for them to execute along with the more difficult problems which challenge their abilities. (5)

The "whole person" concept. Finally, the *"whole person" concept* should be considered when matching people and jobs. When an employer selects an employee, the whole person is selected with all of the strengths and weaknesses, assets and liabilities, judgments and foibles, personal problems and failures, and the motivations to work, as well as the nonproductive tendencies which are found in all people. Empirical evidence shows that it is impossible to separate the positive factors that lead to productivity in an individual from the negative elements that result in a lack of productivity. (6) However, employees, when properly motivated, may compensate for their weaknesses by concentrating on, and developing, their strengths, in which case they should become more effective employees.

Using same or differentiated procedure?

Research and experience have shown that it is usually more effective to use different selection procedures for different sizes and types of institutions, occupations, and level of employees sought.

Size of firm determines procedure used. First, the tendency is for the number and variety of selection instruments used to increase with increases in organizational size. In the NICB survey, size and use of selection techniques correlated. For example, 81 percent of the firms with 5,000 or more employees used tests in selection and placement, but only 68 percent of the smaller companies used them. An analysis of employment procedures used by Canadian manufacturing firms found similar results. (7) Only 7 percent of firms with less than $500,000 sales used "four or more" selection instruments in their employment procedure, but that many were used by 40 percent of the companies with sales of over $50 million.

Occupation and level of job determine procedure used. Different procedures must be used to select blue-collar and clerical personnel than is used in choosing professional, technical, and managerial personnel.

> The employment office of a large chemical firm processes all applicants for production and clerical personnel, performing all the steps except the medical exam. The people chosen are put on a "wait list." When a person is needed by one of the producing departments, a requisition is sent to the employment office. The employment supervisor, or an assistant, telephones the top candidate (in qualifications) on the list to come in for an interview with the manager in production who will supervise the new employee. If the person is acceptable, and passes the "physical," he or she is put on the payroll.
> The same procedure is followed for clericals.
> Conversely, the production (or research and development) managers recruit

at colleges for technical and professional personnel. Only when someone is invited to the plant for an interview does the employment officer become involved and then only in a service capacity.

SECOND STAGE: IDENTIFYING AND CHOOSING SELECTION CRITERIA

There have been many efforts in the past to select people on the basis of some form of character analysis. At one time, *phrenology,* the study of the head's shape, bumps, and irregularities, was used. In Germany and certain other continental countries, *graphology,* or the interpretation of handwriting, is now extensively used in the selection of managerial personnel. (8) *Astrology* and the more esoteric criteria for selection have been used in France and some other European areas. Other efforts have been made to study the body structure and so forth. However, these abstractions are beyond the scope of this study, and attention will be given in this chapter to the more ordinary and practical selection procedures using the more acceptable predictive factors.

Identifying criteria of successful performance

One of the important questions facing personnel specialists at the present time is which personal characteristics are valid predictors of successful job performance. Considerable effort is now being expended to determine what *selection criteria are valid predictors of job success* and can be used in making selection decisions. Present research findings are inadequate and sometimes even contradictory. For example, an evaluation of research conducted to determine the reliability of selection criteria found four studies with *scholarship positively correlated with success;* one found it to be *indeterminate;* and two found it *not related (or even inversely related)* to success. (9)

Some of the problems involved in setting up selection criteria are whether to use a single criterion or multiple criteria. Also, the problem of validating and revalidating the criteria over a period of time is important. Another problem area is providing specific criteria for specific organizations, instead of finding criteria which are generally applicable.

Characteristics of a desirable criterion. If personnel executives are looking for usable *performance criteria* that truly measure productivity and *selection criteria* that accurately predict success or failure on the job, they must use selection instruments which will identify those individuals who, when hired, will be most likely to have high productivity. This is called *validity.* Also, the yardstick must give consistent results when used by different people and at different times. This is called *reliability.* In addition to validity and reliability, a criterion must be: (*a*) defined operationally; (*b*) relevant; (*c*) acceptable to users; and (*d*) free of bias. (10)

Types of performance criteria. The most valid criterion of successful job performance is the individual's performance on the job. Some other useful criteria are output per unit of time, quality of production, time lost by employees, labor turnover, time required for training, employee promotability, and employee satisfaction. (11)

Criteria may also be classified as *objective* and *subjective*. The *objective criteria* deal with some form of measurable productivity, either quantitative and/or qualitative. Another criterion is using a job sample, which is a test of job performance done under carefully controlled conditions.

Subjective criteria are needed as it is not always possible to obtain objective measures of performance. These criteria attempt to assess performance based upon subjective estimates of employee proficiency. These are obtained by some form of rating by supervisors and managers.

Identifying predictors of success

While it might be desirable to have one criterion which would correlate sets of personal characteristics with job success and, therefore, be able to pinpoint those characteristics which most likely would lead to successful job performance, this is not possible for most jobs are multidimensional and perhaps even curvilinear. (12) This necessitates including these dimensions in the criterion which is used for selecting supervisors. According to Siegel and Lane, there are two ways of doing this, namely, developing multiple criteria for each job or combining such multiple criteria into a single index of overall employee effectiveness. (13)

Another problem involved in establishing selection criteria is to isolate *predictors* which can be identified through the use of selection instruments—such as tests, interviews, references, and so forth—which will later correlate with the criterion scores of successful performance. If the predictor correlates highly with the criteria, then there is *predictive validity* and that predictor can be successfully used in hiring future personnel with the assurance that they will perform successfully.

These ideals of setting up criteria and predictors must be modified by the *selection ratio*. This ratio is simply:

$$\frac{\text{The number of applicants hired}}{\text{The number of applicants available for hiring}}$$

The higher this ratio, the less selective the personnel officer can be; conversely, the lower this ratio, the more stringent can be the passing scores for any of the "tests" used in the employment procedure. When the ratio is high, the organization must hire most applicants regardless of their performance in the selection procedure.

Determining selection criteria

In general, successful job performance is largely determined by the employee's innate abilities, i.e., intellectual and physical capacities; the modification of these abilities by the total environment, including education, training, and experience; and the person's motivation to success, or the willingness to pay the price of success. (14) It can be concluded that in many cases ability and motivation are far more meaningful to success than is education. This was the conclusion I reached in a 1961 study for the Small Business Administration concerning the selection of management talent for small businesses.

Specific qualities sought in employees. As previously indicated, to be most successful in selecting the right person for employment, the personnel executive needs to determine through research which personal variables are the best predictors of successful performance for specific jobs, (15) establish these as the characteristics to be sought in prospective employees, and then design a selection procedure which will enable the personnel executive to ascertain to what extent a given applicant possesses them. It is possible to design a rating scale which can be used to evaluate applicants successfully if the requirements of the job are known, if the degree of importance of each requirement to the total position is known, and the accuracy of the predictive variables are validated. (16) (See Table 9–1 for some of these variables.)

The *personal background* data sought include such items as place and date of birth; educational institutions attended and courses of study pursued; the number of dependents; military service; experience with different tools, machines, or equipment; and work history. These data are considered important as indicators of past performance and as potential predictors of future performance.

Information on *aptitudes* and *interests* is sought, for these indicate our inclinations, including our natural abilities and capacities for learning, as well as potential abilities to do certain jobs.

The *attitudes* and *needs* of an applicant are sought as indicators of the frame of mind, emotional and mental maturity, and a sense of responsibility and authority—as well as keys to future motivation.

As our *analytical* and *manipulative abilities* indicate our thinking processes, they provide parameters of our intelligence, as well as our ability to use knowledge effectively and readily in performing assigned tasks.

Acquired *skills* and *technical abilities* indicate the ability to perform specific manual operations, as well as technical aspects of a job. These are products of education, training, and experience and, therefore, tend to predict *what one can do* if properly placed, oriented, developed, and motivated.

As *health, energy,* and *stamina* are essential for the successful performance of most jobs—especially those involving manual and managerial duties—they indicate our *physical* ability to perform the assigned tasks satisfactorily.

Our *value system* provides clues to our motivation—especially goals and objectives—work values, perseverance, and conscientiousness.

There are, of course, other qualities and characteristics which may be considered to be significant or desirable, but no effort is made to include all of them.

Some limitations on use of predictors and criteria. Some words of caution are in order relative to seeking out these items of information. First, the details of some of this information may be in violation of public policy, especially if

TABLE 9-1
Personal characteristics sought in prospective employees and source of information about them

Personal characteristics needed to perform job adequately	Sources of information upon which to evaluate if characteristic is present
Personal background	Application blank Preliminary interview School records References Diagnostic interview
Aptitudes and interests	Application blank School records Psychological tests References Interviews Work records
Attitudes and needs	Interviews Psychological tests References
Analytical abilities	School records Psychological tests Diagnostic interview Work references
Skills and technical abilities	School records Training records Interviews Work references Performance tests
Health, energy, and stamina	Medical examination Diagnostic interview Work reference
Value system	References Diagnostic interview

used in conjunction with other data or criteria in such a way as to suggest prima facie evidence of intent to discriminate against any of the protected groups.

Second, as no individual will possess *all* qualities considered to be desirable, and as they will not appear in the proper quantity and quality sought, an acceptable combination of maximum and minimum cut-off points should be predetermined.

Finally, a criterion which is generally accepted at one point in time may prove to be arbitrary or indefensible at another time or place. For example, ethnic background has been considered a basis for selection or rejection. Now, managerial philosophy and research findings (17)—as well as public policy—restrict the use of this variable in selecting personnel.

THIRD STAGE: GATHERING INFORMATION ABOUT POTENTIAL EMPLOYEES

The information-gathering stage involves several steps. At each step, various selection techniques—or instruments—are used to obtain meaningful information, from which the selection decision will be made. These instruments and their application are shown in Table 9–2.

As can be seen, the information-gathering stage begins with the available applicants who have been recruited as potential employees. As each instrument is used, some of the applicants are eliminated for the reasons shown. (This makes sense, for if a person is obviously unqualified for the jobs or is disinterested in the job or the organization, there is no need to waste anyone's time further.) Finally, the person left is selected for the job. However, if there is more than one qualified candidate remaining, a personal value judgment must

TABLE 9–2
Instruments for gathering information about potential employees

Instruments used to gather data	Characteristics to look for	Applicants who are available as potential employees
Preliminary interview	Obvious misfit from outward appearance and conduct.	
Biographical inventory from application blank, BIB, résumé, etc.	Lacks adequate educational and performance record.	
Testing		
Intelligence test(s)	Fails to meet minimum standards of mental alertness.	
Aptitudes test(s)	Lacks specific capacities for acquiring particular knowledges or skills.	
Proficiency, or achievement test(s)	Unable to demonstrate ability to do the job.	
Interest test(s)	Lacks significant vocational interest in job.	
Personality test(s)	Lacks the personal characteristics required for the job.	
In-depth interview	Lacks necessary innate ability, ambition, or other qualities.	
Verifying biographical data from references	Unfavorable or negative reports on past performance.	
Physical examination	Physically unfit for the job.	Persons left for selection

Source: Adapted from L. C. Megginson, *Providing Management Talent for Small Business* (Baton Rouge, La.: Division of Research, College of Business Administration, Louisiana State University, 1961), p. 108.

be made in selecting the one person from among those remaining. This aspect of selection will be covered in detail later.

As the data from various sources are often contradictory, a personal judgment must be made at each step in selecting the specific individual for the specific job.

Authorization to hire

It should be kept in mind while studying each of these stages that we are really referring to methods of collecting information from which to judge whether or not a given applicant has the personal qualifications found to predict the successful performance of a given job. The latter information is obtained from the *authorization to hire,* which has been received from some division within the organization. It contains a statement of the *job's specifications,* including the *personal characteristics* that have been predetermined to lead to successful job performance.

Initial contact with potential employee

The steps in the selection procedure will be determined by the recruiting method used. For example, in college recruiting, the initial contact is usually the preliminary interview. If advertising is the recruiting technique used, very likely the initial contact is the letter of application. For "drop-ins," there is an initial contact which will result in either a preliminary interview or the completion of an application blank. For higher-level personnel, such as managers, recruited by consultants, the initial contact might even be at the employment interview.

A study of 155 personnel managers in the greater Los Angeles area indicated the diversity of initial contacts. Over 53 percent of the managers said applicants should send in a letter of application and a résumé; 46 percent indicated that the applicant should apply in person; while less than 21 percent wanted them to phone for an interview. (18)

For purposes of this chapter, it will be assumed that there has been some form of initial contact and the decision has been made to have a preliminary interview.

Preliminary interview

Whether formal or informal, there is always some form of preliminary screening of applicants early in the procedure. This elimination is usually done in the preliminary interview, but it may be based upon the application form.

The preliminary interview is designed to eliminate individuals who are obviously disqualified because of poor appearance, physical disability, unavailability for employment, lack of serious interest in the job or the opportunity it provides, and so forth. By eliminating obvious misfits, the personnel manager can concentrate upon evaluating the other applicants.

This step deals with the obvious factors that affect an individual's relationships with others, such as voice, dress, physical appearance, personal grooming, educational background, professional training, and—to a limited extent —experience. It ought to be obvious that the applicant should also know something about the company, its products and personnel, if one is to be adequately prepared for the preliminary interview.

As this interview is *preliminary* and is usually done by only one person, there is the danger that the interviewer might empathize excessively with the interviewee. This tendency may cause a decision to be made on the basis of *selective perception* rather than on a more objective basis.

> While doing a case study of an employment agency, I observed that one interviewer had selected significantly more applicants with mustaches than the other interviewers. It turned out that the interviewer also had a mustache.

There are many ways of overcoming this selective perception but the most important ones are by using group interviews and establishing definite criteria for selection.

Regardless of the job being filled and regardless of the intensity of the first interview, this is where many organizations get into trouble by asking questions directly related to sex, race, color, religion, age, or national origin. Unless there are what the EEOC calls "bona fide occupational qualifications," questions which would either directly or indirectly elicit information about those characteristics might be deemed discriminatory. As you are faced with the problem of not only *intent,* but also of *consequences,* ask no questions that could be construed to be a basis for discrimination. A representative of the EEOC put it this way, "It is not so much the questions that you ask which get you into trouble, but what you do with the answers."

As charges by EEOC and OFCCP can be based upon suspected subtle discrimination in the form of increased qualifications for a job, there is danger of litigation in asking questions dealing with foreign addresses, membership in organizations, name and address of relatives, type military discharge, aca-

© 1971 Chicago Tribune—New York News, Inc. World rights reserved.

demic background at private schools, arrests and convictions for misdemeanors, social security status, height, weight, marital status, and ownership of a house or car. Also, you cannot ask for a photograph or ask if the person *can* receive a recommendation from a former employer. (19)

Biographical inventory

The preliminary screening mentioned above usually involves an analysis of background, environment, education, and experience. Personnel executives are now looking for tangible evidence of performance in a person's record, rather than basing their decisions upon such intangible factors as opinion or assumption. Instead of emphasizing interviews, appearances, or related impressionistic factors alone, those doing the selecting are becoming more interested in the data revealed by *past performance*. These data are available from *application blanks, personal data sheets, work records, school records, military records,* and similar sources. If the position under consideration is of a fiduciary nature, information concerning the applicant's financial condition should also be investigated.

Application blank. The application blank is the classical instrument used for obtaining biographical information, such as previous education, including schools, subjects, degrees, and grades or standing; specialized training programs; previous work experience, including employer, location, when employed, duties and responsibilities, salary, and reasons for leaving; membership in job-related associations; convictions for felonies; number of dependents; whom to notify in case of emergencies; and health history.

Practically all organizations use the application blank. However, organizations will sometimes use different forms for different jobs, for different divisions, and for different purposes, such as the preliminary interview as opposed to the employment interview. Also, the form may be weighted to emphasize certain items as predictors of success.

Considerable progress has been made as a result of public policy to encourage continuous revision and upgrading of these forms. Much closer relationship between the questions asked and the information sought and the job to be filled is now observed.

Other sources of biographical data. There are two variations of these forms and records which are important in some areas. First, the biographical information blank (BIB), a refinement of the weighted application blank (WAB), is used extensively to do research on the relationship between factors in the employee's tasks and the current level of performance. Then this information is used for prediction purposes to see if future applicants will meet the established criteria for job performance.

The other variation is a personal résumé. While the organization designs the form to gather most biographical information, the applicant designs the format and content of the résumé. An employment agency executive indicated the emphasis given to this instrument by saying, "The résumé is the most important document the applicant may ever write."

How used. Personnel professionals can use these biographical forms in more ways than they realize. As the forms are almost always completed in long hand, they serve as a simple literacy test to see if the person can read, write, and organize and present facts and thoughts clearly; they can also be used to verify information obtained by means of the other instruments and provide the data for employee's permanent record—if hired.

Figure 9–4 is a well-designed form, free of any questions which presuppose an intention to discriminate in employment. Notice the questions *not* asked!

Testing

Probably no other area of personnel-human resources administration has provoked as much controversy as employment testing. While many people think of employment tests as being *synonymous with the selection procedure,* tests can be used by organizations for at least four purposes, namely: selecting and placing new employees; transferring present employees; evaluating and appraising employees for rewards; selecting individuals for training and development programs; and as a basis for counseling problem employees.

Tests are important in selection as they provide a more objective means of obtaining information concerning the qualifications of job applicants, as well as from employees who are candidates for transfer, training, promoting, or rewarding. They are particularly valuable in uncovering talent, abilities, and qualifications that would not be found through interviews or biographical information forms. Also, testing tends to eliminate the bias of interviewers or others making selection decisions. Instead, emphasis is placed upon potential ability of the individual being tested.

Extent of use. At present, the extent of testing and its use in selection are—at best—conjecture because of the effects of EEOC and OFCCP guidelines and policies. The NICB studies found 70 percent of manufacturing firms using tests for both blue- and white-collar employees, while 26 percent used them only for white-collar personnel. Their use by other industries varied as follows: utilities, 93 percent of nonexempt personnel; insurance, 88; banks, 87; wholesale trade, 84; and retail trade, 83 percent. In general, the larger firms tended to use tests more frequently and extensively than the smaller ones.

Testing, however, received a setback in 1971 when the Supreme Court ruled in *Griggs* v. *Duke Power Company* that employment tests could be used only if they were culturally unbiased and job-related, as evidenced by valid studies at the place and time where the tests were being used. Less than three years later, a study of 60 companies in a variety of industries indicated that of the 53 using test programs at the factory, clerical, or managerial/professional levels before *Duke Power,* eight, or 15 percent, dropped them altogether. (20) As would be expected, those dropping the tests were among the smallest firms polled. Of greater significance, though, was the fact that before the ruling, 14 of the 53 firms using testing did no validation of any factory-level tests; 15 did not validate their clerical tests; and 10 did not validate managerial/profes-

9 / The selection procedure 207

FIGURE 9-4

APPLICATION FOR EMPLOYMENT

EXXON

Exxon Corporation and affiliates

EQUAL OPPORTUNITY EMPLOYERS

PLEASE PRINT

[Form fields include:]

PERSONAL: Name (Last, First, Middle); Contact Phone No.; Alternate Phone No.; Time to Call (A.M./P.M.); Present Address; Permanent Address (if different from above); Contact Phone No.; Social Security No.; Do you have relatives with Exxon? (Name, where, relationship) Yes/No; Have you applied to Exxon before? (Which company - when); U.S. Citizen Yes/No; Non-U.S. Citizen — please indicate U.S. visa status: Permanent Visa, Student Visa, Exchange Student Visa, Visitors Visa, Other Visa Explain; Alien Registration No.; Have you ever been deported from the U.S.? Yes/No

EDUCATION: Name and Location of High School; Grad. Date (Mo./Yr.); Your Class Standing in Your Major; Your Overall Gradepoint Average; College Name and Location; Date (Mo./Yr.) From/To; Fields of Study Major/Minor; Graduation Degree, Date (Mo./Yr.); My Stdg. is 1st in class of 60 Example: 1/60; My Avg. all A's 4.0 Example: 3.7/4.0

*Insert number of college credit hours completed if no degree obtained.

College Financing: % G.I. Bill, % Own/Work, % Scholarship Explain, % Other Explain

Employment Desired: Permanent/Summer; Date Available for Work; Location Preference (if any); Salary Expected; Type of Work Desired Initially; Type of Work Desired Eventually; Is there some division or function in which you are especially interested? Is there a specific project or study that you would like to do?

EMPLOYMENT: Employer Name, Address & Phone No. (include graduate assistantship & summer jobs); Date (Mo./Yr.) From/To; Your Job Title and Duties; Supervisor's Name and Job Title

U.S. MIL: Branch of Service; From (Mo./Yr.) To (Mo./Yr.); Rank on Entry; Rank on Discharge; Type of Duty (especially if professional)

ACTIVITIES: Subjects of special study or research, college or other; Honors, honor societies, scholarships, extra curricular activities - offices held or responsibilities (exclude those which indicate race, color, religion, sex, or national origin)

ADDITIONAL INFORMATION:
Have you been convicted under any criminal law within the past 5 years? (Excluding minor traffic violations) Yes/No
Have you ever been imprisoned as a result of a criminal conviction? Yes/No
If the answer to either of the above questions is "YES", please give details on back.

Are you or have you ever knowingly been a member of the Communist Party or any organization which advocates overthrow of the United States Government by force or any illegal or unconstitutional method? Yes/No If "YES", please give details on back.

Are you under technical contract or restriction with a former employer? No/Yes — With whom?
May we call your present employer? Now - Yes/No After Visit - Yes/No Comments

I authorize investigation of all statements contained in this application for employment. I understand that misrepresentation or omission of facts called for hereon will be sufficient cause for cancellation of consideration for employment or dismissal from the Company's service if I have been employed. I understand that my employment is subject to a physical examination in which my health is found to be satisfactory to the Company. I understand that if I am employed evidence of U.S. citizenship or U.S. resident status and a birth certificate or other evidence of date of birth will be required.

X SIGNATURE   DATE SIGNED

This is to inform you that as part of our procedure of processing your employment application it is understood that an investigative report may be made whereby information is obtained through personal interviews with third parties. This inquiry includes information as to your character, general reputation, personal characteristics, and mode of living, whichever may be applicable. You have the right to make a written request within a reasonable period of time for a complete and accurate disclosure of additional information concerning the nature and scope of the investigation.

(PLEASE GIVE US ANY ADDITIONAL INFORMATION ON SCHOLASTIC ACHIEVEMENT OR EXPERIENCE ON A SEPARATE SHEET OF PAPER)

sional testing. Yet, after the ruling, of the 45 companies still testing, only two companies were not validating factory-level tests; four, clerical tests; and three, managerial/professional tests. (21)

Of the Los Angeles personnel managers polled, 37 percent gave some form of test.

> In the summer of 1975, Prentice-Hall studied 2,500 firms for the American Society of Personnel Administration. The study disclosed that 36 percent of the firms do no testing, although many did not test before the *Duke* ruling either. Of the firms still using tests, three out of four have reduced their use, and nearly 14 percent planned to stop testing entirely. (22)

Use of the polygraph. The polygraph, a form of "test," is being used with increasing frequency by business to meet the surge of white-collar theft. The primary purpose of the "lie detector" in business is to declare the innocence of those under suspicion. To keep the white-collar thief out of business in the first place or to find him out once a crime occurs, three examinations have been devised using the polygraph. They are the preemployment security clearance examination; a specific loss examination; and the periodic examination.

The test that has been most helpful to businesses is the preemployment examination. Companies request applicants in certain areas to take a polygraph examination to determine their integrity and character. They are asked about their past performance on jobs, their physical and mental condition at the time of the test, and their integrity. The biggest asset to the business is that they cull out potentially bad employee risks before they get in.

In-depth interview

The in-depth interview—variously referred to as the employment interview, the preemployment interview, and the diagnostic interview—is probably the most important part of the whole selection procedure, for all the relevant information is brought into focus at that point. Often the final decision to hire an individual is made during that interview.

The factors of aptitude, proficiency, and personality, as measured by energy, drive, social adaptability, emotional control, and conscience, are related to an employee's productivity. These subjects should be openly discussed during this interview. Primarily the interviewer seeks to ascertain the applicant's level of maturity, ability to persevere, and degree of self-discipline. Secondarily, the interviewer searches for the right attitude, knowledge, and skills needed for successful performance on the job. In summary, the interviewer attempts to evaluate the person's ability to utilize available resources in solving complex problems.

Verifying background information

Somewhere in the information-gathering stage, the previously gathered information should be verified. If this is not done and it becomes known, questions are raised about the integrity of the whole selection procedure. Also, if the data are not checked, there is a question as to the validity of using so much of the applicant's time in providing the information. Finally, the data should be verified as a predictor of success on the new job.

A survey of 38 manufacturing and service-type organizations showed that 43 percent of them used background checks merely to verify information; 34 percent indicated that it gives additional information about the applicant; and 13 percent believed that it uncovered information which would not be otherwise uncovered. (23) Three out of four respondents said the verification occurred after the interviews.

Sources used to verify data. The data can be verified by checking references given, doing a credit check, and/or contacting educational institutions.

References. There are essentially three kinds of references—personal, academic, and past employment. The first of these is relatively insignificant, as it invariably is biased in favor of the applicant. The second is of considerable value if the organization develops a relationship with the teachers based upon mutual respect and interest.

By far the most important references, though, are those from the applicant's previous employers. A measure of the person's actual accomplishments, including productivity, the ability to "get along with others," and weaknesses and strengths, may be obtained this way. Work references can give an indication of a person's possible future success on the job by showing what he or she has done in the past. Yet, there is the danger that "spite references" will belittle a qualified candidate. The opposite tendency is also prevalent, as former employers often fail to reveal shortcomings of a worker out of sympathy, if one has problems and quits voluntarily; or out of a sense of guilt if the worker is discharged for cause.

Credit check. Although they are declining in popularity because of changing public policy, credit checks still provide a useful source of verification of data given, as well as a source of new information. These credit reports are now subject to the *Fair Credit Reporting Act, 1970.* An applicant must be notified in writing that such information is being sought and is then entitled to "full disclosure" from the report received.

Transcripts. Nearly three out of four firms in one survey attempt to obtain complete transcripts of job applicants' educational backgrounds. This information is useful in seeing if there is a "pattern" of grades in given courses or subject areas. I have found that this is a good predictor of success for students going into specialized jobs.

How extensively is verification used? The NICB study found that 99 percent of the manufacturing firms checked work references; over 65 percent checked school and personal references; while 36 percent asked for credit checks. Over 94 percent of the service organizations checked work references; but the percentage doing credit checks varied from 18 for wholesale to 54 for banks.

As with the other selection instruments, references are declining in use because of the *Fair Credit Reporting Act* and equal employment guidelines.

National Bank of Detroit will only "confirm dates and nature of employment. We try not to make judgments or go beyond the basic facts."

General Electric will say whether it would rehire a discharged employee, but it won't elaborate.

Uniroyal and ACF Industries try to ease the problem by asking written permission of applicants to check references.

A large utility worries that concern about privacy is "protecting the crooks. We have to hire meter readers who are going into people's homes and we can't get background information on anybody." (24)

What method used to verify? Information can be verified in person, by phone, by letter, or by a prepared questionnaire. As the in-depth, in-person verification is used infrequently and as it is so costly, it will not be discussed further.

Phone. If a personal visit with the reference giver is not feasible, a personal phone call should gain the most valuable and accurate information available. With this method, you can listen to the tone of voice, notice pauses or hesitancies, and follow up quickly on questions, intimations, or inferences which indicate a problem area. It is the most frequently used method of verification. However, there seems to be no research demonstrating its superiority over the other methods of obtaining references. (25)

Letter. While letters are still being used, their validity and return rates are low, and they tend to be biased toward favorable responses.

Questionnaire. Nash and Carroll found that the response rate increased from 35 percent to 85 percent when they used a one-page, objective questionnaire with an individually typed letter signed by one of the authors as "Director of Personnel." (26) While this worked with former employers of clerical applicants at the University of Maryland, it did not work satisfactorily with former employers of maintenance and custodial applicants. The most effective form was found to be the forced choice rating form.

How valid are reference checks? The research just mentioned found that organizations can improve the usefulness of the reference check when selecting personnel by giving careful attention to who gives the reference and the method used to obtain the reference.

Only references from former supervisors of the job applicant are predictive of success in a new job. Even then, references from supervisors who have had recent—and sufficient—opportunity to observe the applicant working in a job similar to the one being sought and who are of the same sex, race, and national origin as the applicant will be predictive of job success. (27)

A forced choice form (sent with a personally typed and signed letter to increase the rate of return) can be predictive of job success.

Medical examination

The final step in the information-gathering stage is some form of medical examination. Some organizations will use a thorough medical history, plus careful observation during interviews, instead of a thorough physical. However, the NICB study found 71 percent of the manufacturing firms gave preemployment physicals to both blue- and white-collar employees, while another 14 percent provided them only for blue-collar employees. The percentage in the service industries varied from 30 in wholesaling to 95 in utilities.

Although a physical is usually given as part of the preemployment procedure, it really has several purposes. First, it is designed to screen out individuals who might not be physically capable of performing the assigned duties effectively. Thus, the intent is to protect prospective employees from possible injury caused from performing a job for which they were not capable of doing. Second, this instrument can be used to prevent the employment of individuals who might have a high incidence of absenteeism, illness, or accidents. (As shown in Chapter 23, this is particularly true in the case of chemical dependency.) Third, it can prevent hiring people with communicable diseases. Finally, it can be used as a defense in case of unwarranted claims under worker's compensation laws or in suits for damages.

As current personnel policies are designed to hire more handicapped workers, this poses a dilemma for those doing the selection. However, many states have faced up to the reluctance of employers to assume the potentially higher liability caused by hiring those with existing physical impairments. Many states have now passed laws with "second-injury" provisions. Under these laws, the present employer's liability is limited only to those injuries resulting from the present job, as another fund—usually administered by the state—will provide for earlier injuries.

It is surprising how many applicants are rejected on the basis of physicals. Apparently our new life-styles are partially responsible.

> While doing a case study of a chemical plant in New England, we were told that "over 40 percent" of blue-collar applicants who reached the physical exam stage of the employment procedure were rejected for "back ailments." Many of the problems resulted from "poor posture."
>
> In Los Angeles, an energy firm found "a substantial proportion" of young applicants were rejected because of "hearing problems." This was particularly true of former employees of places where music was played.

FOURTH STAGE: EVALUATING INFORMATION AND ASSESSING APPLICANT

This stage involves an in-depth analysis and rigorous evaluation of the information received. Particular attention is now being given to biographical data as predictors of success. Also, information from testing and interviewing provides valid clues to success.

Because of the complex and technical nature of these procedures, they will be discussed in detail in the next chapter.

FIFTH STAGE: MAKING THE DECISION TO ACCEPT OR REJECT APPLICANT

The next step in the selection procedure is choosing the desired candidate from among the remaining available alternatives. Whether the selection procedure is regarded as positive *selection* or as negative *rejection,* the truth is evident that many decisions are made concerning the individual's actual and potential abilities at each stage of the procedure.

How is the decision made?

So far, we have looked at the process of gathering information and evaluating it in terms of the applicants' abilities relative to the job to be filled. While decisions had to be made at each step of the way, there comes a time when all the information—often contradictory—must be pulled together and a decision made to accept or reject the applicant being considered.

There are two ways of making this decision. First, some mechanized method can be used, whereby the quantifiable data are fed into a computer which is programmed to make the decision. The technology is now available for the computer to make better decisions than personnel specialists—at least for certain jobs.

Finally, however, a value judgment must be made, using personal knowledge obtained from the various evaluative techniques rather than from objective data provided by the computer or other device. (28) This evaluation occurs when the decision is made as to whether the person will be hired or not. (Although not always true, the tacit assumption is made that there are multiple candidates for each job.)

The paradox involved in this step is that the practical art of weighing and evaluating human virtues and limitations finally must reside with an individual who may have many of the same strengths and weaknesses. This most important step in the selection process, then, is made by a fallible person. The saving factor is that the chances of success are enhanced if the procedure has been effectively handled up to that point, thus furnishing a store of evidence to serve as a guide to action. Also, most jobs have some crucial indicator or critical factor, which is based upon research, that serves as the focal point for making the decision.

Who makes the decision?

As shown in Chapter 2, employment is one of the primary functions of the personnel department. However, the decision to hire is relatively low on the functions desired of the personnel department by line managers and even lower by the personnel executives' supervisors. As the department tends to have staff or functional authority, the final decision to hire is usually left up to operating executives, except for low-level, routine jobs.

A shared responsibility. There is a division of labor, however. The personnel executives can: (*a*) do research to establish performance criteria and determine the validity of the selection instrument in predicting the criterion; (*b*) advise on hiring standards; and, in case of public policy, even set hiring guidelines.

In most organizations, the division of labor works this way:

1. The personnel department does the recruiting; handles the details of the selection instrument, except the final employment interview; and then recommends to the operating department that a given individual(s) be interviewed for final selection; and
2. The operating executives do the final interviewing, and make the final decision to select or reject a given applicant.

There are modifications of this procedure, as will be seen from the case problems at the end of this part. Increasingly operating executives are doing college recruiting and preliminary interviewing for scientific, technical, and professional personnel. In that case, the personnel department takes over and processes the information.

Current practice. According to the previously mentioned NICB studies, current practice is for the employment office to do the initial screening and the various departments to do a follow-up interview and make the hiring decisions.

From personal observations and case research, personnel executives are increasingly brought in on the final decisions because of public policy and their expertise in the matter. Also, these administrators are having an important input into the position, salary, and benefits to be offered to individuals.

SIXTH STAGE: COMMUNICATING THE DECISION

When the decision is made not to make a job offer, the rejection may be done by either the personnel office or the operating executive. (29) Usually it is done by the personnel department.

When the decision is made to employ the applicant, the job offer may be made by the operating department, but the personnel department usually must give its approval to the terms and conditions of employment.

Ironically, even when the job offer is made, the possibility is always present that the applicant will reject the employment offer. A NICB survey found the average percentage of offers made by companies to college graduates being accepted by 43 to 59 percent of those selected. (30)

It has also been shown empirically that applicants tend to have a mental ideal job model involving: (*a*) opportunity for advancement; (*b*) challenge of the job; (*c*) salary and economic benefits; (*d*) prestige of the position; (*e*) geographic location; and (*f*) job content. When a job offer is received, the applicant compares it to the "ideal offer." The closer the actual offer is to the ideal, the greater are the chances of acceptance. (31)

IMPLICATIONS AND APPLICATIONS FOR PERSONNEL EXECUTIVES

Several hypotheses can be derived from the research findings presented. They are:

1. *Employees work best and accomplish most when they are assigned definite jobs for which they are mentally, emotionally, and physically suited, which is of sufficient difficulty to challenge their best effort and which is to be completed in a given period of time.* (32)
2. *The lower the level of the job, and the more routine its nature, the greater the use of a single criterion as a predictor of job performance and, therefore, its use as a rejection factor.*
3. *The higher the job level and the greater its use of interaction of variables, the greater the use of multiple-correlation procedures to evaluate the validity of each selection criteria and the magnitude of the intercorrelations between them as predictors of success.*
4. *The lower the level of the job, the greater the tendency to hire the person for an individual job, but, for higher positions, individuals are hired for career development or for occupational growth and development.*

The only generalization that can be made concerning the correlation between *intelligence* and success in performing most nonmanagerial jobs is that some minimum level of intelligence is necessary for achievement; but this alone is not sufficient. Above the minimum level, the relative importance of this factor is determined by the degree of sophistication and complexity of the job to be done and management's wishes.

Other general success indicators to look for in potential employees are *imagination, logic, insight into human nature, ability to attack and solve difficult problems.* These enumerated characteristics are only a few of the significant ones looked for in selection, but they are illustrative of the type of qualities one should seek in job aspirants.

Small organizations have some advantages when it comes to selection. They are able to offer job flexibility, work modification, and greater challenges. Also, selection and job performance are more closely related. Some disadvantages are a general lack of promotable people, the crucial nature of each appointment, the inability to spend much time and money on selection, and lack of expertise—as hiring is done infrequently. Also, the more individualized nature of jobs makes it difficult to prepare uniform job specifications.

There are things that can be done to improve selection in these organizations. Formal policies concerning qualifications, salary, and advancement can be established; budget a substantial amount for advertising; rely heavily on *detailed* application blanks; do intensive check of references; have an effective, personalized placement and orientation system, and adhere to a rigid probationary period. (33)

DISCUSSION QUESTIONS

1. Do you think the selection procedure is one of *selection* or *rejection?* Explain your answer.

2. What is the relationship between employee attitudes and productivity? How does this relationship apply to selection? Explain.
3. What is meant by the statement that "the matching procedure begins with and is predicated upon an evaluation of the employee's assets and liabilities."
4. Discuss the main personal characteristics which are associated with successful job performance and the implications of each of the selected function.
5. How does public policy affect selection?
6. Discuss the stages in the suggested selection procedure. Would you recommend any revision in the stages? If so, what revisions?
7. A prevalent opinion among first-line managers is they, because of their interaction with the work group, should have complete authority over the selection process. Comment on this opinion.

REFERENCES AND SUGGESTIONS FOR FURTHER STUDY

1. Much of the material in this chapter is based upon Lawrence Siegel and Irving M. Lane, *Psychology in Industrial Organizations,* 3d. ed. (Homewood, Ill.: Richard D. Irwin, Inc., 1974). This conclusion was reached after studying Part II of that book.
2. Ibid., pp. 52, and 134–35.
3. A. Polin, R. J. Morse, and J. H. Zenger, "Selecting Programmers from In-Plant Employees," *Personnel Journal,* vol. 41, no. 8 (September 1962), pp. 398–99, 412.
4. Francis O. Harding and Robert A. Bottenberg, "Effect of Personal Characteristics in Relationships between Attitudes and Job Performance," *Journal of Applied Psychology,* vol. 45, no. 6 (December 1961), pp. 428–30.
5. C. F. Carter, "The Economic Use of Brains," *Economic Journal,* vol. 72, no. 285 (March 1962), pp. 1–11.
6. Sheila Jordan, M. Zieden-Weber, and Fred Ripin, "What Makes Him Tick?" *Institute of Applied Psychology Review,* vol. 3, no. 1 (Winter 1963), pp. 14–17.
7. See Harish C. Jain, "Managerial Recruitment and Selection in the Canadian Manufacturing Industry," *Public Personnel Management,* vol. 3, no. 3 (May–June 1974), p. 212, for other results of the study.
8. Phillip Miller, *Einfuhrung in die Graphologie* (West Berlin: Ullstein Bucher, 1960. Advocaters of this evaluation technique believe that while it can not reveal the content of a person's thoughts, it can indicate the degree of energy, inhibitions, and spontaneity, as well as suggesting certain idiosyncrasies and personality characteristics. For further details, see Jitendra M. Sharma and Harsh Vardhan, "Graphology: What Handwriting Can Tell about an Applicant," *Personnel,* vol. 52, no. 2 (March–April 1975), pp. 57–63.
9. Robert A. Martin, "Our Primitive Employment Process," *Personnel Journal,* vol. 49, no. 2 (February 1970), pp. 177–22.
10. For further information, see Bryant F. Nagle, "Criterion Development," *Personnel Psychology,* vol. 6, no. 3 (Autumn 1953), pp. 271–89, which summarizes around 30 studies of criterion development.
11. R. J. Wherry, "Criteria and Validity," in D. H. Fryer and E. R. Henry, eds., *Handbook of Applied Psychology* (New York: Holt, Rinehart and Winston, 1954), chapter 27.

12. See W. W. Ronan and E. P. Prien, *Toward a Criterion Theory: A Review and Analysis of Research and Opinion* (Greensboro, N.C.: Richardson Foundation, 1966).
13. See Siegel and Lane, *Psychology in Industrial Organizations,* pp. 67–87.
14. I. L. Janis, "Psychological Preparation for Post-Decisional Crises," in T. W. Costello and S. S. Zalkind, eds., *Psychology in Administration: A Research Orientation* (Englewood Cliffs, N.J.: Prentice-Hall, Inc., 1963), pp. 188–89.
15. For example, for a discussion of research findings on some criteria of success and the variables which will predict successful job performance for *medical-surgical nursing aides,* see E. J. Kelleher, W. A. Kerr, and N. T. Melville, "The Prediction of Subprofessional Nursing Success," *Personnel Psychology,* vol. 21, no. 3 (Autumn 1968), pp. 379–88; for *salesmen,* see James C. Cotham, "Selecting Salesmen: Approaches and Problems," *MSU Business Topics,* vol. 18, no. 1 (Winter 1970), pp. 64–72; for *policemen* and *firemen,* see J. D. Matarazzo, B. V. Allen, G. Saslow, and A. N. Wiens, "Characteristics of Successful Policemen and Firemen Applicants," *Journal of Applied Psychology,* vol. 48, no. 2 (April 1964), pp. 123–33; and for *repetitive jobs,* see T. O. Prenting, "Better Selection for Repetitive Work," *Personnel Journal,* vol. 41 (September 1964), pp. 26–31.

    It is interesting that the last of these articles shows that some people do not like "larger" jobs but actually enjoy repetitive work. Thus, the efforts of *job enlargement* to alleviate the boredom and monotony of repetitive work may be in vain, especially for middle-aged—or older—workers, with a tendency toward introversion, who are psychologically stable, persevering, and calm. This conclusion was also reached by the author in a study of Pheol Manufacturing Company in Chicago in 1952. Older women were found to have a high degree of productivity, a well-developed social system, and high morale while inspecting nuts, screws, and bolts for long periods of time.
16. Owen N. Rabourn, James H. Schilz, and Charles W. Holland, "A Successful Selection Technique," *Personnel Journal,* vol. 46, no. 4 (April 1967), pp. 211–13.
17. A recent study attempted to determine if selected subcriteria of overall job effectiveness could differentially account for variations in an overall criterion for black and white employees working on the same job. While no significant differences were found between the two ethnic groups on most of the training, job performance, and personnel rating subcriteria, there was a consistent trend toward slightly lower mean scores and less variability around the means for black employees as far as the latter two factors were concerned. A second observed trend was toward greater absences and tardiness by this group and a tendency toward more disciplinary warnings and wage attachments. However, the researcher concluded that these findings were partially explained in terms of differences between the subgroups on several demographic variables. See Brain C. Arnold, "Comparison of Caucasian and Negro Subgroups on Criterion Indices of Overall Job Effectiveness," *Dissertation Abstracts International,* vol. 30, no. 2–B (1969), p. 881.
18. See Marshall Keyser, "How to Apply for a Job," *Journal of College Placement,* vol. 35, no. 1 (Fall 1974), pp. 63–65, for other suggestions.
19. Specific questions pertaining to these characteristics are presented and discussed by Lipman G. Fels, an attorney, in "15 Questions You Dare Not Ask Job Applicants," *Administrative Management,* vol. 53, no. 6 (June 1974), pp. 20, 21, 80, 82.

A major California firm prepared an interview guide for its managers and supervisors showing what they could and could not do or ask. For details, see *Business Week* (May 26, 1975), p. 77.

20. Donald J. Peterson, "The Impact of Duke Power on Testing," *Personnel,* vol. 51, no. 2 (March–April 1974), pp. 30–37.
21. The Industrial Psychology Division (division 14) of the American Psychological Association has released a booklet titled, "Principles for the Validation and Use of Personnel Selection Procedures." APA cautions readers of the booklet that it "is prepared as a technical guide (and) is not written as law. However, the guidelines can be followed when conducting validation research."
22. Hal Lancaster, "Job Tests Are Dropped by Many Companies Due to Antibias Drive," *Wall Street Journal* (September 3, 1975), p. 1.
23. This study by George M. Beason and John A. Belt, "Verifying Job Applicant's Background," *Personnel Administrator,* vol. 14, no. 8 (November–December, 1974), pp. 29–32, provides much research data for this discussion.
24. *Wall Street Journal* (January 6, 1976), p. 1.
25. H. C. Pyron, "The Use and Misuse of Previous Employer References in Hiring," *Management of Personnel Quarterly,* vol. 9, no. 2 (Summer 1970), pp. 15–22.
26. See Allan N. Nash and Stephen J. Carroll, Jr., "A Hard Look at the Reference Check," *Business Horizons,* vol. 13, no. 5 (October 1970), p. 47, for further information.
27. Ibid., p. 44.
28. Robert M. Guion, "Criterion Measurement and Personnel Judgments," in H. W. Karn and B. von Haller Gilmer, eds., *Readings in Industrial and Business Psychology,* 2d ed. (New York: McGraw-Hill Book Co., 1962), pp. 108–15.

    However, efforts have been made to reduce the judgmental factor. See Robert D. Smith, "Models for Personnel Selection Decisions," *Personnel Journal,* vol. 52, no. 8 (August 1973), pp. 688–95, for a discussion of an experimental computer model, where the computer printed out the same final selection decision as an independent consulting psychologist on whether or not to hire seven out of eight applicants for clerical positions.
29. The rejection letter is a point of contention with college graduates, especially MBAs. See Harry Steinberg, "Those Finely Tuned Rejection Letters," *MBA,* vol. 9, no. 6 (June 1975), pp. 24–25, for an interesting article comparing rejection letters from 60 companies. The author has constructed a hypothetical rejection letter, using the phrases which are similar in most of the letters.
30. "College Recuiting in 1960," *Management Record,* vol. 22, no. 1 (January 1960), pp. 11–13.
31. See Raymond E. Hill, "An Empirical Comparison of Two Models for Predicting Preferences for Standard Employment Offer," *Decision Sciences,* vol. 5, no. 2 (April 1974), pp. 243–53, for details on how the ideal job offer compares with the "utility model."
32. Findings similar to this hypothesis were found in a research study which showed that the average man would produce 800 units per day but a theoretically perfectly selected man would produce 1,200 units. See Charles Bahn, "Economy of Scientific Selection," *Personnel Journal,* vol. 49, no. 8 (August 1970), pp. 651–54.
33. See Roger Holdsworth, "Selection Tips for Small Firm Managers," *Personnel Management,* vol. 7, no. 3 (March 1975), pp. 31–33, for further suggestions.

Chapter 10

Evaluating information and assessing applicants

Requirements for effective use of selection techniques
    How valid is the technique?
    How reliable is the technique?
    How accurate is the information received from applicants?

Evaluating biographical inventories
    Methods of obtaining data
    Methods of evaluating data
    How valid is this technique?
    Requirements for effective use of biographical inventories

Evaluating test results
    Criticisms of tests
    Arguments in favor of tests
    Types of tests
    Requirements for effective testing

Using the interview to evaluate applicants
    Uses in selection procedure
    Methods used in interviewing
    Constraints on the use of the interview

Implications and applications for personnel executives
    Using biographical inventories
    Using tests
    Using interviews

10
Evaluating information and assessing applicants

A man who qualifies himself well for his calling, never fails of employment.

THOMAS JEFFERSON

Some years ago, a recruiter would visit our campus, interview engineering students, select the best one, and take him out to eat. He observed the young man to see if he tasted his food before salting it. If not, he was rejected for "jumping to conclusions" and not being "analytical."

This true case illustrates one technique for identifying predictors of success. But it is *not* suggested for general use! Instead, it was shown in the previous chapter that there are certain *performance criteria* which can be used to measure success on the job; there are *predictors of success* which determine if a potential employee will likely perform well; and these predictors, which serve as selection criteria, can be identified by some common *techniques,* or *selection instruments.** These were briefly mentioned in the context of the overall selection procedure itself.

In this chapter, we will do in-depth analyses of the three most valid instruments for obtaining and evaluating information about prospective employees, namely: (*a*) biographical inventories, obtained from application blanks, biographical information blanks, and résumés; (*b*) psychological and employment tests; and (*c*) interviews. We will also see how the information obtained from them is used to assess applicants for employment.

REQUIREMENTS FOR EFFECTIVE USE OF SELECTION TECHNIQUES

However, before considering using these techniques, personnel executives should look at some problems which are common to all of them. They should probe to see: (*a*) how effective is the instrument in predicting success on the job; (*b*) does it obtain the same results when used by different individuals, at varying times, and under dissimilar conditions; and (*c*) how accurate is the information obtained from the prospective employee?

---
* While the proper word is probably "instrument," it will be used interchangeably with "technique" to avoid repetition.

How valid is the technique?

Validity, or the effectiveness of the instrument in predicting success on the job, is the first problem to be considered. (1) It will be defined and classified as to types, and then an explanation of the validation process will be given.

What is validity? When making selection decisions, personnel executives try to choose from among all the applicants only those who will most likely perform successfully when placed on the job. This poses the problem of predicting job behavior before it can occur. This can be done by correlating the results obtained from using a selection instrument, or technique (such as a test), on all job applicants with their scores on actual job performance criteria later on. If the correlation is sufficiently high and the applicants who receive high "scores" from the selection technique also perform successfully as employees on the job, the technique is considered to be valid as a predictor of success.

In essence, a selection technique is valid if *it measures the qualities or characteristics which it purports to measure.*

Types of validity. While there are several types of validity, the ones the personnel professionals are interested in are: (*a*) concurrent validity; (*b*) predictive validity; (*c*) face validity; and (*d*) synthetic validity.

Concurrent validity. This is sometimes referred to as the *present-employee* method. In effect, it is the extent to which the results obtained with a selection technique (such as a test) are statistically related to the performance of employees currently on the job. This approach permits the immediate determination of the usefulness of that selection instrument.

Predictive validity. This validity, sometimes referred to as the *follow-up* method, is arrived at by using the selection technique on *all* applicants who apply for the job. As the instrument itself is being tested, *acceptances or rejections should not be made on the basis of the results* ("scores"), but hiring decisions should be made on the basis of other selection techniques. After the new employees have been on the job sufficiently long to obtain a true measure of their performance, a statistical correlation is prepared between their earlier "scores" on the instrument and the criterion used to measure successful performance. The most frequently used criterion is supervisory evaluations.

This validation technique requires considerable time before it can be known for certain whether the instrument is useful in predicting success. As a result, *concurrent validation* is used most frequently in employment procedures.

Face validity. Prospective employees are more willing to accept the results of a selection technique that seems logical and valid to them, regardless of whether the results are valid or not. This validity, then, refers to whether the information being sought *appears to be "fairly" related to the job* in question. It cannot be measured statistically, and an instrument which may *appear* to have face validity may be found *actually* to have a poor statistical correlation with the criterion.

Synthetic validity. Because of public policy, as well as the desire of the new type of employees for "face validity," considerable effort is now being made to find some generalized procedure that will permit the application of relevant validation information about an instrument from one setting to another. One of the most promising approaches to this problem is a form of synthetic validity known as *job component validity.* (2)

Small companies particularly attempt to find synthetic validities, for their size makes it difficult for them to establish the more desirable predictive validities of their own. (3)

Effects of public policy on validation. In addition to the professional interest in validation as a means of improving selection techniques, public policy has forced personnel executives to validate their selection instruments. This generalization is especially true of testing but also of the biographical inventories and interviewing.

While *Title VII* specifically permits testing which is nondiscriminatory, professionally prepared and administered, and job-related, a series of court interpretations have led to such a strict interpretation of these requirements that many organizations are now dropping tests as shown in the previous chapter. In *Myart* v. *Motorola,* a black applicant was denied a job because of a low score on an intelligence test. The court said the test could be used *if the company could show the test predicted success,* but as researchers have shown that tests and other instruments may not be equally predictive of success with black, Spanish-surnamed, and white workers because of differing values, (4) this is difficult to do. In *Griggs, et al.* v. *Duke Power Company,* the Supreme Court ruled unanimously in 1971 that the company could not require applicants to take the Wonderlic Personnel Test and the Bennett Mathematical Aptitudes Test—nor require a high school diploma, as a basic measurement of the prospective employee's ability to learn or to perform a job or job category. (5) In essence, the Court laid down the guideline that: *Any selection criterion must be related to the applicant's ability to perform the job being sought.* The Court said, "The act proscribes not only overt discrimination but also practices that are fair in form, but discriminatory in operation. The touchstone is business necessity. If an employment practice which operates to exclude Negroes cannot be shown to be related to the job performance, the practice is prohibited."

The Court upheld *Griggs*—and even strengthened it—when it held in *Moody* v. *Albemarle Paper Co.* (6) that, although the firm's hiring and promotion tests had been validated *for content,* they did not follow EEOC guidelines, (7) which were entitled to "great deference."

It can be inferred from these and other decisions that a valid selection instrument—especially tests—must fairly measure the knowledge or skills required by the particular job or class of jobs which the applicant seeks, or fairly afford the employer a chance to measure the applicant's ability to be *trained to perform a particular job or class of jobs.* (8)

How reliable is the technique?

A selection technique must also have reliability in the sense that it gives consistent results under the same, or similar, circumstances and when administered and interpreted by different people. This means that each time the instrument is used, the same relative appraisal should result. One problem that must be overcome is the transparency of some of the questions on some tests which allows intelligent persons to fake their answers to the questions. A similar problem exists with biographical inventories and interviews. In practice, validity and reliability are actually interrelated, for a selection technique which gives consistent results usually has a high validity.

How accurate is the information received from applicants?

A technique is only as valid in predicting success as the information obtained from the prospective employee. Several studies indicate that information obtained from biographical forms and during the interview tends to be biased in favor of the applicant, particularly on information considered to be socially acceptable. One study found that this tendency was not necessarily caused by poor memory, as the bias was also present in information given about the present job held by the applicant. (9)

Another study of nurse aides found substantial disagreement between the applicant's statement and the reference checks on duration of previous employment, reasons for leaving, and salary. In fact, 15 percent of the applicants had never worked for the employer shown on the form. (10)

EVALUATING BIOGRAPHICAL INVENTORIES

There is considerable research indicating that a careful evaluation of biographical inventories can result in the selection of qualified employees better than other instruments and can also reduce labor turnover. The implicit assumption can be made that—in general—information about the applicant's past performance and personal characteristics tend to predict future success —or lack of success—on the job. These inventories not only gather valuable information systematically, but they do it effectively and inexpensively. (11) In fact, *one research study indicated that biographical inventories showed higher validities in predicting job proficiency than psychological tests.* (12)

Methods of obtaining data

The usual method used to obtain biographical inventories is the *application blank*, which may be short or long, simple or complex. The latter usually takes the form of a weighted application blank (WAB). Another form is the *biographical information blank* (BIB), which is sometimes called a "life history antecedent questionnaire" or "personnel information blank." The third method of obtaining background information is the *résumé*. The form and content of the first two are determined by the organization, while those of the latter are determined by the applicant.

Methods of evaluating data

Biographical data can be evaluated either by using the analytical, clinical approach, or a statistical analysis and correlation can be done.

In using the *clinical approach,* the analyst studies the answers to the questions in an attempt to find meaningful "patterns" which might predict whether the person will successfully perform the job to be filled. A properly trained and experienced analyst should be able to determine if there is a "progression" in education pursued, positions held, and other work-related items which might predict success.

The second method uses *statistical analysis.* Because of the great amount of research and statistical correlation which has been done since the development of the 1920s, this method is now preferable.

Any attempt to explain this approach in detail would require more room and time than is warranted in this presentation. *In general,* using standard research procedures, the investigator must determine the extent—if any—of the relationship between the applicant's responses to the items on the blank to some predetermined criterion of successful job performance—such as volume produced or supervisor's appraisal. The items which are shown to be predictors of success, as measured by the criterion, are given a weight to reflect the extent of that relationship. After the results are validated against external criteria, the form is developed and used in the selection procedure. The total form is scored by summing the weights of each of the responses to the individual items. There is a "cutting" score which determines whether an applicant will be accepted or not. (13)

The computer is also used. The Metropolitan Life Insurance Company developed a program to examine all possible combinations of 25 intervals of six background factors to identify the predictive ability of those factors. The application of the technique to 1,525 sales personnel found "previous income" as the most important variable; number of dependents was next. As seen in Figure 10–1, the first "cutting score" was "$90 or more"; the second was "$130 or more"; and the third was "3 or more" dependents. (The performance criterion was "remaining on the job at least four quarters.")

How valid is this technique?

Apparently this technique can be quite valid as a predictor when used properly and when correct information is obtained from the applicant.

Validity of the weighted application blank as a predictor. As indicated, the WAB has been shown to be quite valid in predicting the rate of turnover and the length of tenure of employees. For example, selected background data from the WAB have been found to be related to job success in the following occupations and can *possibly be used for predictive purposes:* (14)

a. *Unskilled females* in the *canning industry*—living close to the plant, and having family responsibilities;

FIGURE 10-1
Results of pattern analysis predictors of sales production

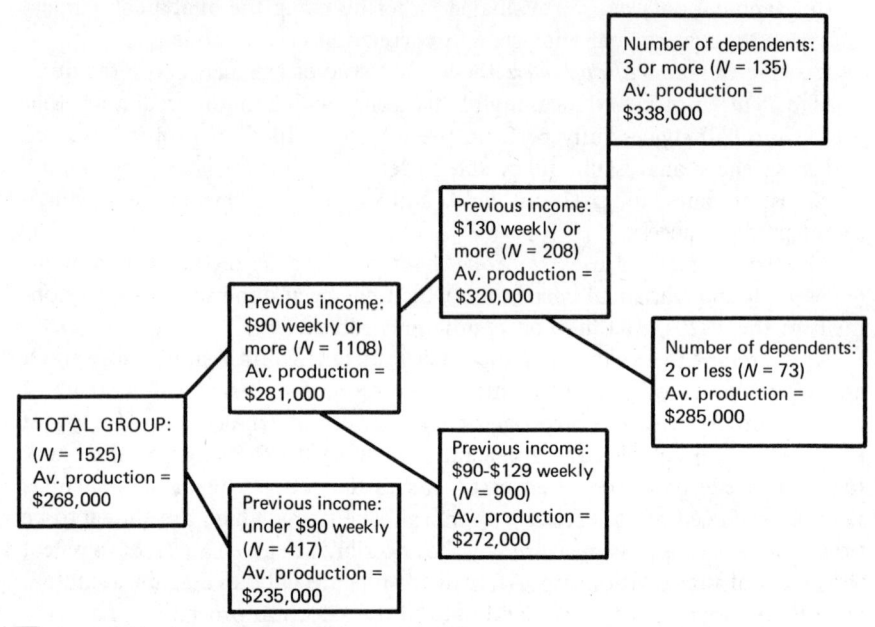

```
                                              ┌─────────────────────────┐
                                              │ Number of dependents:   │
                                              │ 3 or more (N = 135)     │
                                              │ Av. production =        │
                                              │ $338,000                │
                                              └─────────────────────────┘
                                         ┌─────────────────────────┐
                                         │ Previous income:        │
                                         │ $130 weekly or          │
                                         │ more (N = 208)          │
                                         │ Av. production =        │
                                         │ $320,000                │
                                         └─────────────────────────┘
                     ┌─────────────────────────┐
                     │ Previous income:        │           ┌─────────────────────────┐
                     │ $90 weekly or           │           │ Number of dependents:   │
                     │ more (N = 1108)         │           │ 2 or less (N = 73)      │
                     │ Av. production =        │           │ Av. production =        │
                     │ $281,000                │           │ $285,000                │
                     └─────────────────────────┘           └─────────────────────────┘
 ┌─────────────────┐                          ┌─────────────────────────┐
 │ TOTAL GROUP:    │                          │ Previous income:        │
 │ (N = 1525)      │                          │ $90-$129 weekly         │
 │ Av. production =│                          │ (N = 900)               │
 │ $268,000        │                          │ Av. production =        │
 └─────────────────┘                          │ $272,000                │
                     ┌─────────────────────────┐ └─────────────────────────┘
                     │ Previous income:        │
                     │ under $90 weekly        │
                     │ (N = 417)               │
                     │ Av. production =        │
                     │ $235,000                │
                     └─────────────────────────┘
```

Source: R. Tanofsky, R. R. Shepps, and P. J. O'Neill, "Pattern Analysis of Biographical Predictors of Success as an Insurance Salesman," *Journal of Applied Psychology*, vol. 53, no. 2 (April 1969), p. 137.

b. *Seasonal workers* in the *canning industry*—distance between plant and worker's home, marital status and number of dependents, a telephone in the home, and veteran status;
c. *Drivers*—absence rate per year;
d. *Chemists* and *engineers*—previous work experience, amount and type of extracurricular activities in college, and membership in honor societies;
e. *Sales representatives* and *district managers*—family and fiscal responsibilities, and stability of tenure;
f. *Young executives*—education;
g. *Female managers* of *convenience stores*—length of service—in days—of last job;
h. *Managers* of *AT&T*—rank in graduating class, "quality" of college attended, and extracurricular achievements; and
i. *Consultants*—attendance at private prep school or small private college, graduate degree from prestigious college or university, service in the Air Force or Navy, and manager in a private business firm.

Finally, an intensive study of several groups of employees—such as secretaries, female dietary aides, male nursing attendants, and staff nurses—found indications that the WAB not only improved the selection decisions, but also lowered turnover costs. The weighted information used on the form for selecting secretaries is shown in Table 10–1.

Validity of the biographical information blank as a predictor. The BIB consists of a series of statistically correlated and weighed questions concerning the applicant's background. Usually developed and validated by trained professionals, these blanks can be scored and interpreted in much the same manner as other objective instruments. The BIB is usually used to obtain information for predicting success in a given type job or occupation.

This instrument has been found particularly effective in selecting sales,

TABLE 10–1
Information included in weighted application blank used to select secretaries

Item	Percentage Short-term	Percentage Long-term	Weight
Age			
20 or under	10	0	0
21–25	50	12	−4
26–30	20	12	0
31–35	10	23	0
Over 35	10	53	+5
Marital status			
Married	20	47	+2
Single	63	41	−1
Widowed	0	0	0
Divorced	10	6	0
Separated	7	6	0
Education			
Attended grade school	0	0	0
Grade school graduate	0	0	0
Attended high school	0	12	0
High school graduate	33	41	0
Attended college	40	41	0
College graduate	27	6	−1
Business school	10	29	0
Years on last job			
Less than 1	50	0	−5
1–1½	7	35	+2
1½–2½	37	12	−1
2½–3	0	6	0
More than 3	10	35	+2
Years of experience			
0	3	18	0
Less than 1	20	0	−1
1–2	20	0	−1
2½–3	30	0	−3
More than 3	27	71	+5

Use of the cutting score of +2 would have eliminated 83% of the short-term employees and 13% of the long-term employees.
Source: Stanley R. Novack, "Developing an Effective Application Blank," *Personnel Journal*, vol. 49, no. 5 (May 1970), pp. 421–22. Reprinted with permission of *Personnel Journal*, copyright May 1970.

technical, and managerial personnel. (15) In fact, many companies have found the BIB to be the single best predictor of success for specialized occupations. After considerable experimentation, Standard Oil of Indiana dropped its testing procedure in favor of this form for many of its positions. (16)

Validity of the résumé as a predictor. Research has also shown that considerable improvement in selection can be achieved through learning how to evaluate a personnel résumé. (17) Some clues to seek are: a record of achievement, such as upward movement in one firm or progressive horizontal movement between firms; responsibility, as shown by positions held; sudden shifts in career movement which might indicate lack of maturity or changed aspirations; degree of mobility, as shown by the number of jobs held *vis-a-vis* years of employment; and reason for wanting the job.

Information on personal data sheets can also be used to predict job stability and reduce turnover. (18) Now, efforts are being made to seek *attitudinal information* on the application blank which can be used in subsequent interviews. (19)

Requirements for effective use of biographical inventories

The use of this instrument for selection purposes can be improved by using different forms at different steps in the procedure. For example, a short, simple application form can be used for preliminary screening, a longer WAB or BIB can be used for later, more intensive analysis. Different forms could be used for different occupations. In any case, the *information must be cross-validated with other predictors and criteria.*

To be valid, the information must be updated, for one survey showed consistent decrease in the predictive value of the application blank with the passage of time. (20)

EVALUATING TEST RESULTS

When the word "testing" is used, most people immediately think of selection and *predicting* subsequent job performance. Yet, more companies *do not use* tests than do. Also, tests are used for other purposes, such as *evaluating* the performance, abilities, knowledge, and other attributes of present employees.

In spite of their controversial nature, tests are still one of the major methods of uncovering qualifications and talents that would go unnoticed in interviews, biographical inventories, and other instruments of selection. (21)

This section will look at some criticisms of testing, arguments in favor of tests, types of tests, and some requirements for effective testing.

Criticisms of tests

Among the major criticisms of testing, the following are the most frequent and—from the personnel executive's viewpoint—the most relevant. It has been found that tests: (22)

a. Do not show a particularly impressive correlation with actual performance;
b. Any intelligent person can fake the answers on some tests to produce whatever pattern of score desired;
c. Tests are an "invasion of privacy," for they pry into matters that are of no concern to anyone except the applicant, and, by so doing, they encourage undue conformity; and
d. Because they are numerically scored, they tend to acquire an aura of finality and objectivity that is unwarranted by the results obtained.

Only the last two of these criticisms will be discussed at this time.

Tests are pseudoscientific. The last mentioned criticism implies that testing often only makes the selection process *appear* to be more scientific, while in fact it is claimed that many of the earlier tests had very little validity. It has been said that the public guidelines have not had that much effect because "much of what was lost without personnel tests was never there in the first place." (23)

Tests are an invasion of privacy. The "invasion of privacy" argument is becoming much more heated at the present time. This issue was raised by William H. Whyte, Jr., when he suggested that personality testing was an invasion of privacy. He even provided some guidelines to enable an applicant to "pass" any personality test and, thus, evade the privacy issue. (24)

How valid is this criticism? Apparently there is considerable concern, for a recent study found general sensitivity against questions dealing with religion and racial or ethnic background (which are now illegal to ask anyway); finances, particularly other sources of income, savings, budgeting, and loans; and members of the family. Specifically *female employees* were concerned with subjects dealing with their past history; *younger employees* were more concerned with questions about their value systems; and the *more educated* were concerned with questioning of their personal finances. (25)

What are personnel executives doing about this charge? The following case is one example.

> IBM, as a result of generally enlightened personnel policies and because the computers they produce have a great ability to invade privacy, recently dropped personality tests for job applicants and existing personnel. They also dropped the use of outside investigative agencies to check references or credit standings. (26)

Arguments in favor of tests

Among the arguments in favor of tests, the following are most pertinent. It has been found that: (27)

a. The abuse of privacy and the damage to individual careers are not inherent in testing but result from its unscrupulous use;
b. The use of tests to weed out individualists springs from an oversimplification of—and obsolete notion about—how test scores should be interpreted;

c. Sophisticated testers recognize that in most institutions success can be achieved in more ways than one and by more than one kind of person. (Thus, tests can be used to screen out job applicants who will pass other forms of evaluation but who will fail in the training period or shortly thereafter; the reverse of this can also be true.);
d. Since a person's opinion of another individual may involve some bias, it will tend to differ from the opinion of other observers, so testing provides one of the few available selection instruments with objectivity; and
e. There is research evidence that individuality can be assessed and measured with accuracy, and, thus, recognition can be given to real merit.

Types of tests

While *it is essential for each organization to validate* the tests it uses with its own staff, with different groupings of its own personnel, and for specific jobs, there is no need for it to develop its own tests. There are over 1,000 tests commercially available, most of them distributed by a few firms that specialize in developing and using tests. (28)

The types of test can be classified according to *format* or *characteristics* measured. (29)

By format. As for format, tests can be classified as subjectively or objectively scored, speed versus power, group versus individual, or performance versus "paper-and-pencil."

Subjectively versus objectively scored. Although some tests can be scored subjectively, most selection tests are objective because of ease of administering and grading, as well as being more reliable.

Speed versus power. *Speed tests* have a fixed time limit for the respondent to answer all the questions. A *power test* is administered without time limits, for the results are dependent upon the ability to provide the answers, regardless of time.

Group versus individual. Individual tests are used extensively in clinical and vocational guidance activities. But, for selection purposes, particularly if there are a large number of applicants, it is more economical and objective to give the test in groups.

Performance versus "paper-and-pencil." Performance tests involve manipulation of some type of apparatus or equipment, or doing a specific job. The "paper-and-pencil" tests require the applicant to make marks or write answers on an answer sheet.

By characteristics measured. Tests can also be classified on the basis of personal characteristics sought from the applicant, including intelligence, aptitudes, interests, personality, and achievement (proficiency).

Intelligence. These tests have been widely used as a selection instrument to measure mental ability or general learning ability. There is no generally accepted definition of intelligence because there is such a diversity of concepts as to what is included. However, Thurstone has isolated the specific types of mental abilities that most of these tests attempt to measure, namely, inductive reasoning, memory, numerical facility, spatial visualization, speed of perception, and verbal comprehension. (30)

Regardless of the definition, the outstanding feature of these tests is the ability to predict the general capacity for learning and/or problem solving.

Sometimes these tests are used to measure the abilities of children and youth, in which case they are frequently stated in terms of *intelligence quotients* (IQ), or the ratio of mental age, which is defined by test performance, to chronological age. These IQs are less meaningful, so percentile ranks are used.

The most popular intelligence tests are the *Wonderlic Personnel Test* (31), *Otis Quick-Scoring Mental Ability Tests* (32), and *Thurstone Test of Mental Alertness* (33).

Aptitudes. In general, aptitude tests measure the specific capacity of an individual to learn a given job, provided there is adequate training. While there are several types of aptitudes or capacities for which tests are available, the personnel executive is more interested in those dealing with clerical and mechanical aptitudes.

Clerical aptitude tests include the *Short Employment Tests* (SET) and *Minnesota Clerical Tests.* (34) The *mechanical aptitude tests* include the *Bennett Test of Mechanical Comprehension* and the revised *Minnesota Paper Form Board Test.* (35)

Probably the most widely used general inventory of aptitudes is the *General Aptitude Test Battery* (GATB), developed by the U.S. Department of Labor for use by state public employment offices. (36)

How valid are aptitudes tests in predicting "trainability" and job proficiency? Ghiselli did a very comprehensive study of the findings of other studies regarding the validity of these tests, using the Pearsonian Coefficient of Correlation. For managerial occupations; clerical operations; sales; protective service; vehicle operators; trades and crafts; and industrial occupations, the aptitudes tests proved to be of value in predicting success. (37)

Interests. While intelligence, aptitude, and achievement tests are basic to most personnel selection programs, they rarely yield validity coefficients sufficiently high. Therefore, as some job applicants selected on the basis of these test scores alone will fail as employees, the validity of their cognitive value can be supplemented with tests of employee interests and personality. Interests are derived from both hereditary and environmental factors. Therefore, they should help predict a person's success on the job if the interests and the jobs are matched.

The more popular interest tests are designed to discover patterns of individual interest which are associated with success in various types of jobs. The most widely used ones are the *Kuder Preference Record* (38) and Strong's *Vocational Interest Blank.* (39)

Personality. Some personnel specialists tend to regard "personality" as a basic prerequisite of success, especially in supervisory or managerial positions. They feel that selective personality characteristics may be even more important than job knowledge or skill, as emotional maturity influences the ability to withstand stress and strain, to be objective, and to gain the respect and cooperation of others.

There are two types of these tests, namely, questionnaires and projective techniques. The first are essentially an inventory of characteristics to be completed by the individual. The projective techniques ask the individual to interpret human behavior—either real or simulated. This tends to project the individual's personality for examination, evaluation, and assessment.

Among the more popular of the projective tests are the *Rorschach Test* and the *Murray Thematic Apperception Test* (TAT) and a modification known as the *Thematic Evaluation of Managerial Potential* (TEMP).

Siegel and Lane have concluded that for most employment positions, personality assessment is of "dubious validity and, therefore, may constitute an unwarranted invasion of privacy." (40)

After investigating 95 different validation studies on 15 leading personality inventories, 11 validation studies on 6 projective tests, and 11 validation studies on 3 special inventories, it was concluded by Guion and Gottier that "it is difficult in the face of this summary to advocate, with a clear conscience, the use of personality measures in most situations as a basis for making employment decisions about people." (41)

Achievement or proficiency. Most of the tests described have measured *potential.* Yet, personnel executives are often looking for seasoned, experienced workers with a knowledge of a given job. In other words, if the personnel department is looking for someone who knows how to do a certain job—now—one of these trade tests is probably preferable. Most of the *trade tests* currently being used are not for general distribution, as they have been developed for, and are used by, individual organizations. However, some tests have been published in areas such as stenographic proficiency, blueprint reading, industrial electricity, machine shop tool handling, and procedures proficiency. In addition to identifying abilities to perform the job, these tests are sometimes convenient in spotting "trade bluffers," or people who claim knowledge and job experience they do not possess. (42)

A specialized form of achievement test is *work sampling,* or *work previews.* Such a test consists of having the prospective employee do a task that is representative of the work actually to be done on the job. It must include the more crucial aspects of job performance in order to be valid. In addition to seeing whether the prospective employee is able to do the job, it also provides the latter with realistic job expectations. (43)

Requirements for effective testing

Assuming that an organization is going to use tests, the testing program can be made more productive and rewarding by accepting the following suggestions.

Test the tests. Every testing program should be subjected to frequent critical review and should be a potential candidate for replacement. In other words, the tests should be thoroughly tested themselves. (44)

Use only with other instruments. Having established the fact that individuals differ in many characteristics, personnel executives realize that these differences are more important in selecting employees than are the similarities, even though the latter are more numerous. Certain of these abilities and characteristics can be measured more accurately and economically by tests than by any other means. Thus, the recruitment program can become more systematic, and selection can be improved through the use of testing. However, it must be *used with discretion* and *only in conjunction with the other selection techniques.*

Use battery of tests. Except when using proficiency tests to determine an applicant's ability to perform a specific job, it is more effective to use a battery of tests rather than relying upon a single one. If the applicant takes several tests measuring the characteristics discussed earlier and if those test scores are grouped into a *profile,* it will better indicate whether the applicant's characteristics fit the job requirements than if a single test score is used.

Use only validated tests. Whether an organization designs its own tests or uses commercially available ones, they should be validated with the institution's own work force before being used as a selection instrument. Only when the test itself is tested can there be any degree of confidence placed in its ability to predict job performance successfully. (45)

Use discretion in scoring. There are two or three thoughts which are applicable at this point. First, testing can make the greatest contribution in situations where it is relatively difficult to obtain satisfactory employees by using the other selection instruments, such as biographical data or interviews. Thus, testing would probably not be useful in selecting unskilled labor for routine, well-defined jobs.

Second, tests probably do a more commendable job of separating individuals at the extreme of the normal curve of distribution rather than selecting *one individual for a given job.* In other words, they are more useful in selecting *groups of people* from which other techniques can be used to select *the specific employee(s).* (46)

Third, while most tests can be easily scored by trained clerks using a *key,* or a *template,* laid over an answer sheet, the *raw* score so obtained is relatively meaningless until interpreted. Also, a *critical,* or *cut-off,* score is usually predetermined. However, this is not a totally fixed score, as it tends to vary up or down depending upon the number of available applicants relative to the need for their services. While the raw scoring can be done by a skilled clerk, the interpretation should be done only by a personnel specialist.

Others. Other requirements for effective testing are: (a) cost, which is not great for even high-quality tests; (b) time, with a preference for shorter tests; and (c) ease of administration and scoring, as those requiring the service of expert testers may not be feasible.

USING THE INTERVIEW TO EVALUATE APPLICANTS

The interview is probably the most widely used personnel technique, particularly in the selection procedure. Surveys show that almost all personnel managers use this method at some stage in the selection procedure. It is also used for other purposes, such as appraisals, counseling, merit rating, handling grievances, and as an exit interview to gather information when employees leave the organization.

Uses in selection procedure

The main reason for using the interview in selection is to permit the personnel manager to meet the applicant in a personal relationship in order to evaluate characteristics of the applicant which cannot be evaluated elsewhere.

Why used? There are two characteristics of interviewing which set it aside from the other instruments. First, it is *quite flexible* and can be used for many different types of jobs and applicants. Consequently, there can be a division of labor. For example, the personnel executive can attempt to evaluate "personality," including motives, attitudes, and other personal characteristics which would indicate the applicant's compatibility with the organization; the operating managers can try to determine technical abilities, experience, and expertise.

A second characteristic of the interview is its *two-way nature;* it permits the interviewer to learn more about the job applicant, while permitting the applicant to learn about the opportunities, challenges, and limitations of the organization. This information exchange characteristic is particularly important for college recruiters. Also, this characteristic is present in orientation and termination interviews. This instrument is the only one which provides this two-way communication.

How used? The selection interview can be used either (*a*) to supplement biographical data, test scores, or references and physical examinations, or (*b*) as a selection instrument itself.

If it is used as a *supplement to other instruments,* all available data should be made available to the interviewer in advance. Therefore, the interviewer can have reached some *tentative* conclusions prior to the interview, based upon the other data.

If used as a *selection instrument,* it will probably be more effective if the interviewer has very little information about the candidate in advance. Information concerning biographical data, attitudes, and belief systems should then be obtained directly from the applicant by the interviewer independently of the other sources of information.

Methods used in interviewing

The methods used in interviewing (47) can be classified in several ways, including: (*a*) the degree of structure; (*b*) the degree of depth; and (*c*) the number of interviewers used.

Degree of structure. Interviews may be either structured or unstructured, directed or nondirected, guided or unguided, and patterned or unpatterned. As each of the types of interviews has advantages and disadvantages, the one used will depend upon where it occurs and how it is used in the selection procedure. Regardless of the term used, the primary differences are in the type information sought, the way the questions are asked, the way the answers are interpreted, and the extent to which the questions are related to the specifications of the job to be filled.

Unstructured interview. In the unstructured interview, the patterns of questions asked, the circumstances under which the questions are asked, and the bases for evaluating the replies—relative to the job being considered—are not standardized. As these factors vary between interviewers and between applicants, this type interview is highly subjective, which may lead to quite diverse conclusions concerning the suitability of a given applicant.

There is no such thing as a *totally unstructured* interview, for any experienced interviewer approaches the assignment with some objective in mind and some general understanding as to how to achieve the objective. However, in this type interview, the main thrust of the discussion is for the applicant to do most of the talking and asking of questions. The interviewer is to provide the stimuli needed to bring forth the desired information. This approach to interviewing was an outgrowth of the counseling technique developed by Carl Rogers. (48)

An advantage of this method is the possibility of the applicant volunteering information which might be valuable in making an employment decision which might not be forthcoming otherwise.

In addition to the problems of reliability and validity inherent in this method, which will be discussed later, there is the unique problem that the interviewer might talk too much during the interview. Research shows this tends to lead to a higher rating of the applicant. (49) This tendency seems to be particularly true in college recruiting, for one study found that most of the students thought the interviewer talked too much. In an examination of 31 tape-recorded interviews, the interviewers did 60 percent of the talking. (50)

Structured interview. Structured interviews are typically developed for particular jobs in specific organizations. These interviews are both *standardized* and *controlled* relative to the questions to be asked, the sequence in which they are asked, the interpretation of the replies, and the weight to be given to critical factors to be considered in making the value judgments.

The most popular patterned interview guide is the *McMurry Patterned Interview Form,* shown in Figure 10–2. The questions to the left of the blanks are to be asked of the applicant during the interview, while those below the line are to help the interviewer evaluate the information being presented and to use it in making the employment decision.

One survey of 273 firms found only 26 percent of them using a patterned interview. (51)

Degree of depth. The depth of questioning varies from the superficial preliminary interview looking for obvious differences between the applicant

FIGURE 10–2
McMurry patterned interview form

S U M M A R Y	Rating: 1 2 3 4 Interviewer _____ Date _____
	Comments (List both favorable and unfavorable points) _____
	In making final rating, be sure to consider not only the man's ability and experience but also his stability, industry, perseverance, ability to get along with others, loyalty, self-reliance, and leadership. Is he mature and realistic?
	Is he well motivated for this work? Are his living standards, finances, his domestic situation, and the family influence favorable to this work?
	Does he have sufficient health and physical reserve?
	_____ Position Considered for _____

Name _____ Telephone Number _____ Is it your phone? _____
Present Address _____ City _____ State _____
Will this location affect his attendance? Is this a desirable neighborhood? Does it appear consistent with income?
Date of your birth _____ Age _____ Have you served in the Armed Services of the United States? ☐ Yes ☐
In some States, legislation forbids discrimination because of age.
(If yes) What were the dates? _____ 19 __ to _____ 19 __ If rejected or exempted, what were the reasons? _____
Discuss military service as a job in chronological order with other jobs. Will this affect his performance on our job?
Why are you applying for this position? _____
Are his underlying reasons practical? Does he have a definite goal?
Are you employed now? ☐ Yes ☐ No;   (If yes) how soon available? _____
What are relationships with present employer?

WORK HISTORY: LAST OR PRESENT POSITION   Dates from _____ 19 __ to _____ 19 __
If out of work—how long?
Company _____ Division _____ Address _____
Does this check with application?
How did you get this job? _____
Did he show self-reliance in getting this job? Stability of interests? Perseverance?
Nature of work at start _____ Earnings at start _____
Did this work require energy and industry? Close attention? Cooperation?
How did the job change? _____ Earnings at leaving _____
Was progress made? Any indications of strong motivation? Is this in line with what he can earn here?
What were your duties and responsibilities at time of leaving? _____
Did he accept them? Indications of industry? Self-reliance? Perseverance? Leadership?
Superior _____ Title _____ How was he to work with? _____
Was this close supervision? Are there indications of loyalty? Hostility?
What did you especially like about the position? _____
Has he been happy and content in his work? Indications of loyalty, ability to get along with others?
What did you especially dislike? _____
Did he get along well with people? Is he inclined to be critical? Were his dislikes justified?
How much time have you lost from work? _____ Reasons _____
Is he regular in attendance on the job? Are there other interests?
Reasons for leaving _____ Why right then? _____
Are his reasons for leaving reasonable and consistent? Do they check with records?
Part-time jobs during this employment _____
Does this indicate industry? Ambition? Lack of loyalty? Lack of interest in duties of position?

NEXT TO LAST POSITION   Dates from _____ 19 __ to _____ 19 __
Any time between this and last job?
Company _____ Division _____ Address _____
Does this check with application?
How did you get this job? _____
Did he show self-reliance in getting this job? Stability of interests? Perseverance?
Nature of work at start _____ Earnings at start _____
Did this work require energy and industry? Close attention? Cooperation?
How did the job change? _____ Earnings at leaving _____
Was progress made? Any indications of strong motivation? Is this in line with what he can earn here?
What were your duties and responsibilities at time of leaving? _____
Did he accept them? Indications of industry? Self-reliance? Perseverance? Leadership?
Superior _____ Title _____ How was he to work with? _____
Was this close supervision? Are there indications of loyalty? Hostility?

Source: Published by the Dartnell Corporation, Chicago. First page only is reproduced with permission. © The Dartnell Corporation, Chicago.

and the job to be filled, to the in-depth interview covering different areas of the applicant's personal, family, social, educational, economic, and work backgrounds. There are many guides which can be obtained from commercial establishments to be used in asking the questions and evaluating the answers.

The two most popular ones are the *Diagnostic Interviewer's Guide* (DIG) and the *Depth Interview Pattern.* (52)

The *stress interview* was developed during World War II as a method of selecting personnel for espionage activities. While no meaningful research has validated the effectiveness of this technique in selecting individuals in civilian employment, it is still used frequently in choosing managerial personnel. Some forms it takes are:

1. The interviewer will fire rapid questions at the applicant and suddenly stop, fold his arms, and stare at the applicant;
2. The applicant will be invited to draw up a chair and sit down, only to find a cord to a lamp entwined around one of the legs;
3. An applicant will be invited to smoke, only to find there is no ashtray; or
4. A group of interviewers will fire questions at the applicant in an unfriendly, or even hostile, manner.

This method is *not being advocated* but is presented for the reader as a guide in case such a situation is ever encountered.

Number of interviewers. Research has indicated that decisions made by individual interviewers are notoriously unreliable because of the marked differences between the evaluation of the same applicant by two or more interviewers.

In order to overcome these difficulties, many companies now use multiple interviewing. Under this arrangement, the prospective employee is interviewed by two or more individuals in order to obtain the judgment of more than one person. Although this method provides different views and judgments, one individual must ultimately make the final decision to hire while the others can merely advise.

Whether the individual or group approach is used will be determined by the purpose of the interview and the economy in terms of time and effort of the applicant and the executives.

Constraints on the use of the interview

There are both procedural and perceptual constraints on the use of interviewing. The first deals with *how* the interviewing is done; the second involves the *way* both parties view it.

Some procedural constraints. There are at least three constraints on the use of the interview, namely, its reliability, its validity, and environmental factors.

Some reliability problems. By definition, reliability is consistency in measurement. When applied to interviewing, there are two types of reliability—intrarater and interrater reliability, each of which can affect its usefulness in predicting success.

The *intrarater reliability* problems revolve around the ability of the same interviewer to rate the same interviewee the same way during subsequent interviews, or when listening to a tape of the original interview. This type of unreliability seems to pose no insurmountable problem in interviewing, as it can be overcome when the interviewer is made aware of the difficulty.

The *interrater reliability* problems, which tend to involve the ability of two or more interviewers to evaluate the same applicant on essentially the same characteristics used in selection, is more difficult to overcome. The extent of reliability is a function of the amount of information available about the job and the method used in interviewing. A study comparing interviewer agreement in evaluating candidates with and without detailed descriptions of the job to be filled found higher reliability with specific details than without. (53)

The other variable affecting interrater reliability is the degree of structure used. The unstructured interview has been proven to be notoriously unreliable. In an experimental situation, experienced interviewers were asked to evaluate the credentials of 243 hypothetical applicants for a secretarial position. The interviewers not only differed in the weight which should be assigned to each of the factors included in the credentials, but also in their evaluation of the likelihood of job success. (54)

Conversely, structured interviews have shown greater reliability, as well as validity. In general, it can be *hypothesized* that *structured interviews tend to result in greater reliability and validity than unstructured interviews.* In general, this hypothesis has been shown to be valid from the research findings. (55)

Some validity problems. The interview, even when structured and with trained interviewers, still shows questionable validity. After examining over 300 articles on interviewing, Mayfield was critical of its validity as a selection instrument. (56) A different conclusion was reached by Ghiselli, who believed that the validity of the ordinary personnel interview was at least equal to—if not even greater than—the validity of tests. (57)

It can probably be concluded that interviewing validity is enhanced through having structured interviews and separating the collection of the information from the interpretation of the information. (58)

Some environmental factors. As indicated in earlier chapters, public policy dictates what questions can and cannot be asked of individuals seeking equal employment opportunities. Suffice to say, questions that *imply* selection will be based upon sex, race, creed, color, nation of origin, or age cannot be asked. (59)

Some perceptual constraints. In addition to the procedural problems involved with interviewing, there are some perceptual problems. As the interview involves a very dynamic, interpersonal relationship between two individuals, there is the danger of: (*a*) a lack of rapport; (*b*) bias; (*c*) the "halo" effect; and (*d*) the contrast effect. To be most effective, great care must be taken to select and train interviewers to be aware of these problem areas.

Lack of rapport. As practically every person experiences some degree of tension and anxiety during an interview—especially for a desired job, it is up to the interviewer to develop a feeling of warmth, understanding, and relaxation at the beginning of the interview—if valid information is to be obtained.

Bias. A danger in interviewing, which tends not to be present in the other selection instruments, is the tendency of interviewers to let their biases and preconceptions about people influence their decisions as to whether to hire an individual or not. Indeed, one study found that recruiters often consider the applicant's personal appearance as the most important variable in the interview, in spite of the fact that this hypothesis has not been verified by research. (60)

The "halo" effect. There is a tendency for us to generalize from some specific characteristic to a conclusion based upon that characteristic. If the interviewer approves of the way the interviewee knocks on the door, is dressed, or other outward manifestations, the tendency is to use that as a basis for reaching conclusions concerning the applicant's employability.

The converse of this tendency is the *horn effect,* whereby some negative characteristic is used to reach a negative employment decision.

The contrast effect. When groups of individuals are being interviewed, there is the danger that one applicant will be compared and contrasted with the previous one(s). If the previous applicant was "outstanding" and the present interviewee does not *appear* to measure up, there is the danger of rating the individual lower than otherwise. The converse is also possible. This tendency *tends* to come into effect with applicants who have intermediate qualifications, rather than those at the extremes of either "good" or "poor." (61) This research indicated that the contrast effect may account for up to 80 percent of the variation in ratings of the "average" applicants when they follow several exceptionally "poorly qualified" or "well-qualified" interviewees.

The decision-making process. If we know how the decision is made in the employment interview, then we will know how to improve its use. The McGill University studies attempted to ascertain how interviewers reached their decisions. In general, it was found that: (*a*) a bias develops early in the interview and influences the final decision; (*b*) the unfavorable factors have more influence than favorable ones; (*c*) when the interviewers receive all the information concurrently, their judgment is better than when it is received in bits and pieces; and (*d*) the more experienced interviewers tend to be more selective than less experienced ones, but there is a high degree of consistency in the percentage of applicants accepted by the experienced interviewers. (62)

IMPLICATIONS AND APPLICATIONS FOR PERSONNEL EXECUTIVES

Hopefully this discussion of the evaluation stage of the selection procedure has demonstrated the value of evaluating biographical inventories, testing, and interviewing in assessing applicants for employment.

Using biographical inventories

Almost all institutions, from the smallest to the largest, use some form of application blanks as a selection technique. However, the smaller ones *tend* to use the forms only for information gathering, but not so much for evaluation and assessment. Yet, as they tend to use fewer techniques than larger organizations, they should use them more effectively.

As has been shown by research studies, the use of well-developed, statistically validated, and expertly administered biographical inventories—especially the WAB and BIB—can improve prediction in selection. In other words, these instruments can significantly increase the personnel executive's chances of selecting the "right" person for the "right" job. This is particularly true when the results of the analysis of application blanks are related to other selection techniques such as personnel investigations and employment interviews.

Using tests

The basic assumptions underlying the use of testing are that *there are significant differences in the characteristics of individuals,* that *these characteristics can be adequately and accurately measured for comparative purposes,* and that *there is a direct and positive correlation between the extent or intensity of these characteristics and the person's performance on the job.*

From these assumptions, the premise is reached that *future job performance of an employee is determined by the same elements as found in one's test behavior.* Based upon these assumptions and this premise, it can be hypothesized that *one person's performance on a group of reliable tests is a valid predictor of subsequent job performance.*

While testing is still one of the more controversial elements of personnel selection, a careful reading of the court decisions, as well as the EEOC and OFCCP guidelines, indicate that tests which are *culturally unbiased,* which are *job-related,* and which are not used in conjunction with other employment instruments in such a way as to discriminate against minorities, are acceptable instruments for selection.

In essence, properly administered tests are construed to be behavior samples from which inferences as to future behavior and productivity can be made. However, the generalization can be made that a significant number of personnel tests are underdeveloped, and considerably more effort is needed to develop them and improve their use.

While there is a tendency for larger institutions to use testing, there is no reason smaller ones cannot obtain the services of a consultant to use *validated* commercial tests and then evaluate the results for the personnel executive.

Using interviews

As the interview is so universally used, and as it is the technique which provides both the interviewer and the interviewee a chance to get information about the other, and as it is a point in the selection procedure where the other information can be brought into focus, its use should be continued.

Yet, there are procedural and perceptual problems which need correcting for interviewing to be most effective. One problem is the inability of interviewers to reach consistent conclusions concerning applicants. There are many reasons for the poor performance of interviewers. One of these is the careless, slipshod procedure used by many recruiters. Second, the interviewers spend a disproportionate amount of their time selling the company to the applicant as compared to the time spent uncovering information about the prospective employee. As indicated earlier, many interviewers empathize with the interviewee more than they should and, therefore, are unable to reach objective decisions. These weaknesses lead to the third fault, selective perception, whereby the interviewers see only the qualities and obtain only the information that they desire. Experience has verified this weakness by showing that first impressions, which tend to be erroneous, play a large part in the hiring of personnel. Permeating all of these difficulties is the practice of many interviewers of excessive reliance upon intuition: they permit their own emotional reactions to a person, rather than objective criteria, to influence their choice of employees.

In summary, interviews are almost universally used in evaluating and appraising applicants. However, to make its use more effective, the patterned interview should be used, with the information collecting and the evaluation phases being separated. Finally, interviewers should not only be highly selected, but also trained in this art.

DISCUSSION QUESTIONS

1. What are the requirements for effective use of selection techniques?
2. Describe how you would use the biographical inventory as a selection instrument.
3. Are the criticisms against use of tests valid? If not, can you justify the use of tests? Explain!
4. Briefly describe the various tests used in the selection process.
5. What advantages do interviews have over other selection instruments? Can you justify from personal experience that interviewers do most of the talking? (See reference 50).
6. Briefly describe the different kinds of interviews used.

REFERENCES AND SUGGESTIONS FOR FURTHER STUDY

1. This discussion is based upon a seminar conducted by Professor Laurence Siegel and from the book by him and Irving M. Lane, *Psychology in Industrial Organizations*, 3d. ed. (Homewood, Ill.: Richard D. Irwin, Inc., 1974).
2. See Ernest J. McCormick and Angelo S. DeNisi, "An Alternate Approach to Test Validation," *The Personnel Administrator*, vol. 21, no. 1 (January 1976), pp. 56–59.
3. Richard J. Walsh and Lee R. Hess, "The Small Company, EEOC, and Test Validation Alternatives: Do You Know Your Options?" *Personnel Journal*, vol. 53, no. 11 (November 1974), pp. 840–45.

4. See Gene E. Buton, "Some Problems of Minority Recruiting," *Journal of College Placement*, vol. 35, no. 2 (Winter 1975), pp. 71–73, for further results. In summary form, they were:

Job value comparisons between nonwhite and white students

		Nonwhite		White		
Job value	I/E	Rank	Means	Rank	Means	T
Opportunity for advancement..........	I	1	5.909	1	6.486	−2.89‡
Opportunity for self-development	I	1	5.909	3	6.197	−1.44
Freedom on the job	I	1	5.909	5	6.032	−0.62
Job security.......................	E	4	5.818	8	5.564	1.30
Fringe benefits.....................	E	5	5.636	11	5.174	2.33†
Challenge and responsibility..........	I	6	5.545	2	6.436	−4.45‡
Type of work	I	6	5.545	4	6.124	−2.89‡
Salary	E	8	5.364	6	5.908	−2.72‡
Working conditions..................	E	9	5.0	12	4.995	0.02
Working with people.................	I	10	4.818	7	5.90	−5.40‡
Training...........................	I	10	4.818	9	5.353	−2.68‡
Company reputation.................	E	10	4.818	10	5.220	−2.01*
Job title...........................	E	13	4.545	14	4.404	0.71
Location of work	E	14	4.364	13	4.844	−2.40†

I = Intrinsic job value.
E = Extrinsic job value.

* Significant beyond .05.
† Significant beyond .01.
‡ Significant beyond .005.

5. See 401 U.S. 424 (1971).
6. See 422 U.S. 405 (1975).
7. See 29 C.F.R., Part 1607, for these guidelines.
8. For a scholarly analysis of the issues involved in this aspect of employment testing, see Robert M. Guion, "Employment Tests and Discriminatory Hiring," *Industrial Relations*, vol. 5, no. 2 (February 1966), pp. 20–37.
9. D. J. Weiss, R. V. Dawis, G. W. England, and L. H. Lofquist, *Validity of Work Histories Obtained by Interview* (Minneapolis, Minn.: University of Minnesota, Industrial Relations Center, Studies in Vocational Rehabilitation, no. 12, 1961).
10. Irving L. Goldstein, "The Application Blank: How Honest Are the Responses?" *Journal of Applied Psychology*, vol. 55, no. 5 (October 1971), pp. 491–92.
11. Allen J. Schuh, "The Predictability of Employee Tenure: A Review of the Literature," *Personnel Psychology*, vol. 20, no. 2 (Summer 1967), pp. 133–52.
12. James J. Asher, "The Biographical Item: Can It Be Improved?" *Personnel Psychology*, vol. 25, no. 2 (Summer 1972), p. 255 ff.
13. For further information, see George W. England, *Development and Use of Weighted Application Blanks* (Minneapolis, Minn.: Industrial Relations Center, University of Minnesota, 1969).
14. The following citations provide the source of the research findings for each occupation: (*a*) Richard D. Scott and Richard W. Johnson, "Use of the Weighted Application Blank in Selecting Unskilled Employees," *Journal of Applied Psychology*, vol. 51, no. 5 (October 1967), pp. 393–95; (*b*) Marvin D. Dunnette and James Maetzold, "Use of a Weighted Application Blank in Hiring Seasonal

Employees," *Journal of Applied Psychology,* vol. 39, no. 5 (May 1955), pp. 308–10; (*c*) Dale Zechar, "Auto Insurance Rating: Measure of the Man?" *Personnel Journal,* vol. 49, no. 4 (April 1970), p. 315; (*d*) J. R. Hinrichs, "Technical Selection: How to Improve Your Batting Average," *Personnel,* vol. 37, no. 2 (March–April 1960), pp. 56–60; (*e*) Melany E. Bachs and Glenn B. Williams, "Prediction of Sales Success from Factorially Determined Dimensions of Personal Background Data," *Journal of Applied Psychology,* vol. 52, no. 1 (February 1968), pp. 29–30; (*f*) Edwin E. Wagner, "Predicting Success for Young Executives from Objective Test Scores and Personal Data," *Personnel Psychology,* vol. 13, no. 2 (Summer 1960), p. 181 ff.; (*g*) R. Wayne Mondy, Frank N. Edens, and R. Wayne Gober, "Predicting Employment Tenure of Women Managers," The *Spectrum,* accepted for publication; (*h*) William C. Byham, *The Uses of Personnel Research,* (New York: American Management Assn., Research Study 91, 1950), p. 60; and (*i*) John B. Miner, "Success in Management Consulting and the Concept of Eliteness Motivation," *Academy of Management Journal,* vol. 14, no. 3 (September 1971), pp. 367–78.

15. See the following research studies for a discussion of this point: T. W. Harrell, "The Validity of Biographical Data Items for Food Company Salesmen," *Journal of Applied Psychology,* vol. 44, no. 1 (February 1960), pp. 31–33; W. D. Buel, "Biographical Data and the Identification of Creative Research Personnel," *Journal of Applied Psychology,* vol. 49, no. 5 (October 1965), pp. 318–21; and Howard C. Lockwood and Stuart D. Parsons, "Relationship of Personal History Information to the Performance of Production Supervisors," *Engineering and Industrial Psychology,* vol. 2, no. 1 (Spring 1960), pp. 20–26. The last article explained the use of personal history inventories involving early family life, education, finances, health, and social life. The results proved statistically reliable in appraising subordinates and served as stable and valid predictors of performance of production supervisors, at least in that research situation.

16. Byham, *The Uses of Personnel Research.*

17. Pearl Meyer, "How to Read a Résumé," *Dunn's Business Review,* vol. 96, no. 4 (October 1970), pp. 48–52.

18. Gordon C. Inskeep, "Statistically Guided Employee Selection: An Approach to the Labor Turnover Problem," *Personnel Journal,* vol. 49, no. 8 (August 1970), pp. 15–24.

19. Robert Hershey, "The Application Form," *Personnel,* vol. 48, no. 1 (January–February 1971), pp. 36–39.

20. Schuh, "The Predictability of Employee Tenure," *Personnel Psychology,* pp. 133–52.

21. J. P. Hogue, Jay L. Otis, and Erich P. Prien, "Assessments of High Level Personnel: VI—Validity of Prediction Based on Projective Techniques," *Personnel Psychology,* vol. 15, no. 3 (Autumn 1962), pp. 335–44.

22. There are several sources from which these criticisms originate, but, in order to conserve space, only one source is given for each criticism. They are: (*a*) Andrew H. Souerwine, "More Value from Personnel Testing," *Harvard Business Review,* vol. 39, no. 2 (March–April 1961), pp. 123–30; (*b*) Oakley Gordon, "Do You Use Tests? Are They Worth Anything?" *Personnel Administrator,* vol. 9, no. 5 (September–October 1964), pp. 34–35 and 37; (*c*) Joan Zola, "Adventures of a Test Taker," *National Review,* vol. 17, no. 2 (January 12, 1965), pp. 21–23; and

(d) J. G. Phelan, "Projective Techniques in the Selection of Management Personnel," *Journal of Protective Techniques,* vol. 26, no. 1 (March 1962), pp. 102–4.

23. Laurence Lipsett, "Selecting Personnel without Tests," *Personnel Journal,* vol. 51, no. 9 (September 1972), pp. 648–54.
24. *The Organization Man* (Garden City, N.Y.: Doubleday & Co., 1957), p. 48 ff.
25. Bernard L. Rosenbaum, "Attitudes Toward Invasion of Privacy in the Personnel Selection Process, and Job Applicant Demographic and Personality Correlates," *Journal of Applied Psychology,* vol. 58, no. 3 (December 1973), pp. 333–38.
26. Alan L. Otten, "Privacy Pioneer," *Wall Street Journal* (October 2, 1975), p. 14.
27. There are several sources for each of these arguments, but, in the interest of conserving space, only one source is given for each argument. They are: (a) Richard S. Barrett, "Guide to Using Psychological Tests," *Harvard Business Review,* vol. 41, no. 5 (September–October 1963), pp. 138–46; (b) Donald F. Hueber, "Projective Techniques in Personnel Selection," *Personnel Journal,* vol. 42, no. 11 (December 1963), pp. 563–69; (c) Marvin D. Dunnette, "A Modified Model for Test Validation and Selection Research," *Journal of Applied Psychology,* vol. 47, no. 5 (October 1963), pp. 317–23; (d) Richard Hodgson, "Personality Appraisal of Technical and Professional Applicants," *Personnel Psychology,* vol. 17, no. 2 (Summer 1964), pp. 167–87; and (e) Marvin D. Dunnette, "Critics of Psychological Tests: Basic Assumptions: How Good?" *Psychology in the Schools* (January 1964), pp. 63–69.
28. For a discussion of some of the types of tests available, see O. K. Buros, ed., *The Seventh Mental Measurements Yearbook* (Highland Park, N.J.: Gryphon Press, 1972). This is a basic reference book summarizing practically all the developments in the field of testing.
29. This discussion of the types of tests has been heavily influenced by Siegel and Lane, *Psychology in Industrial Organizations,* pp. 157–70, as well as from a seminar in "Current Research in Psychology" taken from Professor Siegel.
30. L. L. Thurstone, *Primary Mental Abilities* (Chicago: University of Chicago, Psychometric Laboratory, 1948).
31. For information concerning this test, contact E. F. Wonderlic and Associates, P. O. Box 7, Northfield, Ill. 60094.
32. Distributed by Psychological Corporation, 304 East 45th Street, New York, N.Y. 10017.
33. These two tests can be obtained from Science Research Associates, 259 E. Erie Street, Chicago, Ill. 60011.
34. These can be obtained from the Psychological Corporation. The Minnesota Clerical Test has been predictively validated on the basis of sex. The results showed a significant difference in predictor means in favor of females, as well as significantly higher predictor standard deviations; but no significant criterion measure differences were found. See John A. Fossum, "Subgroup Validation by Sex: Clerical Aptitude and Performance" in *Proceedings of the 35th Annual Meeting of the Academy of Management,* New Orleans, La., August 10, 1975, pp. 216–18.
35. Can be obtained from Psychological Corporation.
36. Can be obtained from the U.S. Employment and Training Administration, Washington, D.C. 20212.

37. Edwin E. Ghiselli, "The Validity of Aptitudes Tests in Personnel Selection," *Personnel Psychology,* vol. 26, no. 4 (Winter 1973), pp. 461–77.
38. Published by Science Research Associates.
39. Published by the Stanford University Press, Stanford, Calif. 94305.
40. Siegel and Lane, *Psychology in Industrial Organizations,* p. 170.
41. Robert M. Guion and Richard F. Gottier, "Validity of Personality Measures in Personnel Selection," *Personnel Psychology,* vol. 18, no. 2 (Summer 1965), p. 164.
42. Dale Yoder, *Personnel Management and Industrial Relations,* 6th ed. (Englewood Cliffs, N.J.: Prentice-Hall, Inc., 1970), p. 312.
43. See Michael A. Raphael, "Work Previews Can Reduce Turnover and Improve Performance," *Personnel Journal,* vol. 54, no. 2 (February 1975), pp. 97–99, for a discussion of how this instrument has been used, especially in the insurance business. One company, using this instrument, had 40 percent of its agents surviving for 12 months, as opposed to 13 percent of those not taking the job sample surviving for that long.
44. Rodney C. Cannedy, "The Development and Validation of Psychological Tests to Predict Employee Tenure," *Dissertation Abstracts International,* vol. 30, no. 3–B (1969), p. 1391.
45. In spite of all of the efforts to validate tests, including equal employment opportunity requirements, it has been reasonably estimated that well over one-half of all industrial firms in the nation have been using unvalidated tests. See David E. Robertson, "Employment Testing and Discrimination," *Personnel Journal,* vol. 54, no. 1 (January 1975), pp. 18–21.
46. See Raymond W. Kulhovy, "Personnel Testing: Validating Selection Instruments," *Personnel,* vol. 48, no. 5 (September–October 1971), pp. 20–24, for a description of how to determine whether a high, medium, or low score is the best predictor of success.
47. The following discussion is influenced by Siegel and Lane, *Psychology in Industrial Organizations,* pp. 149–53.
48. For an excellent discussion of this method, see Carl Rogers, *Counseling and Psychotherapy* (Boston: Houghton Mifflin Co., 1942).
49. Daniel Sydiaha, "Bales' Interaction Process Analysis of Personnel Selection Interviews," *Journal of Applied Psychology,* vol. 45, no. 2 (December 1961), p. 399 ff.
50. Calvin W. Downes, "Perceptions of the Selection Interview," *Personnel Administration,* vol. 32, no. 3 (May–June 1969), pp. 8–23.
51. Milton M. Mandell, *The Employment Interview* (New York: American Management Assn., Research Study No. 47, 1961), p. 23.
52. The first of these can be obtained from Wonderlic & Associates. (See note 31.) The second can be obtained from Judd-Safian Associates, New York.
53. J. A. Langsdale and J. Weitz, "Estimating the Influence of Job Information on Interviewer Agreement," *Journal of Applied Psychology,* vol. 57, no. 1 (February 1973), pp. 23–27.
54. E. Valenzi and I. R. Andrews, "Individual Differences in the Decision Process of Employment Interviews," *Journal of Applied Psychology,* vol. 58, no. 1 (August 1973), pp. 49–53.

55. Earlier research on this subject was codified and evaluated by E. C. Mayfield, "The Selection Interview: A Reevaluation of Published Research," *Personnel Psychology,* vol. 17, no. 3 (Autumn 1964), pp. 239–60. Subsequent research has also tended to agree with this reliability. See D. P. Schwab and H. G. Heneman, III, "Relationship between Interview Structure and Interviewer Reliability in an Employment Situation," *Journal of Applied Psychology,* vol. 53, no. 3 (June 1969), pp. 214–17. Subsequent research tended to verify the tendency for structured interviews to yield higher reliabilities than unstructured interviews. See Herbert G. Heneman, III, "The Impact of Interviewer Training and Interviewer Structure on the Reliability and Validity of the Selection Interview," in the *Proceedings of the 35th Annual Meeting of the Academy of Management,* New Orleans, La., August 10–13, 1975, pp. 231–33.

56. Mayfield, "The Selection Interview," *Personnel Psychology,* pp. 239–60.

57. Edwin E. Ghiselli, "The Validity of a Personnel Interview," *Personnel Psychology,* vol. 19, no. 4 (Winter 1966), pp. 389–94.

58. Donald L. Grant and Douglas W. Bray, "Contributions of the Interview to Assessment of Management Potential," *Journal of Applied Psychology,* vol. 55, no. 1 (February 1969), pp. 24–34.

59. The following articles should be read for valuable guidelines on interviewing these individuals: Jeanne B. Driscoll and H. Richard Hess, "The Recruiter: Woman's Friend or Foe?" *Journal of College Placement,* vol. 34, no. 4 (Summer 1974), pp. 42–50, for an analysis of how differently women interviewees perceive the interview; James Johnston and Paula Asinof, "Interviewing Women," *MBA,* (September 1975), pp. 32–35, for some practical guidelines for interviewing women; William Pickens, "The Interview—The Black's Viewpoint," *Business Horizons,* vol. 13, no. 5 (October 1970), pp. 13–22, for an analysis of the tendency to overemphathize with blacks; and Lipman G. Feld, "15 Questions You Dare Not Ask Job Applicants," *Administrative Management,* vol. 35, no. 6 (June 1974), pp. 20–21, 80–82, for a look at some of the legal ramifications of interviewing.

60. S. J. Carroll, "Beauty, Bias, and Business," *Personnel Administration,* vol. 32, no. 2 (March–April 1969), pp. 21–25.

61. K. Wexley, G. Yukl, S. Kovacs, and R. Sanders, "Importance of Contrast Effects in Employment Interviews," *Journal of Applied Psychology,* vol. 56, no. 1 (February 1972), pp. 45–48.

62. Edward C. Webster, *Decision Making in the Employment Interview* (Montreal: McGill University, Industrial Relations Center, 1964), pp. 85–91.

   A recent study tended to refute these findings but, instead, found (*a*) the majority of interviewers tend to make their recruitment decisions during the second half of the interview; (*b*) there is little appreciable difference at the point in time when *either* a negative or a positive decision is made; and (*c*) interviewers take about the same time during the interview whether the decision is positive or negative. See John M. Huegli and Harvey Tschirgi, *An Investigation of the Relationship of Time to Recruitment Interview Decision Making, Proceedings of the Academy of Management,* 1975, pp. 234–36, for further details.

Chapter 11

Selecting supervisory and executive talent

Shortage of managerial personnel
  Declining number of managers
  Increasing demand for managers
  Changed content of manager's job

Some special aspects of managerial planning
  Organizational planning
  Different levels of management
  Determining requirements of manager's job

How to identify managerial talent
  Some problems involved
  Establishing criteria of job success
  Determining valid predictors of job success

Specialized techniques for identifying and selecting
    executives
  Assessment centers
  Computer assistance

Implications and applications for personnel executives

11
Selecting supervisory and executive talent

Try not to become a man of success but rather try to become a man of value.
ALBERT EINSTEIN

All men are ordinary men: the extraordinary men are those who know it.
G. K. CHESTERTON

Do you want to live longer? Then become a top executive. A recent study by the Metropolitan Life Insurance Company indicates that executives who have reached the highest levels in the business community experience a very favorable longevity. "Captains of industry not only live distinctly longer than men in the general population of the United States but also considerably longer than prominent business executives in general." according to a 16-year follow-up study of 1,078 corporate executives of the 500 industrial corporations ranked by *Fortune* magazine as having had the largest sales in 1957. It was concluded that they "recorded mortality only 63 percent of that of their contemporaries in the general population." (1)

It might be surprising in view of the above findings that the basic premises of this chapter is: In general, *the demand for properly qualified persons to assume managerial positions is greater than the supply of persons available.* It is also assumed that the *top management of an organization wishes to consider all qualified candidates in identifying and selecting its executive talent.* If this premise and assumption are true, it should follow that every progressive organization will have a well-planned and well-run program for selecting its managers.*

The underlying objectives of programs for selecting managerial talent are similar to those discussed in previous chapters. However, while the intent of all selection procedures is to predict future success on the job, the problem is compounded in the selection of persons for executive positions, for here the aim is the *early identification* of individuals with executive potential. That is more difficult than other forms of selection.

---

* In this chapter, the terms "manager," "executive," and "administrator" will be used interchangeably in order to avoid repetition.

This chapter explores the shortage of executive talent and then discusses the procedure for identifying and selecting managerial talent.

SHORTAGE OF MANAGERIAL PERSONNEL

It has been assumed that somehow through a process of natural selection and development, there would be assured a continuing supply of managers to meet the increasing demands for leadership. However, during recent years this assumption has proved invalid. Rapid technological expansion throughout the world has produced a group of managerial elite. However, the increasing pace of this growth has resulted in a severe shortage of management talent in the developed, as well as the less developed, countries, and the deficit appears to be growing.

There is reason for concern because genuine excellence in an organization's management is vital to its competence and leadership. Yet there is an acute shortage of people with the skills necessary for managing expanding economic activities.

The shortage of managerial personnel results from several factors which have tended to decrease the number of managers available while increasing the demand for their services.

Declining number of managers

The birthrate during the 1930s was exceedingly low—at least in the United States. This biological default effectively reduced the number of people who would normally be in the upper middle managerial ranks at the present time and in the top levels during the next decade. This deficit in personnel was further increased by World War II, which through death, injury, or removal from the promotional stream, reduced the number of persons who would presently be in the top management group. Consequently, there is now a shortage of people in the 45–64 age group capable of filling top management jobs.

Second, the lack of appreciation for the importance of management succession during past decades aggravated the shortage. This fact, coupled with the consequent failure to provide the developmental programs for potential managers, has further depleted the supply of this scarce resource.

Finally, the traditional selection model, which sought to link predictors to criterion measures through the correlation coefficient, has also reduced the available supply of potential executives. Under this model, potential managers were subjected to several selection instruments (predictors), which were then correlated with a single criterion measure of job performance—usually supervisor ratings, rank, or salary level. While this method was effective in reducing selection errors, it also eliminated many persons who might have been successful executives if given the opportunity and proper development and guidance.

Now, because of public policies emphasizing equal employment opportunities, as well as increased involvement in multinational activities, many progressive personnel managers are searching for more effective—and equitable—identification and selection procedures.

> A U.S. Labor Department study found that only about 15 percent of a group of black and Indian trainees were considered to have management potential under the traditional selection model—using the usual written tests. When the assessment center approach—using simulation techniques—was used, about 50 percent were found to have promotional possibilities. (2)

Increasing demand for managers

There have been several factors which have magnified the demand for managerial personnel. During the last few decades, managerial philosophy has emphasized group decision making rather than the more dynamic and personal type of leadership. Thus, committees and groups of individuals have been used to make decisions that previously had been made singly.

> General Electric Company, Armco Steel Corporation, Honeywell, and Heublein have all adopted one form or other of group management. Typically these groups include six senior executives.
>
> Sears, Roebuck & Company and Transworld Airlines each have a *group of managers* designated as the "office of the chairman" to share responsibilities for decision making.
>
> International Telephone & Telegraph Corporation, Hartford Fire Insurance Company, and Travelers' Insurance Company have an "office of the president," composed of *a group of managers.*
>
> Aetna Life & Casualty set up a four-man "corporate office" in 1972 with a chairman and chief executive officer. (3)

This emphasis on the multiple-management decision-making process, coupled with a concurrent trend toward a narrower span of management, has aggravated the already grave problem of supplying the number of managers needed.

In addition to the above factors, the sheer increase in the number and the size of organizations of all types is leading to a shortage of managers. The growing number of educational, governmental, health, service, military, religious, and other types of organizations requiring executives have competed with business for the limited supply of available managerial talent.

Changed content of manager's job

In addition to the pressures that have decreased the supply of managers and increased the demand for additional personnel, there is a third factor to consider. This is one which affects both of the others and involves changes in the abilities required for performing the managerial function itself.

Managerial jobs are becoming more difficult, complex, and exacting, and it is becoming increasingly difficult to find people capable of becoming managers. Thus, there is not only an absolute shortage of people in the group from which managers come, but a smaller proportion of them has the capacities and capabilities, developed through education, training, and experience, to cope with modern-day problems.

SOME SPECIAL ASPECTS OF MANAGERIAL PLANNING

A complicating aspect of selecting upper-level managerial personnel is the fact that the incumbent's influence on the organization may have been so great that it reflects one personality. Therefore, one of the first requisites in identifying and selecting managerial personnel is to study the organization to see if changes are needed when bringing in new executives.

Organizational planning

As human resource planning was covered extensively in Chapter 7, only those aspects affecting the need for, and supply of, executive personnel are discussed in this chapter.

Determining the need for managerial personnel. Because of the long lead time required in gaining experience and in educating and developing future executives, their need must be anticipated years in advance. While this is not always possible—or feasible—at least some effort should be made to forecast the future needs in terms of personnel required for expansion—or contraction, as well as for replacements caused by deaths, retirements, resignations, transfers, and "failures."

Need for expansion. Many openings resulting from expansion are filled by recruitment from outside. This is particularly true when technological development, innovation, or changing organizational direction bring about the expansion. Currently there seems to be a stabilizing of organizational expansion, except in public organizations—at least in the United States. Yet, each individual organization must determine for itself what the future needs will be for changes in the number of managers required because of expansion or changes in organizational structure.

Need for replacements. In organizations with well-developed human resource planning systems, predicted losses of key managerial personnel can be projected with a substantial degree of accuracy. For example, losses from retirements, promotions, transfers, dismissals, physical disabilities, and substandard job performance can be estimated from past performance, as modified by current situations.

Retirement, the most common type of anticipated need, and other openings occasioned by movement of personnel within the organization are usually filled by promotion.

Determining the supply of potential managerial personnel. As indicated in Chapter 7, a part of any human resource planning system is either a computer or manual inventory of existing managers, as well as potential personnel to replace them. The latter phase involves searching for people within the organization who have the qualifications for further advancement, including education, development activities, and experience. In addition, such an inventory would specify what further training, development, and/or experience would be desirable—or required—to permit the persons to move up in the organizational hierarchy. This inventory should include not only present and *known* potential abilities, aptitudes, and desires, but also those which have previously remained undiscovered. This point is particularly valid as far as minorities and females are concerned, as often their potentialities have gone unnoticed.

Finally, this inventory should take into consideration the motivation of potential managers, including the ability and willingness to do the training, development, and other activities necessary to move into these positions.

> The Canadian National Railways found in its inventory of 7,500 managers in the middle organizational levels that motivation was very important in their potentialities for future development. In fact, it tended to limit the supply of future managers. (4)

Different levels of management

There is a definite hierarchy of managerial jobs. Therefore, although the principles of management are the same at all levels of the management hierarchy, the responsibilities required of individuals toward their job has a definite growth pattern that usually can be clearly delineated as they advance in the organization. For example, individual workers are accountable for their own performance; first-line supervisors are responsible for seeing that their subordinate workers perform their jobs; managers in the intermediate levels are obligated to integrate and coordinate the overall activities and to feel partially responsible for the company's financial success; while the chief executive officers should be accountable for the overall success of the organization.

Differing personal characteristics. At the various levels, there are different job conditions requiring different characteristics of the persons performing each job. The demands associated with the work managers do tend to mount as they ascend the job levels, and the pressures exerted upon the person performing the work subsequently become more severe. For example, selection of individuals at the lower organizational level is based primarily upon the ability to perform the work associated with the job. In the higher echelons, it was found to be based upon factors such as family background, spouse, and social activities, in addition to ability. (5)

Another study, using a specially designed personality test, found that top managers were better adjusted, less emotional, and liked detail less than clerks and factory workers. (6)

In another study designed to measure the abilities of top management, middle management, supervisors, and workers, it was found that the top two levels were more similar in characteristics than were the bottom two. Also, the top two levels were superior to the bottom two in many respects. This was particularly true for intelligence, supervisory ability, initiative, and self-assurance. (7)

Distinction between supervisory and executive personnel. Although everyone who performs the managerial function is a manager, for purposes of providing management succession a distinction should be made between supervisory and executive personnel.

First, there is a *qualitative difference,* as the losses caused by incompetent supervisors are relatively insignificant compared to those resulting from an incompetent executive.

There is also a *content difference* between the jobs of the two groups. Essentially the supervisor is concerned with details, while the executive's work is broad and general and involves the "whole" job. For the supervisor, the persuasion of subordinates is personal, direct, and immediate; but to the executive it is only incidental to the overall program and often does not involve direct contact with the people to be persuaded. The activities to be performed by the supervisor are relatively well defined within comparatively narrow limits; but the definition and determination of the executive's activities are the most difficult parts of the job, as it is so nonrepetitive. The supervisor is concerned with coordinating the work on individual people; the executive coordinates policies, the physical and human factors, and even institutions. The supervisor's contacts with others permit time to win their acceptance, while the executive often has only a short span of time to make a good impression on others.

Also, the two groups of managers tend to have *different backgrounds.* In general, supervisors are promoted from among the rank-and-file employees, whereas executives tend to come from the professional, technical, and scientific personnel, particularly from college recruits hired as management trainees. Consequently, although a good executive could probably perform the work of a supervisor effectively, it by no means follows that a good supervisor could also perform the job of an executive, even with training and experience.

In summary, future organizations will probably have three administrative classifications. The first will be the *supervisor,* who will continue to supervise work and motivate the workers. Second, there will be the *bureaucrat*—who is variously called "middle-level manager," "operating executive," and "junior executive." This manager will administer a system, and will need skills in using judgment in making decisions and carrying out policies, but will still obey the commands issued from the top of the system. The third classification, the *executive,* will deal almost exclusively with decision making, goal setting, and dealing with the future. The requirements for that job are intelligence and behavior flexibility. (8)

Other differences in managerial personnel. There are many other differences among potential managerial personnel, including their managerial philosophy, the degree of autonomy demanded, the degree of authority exercised, the pace of development and drive, the privileges of office demanded, and the degree of creativity and initiative exercised.

These differences assume importance when it is realized that selection and placement are based upon two basic premises, namely, that there are fundamental differences between persons in one occupation and another, (9) and that there are differences between managers who succeed in a given occupation and those who do not. (10) Although the validity of these premises has never clearly been demonstrated, they do have sufficient acceptance to warrant their underlying the decisions made in selection, placement, and promotion.

Determining requirements of manager's job

If needed managers are to be found and developed, it is essential that more be known about the jobs they are to perform. It would be highly desirable to develop detailed descriptions of, and specifications for, each job and find the person with qualifications to match. This is impossible, however, for the position requirements are nebulous and highly variable.

Even though it is difficult to determine job descriptions for managerial positions, there should be at least some understanding of the nature of the job to be filled.

General characteristics. An understanding of management is incomplete without a realization of its universal nature. The management functions are the same anywhere and everywhere, at any and every time. The functions may be applied differently by different people, but they remain the same, because all executives operate by working with people. The type of organization in which they find themselves makes comparatively little difference.

It is hypothesized that *management is also universal because it involves a systematic body of knowledge, applicable to all managerial situations.* This knowledge is valid in all types of organizations and at all levels of management in the same organization. A manager who knows these fundamental principles and knows how to apply them to a given stituation will perform the managerial functions most efficiently and effectively.

An approach to determining position requirements. Most managers seeking to fill a specific managerial opening have some preconceived guidelines as to the type individual needed. However, these preconceptions are too often based upon the characteristics of the previous incumbent, as discussed earlier. These specifications are frequently arbitrary, unachievable, and unrelated to the actual requirements needed to perform the job. Also, this method of determining job specifications focuses on the candidates' past experience and performance rather than their future ability to develop their abilities to fit the job requirements.

What is needed is a statement of qualifications which are "position-focused" and explicitly stated in terms of what the executive will be doing.

Table 11-1 shows an actual example of a "candidate-oriented" position

TABLE 11-1
An actual, versus a hypothetical, list of requirements for a manager's job

Typical candidate-oriented position requirements:

A minimum of ten years' experience at high levels within the industry, plus extensive knowledge of the company's various organizations, goals, and procedures. Must be able to communicate effectively with governmental and industrial groups and with top management.

Position-oriented requirements for same opening:*

Required education: Bachelors degree *Non-English language skills:* None
Desirable education: MBA *Professional certification*
Major field: No preference *required:* None

Position activities	Required skill level
Government relations—national	5
SEC Commission	3
Import/export regulations	5
Interstate Commerce Commission	2
Public relations—general	2
Relations with news media	2
Financial statements analysis	3
Merger and acquisition analysis	3
Public speaking	4
Purchasing practices—general	3
Manufacturing processes—general	3
Marketing practices—general	3
Marketing—environmental protection	4
Environmental protection laws	2

Code: 5 = extensive; 4 = considerable; 3 = some; 2 = very little; 1 = none.
* Hypothetical. For purposes of illustration, no managerial skills or personal qualifications are shown. Naturally they can be included in any position requirement.
Source: Richard T. McNamar, "Building a Better Executive Team," Reprinted from *California Management Review*, vol. XVI, no. 2, p. 63, by permission of the Regents. © 1973 by the Regents of the University of California.

filled by a company in the top 100 of *Fortune's 500*. It expresses the qualifications in terms of what the incumbent will be expected to do. The requirements listed in the top statements would not tell an individual—either the one doing the selection for the job or the one interested in the job—what was specifically required by way of job performance.

Even though this system is only a beginning, at least it shows what can be done by way of specifying actual job requirements, which can then be matched either in person or by using a computer.

HOW TO IDENTIFY MANAGERIAL TALENT

After establishing the requirements of the managerial job, it is desirable to ascertain what personal qualities a person needs in order to perform the job effectively. This process is complicated by the fact that there are an infinite number of successful managers with an inexhaustible variety of qualities. Therefore, it is impossible to detect with certainty the qualities that lead to managerial success. The job of manager requires a curious blending of qualities that constitute the person's total personality. Consequently, when one hires an executive one hires the whole person, with a complex of strengths and weaknesses and not just the qualities needed to perform the job.

Some problems involved

One of the first problems to be overcome is to *define successful job performance*. There are several *criteria* that can be used to measure it: the rapidity of promotions; the person's position in the organizational hierarchy; the relative salary position of the individual in the institution; some quantitative or qualitative measure of managerial effectiveness, obtained through either objective or subjective measures; or performance ratings. Finally, a combination of these can be worked out. Once the criteria for measuring success are established, the decision maker will have a more objective way of estimating whether a person will probably be a successful manager.

A second problem is to *identify and isolate the traits and qualities that can serve as predictors of success,* at least as far as a specific job is concerned. As indicated, the reliability of these predictors is highly subjective and of questionable accuracy.

The third problem is to try to *determine whether a given candidate for the job has those characteristics.* A corollary problem is to predict whether the person *will* develop those traits and become the manager desired, for not all of the ingredients of success are measurable.

Establishing criteria of job success

Earlier selection studies have undertaken to predict managerial effectiveness with very global criterion measurements such as overall performance ratings by supervisors and other superiors or other indices related to salaries or promotions. Subsequent research has shown that it is unrealistic to assume that managerial job performance is unidimensional. Instead, successful managerial performance is now considered to be multidimensional and results from the interaction of factors involving at least ability, personality, motivation, the institution, the environment, and the situation. Therefore, these factors must be included among any criterion measurements used to assess managerial performance.

New selection systems require more effective criteria. As indicated earlier, there is now a movement away from using single criterion measurements toward a systems approach to selection. These new, comprehensive, and more systematic models include individual, job, organizational, and environmental variables. As a result, the management selection process includes not only the identification and selection of managerial personnel, it also serves as a basis for identifying training and development needs and organizational change and development. (11)

Some acceptable criterion measures. Some of the more commonly used criterion measures which will be discussed in relation to managerial selection are:

1. Ratings by supervisors and other superiors, peers, and subordinates;
2. Salary;
3. Rank *or* levels held in the organization;
4. Rapidity of promotions or advancement; and
5. Others, including quality and quantity of output, cost/effectiveness relationship, and turnover, absenteeism, and grievances.

All of these criteria have problems. Some of these problems will be discussed as each criterion measure is discussed.

Ratings. Ratings by supervisors have probably been the most frequently used criterion measure, as it has been assumed that the superior has the best overall knowledge of the manager's job behavior which contributes to the overall objectives of the organization. Some modifications of this rating are to have *both* the manager's immediate supervisor and a higher superior rate the manager. This tends to remove a possible bias, positive or negative, on the part of the supervisor. A considerable amount of research indicates that peer ratings of a fellow worker are relevant as they are in a better position to evaluate how one performs in terms of the horizontal relationships in the organization. Ratings by subordinates are also of value in providing inputs as to the manager's human relationships.

Salary. Salary level, when statistically corrected for age and/or length of service, has proven a valid criterion of success. However, it too has problems, for salaries differ by industry, occupation, and even between different units in the same organization. Also, as wage and salary administration has been so "unscientific," there may be "quirks" which do not adequately reflect success.

Rank or organizational level. Rank, or organizational level, at least shows that the individual has been able to survive and make movement, regardless of the reason. It does have the problem that promotions are sometimes made on the basis of favoritism or "kicking the person upstairs."

Rapidity of promotions. The rate at which a person is promoted or advanced in the organization may be another measure of success. It at least shows *movement,* which is one quality often sought in executives. However, care should be used to discount the effect of any "patrons," or "mentors," who might have contributed to a faster than normal progression. (12)

Others. While not used too frequently as measures of higher-level executive success, the following can be used to measure supervisory success: (*a*) the quantity and quality of output as measured by some quantifiable unit; (*b*) turnover, absenteeism, and grievances; and (*c*) a number of cost-related variables such as return on profits and other ratios.

Use of combined criteria. The previously mentioned single criterion measures tend to be less effective when used alone than when used in combination.

Individually they measure only a small proportion of the variance caused by an individual manager in the overall organizational performance. When these measures are used together, particularly when combined into a single overall index by way of factor analysis and multiple regression analysis, they have proven successful.

> Standard Oil of New Jersey, after spending years studying various criterion measures, statistically combined organizational level of job held, salary history, and general effectiveness ratings into an overall success index. It has turned out to be very effective in gauging how successful managers will become over the course of their careers with the company.

Determining valid predictors of job success

Once the measures of success have been established, the problem becomes one of identifying and isolating the personal traits and characteristics that can serve as valid predictors of future success, using the selected criterion measure.

Regardless of the characteristics sought in potential managers, their performance must ultimately be measured against the objectives of the company. Their qualifications should be reviewed, evaluated, and rated. This evaluation can be either objective or subjective. Some experts claim that the objective method is best. For example, it has been asserted that it is possible to predict fitness for promotion to administrative jobs by using an objective analysis of a person's performance rating, educational level, age, time in job, years of service to the firm, job level, and annual salary. (13) This is especially true if there is an intensive integrative analysis of the responses on all the selection instruments, rather than an uncritical reliance upon numerical test scores.

Other authorities are equally adamant in asserting that subjective judgment and knowledge are necessary in predicting success. (14) Subjective appraisals not only permit a meaningful integration of the individuals' performance in the various aspects of their jobs, but they also permit an evaluation in terms of the demands of the setting in which the jobs take place.

Regardless of whether objective or subjective methods are used, ultimately there must be an analysis of the potential manager's competitive performance. Also, as shown in Chapter 10, a person's *past record* is the best prediction of future achievement, for it shows what one has done with one's capabilities and what probably will be done with them in the future.

Although there is no generally accepted list of qualities necessary to be a successful manager, research shows that some are considered "plus" factors by most executives when evaluating personnel for a managerial position. These qualities are *intelligence; education,* including rank or standing in class, and leadership in extracurricular activities; *interests;* and *various aspects of personality.*

Intelligence. In spite of our emphasis on equality, research shows that managers usually score higher on intelligence tests than does the average person. One study found that the typical executive attained a score between the 95th and 97th percentiles on the *Thurstone Primary Mental Ability Test,* and higher salaried executives were higher in intelligence than lower salaried ones (15); another group of executives had scores on the *Wonderlic Personnel Test* (Form A) that were higher than 96 percent of the universe of industrial and business workers (16); and norms for the *Thurstone Test of Mental Alertness* showed a group of executives at around the 89–90th percentile when compared with groups of supervisors and nonmanagerial personnel. (17)

There is some disagreement on this point, for another study showed that scores of a group of executives on the *Concept Mastery Test* and the *Ship Destination Test* showed no statistically significant relationship to their advancement. (18)

Education. A person's past performance included both academic and work experience, as shown in detail by a Bell System study of 17,000 of its managers who were college graduates. The results indicated a decided correlation between rank in the graduating class and progress in the system. Further, being a graduate of an "above average" college substantially increased promotability, and extracurricular achievements were also related to salary progress, for those with substantial activities and honors fared better than others. There was no appreciable difference between those who earned their way through college and those who did not. (19)

A more recent study has corroborated these findings: of 2,260 persons who were rated as "promotable," 84 percent had attended college and 59 percent had degrees. Conversely, 75 percent of the 942 rated as "nonpromotables" had no college or no degree. Yet the results showed no substantial correlation between major areas of study and success on the job. It was also concluded that age and performance can overcome deficiencies in education. (20)

One of the previous studies found 67 percent of successful managers had college degrees—even before college became popular—and were active in leadership positions in clubs and organizations. (21) A study for *Fortune* found that, on the average, executives were better educated than the public. (22) Finally, when 31 different variables were compared with success criteria, the extent of education was the best predictor of executive success. (23)

As a practical matter, this is one of the major criteria sought by personnel managers when hiring college graduates. Of 20 firms contacted in Atlanta, 10 of them use "academic performance" as one of the primary qualifications sought. (24)

Interests. In general, executives seem to have significantly broader interests than nonexecutives. For example, one of the previously mentioned studies found top executives scored higher on the computational, literary, and persuasive scales. (25) Another group of executives scored substantially higher on the *Strong Vocational Interest Blank* than did nonexecutives. (26)

Various aspects of personality. There are measurable differences between managers and nonmanagerial personnel as far as certain personality variables are concerned. For example, managers have superior skills in dealing with people, as well as more self-confidence and more self-esteem (27); they have better mental health, as well as more confidence and optimism, and are better able to tolerate frustration (28); they have drive and health (29); they tend to be firm, positive, and decisive (30); they possess mental and emotional strength and judgment (31); and they are innovative (32); and they are nonconformists. (33)

Use of multiple predictors. The more successful organizations are now using multiple predictors in selecting managerial personnel. For example, the Sears, Roebuck & Company studies, which are among the oldest such research programs, found a number of significant characteristics and attitudes associated with managerial success. Using a *battery of tests* to measure intelligence, personality, interests, and values, it was found that managers had more orderly thought, overt—or even aggressive—self-confidence, practical and economic personal values. (34)

The previously mentioned study of Standard Oil of New Jersey used a biographical inventory and tests to measure intelligence, personality, and attitudes and found that the biographical inventory was the greatest predictor of success; but that the battery together successfully predicted success in the company. There were correlations as high as .70 between the battery and job-potential measures of managerial success. None of the individual instruments proved that effective.

Some faulty predictors. In any choice of personnel, whether managers or nonmanagers, certain basic assumptions are made. Some of these assumptions are valid and some are not. One of the most invalid is the assumption that an employee who is highly skilled and who has been able to perform technical jobs also has the requirements and characteristics to become a supervisor or manager. This is an invalid assumption, for *a good producer is not necessarily a potential supervisor or executive.*

Another danger is that of *selective perception.* This means that we perceive only what we want to perceive. People tend to notice traits that they think will satisfy their needs and to ignore those that are unfavorable. Managers frequently are hired on the basis of first impressions or because they have physical characteristics that approximate those of the employer.

SPECIALIZED TECHNIQUES FOR IDENTIFYING AND SELECTING EXECUTIVES

The traditional selection instruments tend to be declining in favor in identifying and selecting managerial talent. Interviews have proven to be quite unreliable; tests are declining in acceptability and validity; references are both unreliable and are now suspect under public policy; but the biographical inventory seems to be emerging as the single best predictor of managerial effectiveness, according to research on the traditional instruments.

Other techniques being experimented with are simulation exercises involving in-basket techniques and management games; structured and unstructured group interaction exercises; and peer ratings, subordinate ratings, and even self-ratings.

Assessment centers

A new and exciting basis for making promotion decisions in the assessment center. Probably the best definition of an assessment center *is a place where potential candidates for managerial positions are put through a series of interviews, tests, and simulations to determine their promotability and point out weaknesses which need to be corrected through training and development.*

AT&T probably had the first assessment center in this country. It started its management progress study in 1956 to investigate the relationship between selection techniques and careers of managers. The original purpose of the project was to ascertain if measurements and ratings made in the early phases of a manager's career at an assessment center are valid predictors of subsequent accomplishment in the future. They were measuring, observing, and evaluating a group of potential managers, including college graduates and noncollege personnel who had advanced to the lowest level of management.

The results of the assessments were not made known to operating managers. After about eight years, correlations were made between the predictions from the assessment center and criteria of performance between then and 1965. The original assessments were 78 percent accurate for those expected to move fastest in management ranks; of those judged not likely to reach middle management levels within nine or ten years, the predictions were 95 percent accurate.

At that time, the Bell System established over 50 assessment centers throughout the country, using essentially the same techniques used in the original program.

Because of the success at the Bell System, the larger companies now have assessment centers and probably there are over 150 such programs. It is also estimated that over 70,000 prospective managers have been assessed and currently around 10,000 per year are being assessed in the United States. (35)

While different centers operate differently, in general, five or six managers are gathered into a group, given psychological tests, complete biographical inventories, and participate in intensive interviews with the assessors. Using a variety of criteria to evaluate the potential managers, the managers and consultants make multiple judgments based upon their observations, interviews, and the test scores.

As the information from the centers is used not only in selection, but in training and development, as well as counseling, there are multiple benefits to be derived from this selection technique.

Current results indicate about 30–40 percent of the examinees score in the "Acceptable/Outstanding" category; 40 percent are "Questionable"; and 20–30 percent are "Unacceptable." These ratings are recommendations in the form of briefs prepared on each person and seem to provide relatively valid predictions of managerial ability.

These centers are not an unmixed blessing, for there are some disadvantages. While they are quite sophisticated, this means that they are also quite expensive. Another criticism is the feeling—at least among those who rate low—that a negative rating is "the kiss of death" as far as the individual is concerned in that organization. This leads to the third criticism, the demotivating effect of the centers. While the assessment centers are a more comprehensive approach to the collection and analysis of data, it has been hypothesized that what the centers actually measure are the candidates' skill and sensitivity in interpersonal relationships. (36)

Computer assistance

As mentioned in previous chapters, the computer is being extensively used not only to select nonmanagers, but also managerial personnel.

Richard McNamar, a consultant, has developed a feasible program to be used by larger organizations making several hundred promotion decisions each year. The system, called a *Candidate Identification System (CIS)*, is based upon the use of information which usually already exists. First, when an opening is about to occur, the responsible operating manager obtains from the personnel department *position qualification guidelines,* a list of the explicit requirements for the position, which was previously prepared during human resource planning. This document, which lists the knowledge, skills, experience, education, and other requirements for the job is modified—if necessary—and programmed into the computer. Second, *employee skills inventories,* including educational background, knowledge, skills, experience, interests, and other

"Of the three, I like this fellow."

Look, May 3, 1966

**FIGURE 11-1
CIS inputs/outputs**

- Position Qualification Guidelines
  - Knowledge, skill, experience requirements
  - Other guidelines, e.g., education
- Employee Skills Inventory
  - Educational background
  - Knowledge, skill, experience
  - Background and interest
- Employee Appraisal
  - Performance
  - Promotability
  - Potential
  - Managerial skills
  - Personal qualifications
- CIS Output
  - List of identified candidates
  - Individual résumés

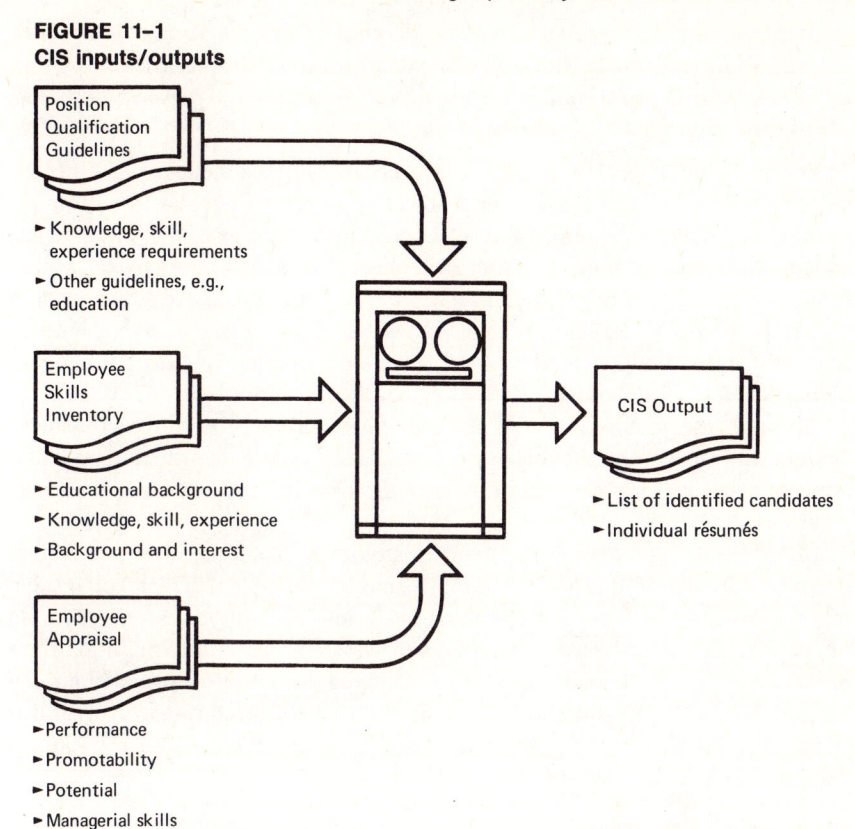

Source: Richard T. McNamar, "Building a Better Executive Team," Reprinted from *California Management Review*, vol. XVI, no. 2, p. 64, by permission of the Regents. © 1973 by the Regents of the University of California.

background data of potential candidates are prepared and also put in the system. Third, various *employee appraisals* dealing with performance, promotability, and managerial skills and potential, and personal qualifications are also fed into the computer. The result is an elimination of obviously unacceptable candidates and the identification—along with individual résumés—of those deemed to be promotable.

From the list—and the résumés—the concerned executives can continue the selection procedure as they choose. See Figure 11-1 for an explanation of how this system works.

IMPLICATIONS AND APPLICATIONS FOR PERSONNEL EXECUTIVES

Based upon research findings which have been mentioned in this chapter—as well as earlier ones—it can be hypothesized that:

1. *In general, there are certain attributes which executives have to a higher degree than does the general public; there are selected predictors which,*

when properly identified, tend to differentiate between successful and less successful executives and between executives and nonexecutives.
2. There is a definite and positive correlation between a person's academic records and objective criteria of success.

While "good looks" and certain aspects of "handsomeness" do, in fact, seem to take precedence over more objective selection criteria in college recruiting, (37) there are more valid selection criteria. For example, intelligence; education, including rank or standing in class, and leadership in extracurricular activities; interest in computational, literary, and persuasive activities; and certain personality variables, such as self-esteem, mental health, drive, innovation, and individualism tend to be found more frequently, and stronger, in managers than nonmanagers.

Through the judicious use of the regular selection procedure, assessment centers, and the computer, these selection criteria can be identified in potential managers and serve as the basis for selecting those individuals for higher-level positions.

Many small institutions may tend to shy away from the idea of a formal program for identifying and selecting managers for fear it will involve them in an elaborate, costly information system. While such organizations often do not need a computer-based personnel data system to select and maintain their moderate-sized managerial staffs, they do need better information than can be found on a "hit-or-miss" basis. Conversely, medium and larger organizations will find the use of a computer-based system efficient and economical because of the sheer size of their staffs.

DISCUSSION QUESTIONS

1. Do you agree with the basic premise of this chapter? Support your answer.
2. Discuss briefly the causes of the shortage of managerial personnel.
3. How would you determine the need for managerial personnel?
4. What differentiates a high-level management position from a low-level one?
5. What are some common criteria for measuring successful job performance? What difficulties do you anticipate in using any single criterion as a measure of successful performance? What merit do you see to the systems approach to management selection?
6. What characteristics differentiate successful and unsuccessful managers?
7. Do you think students with high scholastic grades will make better managers than those with average marks? Explain. Defend your answer.
8. How is the assessment center being used for making promotion decisions?

REFERENCES AND SUGGESTIONS FOR FURTHER STUDY

1. For the exact figures and method used in reaching this conclusion, see "Longevity of Corporate Executives," in Metropolitan Life *Statistical Bulletin,* February 1974, pp. 2–4.
2. See "Where They Make Believe They Are the Bosses," *Business Week* (August 28, 1971), pp. 34–35, for details of this experiment.

3. See "Aetna: Where Group Management Didn't Work," *Business Week* (February 16, 1976), p. 77, for a discussion of these group arrangements to see which are operating effectively and which aren't.
4. See A. T. Mathews, "Keeping Tabs on 7,500 Middle Managers," *Personnel,* vol. 43, no. 3 (May–June 1966), pp. 24–29, for how the organization was able to "keep tabs" on that many people.
5. Reed M. Powell, "Elements of Executive Promotion," *California Management Review,* vol. 6, no. 2 (Winter 1963), pp. 83–90.
6. Henry D. Meyer and Glenn L. Pressel, "Personality Test Scores in the Management Hierarchy," *Journal of Applied Psychology,* vol. 38, no. 2 (April 1954), pp. 73–80.
7. Edwin E. Ghiselli, "Traits Differentiating Management Personnel," *Personnel Psychology,* vol. 12, no. 4 (Winter 1959), pp. 535–44; and "The Validity of Management Traits in Relation to Occupational Level," *Personnel Psychology,* vol. 16, no. 1 (Summer 1963), pp. 109–13.
8. See David H. Reed and J. Rogert Harman, Jr., "Seiecting a Chief Executive Officer," *Trustee,* vol. 28, no. 8 (August 1975), pp. 14–18, for an example of this point in a hospital setting. They conclude that few "number two" people are fully proven as CEOs as the "roles are subtly but sufficiently different."
9. John A. Hicks and Joics B. Stone, "The Identification of Traits Related to Managerial Success," *Journal of Applied Psychology,* vol. 46, no. 6 (December 1962), pp. 428–32.
10. Abraham Zaleznik, C. R. Christensen, and F. J. Roethlisberger, *The Motivation, Productivity, and Satisfaction of Workers* (Boston, Mass.: Harvard Graduate School of Business Administration, 1958), p. 437, especially Hypothesis 21, "The more the worker aspires for job advancement, the more likely he will tend to produce high as a means of realizing this aspiration."
11. See James R. Rawls and Donna J. Rawls, "Recent Trends in Management Selection," *Personnel Journal,* vol. 53, no. 2 (February 1974), pp. 104–9, for a more detailed discussion of these selection suggestions.
12. It has long been known that one good way of progressing in an organization is to find someone up the line who will keep an eye on you—and your career progression. Now, according to Jacqueline Thompson in "Patrons, Rabbis, Mentors—Whatever You Call Them, Women Need Them, Too," *MBA,* vol. 10, no. 2, (February 1976), p. 26 ff., women are discovering the importance of patronage, and they are learning to play the sponsorship game.
13. James W. Walker, Fred Luthans, and Richard M. Hodgetts, "Who Really Are the Promotables," *Personnel Journal,* vol. 49, no. 2 (February 1970), pp. 123–37.
14. David W. Ewing, "The Knowledge of an Executive," *Harvard Business Review,* vol. 42, no. 2 (March–April 1964), pp. 91–100.
15. L. Huttner, S. Levy, E. Rosen, and M. Stopel, "Further Light on the Executive Personality," *Personnel,* vol. 36, no. 2 (March–April 1959), pp. 42–43.
16. Robert M. Wald and Roy A. Doty, "The Top Executive—A Firsthand Profile," *Harvard Business Review,* vol. 32, no. 4 (July–August 1954), p. 45.
17. L. L. Thurstone and T. G. Thurstone, *Examiner Manual for the Thurstone Test of Mental Alertness* (Chicago: Science Research Associates, 1952). Also see E. E. Ghiselli, "The Validity of Management Traits Related to Occupational Level,"

Personnel Psychology, vol. 16, no. 2 (Summer 1963), pp. 109–13, for further evidence that managers have above average intelligence.

18. Allen I. Kraut, "Intellectual Ability and Promotional Success among High-Level Managers," *Personnel Psychology,* vol. 22, no. 3 (Autumn 1969), pp. 281–90.
19. Frederick R. Kappel, "From the World of College to the World of Work," Green Foundation Lecture, Westminster College, April 5, 1962, in *Business Purpose and Performance* (New York: Duell, Sloan & Pearce, Inc., 1964), p. 186.
20. Fred Luthans, James Walker, and Richard M. Hodgetts, "Evidence on the Validity of Management Education," *Academy of Management Journal,* vol. 12, no. 4 (December 1969), pp. 451–57.
21. Wald and Doty, "The Top Executive," *Harvard Business Review,* p. 45.
22. *Fortune* (November 1952), p. 132.
23. Edwin E. Wagner, "Predicting Success for Young Executives from Objective Test Scores and Personal Data," *Personnel Psychology,* vol. 13, no. 2 (Summer 1960), pp. 181–86.
24. See Beaufort B. Longest, Jr., "Criteria for Hiring College Graduates as Management Trainees," *Training and Development Journal,* vol. 27, no. 90 (September 1973), pp. 46–48, for the other qualifications sought.
25. Wald and Doty, "The Top Executive," *Harvard Business Review,* p. 45.
26. Thomas W. Harrell, *Manager's Performance and Personality* (Cincinnati, O.: South-Western Publishing Co., 1961), p. 91.
27. Laurence Siegel and Irving Lane, *Psychology in Industrial Organizations* 3d ed. (Homewood, Ill.: Richard D. Irwin, Inc., 1974), pp. 344–45.
28. Huttner, *et. al.,* "Further Light," *Personnel,* pp. 42–43.
29. See "Young Top Management," *Business Week* (October 6, 1975), pp. 56–68, for a discussion of this and other qualifications exhibited by some outstanding young executives.
30. Wald and Doty, "The Top Executive," *Harvard Business Review,* p. 45.
31. H. D. Meyer and A. J. Fredia, "Personality Test Scores in the Management Hierarchy," *Journal of Applied Psychology,* vol. 43, no. 3 (June 1959), pp. 212–20.
32. Eugene K. Von Fange, *Professional Creativity* (Englewood Cliffs, N.J.: Prentice-Hall, Inc., 1959); and E. A. Fleishman and D. R. Peters, "Interpersonal Values, Leadership Attitudes and Managerial Success," *Personnel Psychology,* vol. 15, no. 2 (Summer 1962), pp. 127–43.
33. Ghiselli, "The Validity of Management Traits," *Personnel Psychology,* pp. 109–13, states that his research showed "that the men who displayed the greatest individuality in managerial behavior were in general the ones judged to be . . . the best managers."
34. Siegel and Lane, *Psychology in Industrial Organizations,* pp. 344–45.
35. Rawls and Rawls, "Recent Trends in Management Selection," *Personnel Journal,* pp. 104–9.
36. See John E. Wilson and Walter Tatge, "Assessment Centers—Further Assessment Needed?" *Personnel Journal,* vol. 52, no. 3 (March 1973), pp. 172–79, for an excellent analysis of these criticisms.
37. See John L. Schlachter, "Criteria for selection and Promotion," *Arizona Business Bulletin,* vol. 18, no. 9 (November 1971), pp. 16–21, for further details.

CASES FOR FURTHER STUDY

III-1. Companywide Seniority

The Welcom Company had a policy of promoting on the basis of companywide seniority, providing the competing employees' qualifications were otherwise equal. Bill was "first machinist" in the firm's Plant A when he was offered the job of "plant foreman" in its Plant B. This job was particularly attractive because Plant B was slightly larger than Plant A and, therefore, carried a higher prestige value. Ralph, the first machinist in Plant B, also wanted the foreman's job. Although he had the most plantwide seniority in Plant B, he was not given the job because he had been with the company six months less than Bill, and Bill, therefore, had six months more companywide seniority.

Bill knew that Ralph had counted on getting the job and that several of his new subordinates considered Ralph next in line and better qualified. Fortunately the previous foreman had talked with Ralph before leaving and had tried to explain why he did not get the job. Even so, Ralph resented Bill's presence in the plant and was not too cooperative.

When a machine broke down, Ralph worked diligently on it and did an excellent job of repairing it. Bill, wanting Ralph to know that he appreciated his work, complimented him in front of the other men. "Ralph, thanks for the fine repair job you did on the machine. You demonstrated outstanding skill, knowledge, and experience, and I want you to know I consider you the best qualified first machinist in the company."

Ralph replied, "I should know how to fix that machine, for I helped install it. In fact, I know more about this whole plant than you do, as I've been here longer. In fact, if this company had a fair promotion policy, I would be plant foreman and you wouldn't be here."

Questions

1. What does this case indicate about the problem of promoting from within?
2. What does it show about the difficulty of using seniority as the basis of promotion?
3. Evaluate the way Bill handled the situation.
4. What would you do now if you were Bill?
5. What does the case illustrate about the source of personnel?

III-2. Outside Help

Because of expansion, the time came for the management of a rapidly growing engineering consulting firm to employ personnel for certain key executive positions. In those firms, the technical qualifications of nonmanagerial employees are normally given more emphasis than their managerial abilities. This eventually leads to a partial vacuum in the executive end of a growing business.

A nontechnical executive from the outside was employed as the assistant to the president. This move was not received very well by the older department heads. It was generally felt that someone from inside the organization should have been placed in the position. Consequently, the new presidential assistant had a hard time obtaining cooperation from his fellow employees.

He remained as assistant to the president for approximately four years, at which time he was made a vice-president. During that period he was able to convince his fellow employees of his managerial abilities and the need for his services within the business. His promotion to vice-president was "generally well received by all."

Questions

1. What does the case illustrate about the relationship between type of organization and source of personnel?
2. Why was it necessary—or at least desirable—to go outside for the new manager?
3. What would you have done if you were the president? Explain.
4. Evaluate the way the presidential assistant handled himself.

III-3. Selection: In Theory and in Practice

The following letter was received from the personnel director of a large chemical company in answer to the question: "What selection techniques do you use?"

> Among the various selection (or rejection) bases we use, the best method for predicting what an employee can and will do is by evaluating what one has consistently done in the past. Therefore, a careful review of an applicant's performance history should provide a forecast of what one probably will do in the future.
>
> The information normally required on employment applications and résumés has been diluted to the point where they provide basic information only.
>
> An important selection technique, which is currently causing much controversy, is preemployment testing. Despite all of the arguments against testing, it is still one of the best measures we have for providing objective results.
>
> Testing, professionally validated, is a tool of great value, but the greatest value of such testing lies in its administration and use specifically related to the job to be filled. Also, greater value of a testing program is in obtaining scores from

a test battery providing the psychological characteristics of the worker to insure compatibility with the job function and the personnel with whom the employee will be associated. The trend of discounting such testing is causing considerable problems in that the techniques of the personnel interview require considerable training and skill—which most interviewers do not have.

Reference investigations are usually of little value because of the hesitancy of former employers to provide information on former employees. This lack of interest in giving requested information is due to the emphasis being given by various governmental agencies on the right of privacy of the worker.

This dilution of necessary information is even reaching into the preemployment physical examination, for we get little information from the doctors to help us make employment decisions.

Questions

1. Evaluate this person's assessment of selection.
2. If you were asked to advise this manager, what suggestions would you make?

III-4. To Do Or Not to Do?

The AAA Corporation was a large national chemical company. The company's research department was located at one of its manufacturing locations on the East coast. The department, charged with the responsibility for providing the new technology needed to stay competitive in that rapidly changing industry, had about 300 employees, 80 of whom were professional employees with degrees in either chemical engineering or chemistry.

The company's employee relations department did all the on-campus recruiting for the company, including the research department. Any department needing personnel would then screen the application blanks, academic records, and interview reports of employment prospects that recruiters had interviewed on the college campuses and choose the individuals it wanted to hire. Because of the high standard of technical expertise that the research department maintained, it made the decision on which candidates to invite to visit the department for further evaluation. During the visit, each candidate was interviewed by at least four of the professionals, including a young engineer, a more experienced technical expert, a middle-level manager, and one of the four top managers in the department. Based upon these interviews, the applicants' academic records, the inexperience level, and the quality of the colleges involved, a decision was made that the candidates were either "qualified" or "not qualified" for the type of work to be done. If a candidate was rated as "outstanding," an offer of employment was made during the visit. Otherwise, offers of employment were made only after reviewing and comparing the evaluations of all the candidates that had visited the department.

The department had a reputation as a top scientific organization because of its record of technical accomplishments during its 30 years of existence. Its top management was "very proud of this record and the reputation for technical excellence that the department enjoys." The manager of the department, Bob Jones, and his three assistants, Fred Smith, Jay Lord, and Bill Shaw, attributed the success in part to "the policy of recruiting only top technical people from highly-rated schools."

Although the size of the technical staff in the department had stayed fairly constant at about 80 for a number of years, the department usually hired three to five new technical personnel each year to replace those employees that had transferred to other parts of the company, had retired, or had left the company. Last year the department needed to hire four chemical engineers.

According to the employer relations manager, "The company has been very active over the last few years in recruiting and hiring female employees." It had an aggressive and successful AAP, as it did a lot of business with the government. The manufacturing plant (where the research department was located) had been successful in meeting their affirmative action goals on hiring both professional and nonprofessional female employees. The research department had also been very successful in hiring qualified women in the nonprofessional jobs. However, the department to date has not been able to hire a female engineer or chemist. They have no women in the total professional staff of 80.

"Recruiting female professionals has been a difficult task as the national proportion of female chemical engineers, the primary degree required in the department, is less than 2 percent. Based upon this fact, we have set a goal of eventually hiring at least two female professionals, with a goal of hiring at least one this year."

Overall, the company was meeting its goals—which had been established in compliance with the laws—of hiring women, so the research department was not receiving pressure from the government on its deficiency of women professionals. However, Bob Jones was receiving pressure from the company's employee relations manager to hire a female professional. Actually the department had made employment offers to two female chemical engineers in each of the last two years, but all of them had declined offers. In fact, one of those two had accepted employment with another department of the firm. The four candidates who had received the job offers were "outstandingly qualified," and the competition for their employment had been intense.

This year, in seeking four new chemical engineers, Bob had invited 25 candidates, including five females, to visit the plant. Several of the women did not appear to be qualified—based on their campus evaluations alone—but Bob had invited them anyway to get a better personal evaluation of their qualifications.

Three of the current candidates—all males—had been rated as "outstanding" and were offered jobs during their visit. All three had accepted the offers. Of the other 22 applicants, seven—including one female, Betty Craig, a senior at a small engineering school in the Midwest—had been evaluated as being "qualified" for employment in the department. Betty was ranked fourth out of the seven.

At that time, Bob called a meeting of his three assistants and the employee relations manager to discuss their views on what action should be taken in filling the other vacancy. With only one opening left, the normal procedure would have been to offer the job to the next candidate that had the highest evaluation. However, because of the conflict between their normal, seemingly objective, procedure and their desire to hire a woman professional, Bob wanted to get their advice before making his decision. Betty had been interviewed by Bob when she visited and indicated to him that she would accept a job in the department if it were offered. So Bob knew that he had a certainty of fulfilling his affirmative action goal if he decided to offer her the job.

Fred Smith, who had been in the department since it was formed 30 years ago, thought that Betty should not get the next offer. If the next three applicants turned down the offer, then he agreed that Betty should get the job. He pointed out that the success of the department and the company had been "based on the high degree of technical expertise that the department has maintained—and that goal should override the affirmative action goal. Thus, the offer should be made to the person who has been objectively judged as being the best qualified of the remaining possibilities. Otherwise, the company will be practicing 'reverse discrimination.' "

Jay Lord, recently promoted into his job, recommended that Betty be given the job as she had been "evaluated as meeting the qualifications and thus could not jeopardize our technical reputation. Also, our evaluation procedure should be changed as it is biased in favor of men and is not distinctive enough to select between candidates rated so close."

The third assistant manager, Bill Shaw, agreed that Betty was qualified, but he concurred with Fred that the three people over her on the list of qualified applicants should be offered the position first. He also expressed a concern that to hire a person near the bottom of the qualified list might cause some future risk of an unusual nature. "If she does not turn out to be a good performer, we might have great difficulty in releasing her as the only female professional in the department. On the other hand, one of the male applicants would pose no problem in releasing if he should happen not to perform satisfactorily." He recommended that they wait and try to hire a woman that clearly was "outstanding" from a well-established college to minimize this problem. He knew that they had been unsuccessful in doing that in the past but suggested that they make an unusually high salary offer to the next clearly outstanding female applicant to ensure their success.

Bob was quiet through most of the discussion. He was in agreement to some extent with both the pros and cons presented but knew that he would have to make the decision himself considering the effect on the company, the department, the applicants involved, as well as the effect on his own career.

Questions

1. Evaluate the firm's recruiting procedure.
2. Would you propose any changes in it? Explain.
3. Discuss the validity of the arguments made by each of the three assistant managers.

4. How would you resolve the apparent conflict of goals imposed by different parts of the company?
5. Do you think the procedure used for selecting professional employees is a fair method? If not, how would you change it?
6. What concepts about female employees surface in the case?
7. Assume that you are the employee relations manager, propose a solution and defend it.

part four

Maximizing personnel potential

12. Personnel development strategies
13. Executive development
14. Career planning and development
15. Maximizing personnel potential

Cases:
  IV–1. Louis Kemp
  IV–2. Sinclaire University
  IV–3. Technical Obsolescence

Introduction

As institutions are a mixture of many individuals with differing abilities, aptitudes, education, and experiences, their success ultimately depends upon the particular contribution of *each* person. Therefore, the eventual effectiveness achieved by the institution is governed by the development and utilization of every member's abilities.

As shown in Figure IV–1, this results from proper human resource planning, recruiting, selecting, and placement, which were discussed in the previous part. Another input into the system, maximizing personnel potential, is covered in this part. It includes training and developing personnel, with special emphasis upon executive development, career planning and development; movement through the organization; and leading and motivating employees in order to maximize their potential.

Employees do not enter an organization in a raw, unformed state, for they are the product of their heredity and environment, as modified by their past experiences. They bring their attitudes, assumptions, beliefs, and preconceptions with them to the work place; and these factors must be considered when attempting to develop people.

The problems associated with developing nonmanagerial employees are

FIGURE IV–1
A system's approach to maximizing personnel potential

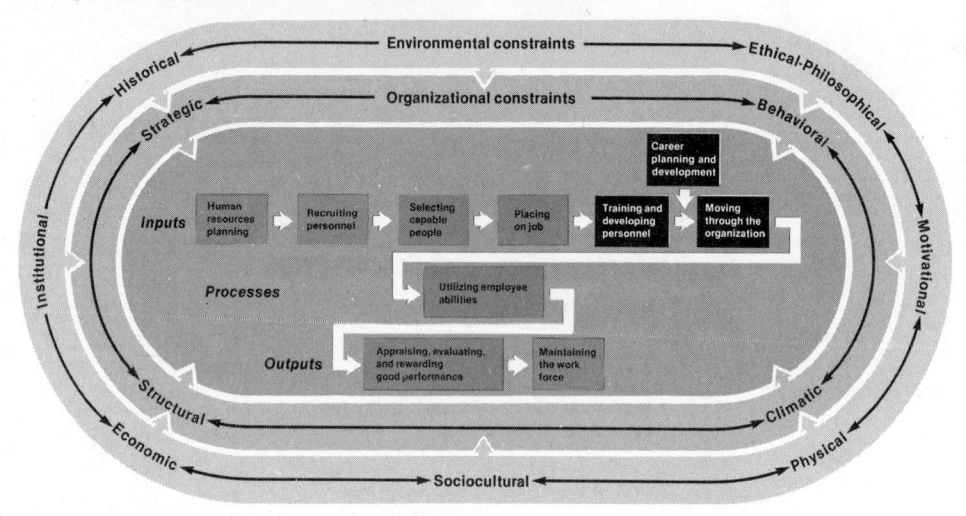

discussed in Chapter 12, while Chapter 13 is concerned with management development.

Chapter 14 looks at the problems of helping personnel plan and develop their careers so organizational and personal objectives can be reached. This includes counseling and providing guidance; upgrading, transferring, and promoting; using employee appraisals; and "management by objectives."

The use of managerial leadership, communications, motivation, and other behavioral techniques to maximize employee potential are discussed in Chapter 15.

Chapter 12

Personnel development strategies

Establishing development objectives
    To meet challenge of technological development
    To fulfill social responsibility
    To provide greater personal satisfaction

Assigning responsibility for development
    Role assigned to society
    Role assigned to the organization
    Role assigned to the union
    The individual's residual responsibility

Assessing development needs
    Specific methods used in assessing needs
    Some generalizations about development needs

Designing development programs
    Some principles of learning
    Applying learning principles to personnel development

Conducting developmental programs
    Who is to do the development?
    What is to be taught?

Evaluating effectiveness of development programs
    Approaches to evaluation
    What is evaluated?
    A cost effectiveness approach

Implications and applications for personnel executives

12

Personnel development strategies

Chance favors the prepared mind.
LOUIS PASTEUR

No man can reveal to you aught but that which already lies half asleep in the dawning of your knowledge.
KAHLIL GIBRAN, The Prophet

Learning maketh young men temperate, is the comfort of old age, standing for wealth with poverty, and serving as an ornament to riches.
CICERO

The great jurist, Oliver Wendell Holmes, once said, "A child's education should begin at least 100 years before he is born."

This truth is exemplified by the attitude of Francis W. Parker, an educator. After a lecture, a woman rushed up and asked:

"How early can I begin the education of my child?"

"When will your child be born?"

"Born?" she gasped. "Why, he is already five years old!"

"My goodness, woman," he cried, "don't stand here talking to me—hurry home; already you have lost the best five years."

These statements emphasize that development involves both heredity and environment. *Heredity* essentially determines people's maximum mental capacity for development, *environment* significantly affects the level to which they have grown—and will ultimately grow—toward achieving full utilization of that total capacity. Consequently, employees' inherent abilities are determined by their heredity, but the actual level of development is determined by their education, training, experience, and motivation, which are functions of their environment.

Much time, effort, and space has been wasted on attempts to delineate the differences between education, training, and development. These attempts are largely useless, for they involve a question of semantics. In reality, the three activities are part of the same concept, namely, developing personnel in the broadest sense of the word. However, if an attempt is made to find some distinctions between them, it can be said that *training* implies the acquisition

FIGURE 12-1
Model for developing personnel and human resources

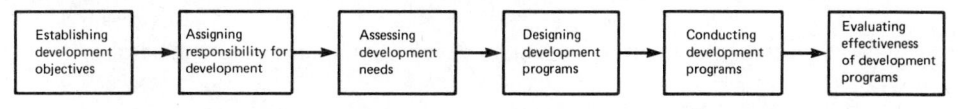

Establishing development objectives → Assigning responsibility for development → Assessing development needs → Designing development programs → Conducting development programs → Evaluating effectiveness of development programs

of specific, detailed, and routine skills and techniques; *education* involves the acquisition of broad generalized knowledge; and *development* is the systematic process of education, training, and growth by which a person acquires and applies information, knowledge, skills, attitudes, and perceptions.

The purpose of this chapter is to explore the development process, especially as it applies to nonmanagerial personnel, as shown in Figure 12-1.

ESTABLISHING DEVELOPMENT OBJECTIVES

One of the basic beliefs of professional managers is that the objective of a business organization should be to produce a good or service for its clients or customers, at a price they are willing and able to pay, and at a cost of production which will permit the owners a reasonable profit. Also, the objective of nonbusiness organizations is assumed to be to provide services for their clients at the lowest feasible cost, corresponding to the quality and quantity of the services provided.

As one of the objectives of personnel administrators is to see that the resources available to their organizations—whether private or public—are used efficiently and effectively, it follows that these managers should be concerned with improving the performance of their employees. This interest is more evident in large, highly profitable, nonunionized, manufacturing firms with a large proportion of social psychologists and consultant teams on their staffs. (1)

To meet challenge of technological development

Because of rapid technological changes, the problem of human resource development is particularly acute. Not only must new employees be trained, but present ones must be retrained and upgraded. It is an alarming fact that such a large number of young people without the necessary education or skills required for today's employment are joining the ranks of the unemployed. It is not that they are incompetent but that there are just not enough jobs for their limited skills. The problem is expected to increase in magnitude and severity.

Research at the Illinois Institute of Technology has put this problem into clear perspective. "A steadily increasing level of educational achievement" and the "acceleration of technological change" are accompanied by "increased stress on formal education" by management. Consequently, there are decreased promotional opportunities for lower-level employees. This leads to difficulty in attracting and retaining managerial personnel at that level, as well as conflict between supervisors and subordinates. The result of these pressures is to institute—and upgrade—formal organizational and developmental programs. (2)

The validity of this conclusion is emphasized by the shortage of persons with the basic skills, such as skilled machinists, auto mechanics, welders, and secretaries. With an unemployment rate of around 8 percent, the U.S. Employment Service's "job bank" listed 244,000 openings at the end of 1975. (3)

To fulfill social responsibility

During the 1960s, there was a change in public policy as well as in managerial objectives, as far as development was concerned. Emphasis was placed upon providing employment and promotional opportunities for everyone. But, as there was such a close correlation between employment opportunities and an individual's level of training and education, considerable emphasis was given to developing minority groups, especially the hard-core unemployed. This policy has led to many successful experiences in expanding the available supply of capable personnel. (4)

To provide greater personal satisfaction

Individual employees also have a stake in development, for they acquire a greater sense of worth, dignity, and well-being as they become more valuable to society. They will receive a greater share of the material gains that result from increased productivity. These two factors will provide a sense of satisfaction in the achievement of personal and social goals. It follows that more highly developed employees will also cause fewer problems and will have greater job satisfaction.

> IBM's "career bend" is a program of "enlightened paternalism" which offers near-total security to its employees. The firm claims that in more than 35 years it has never laid off a worker for economic reasons. It retrains workers not needed in one job and assigns them to another. Since 1970 it has retrained and physically relocated 5,000 employees as part of the most extensive corporate education program in the United States.
> The payoff has been in intangible but real benefits such as "loyalty," "hard work," and "satisfaction." (5)
>
> As another example of this truth, 226 Indians benefited by an average annual increase in earnings of $1,900 as a result of an on-the-job training program provided by nine firms between 1960 and 1967. In addition, while social costs were $1,010, social benefits were $2,034, and each person averaged 3.4 more months of annual employment after the training. (6)

ASSIGNING RESPONSIBILITY FOR DEVELOPMENT

It is generally recognized that a minimum of four parties are responsible for personnel development, at least in our economic system. The first of these, *society*, fulfills its obligation through the regular educational system and extension programs, including adult education. The second party is the *organization* itself, including the owners and managers who are responsible not only for providing the means for individuals to develop, but also for actually performing much of the training and education themselves. The *unions* and other *employee associations*, which are not only interested but also exert significant influence upon development programs, especially through the apprenticeship programs, are the third party. The fourth responsible party is the *individual* directly involved, for, finally, it is the individual who must have the ambition, initiative, character, and perseverance to pay the price required for successful development.

Role assigned to society

In general, the responsibility for general education is assigned to the general public through public and private education. Also, many facets of adult education and generalized training are best performed by public bodies. Because of scientific and technological changes, the increasing proportion of the population seeking an education, and other factors, formal schooling is becoming much more expensive. Each year, society in the United States spends close to $90 billion on all levels of education. (7)

Increasing emphasis on career education. An idea whose "time has come" is *career education*. The premise behind career education is simply that all classroom work, whether academic or vocational in nature, should visibly relate to the individual student's post-schooling ambitions. It has two primary concerns, namely, that students see the relationship between their studies and whatever form of work they will eventually seek; and that work, because it fills a basic human need, should become a meaningful part of every individual's life.

The Comprehensive Employment and Training Act of 1973 (CETA). Beginning in 1937 with the passage of the *National Apprenticeship Act*, the government has worked with organizations to develop employees. With the passage of the *Servicemen's Readjustment Act of 1944 (the "GI Bill")*, the emphasis shifted to assist special groups to become more employable and promotable. With the enactment of the *Manpower Development and Training Act of 1962 (MDTA)*, the emphasis shifted to providing *unemployed* and *underemployed* persons with opportunities for upgrading their skills and providing them with new skills to meet changing job markets. Since then, special programs have been developed to assist occupationally deprived groups, such as minority members, public assistance recipients, the handicapped, Indians, older workers, and migrant and seasonal farm workers. In addition, efforts have been made to provide the criminal justice system with a basis for giving offenders an alternative to prison.

In 1973, Congress passed the *Comprehensive Employment and Training Act (CETA)* to provide for decentralization of these acts to the state and local governments and to eliminate numerous categorical programs. While the funds under the act may be used for supportive services, including recruiting and testing, the major emphasis is on training. Around 80 percent of the funds are to be used by the states under Title I for training programs.

Role assigned to the organization

Developing human resources is also the responsibility of the organization. It can be hypothesized that *the economic returns from development justify the expenditure of scarce resources to develop employees.* The managers of many modern firms feel that increasing job specialization and tightening skill-labor markets not only justify this kind of expenditure for personnel training but demand it. The empirical evidence substantiates this conclusion, for American business spends more than $2 billion yearly to provide formal education courses for 3.5 million employees. This number is approximately equivalent to the total undergraduate enrollment of all U.S. colleges and universities. The widespread acceptance of this responsibility was indicated by a Prentice-Hall research staff survey which showed that 98 percent of the firms surveyed helped their employees financially to advance their education and improve their skills either through company or other educational opportunities. (8)

Role assigned to the union

Another responsible participant in training activities is the labor union, or other types of employee associations. The role of labor organizations is quite formal under apprenticeship training arrangements, as there is a joint responsibility between them and management for administering the programs. The unions are even given the right to administer discipline to laggard trainees.

The individual's residual responsibility

Although society, industry, and employee associations are responsible for developing employees, the residual responsibility for their development ultimately rests with individuals themselves. The necessity for self-development is based upon the basic assumption that *there is a possibility for conflict between personal goals and values on the one hand and organizational goals and values on the other,* for conflicts between groups and members of a group are most frequently caused by conflicts in their value systems.

Regardless of the individual's ultimate responsibility for development, it is essential that there be outside assistance, because "Stimulation and contact—physical, mental, social—are necessary for normal human development (i.e., development into what the members of the society would consider a human being). This holds to some extent even at the biological level." (9)

ASSESSING DEVELOPMENT NEEDS

In general, there are formal and informal types of development programs, but the following discussion involves only the formal ones. Assuming that an organization has a formal development program, it is necessary to determine the development needs, including what types of learning are needed.

Specific methods used in assessing needs

There are numerous methods for determining needs for training programs. However, the most frequently used ones are: (*a*) supervisory recommendations; (*b*) analysis of job requirements; (*c*) analysis of job performance; and (*d*) employee suggestions.

Supervisory recommendations. There are several ways the recommendations from supervisors can come to the training director. First, the supervisor may ask the training department to put on a program for a group of employees or provide training for a specific employee. Either way, the request comes *voluntarily* from the supervisor.

A *training needs survey* might be conducted by asking supervisors to complete their needs on a prepared form. A modification of this is to use the interview method of soliciting training needs from the supervisors.

A third method is through *problem analysis discussions,* whereby a training specialist meets with a group of supervisors from a given job area and asks them to crystalize their specific problems. There is a dual benefit, for not only are the training needs identified, but the supervisors are trained to become more analytical and objective in their study of their problems. See Figure 12–2 for a graphic illustration of how employees learn faster with trained supervisors.

Analysis of job requirements. As a result of the selection procedure, the difference between the abilities of an employee or group of employees and the job requirements may indicate a need for training. The important thing is to concentrate on determining training activities which result from—and are expected to correct—the employees' inability to do a job, to do it well enough, or to correct it when they are doing it incorrectly.

Analysis of job performance. Training needs can be highlighted as a result of employee performance ratings, or other form of performance appraisal, which indicates that an employee is not doing the job properly.

A modification of this method is by using a *personnel progress report,* usually used for new employees. By recording the worker's progress, a need for training is reflected where quality specifications or production schedules are not being met.

Another modification is *work data analysis.* Training directors can study all available reports to determine trends in unit costs, grievances, safety re-

FIGURE 12-2
Employee learning curves

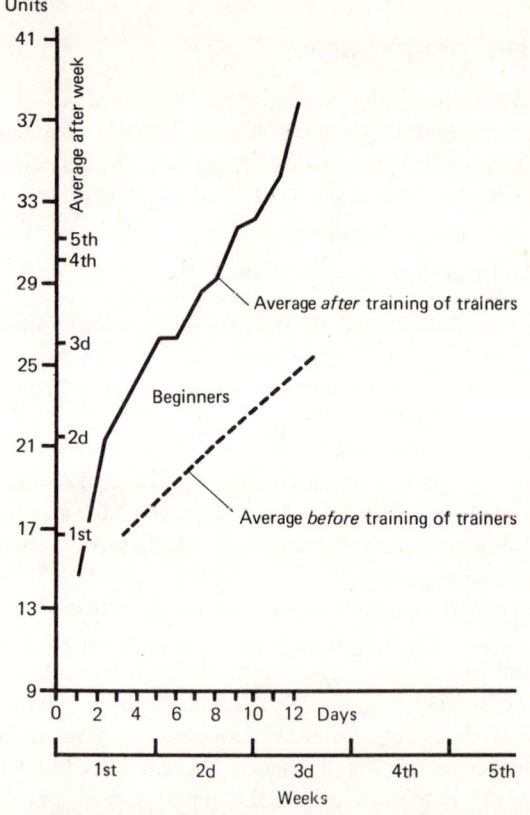

These two groups of employees were trained before and after instructor-training was introduced. Workers who learned stitching operations after the instructors were trained learned more rapidly and achieved much higher proficiency than workers who learned before the training methods were adopted. (Courtesy of A. Bavelas.)
Source: Norman R. F. Maier, *Psychology in Industry*, 3d ed. (Boston: Houghton Mifflin Co., 1965), p. 404.

ports, and other quality of production standards. It might become evident that an employee, or group of employees, is not performing satisfactorily.

Employee suggestions. If it is assumed that employees *wish to do a good job*, which is generally accepted, then it follows that employees who know they are not doing a good job may request training. Also, if the employees wish to progress through transfers or promotions, they may request training as a stepping stone to a better job.

Some generalizations about development needs

Although there is no generally accepted theory which explains how to determine development needs, the following elements are usually included.

Objectives of the development process. The most effective programs have found that the training objectives are: realistically attainable; in harmony with other organizational objectives; oriented toward both the long and short run; designed to provide common meaning to all concerned personnel; and closely related to the personal goals of the learner. (10) These programs are also finding that preoccupation with training based on the kinds of jobs that need to be filled is becoming secondary to *developing the kind of people* that the organization and the economy are going to find necessary for future effectiveness.

Types of development needed. Before students become a specialist of any kind they should first learn to understand what they read, to think for themselves, to express their thoughts clearly, to handle the basic tools of mathematics in their application to daily life, and to grasp some of the realities of their natural and human environment. If they learn these things, they will have *learned how to learn.* Such an education is like a master key that opens many doors, and the person who has it need never fear becoming the prisoner of an obsolete skill.

Adaptability. A basic need today can be summed up in one word: *adaptability.* In our complex economy, specialized skills are as important as ever, but the specialties become obsolete sooner than they used to. Some 70 percent of the skilled trades in American manufacturing in the year 1900 do not exist today. It is a safe prediction that a large proportion of today's skills will become obsolete in a much shorter period between now and the year 2000, which is a period shorter than the average man's working lifetime.

Retraining. A study of technologically obsolete employees indicated that many persons not previously considered eligible for training could be successfully retrained for relatively high-level technical jobs. (11) Apparently the ability to learn did not constitute a major limiting factor in the process, but the educational background of the workers did. The people who enrolled for training were influenced by interest in the work, confidence in their ability to succeed, and the environmental climate created by management.

However, retraining is not a panacea! One problem is the immobility of employees in technologically depressed areas. They often refuse to move to areas where there is available employment. Also, the very employees who most need retraining are the ones who, through lack of education, training, experience, and aptitudes, are unable to become the skilled craftsmen, technicians, or professional workers that are most needed. Finally, they are sometimes difficult to motivate to participate.

DESIGNING DEVELOPMENT PROGRAMS

The next phase of human resource development is to design development programs to satisfy the assessed needs. This step is successful only if based upon well-established principles of learning. (12) These principles can be utilized to accelerate favorable growth in employee behavior, but they do not insure successful development.

Some principles of learning

One shies away from using the word "principles" in generalizing about human behavior. However, there have been developed certain principles to be used in the learning process. For example, several conditions have been identified through research as facilitating the learning process. They are: (*a*) all realms of human behavior are subject to the learning process; (*b*) learning requires reinforcement in the form of rewards and punishments, and rewards are more useful in changing behavior and increasing one's learning than punishments; (*c*) learning is accentuated through feedback concerning the learner's performance; (*d*) training in one activity can be transferred to another if there are similar components or if the learner discovers principles or methods in one learning situation that can be transferred to others; (*e*) repetition, plus reinforcement, tends to facilitate learning, thus practice and reinforcement aid the growth process; and (*f*) learning corresponds to the meaningfulness of the material to be learned and how well it is organized. (13)

Applying learning principles to personnel development

What generalization can be made about these learning principles, as applied to human resource development? In general, it can be assumed that:

1. Development is most effective if it has positive motivation;
2. Continuous development is more effective than intermittent activities; and
3. Effective development utilizes the systems approach; i.e., all elements of the learning process such as site, selection and grouping of learners, teaching methods and personnel, and training aids are interrelated and interacting.

Need for positive motivation. As with all human behavior, there must be motivation before there can be learning. This motivational process is as follows: The learners' objective is self-gratification; to achieve this goal, their predominant need (or needs) must be satisfied; some external stimulus in the form of anticipated needs satisfaction is offered; they then learn by making the desired response in order to attain the thing they desire to satisfy their needs.

Identification. One of the essential aspects of motivation which leads to psychological growth in an organized group is *identification,* and this identification process continues to be a mechanism for growth (or regression) throughout a person's life. These relationships should have the quality of encouragement and affection which facilitates identification. This sound principle is based upon the assumption that a person must identify with someone who has more experience, skill, and power than oneself.

Law of Effect. In motivation to learn, it is generally accepted that superiors are constantly training their subordinates through the *law of effect.* (14) This law, simply stated, is that behavior which appears to lead to reward tends to be repeated, while behavior which appears not to lead to reward, or appears to lead to punishment, tends not to be repeated. Consequently, superiors are constantly using the law of effect to shape the behavior of subordinates through the allocation of rewards and punishment. Therefore, supervisors cannot abdicate their role as developers of *their* subordinates, for even though they may consciously ignore that role, they continue to function thus.

Development must be dynamic and continuous. Learning is, indeed, a lifelong process! Although fantasy, *Through the Looking Glass* reminds us of the rapidly changing tempo of the world when the Queen says: "It takes all the running you can do to stay in the same place." In more academic terms, the noted anthropologist Margaret Mead vividly expressed the idea of continuing education when she wrote: "No one will live all his life in the world into which he was born, and no one will die in the world in which he worked in his maturity. . . . Learning of this kind must go on not only at special times and in special places, but all through production and consumption. . . . " (15)

Therefore, although the need for developing *new* employees is generally recognized and practiced, it is now also recognized that development is a continuous need and that *all* employees need it. Industry cannot be static; it *must be dynamic* in evolving programs, both qualitative and quantitative, to meet the increasing needs for capable personnel. This statement is based upon the finding that: Human behavior is far more variable and, therefore, less predictable than that of any other species. The repertoire and range of behavior available to any given man, as well as the range that exists across men, is far broader than anywhere else in the animal kingdom. (16)

Development involves the systems approach. As indicated, all aspects of development, including the learner; teaching personnel, methods, and content; the physical surroundings; the psychological environment, including the organizational climate, the role of the superior, and the motivators used, and the condition to which the learner returns affect the success of development.

One special aspect of the systems approach is whether to try and train employees in only one phase of the job or teach the entire job. Researchers have compared the effectiveness of the following methods of learning: teaching employees to learn the parts of the task as opposed to the whole task; having them learn the whole job at one time; and using a combination of the whole and part types of learning. Contrary to the commonly held opinion, the result of their research showed that the whole method (or a combination of part and whole) was superior to the pure part type of learning. (17) In other words, the more nearly you can train workers to perform the whole job, the more effective they should be.

CONDUCTING DEVELOPMENTAL PROGRAMS

There are three interrelated questions involved in the action phase of development, namely, who is to do the developing, what is to be taught, and how is it taught.

Who is to do the development?

The NICB study of manufacturing firms found the majority of the firms using personnel staff members or full-time training instructors to train both blue- and white-collar employees. In fact, 78 percent of the firms used personnel staff members to train some or all of these employees. Yet, 93 percent of them used foremen, supervisors, or executives to do the training. Smaller proportions used vocational, technical, or business school teachers; or university and college professors to do the training. The other developmental activities were carried on by company suppliers of equipment or high school teachers.

Line-management's function. The middle- and top-level line management are responsible for establishing a climate in which personnel can grow by building an atmosphere of confidence between management and employees and by encouraging creative interaction among them.

Many line executives actually teach in formal programs, especially orientation and management development. An individual *supervisor* has great influence upon subordinates' development. Although the employees' desire for knowledge, coupled with their desire for usefulness, should motivate development, the supervisor can enhance this motivation by immediately communicating with employees when their performance is not conforming to management standards. Thus, if employees are apprised of their contribution to the organization when they are doing a good job, it should stimulate pride of accomplishment in them. This is called *reinforcement.*

Supervisors also participate in the actual development of subordinates. This statement is based upon the assumption that *a supervisor inevitably trains and induces development, either good or bad, in subordinates.*

Staff specialist's function. The personnel staff specialist's function is to provide formal training programs and to maintain the related records. However, it is axiomatic that good training directors don't usurp the line-manager's responsibility for training; instead, they help the other managers fulfill that responsibility. In essence, the responsibility for the total program for employee development is a joint responsibility, with the personnel staff performing the activities it can best perform and line managers implementing those which they are best equipped to handle.

What is to be taught?

The NICB study found job skills, company orientation, safety, first aid, presupervisory training, and economics—in that descending order—being taught in formal training programs. In essence, job skills, safety, first aid, and presupervisory training were emphasized with blue-collar workers; while company orientation was emphasized more to white-collar workers.

For purposes of this discussion, development will be discussed according to where it occurs—either on-the-job, or off-the-job.

On-the-job techniques. Although it is desirable to learn theory and principles, ultimately the employees must apply that knowledge to learning the practical aspects of their job. This process involves being instructed in the methods and techniques of actually performing the work and, thus, enhancing their skill level.

There is currently a renewed interest in vocational education, training, and development. For example, the U.S. Census Bureau reports that from 1964 to 1969, the number of young Americans enrolled full-time in vocational or technical training courses above the high school level zoomed from 150,000 to about 2 million, or a 13-fold increase. This emphasis upon vocational training and manual work may prove advantageous to employees and employers, for research has shown that vocationally trained workers have a higher labor force participation rate, a higher mean occupational mobility, and a lower mean unemployment rate. (18)

Orientation. New employees' development begins with their placement on the job for which they were selected. This involves being introduced into the organization through some form of orientation procedure. Orientation is quite important, for it often means the difference between success or failure in retaining productive employees, as employee turnover tends to occur primarily during the early period of employment. This is often a "trial" period for the newcomer, for one will be accepted or rejected by other employees; also, the worker decides whether to "accept" or "reject" the organization itself.

A research project at Ohio State University indicated that orientation of new employees may be an even more important factor in employee satisfaction and turnover than commonly recognized. A study of 15 supermarkets examined eight dimensions of employee job satisfaction and five dimensions of the employee's work group. The study isolated job orientation as a new and important independent variable affecting work group dimensions and employee satisfaction. (19)

This problem is particularly acute among scientific and technical personnel. Their technical curricula seem to arouse expectations and to emphasize values and goals inconsistent with the realities of corporate life. The result is widespread dissatisfaction among large numbers of scientific and technical employees when they enter industry. (20)

Special problems are encountered in placing minority members—especially the hard-core unemployed—on jobs for which they have been selected. Work relationships, housing, schools, and the host of other problems that usually are associated with a new job are sometimes almost overwhelming for these new employees and tend to be more of a problem than the actual fight for the job. (21)

There are a number of positive actions that personnel executives can take to reduce the undesirable aspects of orientation, to shorten the adjustment period, and to enhance the new member's growth and development. First, assign a mentor to the newcomer; next, have a formal indoctrination program to describe the overall activities of the organization; encourage individual recognition; provide pleasing work conditions; and train direct supervisors in human relations. (22)

On-the-job training. The most universal form of employee development is on-the-job training (OJT), the actual performance of work duties under the supervision and guidance of a trained worker or instructor. Thus, while learning how to perform the job, one is also a regular employee producing the product or service that the firm sells. This form of training always occurs, whether consciously planned or not. (23)

The primary advantages of OJT are that it results in low out-of-pocket costs, production is carried on during training, and there is no transition from classroom learning to actual production. However, poor instruction, excessive waste caused by errors, and the poor learning environment provided by the production area are disadvantages of this type of training.

Apprenticeship training. Apprenticeship training blends the learning of theory and of methods and techniques. It is used to impart job skills which require a long period of practice and experience and is generally used in trades, crafts, and other technical fields. If proficiency can only be acquired after a long period of classroom instruction and actual learning experiences associated with the job, this training method should be used. The extent and intensity of training vary among the types of apprentice programs, but they usually consist of 144 hours per year spent studying theory in formal classes and around 2,000 hours of supervised work experience where the skills in application are learned.

Apprenticeship has not been the total answer to craft training. It has been supplemented by the companies through hiring "helpers" who are upgraded to craftsmen. Also, with the complex and dynamic nature of present production jobs, some firms are instituting their own classroom programs in which the teaching of theory and principles supplements the regular job training. It is felt that this method will become prevalent in the future.

Internship training. Internship training (sometimes referred to as *cooperative education* or *coop ed*) is another method of coordinating the two types of learning, especially for professional, managerial, clerical, and sales personnel, in conjunction with an educational institution's teaching program. Usually selected students enrolled in a regular academic program are introduced into a company for a designated period of time to gain employment experience. By this training, students gain a better understanding of the relationship between the theory they learn in school and its application. It also gives them a chance to determine if they like the chosen type of work. But it is such a slow developmental process that both parties should have patience if they expect to achieve the greatest benefit from it.

Off-the-job techniques. Essentially there are two types of learning involved in employee development, namely, learning theories, concepts, and principles, and learning their application. Obviously some types of training bypass the theoretical aspects and concentrate on the practical requirements for performing the job. This trend will probably be reversed as jobs become more complex and technical. Technological development is exerting pressure upon employees to learn the whole job, that is, not only learning how the work is done but why it should be done in a given way.

The two types of learning are not mutually exclusive and do not have to be separated.

Assuming that a knowledge of theoretical concepts is desirable for the employees' use in adjusting to changes in the job requirements, how can they best be learned?

Vestibule training. An effective method related to OJT is "vestibule training," which is designed to give new employees some preliminary learning experience prior to any actual shop or office practice. It attempts to duplicate OJT under simulated work conditions in a room near the production area which is furnished with equipment similar to that which the employees will later be using. While employees are learning, output is not a major objective, but the acquisition of the necessary skills and instructions is the goal. As a result, they will be able to do the actual work more effectively when assigned a job. (24)

This method has the advantage of training large numbers of employees in a short period of time without disturbing the actual production routine. It also gives employees a chance to gain preliminary knowledge about the job so they will have confidence when they begin working. However, since this method requires special instructors and the duplication of shop or office facilities, it is relatively expensive.

Classroom instruction. There is still no feasible substitute for the student-teacher relationship found in the classroom, where knowledge is transmitted from the instructor to the learner by some form of oral or visual exchange of ideas. Many firms now have training classrooms in which to teach employees the theoretical and background information that is needed for successful job performance. There, away from production pressures, the teacher and learners can concentrate on the education experience.

Programmed instruction. One of the newer training methods for learning theory, principles, and concepts is programmed instruction. This type of instruction sometimes involves what are colloquially called *teaching machines.* In essence, the method involves presenting material organized in a sequential order on film or printed matter. The learners are not allowed to proceed beyond a given point until they have mastered the necessary information to permit them to perform the job. In other words, they must learn one part of the training program before continuing to the next. For this method of instruction to be used effectively and efficiently, it should be based upon material that will remain relatively static and can be taught to a large number of individuals over a substantial period of time.

In a study of the effectiveness of this learning device, it was found that typing efficiency in an office increased 32 percent; in another, errors were decreased 60 percent and speed increased 53 percent. (25) One study showed that training expenses could be reduced by about 40 percent while the amount of information retained by the trainees increased measurably. (26) In summary, in experiments at over 1,500 companies, programmed learning seems to offer improved learning at lower cost. (27)

Educational television. Another emerging method of training is educational television, whereby either ordinary television or closed-circuit television is used for learning purposes. This method has the unique advantage of being available to practically unlimited numbers of persons, and the cost per person can be decreased commensurately. To the extent feasible, television can permit personnel managers to do for training and development what industry has done with production, namely, provide mass development on the assembly-line basis, with quality control, at a low unit cost per person. (28)

Extension courses. Extension courses, including *correspondence courses,* are widely used in industry as an alternative to classroom instruction. Some companies pay all or part of the tuition for the job-related courses. (More than 5.2 million students are enrolled in correspondence courses, according to the National Home Study Council.)

Another variation of this training method is for a regular academic instructor to go to the firm's premises and conduct regular or special courses for employees.

Some firms provide paid leave for their employees to earn a degree or upgrade their knowledge at the company's expense.

Assistance from manufacturers, trade association, and professional organizations. Many organizations receive outside assistance from manufacturers of specialized equipment, trade associations, or other professional organizations which provide specialists for training the employees of their customers and members. This is particularly true of technical jobs and activities involving special skills or knowledge. Some computer manufacturers train the personnel of companies that purchase or lease equipment.

EVALUATING EFFECTIVENESS OF DEVELOPMENT PROGRAMS

It is necessary to evaluate the effectiveness of formal training programs in achieving development goals, for training does not always train! An examination of any range of development attempts would reveal a high proportion of failures, which could be attributed to such factors as having the wrong objective, using the wrong method, poor instruction, poor training material, and resistance to training.

At best, consequences of ineffective development programs may be merely a waste of time, effort, and money. At worst, ineffectual training results in failure to develop knowledge and skills, which may lead to organizational and personal decline. Essentially the payoff is reflected in the application of the improved development which results in better performance.

Approaches to evaluation

Probably no other area of the personnel function has been given more attention than evaluating training efforts. There are many techniques that can be used to increase effectiveness and impact of development upon the organization. (29) Fortunately the costs and benefits are not too difficult to approximate and evaluate.

In evaluating the results of development, there should be a repetition of the measures employed previously in analyzing training needs. For example, if statistical analyses were used to determine the need for developing employees, then essentially the same techniques should be used to determine the effectiveness of the program. In making the evaluation, a distinction must be made between short- and long-range benefits. Some developmental programs may show immediate results, particularly if they involve routine learning of skills. Conversely, some results may not become evident for years if it is the educational type of development, based upon the acquisition of general knowledge. Another evaluation problem is whether there is objective evidence of improvement or whether qualitative judgment must be made. When objective evidence is available, it should be used; if not, then a qualitative judgment must be made.

However, there are complicating variables. First, there are some intangibles which are not capable of measuring, such as attitudes, opinions, beliefs, and the long-run consequences to the individual and to the organization. Also, there are many contaminating factors. Formal and informal development activities may coincide and even conflict.

> A training program was conducted at a hospital to improve supervisory performance. Opinion surveys of the experimental and control groups were done before and after the training. However, during the two months of the program, the board separated merit increases from cost-of-living, granted a 5 percent across-the-board increase, and gave supervisors greater flexibility and discretion in granting the merit increases.

What is evaluated?

Most valid evaluation efforts attempt to evaluate four things, namely:

1. Reaction—did the participants enjoy the program and think it was effective;
2. Did learning occur—how well did the participants learn the facts, skills, techniques, and so forth;
3. Job behavior changes—how did behavior change on the job after the program; and
4. Tangible results—increased output and improved performance; reduced costs, errors, turnover, absenteeism, and so forth. This approach is results-oriented.

A cost effectiveness approach

Assuming that the objectives of a development program are specifically stated, the evaluation procedure should try to determine the cost of the devel-

FIGURE 12-3
A model for evaluating effectiveness of developmental program

Group	Time period		
	1 Preprogram	2 Program	3 Post program
Control............	Test —————————————————→		Test
Experimental......	Test ————→	Development ————→	Test

opment program and the benefits derived. This cost effective approach would involve several steps using the experimental method.

First, the total development costs are obtained by adding the *direct costs* of the trainers, materials, lost output of employees during the training program to the *indirect costs,* which are a share of the administrative and personnel departments' overhead.

Second, experimental and control groups are set up. Each group is structured to be as nearly similar as possible as far as intelligence, education, experience, and job level are concerned. Each group is then tested, using appropriate testing instruments based upon the objectives of the training and the type groups being developed.

Third, the experimental group is provided the training, while the control group is held as nearly constant as feasible.

Fourth, after the program is over, both groups are again tested to see if there were measurable benefits derived from the training. Other ways of determining these benefits are through opinion surveys, trainer evaluations, and measurement of job performance or productivity after the training.

By comparing the before and after performance of the experimental group with that of the control group, an approximation of the effectiveness of the

FIGURE 12-4
Mastery attainment by experimental and control groups

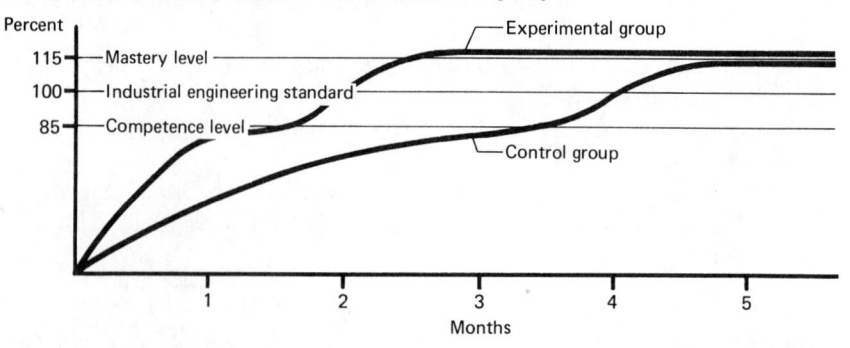

Source: Earl R. Gomersall and M. Scott Myers, "Breakthrough in On-the-Job Training," *Harvard Business Review,* vol. 44, no. 4 (July–August 1966), p. 69. Copyright © 1966 by the President and Fellows of Harvard College; all rights reserved.

training can be obtained. The model for evaluating change resulting from development is shown in Figure 12-3. An example of this type of evaluation was a Texas Instrument experiment with a one-day "anxiety-reducing" orientation program which showed reduced training time, costs, absenteeism, tardiness, waste, and rejects. Figure 12-4 shows improvement in job performance of the experimental group, as compared to the control group.

In summary, most evaluation studies show training and development pay for themselves through improved performance, higher productivity, lower turnover, less absenteeism, and higher personal satisfaction. (30)

IMPLICATIONS AND APPLICATIONS FOR PERSONNEL EXECUTIVES

It cannot be emphasized strongly enough that *an organization pays the cost of development whether it has a formal program or not.* It pays for inadequate or nonexistent training through waste, scrap, and damaged production, or through absenteeism, high turnover, lower job satisfaction, slowdowns, complaints, and grievances, and, in general, poor performance. It also must use the funds saved by not having a formal program in raising wages and salaries sufficiently to lure already trained employees away from competitors, a practice that presently is discouraging real training programs for many companies. Consequently, some type of development goes on in every institution, whether it is formalized and directed or not. This conclusion is based upon the hypothesis:

1. *Human learning and human adaptive behavior are communicated and, therefore, cumulative. Members of other species also learn but only through immediate, personal experience.*

Everyone is constantly learning new information and acquiring new skills, habits, attitudes, and beliefs, either consciously or unconsciously. The vice president of a large organization once stated to me, "I've never worked for anyone who didn't contribute at least a little bit to my knowledge. But some of them contributed in a way they would be very unhappy to know about. They taught me what *not* to do rather than what to do."

A second hypothesis is:

2. *Development is a result of both heredity and environment; heredity determines employees' maximum mental and physical capacity for development, while their total environment greatly affects the level to which they have grown and will grow toward achieving their total potential through education, training, experience, and motivation.*

Another basic hypothesis of this book is that:

3. *Individual effectiveness is increased through programs of education and training which develop the inherent capabilities of individual employees.*

A corollary hypothesis is:

4. *Human behavior is more dependent upon learning and less regulated by instinct or other innate behavioral predispositions than the behavior of lower creatures.*

This truth signifies that the behavior of an individual is directed toward achieving a desired and unattained goal or satisfying an unfulfilled need. As an employee's behavior results from the combined force of these motivations, any change in one's behavior will be the result of an attempt to increase satisfaction of one's needs or to avoid a decrease in the possibility of attaining satisfaction. If the above hypothesis is valid, personnel development is an attempt to *change the behavior pattern of employees,* preferably with the consequence that their performance will increase.

Therefore, assuming that *human behavior is a function of learning, which changes the behavior pattern of employees into the desired direction,* the basic hypothesis of this chapter is:

5. *A nation or organization's supply and caliber of human resources can be effectively increased and enhanced through education, training, and personal development.*

A hypothesis that needs testing is:

6. *All trainees resist training to some degree, and the degree varies from very little to a great deal.*

There are several important conditions upon which successful development is based. First, learning should be a continuous process, because cultural and technological changes demand *constant development.* Second, *every aspect of* human *behavior* should be subject to the learning process, because every human faculty and element is related to an individual's behavior. Third, development requires *dynamic reinforcement* in such forms as rewards and punishments, because the needs of employees are dynamic and various and the use of only one approach cannot meet our training needs. Fourth, the *participant's attitudes and motivation* should be *favorable* in order to facilitate the development process.

The following comments by a practicing personnel executive illustrate this last point.

> In some of our operations, on-site educational programs are provided on a scheduled or nonscheduled basis and are, in most cases, voluntary and selective. In most cases, the programs are centered around the first- and second-line management function.
>
> A great many companies provide a tuition program off-site that is job-oriented and is obtained from an accredited institution. This program is paid for by the company on the basis of the grades earned by the employee. *There is a surprising lack of interest by employees in these programs.*

DISCUSSION QUESTIONS

1. What are the usual objectives of development programs?
2. Comment on the following assumption: "You cannot teach people anything; they must learn it for themselves."
3. In your own words, what are some principles of learning underlying employee development?
4. How would you evaluate a specific development program?
5. What is the relationship between personnel development and social responsibility?
6. Why is self-development so important?
7. Explain how you would determine the development needs of a given organization.
8. Explain the *law of effect*.
9. What are some of the training techniques used in development?

REFERENCES AND SUGGESTIONS FOR FURTHER STUDY

1. The National Industrial Conference Board (NICB) survey gave corroborating evidence for this generalization. It found that the percentage of manufacturing firms with formal training programs was a function of size, as follows:

Number employees	Percent with formal programs
250–499	30
500–999	35
1,000–4,999	60
5,000 and over	83

2. See Elmer H. Burack and Peter F. Sorensen, Jr., "Manpower Development and Technological Change; Some Considerations for Revised Strategy," *Journal of Management Studies,* vol. 8, no. 3 (October 1971), pp. 304–14, for further discussion of the need to upgrade and improve the attractiveness of the lower positions.
3. Since only a fraction of all job openings are reported to the USES job bank, government officials estimate that there were as many as a million job openings during the month, partially because of the shortage of basic skills. See "A Million Jobs with No Takers," *Business Week* (January 19, 1976), pp. 16–17, for a further discussion of this problem.
4. See Donald P. Crane, "Guidelines for Minority Manpower Development," *Personnel Journal,* vol. 49, no. 10 (October 1970), for the experience of several firms' training for professional employment.
5. See "How IBM Avoids Layoffs through Retraining," *Business Week* (November 10, 1975), pp. 110–12, for examples of how this program works in practice.
6. L. C. Scott, "The Economic Effectiveness of On-the-Job Training: The Experiences of the Bureau of Indian Affairs in Oklahoma," *Industrial & Labor Relations Review,* vol. 23, no. 2 (January 1970), pp. 220–36. Both private and social benefits were probably underestimated as they included only explicit factors. Areas of

psychological and social benefits, such as an increased feeling of personal worth, lower crime rates, and reduced social welfare and unemployment expenditures were not measured.

7. "Preparing Third Graders for Something beyond Fourth Grade," *Bell Telephone Magazine,* vol. 54, no. 2 (March–April 1975), pp. 13–19.
8. *Personnel Management—Policies and Practices,* Bulletin No. 12 (New York; Prentice-Hall, Inc., December 3, 1963), p. 279.
9. Bernard Berelson and G. A. Steiner, *Human Behavior: An Inventory of Scientific Findings* (New York: Harcourt, Brace & World, Inc., 1964), p. 39.
10. E. Arthur Prieve and Dorothy A. Wentorf, "Training Objectives—Philosophy or Practice?" *Personnel Journal,* vol. 49, no. 3 (March 1970), pp. 235–40.
11. Walter J. McNamara, "Retraining of Industrial Personnel," *Personnel Psychology,* vol. 16, no. 3 (Autumn 1963), pp. 233–47.
12. There are numerous "schools" of learning theory, but the most prevalent are: (*a*) the behaviorist school, which holds that learning is the result of rewards or punishment that follows a response to a stimulus: (*b*) the gestalt school, which feels that learning is more complex than simple stimulus-response relationships. Learning is cognitive and involves the whole personality: (*c*) the Freudian school, which is impossible to capsulize: (*d*) the functionalist school, which takes parts from all schools and views learning as complex: (*e*) the mathematical models school, which feels that learning theories can be expressed in mathematical models; and (*f*) the current learning theory school, which runs the gamut from modifying the others to combining them. See the two-part article entitled, "Learning Theories and Training," by Leslie E. This and Gordon L. Lippitt, published in *Training and Development Journal,* vol. 20, no. 4 (April 1966), pp. 2–12, and no. 5 (May 1966), pp. 10–19, for a discussion of these.

See also O. Jeff Harris, Jr., *Managing People at Work* (Santa Barbara, Calif.: John Wiley & Sons, Inc., 1976), pp. 427–28, for another discussion of learning theory.

13. Timothy W. Costello and Sheldon S. Zalkind, *Psychology in Administration: A Research Orientation* (Englewood Cliffs, N.J.: Prentice-Hall, Inc., 1963), pp. 206–26.
14. See Edward L. Thorndike, *Human Learning* (New York: Century Co. 1931), for a discussion of how this factor works in practice.
15. Margaret Mead, "Thinking Ahead: Why Is Education Obsolete?" *Harvard Business Review,* vol. 36, no. 6 (November–December 1958), p. 34.
16. Berelson and Steiner, *Human Behavior,* p. 39.
17. George E. Briggs and James G. Naylor, "The Relative Efficiency of Several Training Methods as a Function of Transfer Task Complexity," *Journal of Experimental Psychology,* vol. 64, no. 5 (November 1962), pp. 505–12.
18. Roger L. Bowlby and William R. Schriver, "Nonwage Benefits of Vocational Training: Employability and Mobility," *Industrial and Labor Relations Review,* vol. 23, no. 4 (July 1970), pp. 500–09.
19. See B. W. Marion and S. E. Trieb, "Job Orientation—A Factor in Employee Performance and Turnover," *Personnel Journal,* vol. 48, no. 10 (October 1969), pp. 799–804, for the results of the research which indicated that attitudes and

impressions developed during the early days of the job have a lasting effect on employee performance, satisfaction, and turnover.

20. Herbert Holt and Robert C. Ferber, "The Psychological Transition from Management Scientist to Manager," *Management Science*, vol. 10, no. 3 (April 1964), pp. 409–20.

21. See Ulric Haynes, Jr., "Equal Job Opportunity: The Credibility Gap," *Harvard Business Review*, vol. 46. no. 3 (May–June 1968), p. 113 ff., for suggestions on how to help the new employee make the adjustment.

22. See George C. Bucher, "How to Help the New Researcher Adjust to the Organization," *Research Management* (July 1974), pp. 34–38, for further details and suggestions.

23. For example, it was found that 21.5 percent of training in construction, where apprenticeship is so important, was done by actual experience on the job. See Howard G. Foster, "Nonapprentice Sources of Training in Construction," *Monthly Labor Review*, vol. 93, no. 2 (February 1970), pp. 21–26.

24. A recent study showed that this type training gave best results when coupled with on-the-job training. Joel Lefkowitz, "Effect of Training on the Productivity and Tenure of Sewing Machine Operators," *Journal of Applied Psychology*, vol. 54, no. 1 (February 1970), pp. 81–86.

25. A. E. Oriel, "Programmed Instruction," *Advanced Management—Office Executive*, vol. 1, no. 9 (September 1962), pp. 33–35.

26. L. W. O'Donnel, "Programmed Instruction," *Administrative Management*, vol. 25, no. 1 (January 1964), pp. 43–45.

27. John W. Buckley, "Programmed Instruction in Industrial Training," *California Management Review*, vol. 10, no. 2 (Winter 1967), pp. 71–79.

28. For example, several South Carolina companies united and utilized the state's educational TV network for training their middle managers. They used such courses as "Exploring Basic Economics." "TV Teaches Training Plant Bosses Statewide," *Business Week*, no. 1826 (August 29, 1964), pp. 64–66.

29. From a review of the better known and publicly available studies attempting rigorous evaluation of training program effectiveness, it has been concluded that the use of controls of some type, and an attempt to gauge the on-the-job behavior change, has become almost standard procedure. However, beyond that, a great variety of methodological procedures enter in. Improvement is usually measured by before and after performance. The primary weakness of these studies is their lack of focusing evaluation on both short- and long-term effects.

    See Joseph Wolfe, "Evaluating the Training Effort," *Training and Development Journal*, vol. 27, no. 5 (May 1973), pp. 20–27, for an excellent presentation.

30. Maurice Kilbridge, "A Model for Industrial Learning Costs," *Management Science*, vol. 8, no. 4 (July 1962), pp. 516–28; Warren H. Schmidt, "How to Evaluate a Company's Training Efforts," *California Management Review*, vol. 12, no. 3 (Spring 1970), pp. 49–56.

Chapter 13

Executive development

Objectives of executive development
  To achieve organizational goals
  To achieve individual growth

Establishing parameters to executive development
  Role of executives in developing subordinates
  Role of self-development

Determining developmental needs
  Criteria for determining who needs developing
  Criteria for determining what should be developed

Methods used in developing executives
  Some policy decisions
  Methods used to improve technical knowledge and skills
  Methods used to develop administrative skills
  Modifying attitudes and developing managerial philosophies
  Acquiring general, or integrated, knowledge

Appraising and evaluating executive development
  Difficulty of evaluating
  Methodology
  Relating evaluation to objectives

Groups requiring special attention
  Women
  Minorities
  Managers of small businesses
  Personnel executives themselves

Implications and applications for personnel executives

13
Executive development

There are a lot of completely educated people in the world and of course they will resent being asked to learn anything new.
ROBERT FROST

An institution that cannot produce its own managers will die. From an overall point of view the ability of an institution to produce managers is more important than its ability to produce efficiently and cheaply.
PETER F. DRUCKER

The chief executive officer of a large food company recently committed suicide. He not only ran a one-man show, but he failed to prepare a successor. The board searched for an outside replacement while the company was run by two committees.

Drucker's statement and this case illustrate the importance of executive development. Yet, its importance is not always recognized and given the importance it deserves. This is one of the first "costs" cut in a recessionary period.

Some of the principles of learning and the necessity of establishing criteria for evaluating the effectiveness of developmental programs were presented in the previous chapter. The material was oriented toward both managerial and nonmanagerial personnel. In this chapter, the different concepts that must be applied to developing scientific, technical, and professional employees, as well as executive personnel, are discussed.* Figure 13-1 shows the model which can be used in developing such a program and applying it to a given organization.

Management training has increased in the United States over the last four decades in an uneven manner. Yet, it has grown from being used by around 3 percent of corporations in 1935 to around 75 percent now. However, the truly phenomenal growth has occurred in public organizations. (1)

Two of the prime reasons for this increasing interest in executive develop-

---

* The terms "executive," "management," and "managerial personnel" will be used to apply to all scientific, technical, and professional personnel. The rationale for this is the fact that managers almost inevitably will come from among those individuals rather than from the ranks of the skilled, unskilled, or clerical employees. Also, these tend to perform some aspect of the managerial functions of planning, organizing, staffing, directing, and controlling.

FIGURE 13-1
A model for developing executives

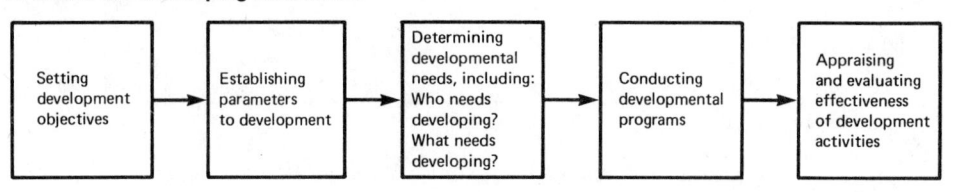

Setting development objectives → Establishing parameters to development → Determining developmental needs, including: Who needs developing? What needs developing? → Conducting developmental programs → Appraising and evaluating effectiveness of development activities

ment are the rapid increases in knowledge, particularly of human behavior, and the fact that today's organizations are operating in a "perpetual state of escalating managerial expectations." (2)

If an executive development system is to be relevant to future organizational problems, it must be a "well-planned, well-implemented, action-oriented, practical program headed up by professionals." (3)

OBJECTIVES OF EXECUTIVE DEVELOPMENT

Much has been said and written concerning the goals of executive development. These goals are described in such comments as: "The company wants to be progressive"; "To be dynamic, the company must develop its managers"; and many similar remarks. However, the actual motives behind the desire to develop managers and related personnel may be quite different. They may include such things as a desire to bend the thinking of subordinates to fit the pattern of the top management; a desire to revolutionize the way the organization operates; a desire to extend the point of view of the present generation of managers to the next; or simply a desire to "keep up with the Joneses."

To achieve organizational goals

Regardless of the overt goal of such programs, their basic aim must be to create within individuals a capacity to manage and administer the affairs of their organization efficiently and effectively. Thus, development should result in individual growth and a greater degree of achievement of organizational goals.

Research has shown that developmental programs conducted within the influence of the organization are more oriented toward organizational identification than are university and other outside programs. (4) The internal programs tend toward transmission of the "company line" or "organizational philosophy." The universities, through their emphasis upon a spirit of investigation and exploration, tend to create potential nonconformists and innovators. Therefore, institutions seeking to maintain the status quo might find it advisable to use their own programs rather than the outside ones.

To achieve individual growth

I believe that most formal executive development programs do little to ensure organizational development in an age of constant and pervasive change. At best, they are useful for developing managers and personnel to perform present activities; but they do little toward preparing them for future operations. At worst, they develop attitudes and habits which preclude change and growth and tend to compound the errors and inadequacies inherent in many organizations that attempt to maintain the status quo.

ESTABLISHING PARAMETERS TO EXECUTIVE DEVELOPMENT

After deciding what the training objectives are, some parameters to that development should be established. These will serve as guidelines, "principles," or boundaries not only delimiting the development activities themselves, but also providing a realistic expectation of what can be achieved through developmental activities.

While no two organizations approach executive development the same way, there are some common threads running through the more effective programs. Some of the factors leading to effectiveness are:

1. They are a deep and integral part of the organizational system, involving all levels of management, reflecting the organizational climate, and affecting the very way the organization works;
2. Support of, and a long-term commitment to, the program by top management are unwavering;
3. Management development is a significant part of every manager's job; (5) and
4. Participants view the program positively and enthusiastically.

Only the last two will be discussed in detail.

Role of executives in developing subordinates

Research has shown that superiors have a considerable influence on the development of their subordinates. (6) The way they treat their followers and their expectations of them will lead to high performance and career satisfaction or vice versa.

Executives not only affect the expectations, development, and productivity of subordinates, but also influence their *perceptions* of their job and themselves. If managers perceive their superiors as incompetent, unskilled, or insensitive to their needs, their performance and growth may be adversely affected. However, if the subordinates perceive that the superior is skillful and has high expectations of subordinates, the latter's self-confidence, development, and capabilities will be high.

Another interesting aspect of the relationship between managers and their superiors was highlighted in a recent study comparing the type of leadership exerted by executives and the growth progress of their subordinates. The results indicated that executives feel they have learned more from "tough bosses" who gave them responsibility and "demanded superior performance" from them than from those who "led" and "guided" their development. In both relationships, the superiors initiated and stimulated the growth of their followers. However, both managerial types were preferable to the dominating boss who stifles growth by overcontrol and failure to delegate and to the indifferent boss who simply neglects developing junior personnel. (7)

Role of self-development

It has been stated in many ways by many people, but the message is the same: executive development is self-development. An organization does not begin with totally raw material and develop it into a desirable manager. Instead, new managers have already grown to a certain level, depending upon their heredity and environment. If they want to succeed, they have the residual responsibility for their own destiny, for no one else can force them to grow, nor should they be required or permitted to do so.

The role of role perception. The point of departure in self-development is to recognize that people have a perception of the role they play as a person, citizen, student, or manager. The developmental process must be geared to enhancing the image of the role played in the organization. If this is not done, their self-image may be destroyed; and, instead of becoming better producers, they may lose all aspiration and initiative.

The results of a recent research study by Esso Research corroborates this.

© 1970 by NEA, Inc. Reprinted by permission of NEA.

The organization's researchers developed a program designed to improve their supervisors' performance. The system was built around the concept that the supervisors, with aid from top management and their subordinates, would strive for self-development. The result was that 60 percent of the supervisors and subordinates agreed that productivity had been favorably affected; 88 percent of the supervisors had tried to change; and 25 percent of the subordinates saw lasting changes in their supervisors. (8)

Importance of unknown factors. An interesting aspect of this discussion is that the unknown factors about executives are as significant in their development as are the knowns. This assumption is a partial explanation of differential achievements from people with apparently the same capacities and aptitudes. The source of these differences is deeply imbedded in a person's conscious and subconscious being, and it is impossible to measure these by tests, interviews, or other methods. These qualities are relatively imperceptible. Therefore, only one person is able to assess them with approximate accuracy and that is the individual person. (It should be understood that everyone does not always understand one's own capabilities and motivations.)

Self-judgment is really the most significant judgment made of an individual. We do not judge ouselves only once; we do so daily. And our conclusions about ourselves are usually concealed within us. Therefore, each individual has a unique personal contribution to make to one's own development. Others can only create the opportunity and atmosphere for development.

DETERMINING DEVELOPMENTAL NEEDS

There are two primary decisions that must be made in determining developmental needs, namely, who and what needs developing.

Before the actual development process begins, an assessment of development needs should be carried out. Management development personnel must take into account the specific needs of individual managers, as well as the organizational climate in which managers will work, for the climate will significantly influence managerial behavior. Some of the commonly used techniques in assessing training needs are: (9)

1. Management appraisals—The rating system allows an objective comparison of the discrepancy between present and desired levels of manager performance. This technique is used by 85 percent of U.S. companies;
2. Surveys—Two types are used, (*a*) ask managers to specify training needs of their subordinates, (*b*) a rate-your-own performance survey;
3. Critical incidents—They are job behaviors which supervisors would consider either "good" or "bad";
4. Job analysis—It outlines the major functions and general expectations of a position;
5. Assessment centers—These are used for identifying management potential and their development needs;

6. Psychological testing—Tests of intelligence, vocational interest, verbal and mathematical skills, and personality are often included as part of the assessment center;
7. Skills inventory—This contains autobiographical information on various employee populations; and
8. Coaching—Here the superiors provide help to their subordinates.

Criteria for determining who needs developing

There is also no easy answer to the question of who should be developed. In any developmental activities, the primary axiom is to start at the top of the organization and work down from there rather than to start at the bottom and work upward. However, it is usually impractical to begin at the top, for training begins at some lower level. Apparently top executives are not prepared to accept the fact that they need further development. As an excuse, they say they are "too busy" or "the organization cannot afford to let them go."

Special groups needing development. According to a study made at Du Pont, those people in the upper end of the managerial spectrum who are thought to be qualified to attain higher management status and those individuals at the lower end who are relatively young employees but who are considered to have substantial capacity for advancement should be included in development programs. (10)

Another study of 60 firms was conducted to determine who had actually been selected to attend management development programs. It was found that 82 percent of these firms sent *managers* who were *newly appointed to a position of increased responsibility* or someone selected for promotion in the near future; 66 percent selected *technicians and specialists* requiring general management "know-how"; and 60 percent *selected personnel who needed a refresher course* in new theories of general management. (11)

Those preparing for career changes. There is a point somewhere in an employee's career when a shift is required from performing the technical aspects of one's job to performing the managerial. The skills required are quite different, but the transition is usually gradual, which permits the person to make the shift satisfactorily.

As can be seen from Figure 13-2, the entry-level workers devote most of their time to using technical skills. However, as they progress into first-line supervision and later into middle management, the need for performing more managerial skills and less technical skills occurs. When upper management and top management levels are reached, the technical skills are subordinated to the managerial skills.

At several places along this spectrum, these managers need development. First, it is needed at the job entry level, as most of the time is spent using technical skills. At the supervisory level, the person needs training in supervis-

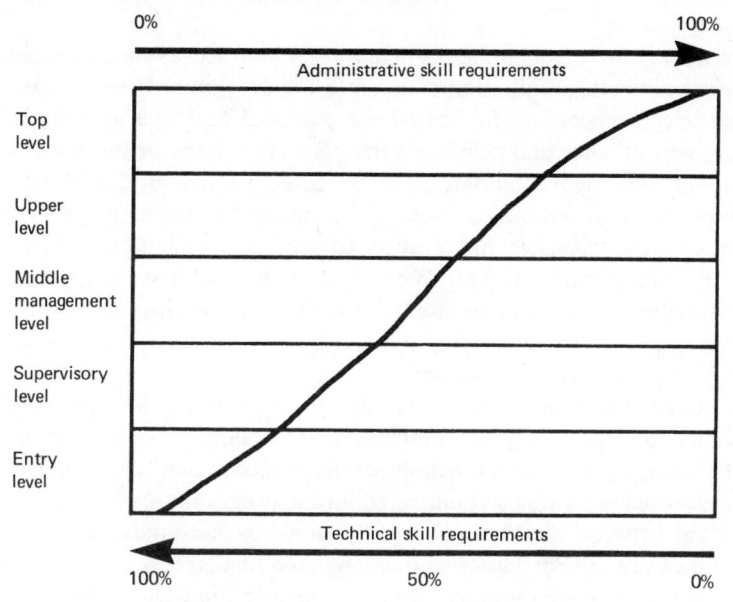

FIGURE 13-2
The progression of management skills

[Figure shows a graph with management levels (Entry, Supervisory, Middle management, Upper, Top) on the vertical axis. Administrative skill requirements increase from 0% to 100% (left to right) as one moves up the levels, while Technical skill requirements decrease from 100% to 0% (right to left).]

ing nonmanagerial personnel. When one reaches the middle management level, another change occurs and one begins to manage other managers which requires more and better administrative skills. This tendency increases the further one rises in the managerial ranks.

Those with technical background. As shown earlier, there has been difficulty in integrating scientific, technical, and professional personnel into the managerial ranks. Because of their specialized education, *technicians tend to think in terms of things,* but *executives must think in terms of people;* the former tend to think in terms of the scientific approach to problem solving, whereas, although managers can utilize the scientific approach in decisions making, they must usually utilize the artistic approach to decisions and in applying the decisions to subordinates involved. Essentially the important thing is that these people need to *learn to think and act like executives.*

The reorientation of these specialists involves three essentials. First, it is necessary to arouse their interest in "people-type" problems. Second, certain roadblocks resulting from their prior training, which limit the extent of their empathy with people, must be removed. Finally, there is a need to train them in areas previously neglected, which is usually interpersonal and intergroup relationships. In this context, "removing the roadblocks" means teaching the individual to arrive at decisions that are not always "right" in the eyes of peers who remain oriented to the research, technical, or engineering areas. The scientist solves problems in the context of *one correct answer;* management must assume that there are *several acceptable answers, no one of which is totally and solely correct.*

Strategies used in selecting participants. There are several strategies used by organizations in nominating candidates for development programs. They may be selected because: (*a*) they have potential and it is hoped that the program will enhance and accelerate their growth; (*b*) the deficiencies in their performance, and their attendance may be corrective in nature; (*c*) the superior may hope that a dismal performance will either lead to the manager's resignation or give the manager justification to ask for a resignation; or (*d*) the manager acts arbitrarily and sends people on a rational basis, i.e., whose turn is it? Regardless of the strategy used, it is felt that those with the responsibility for developing and implementing these programs should make clear the criteria by which nominations are made.

Voluntary or mandatory participation. The question of whether participation should be mandatory or voluntary is important, for it was found in a research study of a Veterans Administrative management development program that when individuals volunteered for the program, there was not a clear delineation between the "better" and "poorer" backgrounds. The results of this failure were mixed. Those who volunteered tended toward a higher level intellectually and educationally and had a greater knowledge about supervisory practices in the organization. However, the volunteers tended toward "depressive reactions and, to a lesser extent, toward somewhat greater constriction of thought and action." (12)

Participants' perception of program. There is another practical element which must be considered in choosing people for formal development programs, namely, the *perception* the participants and their peers have of the purpose of the selection. Inevitably there is the problem of jealousy among fellow workers for they may consider the possibility that the employee selected for development will be considered a "crown prince," being groomed for promotion over them. This problem is also present in the immature superior who feels that once a subordinate is developed the subordinate will replace him. There is another perception that is diametrically opposed to this one. Sometimes an individual may get the impression that she has done something wrong, or is being punished for some error or deficiency. If either of these elements is present to a significant degree (they will always be present to a slight degree), the effectivess of the development will be restricted. This is particularly true if the participant enters the training program believing she is being punished, for research indicates that when this occurs little learning takes place. (13)

Another research study was conducted in order to relate personal and situational characteristics of participants in a development program to their reactions to the development activities. It was found that the participants' liking for the training was correlated only slightly to their perception that it would be helpful in performing job duties. However, they viewed the program as being more helpful when they perceived that higher-level executives were interested in, and supported, the training program. Finally, the group responded favorably to the training when they saw a relationship between using their training and obtaining various types of rewards corresponding to their interests and goals. (14)

Predictors of success as participants in development programs. Regardless of who is chosen for formal development programs, the individuals who are selected for future managerial positions in an organization must have the qualities necessary for them to grapple effectively with the constant upheaval that has supplanted the comparative tranquility of the past. As shown in Chapter 10, those qualities would include *intelligence,* including the ability to absorb, understand, and use the information being presented; *adaptability,* or openness to new knowledge or situations; *motivation* to learn, and a *favorable attitude* toward the material taught in the program; and *willingness to take risks.* (15)

Other research has shown that the requirements for success in developing programs are primarily *intellectual,* with special emphasis being given to *reading* and *mathematical abilities.* Personality factors have not been found to be valid predictors of success.

A study of the largest sales organizations in 1964 found all of the respondents ranking intelligence as the most vital prerequisite to success in management training programs. *Maturity* and *interpersonal skills* such as *empathy* and *communications* followed in importance. (16)

Criteria for determining what should be developed

Probably the oldest, most prevalent, and most frustrating question asked in this important area is what should be developed in executives. Although there is no consensus among the authorities as to the theoretical concepts or specific content of these formal development programs, (17) it is assumed that essentially four things should be developed in present and future executives. They are shown in Figure 13–3.

Improving technical knowledge and skills. Executive development consists not only of helping individuals to overcome the blind spots and habits of wishful thinking that prevent them from achieving their fullest potentialities, but also of giving them specialized training in specific skills.

Although it is not essential for managers to be able to perform every job under their supervision, it is highly desirable that they know how each job should be performed. Consequently, they should have a sufficient grasp of the details, techniques, and technicalities of all phases of their profession and specialty so as not to be embarrassed when subordinates ask questions concerning the operations in their field of activity.

Developing administrative skills. In executive development, as in any other phase of life, it is good policy to rely on sound fundamental principles. There are certain basic principles of management which rest upon a systematic

FIGURE 13-3
The content of executive development activities

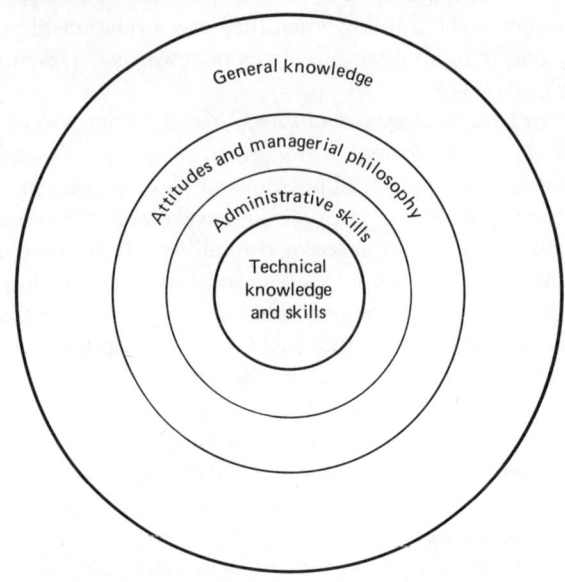

(Concentric circles, from outer to inner: General knowledge; Attitudes and managerial philosophy; Administrative skills; Technical knowledge and skills)

body of knowledge; these are believed to be true in all managerial situations, at all levels, and in different organizations. (It is a truism that people may learn all about the administrative skills without ever learning to manage or to apply the knowledge effectively.)

Modifying attitudes and philosophies. In general, this type of development is directed toward indoctrinating the participants with the organization's philosophy. Indoctrination in this instance is an attempt to impart a set of values that will result in automatic reflex responses to environmental stimuli. It has been demonstrated that unless there is a change in attitudes, there cannot be a change in job performance. (18)

Empathy. In essence, changing the attitudes of new, or existing, managers involves teaching them to have a perceptive consciousness of their impact upon other people and vice versa. This is the ability to put ourselves in the position of others and to view problems from their frame of reference. (19) If this awareness of one's self and one's relationship to others is to prevail, executives must establish an "executive culture" in which spontaneous and full feedback to one another is not only possible but is rewarded.

Values. A basic problem constantly faced by the CEO is inducing new managers to *think* like an executive. New managers must change their philosophy when they move from a nonmanagerial to a managerial position. The common denominator of nearly all organizational problems is to be found in the area of values. Although the existence of differing values between different cultures and peoples is recognized, the influence of value differences on individuals' thinking and acting is greatly underestimated.

Importance of self-perception. There is the ever-present danger that new managers will tend toward one of two extremes; either to "live and let live" and continue to be oriented toward one's peers rather than toward higher management, or to become the "hard-nosed manager" because of the formal authority that is suddenly conferred upon them. This latter type implies to his subordinates, through words or actions, that he was promoted over them and that because of their deficiencies he is now their superior. These managers usually become more company-minded and production-minded than even the highest levels of the managerial hierarchy.

Developing the team concept. The goal of organizational training is to perfect the operation of individuals as team members rather than as isolated units functioning independently or even competing with each other. This should prevent the emergence of intergroup conflicts within the organization.

This thought has also been expressed in a different way by a group of research psychologists. They questioned the assumption that training individual members of management in isolation from the other members of their work team can result in each person being able to bring what each has learned to bear on executive team action. (20) Yet, most conventional training methods seek to improve team action by training individuals rather than by training the team as a unit. As we will soon see, organizational development (OD) is attempting to overcome this deficiency.

Acquiring general knowledge. As one of the objectives of executive development is to enhance their general abilities, it follows that acquiring generalized knowledge should be included in those programs. Such learning may or may not be applied directly on the job, but it does help the executive to "grow."

METHODS USED IN DEVELOPING EXECUTIVES

There is an infinite variety of methods that can be used to develop executives. There are also numerous ways that these methods can be classified for discussion purposes. The usual method is to discuss those that are job-related and those that are done away from the job. For the following discussion, the methods will be classified according to how the content of development activities can be acquired, as shown in Figure 13–3.

While recognizing that the methods of development cannot be so neatly identified, isolated, and compartmentalized, at least for discussion purposes, that will be the order of classification.

You might want to review Chapter 12 to see how these methods fit into the overall development scheme.

Some policy decisions

There are at least two policy decisions which must be made at this time if an organization is seriously to become involved with executive development.

Formal or informal programs? The first decision, involving methodology is whether to have formal or informal programs, or a combination of both.

The previously mentioned study of the largest sales organizations showed 45 percent using formal programs; 33 percent used informal activities; while 22 percent used both. (21) On-the-job training and conference discussions were the most popular learning methods, with job rotation, attendance at external management development programs, and case analysis and problem-solving sessions following in favor.

On premises or off? If the decision is to have formal programs, the next decision is whether to conduct it internally on the premises, using the organization's staff, or to conduct it externally, probably using outside personnel.

Both sites have their advantages and disadvantages; almost invariably both are used in combination. The generalization can be made that the higher the position of the participant in the hierarchy, the greater are the chances the training will be done externally. However, there are exceptions.

A study of 34 firms in California showed two-thirds of them preferring off-site locations. The reasons offered for this preference were psychological and empirical. (22)

Methods used to improve technical knowledge and skills

Some of the more frequently used methods for improving technical knowledge and skills are: on-the-job learning experiences; coaching and counseling; and others, including lecturing, workshops, and conferences.

On-the-job learning experiences. Experiential learning is still one of the most effective ways of learning the content and methodology of a job.

The reasons for using this method are: its convenience, as little extra effort is required; its inevitability, for learning takes place whether it is positive or negative, effective or ineffective, or constructive or destructive; and its "out-of-pocket" costs are negligible, although actual costs may be high.

Some of the disadvantages of this method are: its inefficiencies, as the learner is primarily a producer; its wastefulness, for errors in learning are carried over into performance; and it is time-consuming and static, as it tends to perpetuate existing knowledge, skills, and practices.

In conclusion, while this method of learning, used alone, is inadequate, (23) it is an effective method of learning for some groups, especially scientific and technical personnel. (24)

Coaching. Every organization uses some form of on-the-job management training. One of these is coaching, which consists of the superiors at all levels providing guidance and counsel to the subordinates in the course of their regular job performance. Another version of this method is the "buddy system." The training department gives little assistance in this respect, for the success of this method depends upon the willingness and abilities of the executives themselves. A unique and interesting form of this development was engaged in by one administrator who invited her young subordinate to her home four or five times a week to discuss the events of the day with her. During the discussions, she suggested ways for the young woman to grow.

Coaching is successful because most people look up to someone in authority who is an advisor and counselor. The basic idea is for the junior executive to pick up some of the qualities which have made the senior executive a senior executive.

Methods used to develop administrative skills

Administrative skills involve learning the managerial functions of planning, organizing, staffing, directing, and controlling. Also, permeating all of these is using the scientific method to make decisions and the artisitic approach in implementing and applying those decisions. Some effective methods of developing these skills are case analysis; simulation, including "business games," in-basket technique, and role playing; planned progression; job rotation; temporary or anticipatory assignments; management internships; and multiple management.

Case analysis (25). Almost two decades ago, two comprehensive studies of academic preparation for executive positions emphasized the need to increase the intellectual rigor of management programs. (26) Such preparation should focus on the problems to be faced by the administrator rather than on descriptive training in institutions, practices, and techniques. Both studies urged the use of the case method for a significant part of the education offered toward reaching that goal.

While no two people define and use the case method in the same way, the essential features are: the learning vehicle is a written, oral, or visual presentation of actual situations, involving real people acting and reacting in a true situation, and including some extraneous material but not including some essential material; the teacher either plays a neutral role of directing the discussion or, in a more passive way, leads the participants to develop generally useful concepts; and the learning can either be illustrative of some concept to be learned, an analytical evaluation of some administrative action, or action-oriented in the form of reaching and implementing a decision.

This method has been criticized on the grounds that it tends to be passive, and does not develop theoretical concepts; it is not based on rigorous analysis research, and is not experimentally based; and later techniques have diminished its usefulness.

In summary, while it is not the most effective method of presenting well-structured material, such as quantitative methods, encyclopedic data, and theoretical concepts, when *used effectively* by a well-trained leader, it can be effective for developing administrative skills in decision making and implementing, in marketing, and in organizational behavior.

Simulation. Simulation, an outgrowth of the case method, tends to be more realistic than the predecessor method and leads to greater involvement. It can be thought of as a form of vestibule training, where the participants perform —or act out—simulated business behavior in reaching decisions and implementing them.

Role playing. One of the earliest forms of simulation was role playing. It was extensively used in human relations training and is now used in *experiential learning* to acquire skills in *organizational behavior* and *team building.* (27)

In essence, the participants act out the role implied in a given situation. Then they switch roles, play the other roles out, and evaluate each other's performance. The learning takes place not only in the playing of the roles—which must be realistic and credible in order to be a learning vehicle—but learning also takes place in the evaluation of the role playing.

From experience, I have found role playing to be more effective as the basis of a class discussion, rather than as a learning vehicle itself.

Business games. Business gaming is used to learn decision making and implementation. The learning involves taking a simulated business situation, dividing the participants into groups, and letting the groups organize into simulated organizations. Then the groups begin to make decisions, the computer analyzes and presents the results of each team's decision, and on the basis of the print-out the teams make further decisions until the game is terminated.

The advantages of this method are its involvement, for the participants begin *actually to run the business;* it dramatically shows the need for organization; and it dramatizes the use of feedback as an input into decision making.

The disadvantages are its cost in terms of time and money (it takes from one to three hours for the teams to make their decisions, after taking several hours to be introduced to the game and to organize. It also requires about 30 minutes of computer time to analyze and print out the results.); there is a tendency for the participants to "play the game," as they know it will terminate, and they can guess what is necessary to "win" at termination; and there is some question as to the transferability to the job of the knowledge acquired during the learning session.

In-basket technique. As shown in Chapter 10, this technique is used in assessment centers as a technique for selecting managers. However, it also grew out of the case method as a learning technique. The participant is presented background material on the simulated organization, including details on its product, personnel, and organizational structure. Then the learners are given a basket full of assorted information, memoranda, requests, complaints, grievances, and other activities requiring managerial action.

Learning occurs or takes place in the following forms: ordering of priorities, decision making and implementation, interpersonal relationships, and use of time.

Planned progression. A system of planned progression is utilized when an organization blueprints the path of promotions that lie ahead of the developing executives. This is frequently charted through successive levels of the functional organizational structure. If the institution considers it overly optimistic to chart the progression specifically, it may have a committee to outline the alternative positions the individuals could occupy.

Job rotation. In general, job rotation is a procedure whereby managers receive diversified training through performing various and differentiated jobs.

This may take the form of rotation in nonsupervisory work, in observation assignments among managerial training positions, in middle-level "assistant" positions, and in unspecified rotation in managerial positions.

interesting

Temporary, or anticipatory, assignments. A quite prevalent development method is to put the learners on a short-term, temporary basis in some position where they can learn to grow into higher-level positions. Other assignments may be made on a more permanent basis but still anticipating that the learners will grow into the next higher job.

The most frequently used of these techniques are the "assistant to" position, understudy, and temporary promotion.

Management internships. While few doubt that today's colleges and universities are turning out the best qualified management talent, there are many who feel that these young people need to be more familiar with the pragmatic practicalities of the actual organizational world. To avoid these difficulties, numerous universities now have "professional practice programs," or *cooperative work programs,* worked out with participating firms. The objective is to provide actual management experience along with academic preparation.

Modifying attitudes and developing managerial philosophies

The methods used in this type development try to modify the attitudes of the participants and develop in them more desirable managerial philosophies. The subject matter deals with empathy, self-perception, interpersonal relationships, team building, and value systems. These tend to be the newer techniques and have become popular as the behavioral scientists have developed their techniques and expertise.

Laboratory training. Laboratory training is, in effect, laboratories in which executives learn by experimenting on themselves and modify their attitudes from unstructured discussions, analyses, and observations. (28) This training method is one of the most controversial, (29) yet it is one of the most frequently used development techniques. (30)

This type training is also known as *T-group training* and *sensitivity training.* The term, *T-group training,* refers to all those laboratory methods where small groups of 10 to 15 learners are confronted with unstructured learning activities. While all T-group training takes the same essential form, the trainers, who are known as *consultants* or *change agents,* emphasize different aspects of learning. One group focuses upon *individual emotions,* while others are more concerned with *interrelationships* between members of the group. The ones emphasizing individual emotions tend to call their programs *sensitivity training.* It tends to be a deeper form of training and is related to encounter groups and even psychotherapy.

Goals. Among the many goals of this type of training are: (*a*) to increase self-insight and self-awareness of one's own behavior; (*b*) to become more sensitive to, and increase one's empathy for, the behavior and feelings of others; and (*c*) to increase one's communicative and interpersonal abilities.

Methodology. The groups are usually unstructured, have no set agenda, practically no guidance from the leader, and use many of the other techniques such as *experimental learning, role playing, recording and playing back discussions,* and an occasional *lecturette.* As "nature abhors a vacuum," someone begins to assume the leadership position after the program is initiated by the trainer. As the discussions progress, each person evaluates, records, and feeds back their assessment of the behavior of others.

As the sessions progress, groups go through periods of shock, frustration, hostility, and understanding. In the first period, there is usually an unfreezing, whereby the participants become dissatisfied with their behavior; frustration, in which they search for better forms of behavior; and refreezing, whereby the selected behavior patterns become a part of the person's commitment to do a better job as an executive.

© 1971 by NEA, Inc. Reprinted by permission of NEA.

Evaluating research findings. The proponents of this method claim that it improves self-understanding, a tolerance and understanding of others, improved communications and interpersonal abilities, and more effective personal leadership.

The critics claim that it is so traumatic that it can destroy self-confidence; it is costly; the new values, such as openess and trust, may not lead to executive advancement, but the newly acquired acceptance of confrontation may lead the individuals to become more dogmatic; and even if the person changes, it may not carry over to improved managerial effectiveness.

Many research efforts have been made to ascertain the effectiveness of these programs. In one of the most exhaustive efforts, 26 studies of the effect of these sessions were analyzed. It was concluded that these sessions do result in attitude changes—as measured by the participants' self-perceptions; but there was no clear evidence that those attitude changes resulted in improved job performance. (31) One study found more detrimental effects on performance than positive changes. (32)

It can be concluded that even where there are changes in interpersonal behavior and self-perception, there is no established relationship between such changes and increased job effectiveness. (33)

Organizational development. As executives were developed in laboratory training programs, they were frustrated when returning to the same organizational climate they had left. Much of what they had gained in improved behavior was wasted in the new organization. Consequently, organizations began to search for a broader, more eclectic, and more integrative form of management *and* organizational development. These efforts were called "planned change," "organizational renewal," and "applied behavioral sciences." However, they are now generally called OD, or organizational development.

Conceptual framework. When the question was asked, "What should be the primary target for change, the executive or the organization?" the answer was, "Both!" Whereas other management development activities focused on the development of individual managers, OD looks at the *overall* development of organizational units, including structural relationships, the choice and development of people, and the interaction and interrelationships between individuals within groups.

Methodology. OD can be defined as the *conscious activity, undertaken by top management, to increase the health and effectiveness of the entire organization, through planned innovation in the organization's processes.* It can be seen that there are three steps involved in this process. They are: (*a*) a diagnosis of the problems keeping the organization from reaching its objectives; or (*b*) intervening to combat those problems through executive development and organizational change; and (*c*) evaluation of the results.

OD builds upon the Theory Y assumptions of Douglas McGregor (34) and proposes alternative normative models for explaining executive behavior in organizations. Stress is placed upon interpersonal competence, collaboration and teamwork, and group dynamics skills. Attempts are made to gain increased effectiveness and adaptability from employees by freeing them from the limitations and restrictions of highly structured and authoritarian organizations. It seeks to build upon the foundations of greater employee participation and more collaborative decision making and problem solving.

Evaluation of results. Some of the criticisms of OD are: (*a*) an overemphasis upon personal sensitivity and interpersonal relationships, rather than attacking structure, reward system, and other organizational constraints which can be achieved more effectively using other techniques; (*b*) OD "graduates" become so engrossed with establishing new behavior patterns that they tend to ignore the responsibilities of their job; and (*c*) the organization is called upon to fit itself into the OD package, whereas the package should be tailored for each organization, depending upon its needs. (35)

Proponents of OD claim that these are not valid criticisms. Whereas the organization can begin either from within or from without, at least it makes an attempt to improve both executives and the organizational climate to which they return from developmental activities. (36)

What conclusions can be reached? First, evaluation of this effort should be incorporated into the original plans for the method, not at the end. Apparently this method of training is improving both the organizational climate and the performance of executives.

Managerial grid. In reality, the managerial grid is probably the best known OD method in use. Using various stimulations, the executives being trained are forced to confront the difference between their own behavior and their idealized behavior. It probably is effective in effecting both short-run and longitudinal changes in the attitudes of managers.

Acquiring general, or integrated, knowledge

In addition to the executives' academic preparation, generalized knowledge can be obtained through attending university executive development programs, sabbatical leaves, and selected readings.

University executive development programs. From research findings, as well as my own experience, I conclude that a well-conceived, well-developed, and well-taught program of this nature is probably the most effective management development program available. (37) Although this method of development is numerically insignificant in as far as the total number of executives developed for U.S. institutions, its influence is disproportionately significant, for the executives trained by this method tend to become the top managers of their organizations. (38) Also, it tends to be the most progressive and dynamic of all the developmental techniques, for "He who learns from one occupied in learning drinks of a running stream. He who learns from one who has learned all he has to teach drinks the green mantle of the stagnant pool." (39) The curriculum usually consists of business policy; behavioral aspects of administration; the management process itself; and communications, as well as a simulation exercise.

These programs are also both praised and criticized. The praise centers around its dynamic and progressive nature, as well as results—for top managers tend to go to them, and, conversely, those who attend these programs tend to become the chief executive officers.

Some of the criticisms were highlighted in a recent study of 93 of the largest United States business corporations who are regular users of these programs. It was found that the majority of the participants receive no preprogram orientation; selection of participants was made primarily by staff executives rather than by the line executives most responsible for the performance of those selected; and over half the participants were uncertain whether the program had any impact upon the productivity of the group. (40)

Sabbaticals. Sabbaticals promise to be an excellent developmental technique for persons in the higher levels of the organization. The objective is to help the executives' performance by refreshing them and expanding their capabilities for learning. While on such leave, the individuals usually study in an area other than, but related to, their specialty. To be most effective, these leaves usually last from six months to one year.

APPRAISING AND EVALUATING EXECUTIVE DEVELOPMENT

Any formal executive development program should be based upon the expectation that continued outlays of money and human resources will result in improved performance. Unfortunately definitive estimates of the effectiveness of such programs are lacking, for companies have not yet developed evaluation techniques sufficiently to ascertain whether they are getting full value from their education investments. These programs usually produce maximum benefits only over a long period of time and, therefore, cannot be expected to induce significant changes in the manager's attitudes and skills that will be immediately perceived in job performance. (This problem constitutes one of the primary research opportunities for the future.)

While there have been many criticisms of the methods used, (41) there have also been criticisms of development programs themselves. For example, from analyzing the results of 400 experimental studies concerned with management development, Robert House became disappointed and disillusioned and concluded that "several management development programs have actually *caused problems and undesirable behavior.*" (42)

Difficulty of evaluating

The very nature of executive development makes it difficult to evaluate results. First, the very nature of the executive's job makes it difficult, for it is intangible and separated from actual performance so that it is difficult to show a cause and effect relationship between development and subsequent organizational performance. Second, the evaluations tend to be done by the participants themselves. And, as attendance at such a program usually signifies that the participant is a "comer" or "crown prince or princess," there is an inherent tendency for the participants to say that the program was effective. They are afraid to say that the learning did not "take," for this might be construed as a weakness on their part rather than on the program's part. As an example, 94 percent of participants in one program rated the experience as "valuable," and over 50 percent indicated it had "high value." (43)

In spite of these difficulties, evaluation is feasible!

Methodology

An evaluation program should have as its objective maximizing the return on investment in human resources. This means that in appraising the programs one should look for job-related performance changes. Some specific criteria for an effective evaluation system are to: (*a*) provide for a systematic and unbiased feedback; (*b*) be administratively feasible, that is, practical to apply within the resources in terms of expense and personnel; (*c*) provide data on the relative achievement of established program objectives; and (*d*) provide information for selectively improving the program.

Evaluation is based upon *measuring the effects* of the learning which has taken place. This can be done with testing before and after training in order to measure knowledge, attitudes, and technical knowledge. The performance part is usually measured by performance evaluations before, immediately after, and a considerable time after the training. The evaluations can be done by the participant's supervisor, peers, and/or subordinates. However, the evaluations are usually contaminated because the ones doing the evaluations know the executive has been subjected to training, and, therefore, they *expect* improvement. These evaluative techniques are improved when there is a control group against which the participants' performance improvement can be measured.

Yet, there are some problems even with this method. One of the inconsistencies inherent in executive development programs is that these courses should help executives focus on improving their personal behavior. Yet one researcher found that none of the programs studied seemed to have this as one of their purposes. Although they produced much self-involvement, they failed to analyze the individual executive's own chosen course. (44)

Yet, an experimental study evaluating a training course in problem solving and decision making involving three levels of management found the participants overwhelmingly recommending the course as they thought it was so worthwhile; yet, the experimental evaluation showed that whatever losses and gains occurred in the experimental *and* control groups were not statistically significant. (45)

A later study of the effectiveness of training to improve leadership styles showed in the evaluation at the completion of the program that no significant difference between the control group and the experimental group existed. (46)

Yet, using a results-oriented questionnaire evaluation in a British firm, it was found that a vast majority of participants thought it had helped them perform in specific areas. Six months later, the superiors were interviewed concerning the managers' performance. Half of them perceived positive changes in their subordinates in the areas of study; one-fourth indicated that the techniques used in the program had been introduced into their division by the participants. (47)

Relating evaluation to objectives

The usual objectives of executive development are to improve knowledge, attitudes, abilities, job performance, and operation results. Some means of evaluating these are:

1. For knowledge, pen and pencil tests could measure achievement;
2. Attitudes can be measured by questionnaires, interviews, and direct observations;

3. Abilities can be measured by simulating actual work conditions;
4. Job performance can be measured by direct observation by the participants' superiors, peers, and subordinates; and
5. Operational results can be measured by performance records.

GROUPS REQUIRING SPECIAL ATTENTION

There are at least four groups which require special attention as far as executive development is concerned. They include women, minorities, managers of small businesses, and personnel executives themselves.

Women

Much has been written about "the empty pipeline" into top positions for women. Yet, any education or training program for *women executives* must include "confidence-raising and definitions of professional behavior as well as effective management techniques." (48)

Consequently, executive development programs must contain these essential elements if the programs are to satisfy the needs of women. This concept was dramatized by a training program for women managers at the University of Minnesota. The objective of the program was to try to get each woman to understand herself, both as a woman and as an achiever, and to accept the premise that these two qualities are not incompatible. After the residential seminar was over, the women were interviewed three months later. The effects most often mentioned were "better self-awareness and increased self-confidence." (49)

Minorities

The second group requiring special attention is *minorities*. For example, at the end of a training program of 44 minority men and women supervisors, it was found thast their classroom scores on cognitive content areas, such as problem solving, were not later associated with their employer's appraisal. Instead, the appraisals tended to be based upon nontask related behavior. (50)

Managers of small businesses

The third group needing special consideration is *small businesses*. They have many problems that cannot be solved without tailor-made programs of development. In general, those programs must be geared to setting achievement goals for the individuals as well as the organization. Yet these are the very organizations which cannot afford even the regular programs.

Personnel executives themselves

The next group requiring special attention is *personnel executives themselves*. In most cases, while the personnel executives are charged with the coordinating responsibility for executive development programs, all too often the organizations have no special training programs for those executives. However, the Philips Company instituted a program in 1950 to assure that personnel people were themselves adequately trained. (51)

IMPLICATIONS AND APPLICATIONS FOR PERSONNEL EXECUTIVES

Based upon the previous discussion, it can be concluded that the basic assumption underlying executive development is: *Such development programs are capable of bringing about improvement in managerial knowledge, attitudes, skills, job performance, and/or operational results.*

Based upon that assumption, the following hypotheses underlying executive development can be formulated.

1. *The type and degree of changes resulting from executive development are functions of: the abilities and characteristics of those to be developed; the attitudes, behavior, and degree of commitment of their superiors; the organizational climate; the attitudes and work concepts of the participants' peer group; and the character and quality of the developmental techniques employed to induce change.*
2. *As successful managerial performance results from the interaction of individual abilities, the job being performed, and the environment in which the job exists, job performance can be improved by changing any one or a combination of the three.*

Executive Development programs usually attempt to improve abilities, without considering the other two. One exception is OD. It is felt that future developmental activities will attempt to integrate all three of these in developmental activities.

3. *Executives' perception of the significance of success influences their attempts to achieve it.*

If they think success is not only desirable but attainable, they will attempt to achieve it; if not, they will not attempt it.

4. *While extrinsic variables determine the degree of resistance, all managers tend to resist development.*

This hypothesis in not new, for one of the shocking discoveries of the early pioneers of management training was the tendency of managers and supervisors to exhibit an almost antagonistic resistance to training. (52)

A basic premise of executive development is that managers react to development according to *who they think they are*. This premise is the basis of an important hypothesis:

5. *If employees think they are important, they will give a greater degree of responsibility to the job; if they think they are unimportant, they will tend to give little responsibility to the position.*

Successful executive development activities stress acquiring technical knowledge and skills, developing administrative skills, modifying attitudes, and acquiring general knowledge. Inherent in the methods used to achieve that learning is the idea of movement, either temporary or permanent. Herein is a problem which is growing more acute, as shown in the following letter from a practicing personnel executive:

> Larger organizations are attempting to "thin out" their operational sites so that there are beginning to be many small operations located throughout the world. This change is having an adverse impact on the tried and true methods of management development. Rotation through various job classifications and at different levels is becoming difficult due to reduction in the size of staffs. Also, moving employees from one location to another, either for training purposes or promotional reasons, is becoming less acceptable.

DISCUSSION QUESTIONS

1. What is executive development? Explain fully!
2. What does a manager do when he knows that through developing a talented and ambitious subordinate, he puts himself in serious danger of losing his relative position to that subordinate?
3. "In essence, everyone who is in a managerial position or is expected to be in one in the future should be developed." Comment!
4. Are there any special problems that arise in developing technical people? If there are, how can they be resolved?
5. In an environment of continuous change, are there any stable propositions upon which executive development programs should be based? Explain!
6. Discuss some of the methods of development.
7. How would you determine the developmental needs of an organization?
8. What role does perception have in management development?

REFERENCES AND SUGGESTIONS FOR FURTHER STUDY

1. Martin J. Gannon, "Attitudes of Government Executives toward Management Training," *Public Personnel Management,* vol. 4, no. 1 (January–February 1975), pp 63–69.
2. Charles P. Bowen, Jr., "Let's Put Realism into Management Development," *Harvard Business Review,* vol. 51, no. 4 (July–August 1973), pp. 80–87.
3. James D. Somerville, "A Systems Approach to Management Development," *Personnel Journal,* vol. 53, no. 5 (May 1974), pp. 367–71.
4. Reed M. Powell, "Management Development—The Plus Factor in the Survival of the Firm," *Training Directors,* vol. 17, no. 1 (January 1963), p. 25.
5. It is hardly coincidence that companies dominant in their industries—such as AT&T, Citicorp, Exxon, and IBM—often have the most effective programs. In fact, the chief executive officers of these firms all have 20 years or more of service in their firms and are products of the programs. See "How Companies Raise a New Crop of Managers," *Business Week* (March 10, 1975), for statements of their management development philosophies.

6. J. Sterling Livingston, "Pygmalion in Management," *Harvard Business Review,* vol. 47, no. 4 (July–August 1969), pp. 81–89. See also Harry Levinson, "The Obsolescent Executive," *Personnel Administration,* vol. 33, no. 3 (July–August 1970), pp. 8–13.
7. R. L. Randall and Louis Cassels, "Survey Shows How to Succeed," *Nation's Business,* vol. 50, no. 7 (July 1962), pp. 38–39.
8. P. W. Maloney and J. R. Hinrichs, "A New Tool for Supervisory Self-Development," *Personnel,* vol. 36, no. 4 (July–August 1959), pp. 46–53.
9. Fred Wessman, "Determining Training Needs of Managers," *Personnel Journal,* vol. 54, no. 2 (February 1975), pp. 109–25.
10. R. Carter Wellford, "Development Managers in a Product-Type Organization," *Management Record,* vol. 22, no. 4 (April 1960), p. 22.
11. S. G. Huneryager, "Executive Training Courses: Problems and Practices," *Management Review,* vol. 50, no 4 (April 1961), p. 29.
12. Daniel N. Wiener, "Evaluation of Selection Procedures for a Management Development Program," *Journal of Counseling Psychology,* vol. 8, no. 2 (Summer 1961), p. 217.
13. Edgar H. Schein, "Management Development as a Process of Influence," abridged in Timothy W. Costello and Sheldon S. Zalkind, eds., *Psychology in Administration: A Research Orientation* (Englewood Cliffs, N.J.: Prentice-Hall, Inc., 1963), pp. 299–309.
14. S. J. Carroll and A. N. Nash, "Some Personal and Situational Correlates of Reactions to Management Development Training," *Academy of Management Journal,* vol. 13, no. 2 (June 1970), p. 187 ff.
15. Robert J. House, "A Commitment Approach to Management Development," *California Management Review,* vol. 7, no. 3 (Spring 1965), pp. 15–28.
16. Wayne J. Foreman, "Management Training in Large Corporations," *Training and Development Journal,* vol. 21, no. 5 (May 1967), pp. 11–17. See also L. W. Gruenfeld, "Selection of Executives for a Training Program," *Personnel Psychology,* vol. 14, no. 4 (Winter 1961), pp. 421–31.
17. Roger P. Sonnabend, "Executive Education," *Advanced Management—Office Executive,* vol. 1, no. 9 (September 1962), pp. 16–21.
18. Edward C. Andler, "The Promotional Ladder," *Personnel Journal,* vol. 44, no. 2 (February 1965), pp. 68–71.
19. An American Indian proverb expresses it this way: "Grant that I may not criticize my neighbor until I've walked a mile in his moccasins."
20. Robert R. Blake, Jane S. Mouton, and Michael G. Blansfield, "How Executive Team Training Can Help You," *Training Directors,* vol. 16, no. 1 (January 1962), pp. 3–7.
21. Foreman, "Management Training in Large Corporations," *Training and Development Journal,* pp. 11–17.
22. John E. Wilson, "Location of Management Training Conferences," *Training and Development Journal,* vol. 20, no. 1 (January 1966), pp. 52–55.
23. Fred Fiedler found a minus correlation between length of experience and measures of effectiveness for 385 managers in five organizations. See "Leadership

Experience and Leader Performance: Another Hypothesis Shot to Hell," *Organizational Behavior and Human Performance,* vol. 5, no. 1 (January 1970), p. 10 ff.

24. Two researchers found in a study of 290 scientists and engineers engaged in research and development that interaction with fellow professionals on the job was a major source of information and motivation. See Newton Margulies and Anthony Raia, "Scientists, Engineers, and Technological Obsolescence," *California Management Review,* vol. 10, no. 2 (Winter 1967), p. 44 ff.

25. The following material has has been heavily influenced by my experiences with Andrew R. Rowl, former director of the Intercollegiate Case Clearing House, Graduate School of Business Administration, Harvard University, for 17 years. Anyone seeking more knowledge of the use of the "case method" in executive development should see his book entitled *To Study Administration by Cases* (Boston, Mass.: Harvard Graduate School of Business Administration, 1969).

26. Frank Pierson, and others, *The Education of American Businessmen* (New York: McGraw-Hill Book Co., 1959); Robert Gordon and James Howell, *Higher Education for Business* (New York: Columbia University Press, 1959).

27. This technique has been found effective in developing administrative skills in inducting employees into the organization, giving recognition to an employee, performing employee appraisals, and in other interpersonal areas. See Melvin Sorcher and Arnold Goldstein, "A Behavior Modeling Approach in Training," *Personnel Administration,* vol. 35, no. 2 (March-April 1972), pp. 35–40.

28. This discussion is heavily influenced by Laurence Siegel and Irving Lane, *Psychology in Industrial Organizations,* 3rd ed. (Homewood, Ill: Richard D. Irwin, Inc., 1974), pp. 347–52.

29. See Frank T. Paine, "Management Perspective: Sensitivity Training: The Current State of the Question," *Academy of Management Journal,* vol. 8, no. 3 (September 1965), pp. 228–32, for an excellent analysis of the pros and cons of this training method.

30. See Raymond E. Miles and Lyman W. Porter, "Leadership Training—Back to the Classroom?" *Personnel,* vol. 43, no. 4 (July–August 1966), pp. 27–35, for a possible reversal of this trend.

31. J. P. Campbell, *et al., Managerial Behavior, Performance, and Effectiveness* (New York: McGraw-Hill Book Co., 1970).

32. William J. Underwood, "Evaluation of Laboratory Method of Training," *Training Directors Journal,* vol. 19, no. 5 (May 1965), pp. 34–40.

33. For evaluations of this method, see Stokes B. Carrigan, "A Plug for Non-T-Group Confrontation," *Journal of Applied Behavioral Science,* vol. 3, no. 4 (October–December, 1967), pp. 548–50; Robert J. House, "Leadership Training: Some Dysfunctional Consequences," *Administrative Science Quarterly,* vol. 12, no. 4 (March 1968), pp. 556–71; Paul C. Buchanan, "Laboratory Training and Organization Development," *Administrative Science Quarterly,* vol. 14, no. 3 (September 1969), pp. 466–80; and Robert Fulmer, "Making Sense of Sensitivity Training," *Association Management,* vol. 22, no. 6 (May 1970), pp. 48–52.

34. John J. Morse and Jay W. Lorsch, "Beyond Theory Y," *Harvard Business Review,* vol. 48, no. 3 (May–June 1970), pp. 61–68.

35. See Larry E. Gruiner, "Red Flags in Organizational Development," *Business Horizons,* vol. 15, no. 3 (June 1972), pp. 17–24, for these and other criticisms.

36. See Daniel L. Kegan, "Organizational Development: Description, Issues, and Some Research Results," *Academy of Management Journal*, vol. 14, no. 4 (December 1971), pp. 453–62; and Guvenc G. Alpander, "Planning Management Training Programs for Organizational Development," *Personnel Journal*, vol. 53, no. 1 (January 1974), pp. 15–25, for other benefits.
37. In 1970, an estimated 3,500 executives attended programs at 53 graduate schools of business. The majority were senior executives and they averaged 43 years of age, with 17 years of service, and a minimum salary of $35,000. They spent about $7.5 million in tuition and $8 million in travel and other expenses. See Alvin A. Butkus, "Should Executives Go Back to School?" *Dun's Review*, vol. 96, no. 9 (September 1970). pp. 38–40.
38. See "A Guide to Executive Education," *Business Week* (March 8, 1976), pp. 79–85, for further discussion of this method, including a discussion of the "best ones."
39. A mid-Victorian educator quoted by Mary E. Murphy in "The Teaching of Social Accounting: A Research Planning Paper," *Accounting Review*, vol. 32, no. 4 (October 1957), p. 637.
40. Reed M. Powell and Charles S. Davis, "Do University Executive Programs Pay off?" *Business Horizons*, vol. 16, no. 4 (August 1972), pp. 81–88.
41. John H. Zenger, "Third Generation Manager Training," *MSU Business Topics*, vol. 22, no. 3 (Summer 1974), pp. 23–27.
42. House, "Leadership Training," *Administrative Science Quarterly*, p. 15.
43. Reed M. Powell, "Two Approaches to University Management Education," *California Management Review*, vol. 5, no. 3 (Spring (Spring 1963), pp. 87–97.
44. Chris Argyris, "Puzzle and Perplexity in Executive Development," *Personnel Journal*, vol. 40, no. 4 (April 1961), pp. 463–65, 483.
45. Dannie J. Moffie, Richard Calhoon, and James K. O'Brien, "Evaluation of a Management Development Program," *Personnel Psychology*, vol. 17, no. 4 (Winter 1964), pp. 431–39.
46. Herbert Hand and John Slocum, Jr., "A Longitudinal Study of the Effects of a Human Relations Training Program on Managerial Effectiveness," *Journal of Applied Psychology*, vol. 56, no. 5 (October 1972), pp. 412–17.
47. S. Thobley, "Evaluating an In-Company Management Training Program," *Training and Development Journal*, vol. 23, no. 9 (September 1969), pp. 48–50.
48. Mildred E. Buzenberg, "Training and Development of Women Executives: A Model," *Collegiate News and Views*, vol. 29, no. 1 (Fall 1975), pp. 19–22.
49. J. Stephen Heinen, et al., "Developing the Woman Manager," *Personnel Journal*, vol. 54, no. 5 (May 1975), pp. 282–86.
50. Richard W. Beatty, "Blacks as Supervisors: A Study of Training, Job Performance, and Employers' Expectations," *Academy of Management Journal*, vol. 16, no. 2 (June 1973), pp. 196–205.
51. Sussane Laurence, "Personnel Management Training on the Job," *Personnel Management*, vol. 6, no. 9 (September 1974), p. 33.
52. Willard E. Bennett, "Master Plan for Management Development," *Harvard Business Review*, vol. 34, no. 3 (May–June 1956), pp. 71–84.

Chapter 14

Career planning and development

Using performance appraisals for developmental purposes
    Purposes of appraisals
    Theory underlying performance appraisals
    The problems of validity and reliability
    Methods of appraisal
    Making performance appraisals more effective

Using counseling in career planning and development

Providing progression within the organization
    Upgrading
    Promoting
    Transferring

Using "management by objectives" in career development
    Underlying concepts
    Requirements for successful use
    Evaluating MBO's effectiveness

Groups needing special attention
    New entrants into management ranks
    Managers with special problems

Implications and applications for personnel executives

14

Career planning and development

Every great man is always being helped by everybody, for his gift is to get good out of all things and all persons.

JOHN RUSKIN

To a person who has been in the same job for a long period of time, career development might mean the opportunity to go to a conference. To someone else, it might mean a sabbatical to be used for an executive development program or for independent study. To the young woman or minority person, it might mean a realistic career ladder.

This statement by Fred Foulkes summarizes well the role of career planning and development.* This personnel activity is becoming increasingly important because of the new entrants into the work force—especially into management positions; the slowing down of organizational growth, which is limiting the upward progression of many capable people; and the high expectations of today's employees.

A model for career planning and development is shown in Figure 14–1.

While the *primary* responsibility for career planning and development must rest with the individual, the organization can help employees grow and develop by making various growth aids available. For a number of years, several companies have engaged in career counseling, and many have recently begun *career development workshops*. At these workshops, individuals are given assistance in evaluating their own abilities and interests, as well as information about various job and career possibilities within the company.

Some organizations are now asking their managers and expected future managers to state their career goals in writing. In fact, one company has asked its people to define their next two jobs in the company (a very hard but worthwhile assignment for most managers, particularly women). Then the personnel executive and staff assist the individual in achieving that career goal. Other companies are offering "life planning" courses to employees in their forties so that they can plan more thoughtfully for the future. (1)

---

* Several terms are used to refer to this activity, including "career planning," "career guidance," "career development," and "career management." The designation I prefer is "career planning and development," but the others will be used interchangeably to avoid repetition.

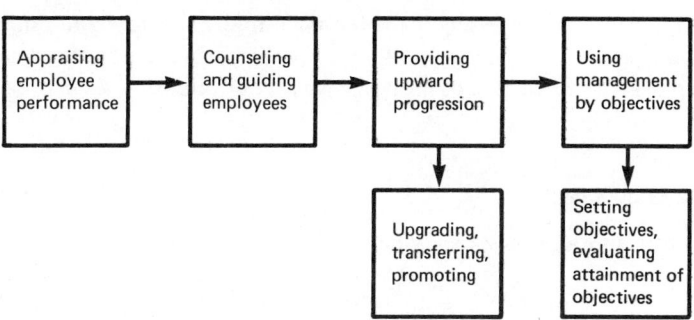

FIGURE 14-1
A model for career planning and development

```
Appraising      →  Counseling    →  Providing      →  Using
employee           and guiding      upward            management
performance        employees        progression       by objectives
                                       ↓                  ↓
                                   Upgrading,         Setting
                                   transferring,      objectives,
                                   promoting          evaluating
                                                      attainment of
                                                      objectives
```

These workshops are particularly important to new entrants into management ranks, for as a group they have a very low perception and expectation of how far they can rise in the organization. While most entrepreneurs and executives have a high achievement drive and possess a need for power, minorities, women, the disabled, and older workers need to have these traits instilled into them—as they may have been denied the exercise of these traits in the past. This is one of the functions of these workshops.

One of the better known of these programs is that of TRW, Inc. Based upon the concept of developing a "need for achievement," TRW set up a career achievement workshop emphasizing the need of individuals to make decisions concerning their own career, based upon building upon their strengths. Instead of the conventional concept of working on one's weaknesses, participants in these workshops are encouraged to work on their strengths, which enable them to expand upon their uniqueness and behave with more self-confidence and self-esteem. A corollary objective is to instill in them the willingness to take more prudent risks. (2)

Apparently the workshops are proving to be successful, as 80 percent of the employees who have attended did something later to advance their careers. In fact, 20 percent of them received promotions within eight months of attendance. A peripheral benefit was a reduction in turnover of employees.

USING PERFORMANCE APPRAISALS FOR DEVELOPMENTAL PURPOSES

Of all the techniques at the disposal of the personnel executive, performance appraisals would seem to be the greatest aid to improving employee growth, development, and productivity. It is also one of the universally used techniques. According to a survey of the Bureau of National Affairs, 93 percent of the firms have appraisal programs. Yet, only 10 percent of the personnel executives of those firms felt that their appraisal programs were effective. (3)

Although the terms *merit rating, efficiency rating, service rating, employee* rating, performance rating, personnel rating, performance appraisal, and *employee appraisal* are used interchangeably in this text, the term *performance appraisal* is preferred. In essence, the term "rating" is narrow and limited; the words "appraisal" and "evaluation" are broader and include the concept of comparing the performance of individuals and of evaluating their possibilities for growth.

Purposes of appraisals

Employee appraisals serve a wide variety of purposes. First, *new employees* are appraised as a basis for hiring and for establishing their beginning wage rate. An effort is made to evaluate their capabilities and potentialities, as modified by their aptiudes. These are called *selection appraisals*.

Present employees are evaluated to determine layoffs, transfers, promotions (demotions), pay changes, and for other reasons. These appraisals, which are made to prove to the employees that they have been evaluated upon the basis of demonstrated merit rather than influence of favoritism, are called *performance appraisals*.

Motivation. The mere process of appraising has a motivational effect upon employees; it fosters initiative, develops a sense of responsibility, and intensifies the employee's effort toward achieving organizational goals. Performance evaluation is also beneficial to employees in that it gives them a better understanding of job responsibilities, of relationships with co-workers, of the work expected of them, and of their training needs. The process also aids the appraisers by providing them with a greater understanding of their subordinates' job behavior, the job itself, and each employee's strengths and weaknesses. And, finally, performance evaluation improves teamwork.

Yet, in all fairness, it must be emphasized that employee appraisals which are not based upon objective measures of actual performance are highly subjective and tend to be imperfect. In other words, the greater the reliance upon some objective measurement of actual performance, the greater is the validity of the evaluation; the greater the use of appraisals of subjective criteria, the more imperfect become the evaluations and the less becomes their validity as a basis for making judgments about training needs and career development.

> The findings of a study of three groups of salespersons chosen from 20 randomly selected departments in a retail store indicated that there was no relationship between dollar sales volume (the success criterion used) and any functions of the job upon which the employees were rated. (4)

Administrative versus employee development. In general, the purposes of appraisal can be classified into two major categories, "administrative" and "employee development." As the administrative purposes include merit salary adjustments, promotion and transfer decisions, and reduction-in-force decisions, appraisals performed for this purpose are conducted primarily for use by management. When used as a basis for employee development, appraisals provide employees with information regarding the performance expectations (standard of performance) of their supervisor, feedback to them regarding subsequent performance, and advice, coaching, or counseling to help employees meet expectations that have not been achieved.

The purpose of performance appraisals will determine the bases for comparison, the techniques to be used in appraisals, the role of the supervisor, and the distribution to be made of the evaluations. A summary of these can be seen from Table 14–1.

TABLE 14–1
Differences between administrative and employee development appraisals

	Purpose of employee performance appraisal	
	Employee development	Administrative
Definition of purpose	Performance improvement through advising employee what is expected	Information for decisions re: salary adjustments transfers promotions reduction-in-force
Basis for comparison	Performance relative to predetermined standards of performance (absolute standard)	Performance relative to other similar employees (relative standard)
Technique of appraisal	Results-oriented appraisal	Employee ranking
Role of supervisor	Counselor	Judge
Distribution of evaluation information	Employee and supervisor	Employee, supervisor, personnel folder, others involved in admistrative actions listed above

Source: Robert J. Hayden, "Performance Appraisal: A Better Way," *Personnel Journal*, vol. 52, no. 7 (July 1973), p. 610. Reprinted with permission, *Personnel Journal*, copyright July 1973.

Theory underlying performance appraisals

The theory underlying performance appraisals includes several assumptions. First, *if production can be measured, there is less need for employee appraisal, for each person can be judged according to the amount produced; if the work performed cannot be measured, the personal characteristics which lead to increased productivity and contribute to employee performance must be determined.*

The theory assumes that there are traits and characteristics which lead to productivity; they can be perceived and isolated; they can be measured; and they can be evaluated. Although there is no unanimity as to which personal characteristics are meritorious, the following are generally accepted as bases for appraisal: work quality, reliability, cooperation, job knowledge, initiative, attitude, safety consciousness, attendance, learning ability, health and physical condition, adaptability, judgment, and responsibility.

In theory, performance appraisal pertains only to the characteristics which affect employees' performance. Therefore, *in evaluating employees, the factors measured should be the characteristics, qualifications, traits, capacities, proficiencies, and abilities of the individuals themselves,* and not the job being performed. They should be considered separately and distinctly from the characteristics and requirements of the job itself.

A second assumption is that *objective ratings, or rankings, of employees' productive contribution can be made on the basis of their performance characteristics.* It is further assumed that these can be correlated with specific characteristics of job performance to show a cause and effect relationship between employee characteristics and productivity on the job. One of the most cogent criticisms of employee appraisals is that this objective appraisal cannot be made, as the ratings are usually subjective and do not necessarily deal with the characteristics that lead to improved performance. Not many rating plans even attempt this form of scientific precision; most plans use variables which presumably lead to an estimation of the employee's overall contribution to the enterprise. (5)

The problems of validity and reliability

As with most other personnel techniques, performance appraisals have the problems of validity and reliability. (6)

The validity problems. Performance appraisals are intended to evaluate the performance and potential of employees. Yet, they may not be valid indicators of what they are intended to assess because of a variety of limitations on their use.

The most common sources of error are the halo effect, bias, inflation of ratings, and central tendency.

The halo effect. The "halo effect" (and its counterpart, the "horn effect") is the tendency of evaluators to base assessments of *all* individual characteristics—which are presumed to be independent of each other—on the raters' *overall* impression of the person being evaluated. In essence, the halo effect is the tendency to generalize from a predetermined overall impression to the appraisal of specific traits and characteristics.

While the halo effect applies to almost all methods of appraisal, it seems to apply less to the forced-choice method.

Bias. Many otherwise valid appraisals are invalidated because of bias on the part of the appraiser. The bias may occur for many reasons, including racial, religious, or interpersonal conflict. Also, an evaluator may just not like the person being evaluated. While it is difficult to deal with bias, the more descriptive methods offer less chance for overt bias. Bias may also be a factor of time. Recent impressions are also likely to bias appraisals, as there is a tendency to forget or overlook more distant events. Consequently, recent information about an individual may have an undue influence on evaluations. This problem may occur with all evaluation methods.

Inflation of ratings. Another limitation on appraisals is the tendency to inflate ratings. Sometimes there is a gradual inflation of ratings over time. In other organizations, inflation may occur on the part of certain raters at all times.

Central tendency. There is also a tendency for evaluators to avoid using the extremes of rating scales. In other words, there appears to be a tendency for ratings to cluster around the midpoint, or center, of the rating scale.

The reliability problems. Appraisals may lack reliability as well as validity because of the inconsistent use of differing standards, lack of training in appraisal techniques, and failure to follow on the use of appraisals.

Methods of appraisal

It is ironic that after over half a century of experience with performance appraisals, there are still no commonly accepted and utilized norms. The method used in rating and evaluating employees still tends to be the weak point in the entire procedure of career planning and development.

Also, there is no generally accepted standard as to what method of evaluation produces the best results. There is not even uniformity as to what these methods are called; they are referred to as "types," "plans," "systems," and "scales," as well as "methods." The only essential thing agreed upon is that there be some kind of a measuring device or scale, or processing procedure, and some form on which to record the results.

Among the numerous methods of appraisal, the following are most popular today:

1. *Ranking methods*—The rater judges competence by ranking employees from top to bottom, presumably by comparing the worth of each rather to all others;
2. *Rating methods*—Competence is estimated by rating persons along a theoretical standard sometimes denoted by a line or series of boxes;
3. *Essay methods*—The appraiser describes the competence of ratees by recalling past performance; and
4. *Checklist methods*—The rater diagnostically reports the competence of people by identifying those behaviors one has observed from among a group of behaviors representing competence.

Ranking methods. The three most popular ranking methods are: peer, or buddy, ranking; paired comparison; and forced distribution.

Peer or buddy rating. The peer, or buddy rating, method is frequently called the "mutual rating system." In effect, it consists of each employee evaluating, by secret ballot, each of the other members in the work group.

A modification of this system is used at TRW, Inc. Performance evaluations are made by the executives' supervisors, as well as by their peer groups. Before making the judgment about an executive's need for development, possibilities for promotion, or other reason, the supervisor talks to the people who regularly work along side the executive to see what they think about his or her performance. (7)

Paired comparison. Under the paired comparison arrangements, every employee is "paired" with every other worker in the group. Then, the supervisor must decide which of the two subordinates in each pair is more valuable to the firm. This procedure is repeated until each person has been paired with every other employee and each one's rank relative to every other person has been ascertained. The main disadvantage of this system is its complexity and the volume of work involved. Yet research on the reliability of this method has found it more reliable than simple ranking.

Forced distribution. Under the forced-distribution method, the rater is forced to distribute the ratings of the employees along a scale from the "most valuable" to "least valuable." In effect, this is rating each employee vis-a-vis all other employees. The purpose of this technique, which is analogous to "grading on the curve," is to evercome any tendency for evaluators to be either too lenient or too severe in their ratings. However, it can lead to an invalid assessment unless the group of individuals actually comprise a "normal distribution" in performance and/or potential.

The advantage of this method is that all the values cannot be stacked at one end of the scale; there must be a distribution of the individuals over the entire curve, from "best" to worst." Also, this system forces the rater to consider and evaluate each employee in relation to the other employees. At a progressive hospital, the evaluators must allocate no more than 20 percent to the highest category on the scale, around 70 percent to the middle of the scale, and about 10 percent in the lowest class on the scale. Western Electric has recently begun insisting that supervisors award "outstanding" evaluations to not over 20 percent of their subordinates. (8) This forces an annual "weeding out" that makes it difficult for someone who was once an outstanding performer to coast along on the strength of earlier ratings.

Rating methods. The most frequently used of these ratings are the "yes-no" scales and the graphic rating scale.

"Yes-no" scale. The "yes-no" scale is the simplest method of rating employees. The rater simply indicates with a yes or no whether the employee has each of the characteristics listed, such as cooperation, initiative, or attitude. However, this method is becoming unpopular because it assumes that human behavior is dichotomous, i.e., either "good" or "bad," rather than distributed all the way from one extreme to the other.

Graphic rating scale. The graphic rating scale usually consists of a line with varying degrees of each characteristic or qualification upon it. The rater indicates the degree of each person's qualifications by the point checked on the line. This scale is a continuum from one extreme, which is assumed to be negative, to the other, which is supposed to be positive. The midpoint should be average. However, as there is a human tendency to attribute a negative connotation to anything which is average, there is a constant pressure to rate people between average and superior, rather than along the entire scale.

Evaluation of the ranking and rating methods. These methods of rating have built-in possibilities for error, such as the rater being: (*a*) against some personal attribute of the ratee; (*b*) untrained or inexperienced in evaluation; (*c*) unable to translate estimates of competency to a scale or number; and (*d*) unable to translate value judgments into numeric or points on a scale. Research has shown that these methods have many errors built in. (9)

Essay method. This method of appraisal was developed to avoid many of the difficulties with the previous two methods. It uses an essay to describe aspects of a person's performance, usually without a prescribed format. The evaluator may be asked to describe a person's "strengths" and "limitations" or simply to describe competence sometime after performance is over. While it is helpful in the development process, it is less useful in providing a basis for administering reward systems for it does not provide a convenient basis for comparison with other employees. The essay method may be used with virtually all sources of evaluation, including self-assessments.

Research shows that this method also has some serious inherent difficulties. Raters vary greatly in their ability to write; some have better powers of recall of past performance than others; and all are subject to losses in recall over long periods of time. Finally, raters tend to become confused because there usually are no guidelines as to what content should and should not be included in their essays. (10)

Checklist methods. The checklist methods require appraisers to admit having observed specific behavioral incidents in their working relationships with the individuals being rated. They are not required to judge the value or importance of the incidents, nor do they have to summarize their observations descriptively or numerically. They simply report the incidents in such a way that the combination of incidents reported represents the profile of the individuals being rated. The three most popular forms are the forced-choice rating scale, the critical incidents checklist, and the specimen checklist.

Forced-choice rating scale. The forced-choice rating method is most favored at present. Although its specific applications differ, in general this plan includes an arrangement of several pairs of statements concerning the job performance of each employee. There are two comments which appear to be equally favorable and two which appear to be equally unfavorable. These two sets of statements and one other irrelevant statement are placed together in a group. From this group of observations, the rater must choose one statement that is most descriptive of the person under consideration and one which is least descriptive.

Although the rater does not know it, only one of the statements which appears to be favorable is really meaningful as far as job performance is concerned, and only one of the apparently unfavorable ones really counts against the employee. These results have been predetermined from research with similar jobs and employees and have been found to be valid predictors of success. Because the rater does not know which of these apparently favorable responses really counts in favor of the employee, nor which of the factors that appear to be unfavorable are really detrimental to the worker, there is less bias in the ranking procedure. Therefore, theoretically the person doing the rating would choose the respective comments which are truly most descriptive of the person under consideration.

Besides tending to eliminate the factor of bias more than any other method, the forced-choice, rating scale also eliminates the "halo" effect whereby the rater gives the subordinate a "good" rating, and the "horn" effect whereby one receives a poor rating.

The forced-choice rating scale does have disadvantages. Because it is so complex and involved, it is difficult to use the findings as a basis for counseling employees. Also the construction of this list causes some unique errors. (11) Also, informed raters can "see through" the form and still bias their evaluations. Another problem is that appraisers object to the intended secrecy of the method and try to bias their appraisals in order to fight the system. Finally, the format tends to use only behavioral incidents which can be paired with others, and, if a behavior cannot be paired, then it cannot be used.

Critical incidents checklist. This method was designed to maximize objective rating, as it involves recording significant, or critical, incidents of positive or negative performance as a basis for appraising performance. It is related to the essay method, as it is intended to describe actual performance. As there are no guidelines or criteria for determining what constitutes critical incidents, the evaluator's judgment must determine them. Sometimes a list of categories of job requirements may be provided. While this method is intended to provide an "objective" basis for evaluating performance, the choice of incidents to record as "critical" is subjective. However, as this method focuses upon actually *observed behavior,* it can be useful in the development and career planning processes. Unless the incidents relate to characteristics required for promotability, it may not be particularly useful in making promotion decisions.

Some of the problems of this method are: Critical incidents tend to be committed at infrequent intervals so that reliability suffers as the employee's evaluations may vary considerably over two time periods; supervisors tend to shy away from recordkeeping and may forget these incidents; as the guidelines call for only *outstandingly* effective or ineffective incidents, most behavior is not recorded, and, finally, employees tend to view this method as a "surveillance system" and a threat.

Specimen checklist. This method is a modern version of the critical incidents checklist. The appraiser checks those behaviors he has witnessed in the ratee during a specified time period. The list of behaviors for which selections are chosen is constructed by interviewing or surveying superiors, peers, subordinates, or any combination thereof, who have been associated with workers occupying a given job and are required to appraise their performance. They are asked to consider each worker they knew who had performed the job and then recall at least one incident which caused them to feel the worker was particularly effective or ineffective at the time. For the average job, listings usually consists of 100 to 200 distinct behaviors, about evenly divided between effective and ineffective specimens. Figure 14–2 illustrates 30 incidents from a 141-item checklist for the appraisal of lower management personnel in a large processing plant.

This type of checklist has been used successfully to appraise job perform-

FIGURE 14-2
Sample items from a managerial checklist

___Refused to make an unpleasant decision or reprimand in his own name; named his superior as the responsible one.
___Resisted pressure to start a job without sufficient advanced thought and planning.
___Refused to accept job instructions without a prolonged discussion or argument.
___Reported findings on a problem in a fashion which expedited an effective solution.
___Failed to consider alternate ways of performing a job when available information indicated he should.
___Apologized to subordinate when wrong.
___Performed ineffectively on a project because of failure to plan sufficiently.
___Demonstrated the ability to place proper priorities on jobs.
___Planned for long-range requirements and coming developments with unusual effectiveness.
___Acquired thorough knowledge of equipment for which he was not responsible, but which related to his job.
___Made unrealistic demands of his group in terms of time and effort.
___Studied a current operating procedure and made effective recommendations for improvements.
___Required prodding on jobs outside of his major responsibilities.
___Displayed ingenuity in cutting corners to meet a deadline.
___Placed the blame for his own mistakes on his subordinates.
___Demonstrated inability to get along with other employees on the same level.
___Misinformed his superior concerning an important matter.
___Failed to prepare requested report on time.
___Recognized the abilities and weaknesses of his subordinates and made job assignments accordingly.
___Insisted on using equipment that could not be justified economically.
___Failed to keep superiors informed about important job developments affecting other departments or divisions.
___Refused to accept substandard work from subordinates who were capable of better performance.
___Refused to follow instructions, even though they were clearly spelled out.
___Made excellent and reliable reports on important matters.
___Performed a difficult task which was outside his regular duties without being told to do so.
___Ignored the results of a study revealing defects in a proposal he submitted.
___Appropriated the good ideas of subordinates as his own.
___Ignored important facts in giving merit increases or promotions.
___Instituted effective procedure for controlling expenses in his department.
___Failed to clearly communicate the duties and responsibilities of a job to his subordinates.

Source: Barry M. Cohen, "A New Look at Performance Appraisal: The Specimen Checklist," *Human Resource Management*, vol. 11, no. 1 (Spring 1972), p. 21. Graduate School of Business Management, University of Michigan, Ann Arbor, Michigan.

ance for technical, supervisory, and even teaching personnel. Also, its reliability has been consistently high, as it results in as full a report of performance as the appraiser can recall. (12) However, a serious problem with this method is the possibility that appraisers may not be willing to admit to themselves that they have witnessed certain incidents concerning their subordinates.

Self-appraisal. A new trend is to let subordinates evaluate themselves. At the First National City Bank, a senior vice president simply hands his subordinates their own blank evaluation forms and asks them to fill in their ratings themselves. According to him, "It's amazing how honest people are. They put things in that are detrimental to their own progress and promotion." (13) The procedure has a built-in safeguard, as the vice president makes a final review of the ratings himself.

Making performance appraisals more effective

If performance appraisals are to be used successfully for career planning and development, they should be based upon performance standards, result in a face-to-face performance review, be based upon multiple assessments, and integrated into the work cycle.

Appraisal followed by a performance review. A second requisite for improving the developmental effect of performance appraisals is for the supervisor to compare subordinates' actual performance with the predetermined standards in order to determine how well—or how poorly—each employee has performed. This analysis is then conveyed to each employee through an appraisal interview, or performance review.

These interviews have not been very effective in the past. Yet, the skill with which the supervisor handles the appraisal feedback is the key factor in determining whether the performance appraisal program is an effective motivational factor in changing employee behavior or not. For example, research has indicated that among middle managers in a large manufacturing firm those who took some form of constructive action as a result of performance appraisals did so because of the way their superiors had conducted the appraisal feedback interview and discussion. (14) Consequently, while this procedure may be continuous or periodic, formal or informal, it must be performed. It has been suggested that one way of improving the performance reviews is to use the "group system" instead of having only the superior and subordinate meet together. (15) It is claimed that the group method leads to greater openness, less tenseness, and higher subsequent productivity.

Using multiple appraisals. Because of the previously mentioned bias and halo effect, it may be more useful to use multiple ratings rather than single evaluations. While the rating of one supervisor may not be valid, the overall pattern of several ratings do provide an indication of overall performance and potential for development. Therefore, the use of multiple ratings enables the organization to interpret the ratings of each appraiser who may be known to be typically "easy to please" or "difficult to please." In one hospital, the supervisor, department head, and the vice president evaluate each employee as a basis of training and development activities.

Integrate appraisals into the work cycle. A problem commonly found in the appraisal process is the differing perceptions of the supervisor and employee concerning the latter's job performance. As few employees consider their performance to be unsatisfactory, changes in behavior do not often result when a negative appraisal is given to an employee. One research study has suggested that this problem can be overcome by integrating the appraisal process into the work cycle with the understanding that both parties have roles and expectations which must be fulfilled if the appraisal process is to be successful as a developmental tool. This model is based upon the establishment of an interpersonal contract (sometimes referred to as a "psychological contract"), developing a helping relationship between the two; using the appraisal interview formally to apprise employees of their job performance; and to set goals and plans for self-development. This model is shown in Figure 14–3.

It has also been hypothesized that a primary problem of performance appraisals is using one "closed system" of appraisal for all employees, regardless of their abilities or level in the organization. What is needed is an "objective focused" or "open system" which differentiates groups and types of employees. (16)

FIGURE 14–3
Performance appraisal task model

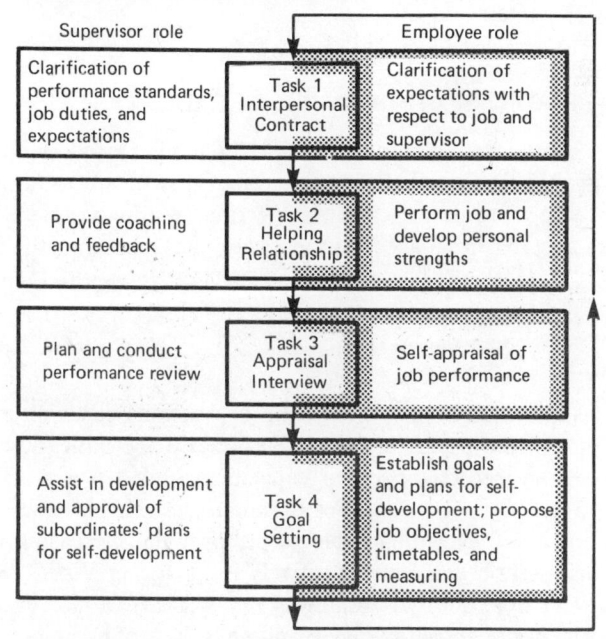

Supervisor role		Employee role
Clarification of performance standards, job duties, and expectations	Task 1 Interpersonal Contract	Clarification of expectations with respect to job and supervisor
Provide coaching and feedback	Task 2 Helping Relationship	Perform job and develop personal strengths
Plan and conduct performance review	Task 3 Appraisal Interview	Self-appraisal of job performance
Assist in development and approval of subordinates' plans for self-development	Task 4 Goal Setting	Establish goals and plans for self-development; propose job objectives, timetables, and measuring

Source: John D. Colby and Ronald L. Wallace, "Performance Appraisal: Help or Hindrance to Employee Productivity?" *The Personnel Administrator*, vol. 20, no. 6 (October 1975), p. 38. Reprinted with permission of *The Personnel Administrator*; copyright 1975, The American Society for Personnel Administration.

USING COUNSELING IN CAREER PLANNING AND DEVELOPMENT

Counseling is involved in all aspects of the employer-employee relationship. It begins with the employment procedure and does not terminate until the worker leaves the company—if then. The primary question facing personnel executives, then, is not whether to provide this function or not, but where to draw the line of demarcation between what is considered to be valid influence over another's personal, as well as professional, behavior.

While the events of the past three decades have led personnel executives to engage in this activity at an increasing rate and while most managers think this is a valid part of their job to be readily accessible to give advice to subordinates, the practice can be costly. A U.S. Court of Appeals forced a firm to pay the estate of an employee more than $40,000 because the employee had followed the advice of the company's president and lost that amount. The decision stated that it was not enough that the executive had acted in good faith and had given the correct information, but the executive was bound to "take account of the frailties of human understanding." (17) This decision sets a dangerous precedent, for any question of an employee that is answered by an executive or a specialist working as one of the firm's representatives can have similar consequences. Thus, the question of counseling takes on new significance.

While counseling is not new (the greatest stimulus to counseling was the "Hawthorne experiments"), it has been improved as our knowledge of human behavior has expanded.

PROVIDING PROGRESSION WITHIN THE ORGANIZATION

A third phase of career planning and development is providing progression within the organization itself. Progression and growth are usually provided through upgrading, promoting, and transferring. While the selection aspects of these were covered in Chapter 8, the career development phases are now discussed.

Upgrading

Increasing skill requirements often lead to situations in which present job holders can no longer perform their jobs because the educational or skill demands have increased beyond their capacities. Such virtually vacant positions can be "filled" by upgrading present employees. This involves retraining the workers so that they will be able to perform the increasingly complex functions. This method was very effectively used during World War II. At present, however, there are two limitations on its use; (*a*) a lack of motivation on the part of many of those involved; and (*b*) a lack of adequate and easily performed procedures for selecting candidates for upgrading. Where these restrictions can be overcome, however, this procedure results in improving and enhancing the individual's productive abilities.

An organization kept its books using conventional ledgers, journals, and office machines. It decided to use a computer service. The woman keeping the books was not qualified to perform the new job. She was given a leave of absence to attend the local university to take courses to prepare her to learn the new system. When the change was made, she successfully made the transition.

Promoting

Although increases in salaries are sometimes misconstrued to be promotions, this is not necessarily true. For there to be a promotion, there must be movement of workers to higher positions in which responsibilities are increased and in which there is greater status or prestige. Frequently promotions result in higher titles or job classifications.

Why use it? Promoting from within acts as a powerful motivational factor among employees. Some organizations take pride in providing opportunities for their workers to develop and advance. This tends to satisfy the egoistic needs of the employees by permitting them to enjoy the rewards which come from doing more challenging and interesting work with higher pay and better working conditions. Research has shown that advancement opportunities usually precipitate higher productivity. (18) As employees have little motivation to work harder if the better jobs are to be filled from outside, it is the personnel executive's responsibility to seek, train, and reward meritorious service. (19)

Bases for promoting. Promotions may be based upon *seniority*, which refers to an individual's length of service; *merit*, which refers to people's ability and capability to perform a job better than others; or a *combination* of the two.

Using "merit" as basis of promoting. In theory, promotions based upon merit are more desirable from a motivational and developmental point of view, for they induce employees to produce more in order to demonstrate their "merit." Merit promotions are based upon managerial judgment and formal or informal appraisals. One survey showed that "judgment" was the most frequently used basis for promotion, "formal appraisal systems" were second, and "personal characteristics" of the employee ranked third. (20)

Using seniority as basis for promoting. However, for low-level jobs, particularly where unions or public policy are involved, seniority is becoming the more frequently used basis for promotion. The reason for this trend is that seniority is more objective, does not involve as many value judgments, and does not lead to as many personal conflicts as do the other bases for promoting.

Yet, there are problems involved, for there are many types of seniority and many ways it can be lost or modified. It can date from the first day hired; it can include only those times worked, but not include times away because of layoffs, leaves of absence, or other reason. Seniority may be on a spatial basis, such as *companywide* or *only departmental,* or it can be on an occupational classification. Finally, there is *super-seniority,* often given to union officials and some minority groups, and *synthetic-seniority,* often given to workers on military leave.

Transferring

Positions can also be filled internally by transferring employees from a similar organizational level elsewhere in the organization. This is usually done when a person has greater capabilities than those required by the position held or when the transfer puts that individual in line for greater potential advancement. Essentially, a transfer involves the movement of an employee without special regard for either a change in pay or increased responsibilities—although these may occur.

A study of around 500 midwestern business executives indicated a positive reaction to transfers. According to the study, the typical manager first moves at the age of 27–28; while the next one occurs at age 34. While 64 percent of the managers were neutral concerning transfers, they ceased to be neutral with the second move. (21) In general, the reaction to transfers is more favorable by the managers with a great desire to reach the top, those in the higher organizational ranks, and those who have moved more often. Finally, the respondents felt that their transfers *were not a part of careful career planning* and they were *not* adequately consulted prior to the transfer.

Another common type of transfer which appears to be growing in frequency and complexity is cross-function transfers. About 68 percent of respondents from 250 large manufacturing firms indicated that transfers from one function to another within an organization had increased in recent years. (22) In general, it seems that cross-function transfers typically progress from specialized to more generalized functions, although this differs between industries.

USING "MANAGEMENT BY OBJECTIVES" IN CAREER DEVELOPMENT

Since its introduction in 1954 by Peter Drucker, the concept of "management by objectives" (MBO), or "management by results" as it is frequently called, (23) has become so popular as a method of planning, setting standards, motivating, and appraising performance that an organization cannot claim to be modern if it does not profess to practice MBO.

Underlying concepts

MOB's success is predicated upon two underlying hypotheses. First, *one who is strongly attached to a goal is willing to expend more effort in order to reach it than if one were less attracted to it.* The second hypothesis, the *self-fulfilling prophesy,* states that *whenever we predict something will happen, we will do everything possible to ensure that it happens.*

These hypotheses explain why this method is having such success in motivating employees. Another reason for its success is that it tends to incorporate the better parts of the various motivational theories. For example, it incorporates Maslow's *self-fulfillment need;* McGregor's *Theory Y;* Herzberg's *moti-*

vational factors of achievement, recognition, challenging work, and responsibility; and McClelland's *need for achievement* (Nach). It is also based upon the concept that people prefer to be evaluated according to *criteria* which they perceive to be realistic and *standards* which are viewed as being reasonably attainable. Under this method, people participate in setting the goals and identifying the criteria which will be used to evaluate them. Some of the goals may be measurable in quantitative terms (such as sales—or production—volume, expenses, or profits), while others may be assessed qualitatively (such as customer relations, a marketing plan, or employee development).

Requirements for successful use

Regardless of how deeply committed management is to the use of MBO and regardless of the form it takes within a given setting, management by results requires a unique approach to the appraisal of managers. That approach is geared to assessing their *managerial performance* rather than an evaluation of the *personal qualities and potentials* of the people themselves.

Elements of an MBO program. In essence, management by objectives stresses the importance of managers setting (with the aid and concurrence of their immediate superior) specific objectives which they intend to reach in the next period and then measuring performance against the standard of those preset objectives. In the more successful applications, the approach extends beyond a focus upon the objectives-results-objectives applications cycle into a process of ongoing career planning and development, carefully integrated into the institution's overall development program. In such cases, the approach has often highlighted the need for careful self-analyses into the nature of meaningful objectives, more extensive formulation of policies, and even adjustments in organizational designs and control systems. For example, reports of the most successful MBO programs indicate a turning in the direction of establishing organizational units more on the basis of homogeneous objectives rather than uniformity of activities, and the setting up of more direct and faster information systems to enable managers to control their own operations.

In general, the process involves the top manager's setting *organizational objectives;* these are translated into *goals* by the managers at the next lower organizational levels; the managers at the next lower level *develop* their *own specific goals* and submit these to their supervisors for mutual discussion to see if they are feasible and how they will be achieved; at the end of a given period of time—usually a quarter or a year—each subordinate's *actual performance is compared with predetermined goals;* an *appraisal of* each person's *performance* is made and discussed with each; one is *rewarded*—financially and/or otherwise—on the basis of the goal and the extent to which it was achieved.

When used for development purposes, MBO usually consists of the following elements:

1. Individual managers review the nature of their responsibilities, past performance, and planned activities and determine the primary objectives they hope to achieve in the period ahead;
2. They and their superiors confer about the proposed goals and make any necessary adjustments on the basis of additional inputs by the latter. (The crucial factor here is what the superior needs to do to assist the subordinate manager in accomplishing the agreed-upon objectives);
3. The managers ascertain the methods to be used in achieving the objectives, as well as receiving any training needed;
4. The managers begin to perform those activities necessary to reach their targets, sometimes feeling free to move on to contingency alternatives and always discussing with their superiors any revisions based upon early detection of unforeseen events; and
5. At the end of the period, the managers' performance is appraised and rewarded on the basis of the results obtained relative to the standards of performance previously set. On the basis of this review, objectives for the next period are then set.

Advantages and disadvantages. The advantages of using MBO to develop subordinates appear to far outweigh the disadvantages. While both sides are presented, only the highlights are covered.

Advantages. The primary advantage of MBO evolves around its appeal to employees' needs for creative expression, recognition, new experiences, and self-esteem. It challenges subordinates' *creativity* through inducing them to find better ways to perform their activities. Their *recognition* is a function of how high their goals were and the extent to which they achieved them. *New experiences* can be encountered through using the new methods developed to achieve the goals and objectives. *Self-esteem* results from the sense of challenge in setting the goals and the feeling of achievement which comes from meeting challenges.

In addition to those advantages, employees tend to increase their efforts when they know their performance is being appraised and rewarded; the existence of specific, clear-cut goals makes it easier for management to appraise and reward performance; and management is able to spot deficiencies in the organization sooner.

Disadvantages. The disadvantages revolve around the possible overemphasis upon the individual rather than the group. This tendency may encourage undue competition, "buckpassing," and short-range production to the detriment of group cohesiveness, managerial responsibility, and such intangibles as morale, employee development, and long-range organizational development.

Evaluating MBO's effectiveness

While MBO is still very popular, there are some indications that it is not the panacea it was supposed to be. Yet, where tried conscientiously, it does seem to lead to improved management. In one study of managers who were trained in a MBO system, there was a test before the program and a retest two years later measuring (*a*) responsibilities and goals, (*b*) delegation, (*c*) knowledge of performance, (*d*) assistance as needed, and (*e*) motivation. Using the accumulated data, the researchers concluded that irrespective of the organizational level of the supervisors and subordinates involved, the use of MBO led to increased managerial activity and favorable results. (24)

In spite of those impressive results, a recent survey revealed that only 181 of the *Fortune* 500 claimed to use MBO. Of those, less than 10 percent—somewhere between 36 and 50 companies—have MBO-based programs that are considered to be successful; and only 10 companies—or 2 percent—have programs that are considered "highly successful." (25)

GROUPS NEEDING SPECIAL ATTENTION

There are several groups needing special career guidance and counseling. They include the new entrants into management, including youth, minorities, and women; and managers with special problems, including the "fast-track" executives, the "supermobiles," and the "plateaued" executives.

New entrants into management ranks

The newer entrants into management ranks, while being quite dissimilar, have certain characteristics in common. These young people, minorities, and women *tend* to have different expectations, goals, and value systems from previous managerial groups. Personnel executives will need to give much time and effort in the guidance of the careers of these three groups, for they will be an integral part of management in the future.

Young people. It is difficult to draw firm conclusions concerning the young people entering management ranks today. While they tend to be college graduates and while they have certain similar characteristics, the changing economic environment may be changing many of the conclusions previously reached.

These new managers' attitudes, motivational patterns, and values are significantly at variance with those of previous members. The previous reward systems, including money, praise, and promotion, do not appear to be working adequately with this group. Their commitment to an individual organization, with the accompanying performance efforts, appear to be replaced by an identification with their profession, regardless of what it is. The organization is merely a stepping stone to achieving success in their occupation or profession. While these employees are generally well-educated, they are beginning to question the value of their education, as well as some of the things they learned. As a group, they are more mobile and less inclined to remain with one organization very long. However, they want this mobility to be on their own volition and reject transfers, particularly to less desirable jobs and locations.

This group needs guidance in making their expectations conform more to the realities of the economic and organizational environments. They need to be encouraged to think and act like executives and to accept the organizational climate in which they are to work.

Women and minorities. Based upon several years of case research, I have reached the conclusion that there are certain "pivotal" positions which lead either to the top or to stagnation. Along with the pivotal jobs, there are committee assignments, public relations activities, and training and development programs which tend to be predictive of upward mobility in the same organization. The more progressive organizations are now using career planning, guidance, and development to see that women and minorities are given the opportunity to grow into these pivotal positions.

According to one study, many *black professionals* may be limiting their career progression through an unwillingness to be mobile enough to take advantage of better opportunities. (26) Because of a sense of "community," security, belonging, and isolation, many of these professionals tend to concentrate in large metropolitan areas where there is a large black population.

As *women* have for so long been put into sex stereotyped jobs, they have been found to lack expectations equal to their present upward mobility. It has been found that when executive jobs become available, many women do not even apply for the jobs as they do not feel they will get them or are not adequately prepared for the job.

What can the personnel executive do to help guide and develop the careers of these groups? First, they can encourage the black professionals to be more flexible, mobile, and prepared for advancement. These individuals need to be shown that in order to reach a given goal or objective it may be necessary to "endure" less desirable locations, positions, and developmental activities. Much of the career guidance for women now involves raising their expectation level and making them dissatisfied with the position they hold.

Managers with special problems

The second broad group needing special attention in career development are managers with special problems, including those with special abilities who are being groomed for fast promotion, those with unwarranted expectations who tend to be overly mobile, and those who have plateaued in a given position.

The "fast-track" executive. Several leading companies have initiated special programs to identify, develop, appraise, and accelerate the progression of "bright young people" with potential for becoming top executives. These programs usually involve instituting quicker promotions for these individuals, offering them the kind of challenge, recognition, and ego satisfaction that these aggressive young people seek.

A study of personnel planning practices in 220 major U.S. corporations indicated a high degree of interest in the fast-track programs as personnel planning and career development techniques. Over 31 percent of the organizations had such career progression programs, while 42 percent recommended the use of this technique. (27) An interesting finding was that the greater the experience with employee planning, the greater the use of fast-track career progression. While only 16 percent of those with less than one year's experience had these programs, 58 percent of those with over 10 years' experience used them.

While the technique has pitfalls, the effectively designed and implemented programs do provide benefits to both the organization and the individuals. The evidence shows that the technique is both a practical and viable method for providing the needed talent for future growth and development.

The "supermobile" executive. A second group needing particular attention are the "supermobiles," who tend to be an outgrowth of the previous group mentioned. They have the "rising expectations" syndrome, whose expectations increase faster than the organizations can fulfill them. The ambitions of this group are formed before entering the corporation, but many development programs inadvertently encourage and polish these ambitions. While these executives are more easily developed than others, they are also more difficult to retain. This group is usually composed of MBAs selected from "some 220 universities favored by large breeder firms." (28)

The personnel executive can be of assistance to this group by helping them to keep their expectations in line with reality. Also, this group needs to be guided in coping with the stress resulting from lack of relationship between expectations and achievement.

The "plateaued" executive. Career planning and development are especially important during a period of "no-growth" or "slow-growth," such as has been occurring during the last few years. Organizational growth during the 1950s and 1960s tended to solve the morale problem of most business organizations as an expanding work force provided for the expanding quantity and quality of young executives, but this is not necessarily occurring now. (29)

A recently completed research project in nine companies by E. Kirby Warren, Thomas P. Ference, and James A. F. Stoner found a large number of managers who, in the judgment of their organizations, had "plateaued." (30) These individuals had little or no likelihood of being promoted or receiving substantial increases in duties or responsibilities. These long-service employees are of increasing concern to personnel executives, as such plateauing is taking place more markedly, frequently, and earlier than in recent years. A negative result of this trend is a decline in motivation and quality of performance.

While plateauing is inevitable and occurred in previous periods, it was a more gradual process whereby those seeking advancement had opportunity to do so, while those who did not desire to rise could be gradually bypassed by their more ambitious colleagues. Today the declining rate of corporate growth, an ever-increasing number of ambitious candidates have increased the competition for a stabilizing—or even decreasing—number of positions.

Consequently, the managers who advanced rapidly during the growth period of the 1960s are now in the middle and upper middle levels of management, competing for the relatively few positions at the top. The dilemma is that these individuals still have many years before normal retirement with many productive years to go, and yet their career progress has been slowed through no fault of their own.

The researcher, who found this same situation in more than "90 situations" in three years of research and consulting, proposed five kinds of solutions, each with several variations. These vary from "benign neglect," reorganizations, transfers, resignations, and counseling and upgrading. As indicated earlier in this chapter and the one to follow, the personnel officers must use these techniques for helping this group progress.

IMPLICATIONS AND APPLICATIONS FOR PERSONNEL EXECUTIVES

According to a Chinese proverb, "Behind an able man there are always other abler men." This is true of career planning and development, which is becoming one of the most important phases of personnel and human resources administration. First, it helps meet organizational and individual goals. Second, it tends to enhance employee satisfaction and increase their sense of dignity. Finally, it tends to reduce labor turnover and lower personnel costs.

While the methods used vary, in general they include counseling, performance appraisals, movement and progression in the organization, and management by objectives.

Performance appraisals are always used either formally or informally for developmental purposes. Formal appraisal systems are more effective, and their primary value is enhanced when they are used as a motivator of employee performance and as a guide to career development. Performance appraisals are used primarily among the white-collar and salaried personnel, especially the scientific, technical, professional, and managerial employees.

Finally, merit ratings, as such, are being abandoned in favor of goal-setting and performance appraisals, such as "management by objectives" programs. In essence, more emphasis is being given to evaluating the employee's actual past performance relative to preestablished work standards, rather than to appraising the personal characteristics which should lead to anticipate future productivity.

It must be strongly emphasized that the traits used in performance rating must be validated for the individual organizations and jobs involved and cannot be applied on an organizationalwide basis.

Finally, many of the demands of today's recruiting are less formal, more geared to accomplishment, and demand greater creativity and individuality. These demands particularly help the small business. Therefore, the executive officers in a small business should give considerable attention to career planning, guidance, and development of their personnel.

DISCUSSION QUESTIONS

1. Discuss the importance of career planning.
2. What are the advantages and limitations of performance appraisals as a tool of career development? Discuss.
3. What purposes do performance appraisals serve?
4. Describe the popular methods of performance appraisal in use today.
5. Do you see any potential abuses in the counseling method? Discuss.
6. Should seniority or merit be used as a basis for promotion? Defend your answer.
7. Evaluate the use of MBO for career guidance and development purposes. Do you think this method is superior to the others? Defend your answer.

REFERENCES AND SUGGESTIONS FOR FURTHER STUDY

1. Fred K. Foulkes, "The Expanding Role of the Personnel Function," *Harvard Business Review*, vol. 53, no. 2 (March–April 1975), pp. 71–84.
2. R. D. Brynildsen and W. S. Curra, "Program Aims to Mesh Company's, Employees' Goals," *Industry Week*, no. 176 (March 22, 1973), pp. 46–50.
3. John D. Colby and Ronald L. Wallace, "Performance Appraisal: Help or Hindrance to Employee Productivity?" *The Personnel Administrator*, vol. 20, no. 6 (October 1975), p. 38 ff.
4. See Robert J. Paul, "Employee Performance Appraisal: Some Empirical Findings," *Personnel Journal*, vol. 47, no. 2 (February 1968), pp. 109–14.
5. E. H. Conant, "Worker Efficiency and Wage Differentials in a Clerical Labor Market," *Industrial and Labor Relations Review*, vol. 16, no. 3 (April 1963), pp. 428–33.
6. Much of the material in this section is based upon Laurence Siegel and Irving M. Lane, *Psychology in Industrial Organizations*, 3d ed. (Homewood, Ill.: Richard D. Irwin, Inc., 1974), pp. 72–83.
7. Herbert E. Meyer, "How They're Doing," *Fortune* (January 1974), pp. 106.
8. Ibid., p. 111.
9. Thomas L. Whisler and Shirley F. Harper, eds., *Performance Appraisal* (New York: Holt, Rinehart, and Winston, 1962).
10. M. Joseph Dooher and Vivienne Marquis, eds., *Rating Employee and Supervisory Performance* (New York: American Management Assn., 1950).
11. James R. Berkshire and Richard W. Highland, "Forced Choice Performance Rating: A Methodological Study," *Personnel Psychology*, vol. 6, no. 3 (Autumn 1953), pp. 355–58.
12. See Gerald H. Whitlock, "Application of the Psychophysical Law to Performance Evaluation," *Journal of Applied Psychology*, vol. 47, no. 1 (February 1963), pp. 15–23.
13. Meyer, "How They're Doing," *Fortune*, p. 104.
14. H. H. Meyer and W. B. Walker, "A Study of Factors Relating to the Effectiveness of a Performance Appraisal Program," *Personnel Psychology*, vol. 14, no. 3 (Autumn 1961), pp. 291–98.

15. Robert Cherry, "Performance Reviews: A Note on Failure," *Personnel Journal,* vol. 49, no. 5 (May 1970), pp. 398–403, See also Lawrence R. Zeitlein, "Planning for a Successful Performance Review Program," *Personnel Journal,* vol. 48, no. 12 (December 1969), pp. 957–61, for other suggestions for improving these interviews.
16. Paul H. Thompson and Gene W. Dalson, "Performance Appraisal: Managers Beware," *Harvard Business Review,* vol. 48, no. 1 (January–February 1970), pp. 149–58.
17. Robert S. Holzman, "The Price of Advice," *Management Review,* vol. 55, no. 1 (January 1966), p. 7.
18. F. Herzberg, B. Mausner, and B. B. Snyderman. *The Motivation to Work,* 2d ed. (New York: John Wiley & Sons, Inc., 1959), p. 80.
19. Walter Kleinschord, "Human Resources Matrixing: Motivation, Control," *Administrative Management,* vol. 37 (January 1976), pp. 22–26
20. W. R. Noe, Jr., "Selecting the Right Employees for Promotion," *Administrative Management,* vol. 24, no. 10 (October 1963), p. 76.
21. William F. Glueck, "Managers, Mobility and Morale," *Business Horizons,* vol. 17, no. 6 (December 1974), pp. 65–70.
22. David E. Robertson, "Cross Function Transfers: Rates and Patterns," *Human Resource Management,* vol. 11, no. 3 (Fall 1972), pp. 14–19.
23. Peter F. Drucker, *The Practice of Management* (New York: Harper & Brothers, 1954), pp. 121–36. See his book, *Managing for Results* (New York: Harper & Row, 1964), for practical applications of the concept.
24. P. P. Fay and D. N. Beach, "Management by Objectives Evaluated," *Personnel Journal,* vol. 53, no. 11 (October 1974), pp. 767–69.
25. Fred E. Schuster and Alva F. Kindall, "Management by Objectives—Where We Stand Today, A Survey of the Fortune 500," *Human Resource Management,* vol. 13, no. 1 (Spring 1974), pp. 12–13.
26. Carl A. Benson, "The Question of Mobility in Career Development for Black Professionals," *Personnel Journal,* vol. 54, no. 5 (May 1975), pp. 272–74.
27. James W. Walker, "Tracking Corporate Tigers in the Seventies," *Human Resource Management,* vol. 62, no. 5 (Winter 1972), pp. 18–24.
28. Eugene Emerson Jennings, "The Supermobile," *Human Resource Management,* vol. 11, no. 1 (Spring 1972), pp. 4–17.
29. The following headlines dramatize this problem. The headings will be given without comment.
    "The Sudden Surplus of Middle Managers," *Business Week* (February 23, 1974), p. 28.
    "Firms Fight an Effect of 1950s Baby Boom: Young Executive Glut," *Wall Street Journal* (August 18, 1975), p. 1.
    "In Demand Again—Seasoned Executives," *U.S. News & World Report* (November 17, 1975), p. 94.
    "The Times Stay Lean for Middle Managers," *Business Week* (December 15, 1975), p. 21.
30. E. Kirby Warren, Thomas P. Ference, and James A. F. Stoner, "Problems in Review," *Harvard Business Review,* vol. 53, no. 1 (January–February 1975), pp. 30–38, 146–48.

Chapter 15

Maximizing personnel potential

Enhancing an individual's self-perception
  Role of the individual
  How personnel executives can help individuals grow

How leadership style affects employee growth
  Factors affecting leadership
  What causes a manager to be an effective leader?

How motivation can affect employee growth
  The role of motivation
  Some prevailing theories of motivation

Implications and applications for personnel executives

15

Maximizing personnel potential

Always dream and shoot higher than you know you can do. Don't bother just to be better than your contemporaries or predecessors. Try to be better than yourself.

WILLIAM FAULKNER

Any use of human being in which less is demanded of him and less is attributed to him than his full status is a degradation and a waste.

NORBERT WIENER

In the play, *My Fair Lady,* Professor Doolittle takes Liza, a flower girl from the gutters of London, and through personal coaching and guidance converts her into a beautiful and cultured lady. Then he tries to send her back to the gutter, but she refuses.

The modern analogy of the first part of that play is Doris Smithers who began working as a cashier in a supermarket. The manager recognized her potential and trained her for bookkeeping. She then badgered her boss into a management training program. Afterwards she was given more and more responsibility, even before she thought she was ready for it. Eventually she became the first woman manager of Shopwell Grocery Store and is now a highly successful businesswoman. (1)

That's what this chapter is all about—developing the potential within employees so that the organizational goals are reached and the individuals grow to their full potential.

While the previous three chapters have dealt with organized programs for developing personnel, this chapter will deal with the more informal relationships involving superior-subordinate relationships, as shown in Figure 15–1.

ENHANCING AN INDIVIDUAL'S SELF-PERCEPTION

Organizations are now a way of life in industrialized societies. Therefore, while we tend to glorify individualism, in reality we are talking about *relative* degrees of organizational control over individual activities. One of the principles of organization is that effective organization achieves productivity far in

**FIGURE 15-1
A model for maximizing personnel potential**

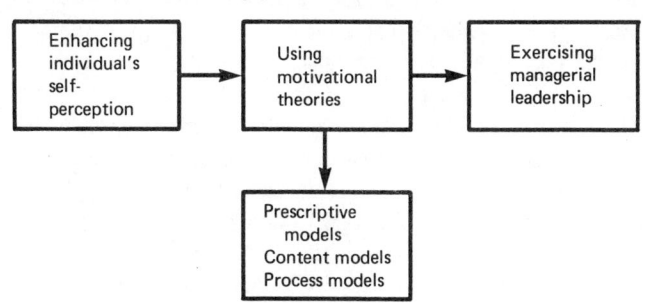

```
┌─────────────┐     ┌─────────────┐     ┌─────────────┐
│ Enhancing   │     │ Using       │     │ Exercising  │
│ individual's│ ──▶ │ motivational│ ──▶ │ managerial  │
│ self-       │     │ theories    │     │ leadership  │
│ perception  │     │             │     │             │
└─────────────┘     └──────┬──────┘     └─────────────┘
                           │
                           ▼
                    ┌─────────────┐
                    │ Prescriptive│
                    │ models      │
                    │ Content models│
                    │ Process models│
                    └─────────────┘
```

excess of the sum of its individual parts. The principle involved is: Individual effort is multiplied when it is combined, carefully planned, and skillfully directed toward the accomplishment of a common goal, yet even in organized activity there should be consideration of the individuality of the participants.

Role of the individual

Healthy organizational growth results from individual creativity. In spite of declining individuality, healthy changes in organizational performance and productivity still result from individual creativity. (2)

Not only is production and performance improved through creative individuality, but also the reliability of production is enhanced. For example, it has been shown that the nonconformist innovator, rather than the "organization man," generates the ideas necessary for progress and success in business operations. (3)

Yet individual creativity enhanced by group interaction. It is a generally accepted principle of human behavior that groups have greater problem-solving ability than do individuals. The supposed reason for this is that groups afford the opportunity for energizing ideas, providing group motivation, and stimulating interactions that arise out of joint effort. A study conducted to test this hypothesis substantiated the hypothesis that group solutions average out to be superior to individual solutions. (4) However, it was noted that the group members who combined their efforts did not incorporate or even summarize the best ideas its members had had prior to the group action. Also, it appeared likely that the group's superiority in problem solving was usually based upon the ability of one talented member.

How personnel executives can help individuals grow

If people are so important, what can personnel executives do to help them grow—as individuals? There are several things which can be done, including developing a more enlightened attitude toward the role of individuals in an organization. While these attitudes have been called by many names, the most frequently used are the "factor-of-production," the "human relations," and "human resources" philosophies. The last one, which is now generally accepted by scholars and personnel administrators as the predominant approach to dealing with employees, tends to incorporate the better elements of the previous two systems of thought.

The factor-of-production approach. The "classical," or "scientific management," approach which regarded employees as merely another economic factor of production reached its peak of acceptance during the 1930s. It tended to be used by the owner-entrepreneurs of some business firms, as well as by many managers of nonbusiness activities, such as governmental units. Employees were treated the same as the other factors of production and had no special preeminence over them. Workers were to be used as intensively as feasible and then discarded when their productive abilities were terminated. The results were that employees often worked long, hard hours for low wages in order to achieve maximum production, as measured by the economic criteria of efficiency and effectiveness.

This approach failed because it was inadequate as a basis for performing the personnel function when individual and national productivity were above the subsistence level. Therefore, during the 1940s and 1950s, when there was high material production, this indifferent approach failed as a basis for explaining, predicting, and influencing human behavior.

To a certain extent, this system of thought provided the background for Douglas McGregor's "Theory X," which stated that the average human being was lazy, disliked work, shunned responsibility, and had to be coerced into effective performance. (5) Most personnel executives have abandoned this concept along with any conclusions they may have drawn concerning its relevance to employee behavior.

The human relations approach. As shown in Chapter 1, the Hawthorne experiments and early research by the behavioral scientists emphasized the concept that "people are human and would like to be treated as such."

The belief *that the goal of personnel administration should be to provide the workers with job satisfaction,* which would result in greater productivity, became generally accepted by enlightened managers. The model for this management method was:

Employee participation → → Job satisfaction → → Increased productivity

In its purest form, this model was similar to McGregor's "Theory Y," which stated that it is generally accepted that work is normal, that people need and desire to work, and that the intellectual and the productive capabilities of employees are only partially utilized.

> Female secretarial and clerical workers and their office managers in a large retail firm were tested on their perceptions of human behaviors. Each subordinate was asked to respond twice—once according to her own attitude preference and once according to her perception of her supervisor's attitudes. The supervisors were to respond only once, according to their own attitudes.

Subordinates who perceived their supervisor as possessing "Theory Y" assumptions of employee behavior tended to be more satisfied with their jobs. (6)

Voluminous research has been done in an effort to identify and measure the extent to which attitudinal variables are related to job performance and employee satisfaction. The accumulated evidence reveals job satisfaction to be very illusive as the variables relate differently to productivity and satisfaction in different organizations and in different individuals. However, it is no longer valid to assume that "happy employees" are productive workers, because their output depends upon so many factors. (7)

Research studies, conducted by Lawler and Porter, found that good performance leads to rewards, which in turn lead to job satisfaction, rather than the reverse. (8) My own research indicates that the better producers tend to be slightly dissatisfied and less than totally pleased with the environment in which they find themselves.

One of the best studies of the possible connections between job attitudes—particularly job satisfaction—and various job behaviors was done by Donald Schwab and Larry Cummings. An extensive search of the literature and research findings led them to conclude that "studied alone or together, they are associated with a number of covariants." (9) They were pessimistic about the value of further theorizing about the satisfaction-performance relationships.

When personnel administrators, in a competitive situation, had to evaluate personnel policies in terms of productivity, cost of production, and profitability, this method was found lacking. Because of numerous misconceptions and abuses to this personnel management philosophy, it declined in popularity when it was forced to meet the economic criteria of efficiency following the "recession" of 1957–58. (10)

The human resource approach. Now, the human resource approach, which views the productivity of employees as being an economic resource of an organization, is popular. While *their performance is measured by the economic criteria of productivity, efficiency, effectiveness, costs, and profitability, employees themselves* in their relationships to other members of the organization *are viewed as having dignity, worth, and value.* (11) Therefore, the *economic aspect* of personnel administration, which is judged in terms of economic analysis, is adhered to, while the *philosophical aspect* of recognizing and respecting the personal dignity of each human entity is also given credence.

This conclusion has been confirmed by research. When 254 managers were given a test to determine how they felt about the present attitudes of employees, most responded that employees tend to resist change and that *the behavior of today's employees is influenced by a complex blend of social, economic, psychological, and biological factors.* Most employees were perceived to be more concerned with their own needs and objectives than those of their institution, yet they were very ambitious and intelligent. These tests indicated that managers today are perceptive and realistic about their subordinates and do not believe in either Theory X or Theory Y but rather try to combine them to meet various situations. (12)

"What's-his-name here claims I don't pay enough attention to human relations."

Courtesy of Dale McFeatters, creator of Strictly Business, and Publishers Newspaper Syndicate.

Also, the experience of Detroit's auto makers has tended to confirm the validity of the resource theory. A variety of experiments has been tried in order to make life on the assembly line more pleasant and meaningful, while still boosting productivity. Yet, a Ford Motor Company survey found that its workers were primarily concerned with wages, job security, and fringe benefits, and, while workers enjoyed enrichment programs, they resulted in no significant change in productivity. (13)

The *expectancy theory* has developed along with this philosophy. It states that managerial *perceptions* and *expectations* affect subordinates' performance, for the way managers treat their subordinates is influenced, in turn, by what the managers *think* their workers *expect* from them. If managers' expectations of their juniors are high, productivity and development are likely to be excellent; if the expectations are low, results are likely to be poor. Managers not only affect the expectations, development, and productivity of subordinates, but also influence their attitudes toward their job and themselves. (14)

Conversely, what employees *perceive* their superior expecting from them will determine their attitudes and performance.

A study of employee performance in a petrochemical firm found the supervisors' highest expectations of their subordinates were "dedication, hard work, thoroughness, and loyalty." In turn, subordinates desired and expected "overall direction and goal setting and considerable freedom to do our work in our own way." When these expectations were met, there was effective performance; when they were not met, ineffective performance resulted.

HOW LEADERSHIP STYLE AFFECTS EMPLOYEE GROWTH

The way personnel executives view the importance of employees also affects the leadership style used by those executives in helping employees grow. Although there are many aspects of leadership which affect employee growth, only two will be mentioned in this context—the factors affecting leadership, and some of the determinants of effective leadership. (15)

Factors affecting leadership

The theory that leadership success is based upon the traits of the individual leader is called the "traitist theory" of leadership. While many earlier studies emphasized this theory, it is now known that leaders are not born with certain traits and characteristics that preordain them to be leaders. Instead, some individuals acquire certain human, technical, and conceptual skills which enhance their leadership capabilities. These skills are one of the factors that lead to expertise in exercising managerial leadership.

Yet, as Mary Parker Follett discovered, there is not one, but three leadership factors—the leader, the followers, and the situation. "*Leadership* is not a matter of a dominating personality. The leader should be the one most able to secure interpenetration within the group of the best ideas of both leader and led. He must have the insight not only to meet the next situation but to *make* it." (16) All these are causal factors in determining the effectiveness of managerial leadership, and no one of them can be studied in isolation, for each, in turn, affects the others, as shown in Figure 15–2.

Fiedler's contingency model is an attempt to carry leadership theory one step beyond this oversimplified model. He indicates that any leadership theory must account for the interaction between personality and the leadership situation, as well as the way in which the situational changes affect leader behavior and organizational performance. (17)

What causes a manager to be an effective leader?

Some of the variables causing a manager to be an effective leader in developing people are: the leadership style used and the closeness of supervision.

The manager's leadership style. The effective manager will use the leadership style which achieves the organizational objectives, and helps subordinates reach their objectives—while growing and developing as employees.

FIGURE 15-2
Causal relationship between the leader, subordinates, and the situation

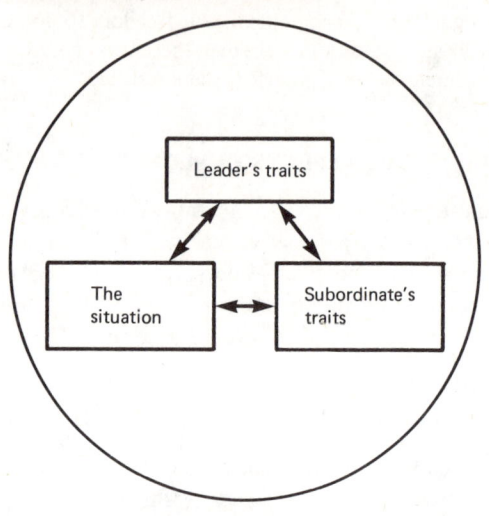

Types of leadership styles. Managerial leadership is often discussed as if managers had certain traits and characteristics which led them to act in a typical way at all times. More accurately, there are leadership styles used by all managers at varying times. These have been called the bureaucratic, authoritarian, participative, and free-rein methods. In reality, though, there are not four distinct styles of leadership, but there is a continuum in the degree of freedom of choice by the subordinates in the organization. Thus, at one extreme employees would have very little, if any, freedom of choice, for authority is exercised primarily by the manager; as one shifts to the other end of the spectrum, the employees exercise practically unlimited discretion. Yet, as seen from Figure 15-3, that freedom is not absolute, for the manager retains the right to withdraw the delegated authority if it is misused.

Recently, Tannenbaum and Schmidt revised an article they had written 15 years earlier. While agreeing with the general concept, as shown in Figure 15-3, they indicated that managers could never shirk the responsibility for making the best decision affecting subordinates. However, the most "democratic" boss is not the one who lets subordinates help decide most of the problems, but rather the one who *lets subordinates participate in solving the most important problems involving them.* (18)

Another authority has emphasized the importance of choosing the leadership style which emphasizes confidence in subordinates and the belief that people will react positively to a leadership style. (19)

The authoritarian approach. Although philosophically and theoretically the democratic approach to leadership may be ideal, from a pragmatic and practical point of view it will not always necessarily work. The dynamics, creativity, and initiative of any managerial position are based upon the au-

FIGURE 15–3
Continuum of leadership behavior

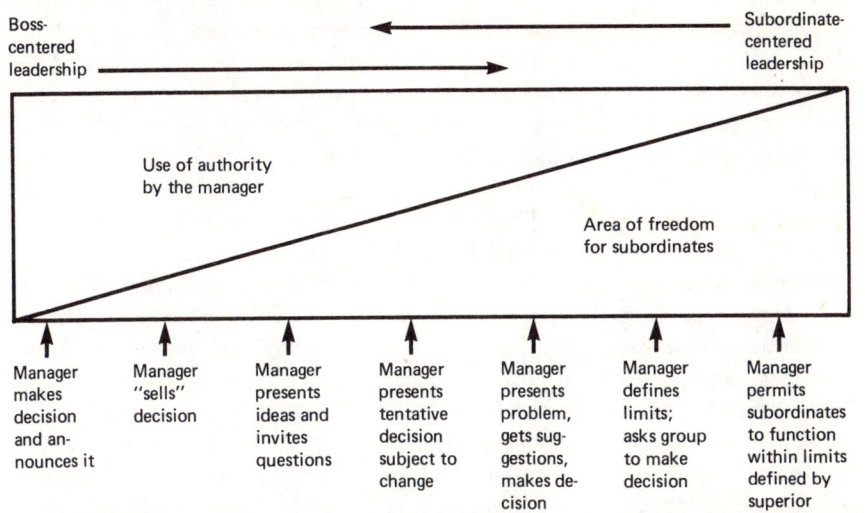

Boss-centered leadership						Subordinate-centered leadership
Use of authority by the manager					Area of freedom for subordinates	
Manager makes decision and announces it	Manager "sells" decision	Manager presents ideas and invites questions	Manager presents tentative decision subject to change	Manager presents problem, gets suggestions, makes decision	Manager defines limits; asks group to make decision	Manager permits subordinates to function within limits defined by superior

Source: Robert Tannenbaum and Warren H. Schmidt, "How to Choose a Leadership Pattern," *Harvard Business Review*, vol. 36, no. 2 (March–April 1958), p. 96. Copyright © 1958 by the President and Fellows of Harvard College; all rights reserved.

thority and responsibility delegated to it, and these cannot be delegated to a collective group but must reside in one individual.

The belief that an executive should not overtly exercise authority but only ask for participation of subordinates was thoroughly dispelled by the late Douglas M. McGregor as a result of his experiences as president of Antioch College. He tried to practice "good human relations" in order to eliminate discord and disagreement and cause the faculty and staff to like him. He hoped to serve as an advisor to the school and avoid some of the unpleasantness of making difficult decisions. However, his desire did not work out in practice, so he had to tell the alumni and faculty in his final message: "I couldn't have been more wrong. It took a couple of years, but I finally began to realize that a leader cannot avoid the exercise of authority any more than he can avoid responsibility for what happens to his organization." (20)

> One of the most dramatic large-scale productivity improvements occurred in a regulated public utility when the company rose from "average" to "one of the best in the industry." The turnabout was attributed to "a clear demand for improved performance that was placed on the company management team." (21)

Research tends to confirm these practical experiences. For example, one carefully controlled study, in which the nature of supervision was systematic and varied, found that "autocratic leadership seemed to lead to improved output, despite its deleterious effect on morale." (22) Another study dealing with large groups showed that groups with leaders who participated with the group in a creative activity had a higher *quantity* of ideas, but the leaders who only supervised the group had higher *quality* ideas. (23)

The participative approach. It has been argued that management performance could be improved by treating subordinates as mature individuals. Thus, subordinate workers were asked to increase their performance and to accept more responsibility, while the manager was asked to assume more responsibility for his area of discretion. (See the earlier discussion of McGregor's Theory Y.)

The free-rein approach. The free-rein approach is based upon the concept that if given a goal and then left alone to pursue their own self-interest, *employees who have the ability, training, and experience to achieve that goal will do so.* It assumes, though, a degree of confidence that is less often justified in dealing with employees in the lower level jobs than with those in scientific, technical, and professional positions. It is felt that this approach will be used with increasing frequency as the caliber of the work force is enhanced.

A laboratory experiment was designed to study the effects differential supervisory role specifications had on work-team performance. The supervisory roles were designed to approximate the authoritarian approach (active monitor), participative (direct participant), and free-rein (laissez-faire) supervisory roles. It was found that the "individual supervisor was a more consistent influence on performance than the particular role each employed." (24) The role played by the supervisors had significance in light of the different performance criteria used. For example, *speed* was greatest under the *laissez-faire type leadership,* while *accuracy* was better under the *other two conditions.* The role played seemed less important than the fact that the supervisors made their intentions known to the team promptly so that the team members could know what to expect and how to react to the supervisor.

In general, this leadership style tends to be preferable for professional subordinates. Research has shown that the effective leader should not give excessive direction to professionals, but rather should *interact with them* and allow them to make their own decisions. (25)

How to determine the style to use. Regardless of the method used, the dynamic managers are those who exercise leadership through helping subordinates grow and develop. They are sensitive to the situation, analyze it, make accurate judgments as to how much authority is necessary—based upon their own and their employees' capabilities. There is no *one* best leadership method.

It has also been shown in an experiment that whereas the customary method of introducing a change is for the leader to describe the new idea and then attempt to persuade the members to adopt it, a problem-solving approach would be more effective. (26) Rather than present a solution and factual evidence pointing to the merits of the change, the leader should pose the problem and share all data that bear on the issue.

Finally, consistency in leadership style appears to be more related to effectiveness than the style used. In a series of opinion surveys, it was found that the manager who failed to show a consistent leadership style was graded far below the ones who were consistent, regardless of the style used. (27)

Participation—a paradox. Executives exhibit a paradox when it comes to managing people. They feel it is important to keep employees informed and to include them in decision making, yet they confess doubts about their capacities for initiative and leadership. A research team at the University of California has found that executives around the world stated that they include subordinates in the decision-making process, but still doubt that their subordinates have enough initiative and leadership ability to benefit effectively from that style. (28)

The manager's "psychological distance." Employees' growth and development also result from the extent of, and the closeness of, the executive's supervision of subordinates. The Sears, Roebuck & Company studies found that wider spans of management and fewer levels of authority resulted in a more effective organizational structure and produced a disproportionate share of promotable personnel. (29) It was also found that managers and employees had a higher level of morale and productivity.

In a large metropolitan insurance firm, it was found that female workers were less satisfied with the supervisor's ability, the reasonableness of her expectations, and the rules she attempted to enforce under close supervision than under general supervision. (30)

Another study has attempted to refine the relationship between managers and other employees. It showed that there are two kinds of close supervision: controlling what and how employees perform their jobs; and issuing orders and checking on performance by giving advice and encouragement. It was found that, in general, the former adversely affects productivity, while the latter does not. It was also shown that close supervision is effective if the manager is considered to be friendly with the group and interested in its welfare. Conversely, if the manager is viewed as being indifferent to the group's welfare, or a hostile outsider, close supervision is met with apathy or resentment. (31)

Finally, a study designed to develop better criteria for selection of postal department supervisors found that *effective supervisors stay psychologically close enough to maintain contact with their subordinates, yet far enough away to deal objectively with poor performance.* (32) Thus, the conclusion is reached that personnel executives should neither become so isolated from employees that they appear indifferent to their welfare nor so close to them that they are hampered by emotional ties.

HOW MOTIVATION CAN AFFECT EMPLOYEE GROWTH

It could probably be concluded from the material so far in this chapter that *management is motivation.* While this is too strong a conclusion to reach from the evidence, it does indicate the importance of the personnel executive using motivational techniques to stimulate employee growth. A similar conclusion was reached by Clarence Francis when he was chairman of General Foods. He said: "You can buy a man's time; you can buy a man's physical presence at a given place; you can even buy a measured number of skilled muscular motions per hour or day; but you cannot buy enthusiasm. You cannot buy initiative; you cannot buy loyalty; you cannot buy devotion of hearts, minds, and souls. You have to earn these things." (33)

This statement illustrates the need for envisioning motivation as more inclusive than the mere application of some specific techniques or device as a stimulant to increase output.

The role of motivation

As shown in Chapter 1, performance results from the interaction of physical, financial, and human resources. The first two are inanimate; they are translated into "productivity"* only when the human element is introduced. However, the human element interjects a variable over which management has only limited control. When dealing with the inanimate factors of production, management can accurately predict the input-output relationship and can even vary the factors as it chooses in order to achieve a desired rate of production. In dealing with employees, however, the intangible factor of will, volition, or freedom of choice is introduced, and workers can increase or decrease their productivity as they choose. This human quality gives rise to the need for positive motivation.

Performance results from ability and motivation. In reality, the level of performance of employees is a function of their abilities and motivation. The first determines what they *can* do; the second determines what they *will* do. If productivity were only a function of ability, the relationship would be simple, for an employee's output would vary directly with increases in ability, as shown by the unitary performance curve in Figure 15–4. This is the performance curve that would result if productivity were based upon ability alone. As ability increased, performance would increase directly and proportionately. However, because of the element of volition, motivation is necessary to enhance output. Thus, the performance curve is related to the type and extent of motivation. It can be seen on the performance curve that where there is a strong positive motivation the employee's output is enhanced at an increasing rate. Where there is a strong negative motivation—or a weak positive motivation—the person's performance level will continue to be low, regardless of changes in ability. (See performance curve 2.)

Motivation is multidimensional. The performance equation and derived performance curves ($P = f[a \times m]E$) is oversimplified. Other factors, such as

---

* What is referred to as "productivity" is likely to be misleading. It is the total output of machines and workers divided by the number of worker hours worked. The total production of a country is obviously the amount of goods and services turned out by everyone. The nation's level of living (scale of living) is determined by the output per person of the entire population, less what is taken by the government for unproductive purposes—from a civilian point of view. From a firm's point of view, it is the total output divided by the number of employees. Another measurement of productivity is the total output divided by the production employees. Regardless of which method of measurement is used, the important thing is to increase the output per worker—hour worked.

FIGURE 15-4

Level of performance (y-axis) vs *Level of ability and intensity of motivation* (x-axis)

- Performance curve 1*
- Unitary performance curve†
- Performance curve 2‡

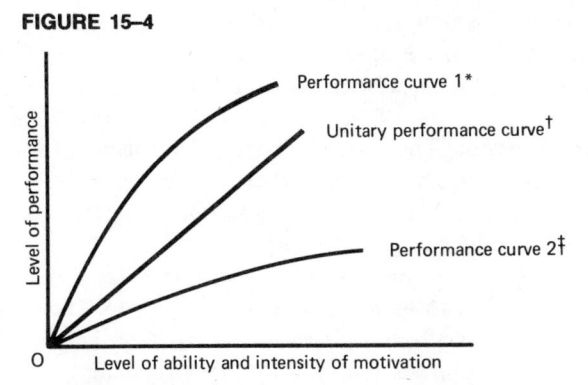

* Result of increasing ability and strong positive motivation.
† Level of performance expected with a given increase in ability but disregarding motivation.
‡ Result of increasing ability but with a strong negative or weak positive motivation.

technology, the social, political, and economic systems, culture, religious beliefs, personal problems, the work environment, the communications system, and other factors, would need to be considered in attempting to answer the question, "Why do people work?" A study was undertaken to determine whether employees perceive any differences in the way these variables affect their job effort or motivation, as compared with their personal satisfaction from those jobs. About 775 scientists and technicians employed in a large midwestern business organization were asked to rank 17 variables for both dimensions on a questionnaire. The results indicated that personal accomplishment, praise for good work, getting along with co-workers, company location, and receiving credit for ideas had a greater impact on *personal satisfaction* than on their job effort. Knowing what is expected of one, having a capable supervisor, having challenging work and responsibility, and being kept informed and participating in decisions were all given more importance for their effects on *motivation,* as opposed to personal satisfaction. (34)

Some prevailing theories of motivation

It is difficult to condense and compare the prevailing theories of motivation as they are based upon different assumptions and often focus on different dimensions of performance. Complicating the problem is that theorists often attach different labels to the same concept.

The theories will be put into three categories for discussion purposes. They are:

1. *Prescriptive models,* which try to tell management *how* to motivate employees. These theories assume there are principles which can be translated into specific instructions for the practitioner to use in motivating employees;

2. *Content models,* which are concerned with the question of *what* causes behavior—such as needs that employees try to satisfy on the job; and
3. *Process models,* which deal with *how* behavior originates and is performed.

Prescriptive models. The earlier behavioral models tended to be prescriptive and were based largely on trial-and-error experience or popular beliefs. The most popular ones were Taylor's "scientific management," the human relations model, and McGregor's Theory Y.

Content models. These models, dealing with individual motivation, focus on the question of what causes behavior to occur and stop. The answers usually center around the *needs, motives,* or *desires* that *drive* employees and their relationship to the *incentives* that *attract* them. The needs or motives are internal to the individual and serve as the motives that cause people to choose a specific course of action in order to satisfy the need. Incentives are external factors which give value or utility to the goal or outcome of the employees' behavior.

The most popular content models are Maslow's *needs hierarchy,* Frederick Herzberg's *two-factor model,* and David McClelland's *needs for achievement model.*

Maslow's hierarchy. (35) This theory is based upon the belief that all forms of animal life will select a beneficial diet if enough alternatives are presented and free choice is allowed. All organisms are self-growing, self-regulated, and autonomous. The constitutional differences in individuals generate differential value systems concerning ways of adjusting one's self to one's cultural environment.

Human beings, as part of their intrinsic constitution, have psychological as well as physiological needs. Thus, all of us have needs or goals which are physiological, safety, social, ego, and self-fulfillment. These needs are related to one another in a developmental way and in a definitely ascending hierarchy. This hierarchy is based upon the order of priority of the need and its strength. All the basic needs may be considered as simply steps along a time path leading to self-actualization, which includes all the other basic needs. (See Figure 15–5 for a modification of this theory.)

Herzberg's two-factor model. (36) Herzberg's theory was based upon the premise that the relationship between job factors—personal attitudes—and effects cannot be studied in isolation but must be studied together. There are two sets of job attitudes and factors. The first-level factors are objective elements of the situation; the second are the employees' perceptions and introspections of themselves, or of their attempts to define their need and value systems.

There are some job factors which, if present, will not lead to motivation, but will lead to job satisfaction. If they are not present, they lead to dissatisfaction and possibly negative motivation. These are: supervision, salary, company policy and administration, benefits, job security, working conditions, and interpersonal relationships with superiors, colleagues, and subordinates.

FIGURE 15-5
A hierarchy of work motivation

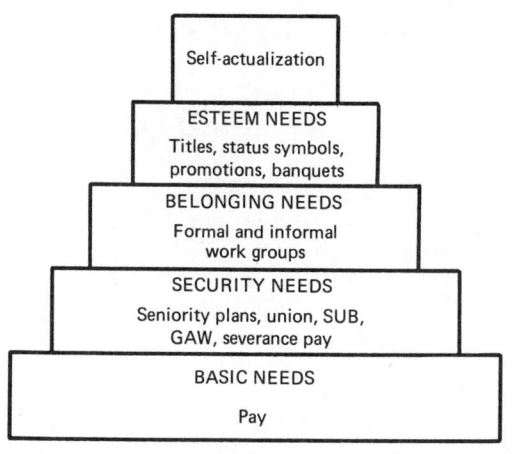

```
            ┌─────────────────────┐
            │ Self-actualization  │
        ┌───┴─────────────────────┴───┐
        │      ESTEEM NEEDS           │
        │   Titles, status symbols,   │
        │    promotions, banquets     │
    ┌───┴─────────────────────────────┴───┐
    │        BELONGING NEEDS              │
    │      Formal and informal            │
    │         work groups                 │
┌───┴─────────────────────────────────────┴───┐
│           SECURITY NEEDS                    │
│      Seniority plans, union, SUB,           │
│          GAW, severance pay                 │
├─────────────────────────────────────────────┤
│              BASIC NEEDS                    │
│                  Pay                        │
└─────────────────────────────────────────────┘
```

Source: Fred Luthans, *Organizational Behavior* (New York: McGraw-Hill Book Co., 1973), p. 486.

Conversely, there are elements that, when present, lead to positive motivation. The most important of these in descending order of strength are: achievement, recognition, creative and challenging work, responsibility, and advancement.

The first set of factors is called *dissatisfiers, maintenance factors,* or *hygiene factors;* the second group is referred to as *motivation factors.* See Figure 15-6 for an approximation of how these factors relate to the job to bring about positive motivation.

McClelland's achievement model. (37) McClelland's theory of motivation is quite extensive and involved. His greatest contribution is in developing the achievement motive. According to him, every motive is a learned one and only two are innate, namely, striving for pleasure and seeking to avoid displeasure or pain. All other motives are acquired. These two factors are at opposite ends of a continuum with one end being an approach to the expectation of pleasure and satisfaction and the other being the negative avoidance of pain or displeasure.

Process models. The previous models focused on the needs that *drive* behavior and the incentives that *attract* behavior. Involved in these is the question of the role of job satisfaction. Much of the human relations model was based upon the theory that satisfaction led to performance. Many of the prescriptive models were then based upon this assumption.

Recent literature has failed to find this link. In fact, one of the most intensive reviews of satisfaction-performance literature found three possible relationships:

FIGURE 15-6

THE JOB

MOTIVATION NEEDS

- **RESPONSIBILITY, RECOGNITION**: Involvement, goal setting, planning, problem solving, work simplification, performance appraisal.
- **GROWTH, ACHIEVEMENT**: Delegation, access to information, freedom to act, atmosphere of approval.

MAINTENANCE NEEDS

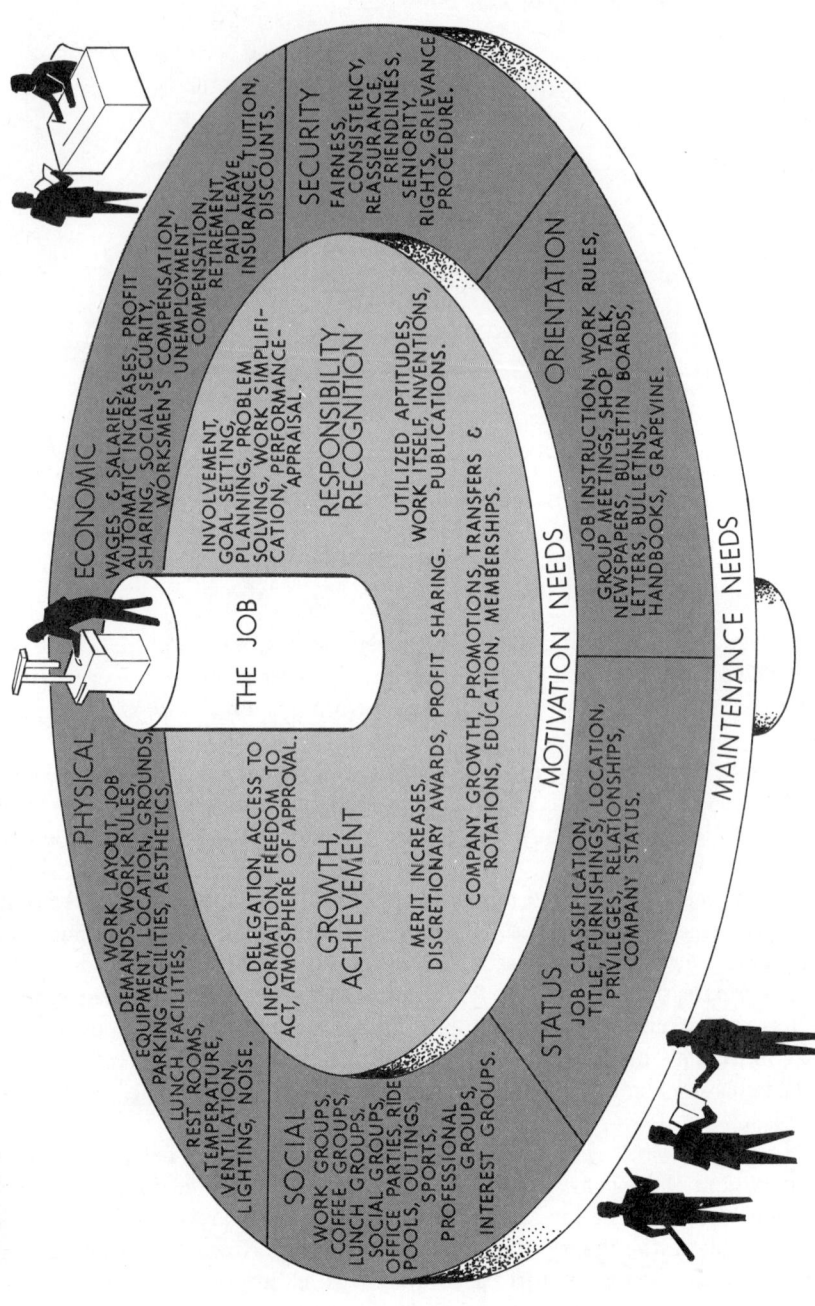

- **PHYSICAL**: Work layout, job demands, work rules, equipment, location, grounds, parking facilities, aesthetics, lunch facilities, rest rooms, temperature, ventilation, lighting, noise.
- **ECONOMIC**: Wages & salaries, automatic increases, profit sharing, social security, workmen's compensation, unemployment compensation, retirement, paid leave, insurance, tuition, discounts.
- **SECURITY**: Fairness, consistency, reassurance, friendliness, seniority, rights, grievance procedure.
- **ORIENTATION**: Job instruction, work rules, group meetings, shop talk, newspapers, bulletin boards, letters, bulletins, handbooks, grapevine.
- **STATUS**: Job classification, title, furnishings, location, privileges, relationships, company status.
- **SOCIAL**: Work groups, coffee groups, lunch groups, social groups, office parties, ride pools, outings, sports, professional groups, interest groups.

Motivation needs (inner ring): Utilized aptitudes, work itself, inventions, publications. Merit increases, discretionary awards, profit sharing. Company growth, promotions, transfers & rotations, education, memberships.

Source: M. Scott Myers, "Who Are Your Motivated Workers?" *Harvard Business Review*, vol. 42, no. 1 (January–February 1964), pp. 85–86.

1. Satisfaction can contribute to, or influence, performance (satisfaction→performance);
2. An uncertain relationship between satisfaction and performance, whereby it could go either direction (satisfaction→?←performance); and
3. Performance itself contributes to satisfaction (performance→satisfaction).

Of the many process models which focus on the question of how individual behavior originates, occurs, and is terminated, only the behaviorist models and the cognitive models will be discussed.

Behaviorist models. An overgeneralization is that the behaviorist models are based upon the *stimulus-response* relationship. B. F. Skinner tested the stimulus-response model and emphasized the *reinforcement* aspect. (38) He distinguished between *reinforcement,* which is the presentation of an attractive reward following a response or the removal of an unpleasant or negative condition following response, from *punishment* which is the reverse of reinforcement.

Training, development, and growth occur through reinforcement or focusing behavioral responses to what should be done.

Management by objectives (MBO) is based upon this learning principle, for it relies heavily on the behaviorist model of motivational principles.

Cognitive models. According to the cognitive models, individuals are viewed as active and conscious decision makers in their environment. Consequently, a person's response to a work-related stimulus results from one's conscious decisions based upon the outcomes one expects from one's response and the value of those outcomes to oneself.

Vroom's expectancy model. One of the best known of these models is Vroom's *expectancy theory.* (39) According to this theory, employees' motivation is the force driving them to achieve some level of job performance. This force or effort depends upon their perception of the probability or likelihood of certain outcomes resulting from their effort, as related to the value they place on these outcomes. For example, if employees believe that if they perform at a high level they will be paid higher wages than if they do not and if the higher income is of value to them, they will produce more. In achieving the high level of performance, the worker has satisfaction which, in turn, influences future efforts. If the employee receives the higher income expected, it will provide satisfaction which, in turn, will tend to make future incomes appear more valuable.

The Porter-Lawler model. This model is also based upon the expectancy theory of motivation. (40) It is a future-oriented expectancy theory, as it emphasizes the anticipated response or outcome. They believe that managers particularly rely upon these future expectations rather than past learning. As can be seen from Figure 15–7, based upon the perceived effort-reward probability, effort is expended; performance is accomplished; rewards are received; satisfaction occurs; and this, in turn, leads to future effort.

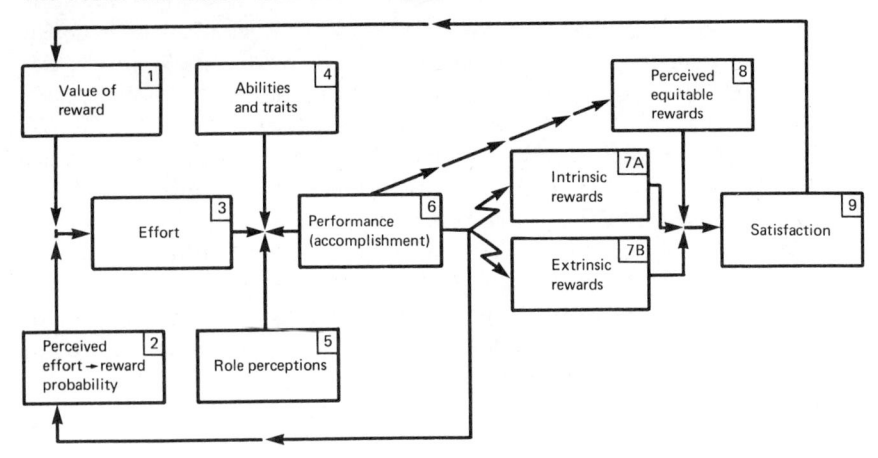

FIGURE 15-7
The Porter and Lawler motivational model

Source: Lyman W. Porter and Edward E. Lawler, III, *Managerial Attitudes and Performance* (Homewood, Ill.; Richard D. Irwin, Inc., 1968), p. 165. Used with permission.

IMPLICATIONS AND APPLICATIONS FOR PERSONNEL EXECUTIVES

The material in this chapter has been based upon the hypothesis that: *Living organisms must grow or die; they cannot remain static. Organizations, being living organisms, must grow or die; organizational growth and creativity is based upon individual growth and creativity.*

Specific emphasis has been given to the role of the personnel executive in developing individual employees. The discussion began with an emphasis upon the role of the individual in improving performance. This relationship should not be underemphasized, for research has shown that individualism itself is a motivator. (41)

The unresolved question facing personnel executives is whether individual employees have traded a satisfaction of the spirit which their work formerly afforded for economic assurances which they did not previously enjoy. That is, have they substituted material compensation for a more intangible satisfaction of indefinable longings?

Next, the hypothesis was developed that: *There is a direct relationship between the kind of leadership style used and executives' effectiveness; in turn, the approach used will be determined by the forces within the executives themselves, their subordinates, and the specific situation.* A corollary hypothesis is that: *The effectiveness of a leadership style depends greatly upon the interdependence of the work group and the interaction of the executives with the subordinates.*

Based upon those hypotheses, it was shown that effective executives are the ones who stay psychologically close enough to maintain helpful contacts with subordinates, yet maintain sufficient distance to deal objectively with poor performance. Those executives will also use the leadership style demanded by the interplay and interaction of the situation, the subordinates, and their own abilities and characteristics which seem to be most effective in motivating improved performance.

It was finally shown that for an organization to be most successful, its personnel executives need to use various motivational theories to develop the full potential of the members of the organization. In essence, the goal of motivation is to create in employees a sense of pride in past performance and a feeling of hope and expectation for future accomplishments.

It is the personnel executive's responsibility to understand the factors that motivate employees and to create a motivational environment where those factors can be organized into a stimulating force that will integrate individual goals with organizational goals. It has been shown by research that higher rewards do not necessarily cause a person to have a correspondingly high commitment to the organization, but the greater the obstacles an employee has overcome in order to obtain the organization's rewards, the greater is the commitment. (42)

DISCUSSION QUESTIONS

1. (*a*) Is group productivity greater (better) than the sum of its individual productivity? (*b*) Explain.
2. (*a*) If group action is a critical part of organizational efforts, why is individualism so important in organizations? (*b*) Explain.
3. (*a*) Why does one individual act, or behave, similar to others? (*b*) Why does one not? (*c*) What are the determinants of behavior?
4. (*a*) Explain how an individual's goal may conflict with the organizational goal. (*b*) How may it be compatible?
5. (*a*) Do you believe creativity is a product of an individual? (*b*) Explain your answer. (*c*) How does a creative product come about in modern organizations?
6. (*a*) What are the factors that affect a given leadership situation? (*b*) Discuss the relationships between each of the factors.
7. (*a*) What factors lead to effective leadership? (*b*) Discuss each.
8. What role is played by *expectations* and *perceptions* as far as leadership is concerned?
9. What are the main themes of the following selected motivational theorists: (*a*) Maslow? (*b*) Herzberg? (*c*) McClelland? (*d*) Vroom? (*e*) Porter and Lawler?

REFERENCES AND SUGGESTIONS FOR FURTHER STUDY

1. Doris Smithers, "How I Got My Job," *Redbook,* vol. 146, no. 5 (March 1976), pp. 80–82.
2. It is difficult to isolate the causes of productivity in work groups, for variation in such performance and interaction processes "can be accounted for by approxi-

mately nine separate dimensions." See Frank Friedlander, "Performance and Interaction Dimensions of Organizational Work Groups," *Journal of Applied Psychology*, vol. 50, no. 3 (June 1966), pp. 257–65.

3. John J. Corson, "Innovation Challenges Conformity," *Harvard Business Review*, vol. 40, no. 3 (May–June 1962), pp. 67–74.

4. Jacob Tuckman and Irvin Lorge, "Individual Ability as a Determinant of Group Superiority," *Human Relations*, vol. 15, no. 1 (February 1962), pp. 45–51.

5. If you have not already read it, you should read Douglas McGregor, *The Human Side of Enterprise* (New York: McGraw-Hill Book Co., 1960), pp. 33–47, for a fuller explanation of Theory X and Theory Y.

6. Further results and analyses can be found in Byron G. Fiman, "An Investigation of the Relationships among Supervisory Attitudes, Behaviors, and Outputs: An Examination of McGregor's theory Y," *Personnel Psychology*, vol. 26, no. 1 (Spring 1973), p. 95.

7. Dr. Kae H. Chung of Wichita State University identified many of the variables affecting the motivation of employees. It should prove interesting to read *Developing a Comprehensive Model of Motivation and Performance*, Louisiana State University Doctoral Dissertation, 1968.

8. Edward E. Lawler, III, and Lyman W. Porter, "The Effects of Performance on Job Satisfaction," *Industrial Relations*, vol. 7, no. 1 (October 1967), p. 5 ff. While they were not the first to reach this conclusion, they have developed it more than others.

9. Donald Schwab and Larry Cummings, "Theories of Performance and Satisfaction," *Personnel Administrator*, vol. 18, no. 2 (March–April 1973), pp. 39–46; and Schwab and Cummings, "Theories of Performance and Satisfaction: A Review," *Industrial Relations*, vol. 9., no. 4 (October 1970), pp. 408–29.

10. See E. Wight Bakke, "The Human Resources Function," *Management International*, vol. 1, no. 2 (March–April 1961), pp. 16–24, for some of these misconceptions.

11. This is an oversimplified model of the human resource approach to human administration. For a more intensive and explicit presentation of this approach, see Raymond E. Miles, "Human Relations or Human Resources?" *Harvard Business Review*, vol. 43, no. 4 (July–August 1965), pp. 148–63.

12. This research was reported by Louis A. Allen in "M for Management: Theory Y Updated," *Personnel Journal*, vol. 52, no. 12 (December 1973), pp. 1061–67.

While attending the Summer Case Workshop at the Harvard Business School in July 1958, several of us heard the late Douglas McGregor say essentially the same thing. He said he wished he had never written the two theories, as they had been so misunderstood. Most workers did not fit into *either* the "X" *or* the "Y" category but had some characteristics of each, and their behavior tended to vary from the one to the other over periods of time. He said he intended to write "Theory Z," but he died before succeeding.

13. The results of this study are reported in Richard D. Denzler, "People and Productivity: Do They Still Equal Pay and Profits?" *Personnel Journal*, vol. 53, no. 1 (January 1974), pp. 59–63.

14. An excellent presentation of this theory can be found in Paul R. Lawrence and

Jay Lorsch, "Differentiation and Integration in Complex Organizations," *Administrative Science Quarterly,* vol. 12, no. 1 (June 1967), pp. 1–47.

15. See Larry L. Cummings, "Managerial Effectiveness I: Formulating a Research Strategy," *Academy of Management Journal,* vol. 9, no. 1 (March 1966), pp. 29–42, for a research model for identifying, measuring, and predicting managerial effectiveness.

16. Mary Parker Follett, *Freedom and Coordination* (London: Management Publications Trust, Ltd., 1949), pp. 47–60; and L. Urwick, ed., *The Golden Book of Management* (London: Newman Neame Ltd., for the International Committee of Scientific Management [CIOS], 1956), p. 133.

17. Perhaps the best explanation of this theory is in Fred E. Fiedler and Martin M. Chemers, *Leadership and Effective Management* (Glenview, Ill.: Scott, Foresman and Co., 1974). For a later explanation of the theory, as tested by further research and applied particularly to the management of managers, see Fred E. Fiedler, "New Concepts for the Management of Managers" in E. L. Cass and F. C. Zimmer, eds., *Man and Work in Society* (New York: Van Nostrand Reinhold Co., 1975), pp. 207–19.

18. Robert Tannenbaum and Warren H. Schmidt, "How to Choose A Leadership Pattern," *Harvard Business Review,* vol. 51, no. 3 (May 1973), pp. 162–80.

19. Aubrey C. Sanford, "Implementing Leadership Theory, Training, and Staffing Implications," *Personnel Administration/Public Personnel Review,* vol. 1, no. 1 (July–August 1972), pp. 26–27.

20. Douglas M. McGregor, "On Leadership," *Antioch Notes* (May 1954), p. 3.

21. See Robert H. Schaffer, "Demand Better Results—and Get Them," *Harvard Business Review,* vol. 52, no. 6 (November–December 1974), p. 91 ff. The author goes on to state that many managers fail to reach their productivity potential because they fail "to establish high performance improvement expectations in ways that elicit results."

22. Frederick Herzberg, Bernard Mausner, and Barbara B. Snyderman, *The Motivation to Work,* 2d ed. (New York: John Wiley & Sons, Inc., 1959), pp. 9–10.

23. Lynn Anderson and Fred E. Fiedler, "The Effect of Participatory and Supervisory Leadership on Group Creativity," *Journal of Applied Psychology,* vol. 48, no. 4 (August 1964), pp. 227–35.

24. Warren G. Bennis, "The Revisionist Theory of Leadership," *Harvard Business Review,* vol. 39, no. 1 (January–February 1961), pp. 26–28, is an excellent discussion of the leadership methods.

25. John W. Slocum, Jr., "Supervisory Influence and the Professional Employee," *Personnel Journal,* vol. 49, no. 6 (June 1970), pp. 484–88.

26. Norman R. Maier and Marshall Sashkin, "Specific Leadership Behaviors That Promote Problem Solving," *Personnel Psychology,* vol. 24, no. 1 (Spring 1971), pp. 35–44.

27. Phillip Sadler, "Leadership Style, Confidence in Management, and Job Satisfaction," *Journal of Applied Behavioral Science,* vol. 6, no. 1 (March 1970), pp. 3–20.

28. "How Bosses Really Feel," *Business Week,* March 2, 1963, p. 58.

29. James C. Worthy, "Organizational Structure and Employee Morale," *American Sociological Review,* vol. 15, no. 2 (April 1950), pp. 169–79.

30. Nancy C. Morse, *Satisfactions in the White Collar Job* (Ann Arbor: Survey Research Center, University of Michigan, 1953).
31. Martin Patchen, "Participation in Decision Making and Motivation: What Is the Relation?" *Personnel Administration,* vol. 27, no. 6 (November–December 1964), pp. 24–31.
32. F. M. Carp, B. M. Vitola, and F. L. McLanathan, "Human-Relations Knowledge and Social Distance Set in Supervisors," *Journal of Applied Psychology,* vol. 47, no. 1 (February 1963), pp. 78–80.
33. Reprinted by permission from *Management Methods Magazine,* copyright 1952 by Management Magazines, Inc.
34. P. F. Werniment, P. Toren, and H. Kapell, "Comparison of Sources of Personal Satisfaction and of Work Motivation," *Journal of Applied Psychology,* vol. 54, no. 1 (February 1970), pp. 95–102.
35. Abraham H. Maslow, *New Knowledge in Human Values* (New York: Harper & Bros., 1959).
36. Frederick Herzberg, et al., *The Motivation to Work,* 2d ed. (New York: John Wiley & Sons, Inc., 1959).
37. David C. McClelland, *Studies in Motivation* (New York: Appleton-Century-Crofts, 1955).
38. B. F. Skinner, *About Behaviorism* (New York: Alfred A. Knopp, 1974).
39. Victor H. Vroom, *Work and Motivation* (New York: John Wiley & Sons, Inc., 1964), pp. 192–210.
40. Lyman W. Porter and Edward E. Lawler, III, *Managerial Attitudes and Performance* (Homewood, Ill: Richard D. Irwin, Inc., 1968).
41. Lawrence N. Soloman, Betty Berzon, and David P. Davis, "A Personal Growth Program for Self-Directed Groups," *The Journal of Applied Behavioral Science,* vol. 6, no. 4 (October–December 1970), pp. 427–53.
42. Oscar Grusky, "Career Mobility and Organizational Commitment," *Administrative Science Quarterly,* vol. 10, no. 4 (March 1966), pp. 488–503.

CASES FOR FURTHER STUDY

IV-1. Louis Kemp

The personnel officer of a division of the state government received a phone call from the manager of a local office, who was having a problem with Louis Kemp.

Earlier the manager had engaged in extensive recruitment efforts to fill a vacancy in her operations. Finally, the personnel officer had recommended a Mr. Kemp after interviewing him in the home office. After an interview with the local manager, Mr. Kemp was hired at the usual rank and salary for that position.

The new employee had a B.A. degree in social science, was 29 years old, and at the time of his employment was unmarried. His experience during the preceding four years had been wholly on jobs that required little or no responsibility. He had worked on a seismograph crew "off and on" for the past two years as a rodman. He had been employed at a cotton gin as a ticket clerk helper for two seasons prior to his employment with the seismograph company.

As the office was small, the manager had only three subordinates, and the line of supervision was direct from her to the employees. After Kemp was employed, he was reluctant to talk to the manager or other employees about the operations of the office and other matters pertaining to the job. For that matter, he was reluctant to talk about any other subject with them. At the completion of his initial training period, the quality and quantity of his work failed to meet the minimum standards set by the manager. She discussed the problem with Kemp and attempted to offer assistance in solving his problem. In the meantime, Kemp had married the daughter of one of the local businessmen.

It was soon apparent to the manager that Kemp needed further training. His lack of knowledge about the activities of his new employment lengthened the time required for him to meet the expected job standards. Therefore, a program of training and development was designed with this factor in mind. However, after three or four months the manager decided that this was not the answer.

Kemp continued to insist that he liked his work but would give no reason for not meeting the expected job goals. The manager requested the aid of her district supervisor and assistance from the staff personnel at the home office. After they interviewed Kemp, a joint conference was held with the manager. This interview and the conference resulted in a decision to try an entirely new approach with the recalcitrant employee. Kemp would be given free rein and full responsibility of the job; the manager and supervisors would follow up on the results of the experiment after a period of several months. The results showed no improvement.

During this two-year period of employment Kemp was sometimes assigned other office duties which were entirely different from his routine ones. It was noted that his attitude on these days seemed somewhat better. After 30 months, it was evident that some decisive action was necessary.

Questions

1. As manager, what would you do now?
2. Upon what criteria should a person be selected and developed?
3. What is the relationship between selection, development, and motivation?
4. Evaluate the development program utilized by this manager.
5. As personnel officer, what would you recommend to the manager?

IV-2. Sinclaire University*

Mr. James Archer, the new director of Computer Services, had been particularly pleased with his first six months at Sinclaire University. In fact, the only work remaining before he headed for his two-week vacation was to respond to a letter from Wayne Ely, his development director, concerning performance evaluations. However, this appeared to be rather perfunctory since he had already spoken with the other directors on this topic.

July 6, 1975

Mr. James Archer,
Director, Computer Services,
Sinclaire University,
Bethesda, Florida.

Dear Jim:

First, I would like to point out that I don't consider the "personnel evaluation," which happens annually in my department, as the complete evaluation process.

It is understood that personnel are welcome to come to me with problems, gripes, suggestions, and so forth. Beyond this, I afford them with an opportunity to open up by personally dropping in on them periodically to see how they are getting alone.

At any time that a person does a job beyond the ordinary, I write a memo commending him or her; with a copy to his or her personnel file, to the director of computer services, and to the director of information services.

If he really "fouls up," I write a memo telling him so, with a copy to his personnel file only. In both cases, I give the employee the letter in person, so we have a chance for discussion.

---

* Prepared by Donald S. Bolon of Miami University and Thomas W. Johnson of Ohio University.

EXHIBIT 1

CONFIDENTIAL
PROGRAMMER EVALUATION SUMMARY

NAME _Harry Winkler_   TITLE _PA VIII_
PRESENT SALARY _$12,050_

		W. Ely	J. Fain	B. Park	W. Stewart	Summary
1.	Attitude	5	5	2	2	3*
2.	Availability	4	5	3	3	3
3.	Overall grasp	4	4	3	2	3
4.	Program analysis	3	5	3	1	3
5.	Realistic estimates	4	4	2	3	3
6.	Coding skills	5	4	3	2	3
7.	Program testing	4	3	2	2	2
8.	Debugging skills	4	4	2	1	2
9.	Documentation preparation	5	5	3	2	3
10.	User interface	4	4	4	4	4
11.	Overall evaluation					3
12.	Recommended for next higher level (✓)†					

Recommended salary _$12,800_   Title _PA VIII_
Wayne Ely   _6/30/75_
         Signature   Date

EMPLOYEE'S ACKNOWLEDGEMENT (Signature indicates only that employee has reviewed the report, not necessarily that he is in agreement with it.)
Signature _Harry Winkler_   Date _7/3/75_

* These members and their meanings are shown below:

  0 = Not applicable or you are unwilling to make an objective evaluation for this category.
  1 = Poor
  2 = Below average
  3 = Average/competent
  4 = Above average
  5 = Very good

† Comments from Personnel Evaluation completed by Wayne Ely contained the following:
Comments: _Always willing to assist others_
Suggestions for improvement: _Needs more self-confidence_

My personnel are programmer analysts and range from levels I through VIII. We have two group leaders, and some of the more experienced programmer analysts function as group leaders at times. I assign all personnel to the various activities, sometimes under the supervision of one of the group leaders. When a person has been assigned to a group leader for at least a month, the group leader must complete an evaluation form on the subordinate. Also, the leader completes the form at the end of the assignment or in time for the annual evaluation, whichever is first. I also complete an evaluation form for all employees. In this way, several evaluation forms may be completed for each individual. I average all the forms and use this average as the final evaluation. Hopefully, this method decreases the effect of playing favorites or personality conflicts.

The day before the evaluation is to be reviewed, I advise the employee and ask that some thought be given to the employees' past performance and to any suggestions concerning the person's professional growth, the department, and other suggestions. On the day of the evaluation, I advise the secretary that I'm not to be disturbed during that time. The evaluation is conducted in private with more than enough time allocated to do a thorough job.

I have determined that there are ten areas to be included in evaluation. The last eight of these ten will have different competency requirements depending upon the level of programmer. I would appreciate any comment or criticism. Thanks.

Wayne Ely
Director, Administrative Systems

em

Att: Both the summary ratings and the individual rating forms for all analysts are attached for your perusal. (*Author's note. In order to save space, the form of only one representative analyst is included.*)

IV-3. Technical Obsolescence

Henry Hiller, a 20-year employee with the Green Thumb Chemical Corporation, assisted in coordinating requests for technical assistance from field salesmen. His work assignments were screened by his immediate supervisor to eliminate those requiring significant technical effort on Henry's part, as his technical education essentially terminated 20 years ago. All of Henry's work had to be closely supervised. The net result was that about one and one-half worker-hours were spent to accomplish one worker-hour of work.

Henry's new supervisor, John Jones, felt that the situation had gotten out of hand, and, searching for some reasonable solution, he discussed the case with Bob Smith, the personnel manager.

Mr. Smith believed that the main reason for Henry's limited usefulness was his limited technical ability. Yet should not the company share some of the blame for this? When Henry was hired, the company was not technically-oriented. Its technical processes had been developed over the years on a "cut-and-try" basis. Technical personnel had not been effectively used and, indeed, were scorned by most of the old hands, including most of middle management.

After Henry had been with the company about five years, an influx of new upper management personnel resulted in increased emphasis on research and development and the technical approach to problem solving. With this change, Henry's position began to deteriorate, and he was given some minor lab assignments in which he did only a mediocre job. The main problem was he was unable to work satisfactorily with either technical or nontechnical personnel. At that time Henry was transferred into his present group and given an assignment of monitoring certain plant data. The results of his work were usually filed and never looked at again. Only occasionally did he make a meaningful contribution to the company's productivity and profitability. For about ten years this essentially meaningless assignment continued.

About five years ago, Jones's predecessor had decided to stop this wasted effort and moved Henry into his present assignment. From the beginning, Henry resented the move but periodically agreed to try to do better. Yet he continued to make no real effort to update his technical know-how. Instead, he said, "I'm too old to start that again."

Smith resolved to avoid similar cases in the future by taking several steps. First-line supervision must be made more aware of their responsibilities in educating, training, and developing new employees. New employees would be encouraged to take survey courses at the plant and enroll for graduate courses in the evening at a nearby university. The in-plant courses could be designed both as refresher courses and as a means of permitting the workers to keep up with advances in various scientific and technical areas. Those persons who did not "find themselves" after about three to five years of encouragement would be made aware of the consequences of their lack of continued personal development.

With respect to Henry Hiller, there were several alternative courses of action available. The first and easiest was to maintain the status quo, justified on the basis that the company had an obligation to Henry as a result of management's acceptance of poor performance and meaningless job performance for extended periods in the past. Another solution might be the usual transfer to another group which would get Henry off Mr. Jones's back. However, it was doubtful that a satisfactory transfer could be found in view of Henry's reputation. The most satisfactory course of action would be to get Henry motivated to update his knowledge and improve his work quality and quantity. The chance of achieving this at this stage was essentially nil, however. The last alternative would be to retire Henry as soon as possible, a procedure used by many companies in similar situations.

Questions

1. Evaluate Henry's comment about training, "I'm too old to start that again."
2. What factors must a new manager take into consideration when one comes into a situation with long-standing (and accepted) problems?

3. Who is responsible when employees find themselves in a predicament such as Henry was in? Explain.
4. Evaluate the steps taken by the personnel manager to prevent a recurrence of the problem.
5. What would you do with Henry if you were the personnel manager?

part five

Effects of reward and penalty systems on personnel effectiveness

16. Determining overall compensation policies
17. Using compensation to provide equity
18. Using compensation to reward performance
19. Using employee benefits to reward loyal service
20. Using discipline as a penalty system

Cases:
V–1. What Determines Wages?
V–2. Ward Chemical Company
V–3. Mid-Western Printing, Incorporated

Introduction

Wage and salary administration* is highly subjective, and many value judgments are involved in determining what "should" be paid employees as remuneration for their expenditure of knowledge, education, training, time, and effort. The equitable determination of a person's rate of pay constitutes economic, psychological, and philosophical problems which defy the application of rigid rules and policies.

Professor John Dunlop stated two "laws" of wages when he was Secretary

---

* The term "wage(s)" has at least two meanings. The word signifies the payment, usually of money, for labor or services. It also refers to the money which is usually paid on an hourly, daily, or piece rate basis for chiefly physical work. A "salary" is usually paid for services requiring special training or abilities, in a fixed amount, and for a longer period of time, especially by the month. However, in this book the term "wage" is used to refer to the general idea of pay for service, unless otherwise indicated. That is, it is used in the general sense of income, not the restricted sense of pay to hourly employees.

FIGURE V-1
How reward and punishment systems fit into the overall personnel system

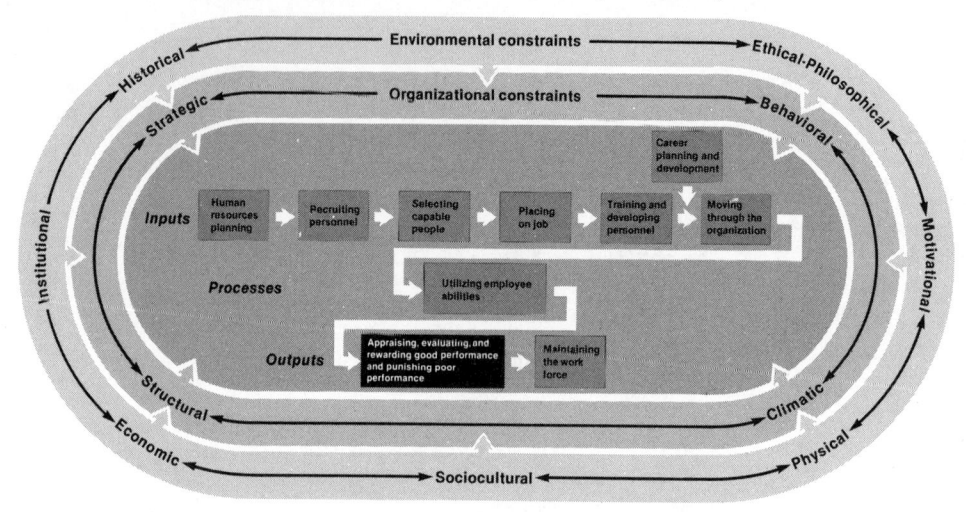

of Labor. The first is: "They go up." The second is: "The most important fact in wage determination is the relative position of wages."

These two statements tend to exemplify the basic problem of wage and salary administration. For, as mysterious as they may sometimes appear to employees and the public, the tools and techniques of wage and salary administration have as their primary objective *the creation of a system of orderly payments which is equitable both to the employee and to the employer and which motivates each person to exert an acceptable effort in the performance of one's job.* Implicit in this objective is the assumption that the primary function of wages is to *integrate individual performance, job worth,* and *external market forces* and, by juggling these three factors, to *arrive at specific wage or salary rates for all personnel.* If this aim is to be achieved, there must be an efficient and effective program of compensation which is *internally equitable* and *externally competitive.* Also, the framework of the compensation program should consist of a system of rewards—financial and otherwise—for all members of the organization.

See Figure V-1 for how reward and punishment systems fit into the overall personnel system.

Several steps are involved in accomplishing this goal. First, management needs to have a well-conceived and clearly understood wage philosophy, including an estimate of how much should be paid to employees as earnings.*

---

* Although it is recognized that total compensation is based upon the interaction of the basic wage rate and the length of time worked (or the units of production, in case of incentive systems), this section will deal only with the wage rate and/or total compensation and will not become involved with the period of time worked, or the units produced, except in Chapter 18.

FIGURE V-2
Steps involved in determining an individual's wage rate

Step 1	Step 2	Step 3	Step 4	Step 5	Results
Management's wage philosophy	+ Wage theory	+ Overall general wage rate	+ Job wage rates or ranges	+ Performance appraisal	= Each individual's wage rate
Assumptions are made concerning what and how much remuneration should be, and when increases should be given.	+ Management has a theory concerning the source of funds from which wages can be paid.	+ Philosophy and theory are modified by the interaction of the law of supply and demand, governmental factors, comparable wages, standard and cost of living, collective bargaining, and ability to pay.	+ Job analysis is performed, which results in job specifications, which are then evaluated to determine the job's worth to the organization.	+ Performance standards are established and each individual's actual job performance and personal characteristics are evaluated and appraised by means of some form of employee appraisal.	

Second, the source from which the compensation is to be paid should be based upon a defensible theory of wages. Third, an overall compensation policy and a general wage rate should be established. Fourth, wage differentials are determined for the various jobs and job ranges. These steps should result in a specific wage rate or wage range for all jobs. Fifth, an appraisal of each employee's performance determines each rate within the wage range.

See Figure V–2 for a summary of these steps.

Chapter 16 explains how an organization determines its *overall compensation policies* and basic wage rate.

The different types of *wage differentials* and the touchy issue of *setting individual rates* of pay are discussed in Chapter 17. Special attention is given to the less acceptable variations in pay based upon sex, race, and age and the methods being used to correct them.

Based upon the assumption that wages do not have a motivational effect upon productivity, a *motivational theory of wages* is developed in Chapter 18 and is then applied to the use of incentive wage plans, profit-sharing plans, bonuses, and merit wage increases to test the effect they have on improving performance.

The background, objective, definition, and extent of utilization of *employee* benefits are covered in Chapter 19.

Chapter 20 explains the different types of discipline, or negative rewards.

Chapter 16

Determining overall compensation policies

Functions of compensation
  The equity function
  The motivational function

Factors affecting an organization's compensation policies and practices
  *What the organization is **willing** to pay*
  *What the organization is **able** to pay*
  *What the organization **must** pay*

Implications and applications for personnel executives

16

Determining overall compensation policies

Man . . . (does) not live by bread alone—but he could not live without it.
MORRIS L. WEST

A fair day's wages for a fair day's work: It is as just a demand as governed men ever made of governing. It is the everlasting right of man.
THOMAS CARLYLE

Between 1966 and 1972, employee compensation in the private nonfarm economy rose 52 percent—from $3.44 to $5.23 an hour, while consumer prices rose 29 percent, and productivity rose 13 percent. This yielded an 18-percent gain in the purchasing power of the compensation package. (1)

The above figures emphasize how complex—but important—compensation is to personnel executives. Of all the areas with which they deal, the remuneration of employees is perhaps the most difficult and perplexing one, for while it is based upon logical reasoning, it also involves many emotional factors.

This chapter will look at the functions of compensation, discuss some types of wage rates, look at the factors affecting the organization's compensation policies and practices, and discuss the wage theories affecting the long- and short-run determination of compensation.

FUNCTIONS OF COMPENSATION

Employees are primarily compensated for two reasons: as a reward for past service to the organization and as a stimulus to improved performance in the future. There are several other services performed by compensation, including attracting better employees, reducing labor turnover, and compensating employees for performing work they otherwise would not do.

The equity function

The most easily understood function of remuneration is to serve as a yardstick for measuring the employee's past performance and present effectiveness. According to this concept, a person's earnings would correlate one's ability and motivation with the work performed. Thus, income serves as a reward for past productive performance.

It has been shown that to work effectively the members of an organization must feel that its reward system—consisting of salaries, wages, bonuses, dividends, interest payments, and so forth—yields them satisfactory remuneration for their efforts and contributions. (2)

To employees, a major consideration in equity determination comes from a comparison of the rewards received from their investment in the job with the rewards others receive from their investments in their jobs. The process by which equity or inequity is perceived involves the inputs and outcomes of the individual and "others."

Possible inputs are: education, experience, training, skill, seniority, age, sex, ethnic background, social status, effort, appearance, health, and spouse's characteristics. This list emphasizes personal traits rather than items related to the job, which is where the primary emphasis is in current compensation administration. Possible outcomes are the individual's receipts from the exchange and include pay, benefits, satisfying supervision, congenial colleagues, status symbols, perquisities, and intrinsic rewards.

The motivational function

In addition to serving as a reward for past performance, compensation serves as a motivator to future initiative and effort. However, there are many motivational factors influencing employee behavior, and it is impossible to identify and isolate any one variable as the specific stimulus to motivated behavior. (3) However, the motivational role of compensation is based upon the "law of effect," which states that *employee behavior which appears to lead to reward tends to be repeated, while behavior which appears not to lead to reward, or seems to lead to punishment, tends not to be repeated.* (4)

Evaluation of research findings. Many classical writers as well as contemporary theorists have emphasized the motivational value of wages. The consensus is that there is a direct and positive relationship between expected compensation and employee productivity. Research studies on this subject have shown that employee remuneration is a strong stimulus to production. Yet, there are also some contrary findings, which will also be presented.

Compensation has a positive effect. One research project showed that when people believe their efforts will lead to the desired reward they will produce; also, it showed that few individuals would engage in extended activities unless they believed that there was a connection between what they did and the rewards they received. (5)

A researcher in England found that the financial drive is still strong as a motivator there also. When the base of any group of employees did not permit satisfaction, the workers turned to overtime, slowdowns, and other means of meeting their needs. (6)

In China, many material and nonmaterial systems have been used in an attempt to increase employee productivity. While work incentive policies have changed with the government's economic development strategy, material rewards seem to be the major method of organizing and motivating the labor force. (7) Also, the one-acre private plots, which account for only 3 percent of the total land area cultivated in the U.S.S.R., provide almost 60 percent of all eggs and 40 percent of all the meat and milk produced in that country. (8)

A study of factors leading to job satisfaction in Australia found that unskilled workers emphasized *pay* at the expense of self-actualization needs. (9)

An empirical study of our low-income families showed that with an *income maintenance program,* workers have more incentive to reduce their hours of work and less incentive to increase them. Thus, the workers are prone to produce less per hour than other employees without such a program. (10)

A Ford Motor Company survey revealed that its employees were primarily concerned with wages, job security, and fringe benefits. An experiment with job enrichment at a Ford plant involved 28 employees showed no change in absenteeism or quality, and, moreover, these workers were ready to swap their "enriched" jobs for "another nickel an hour." (11)

A survey of 2,535 sewing machine operators in 17 plants across the country discovered more concern with pay and job security than with any other factor. The jobs were highly engineered, rigidly structured, and very routine and repetitive. Pay was based on a guarantee, plus a direct productivity incentive. The operators objected strongly to any suggestion of a change in their jobs which might reduce their productivity and, hence, interfere with their earnings potential. The study concluded that the cause of workers' discontent might be their compensation instead of dull jobs. (12)

As indicated in Chapter 15 it is becoming increasingly clear that there is *no necessary relationship between the motivation to perform and job satisfaction.* High motivation and performance can be associated with high satisfaction, but they can also be associated with low satisfaction—or entirely unrelated to satisfaction. A recent study by Schwab found that the type of pay system may have a *positive impact on motivation,* but a *negative one on satisfaction.* (13) This research indicates that the personnel executive's job is more complex than previously conceived. As a policy change may have conflicting impacts on different employee attitudes and behaviors, these executives must become concerned with establishing personnel priorities. For example, to what extent is the organization willing to trade off decreased employee satisfaction for higher motivation to perform?

Compensation does not have a positive effect. In many instances, the economic motive is no longer considered important. The belief is held that employees have risen above the mundane demands of a physical existence and now have higher desires. For example, one outstanding authority said, "In the terms in which we are speaking there is no such thing as an economic motive." (14) A British sociologist concluded that it was impossible to find a direct statistical relationship between the application of incentive schemes and increased outputs. (15)

In a classical treatment of incentives, a leading economist concluded that there were five reasons why people work, and only one pertains to money. (16)

It has been claimed that in actual organizational and experimental laboratories psychological rewards may be more significant than material incentives, (17) even among members of the Academy of Management. (18)

It has also been pointed out from an anthropological point of view that in most cultures people work for some reason other than material reward. (19) This generalization was corroborated in a study of pottery makers in Madagascar, where it was found that lowering wages did not curtail the supply of labor. (20)

Conclusion. There is no simple "yes" or "no" answer to the question, "Does money motivate?" Instead, the conclusion is reached that *until employees satisfy their physiological needs, compensation does serve as a motivator.* Wages and employment security *may even motivate through the safety needs. Above that level, wages* (especially day wages) *tend to decline in importance as stimulants to productivity, and other stimulators achieve greater significance.* (21) Alfred Marshall expressed this truth in economic terms when he stated that, "A man will work up to the point where the marginal utility of the income he derives from his work equals the marginal disutility he incurs in the effort to acquire it." (22)

A recent study was conducted to determine employees' perceptions of the importance of, and the degree of satisfaction with, selected intrinsic and extrinsic variables which typically constitute an organization's reward system. The intent of the study was to determine to what extent management could rely on either intrinsic or extrinsic rewards to sustain job satisfaction and productivity. It involved six organizations and 354 men and women representing all organizational levels and functional areas. The results, shown in Table 16–1, indicate the employees perceived direct and indirect economic (extrinsic) rewards are more important than the intrinsic ones. Three of the four categories

TABLE 16–1
Importance and need dissatisfaction means by reward category (ranked in order of importance)

Reward category	Importance Mean	Rank	Need Dissatisfaction Mean	
Working conditions	6.384	1	1.828	4
Self-actualization	6.279	2	1.625	5
Security	6.274	3	1.452	6
Compensation	6.254	4	2.219	2
Autonomy	5.750	5	1.444	7
Social	5.696	6	0.661	9
Esteem	5.688	7(tie)	1.109	8
Direct economic benefits	5.688	7(tie)	2.568	1
Indirect economic benefits	5.535	9	1.880	3

Source: William E. Reif, "Intrinsic versus Extrinsic Rewards: Resolving the Controversy," *Human Resource Management,* vol. 14, no. 2 (Summer 1975), p. 7.

judged most important—working conditions, security, and compensation—are extrinsic, while the only intrinsic reward was self-actualization.

It can be summarized that people who have high achievement needs will be high producers with or without financial incentives; those with low achievement needs must have the monetary stimulus. (23) Finally, monetary rewards apparently are greater stimulants to males than females. (24)

FACTORS AFFECTING AN ORGANIZATION'S COMPENSATION POLICIES AND PRACTICES

An organization's compensation policies and practices are determined by the interplay of three factors, namely, what it is *willing* to pay, what it is *able* to pay, and what it *must* pay. The first of these factors is established by the inherent managerial philosophies of the owners and/or managers; the second is limited by the underlying wage theories which explain the source and determination of wages; and the third results from the interaction of internal and external pressures which in their totality determine what rate must be paid in order to remain competitive and maintain an effective work force.

What the organization is *willing* to pay

In the long run, the amount of compensation paid employees is determined by inexorable laws of economies—as stated in the various wage theories. However, in the short run, the amount and timing of wage and salary increases are based upon a complex interplay between economic, sociological, psychological, philosophical, and political factors.

Therefore, one of the first considerations in establishing wage rates is determining *what the wage level should be* and *whether increases should follow or precede increases in output.*

In trying to determine how high overall wage rates should be and when raises should be granted, the personnel executive has an infinite variety of philosophies to choose from. However, the two extremes are the *productivity philosophy* and the *purchasing-power philosophy,* with a continuum of possibilities in between.

The productivity philosophy. The productivity philosophy tends to be held by management personnel and determines their thinking about wages. Proponents of this philosophy claim that it is the best approach for a company to follow in a capitalistic economy, as it leads to the greatest benefit to the customers, employees, and owners. These benefits include more and better goods, lower prices, increased earnings, and the higher profits that are essential for upgrading the work force and expanding technology.

The purchasing-power philosophy. The purchasing-power philosophy is based upon the assumption that an expansion of effective purchasing power is essential to create mass purchasing power to absorb the output of the expanded industry, thereby assuring continued national prosperity.

Some economists maintain that in order to keep the total economy operating near full employment, the purchasing power of employees must be high enough so that they will be able to furnish a stimulant to current and future production by buying the output of industry. Rising wages and earnings are therefore held to be a desirable goal.

Evaluation of philosophies. In addition to the variation in how much can be paid to employees, an inherent different between the two prevailing philosophies is a matter of time and approach, i.e., whether the wage increase should precede the increased productivity or follow it. Management believes that it is essential to increase productivity first and increase wages by at least the same amount afterwards, thereby putting the primary emphasis upon increasing capital goods. Therefore, the productivity philosophy has been followed by many companies who have expanded their facilities out of retained earnings, rather than attempting to provide new funds by selling securities.

The amount of goods and services that employees' money will buy—at a given price level—is the important thing, and, if wage increases were expected to raise living standards, the pay raises must be met out of increasing output per employee.

The latter is a particularly pertinent point, for various studies have shown that physical productivity has been increasing for a long period of time, and this increase is reflected in employee earnings. From 1820 to 1928, real wages increased at the rate of about 1 percent per year; between 1929 and 1959, at about 2.5 percent per year; and from 1948 to 1964, at about 3 percent. (25) During the latter period, productivity *rose 51 percent and real weekly earnings of factory workers increased by 50 percent.* However, from 1948 to 1972, the average annual percentage increases were: compensation, per worker-hour, 5.5; output, 3.1; consumer price index, 3.1–5.4. Consequently, real wages declined over the period.

Regardless of which system is more explanatory, the productivity philosophy apparently more nearly approximates the prevailing management attitudes in this country. It is also felt to have more validity in the long run.

What the organization is *able* to pay

Regardless of all other factors, an organization's long-run wage rate is ultimately dependent upon its ability to pay. As previously indicated, wages constitute the most important cost item for an institution. It has also been pointed out that employees tend to receive a relatively fixed proportion of gross national product and of revenue. Therefore, there must be revenue before there can be wages; ultimately there must be profit to the owners if wages are to continue.

Law of wage share. The above statement is based upon the immutable economic "law of the wage share," which states that in spite of wars, depressions, inflation, and unionization, the *ratio of employee wages to total business income has remained practically constant at approximately 50 percent since the* turn of the century. (26) Therefore, the primary source of increased wages to employees is through increasing the company's sales and profits. Although decreasing dividends and other business "expenses" could provide for these wages, in the long run, expenses can be lowered only so much, whereas sales and productivity can be expanded to a greater extent.

Marginal productivity theory. The marginal productivity theory is recognized by many economists as the most valid explanation for the wage phenomenon. According to this theory, wages are based upon the entrepreneur's estimate of the value that will probably be produced by the last, or marginal, worker. Therefore, alert entrepreneurs will tend to use each factor of production up to, and including, the point at which they will make no further gain from using an additional unit of it. At that point they will gain from transferring a small part of their expenditure to another factor of production. Employers will hire additional workers at any given wage as long as the incremental value of the product that results from the efforts of each new employee is at least equal to wages paid. Therefore, each factor of production will tend to receive compensation equal to its contribution to the production process.

In essence, this theory is based upon the law of supply and demand, which assumes that wages depend upon the demand for, and supply of, labor. Consequently, workers will be paid what they are economically worth.

As previously indicated, this theory more nearly approximates the actual working of the economic system, as far as the source of wages is concerned, than any other theory. This theory is prima facie valid, particularly if the unit of production is considered to be a crew of workers, a department, or a plant, instead of the individual employee. For example, a plant will shut down one unit of production, such as a still, an assembly line, or an oil well, when the cost of running it exceeds the value of the production from it. A chain will close one store when its productivity is exceeded by the cost of running it. One factory will be closed when it becomes a "high-cost producer." Also, when the minimum wage is increased, some employees become marginal and are eliminated. Finally, some skills become nonproductive and are no longer demanded when some other skill or machine can perform the job more efficiently and effectively.

This theory has also been proven valid in Japan where a dual wage structure has existed since World War II. (27) The larger, more productive companies hired the educated and more productive employees and paid them superior wages. The smaller firms and agricultural activities used the other workers, but paid them a much lower wage. Now, increased industrial productivity, coupled with more education and a decreased population, is tending to change this setup.

What the organization *must* pay

The third factor affecting an organization's compensation policies and practices is what it must pay, which, in turn, is affected by the interplay of internal and external pressures. Some of the *internal pressures* are: employee needs, desires, and demands; and the extent of automation and technological development. (28) The *external pressures* include: *governmental factors,* such as rules, regulations, executive orders, and laws; relative power of the union and company in the *collective bargaining* procedure; the *standard and cost of living; comparable wages;* and the *supply and demand* for workers.

It is axiomatic that no one of these factors operates alone as a criterion for determining the overall rate. Instead, they all operate concurrently; some in one direction; others in the opposite direction. Thus, the rate selected is the result of all the criteria operating in various directions.

Government factors. One of the strongest and most persistent criteria upon which compensation policies and practices are determined is the large number of government rules, regulations, executive orders, and laws, as discussed in Chapter 4. All states have some type of laws pertaining to unemployment compensation, worker's compensation, and other aspects of employee remuneration, including the maximum hours to be worked and the minimum wage legislation.

Wage and hour laws. At the national level, there are many such laws, including the *Davis-Bacon Act of 1931,* covering employees of construction contractors and subcontractors with government contracts in excess of $2,000; and the *Walsh-Healey Act of 1936,* also called the *Public Contracts Act,* pertaining to employees of any employer with a government contract in excess of $10,000. These laws set labor standards which require the payment of "prevailing wages"* to covered workers, as determined by the Secretary of Labor. Employees must also be paid not less than one and one-half times the employee's basic rate for over 8 hours worked in one day or over 40 in a week.

The basic wage and hour law is the *Fair Labor Standards Act of 1938,* as amended. This law sets a specific minimum wage for all employees engaged in interstate commerce or in the production of goods for interstate commerce, and for federal employees. The minimum was originally 25 cents per hour, the basic workweek was 40 hours per week, and "one and one-half times the rate of pay" was to be paid for all hours over 40 per week. The 40-hour week still prevails, but amendments have increased the wage to $2.30.

The general effect of legislating a minimum wage or of increasing the level of an existing minimum follows the "domino theory" by enhancing the factor cost of labor. Specifically the pay level of all employees increases—including "exempt" personnel,† for differentials must be maintained. Also, the marginal

---

* There are two phrases which are confusing, namely, "prevailing wages" and "going wages." Most personnel executives in business firms distinguish between "going wages," or those currently being paid because of the condition of the labor market, and "prevailing wages," or those set by the Secretary of Labor, based upon the prevailing union rates in the area. This distinction is not made by governmental organizations, which use the term "prevailing wages."

† "Exempt" personnel are those exempted from coverage of the law, particularly scientific, technical, professional, and managerial personnel. Those covered by the law are referred to as "nonexempt."

workers are forced out of the labor force, for not everyone can afford to pay them the higher wage since their productivity does not warrant it. (29) Third, the marginal producers are eliminated from the affected industries, for they cannot produce at a level where income will provide for the higher wages. Finally, there are modifications of production techniques, improvements in labor and managerial efficiency, and of the use of substitute productive factors. In fact, it has been shown that there is a definite correlation between changes in factor costs and minimum wage changes in low-wage industries. (30)

Government wage and salary administration. As shown in Chapter 4, the fastest growing industry is government, which is demanding an increasing proportion of total employed persons. This practice creates a demand for labor which has an impingement on its factor price. Also, with the Coordinated Federal Wage System, there is active union participation in setting wage rates, especially of the wage-and-hour personnel. Finally, the salary structure of the federal government is not only competitive with private business, but is often even higher—especially for the lower job levels.

Collective bargaining. The collective bargaining criterion permeates all the other factors involved in determining the overall wage rate. When a union is involved, basic wages, fringe benefits, job differentials, and individual differences tend to be determined by the relative strength of the organization and the union as tested through the collective bargaining process.

Yet, there is considerable controversy about the influence unions actually exert over the amount of total wages received. For example, one study found that from 1952 to 1958 there was a correlation between union power and wage changes. The correlation was particularly high in industries with only a few producers in which there was a high degree of profitability. (31) Another study indicated that unions had widened the ranges of pay between skilled and nonskilled employees. (32) It found that generally the very highly skilled workers and the very low skilled workers have gained more from unions than the intervening groups.

There are many who reason that the gains in employee productivity achieved through mechanization (as well as a shortage of skilled personnel), not union activity, led to remuneration increases. It was concluded in one study that, "The most important factor in determining if and by how much wages rise is the extent to which revenue productivity rises." (33) The corollary of this conclusion is that collective bargaining, as such, is not generally responsible for the size of any wage increases granted. These increases must be justified on the basis of increased revenue productivity by the wage earners themselves.

Another study of wage increases under union and nonunion conditions showed that wage behavior under the two conditions was very similar. (34) However, it was clear that wage changes under union conditions are less sensitive to high unemployment than under nonunion conditions. Regardless of the role unions play as determinants of wage rates per se, collective bargaining does seem to cause the basic wage rates in a community to become more nearly uniform. The union philosophy of equal pay for equal jobs, which tends to disregard ability and performance judgments as factors in individual pay, leads to this result. Thus, merit rating is minimized and seniority looms even greater, for a second union tenet is the concept that senior employees should be rewarded for their services according to their experience and years of loyalty to the institution.

Standard and cost of living. No discussion of wage policies could be complete without considering the criterion of the employees' standard and cost of living. Although a person's *living standard* is a highly subjective and individualistic concept, it is easy to understand from a practical point of view. If one individual's standard of living is high, one will demand higher remuneration than another whose standard is low.

Closely related to the standard-of-living criterion are changes in the *"cost of living."* During the post-World War II period, employees often received wage increases only to have their effectiveness nullified by rises in living costs. Consequently, the United Auto Workers (UAW) signed an agreement with

CARNIVAL   By Dick Turner

"I believe they've finally done something about inflation! This last raise didn't cost me a cent!"

General Motors (GM) in 1948 which provided for automatic adjustments to wage rates as the cost of living changed. These adjustments (called "escalator clauses"), based upon the changes in the consumer price index (CPI) are made every three months. This arrangement attempts to assure that the employees' income increases as fast as, or faster than, their living expenditures rise. (35)

The number of these wage agreements increased at a rapid rate during the 1950s. However, their popularity then declined because employees sought wage increases that were higher than changes in the cost of living. Now, because of rapid increase in the price level, these arrangements are again popular and will probably remain so for the rest of this decade. According to one survey, only 15 percent of manufacturers have a formal plan for adjusting wages to changes in the cost of living, but another 73 percent provide some form of cost-of-living adjustments (COLA). (36) Possibly 6 million working people now have their incomes directly related to these escalator clauses. Included are: automobile, communications, manufacturing, and railroad workers; teamsters; government employees—including Congressmen; and others.

There are benefits to these arrangements. For employees, it provides a measure of equity by assuring them that their *real wages* are maintained. For employers, it reduces the possibility that employees will withhold performance in order to match production with perceived income.

Yet, there are many difficulties—from an equity point of view—in using this method of income determination. First, the construction of the CPI insures inequity for some as it is designed for urban, manual, and clerical workers, which means it does not apply to a large group of others. Second, as it is an abstract measurement, there is little assurance that it *actually* measures "cost of living." Third, it provides a *common* adjustment for employees covered, regardless of their performance, which means it is inequitable to the better producers. Finally, it implies a constant standard of living, whereby the employees merely maintain their existing positions.

Comparable wages. The most widely used wage criterion is comparable wages. An organization's compensation policies and practices will, voluntarily or involuntarily, tend to conform to the wage pattern in the industry and in the community.

Industry rates. An organization will tend to conform to the wage pattern in its industry for several reasons. First, competition demands that competitors adhere to the same relative wage level. Second, various government laws and administrative and judicial decisions tend to result in conformity. Third, unions encourage this practice so that their members can have "equal pay for equal jobs" and in order to eliminate geographical differences. This uniformity is also a natural result of industrywide bargaining. Fourth, trade associations encourage uniform wage structures through the dissemination of wage information, including wage and salary surveys, to their members.

Finally, the inherent economics of related industries result in uniform wages. Functionally related firms of comparable size in the same industry require essentially the same quantity of employees with the same skills and experiences. This reality results in considerable uniformity in wage and salary rates and in compensation practices within a given industry and considerable diversity between industries. However, some industries do appear to be "high-wage" industries, while others appear to be characterized as "low-wage."

Area rates. A factor related to, but often opposed to, rates is conformity in area wages. It is difficult for an organization to pay rates that are substantially lower—or even higher—than those paid by other employers in the same vicinity. The pressure for this type of uniformity is greater when labor becomes scarce than when it is plentiful.

The factor of geographical specialization is also prevalent in two other forms. First, some cities or regions become known as high-wage areas, while others are known as low-wage centers. Second, some individual firms desire to become known as wage leaders and achieve a feeling of superiority through paying higher remuneration than others in the area or industry. The high-wage areas tend to attract the workers that they need easier than the low-wage centers. Thus, the region begins to have a concentration of a given type of labor. The firms which pay higher wages also tend to attract the more capable employees. However, there is a danger that the firm will tend to price itself out of the market.

Occupational rates. It is also important that an organization's compensation package be related to, and comparable with, the various occupations. This is particularly true with managerial and administrative personnel, professional and technical workers, sales personnel, and—to a certain extent—clerical employees.

Probably the classical example of using occupational rates is the practice of the federal government to tie the wages and salaries of its employees to comparable wages in similar occupations around the country.

The availability of potential employees. The basic laws of economics, including the law of supply and demand, must be considered in establishing wage rates. Regardless of the other factors involved, the overriding one is the supply of employees relative to the demand for their services. Ultimately this relationship will determine the institution's wage rates, for that is the price it will be required to pay for the scarce economic factor—labor.

This tendency, which is referred to as "paying the market" or paying "what the market will bear," presents problems to the personnel executive. With limited supplies of *qualified, capable,* and *available* workers, the executive must decide whether to raise the "going rate" in order to attract the people needed or to "pay the going rate" and accept less qualified people. In a declining industry or organization, the latter course will probably be followed; in a growing organization or industry, the former will probably be used.

IMPLICATIONS AND APPLICATIONS FOR PERSONNEL EXECUTIVES

The effective personnel executive will perceive that wages have become possibly the most effective common denominator of productivity and job worth in our society. This premise forms the background for wage and salary determination and administration.

Primarily compensation performs the equity function by rewarding employees for past contributions to the organization and provides them with a stimulus to future performance. Thus, the compensation method provides the greatest motivation if it is established so that the system of rewards will be perceived as being equitable by all interested parties and will induce employees to exert extra productive efforts.

There are essentially three sets of factors affecting an organization's compensation policies and practices. They are: willingness to pay, ability to pay, and requirements to pay.

The *willingness* to pay is a reflection of the organization's overall compensation philosophies. It reflects management's attitudes toward what is a "fair wage," how much of the increase in productivity should be shared with employees, and when the increases should be given, before or after improved performance.

An organization's *ability* to pay is a function of two things, namely, its income, or revenue, and the marginal productivity of its employees. No organization is able to pay more than a proportionate share of its revenue, as determined by the industry it is in. Also, in a profit-oriented company, management cannot long pay more than the employees are able to produce. Thus, the marginal productivity theory sets long-range maximum rates which can be paid.

The factors affecting what an organization is *compelled* to pay include governmental factors, collective bargaining, standard and cost of living, comparable wages, and the supply and demand for workers.

The actual compensation policies and practices of an organization will be determined by the interaction of all three of these factors.

DISCUSSION QUESTIONS

1. Can a satisfactory solution ever be found to the compensation problem, i.e., one considered "equitable" by all concerned? Explain.
2. What functions are performed by compensation in a reward system?
3. Discuss the role of peoples' perception about their compensation and explain the effect it has upon their motivation.
4. "An organization's compensation policies are determined by: willingness to pay, ability to pay, and what it has to pay." Isn't the third factor the only really important one? Explain.
5. What possible disadvantages might be contained in cost-of-living clauses in wage agreements? Is such an agreement equitable to the employee? The company?
6. "There must be profits before there can be wages." Discuss the validity of this concept as applied to a private business.
7. Defend *or* refute the marginal productivity theory of wages.
8. Do unions determine wage rates? Explain.

REFERENCES AND SUGGESTIONS FOR FURTHER STUDY

1. See Paul L. Scheible, "Changes in Employee Compensation, 1966 to 1972," *Monthly Labor Review,* vol. 98, no. 3 (March 1975), pp. 10–16.
2. Rensis Likert, *New Patterns of Management* (New York: McGraw-Hill Book Co., 1961), p. 116.
3. Bernard Berelson and Gary A. Steiner, *Human Behavior: An Inventory of Scientific Findings* (New York: Harcourt, Brace & World, Inc., 1964), p. 101.
4. Mason Haire, *Psychology in Management,* 2d ed. (New York: McGraw-Hill Book Co., 1964), p. 115.
5. Melvin J. Lerner, "Evaluation of Performance as a Function of Performer's Reward and Attractiveness," *Journal of Personality and Social Psychology,* vol. 1, no. 2 (April 1965), pp. 355–60.
6. Sylvia Schimmin, "Extramural Factors Influencing Behavior at Work," *Occupational Psychology,* vol. 36, no. 3 (July 1962), pp. 124–31.
7. Charles Hoffman, "Work Incentives in Communist China," *Industrial Relations,* vol. 3, no. 2 (February 1964), pp. 81–98.
8. Charlotte Saikowski, "Soviets Wink at Private Farms," *Christian Science Monitor* (December 1, 1970), p. 7.
9. Norman F. Dufty, "Blue Collar Contrast," *International Journal of Comparative Sociology,* vol. 8, no. 2 (September 1967), pp. 209–17.
10. Christopher Green and Alfred Tello, "Effects of Nonemployment Income and Wage Rates on the Work Incentives of the Poor," *Review of Economics and Statistics,* vol. 51, no. 4 (November 1969), pp. 399–408.
11. Richard D. Denzler, "People and Productivity: Do They Still Equal Pay and Profits?" *Personnel Journal,* vol. 53, no. 1 (January 1974), pp. 59–63.
12. Ibid.
13. Donald P. Schwab, "Conflicting Impacts of Pay on Employee Motivation and Satisfaction," *Personnel Journal,* vol. 53, no. 3 (March 1974), pp. 196–200.
14. Haire, *Psychology in Management,* p. 34. Italics added by author.
15. Hilde Behrend, "Financial Incentives as the Expression of a System of Beliefs," *British Journal of Sociology,* vol. 10, no. 2 (June 1959), pp. 137–47.
16. Clark Dickinson, *Compensating Industrial Effort* (New York: Ronald Press Co., 1937).
17. Stanley Sloan and David E. Schrieber, "Incentives: Are They Relevant? Obsolete? Misunderstood?" *Personnel Administrator,* vol. 33, no. 1 (January–February 1970), pp. 52–57.
18. Louis J. Shuster, "Mobility among Business Faculty," *Academy of Management Journal,* vol. 13, no. 3 (September 1970), pp. 325–35.
19. Melville J. Herskovits, *Economic Anthropology* (New York: Alfred A. Knopf, 1960), pp. 122–23.
20. Ralph Litton, *The Study of Man,* student's ed. (New York: Appleton-Century-Crofts, 1936), p. 117.
21. See D. W. Belcher, "Toward a Behavioral Science Theory of Wages," *Journal of the Academy of Management,* vol. 5, no. 2 (August 1962), pp. 102–15, for an excellent discussion of this point.

22. J. R. Hicks, *The Theory of Wages* (London: Macmillan & Co., Ltd., 1932), p. 96.
23. David C. McClelland, "Achievement Motivation Can Be Developed," *Harvard Business Review,* vol. 43, no. 6 (November–December 1965), pp. 6–16.
24. Thomas Crawford and Joseph Sidowski, "Monetary Incentive and Cooperation/Competition Instructions in a Minimal Social Situation," *Psychological Reports,* vol. 15, no. 1 (August 1964), pp. 233–34; and C. G. Cameron, "Job Satisfaction of Employees in a Light Engineering Firm: A Case Study," *Personnel Practices Bulletin,* vol. 26, no. 1 (January 1970), pp. 34–41.
25. Chester A. Morgan, *Labor Economics* (Homewood, Ill.: Dorsey Press, 1962), p. 115: and *Current Wage Developments,* No. 200, U.S. Department of Labor, Bureau of Labor Statistics for others.
26. Sidney Weintraub, "A Law That Cannot Be Repealed," *Challenge,* vol. 10, no. 7 (April 1962), pp. 17–19.
27. Kozo Yamamura, "Wage Structure and Economic Growth in Postwar Japan," *Industrial and Labor Relations Review,* vol. 19, no. 1 (October 1965), pp. 58–69.
28. It is recognized that this factor is not solely an internal factor as it is often imposed from without the organization. However, as of a moment of time when the overall rate must be set or modified the firm's type and extent of automation become a given internal factor as far as skills, mental and physical effort, organizational relationships, and managerial responsibilities are concerned. See Julius Rezler, "Effects of Automation on Some Areas of Compensation," *Personnel Journal,* vol. 48, no. 4 (April 1969), pp. 282–85, for an excellent analysis of how automation has led to improvements in compensation.
29. A research study indicated that there might be a correlation between increases in the minimum wage and the high unemployment rate of youth. See Thomas W. Gavett, "Youth Unemployment and Minimum Wages," *Monthly Labor Review,* vol. 93, no. 3 (March 1970), pp. 3–12.

    This study was corroborated in a report by the Center for Study of American Business at Washington University, St. Louis. It found that more than 300,000 jobs for teenagers were priced out of the labor market by recent hikes in the federal minimum wage. Quoted in *U.S. News & World Report* (May 10, 1976), p. 8.
30. See David E. Kaun, "Minimum Wages, Factor Substitution and the Marginal Producer," *Quarterly Journal of Economics,* vol. 69, no. 3 (August 1965), pp. 478–86, for an excellent analysis of these factors. Also, see "What Happens When Minimum Wages Go Up," *Business Week,* no. 1747 (February 23, 1963), pp. 124–26, for a discussion of the effects of the 1961 boost in the federal minimum wage.
31. Martin Segal, "Unionism and Wage Movements," *Southern Economic Journal,* vol. 28, no. 2 (October 1961), pp. 174–81.
32. Sherwin Rosen, "Unionism and the Occupational Wage Structure in the United States," *International Economic Review,* vol. 11, no. 2 (June 1970), pp. 269–86.
33. It has been concluded that unions are losing their hold on the national wage structure because the percentage of the national income going to wages and salaries is remaining stable. See Kenneth O. Alexander, "Unionism, Wages, and Cost-Push," *American Journal of Economics and Sociology,* vol. 24, no. 4 (October 1965), pp. 383–95.

This may now be changing for employee compensation currently accounts for over 74 percent of the nation's income. This is a drastic change from 1929 when it accounted for only 58 percent of the total; and 1965, when it was 70 percent.

34. Robert R. France, "Wages, Unemployment, and Prices in the United States, 1890–1932, 1947–1957," *Industrial and Labor Relations Review,* vol. 15, no. 2 (January 1962), pp. 171–90.

35. From a practical viewpoint, this is a measurement of the *average change* in the cost of a comprehensive mixture of goods and services consumed by *urban manual and clerical workers* and their families. See the *Consumer Price Index* issued monthly by the Bureau of Labor Statistics for further definitions.

    The 1973 negotiations between the UAW and GM resulted in a shift *to* the 1967-based CPI from the 1957–59 one. Also, the workers were to receive $.01 increase for every 0.3 percent increase in the index. In its 1976 strike against the trucking industry, the teamsters union built an inflationary potential into their contract by winning a cost-of-living clause with *no limit on the increases it could generate* in the second and third years. This will encourage other unions to hold out for an "uncapped" cost-of-living escalator.

36. *Wage and Salary Administration* (Washington, D.C.: Bureau of National Affairs, Personnel Policies Forum, Survey No. 97, 1972), p. 18.

Chapter 17

Using compensation to provide equity

Establishing compensation policies
    Types of wage rates?
    Pay for the time worked or for performance?
    Using a "fixed" or "variable" package?
    Salaries for everyone?
    Secret or open pay policies?

Types of wage differentials
    Acceptable differentials
    Less acceptable variations
    Wage and salary "compression"

Determining job rate differentials
    Some problems in using job evaluation
    Steps in the evaluation procedure

Determining individual rates of pay
    Using performance appraisals
    Converting employee appraisals into pay rates
    How merit rating operates in practice

Special problems of managerial remuneration
    Trend toward individualized plans
    Research findings affecting managerial compensation
    Relationship of compensation and profit
    Timing of increases
    Some useful generalizations

Implications and applications for personnel executives

17

Using compensation to provide equity

> He got a fair raise; or, to be precise,
> Just half what he estimated
> He well deserved—and easily twice
> What the boss believed he rated.
>
> G. S. GAILBRAITH*
>
> What have workers wanted through the ages?
> Shorter hours and higher wages.
> What have employers wanted for aye?
> Longer hours and lower pay.
>
> SAMUEL PEPYS†

The first poem illustrates the basic problem involved in setting individual rates of pay, namely, they are usually too low for the employees and too high for their employers. And, as shown in the second poem, this is nothing new, for the wage-setting process is an ageless issue.

It has already been shown that this process begins with setting the overall wage rate. However, this general rate is meaningless until it is translated into specific rates (or ranges) for each job and, finally, for each employee.

There are many differential rates which must be provided for. These differentials are explained in this chapter. Then the procedure for determining rates (or ranges) of pay for different jobs and individuals are discussed. Finally, some problems with executive pay are explored.

ESTABLISHING COMPENSATION POLICIES

There are several policy decisions the personnel executives must make at this point. They include: (*a*) what type wage rates to use; (*b*) whether to pay by time worked or level of performance (or productivity); (*c*) to provide a "fixed package" of compensation to all employees, or to use "variable (or

---

* George S. Galbraith, "Salary Adjustment," *Management Review*, vol. 52, no. 5 (May 1963), p. 17. Reprinted by permission of the publisher from *Management Review*, May 1963, © 1963 by American Management Association, Inc.

† *The Diary of Samuel Pepys.*

"flexible") packages" for different individuals; (*d*) should salaries be paid to all employees; and (*e*) whether to try to keep salaries "secret" or have an "open policy."

Types of wage rates?

The Bureau of Labor Statistics found that *rate ranges* are used for the vast majority of office workers and most plant workers. (1) Almost all government workers are paid this way and prefer it. The rationale for ranges is: If the job permits differential performance and if employees perform the job differently, they should be paid differently.

The use of *single rates* is growing in many industries—such as automobiles, trucking, steel, trade, and services; and occupations—including the crafts, production workers, and maintenance personnel. (2)

Pay for time worked or performance?

Essentially there are only two methods of compensating employees. One is to pay for the amount of time the worker spends on the job, or the *input of time into the job;* the other is to pay for the amount of goods and services produced, or the *output from the job.* The first of these is called *time wages* (or *daywork*) and tends to perform the equity function; the second, *incentive wages,* tends to perform the motivation function.

Under *time wages,* the employer pays for the physical presence of employees and assumes that productivity will result from their presence. Under a system of *incentive wages,* the employer compensates employees in direct proportion to their production in excess of a certain predetermined amount, when the extra productivity is the result of the worker's added skill and/or concentration.

Using a "fixed" or "variable" package?

During the last quarter century, the use of wages and salaries alone to reward employees has given way to compensation "packages," in which benefits and nonwage items account for around one-third of the total. Under this arrangement, each employee is given a stated amount for compensation and then must determine how the dollars are to be allocated for salary and for each type of benefit. (3)

The philosophy behind the concept is that employees will be better motivated and more satisfied if they have an opportunity to take more than a passive role in developing their income arrangements. Indications are that employees favor this approach. A study in a large aerospace firm found that over three-fourths of the workers would change the composition is they could. (4)

Salaries for everyone?

An extension of the "equal pay for equal job" argument is being used by some union leaders to justify paying hourly paid workers a guaranteed salary, the same as the present salaried personnel. They argue that it is inequitable for some employees to receive steady income by the month or year while others are entitled "only to payment by the tenth of an hour or by the piece." (5)

As indicated in the preface, this seems to be "an idea whose time has come." In fact, several such plans are already in effect.

A recent study described some of the problems involved in—and effects of—making the change in five major plants. (6) Initially, the absence rate increased around 15 percent, as shown in Table 17–1. This was about 1 percent of the firms' payroll. However, at Gillette, the rate for blue-collar workers was 4.7, as compared to 3.5 for white-collar employees.

It was also found that while the supervisors were initially reluctant to assume added responsibilities—they had to administer the program—the change was taken in stride. In fact, Avon claimed that the changes enhanced the desirability of accepting supervisory positions.

According to Black and Decker's experience, the objective of developing a sense of unity among employees was reached along with the achievement of historically good management-employee relations. Other evidence is impressive. At one plant, a 5-percent increase in employment since 1966 was matched by an 80-percent increase in productivity.

Secret or open pay policies?

It is now generally assumed that *money can be a motivator,* but the crucial factor in determining whether or not it does appears to be the employees' perception of the fairness of their pay relative to others with whom they compare themselves. Consequently, openness, or the availability of pay policy information, becomes very important. If such a policy results in more equitable pay policies, it would pay a company to be more open.

Many believe that more openness in these policies would result in higher motivation by bringing about more equitable pay systems. However, a survey by the Bureau of National Affairs, Inc. (BNA), found that among the 184 organizations responding, nearly three-fourths did have a written statement of their basic compensation policies (concerning such matters as paying competitive salaries, pay raises and when they can be expected), but only two-thirds of these firms make their policy known to all employees. (7)

Yet, another study shows a direct relationship between type of pay system and pay satisfaction. (8) Satisfaction declined as the amount of available information declined. In the secret pay group, only 12 percent were satisfied with their pay.

TABLE 17-1 Some results of changing from wage to salary basis of paying blue-collar employees at selected companies

Company	Union status	Date of change over	Objective of changeover	Treatment of time clocks	Absence rate for workers affected by plan* Before	After	Current	Employee reaction	Employer appraisal
Avon Products	Nonunion	1972†	Eliminate distinctions in treatment of office and factory employees	Removed	4.1%	4.4%	4.2%	Some preimplementation resistance from management; favorable postimplementation reaction, including that of supervisors	There were no specific gains, but management is satisfied that the approach is an essential part of its philosophy
Gillette	Nonunion	1955	Provide a logical alternative to improved sick leave	Retained	4.6	4.7	4.7	Generally favorable reaction, but initial minor concern about loss of status of clerical employees	Management is satisfied with the results
Black and Decker	Nonunion	1971	Improve employee relationships, with consequent benefits to operational effectiveness	Removed	1.5‡	2.3	2.0	Introduction of plan a contribution to favorable attitudes; some supervisory concern over payment decisions	Response generated by the plan has enabled continued productivity improvements
Kinetic Dispersion	Union (UAW)	1962	Eliminate distinctions and provide security of income	Retained	§	§	§	Plan welcomed, but misused initially	Management is reasonably satisfied, although problems were far more severe than anticipated
Polaroid	Nonunion	1966	Unify hourly and salaried employees	Retained until 1972	5.0	6.0	6.0	Benefits of plan well accepted, but no fundamental change of attitude	Management is not unhappy and considers program now controlled

* Basis of measurement may vary, so figures are not comparable between companies.
† Weekly salary plan was introduced in 1972, but 1968 changes equalized treatment in most cases.
‡ This applies for sickness only.
§ Rates were not measured; substantial increase occurred after changeover.

Source: Robert D. Hulme and Richard V. Bevan, "The Blue-Collar Worker Goes on Salary," *Harvard Business Review*, vol. 53, no. 2 (March–April 1975), p. 108. Copyright © 1975 by the President and Fellows of Harvard College; all rights reserved.

TYPES OF WAGE DIFFERENTIALS

Employees ordinarily judge the fairness of their pay by comparing it with that of other employees in the organization and with employees doing similar types of work in the industry or the labor market. Whether they think their income is "fair" or not will depend upon how they *perceive* its value relative to the remuneration received by other employees. Consequently, most of the openly expressed dissatisfactions concerning the compensation problem are over variations in rates of pay between jobs and individuals.

There are several important types of differentials the personnel executive must deal with. However, for purposes of this discussion, only the more important ones will be considered. These will be grouped according to their acceptability to management, the employees, and society.

Acceptable differentials

Some bases for differential wage payments are accepted by employees and society while others are not. These groups will usually concede the necessity of paying higher wages for jobs *requiring greater responsibility, ability,* and *knowledge.* To a lesser extent, workers will grant the equity of paying more to those workers who are more productive on a given job. In fact, a study of a group of machinists indicated that the desires paramount in employees' minds are security and stability of earnings and a "limited differential between earnings of members of the group." (9)

It will probably be acceptable that abilities and skills which are temporarily in short supply should receive a greater reward. Also, differentials based upon *occupational differences, skill variations, managerial activities,* and *definable job divergencies* will be tolerated. However, workers will bitterly resent the payment of a wage which cannot be justified on one of the above bases. Their resentment will probably cause them to withhold their best effort and voluntarily restrict output. In the extreme, they may even resign from the organization. This is not only true of the average wage employee but of professionals also. "A professor may be unconcerned about the fact that he earns less than a bricklayer, but still he may become enraged if Professor X across the hall, with six less publications than he, gets a salary increase while he does not." (10)

It is almost universally accepted that the added responsibility for supervising the activities of others should be rewarded by means of added income. In a survey by the National Foremen's Institute, it was found that although it was possible (but not probable) for some first-line supervisors to receive less compensation than their subordinates, most industries maintained around *a 25-percent differential between the income of the supervisor and that of his subordinates.* (11)

The significance of this type of incremental pay cannot be overemphasized, for unless it prevails, the prestige and status of the managerial position is destroyed. In a survey of members of management in five companies, it was found that an equitable pay relationship between oneself and one's subordinates appeared to be of critical importance to satisfaction with pay. (12)

Less acceptable variations

Some less acceptable compensation variations are those based upon the factors of *sex, ethnic groups,* and *race.* While these differentials may contain elements of unwarranted discrimination, there are also economic elements to be considered. There has been a tendency for employees in the aforementioned groups to be concentrated in relatively low-paying jobs because they lack the skills, education, training, and experience to move to higher paying positions. Also, there is a high turnover rate among employees in those categories which further militates against higher earnings.

Differentials based upon sex. As an indication of pay differences, it was found in an early study that the median wage and salary income of employed women was only 58 percent of that of men. (13) There was a 24-percent difference even on the same jobs. However, the men, who were in higher paying occupations, were older and worked longer hours than their feminine counterparts.

As can be seen from Figure 17–1, women who work at full-time jobs the year round still earn around $3 for every $5 earned by similarly employed men. While the ratio varies from year to year, the gap is now greater than it was two decades ago. The women's median wage or salary income as a proportion

FIGURE 17–1
Black-white, male-female ratios of median weekly earnings, full-time workers, 1967–74

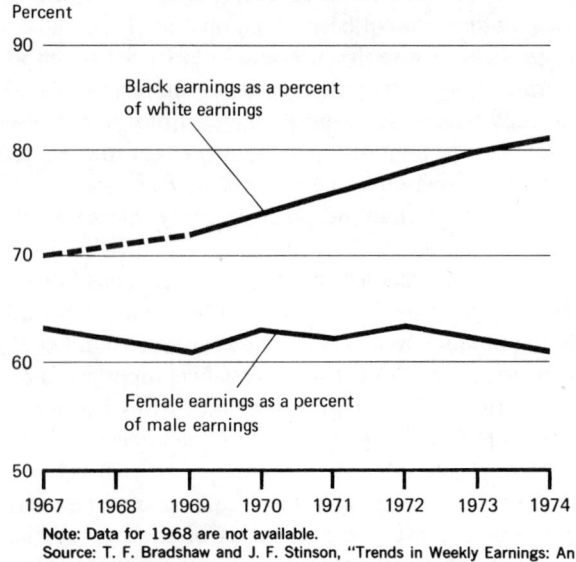

Note: Data for 1968 are not available.
Source: T. F. Bradshaw and J. F. Stinson, "Trends in Weekly Earnings: An Analysis," *Monthly Labor Review,* vol. 98, no. 8 (August 1975), p. 26.

of men's fell from 64 percent in 1955 to 61 percent in 1959, then fluctuated around 60 percent (14) until 1976, when it was 57 percent. Women also receive lower pay in the same occupation. (15)

Differences based upon race. It is prima facie evident that there have been differentials in pay between the nonwhites and whites. For example, a recent study attempted to show what effects changes in discriminatory practices in labor markets may have had on relative earnings of black workers. (16) The results suggest that there was some change and concluded that *nonwhite women* appear to have increased their relative earning position primarily by *movement between occupational categories,* whereas *nonwhite men* have apparently gained by *changes within occupational categories.* An overall impression suggests that the occupational distribution of nonwhites has been improving relative to whites in the sense that nonwhites are moving into the better paying occupations faster than the whites. For example, there were significant relative movements of nonwhites from the labor category into the craft category.

As seen in Figure 17-1, the earnings gap between black and white workers has narrowed significantly over the 1967-74 period. The average earnings of full-time black workers, equal to only 70 percent of the average earnings of white workers in 1967, rose steadily until they were 81 percent by 1974. Black women's earnings rose from about 80 percent of white women's in 1967 to just under 94 percent in 1974. The earnings of black men also increased relative to those of white men, but to a much lesser extent—from 69 to 77 percent.

Efforts to reduce compensation differentials. While it is obvious that these variations do exist and cause many inequities and difficulties, they apparently will be minimized in the future because of the many efforts, discussed in Chapter 4, now being made to correct the causes of this type of discrimination. First, the *Equal Pay Act* made it illegal to pay women less than men (and conversely) for the *same work.* However, a significant breakthrough was achieved when the Third U.S. Circuit Court of Appeals ruled that Wheaton Glass Company had to pay some $250,000 in back wages to its female employees. In rendering the decision, the court said that "women performing the same *general work* as men should receive the same pay." (17)

Also, *Executive Orders 11246 and 11375* and *Title VII* prohibit discrimination in any employment activity based upon race, color, religion, sex, or national origin. While these have been used more as a device for ensuring the selection and promotion of minority groups than in assuring equitable compensation, they are now being used for that purpose and will probably be used even more so in the future.

Wage and salary "compression"

A form of wage inequity sometimes develops when wage employees receive a general wage increase and salaried employees do not and when lower paid persons in the same occupation receive more increases, faster, than higher paid personnel. This variation is not caused so much by inherent divergence in remuneration policies as by diverse methods of computing and paying monetary rewards to various classes of employees. It is primarily caused by placing an upper limit on earnings while continuing to raise the lower levels. Generally, when there are remuneration inequities, the pressure is to correct the lower rate upward rather than the higher rates downward. In the process, the incremental payment is narrowed to the point where it is too small to afford incentive to produce.

Two examples will illustrate the practical inequities of the problem. First, because of the salary spiral, economic prosperity and inflation, and obsolete pay plans, the *real income* of management trainees (with the MBA) rose around 400 percent while that of production workers rose 75 percent and that of professional personnel increased only between 25 and 50 percent. (18) Second, while white-collar employees earned from 50 to 100 percent more than blue-collar workers 40 years ago, the roles were reversed in 1969 when production workers averaged $130 per week but the frayed white collarites earned $105. (19)

DETERMINING JOB RATE DIFFERENTIALS

Research has tended to verify that managers perceive that greater job responsibility and better performance are prerequisites for higher pay. (20) Consequently, *some method must be used to determine the worth of a given job to the achievement of the organizational objectives.* If no valid objective analysis is done, then the value judgment will be done on an informal or arbitrary basis. It seems that job evaluation, with all its weaknesses, is preferable to the arbitrary or capricious method used without it.

Research has shown employees' past experience with, and expectations of, a given pay system determines their preferences for pay systems. The more competent individuals perceive themselves to be, and the more they perceive that they will receive regular pay increases, the more they prefer merit systems. (21)

Some problems in using job evaluation

As with other personnel techniques, the job evaluation procedure has its virtues and limitations. As so much has been written about the values to be gained by using this procedure, that aspect will be minimized herein. Suffice it to say that the advantages of the system outweigh the disadvantages.

Although it has proved feasible to obtain a reasonable degree of equity by utilizing job evaluation, efforts to achieve a greater degree of precision in measurement have not been particularly rewarding. Some specific problems are:

1. The inability to measure precisely the worth of all occupations with the same yardstick;

2. The difficulty of measuring the worth of scientific, technical, professional, and managerial jobs; and
3. The inability to separate the person's contribution from the job being evaluated.

As an example of the last point, one research study found that nonexempt, salaried, clerical, and technical white-collar employees are not significantly different from the managerial and professional groups, and their pay could probably be included in one system. (22)

As satisfaction with one's pay tends to be related to one's preference for a merit system, it can be hypothesized that: *those voicing dissatisfaction with pay are also expressing a lack of satisfaction with the mode of payment as much as the lack of income.*

Steps in the evaluation procedure

This technique has been used for about half a century as a means of minimizing subjective human judgments and of maximizing the objective decisions. Thus, sufficient experience has been acquired to refine and standardize the procedure.

Usually four steps are involved in arriving at the specific job rates. These steps include: performing a job analysis, grading the jobs, assigning a price to each job, and administering the resulting program.

These four steps have the following relationships. The process of *job analysis* results in *job descriptions* which are refined into *job specifications.* These specifications define the personal requirements for performing the work and serve as the basis for hiring personnel. Job specifications are also used in *grading* the jobs. This step involves determining the relative worth of the job and results in job classifications. The *pricing* step uses these grades, plus the company's basic wage rate, to determine the wage range for that job. Then, in *administering* the program, some form of employee appraisal is used to evaluate the performance of each individual worker and to assign each a specific wage rate somewhere between the minimum and maximum rates. This figure becomes the basis for remuneration until each worker is again rated, or the value of the job changes, or there is a general wage increase.

These steps should assure a balance between operating costs and revenue. Every step involves, in turn, a series of procedures, products, and results, which are shown in Table 17-2 and are discussed in the following analysis.

Job analysis. As shown in Chapter 7, job analysis describes the duties, responsibilities, working conditions, and interrelationships between the job as it is and the other jobs with which it is associated. It attempts to record and analyze details concerning the training, skills, required efforts, qualifications, abilities, experiences, and responsibilities expected of a worker.

Job grading. After determining the job specifications, the actual process of grading, rating, or evaluating occurs. A job is rated or graded in order to

TABLE 17-2
Steps in the job evaluation procedure

Step	Procedures and products used	Resulting product
STEP 1: *Analysis*	Job analysis → job description →	Job specifications*
STEP 2: *Grading*	Job specifications + Job evaluation and appraisal of the worth of job → job ratings →	Job grades
STEP 3: *Pricing*	Job grades + company overall wage rate →	Job wage rates, or ranges
STEP 4: *Administering*	Job wage rates or ranges + appraisal of performance or qualities of each employee →	Individual wage rate

* These specifications can be used as the basis for performing the job evaluation procedure, or they can be used to prepare a statement of the personal qualifications needed in a person to perform the job. This statement then becomes the basis of the recruitment and selection procedure.

determine its value relative to all the other jobs in the organization that are subject to evaluation. There are many evaluative methods used, but the most popular ones are the *ranking system,* the *predetermined grading method,* the *factor comparison method,* the *point method,* and the *time-span of discretion.*

Job pricing. Pricing involves converting the relative job values into specific monetary values or translating the job classes into rate ranges. Here again, value judgments must be used, in spite of the statistical techniques used.

Converting job values into pay scales. As indicated in Table 17–2, pricing involves taking each of the job grades and adding it to the company's overall wage rate in order to arrive at a figure that converts the job values established through the grading process into specific rate ranges. Through various analytical processes, the analyst arrives at a specific rate of pay for each job. This figure becomes the beginning wage for any worker who performs the job. More frequently, the analyst sets up a wage rate range, with a minimum and maximum figure for each job grade or classification.

Testing for consistency and competitiveness. After the rates are evolved, they should be tested for internal consistency and external competitiveness. To do this, a limited number of "key jobs" in the organization should be selected and tested to see if they are comparable to the "going rate" for similar jobs in the area. If there is relative comparability, it can be assumed that the other jobs are also competitively priced.

After the "key jobs" are validated, the internal consistency of the rates should be verified. This can be done by using appropriate statistical procedures.

If there is external competitiveness and internal consistency, the assumption can be made that the wage structure is valid and reliable.

Administering the procedure. After the wage range for each job is established, the specific wage rate within the range for each employee must be determined. Through various procedures of performance evaluation, the individual employee progresses over a period of time—usually five years—from the lowest point on the wage scale to the highest. The rate of progression through the wage range depends upon seniority, productivity, or selected characteristics that are assumed to lead to productivity. This procedure involves the very important process of employee appraisal, which was discussed in Chapter 14.

Recognizing role of individual. Although job evaluation and merit rating are separated for purposes of discussion, there is an indefinable relationship between the job and the individuals performing the job that cannot be analyzed separately. One study confirmed that employees who were achievement-oriented and desired responsibility and creative and innovative work also preferred being paid on merit; the security-conscious ones wanted general increases. (23)

The initial wage or salary of each job will be based upon the job itself; but subsequent increments in the wage rate are based upon the individual's performance. In fact, a dual system, with both merit *and* general increases, has proven best. (24)

Recognizing changes in job content. Finally, allowances must be made for variability in work distribution and changes in job content, for no wage plan can provide equitable relationships that will last forever. Jobs change by the addition of new services, reorganization of working components, and introduction of new machines, equipment, and methods. Jobs also reflect the changes wrought by the different employees, for they leave their mark upon the job.

DETERMINING INDIVIDUAL RATES OF PAY

In general, individual wage differences are established by some form of merit rating, either formal or informal. The objective of *formal appraisal programs* is to determine objectively the relationship between the individual's performance and one's wage rate. (25) However, even with only an informal plan in operation, the individual's worth to the organization is inevitably appraised, for when a superior assigns a wage rate to an employee, it is the result of some kind of conscious or unconscious personal evaluation.

Using performance appraisals

Some managers have accepted the concept of the single wage rates (or automatic progression within wage ranges) because of the ease of administering these rates and because of the supervisors' difficulty in defending their judgmental rating before the union or an arbitrator. However, it has been shown that most managers still prefer some variation of payment for performance. (26)

Behind this form of rate setting is the assumption that most employees have the ability to improve their performance through greater effort, experience, or training. Progression toward the maximum rate in the range should serve as a stimulus for them to improve performance. This goal is accomplished by adopting the principle of premium pay for premium performance. This principle implies that wage increases *from the minimum to the midpoint* of the range *should be based upon any improvement in performance, while increases above that should be based upon evidence of superior or excellent performance*

A formal employee appraisal program and the feedback in the form of appraisal discussions contribute significantly more to employer-employee relations than do the more informal programs. This generalization is based upon studies which show that a set of wage ranges, with performance being the determinant of rate range placement, has provided the users with the lowest costs of production. (27)

Yet, research shows that if employee appraisal is not based upon objective measures of actual performance, it is highly subjective and tends to be imperfect. In other words, the greater the reliance upon some objective measurement of actual performance, the greater is the validity of the evaluation; the greater the use of appraisals of subjective criteria, the more imperfect become the evaluations and the less becomes their validity as a basis for wage rate determination. (28)

Converting employee appraisals into pay rates

Once the appraisal of the individual has been completed, it should be converted into a specific rate of pay. Although there are many variations used in performing this function, the ranking received by the employee generally determines where the wage or salary rate will be on the continuum between the minimum rate of pay for the job range and the maximum.

A "normal" procedure is to have five steps in the rate range. Therefore, the usual rate of progression requires five years, at one step per year, before the maximum rate is reached. The employee's beginning rate of pay is important, for variation in the amount of compensation between employees in the same organization tends to increase with increasing tenure. A 20-year research study showed that people who received the largest monetary rewards early in their careers also tended to get the greatest financial rewards as their employment with the firm continued. (29)

Personnel executives tend to oppose having automatic progressions, step by step from the minimum to the maximum, and appraising all the employees on an annual basis. It seems that a better motivational provision would be to vary the time of the performance evaluation so that there would be no connotation of automatic annual increases. Instead, incremental amounts of earnings would vary according to employee merit. The only way this can be accomplished is to have no automatic time period for wage increases nor any automatic amount for step increases. In fact, studies at General Electric clearly indicate that feeding back the results of appraisals and salary actions at the same time is not desirable from both a motivational and developmental viewpoint. (30)

The following letter from a personnel executive illustrates those points.

> Pay practices today seem to be leaning heavily on the theory of paying a specific rate for the job performed but discounting the degree to which it is performed. This practice is acting as a brake on the initiative of the outstanding performers. Merit pay is seldom utilized and is frowned upon in most unionized operations.

How merit rating operates in practice

This wage-setting process is shown in the following example, which illustrates in detail how the procedure works in a small city planning firm.

Step 1: Management sets its overall wage rate based upon its philosophy and theory of wages, as well as external and internal pressures—such as governmental factors, ability to pay, cost of living, and so on. It sets

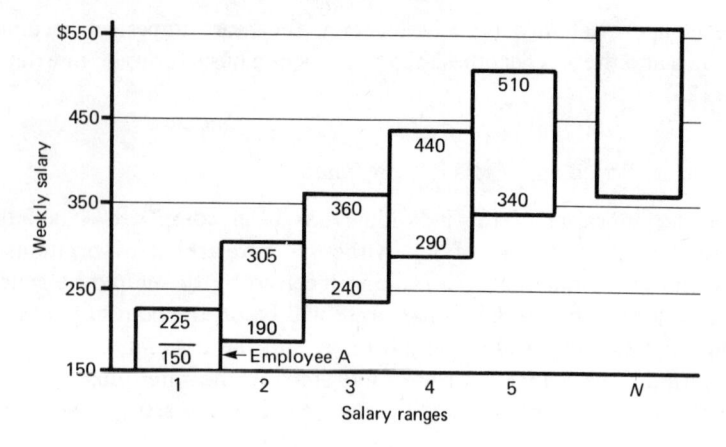

[Figure: Salary ranges chart showing weekly salary ranges 1 through N, with range 1: $150–225, range 2: $190–305, range 3: $240–360, range 4: $290–440, range 5: $340–510. Employee A is marked at range 2 base ($150).]

$3.75 per hour as its basic hourly rate and $150 as its basic weekly salary.

Step 2: Through the job evaluation procedure, salary ranges are established with minimum and maximum rates for each job range, e.g., salary range 1, $150–225; salary range 2, $190–305; and so on.

Step 3: The performance of each employee in each salary range is appraised in order to determine each one's specific rate of pay within the range. For example, employee A, in salary range 1, who was hired at the minimum rate, receives a rating of "superior," which is converted into an increase of $20 per week for a new rate of pay of $170.

SPECIAL PROBLEMS OF MANAGERIAL REMUNERATION

Some special problems involving executive compensation should now be considered. It has been stated as a law of management that the primary financial factors which determine the degree of willingness and enthusiasm with which executives do their work include: (*a*) the rate at which their remuneration has been increasing; (*b*) their prospects for future increases; and (*c*) their fears of receiving less income. (31) While not necessarily agreeing that these generalizations are immutable management laws, one must concur that these are the essential problems relevant to management compensation. At least, research shows that managers with a high need for achievement prefer a merit system, and those wishing security prefer general increases. (32)

Trend toward individualized plans

The tailoring of the executive's income package got its start when personnel executives began to realize that money alone is not what executives seek. Many organizations are now applying the *total income concept* by examining the different values executives may have—the value each one places on time, personal life—as opposed to professional life, and on economic needs. For some executives, it has meant more cash or insurance, time off, or even more support staff. A study of around 300 executives in seven firms found that this method of compensation is far more preferred by executives, even if they must pay more. (33)

Research findings affecting managerial compensation

Earlier research indicated that managers vary systematically by age and education (34); tax considerations, length of service, and children (35) in what they want in a compensation package. At one extreme, the younger, more educated, less tenured managers with below average salaries and family income wanted high pay, as money was important to them. At the other extreme, the older, less educated managers, with older children, longer tenure, and with above average income, family income, and net worth tended to prefer less in salary and more in benefits. It was concluded this group could afford to take chances, while the former group could not. Consequently, they wanted current and individual incentives, while the older ones wanted deferred and group incentives.

It's to Laugh

"I got a promotion that gives me a raise, that puts me in a higher tax bracket, that means we have to economize."

E. LEPPER

Parade, May 30, 1971.

However, the more recent study of 300 executives at all levels of seven firms in several industries found that there was no significant variation by age, income, or tax bracket. (36) Instead, there was a tendency for the executives to overvalue noncash and deferred compensation arrangements.

A fascinating finding of the three studies was that managers want their compensation in the form of salary and want only minimum protection in the form of insurance and pensions. To be sure, preference for other forms of incentive compensation varied among the companies, which seemed to indicate that executive attitudes are situationally influenced.

It was recently found that private executives prefer about 75 percent of their income in cash and 25 percent in noncash and deferred items. (37) (It was believed the present proportion was 85–15.) Another study found that public executives preferred salary to make up "something less than 75 percent of total income." (38)

Relationship of compensation and profit

A study of the compensation of top executives in 420 companies between 1953 and 1964 showed that the relationship between top executives' pay and changes in company profits is becoming increasingly fuzzy. (39)

Another study of 45 large U.S. industrial firms from 1953 to 1959 found that while sales and executive incomes were significantly correlated, profits and executive income were not. (40)

A third study, covering a longer time span and a weighted regression analysis, concluded that "profits appeared to have a strong and persistent influence on executive compensation, whereas sales seem to have little, if any, impact." (41)

Finally, a study of 53 chief executives (CEOs), in office six or more years from 1960 to 1974, found no significant relationship between changes in CEOs' compensation and changes in return on equity. (42)

The conclusion is that the compensation of these managers is beginning to cluster around the "average" both within the industries and industry in general. It seems to be approaching "one pay for one job." Also, recent income tax laws have tended to minimize the effects of some of the more exotic forms of executive payment, such as stock options.

Timing of increases

It can be concluded from research findings that scientific, technical, professional, and managerial employees in the lowest salary ranges—or those whose income is near the bottom of a given salary range, prefer financial increases at regular intervals, comparatively frequently, and of sizable quantities. Conversely, the better paid employees—and those in the upper part of their salary range, prefer increases in a decreasing amount and frequency. One reason for this observation is that money, per se, means more to lower paid people, while the higher paid individuals attach more importance to other factors such as security, autonomy, and esteem. (43) In general, as the amount of pay increases, the satisfaction with it increases; yet, for a given amount of compensation, the amount of satisfaction with it decreases the higher one rises in the levels of management.

Recent indications confirm that managers want cash *now!* They feel they need it to maintain the life-style they prefer.

Some useful generalizations

What generalizations can be made concerning managerial pay?

First, satisfaction with pay is *a function of comparison with other's pay, with downward comparisons having the greatest impact.* It was also found that managers feel that the pay of both superiors and subordinates is too close to their own, so there is insufficient spread for effective motivation. (44)

A second study found that of around 228 executives from five firms, lower-level managers compare with their peers within the firm, while higher-level, more educated, and higher paid managers tend to compare with managers in other organizations. (45)

Those findings tend to confirm my own research with supervisors and executives for the last 15 years. I have consistently found that managers in the middle to upper levels are more likely to compare their income with that of counterparts outside the firm; those in the middle levels are prone to compare their income to that of managers at comparable levels in the same organization; but the lower level managers compare their remuneration with that of their subordinates in the same firm. In general, the higher the educational and organizational level of executives, the more interested they are in making out-of-the-company income comparisons.

Second, *managers' satisfaction with their income and its motivational effect appears to be directly related to anticipated pay raises.* In general, those managers who expect large increases over the next few years apparently are less satisfied with their existing level of income; those expecting little or no increases are more satisfied. Also, a study of 600 middle- and lower-level managers found that the more highly motivated ones said their pay was important to them and that good performance would lead to higher pay for them. (46)

Third, *the choice of merit, as opposed to seniority, as the basis for determining salary rates tends to increase with education and position level.* The actual determinants of pay differentials seem to be job level, supervisory experience, and professional experience. (47)

Fourth, *managerial incentive compensation has tended to become rigid rather than flexible.* (48) If the various compensation media are to be used to motivate managers, there must be a return to greater flexibility and less rigidity.

Finally, *satisfaction* with pay *increased with increased managerial level* and *increases in salary* but *decreased with postgraduate training.* (49)

IMPLICATIONS AND APPLICATIONS FOR PERSONNEL EXECUTIVES

At best, it is difficult to convince employees that their compensation is based upon the *principle of fair pay fairly arrived at.* Yet it is easier to convince them of the "fairness" of their pay if the philosophy upon which it is based is defensible and if the procedure by which differential wage rates are determined seems "fair" and comprehensible to them. Essentially this chapter has tried to do just that.

As job differentials exist in all organizations, there must be some rational method for determining the relative value of each position. This is presently performed most effectively through the process of job evaluation.

Job evaluation is valued only if it can be applied within—and between—groups which are occupationally related; but this is also becoming increasingly difficult because of the growth of new industries requiring new skills, techniques, and methodologies.

The prime interest of lower-level workers is in wages and some form of savings or profit-sharing plan heavily contributed to by the firm. Those employees working a shift schedule are compensated for their inconvenience on a growing scale, so the unhappiness formerly associated with the shift schedule is being eased to the point where it is becoming difficult to get shift employees to accept day supervisory jobs. The 12-hour shift schedule is also increasing in interest particularly among the younger worker because it provides for a greater opportunity for leisure activities and the possibility of increasing income by "moonlighting."

Performance appraisal, as a method of determining individual rates of pay, is practical if it provides for an upgrading of wages rather than a "hold" on a scheduled wage increase. The trend is to schedule wage increases on an annual or 18-month basis and use the performance appraisal—which is done more frequently, to determine how much increases will be—and how frequently they will be given.

DISCUSSION QUESTIONS

1. What is your reaction to granting wage differentials? What are the basic issues involved in the argument?
2. What is the difference between "equitable wage payment" and "equal wage payment"? Discuss the conflict between the two issues.
3. Wage differentials are both an economic and noneconomic motivating force. Explain.
4. From your reading and observation, to what extent are wage differentials based upon race, sex, and age decreasing? To what extent do you think they *should be* decreased?
5. To what extent are managerial responsibility, skill, occupations, and job differentials valid bases for compensation differentials? Defend your answer.
6. What is the best basis for determining wage differentials? Explain.

7. What is the theoretical basis of employee appraisal as a means of deciding the employee's worth to the company?
8. How would you relate job evaluation to employee appraisal? What is the relationship between them?

REFERENCES AND SUGGESTIONS FOR FURTHER STUDY

1. *Area Wage Surveys, Selected Metropolitan Areas, 1968–69* (Washington, D.C.: U.S. Department of Labor, Bulletin No. 1625-90, 1970).
2. John H. Cox, "Time and Incentive Pay Practices in Urban Areas," *Monthly Labor Review*, vol. 94, no. 12 (December 1971), pp. 53–56.
3. System Development Corporation, a computer software firm, has already developed a program to help employees to choose from among several alternatives. See J. R. Schuster, L. D. Hart, and Barbara Clark, "Epic: New Cafeteria Compensation Plan," *Datamation*, vol. 17, no. 3 (February 1, 1971), pp. 28–30.
4. See Jay R. Schuster, "Another Look at Compensation Preferences," *Industrial Management Review*, vol. 10, no. 3 (Spring 1969), pp. 1–18, for further details.
5. See "Should Blue-Collar Workers be Salaried?" *Business Management*, vol. 21, no. 1 (March 1966), p. 43 ff., for these arguments.
6. See Robert D. Hulme and Richard V. Bevan, "The Blue Collar Worker Goes on Salary," *Harvard Business Review*, vol. 53, no. 2 (March–April 1975), pp. 104–12, for more detail than is provided here.
7. Mary G. Miner, "Pay Policies: Secret or Open? And Why?" *Personnel Journal*, vol. 53, no. 2, (February 1974), p. 110 ff.
8. Paul Thompson and John Pronsky, "Secrecy or Disclosure in Management Compensation?" *Business Horizons*, vol. 18, no. 3, (June 1975), pp. 67–74.
9. D. J. Hickson, "Worker Choice of Payment System," *Occupational Psychology*, vol. 37, no. 2 (April 1963), p. 100.
10. George Strauss and Leonard R. Sayles, *Personnel: The Human Problems of Management* (Englewood Cliffs, N.J.: Prentice-Hall, Inc., 1960), p. 581.
11. "How—and How Much—to Pay Your Foreman," *Business Management*, vol. 20, no. 6 (September 1961), pp. 58–60. I remember vividly the humility and frustration of foremen and supervisors in a shipyard in World War II when our subordinates, who received multiple rates for overtime, would walk up to us on payday and say: "Do you want me to cash your check?" It is felt that this practice led to the well-known difficulties that industry experienced with foremen during that period of time. As a result of these practices, the foremen joined the rank-and-file unions along with their subordinates.
12. I. R. Andrews and Mildred M. Henry, "Management Attitudes toward Pay," *Industrial Relations*, vol. 3, no. 1 (October 1963), pp. 29–37.
13. Henry Sanborn, "Pay Differences between Men and Women," *Industrial and Labor Relations Review*, vol. 17, no. 4 (July 1964), pp. 534–50.
14. John E. Burns, "The Earnings Disparity," *Industrial Management*, vol. 14, no. 8 (August 1972), pp. 9–10.
15. In 1975, the average weekly salary for women professionals and technicians was only 73 percent of the average salary for men; for women managers and adminis-

trators, it was only 58 percent of that for men, according to the U.S. Department of Labor, as quoted in *U.S. News & World Report* (April 26, 1976), p. 45.

This is even true of women on the staffs of U.S. senators. A survey by the National Women's Political Caucus showed the median salary for male legislative assistants was $20,082; for females, $15,038. And male press assistants earned a median $26,600, compared with $10,800 for women. *The Wall Street Journal* (June 17, 1975), p. 1.

16. Orley Ashenfelter, "Changes in Labor Market Discrimination over Time," *The Journal of Human Resources,* vol. 5, no. 4 (Fall 1970), pp. 403–30.
17. John E. Burns, "Equality of Women: An Increasing Concern in Labor Relations," *Industrial Management,* vol. 12, no. 8 (August 1970), pp. 15–16.
18. M. Sarni Kassem, "The Salary Compression Problem," *Personnel Management,* vol. 50, no. 4 (April 1971), pp. 313–17.
19. Judson Gooding, "The Fraying White Collar," *Fortune,* vol. 83, no. 6 (December 1970), pp. 78–81 and 108–9.
20. E. E. Lawler, III, "Managers' Attitudes toward How Their Pay Is and Should Be Determined," *Journal of Applied Psychology,* vol. 50, no. 4 (August 1966), pp. 273–79.
21. See Michael Beer and Gloria J. Gery, "Individual and Organizational Correlates of Pay System Preferences," in H. L. Tosi, R. J. House, and M. D. Dunnette, eds., *Management Motivation and Compensation* (East Lansing, Mich.: Division of Research, Graduate School of Business Administration, Michigan State University, 1972), p. 330.
22. Ibid.
23. Ibid.
24. Ibid.
25. For example, one theoretical method of accomplishing this goal has been proposed. The individual's performance would be mathematically determined and converted into an individual performance ratio (I.P.R.) The I.P.R. would be ascertained by dividing the individual's performance rating by the average rating for the group and multiplying by 100, i.e.,

$$\text{I.P.R.} = \frac{\text{Individual's rating}}{\text{Average rating for group}} \times 100.$$

See C. O. Colvin, "A Mathematical Exercise in Salaried Performance Evaluation Theory," *Personnel Journal,* vol. 44, no. 6 (June 1965), pp. 307–13.

26. A survey of the 500 largest industrial firms (*Fortune's 500*) showed that 93 percent of them claimed to subscribe to a merit-reward philosophy of advancing wages and salaries on the basis of job performance. Yet, in fact, relatively few of the firms attempted to implement this policy with an objective measure of employee performance.

Instead, a significant proportion of the companies use single-rate structures to compensate their blue-collar employees, whereby an employee may have a rate advanced by any of three methods: one's job may be reclassified to a higher paying classification; a general wage rate increase may be granted, or bargained for; and one may be promoted from a lower to a higher paying job classification. Advancement within a range on the basis of job performance, or for any other factor, was

usually ruled out due to the nature of the single-rate structure. See William A. Evans, "Pay for Performance: Fact or Fable," *Personnel Journal,* vol. 49, no. 9 (September 1970), pp. 726–31.
27. Walter A. Fogel, "Job Rate Ranges: A Theoretical and Empirical Analysis," *Industrial and Labor Relations Review,* vol. 17, no. 4 (July 1964), pp. 584–97.
28. For example, the findings of a study of three groups of salespersons chosen from 20 randomly selected departments in a retail store indicated that there was no relationship between dollar sales volume (the measure of success used) and any functions of the job upon which the employees were rated. See Robert J. Paul, "Employee Performance Appraisal: Some Empirical Findings," *Personnel Journal,* vol. 47, no. 2 (February 1968), pp. 109–14.
29. Marshall H. Brenner and Howard C. Lockwood, "Salary as a Predictor of Salary," *Journal of Applied Psychology,* vol. 49, no. 4 (August 1965), pp. 295–98.
30. H. H. Meyer, E. Kay, and J. R. P. French, "Split Roles in Performance Appraisal," *Harvard Business Review,* vol. 43, no. 1 (January–February 1965), pp. 123–29.
31. George Copeman, *Laws of Business Management* (London: Business Publications Limited, 1962), p. 61.
32. Beer and Gery, "Individual and Organizational Correlates," *Management Motivation and Compensation,* p. 330.
33. W. G. Lewellen and H. P. Lanser, "Executive Pay Preferences," *Harvard Business Review,* vol. 51, no. 5 (September–October 1973), pp. 115–22.
34. R. P. Meiklejohn, "Financial Incentives beyond Base Pay," *Management Record,* vol. 20, no. 5 (May 1958), pp. 165–70.
35. Thomas A. Mahoney, "Compensation Preferences of Managers," *Industrial Relations,* vol. 3, no. 3 (May 1964), pp. 135–44.
36. Lewellen and Lanser, "Executive Pay Preference," *Harvard Business Review,* pp. 115–22.
37. Ibid.
38. Jay R. Schuster, "Management-Compensation Policy and the Public Interest," *Public Personnel Management,* vol. 3, no. 6 (November–December 1974), pp. 510–23.
39. Arch Patton, "Deterioration in Top Executive Pay," *Harvard Business Review,* vol. 43, no. 6 (November–December 1965), pp. 106–18.
40. J. W. McGuire, J. S. Y. Chiu, and A. O. Elbing, "Executive Incomes, Sales and Profits," *American Economic Review,* vol. 52, no. 4 (September 1962), pp. 753–61.
41. W. G. Lewellen and B. Hunstman, "Managerial Pay and Corporate Performance," *American Economic Review,* vol. 60, no. 4 (September 1970), pp. 710–20.
42. K. R. S. Murthy and M. S. Salter, "Should CEO Pay Be Linked to Results," *Harvard Business Review,* vol. 53, no. 3, (May–June 1975), pp. 66–73.
43. Edward Lawler, III, and Lyman Porter, "Perceptions Regarding Management Compensation," *Industrial Relations,* vol. 3, no. 1 (October 1963), p. 41. Edwin S. Mruk, "And How Would You Like Your Compensation, Sir?" *Management Review,* vol. 63, no. 8 (August 1974), pp. 15–23.
44. E. E. Lawler, III, "Managers' Perception of Their Subordinates' Pay and of Their Superiors' Pay," *Personnel Psychology,* vol. 18, no. 4 (Winter 1965), pp. 413–22.

45. Andrews and Henry, "Management Attitudes," *Industrial Relations,* pp. 29–37.
46. Edward E. Lawler, III, "The Mythology of Management Compensation," *California Management Review,* vol. 9, no. 1 (Fall 1966), pp. 11–16.
47. Kenneth E. Foster, "Accounting for Management Pay Differentials," *Industrial Relations,* vol. 9, no. 1 (October 1969), pp. 80–87.
48. Frank H. Cassell, "Management Incentive Compensation," *California Management Review,* vol. 8, no. 4 (Summer 1966), pp. 11–20.
49. Andrews and Henry, "Management Attitudes," *Industrial Relations,* pp. 29–37.

Chapter 18

Using compensation to reward performance

The underlying theory

Using incentive wages to reward performance
    Definition of incentive wages
    Objectives of incentive wage plans
    Prevalence of incentive wages
    Effects of using incentive wages
    Unions and wage incentives
    Requirements for installing an incentive system
    Requirements for successful use of incentives
    What plan to use
    Evaluating the motivational effects of incentive wages

Using profit-sharing plans as stimulants to productivity
    Objectives of profit sharing
    Definition of profit sharing
    Types of plans
    Extent of usage
    Effects of using profit sharing
    Evaluating the motivational effect of profit sharing

Using merit wage increases as stimulants to productivity
    The logic of merit increases
    Evaluating the motivational effects of merit increases

Using bonus plans as stimulants to productivity

Using companywide productivity sharing systems
    Scanlon Plan
    Rucker Share-of-Production Plan
    Nunn-Bush Shoe Company Plan
    Kaiser Long-Range Sharing Plan
    Evaluating the motivational effects of these
        productivity sharing systems

Implications and applications for personnel executives

18
Using compensation to reward performance

Money motivates most people some of the time and some people all of the time.

SAUL W. GELLERMAN

Ms. Barbara Walters was offered a $1 million-a-year, five-year contract to co-anchor the "ABC Evening News," while the three anchormen of this and other news programs were receiving $300,000. She left NBC's "Today" show to accept.

This case illustrates what has been said in the previous chapters, namely, *while money has rarely been considered as the sole motivational stimulus, it is still a potent one.*

The previous chapters have developed a conceptual framework for determining the organization's overall wage level and for setting wage rates for jobs and individuals. This chapter will develop the proposition that, while time payments are one way of relating earnings to individual employees, there are motivational devices which achieve the same goal, only more equitably.

THE UNDERLYING THEORY

For any theory to be valid, it must be based upon valid assumptions, empirical evidence, and the value judgments of the persons proposing the theory.

It should probably be emphasized at this point that no one of these methods is totally effective in stimulating performance and rewarding productivity. Also, no one of them is the *only* effective incentive. Instead, in any incentive situation, there are pressures to produce and pressures to withhold production. Nonfinancial incentives, especially those related to the higher-level needs discussed in Chapter 15, may be more important as motivators to higher performance and increased productivity than the financial rewards. As shown in Figure 18–1, the rate of production is the interplay between these two sets of factors. The actual level of production can be increased *either* by reducing the effectiveness of the forces above the line or by increasing the effectiveness of the forces below the line.

FIGURE 18-1
Forces affecting rate of production under incentive system

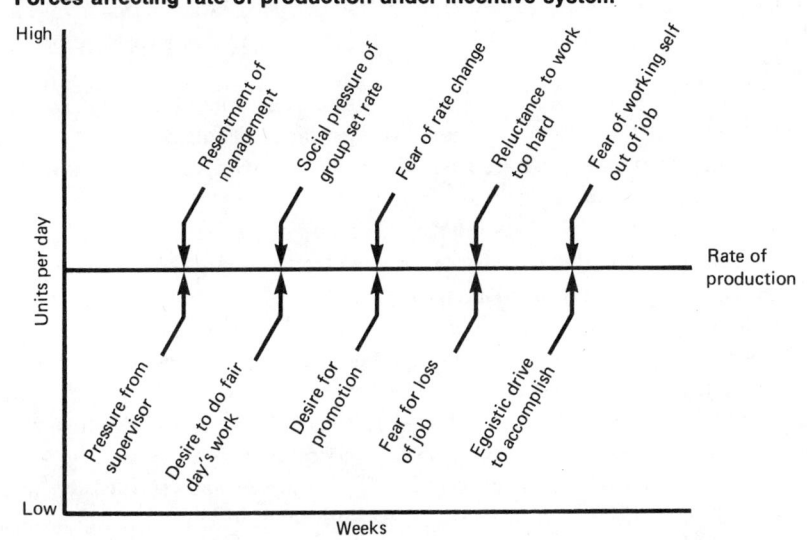

Downward forces (from High): Resentment of management; Social pressure of group set rate; Fear of rate change; Reluctance to work too hard; Fear of working self out of job

Upward forces (from Low): Pressure from supervisor; Desire to do fair day's work; Desire for promotion; Fear for loss of job; Egoistic drive to accomplish

Axes: Units per day (vertical), Weeks / Rate of production (horizontal)

Source: Mason Haire, *Psychology in Management*, 2d ed. (New York: McGraw-Hill Book Co., 1964), p. 167.

USING INCENTIVE WAGES TO REWARD PERFORMANCE

Incentive wage plans are now being subjected to considerable scrutiny as candidates for discard. (1) However, with all their advantages to the employers —as well as to employees, they will be around for a considerable while yet.

The basic assumptions underlying the use of incentive wages as part of the reward system are: work can be measured, quantitative performance standards can be set, above-standard performance can be objectively rewarded monetarily, employees will work harder in order to earn more money, and both the organization and the employees will benefit more from an incentive program than from time wages.

Definition of incentive wages

The fact that there is a great variety of incentive wage plans makes it difficult to define the term precisely. However, a working definition of incentive wages is: *the extra compensation paid employees for all production over a specified standard amount which results from their exercise of more than normal skill, effort, or concentration when performed in a predetermined manner with standard tools, facilities, and materials.*

Objectives of incentive wage plans

Although the objectives of incentive wage plans are manifold, the principal ones are: (*a*) *to lower unit cost by increasing production, especially of direct labor cost;* (*b*) *to increase earnings of employees through individual merit and accomplishment* (if the increase is due to application of one's skill or if one gives more concentrated effort to the task); and (*c*) *to reduce overhead expense per unit produced.*

The use of these schemes is not without difficulties. Therefore, it is expedient to view some of the advantages and disadvantages of incentives.

Advantages of incentive wages. There are many advantages claimed for the introduction of incentive wage plans.

These advantages can be condensed into the one statement: Management profits from the incentive wage system by obtaining greater production, which causes a greater utilization of facilities, which leads to reduced unit cost of goods or services produced, which in turn means greater profits.

There are many advantages to employees, but they all evolve themselves into the one all-inclusive statement: The advantage to the worker of the introduction of incentive wage payments is that it leads to increased earnings which are directly proportional to the worker's increased productivity.

Disadvantages of incentive wages. There are certain serious disadvantages and limitations to the use of incentive wage plans. One very potent limitation to the use of such programs is that they can only be applied in particular cases. It is ill-advised to use them where delays are frequent and beyond the control of the worker or in highly automated plants.

The workers also find disadvantages in the incentive system. Some of these difficulties are superficial; but there are also some fundamental problems, such as:

1. They may produce deleterious effects upon the health of employees;
2. There is the ever-present danger of rate cuts; and
3. The beginning or handicapped workers might not receive a minimum subsistence wage.

Finally, it is always possible that an incentive plan set up to achieve certain purposes may inadvertently achieve the opposite effect. Through errors in the measurement systems, through faulty reward systems, or because of the characteristics of the executives involved, the system may result in decreasing performance rather than increasing it. (2)

Prevalence of incentive wages

During, and immediately following World War II, an increasing number of companies and unions turned to incentive pay plans as a method of improving production and increasing employee income. There has been a slight decline in the percentage of workers on incentive since that time. But the decline is so slight (from 30 to 26 percent) that it could be a sampling error; or it may result from the fact that some industries which cannot use incentives, such as the aircraft and parts industry, were included in later surveys but not in the earlier ones.

Extent of use. The extensive use of incentives was emphasized in a study of 7 million workers in 1945–46. This survey showed that about 30 percent of the plant employees in manufacturing industries were paid on an incentive basis at that time. (3)

In 1958, a similar study was conducted among 11 million production and related employees in *all of the nation's manufacturing industries.* It was found that 27 percent of such workers were paid on an incentive basis. (4) The researchers concluded that the 3 percentage point difference between the use of incentive pay in the 56 industries in 1945–46 and all such industries in 1958 was accounted for, at least in part, by the omission of some major, low-incentive industries such as airframes, printing, and sawmilling from the 1945–46 wage survey program.

From July 1961 to July 1963, the Bureau of Labor Statistics conducted an occupational wage survey in 212 standard metropolitan statistical areas. (5) The study, which covered office and plant personnel in several industries, showed that virtually no nonsupervisory office employees and only one-fifth of the 11 million plant workers were paid on an incentive basis. For comparison purposes, though, 26 percent of the plant workers in manufacturing were on incentive, as compared to 27 percent in 1958 and 30 percent in 1945–46. Only 18 percent of the plant workers in retail, 13 percent in wholesaling, and 12 percent in service industries were paid on an incentive basis.

Trends in use of incentives. In order to examine trend information on the extent of incentive pay, a recent study matched industries, where possible, with those in earlier studies that were similar in industrial coverage. The results showed that proportions of production and related workers paid under incentive wage plans were virtually unchanged over the past several years for most of the matched industries. This was particularly true for industries with a high incidence of incentive plan workers, such as men's apparel and footwear manufacturing, as well as for those having relatively few such workers. As indicated in Table 18–1, there were substantial declines in the proportion of workers who were paid on an incentive basis in cigar manufacturing and in certain machinery manufacturing industries.

It is difficult to determine whether declines in the incidence of incentive workers were caused by changes in establishment policies on method of wage payment, changes in employment among establishments with no policy changes, or by a shift in the ratio of direct to indirect workers, as new and improved methods of manufacturing were introduced.

Effects of using incentive wages

There are so many variables influencing a worker's productivity that it is difficult to isolate the results obtained from using incentive wages and those obtained from other factors. For instance, it was found during the Hawthorne experiments that the Second Relay Assembly Control Group increased its productivity an average of 12 percent when placed on an incentive plan, but

TABLE 18-1
Comparison in percent of incentive-paid production and related workers in selected industries over periods of time*

	Most recent survey		Earlier survey	
Industry	Percent	Year	Percent	Year
Work clothing..................	82	(1968)	80	(1961)
Men's and boys' shirts, except work, and nightwear.........	81	(1964)	81	(1956)
Men's and boys' suits and coats.......................	74	(1967)	71	(1958)
Footwear, except rubber.......	70	(1968)	71	(1957)
Cigars.......................	57	(1967)	75	(1955)
Leather tanning and finishing...	53	(1968)	50	(1959)
Cotton textiles................	34	(1965)	36	(1954)
Farm machinery...............	34	(1966)	32†	(1958)
Wool yarn and broadwoven fabrics.....................	27	(1966)	30	(1957)
Synthetic textiles..............	26	(1965)	29	(1954)
Office and computing machines....................	24	(1966)	31†	(1958)
Service industry machines......	18	(1966)	33†	(1958)
General industrial machinery...	16	(1966)	32†	(1958)
Construction and related machinery...................	13	(1966)	12†	(1958)
Metalworking machinery.......	13	(1966)	24†	(1958)
Industrial chemicals...........	5	(1965)	4	(1955)
Fertilizers....................	1	(1966)	2	(1956)
Cigarettes....................	‡	(1965)	3†	(1958)

* It is not possible to make precise comparisons of the proportions of incentive workers among industries or between the "most recent survey" and the "earlier survey," because the estimates from industry surveys include some sampling error. Thus, differences of a few percentage points should not be considered as real.

† See L. Earl Lewis, "Extent of Incentive Pay in Manufacturing," *Monthly Labor Review*, May 1960, pp. 460–63. Estimates obtained from May 1958 study of the incidence of wage incentives in all manufacturing establishments are not precisely comparable with most recent studies which have a minimum establishment size cutoff.

‡ Less than 0.5 percent.

Source: George L. Stelluto, "Report on Incentive Pay in Manufacturing Industries," *Monthly Labor Review*, vol. 92, no. 7 (July 1969), p. 52.

"It was quite apparent that factors other than the change in wage incentive contributed to that increase. The condition that all other things remain the same had failed of realization." (6) Other factors included were: a selected group with the group spirit, the spirit of competition with a former Relay Assembly Test Group, and better working conditions.

Another illustration of the fact that the importance of financial incentives depends upon subjective factors was shown in a recent research study. It was found that the importance of financial incentives depends upon the intensity of an individual's needs. (7) When the need is great, people will do things for money that they dislike doing. One difficulty of research in this area is that it is practically impossible to simulate this need. Yet without this factor of need, experimental studies cannot approximate reality.

Another researcher found a strong relationship beween output and employee attitude toward the incentive scheme. (8) The connection was true for both individuals and groups. Apparently employees who are favorably inclined toward incentives will exert the extra effort to earn the incentive pay; those who are not, will not. Also, workers who are unable to earn a high bonus soon become disillusioned with the plan. Finally, personnel who feel that they have suffered injustices, such as operating under an impossibly high performance standard or inequitably low rate, will disapprove of the idea of incentive wages.

It has been shown through experimental studies that it is easier to motivate individuals by positive reinforcements. (9) Thus, the newer methods of incentive wage payments now rely upon immediate rewards for increased productivity.

While it is recognized that it is difficult to determine specifically and accurately the effects of using the incentive schemes, an effort is made to approximate their results upon productivity, labor costs, employee earnings, and other factors.

Effects upon productivity. As one of the primary objectives of using incentive wages is to increase performance, the question may rightly be asked, "To what extent *have* they increased employee productivity?"

The practical benefits of production incentives during World War II were reported by the War Production Board in a very conclusive manner: "Considering whole regional areas and including all types of incentive plans, good, bad, and indifferent, they are averaging an increase in productive performance of 25% to 45%." (10)

One of the more comprehensive studies of the effects of incentive plans on productivity was conducted in 1959. The sample for this study included 29 industries and 305 plans, most of which had been installed during the 1950s; the study showed that productivity increased an average of 63 percent. (11)

In California, a farm operator switched from paying machine operators by the hour to paying them by the acre. They boosted their production from "40 to 50 acres per day" to "75 to 85," for a 60-percent increase. (12)

A control study of the effect of piece work on individual operations, average plan efficiency, and productivity per production employee in the corrugated shipping container industry found 16 of 18 operations displayed statistically significant increases in productivity after monetary incentives were installed. Average plan efficiency averaged 58 percent greater efficiency; while productivity per production employee increased 75 percent on the average. (13)

In summary, with a properly developed and administered wage incentive plan, the *output per worker-hour should increase by 20 to 50 percent* and *direct labor* cost decrease 10 to 25 percent as a result of incentives. It has been proved that the output of the individuals in any group of employees on incentives will distribute itself in a pattern which follows the normal distribution curve about the midpoint. This midpoint is generally found at about 130 percent of the standard, or at the 30 percent bonus level.

Increases in production following the installation of an incentive wage plan follow a given pattern. *The rate of increase begins slowly but increases rapidly and then becomes fairly static.* This pattern was true at Western Electric's Hawthorne plant and has been followed in most other installations.

Effects upon employee earnings. Generally, employees operating under an incentive wage plan earn more than employees on a comparable job being paid on the time basis. The differential in earnings between incentive workers and time workers generally varies from 0 to about 40 percent. As shown earlier, incentive earnings of employees are generally 20 percent higher than hourly earnings.

The Bureau of Labor Statistics found that during the postwar period the average hourly earnings of incentive workers in automobile repair shops were 130 percent of the day earnings; in the full-fashioned hosiery industry, the figure was 120 percent; in power laundries, it was 116 percent; in sawmills, it averaged 134 percent; and in the wood furniture industry, the figure was 108 percent.* In the comprehensive study of 1959, the average increase in employee earnings attributed to the influence of incentives was 21 percent. (14)

It can be summarized that incentive wages increase earnings by around 20 percent in most cases.

Other effects of using incentive wages. While there is little evidence concerning the number of grievances occasioned by the installation of such plans, the available evidence indicates that while incentive wage plans *will minimize certain grievances,* they *will also instigate new ones.*

Incentive wages have an effect on labor turnover. The available evidence indicates that the installation of these plans tends to *reduce the rate of labor turnover.* However, since incentive coverage is only one of the many factors involved in the turnover of personnel, the validity of any conclusions drawn from turnover statistics should be judged with considerable discretion.

Other effects of incentive wage plans are: *decreased costs through better methods, smaller number of employees on the payroll, cost control, performance measurement, accurate scheduling, and the pointing out of poor management practices.*

Unions and wage incentives

Unions, in general, are opposed to incentive wage plans, for this type of wage payment has a tendency to differentiate between workers and destroy the group relationship in a shop. Yet, there are wide variations in attitudes toward these wage programs. In the textile, apparel, and (to a limited extent) the metal goods industries, payment by results is the custom and is accepted by the union.

The majority of unions are primarily interested in how the plans are in-

---

* Computed from U.S. Department of Labor, Bureau of Labor Statistics series on "Straight-Time Hourly Earnings for Selected Occupations." These are simple averages, computed by adding the average hourly earnings of the time workers and dividing the result into the total of the average hourly earnings of incentive workers.

stituted and administered rather than in the plan itself. The United Steel Workers Union helped Jones & Laughlin plan and install the equipment utilization incentive plan in many of its plants. (15)

In summary, most unions do not seem to object to incentive wage plans per se. The opposition is to their potentially disruptive effect, for these plans emphasize the individual rather than the group and give management a basis for appraising the work of one worker in relation to that of another. Unions tend to accept the plans that share the gains in productivity arising from all factors, not just the increase in human application. The union must also have a voice in the inception and administration of the plan before it will favor such schemes.

Requirements for installing an incentive system

It would be well to consider the conditions necessary for the introduction of such systems, for they are not universally applicable. First, the *work should be standardized and working conditions uniform;* otherwise there will be inequities in wage payments. Second, the *volume of work performed* by each individual worker, or group of workers, *should be easily ascertainable.* This necessitates defining the units of production clearly and sharply and determining that each unit can be accurately measured either by weighing, counting, or by some other process. Third, *there should be no division of labor within the process for which incentives are paid.* If such were the case, one worker could detain or slow up another so that the first worker's earnings would depend upon the effort of the second person as well as one's own. This would violate the principle upon which the whole incentive wage system is founded; i.e., each worker's reward is directly dependent upon, and proportional to, one's own effort and initiative. Closely related to the last requirement is the one that *production processes should be independent of one another so that one process would not retard the other.* Finally, the materials should come to workers in a uniform condition and in such a manner that *only the worker can control the volume and rate of flow of the work.* This requirement tends to eliminate the use of such schemes in highly automated plants.

Requirements for successful use of incentives

For an incentive plan to succeed once it is installed, it ought to have certain characteristics. First, the *standard of performance should be reasonably attainable* so that average employees can achieve it with "normal" effort. Second, *the rate of pay should be such that employees can achieve an incentive bonus that will make their pay exceed the pay of workers on straight time by about 20 percent.* It has been found that this amount of differential serves as an effective motivator. Third, *the standard of performance and rate of pay per unit should only be modified when technological changes* in the machines, methods, or materials, or changes in living costs *so dictate.* Fourth, *the plan should be installed by an "expert,"* who can prevent some of the problems from occurring. Fifth *management's wage philosophy must be compatible with high employee earnings.* Finally, the plan should be *easily understood,* for research shows that workers' satisfaction with incentive plans is positively related to their understanding of the system. (16) A simple plan will probably be accepted by employees; a complex system may be mistrusted by them.

There are many ways of learning whether your incentive plan is faltering. One method analyzes a normal distribution curve of the average incentive earning percentage of all the employees in your firm. This should be checked on a monthly basis. If the distribution curve is in a normal bell shape, everything is all right. However, if the curve *tends* to approximate a straight line, your incentive program is in trouble. (17)

What plan to use

There are so many plans available that it is difficult to select the one to use. However, they can be classified summarily into two types: (*a*) *payment by the number of units produced,* and (*b*) *payment for time saved in producing a given quantity.* The first is typified by the piece rate plan, the second by the 100 percent premium plan—or a variation.

In a study in two companies using factorially paired comparisons to evaluate employee preferences for alternative forms of job compensation, it was shown that piecework incentives were preferred more by the relatively skilled workers. Also, the incentive value of such plans was greatly enhanced after employees had successful direct experience with them. (18)

Evaluating the motivational effect of incentive wages

Proponents of incentive wage systems have presented evidence that incentive pay systems do serve as stimulants to increased productivity; opponents claim this is not necessarily true. Yet, empirical evidence indicates that incentive systems appear to result in higher productivity than time-based systems. These increased levels of productivity appear to result from a positive motivational effect of the incentive pay systems. However, evidence also indicates a dysfunctional effect on employee satisfaction and group cohesiveness.

The hypothesis has been proposed that *incentive pay systems have a positive impact on employee motivation* (*and, hence, productivity*), *but a negative impact on employee satisfaction.* (19)

Schwab has tested this hypothesis in a large-scale research project in a consumer goods organization in the Midwest which uses three different pay systems for its operative employees—individual piece rates, group incentive rates, and hourly rates. He found that the hourly paid group had significantly greater satisfaction than either of the incentive groups, and employees on group incentives had lower satisfaction than those on the piece rates. Conversely, he found that both valence and the performance-reward probability were highest among the piece rate employees and lowest among the hourly paid workers. In summary, persons paid by the time were most satisfied with their pay, while those paid by the amount of output produced were the most highly motivated to perform.

It can be summarized that a properly developed and administered program should *increase output per worker-hour by around 20 to 50 percent; reduce direct labor costs by 10 to 25 percent;* and *increase earnings by around 20 to 25 percent.*

"A computer breaks down and right away you want a raise!"

The Christian Science Monitor

USING PROFIT-SHARING PLANS AS STIMULANTS TO PRODUCTIVITY

A second financial incentive that can be applied by management to stimulate productivity is the sharing of profits with employees. This device is desirable, for it removes some of the barriers to cooperation between management and nonmanagement groups in a firm. This truth has long been recognized. Alfred Marshall said that "as a rule the relations between employers and employed are raised to a higher plane both economically and morally by the adoption of the (formal) system of profit-sharing; especially when it is regarded as but a step towards the still higher but much more difficult level of true cooperation." (20)

Objectives of profit sharing

The concept upon which profit sharing is based is a combination of ethical idealism and hard practicality. Originally the practice was conceived of as giving employees a creative share in management and the right to share in the profitability of the business. Ethically it links employees' self-interest to the firm's success in an ascending progression. First, there is the wage relationship;

then the profit relationship; and, finally, partnership. Of course, the last stage or two are not always achieved. Managers are often forced to subordinate the ideal and altruistic concepts of this practice to the more practical concern for profitability. This latter can best be achieved through employees increasing their output and efficiency.

Definition of profit sharing

The term "profit sharing" means different things to different people. In fact, the term has been broadened so greatly that it is now a very confusing concept. It is now often used to refer to such plans as cost-of-living adjustments, guaranteed wage arrangements, health provisions, incentive wage plans, bonus payment plans, stock purchase plans, pensions, and production bonus systems. However, it does not mean health insurance, a Christmas goodwill bonus, or any of a multitude of benefit programs. Although it is difficult to define the term, it is in essence a productive system under which all the factors of production in a firm are motivated through sharing—according to a given formula—in the operational gains—as measured by profits.

Regardless of the definition used, there are two tests that can be used in determining whether a given arrangement is a profit-sharing plan. The tests are: Does the extra compensation paid to employees bear some recognizable relationship to the firm's profit? Does management announce to its employees in advance, i.e., at the beginning of the period in question, that profits will be shared with the employees? In view of these two criteria, this study adheres to the definition of profit sharing as *the prearranged distribution of a specified percentage of the firm's profits to the workers, the proportion of earnings to be distributed to them being made known in advance.*

Types of plans

There is a wide variety of plans, but they can be reduced to three: *cash, deferred,* and *combination.* Under the *cash plans,* profits are distributed directly to the employees as current compensation, as soon as profits are determined. The payment may be in the form of check, stock, or even cash, and it may be paid annually, semiannually, quarterly, monthly, or at even shorter intervals, if feasible.

The *deferred plans* are characterized by the incentive earnings being credited to the employees' account, to be paid upon certain contingencies at a later date. These occurrences are retirement, severance, withdrawal from the plan, disability, or death.

Finally, some plans provide for part of the earnings to be in cash and part deferred. These are called *combination plans.*

Extent of usage

It is difficult to state exactly how many plans are in effect or how many personnel are involved, because of the difficulty of classifying the compensation programs. However, it is known that about one-fifth of the companies listed on the New York Stock Exchange (and these are the largest ones) have some such plans. (21) It has been estimated that the number of plans doubled each year from 1951 to 1967 when there were some 125,000 such plans. (22) According to the Profit-Sharing Research Foundation (PSRF), there were between 7 to 8 million employees under these plans in 1971. (23)

According to a National Industrial Conference Board (NICB) study, banks and retail and wholesale establishments use these plans more than manufacturers or insurance companies. (24) In general, *the larger firms use the deferred plans while the smaller firms use the cash programs.* It is felt that the larger firms use the deferred plans as a form of employee economic security, while the smaller companies use the cash programs as motivational devices. The firms with straight profit-sharing features have close to 100 percent of their employees participating in their plans, especially the white-collar workers.

Effects of using profit sharing

Henri Fayol believed that profit sharing would work among the higher managers, and probably among middle management, but not for the individual workers, because the relation between their added effort and the added profit was not understood by most employees. (25) This belief is still held by a large number of managers, but there is a growing belief that the plans are advantageous for all levels of personnel, if profits can be traced to productivity per worker and the time interval is not too long between performance and remuneration.

Benefits. This belief was confirmed in at least one comprehensive, long-range case study of the relevancy of a profit-sharing plan to the survival of an economic firm. Using the objective measures of profits, production, work force, average wages, and wage increments at the American Velvet Company, it was found that the economic status of both management and labor had improved during the 15 years the plan had been in effect. It was also found that profit sharing *accompanied* by effective joint consultation with the union "facilitates introduction of technological change and can partly insulate against the vagaries of adverse economic environment to the survival of an industrial organization." (26)

In another comprehensive study it was shown that over 80 percent of the plans were thought to be "very successful," around 15 percent were considered "so-so," while about 1.5 percent were judged "disappointing." (27)

The PSRF found that profit-sharing firms outperformed other firms by "substantial and widening percentages" from 1952 to 1969. (28)

Limitations. Probably the main limitation of this incentive device is the lack of understanding of what profit is and what causes it. The details of finance and accounting are often not understood by employees; thus, many of them do not appreciate the reason for setting aside reserves for contingencies or other purposes, or the necessity for building up a surplus for future operations. Human nature is such that one often counts anticipated gains or income as actual gains, with the result that if the anticipated gain is not achieved, it is considered as an actual loss. In other words, the workers may anticipate a certain share of the profits, and then when management is required to use large amounts of that profit for the replacement of machinery and equipment, or some other contingency, the workers feel cheated and resentful. Therefore, for any profit-sharing plan to be successful, there should be a close correlation between what the workers expect to receive in a financial way and what they actually receive.

Other limitations are that the rewards vary greatly, depending upon the business and market conditions (and the employees have no control over these variables); and the financial reward is too far removed in time and direct relationship to employee performance to serve as a strong stimulant to productivity.

Studies reveal increasing union involvement in profit-sharing plans (29) even though from 1961 to 1966 unions won only 44 percent of the representation elections at firms having profit sharing, as opposed to winning 60 percent in all other NLRB-directed elections. (30)

Evaluating the motivational effect of profit sharing

In summary, effective profit sharing can be considered as a motivational tool which can raise productivity significantly in our society, through the incentive of increased compensations and participation—the end result being the achievement of higher social goals.

A modification of profit sharing, which will be discussed in greater detail in Chapter 19, is the Employee Stock Option Plans (ESOP). In general, the ESOP borrows money, purchases a large amount of the employer's stock, and allocates it to the employees on the basis of salary and/or longevity. Each year the firm allocates a portion of its profits to be contributed to the ESOP fund, which, in turn, uses the money to pay off the loan. As the employees do not actually receive their shares until they retire or leave the company, the employees do not pay tax on it until they are in a lower tax bracket, and, even then, they must sell the stock before it is taxed as capital gains. The benefits to the company are: It provides a source of needed capital, boosts company cash flow, raises employee morale and productivity, provides new employee benefits, and encourages wider public ownership of its stock.

Some of the possible disadvantages are that, as employees become owners, management may find itself unable to make tough decisions that the workers oppose. Also, the workers may be putting a lot of faith in the employer for which they work, sharing losses as well as gains. However, these plans are now growing in popularity.

> Based upon the concept that the railroad industry is uniquely suited to employee ownership, Northwest Industries sold its Chicago and Northwestern Railroad to its employees in 1969. While it is not possible to quantify the benefits of this employee ownership, it has been claimed that "there is a new spirit in the company which is bound to benefit it." (31)

USING MERIT WAGE INCREASES AS STIMULANTS TO PRODUCTIVITY

As shown in the previous chapter, a policy of granting increases in wages based upon ability and merit, rather than upon seniority or a time interval, has potential incentive value for stimulating employee output and efficiency. When raises are based upon seniority or are automatic, there is a tendency to do just enough to get by and not to exert more effort than is necessary.

The logic of merit increases

Compensation based upon merit was first established on the premise that competition yields the highest benefit in terms of motivation, performance, and productivity. Therefore, merit compensation programs were designed to identify, appraise, and reward employees for making outstanding contributions to the organization's performance. If this be true, then salary increases should be directly related to the individuals' achievements relative to established objectives. Once these objectives are set, merit increase policies can be formulated so that: individuals performing below a "cutoff" line over two or three periods will be removed from the job; those whose performance was below, say, 95 percent would not receive merit increases; while those achieving above 95 percent would be compensated on a pro rata basis with higher merit increases, given at frequent intervals. (32)

The merit wage policy is usually adhered to in the upper brackets of an organization and can reasonably be expected to operate effectively for other levels. There must be some definite criteria upon which to base merit if inequities in rates are to be prevented. Some factors that serve this purpose are training, experience, know-how, absences, tardiness, accident rate, ability to get along with other workers, and production (which reflects the others).

Evaluating the motivational effect of merit increases

While many companies are today turning back to allocating pay on the basis of performance, in most large organizations, particularly public organizations, employees are caught in a highly structured and bureaucratic system where a high degree of individualism is discouraged. Instead, employees are in "lock step" whereby, if they are able to hang on for another year, everyone will receive essentially the same increase.

Yet, if merit plans are kept simple, so that all employees can understand that their compensation is related to their performance; if the plan receives support from top management and supervisors; and if the program is flexible, they should motivate employees to perform, develop positive attitudes, and have greater job satisfaction.

These observations were corroborated by a research study of 25 scientists and 13 research directors. There was great agreement among them that merit salary increases and promotions had "extremely high incentive value." (33)

A large Australian company established a salary administration program based upon counseling and appraisal. All employees worked toward specific goals which they helped establish, and they were regularly given the opportunity to discuss their performance and career interests with their managers. The result was an equal correlation between the employees' performance and pay. (34)

USING BONUS PLANS AS STIMULANTS TO PRODUCTIVITY

Another financial incentive that can be used to stimulate employees to improve performance is any one of numerous bonus arrangements. These vary in differing degrees from profit-sharing arrangements and incentive wage plans, but there are essentially two types. First, there are those tied to production; and, second, there are those which are not prearranged or based upon a proportion of the business profits or directly related to productivity. Included in this latter category are awards for exceeding production quotas; gratuitous payments (not directly associated with production) at Christmas, end of year, or other period; and many others. Usually this bonus arrangement has only an indirect relationship to the employee's productivity, for with the exception of wage incentive bonuses the remuneration is uncertain as to amount and continuity; these details are at the discretion of management.

There are two factors limiting the motivational value of this type bonus. First, if one is granted periodically, the employees view it as a right and take it for granted when it is received; and, if it fails to materialize, resentment is felt. If it is not granted regularly, it is not anticipated and comes as a windfall. In either case, production tends not to be increased as a result of the bonus. (35) However, some plans of this type do have an indirect stimulating effect through improving morale and cooperation.*

The first kind of bonus is one directly or indirectly tied to performance or productivity. For example, a study of 444 firms found around 65 percent paying a salary plus some type of incentive payment, including bonuses, for sales representatives. (36) Other studies found 39 percent of firms having their supervisors participate in bonus plans, and 45 percent of the firms had middle and upper management personnel participating. (37)

Conley Mill Works, employing 22 blue-collar and 5 white-collar people with supporting staff personnel, installed a plan providing a 5-percent bonus based on each worker's "gross earnings for the month" for every 10 percent rise in shipments. Sales have gone up, labor costs have gone down, and earnings have increased for: (*a*) the workers receive the bonus "immediately" after earning it; (*b*) the reward is large enough to be "significant"; and (*c*) the bonus is paid at a time different from the regular salary so that it can be considered as a "special bonus for exceptional performance." (38)

---

* Some companies are now using a bonus system to encourage attendance. If employees put in a full work week, they will receive a fixed bonus, such as 10 percent of their earnings.

USING COMPANYWIDE PRODUCTIVITY SHARING SYSTEMS

With the exception of merit increases, all the systems mentioned have posed difficulties for installing and maintaining. Second, technological change has made it difficult to measure individual or even unit performance. Finally, the pervious systems have *tended* to be based upon competition rather than cooperation between individuals and units.

Because of these factors, interest is now shifting to plans covering the entire plant or organization. (39) The five best known of these plans are the Scanlon Plan, the Rucker Share-of-Production Plan, the Nunn-Bush Shoe Company Plan, the Kaiser Steel Long-Range Sharing Plan, and the Lincoln Incentive Compensation Plan. Only the first four will be described, for the Lincoln Plan is, in reality, a combination of individual piece rate plans and group incentive plans.

These plans tend to be similar in that they offer everyone in the organization a bonus or some form of extra compensation, based on some measure of organizational performance. The bonus is usually a percentage of the base rate of each employee, so that bonuses are equal for those receiving equal wage or salary.

Scanlon Plan

Joseph Scanlon, a union representative, developed this plan in 1937 to help reduce costs in a steel mill. Since then, it has been used in other organizations, including union and nonunion plants. The plan is as much a union-management cooperative venture as a compensation, or motivating, vehicle.

The plans usually have two essential features, namely, a system of departmental and plant screening committees to evaluate cost-savings suggestions, and some direct incentive paid to employees to improve efficiency.

The usual results of these programs are: (*a*) employee willingness to accept technological change, including methods and equipment; (*b*) greater willingness of employees to help one another; (*c*) greater awareness on the part of employees of company problems; (*d*) a better work place and work climate, usually free of loafing; (*e*) less overtime, grievances, and waste; (*f*) better administration of seniority clauses pertaining to promotions, layoffs, transfers, and recalls; and (*g*) more employee insistence on efficient management.

Some problems are: (*a*) management's—particularly supervisory—fear of loss of authority; (*b*) problems caused by changes in product mix, the proportion of direct or indirect workers, and determining the ratio going to employees and the company; and (*c*) the difficulty of installing it in large organizations.

Rucker Share-of-Production Plan

While the Scanlon Plan is difficult to superimpose upon—or replace—incentive wage plans or profit-sharing plans, the Rucker Plan has been successfully added to them. The reason for this conclusion is that the latter plan is a much more sophisticated program based upon a careful analysis of historical relationships between productive value created by the firm and total earnings (direct and indirect compensation) of employees. Also, there are less adjustments in these plans than in the Scanlon Plan because of the careful analysis that goes into the original plan.

Nunn-Bush Shoe Company Plan

One of the oldest and most successful of these plans, and one which served as a kind of prototype of the previous two, was installed over forty years ago as a basis of sharing productivity and guaranteeing annual incomes. The plan has much cooperation between management and employees, although there is no union.

Kaiser Long-Range Sharing Plan

This program was worked out between the union and the company as a means of providing motivation to save on labor, materials, and supply costs. It is similar to the Rucker Plan in that it was based upon a careful study of company costs. The plan is quite complex, having some 16 objectives, including protecting employees against unemployment resulting from technological change.

Evaluating the motivational effect of these productivity sharing systems

It is difficult to evelute the motivational effect of these plans as there are so many of them, they are so varied, and usually there are so many organizational changes made when the plans are introduced. However, under the Scanlon Plan, productivity increases of 60 percent and increases in employee earnings of 50 percent have been reported. (40) In essence, they do increase cooperation but apparently do not have the same degree of motivational value as individual incentive programs because the connection between performance and compensation is broken.

Experience with the Kaiser Plan indicates that productivity increased fairly rapidly at first but tended to decline over time.

A survey of 21 plants having Scanlon Plans indicated employee satisfaction with this way of assessing organizational efficiency and compensating employees for improvements in that efficiency, based upon their hard work. (41)

At Parker Pen Company, bonuses ranging from 5½ percent to 20 percent of payroll have been paid in 142 out of 168 months. (42)

IMPLICATIONS AND APPLICATIONS FOR PERSONNEL EXECUTIVES

The assumptions underlying the motivational theory of wages are:

1. *Management desires to base its wage rates upon the concept of equity and fairness.* If this be true, efforts would be made to see that the employees'

remuneration is equitably related to the competitive market, economic conditions, the value of the job, and the value of the employee's contribution;
2. *Human wants are insatiable while the means of satisfying them are limited.* It is further assumed that these wants are both material and nonmaterial. The financial rewards, such as merit salary increases, incentive wages, and sharing of profits, are limited in supply and can be used only to a restricted extent in motivating employees by promising to satisfy their material needs. Conversely, the intrinsic rewards, such as interesting and challenging work, recognition, and achieving self-actualization, give satisfaction within themselves and can be used to an unlimited extent; and
3. *Employees have divergent capacities for job performance and those capacities are being only partially utilized.* Thus, regardless of the experience, training, or similar factors involved, some personnel will be better performers than others. Therefore, in order to stimulate them to produce at a superior level, remuneration must be provided that is proportional to their performance.

From these assumptions, it can be hypothesized that:

1. *Differential increments of income will produce differential increments of effort.* (43) Consequently, individual performance varies as the economic rewards vary. *The greater the amount of the reward, relative to the employee's economic needs, the greater will be its motivational stimulus to increase productivity and improve performance;**
2. *Individual performance varies according to the perceived value of the rewards and punishments received from management and the group.* (44) It follows that if individuals are rewarded *both* by management and the group they will produce close to the norms set by the group; if rewarded by *management* but not by the group, they will become high performers and approximate the standards set by management; but, if rewarded by the *group* but not by management, they will approximate the norms set by the group. If they are rewarded *neither* by management nor the group, they will be lower producers; and
3. *Employees' perceptions of the "fairness" of their compensation determines its effectiveness as a stimulus to productivity and performance.* (45)

The basic assumptions underlying this theory of the motivational effects of financial rewards needs revising. The concept of the employee as an "economic being" has changed to one of a socioeconomic being. Instead of considering employees as isolated individuals, their behavior must be viewed as part of the intergroup behavior of the organization. Rather than treating employees in a routine, mechanized, and standardized fashion, management must con-

---

* There is a point beyond which absolute financial increases will have a declining and less proportional effect as a stimulus to production and performance.

sider human values. The employee's need for money cannot be viewed in isolation; it must be considered as part of the interplay of various human needs. Finally, the reward, punishment, or stimulus-response system must be modified to consider the complexity of human behavior under complicated situations. (Human behavior is different from the animal response to reward or punishment symbols studied in laboratory experiments. Even in Ivan Pavlov's experiments, the animals failed to respond in the accustomed manner when the symbols were complicated.)

Up to the point of the attainment of a subsistence level, the material incentives do furnish the principal motivations for people, for at that level they think primarily in terms of keeping alive. As the quantity of goods and services available to them passes this subsistence level, the principle of marginal utility comes into play, and the inducement value of the nonmaterial incentives increase. In the higher income levels, the inducement value of money seems to be its prestige value rather than its purchasing power. For example, the editor of *Personnel Administration* was surprised recently to learn that money appeared to be the prime motivator of several electronics engineers who switched jobs. (46) This observation was particularly surprising because the companies that lost the engineers were considered to be among the most "enlightened and progressive." But upon investigating the cause of the switches, it was found that the engineers had not been motivated by money in itself but by its importance as equitable and timely recognition of one's contribution to the firm's total effort.

Conversely, for the rank-and-file production workers, the basic appeal to self-interest is found in systems of financial rewards that enable one to increase one's earnings by increasing output. Even the unintelligent employee, on whom the nonmaterial incentives probably have little effect, can be stimulated to further effort by the prospect of an additional monetary return. In the last analysis, financial incentives are the ones most generally effective. Upon them as a foundation, the rest of the incentive structure can be built; for without a satisfactory wage system, all other incentives lose their force.

In order to be effective in motivating employees to produce more, an incentive system must meet a number of criteria, including: (*a*) that the system be related to some behavior such as better performance (that is, higher production); (*b*) that the reward received through the plan be immediately received; and (*c*) that the employee be rewarded consistently through higher pay (that is, the payment is certain upon displaying a particular behavioral pattern). If these criteria are jointly considered by personnel executives in designing their compensation programs, performance should improve, as shown in Table 18–2.

In summary, as the economic functions of money are to serve as a standard of value, a storehouse of value, and provide purchasing power, compensation does motivate. However, its motivational value is limited for two reasons. First, there are other alternative motivational factors. Second, an organization's monetary resources are limited, so it must use other motivators.

TABLE 18-2
Financial incentives and criteria for improving performance

Type of incentive	(1) Related to behavior	(2) Immediacy of reward	(3) Certainty of reward
Merit increases	Sometimes	Sometimes	Sometimes
Negotiated increases	No	No	No
General increases	No	No	No
Production increases	Sometimes	No	No
Cost-of-living increases	No	No	No
Length-of-service increases	No	No	No
Profit-sharing plans	Sometimes	No	No
Bonuses and commissions	Yes	Sometimes	Yes
Individual incentive plans	Yes	Yes	Yes
Group incentive plans	Yes	Yes	Yes

Source: Reprinted by permission of the publisher from Harold F. Rothe, "Does Higher Pay Bring Higher Productivity?" *Personnel,* vol. 37, no. 4 (July–August 1969), p. 25. © 1969 by American Management Assn., Inc.

DISCUSSION QUESTIONS

1. What is the objective of an incentive wage system? Do you think this type of wage system functions well in contemporary American industry? Why or why not?
2. What are the advantages and disadvantages of the incentive wage system from the company's and the individual's point of view?
3. Why do certain industries use incentive wages more than the others?
4. What is profit sharing and what is the philosophy underlying the scheme?
5. How does money induce people to increase their productivity, and how do people relate their wage to the level of productivity?
6. Why is the concept of *differential* payment important for an equitable and motivational reward system?
7. What is necessary for merit increases to motivate?
8. Discuss the motivational value of companywide productivity sharing systems.

REFERENCES AND SUGGESTIONS FOR FURTHER STUDY

1. For example of this pressure, see R. E. Crandall, "De-emphasized Wage Incentives," *Harvard Business Review,* vol. 40, no. 2 (March-April 1962), pp. 113–16; "Is Incentive Pay Headed for Shelf?" *Business Week,* no. 1817 (June 27, 1964), pp. 51–52; and T. R. Brooks, "Managing Your Manpower," *Dunn's Review & Modern Industry,* vol. 84, no. 6 (December 1964), pp. 45–46.

2. Edwin C. Duerr, "The Effect of Misdirected Incentives on Employee Behavior," *Personnel Journal,* vol. 53, no. 12 (December 1974), pp. 890–93.
3. Joseph M. Sherman, "Incentive Pay in American Industry, 1945–46," *Monthly Labor Review,* vol. 65, no. 5 (November 1947), pp. 535–37. Fifty-six manufacturing industries, including 34,000 establishments with about 5.5 million workers were surveyed. The results included approximately 46 percent of these plants and 58 percent of the workers. Also surveyed were eight nonmanufacturing industries, including 21,000 establishments with about 1.5 million employees. The report included about 35 percent of these establishments and 40 percent of the workers.
4. Earl Lewis, "Extent of Incentive Pay in Manufacturing," *Monthly Labor Review,* vol. 83, no. 5 (May 1960), 460–63.
5. John H. Cox, "Wage Payment Plans in Metropolitan Areas," *Monthly Labor Review,* vol. 87, no. 7 (July 1964), pp. 794–96.
6. F. J. Roethlisberger and William J. Dickson, *Management and the Worker* (Cambridge, Mass.: Harvard University Press, 1939), p. 158.
7. Norman R. F. Maier and L. Richard Hoffman, "Financial Incentives and Group Decision in Motivating Change," *Journal of Social Psychology,* vol. 64, 2d Half (December 1964), pp. 369–78.
8. B. L. White, "Study of Employee Attitudes toward a Wage-Incentive Plan," *Personnel Practice Bulletin,* vol. 15, no. 3 (September 1959), pp. 30–38.
9. Owen Aldis, "Of Pigeons and Men," *Harvard Business Review,* vol. 39, no. 4 (July–August 1961), pp. 59–63.
10. Albert Ramond and Associates, *Bulletin,* June 1945.
11. John D. Dale, "Wage Incentives and Productivity," as reported in "Increase Productivity 50% in One Year with Sound Wage Incentives," *Management Methods,* vol. 15, no. 5 (February 1959), pp. 38–42.
12. Royal Fraedrich, "Incentive Wages Can Boost Production," *Big Farmer,* vol. 44 (February 1972).
13. Donald L. McManis and William G. Dick, "Monetary Incentives in Today's Industrial Setting," *Personnel Journal,* vol. 52, no. 5 (May 1973), pp. 387–92.
14. Dale, "Wage Incentives," *Management Methods,* pp. 38–42.
15. "Steel Answer: Incentive Pay?" *Business Week,* no. 1158 (November 10, 1951), p. 26.
16. Sylvia Shimmin, "Workers' Understanding of Incentive Payment Systems," *Occupational Psychology,* vol. 32, no. 2 (April 1958), pp. 106–10.
17. James W. Nutter, "Don't Let an Incentive System Place a Ceiling on Production," *Industrial Management,* vol. 12, no. 11 (November 1970), pp. 12–13.
18. See Lyle V. Jones and Thomas E. Jeffery, "A Quantitative Analysis of Expressed Preference for Compensatory Plans," *Journal of Applied Psychology,* vol. 48, no. 4 (August 1964), pp. 201–10, for similar statements.
19. Donald Schwab, "Conflicting Impacts of Pay on Employee Motivation and Satisfaction," *Personnel Journal,* vol. 53, no. 3 (March 1974), pp. 196–99. Reprinted with permission of *Personnel Journal,* copyright March 1974. His findings were summarized in the following tables:

TABLE 1
Satisfaction within each pay system

Pay satisfaction	Adjusted* Averages		
	(n = 128) Piece	(n = 84) Group	(n = 61) Hourly
MSQ	7.20	6.21	8.69
JDI	4.10	3.89	6.44

* Averages adjusted for any differences in pay and job level, age, tenure and sex.

TABLE 2
Motivation within each pay system

Motivation	Averages*		
	(n = 128) Piece	(n = 84) Group	(n = 61) Hourly
Pay valance	2.88	2.85	2.24
Performance-reward probabability for pay	4.46	3.95	2.03

* Scaled 1 (low) to 5 (high).

20. Alfred Marshall, *Principles of Economics,* 8th ed. (New York: Macmillan Co., 1948), p. 627. Also see Henri Fayol, *General and Industrial Management,* trans., from French, ed. by Constance Storrs (London: Pitman Publishing Co., 1949), p. 29.
21. "Companies Help Employees Acquire Stock," *Management Review,* vol. 50, no. 12 (December 1961), p. 61.
22. William J. Howell, "A New Look at Profit Sharing, Pensions, Productivity Plans," *Business Management,* vol. 33, no. 3 (December 1967), p. 27.
23. Bert L. Metzer, "Share Profits—Don't Freeze Them," *Personnel Journal,* vol. 51, no. 1 (January 1972), pp. 54–62.
24. National Industrial Conference Board, *Personnel Practices in Factory and Office: Manufacturing* (New York: Studies in Personnel Policy, No. 194); *Office Personnel Practices: Nonmanufacturing* (Studies in Personnel Policy, No. 197).
25. Fayol, *General and Industrial Management,* p. 627.
26. Ram S. Tarneja, *Profit Sharing and Technological Change* (Madison: University of Wisconsin, School of Commerce, Center for Productivity Motivation, 1964), p. 33. The research was done under a Johnson Foundation research grant for a doctoral dissertation at Cornell University.
27. B. L. Metzger, "Profit Sharing: A Cybernetic Response to the Challenge of Cybernation," *Personnel Administrator,* vol. 10, no. 2 (March–April 1965), pp. 26–30.

28. Metzger, "Share Profits—Don't Freeze Them," *Personnel Journal,* pp. 54–62.
29. I. B. Helburn, "Trade Union Response to Profit-Sharing Plans: 1886–1966," *Labor History,* vol. 12, no. 1 (Winter 1971), pp. 68–80.
30. Edgar R. Czarnecki, "Profit Sharing and Union Organizing," *Monthly Labor Review,* vol. 92, no. 12 (December 1969), pp. 61–62.
31. Johyn McClaughty, "Employee Ownership—A New Way to Run a Railroad," *Management Review,* vol. 63, no. 8 (August 1974), pp. 36–38.
32. For an excellent illustration of how this can be used in connection with MBO, see Ronald J. Hundady and Glenn H. Varney, "Salary Administration," *Training and Development Journal,* vol. 28, no. 9 (September 1974), pp. 24–28.

    For further information on how such a program actually works—using variable percentage increases and variable time periods—at Allis-Chalmers, see Roger Hubbell, "Making a Top-Level Performer Out of Your Merit Increase Program," *Administrative Management,* vol. 35, no. 7 (July 1974), pp. 45–48.
33. Albert A. Chalupsky, "Incentive Practices as Viewed by Scientists and Managers of Pharmacuetical Laboratories," *Personnel Psychology,* vol. 17, no. 4 (Winter 1964), pp. 385–401.
34. A. P. Groothuis, "Relating Salary to Performance," *Personnel Practice Bulletin,* vol. 30, no. 1 (March 1974), pp. 61–83.
35. It was found in one study that most employees did not like bonuses. They found it a very unstable way to be rewarded for their efforts because they could not understand the basis of the bonus. "Has the Bonus Carrot Lost Its Savor?" *Management Review,* vol. 58, no. 1 (January 1969), pp. 40–46.
36. Richard L. Smyth, "Financial Incentives for Salesmen," *Harvard Business Review,* vol. 46, no. 1 (January–February 1968), p. 110.
37. Dean Rosensteel, "Supervisory Compensation—An Interim Report," *Personnel,* vol. 33, no. 1 (January 1957), p. 354 ff.
38. Richard I. Henderson, "Money Is, Too, An Incentive: One Company's Experience," *Supervisory Management,* vol. 19, no. 5 (May 1974), pp. 20–25.
39. Based upon David W. Belcher, *Compensation Administration* (Englewood Cliffs, N.J.: Prentice-Hall, Inc., 1974), pp. 328–35.
40. Fred Lesieur and Elbridge Puckett, "The Scanlon Plan Has Proved Itself," *Harvard Business Review,* vol. 47, no. 5 (September–October 1969), pp. 109–19.
41. R. K. Goodman, J. H. Wakeley, and R. Ruh, "What Employees Think of the Scanlon Plan," *Personnel,* vol. 49, no. 5 (September–October 1972), p. 27.
42. R. A. Ruh, R. L. Wallace, and C. F. Frost, "Management Attitudes and the Scanlon Plan," *Industrial Relations,* vol. 12, no. 3 (October 1973), p. 282 ff.
43. Frederick W. Taylor, "Time Study, Piece Work, and the First-Class Man," in H. F. Merrill, *Classics in Management* (New York: American Management Assn., 1960), pp. 67–76.

    Tests were made in a study among the employees of a New York steel products manufacturer to determine whether, in spite of revolutionary social changes and unbelievable advances in technology, Taylor's concept of money as a prime motivator of human efforts is still a viable hypothesis. The results indicate that it is. For details, see H. J. Shapiro and M. A. Wahba, "Frederick W. Taylor—62 Years Later," *Personnel Journal,* vol. 53, no. 8 (August 1974), pp. 574-78.

44. A. Zaleznik, C. R. Christensen, and F. J. Roethlisberger, *The Motivation, Productivity, and Satisfaction of Workers* (Boston: Harvard University, Graduate School of Business Administration, Division of Research, 1958), pp. 436–37.
45. J. Stacy Adams, "Wage Inequities, Productivity, and Work Quality," *Industrial Relations,* vol. 3, no. 1 (October 1963), pp. 9–16.
46. Allan Young, "On the Line," *Personnel Administration,* vol. 29, no. 2 (March–April 1966), p. 60.

Chapter 19

Using employee benefits to reward loyal service

Background

Objectives of benefit programs
    Improve performance by improving job satisfaction
    Reduce labor turnover
    Increase security
    Benefits? Yes! Understanding? No!

What are employee benefits?
    The problem of definition
    The problem of classification

Extent of employee benefits
    Use of fringes
    Cost of programs

Legally required benefits
    Social Security
    Unemployment compensation
    Workers' compensation

Voluntary programs
    Supplemental pay
    Health protection
    Retirement
    Others

Implications and applications for personnel executives

Using employee benefits to reward loyal service

'Sugar in the gourd and honey in the horn, I was never so happy since the hour I was born.''
"Turkey in the Straw," an American folk tune

"Happy Birthday" means different things to different people. To many employees, it means a paid holiday or double pay if they must work that day. A group of supermarkets in the Los Angeles area provide free psychiatric treatment for their clerks and families. Some other benefits now being received are: hairpieces for bald persons; free apartment furnishing for single nurses, steak once a week aboard ships of the U.S. Coast and Geodetic Survey; day-care centers for working mothers; tension-releasing areas, such as gyms and chapels; and dental care, auto insurance, and legal services.

These are only a few examples of the many and varied compensation provisions that are commonly referred to as "fringe benefits."* These items are increasing in importance as part of the compensation package because bigger and costlier benefits continue to be major goals of today's employees.

The purpose of this chapter is to review the background of employee benefits, analyze their objectives, discuss the types of programs, estimate the extent of their use and costs to American business, and explore in depth some of the more important issues involved in this trend.

BACKGROUND

While present-day programs designed to protect employees against the basic hazards of life are relatively new, the inability to produce because of age or disability is not a new problem. Although complex industrial conditions have intensified some of the problems employees now face, the basic hazards have been of concern for hundreds of years.

---

* Although employee benefits have been provided by employers since the period of the guild system in medieval Europe, they began to be consolidated and considered as a separate aspect of employee compensation during World War II. The War Labor Board apparently was the first to use the term "fringe" to apply to the minor benefit awards employers were permitted to grant employees in place of direct wage increases, which were prohibited. Since then, as the number and cost of the benefits have expanded, the term has changed from "fringe benefits" to "employee benefits," or some similar term. Both these terms will be used interchangeably in this book.

The use of employee benefits began when the first *accident and death benefit* plans were initiated by industry in the early 1900s.

The next big expansion of fringes occurred in the 1930s when the government drastically expanded its interest in providing for the *physical and economic security* of employees. Also, as a result of the Hawthorne experiments, it had been concluded that job satisfaction led to increased employee productivity, and, in order to increase productivity, it was necessary to enhance job satisfaction. This premise led to the voluntary introduction of many benefits designed to "make the workers happy," particularly those *paying for time not worked.*

However, the greatest expansion of these benefit programs occurred during World War II, largely as a result of wage rates being frozen, but partly because of the efforts of unions and partly because of current managerial philosophies. Companies, which were desperate for labor, began to compete for the scarce workers by means of expanded employee benefits—usually *extra compensation for some good or service employees needed.* These were granted in addition to the basic wage.

Since then, emphasis has been upon pensions, retirement plans, and insurance provisions; shorter hours of work—for the same pay; and the underwriting of the changing life-styles of employees—including mental health, dental care, legal services, and day-care centers for working parents.

OBJECTIVES OF BENEFIT PROGRAMS

As indicated earlier, many of the more enlightened managers are beginning to take second looks at the employee benefit package. The spiraling costs of the programs are causing managers to wonder whether the purposes of the plans have been attained.

The original objectives of the plans were threefold: to create an atmosphere for improved morale and job satisfaction; to decrease excessive labor turnover costs; and to provide a sense of individual security against some of the employee hazards as well as some of the problems of life.

Improve performance by improving job satisfaction

The basic premise underlying the first objective is now becoming discredited. As has been shown throughout this study, the assumption that there is a direct and positive correlation between job satisfaction alone and productivity is being questioned. Therefore, even if these benefits did *improve morale,* they would not necessarily enhance employee productivity. For example, a study (using a classification scheme based on structural role theory) was done of the reactions of mine workers in Australia to additional benefits in relation to other elements of the work situation. (1) The additional benefits consisted of "excellent" working and recreational facilities, as well as the opportunity to purchase expensive household appliances at a discount—and without cash.

The workers perceived this device as an instrument for controlling the families' economic environment and a tactic for weakening union solidarity. While the employees used the recreational facilities, they compared them with those of competitive firms and treated them with indifference when their demands for better working conditions were not immediately met.

Reduce labor turnover

The objective of *reducing labor turnover* has been reached to an unexpected extent. First, the rate at which production workers are voluntarily switching jobs is less than half of what it was a decade and a half ago. (2) However, there is considerable speculation as to whether this trend is a desirable one. It was shown in an earlier chapter that rank-and-file employees are tending to become less mobile, while scientific, technical, professional, and managerial personnel are becoming more mobile. In many cases, the more proficient employees are leaving, and the ones who remain tend to be the least productive.

Increase security

It is now generally accepted that *security,* the third objective of benefit programs, is probably the most predominant wish of employees. Yet, there apparently is no correlation between the satisfaction of this need and the desire for productivity. There appears to be an inverse relationship, i.e., the greater the degree of security, the less productive the employee. Therefore, this objective seems to be self-defeating. However, recent research findings throw some light on this problem. First, findings permit tentative acceptance of the hypothesis that *the older the administrator, the more likely the belief that it is important for the organization to provide economic security for its employees.* (3) It was also shown that the greater the administrator's educational attainments, the less likely is the belief that security is important. Other general compensation preference patterns have been shown in other research findings. One finding which is germane at this point is that younger workers desire more base salary while older workers seek security. (4) Herein is a dilemma; the managers, who tend to be older, emphasize security, while their employees, who tend to be younger, prefer higher base salaries. Thus, the benefits do not achieve their objective.

Benefits? Yes! Understanding? No!

In view of the above discussion, it is easy to see why so many managers are unhappy with the increasing cost of the programs. Some employers object to the fixed nature of the costs associated with these benefits; others wonder if the advantages offset the costs; and some feel that industry "is encouraging socialism" and that employees should provide some of their own benefits.

Finally, there are so many employees who do not understand the benefits, their cost, or their purpose.

Permeating the above discussion is the unstated assumption that benefits have some motivational value in stimulating employees to greater productivity. Yet, current literature suggests that these programs have little or no incentive value but that they have a great potential for dissatisfaction. (5)

Studies show that employees do not know what benefits are provided or understand their provisions. For example, a study of 36,000 employees of 15 companies found that around 30 percent of them did not understand the company-provided benefits. (6) Although they add around a third to the employer's payroll cost, in nearly every case of poor understanding, it was found that the employees did not appreciate the benefits, nor did they believe they compared favorably with the benefits provided by other firms.

Later research revealed that employees could not even recall an average of 15 percent of the benefits to which they were entitled. (7)

> Shell Oil Company spent $153 million on various benefit programs for its employees, only to find out that they did not appreciate it. It was not that the firm was not spending enough, but it was not taking enough credit for the benefits. Its "Red Book" explained the benefits, but the employees did not read it. A new Red Book was printed clearly indicating to employees the amount the firm was spending on their "invisible paycheck." It also explained exactly what the employees were getting and the cost to them if they had tried to obtain the benefits on their own. (8)

WHAT ARE EMPLOYEE BENEFITS?

Today the employee's "pay package" is no longer easily divisible into "basic pay" and "supplementary benefits." Instead, employee compensation is a complex, integrated bundle in which the components are priced out and may be substituted one for another to arrive at an overall figure. Herein is another dilemma for the personnel executive, namely, determining what can be classified as "benefits," and what as "wages."

The problem of definition

There is no uniform definition for the term "employee benefits." The concept is so broad that it might easily extend from steady employment at fair wages to the payment of tuition for employees attending university management courses; or from comprehensive safety programs to interplant athletics; or from free meals to free psychiatric or legal assistance.

Figure 19-1 dramatizes this problem of definition. The percentage paid for benefits can vary from 33 percent, to 41 percent, to 49 percent, depending upon how you define them. Not including the premium payments as fringes, the average firm paid 33 percent in benefits in 1973. Not counting those payments

FIGURE 19-1
Annual average employee benefits and earnings per employee, 1973

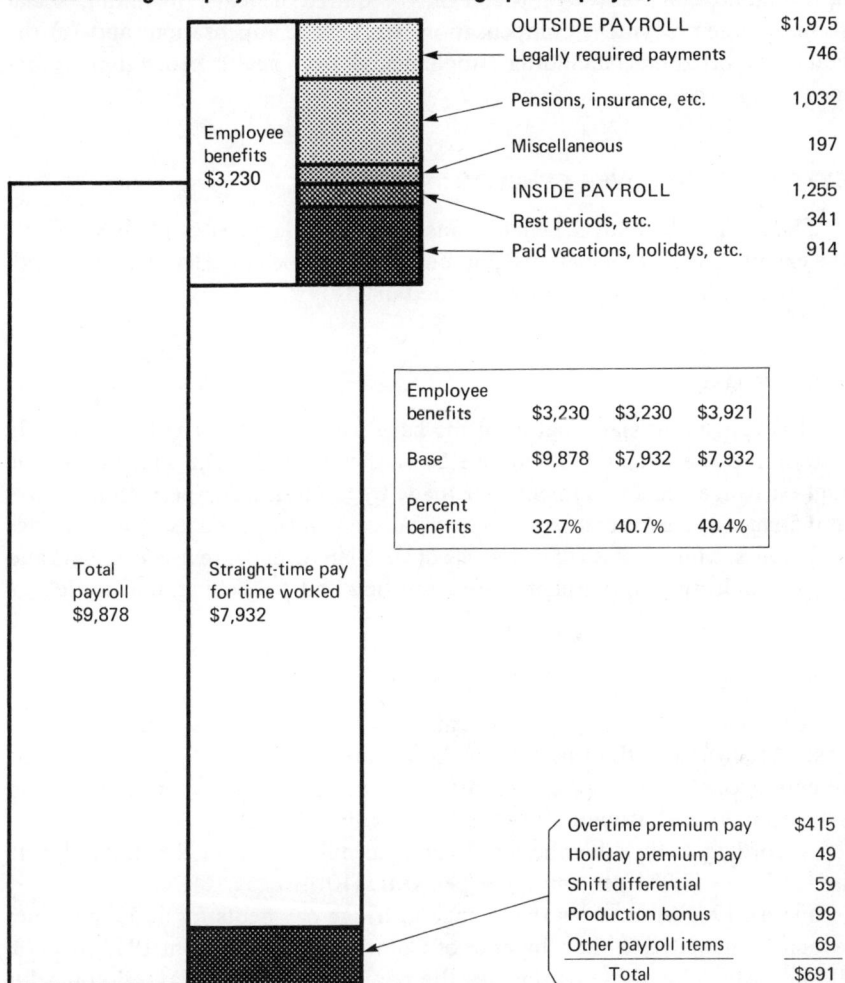

OUTSIDE PAYROLL		$1,975
Legally required payments		746
Pensions, insurance, etc.		1,032
Miscellaneous		197
INSIDE PAYROLL		1,255
Rest periods, etc.		341
Paid vacations, holidays, etc.		914

Employee benefits $3,230

Employee benefits	$3,230	$3,230	$3,921
Base	$9,878	$7,932	$7,932
Percent benefits	32.7%	40.7%	49.4%

Total payroll $9,878

Straight-time pay for time worked $7,932

Overtime premium pay	$415
Holiday premium pay	49
Shift differential	59
Production bonus	99
Other payroll items	69
Total	$691

Source: *Employee Benefits 1973* (Washington, D.C.: Chamber of Commerce of the United States, 1974), p. 26.

as fringes and omitting them from basic payroll, but omitting the payment for time not worked, the average firm paid 41 percent for fringes. Finally, counting the premium payments as fringes, and only using the time actually worked and paid for as the base, the average firm paid 49 percent for fringes.

The problem of classification

There is also no uniform method of classifying employee benefits. Yet, it is desirable to have some procedure for classifying them for comparative and analytical purposes. The system suggested in this text is that of the Chamber of Commerce, namely, (*a*) the legally required benefits, including social security, unemployment compensation, workers' compensation; and (*c*) the voluntary programs, including supplemental pay, health protection, retirement, and others.

EXTENT OF EMPLOYEE BENEFITS

The extent of employee benefits must be analyzed on a two-fold basis. First, the extent to which they are used in business must be considered; and second, the cost of the programs must be ascertained.

Use of fringes

It is realistic to state that all firms have fringe benefit programs; the only question is the extent of their use by individual industries and firms. The highest fringe benefit payments are made by the following: petroleum, banks and finance and trust companies, chemicals and allied products, and insurance companies. Making less extensive use of the plans are: the textile products and apparel industry, department stores, printing and publishing, and trade.

Cost of programs

Another way to gauge the utilization of these programs is through their cost. According to the Institute of the Future, from 1929 to 1967, the costs of employee benefits grew at the rate of 9.6 percent per year while wages and salaries increased around 3.9 percent annually. (9)

According to the Chamber of Commerce study, the cost for all employers in 1975 was $3,984 per employee per year. (10)

Figure 19–2 dramatizes the change in fringe payments for 155 companies which participated in the Chamber of Commerce surveys from 1953 to 1973. It shows that for those companies the percentage of total payroll going for fringe payments increased from 22 percent to 36 percent, the cents per payroll hour increased from $0.41 to $1.81, while the dollar per year per employee increased from $842 to $3,802.

In summary, considering all employers, employee benefits now cost around 26 to 38 percent of total payroll; $0.87–$2.01 per payroll hour; and $1,834–$4,258 per year, per employee.

LEGALLY REQUIRED BENEFITS

First, there are those that are legally required by state and federal laws. These include Social Security, unemployment insurance, and workers' compensation.

FIGURE 19-2
Comparison of 1953-73 employee benefits for 155 companies

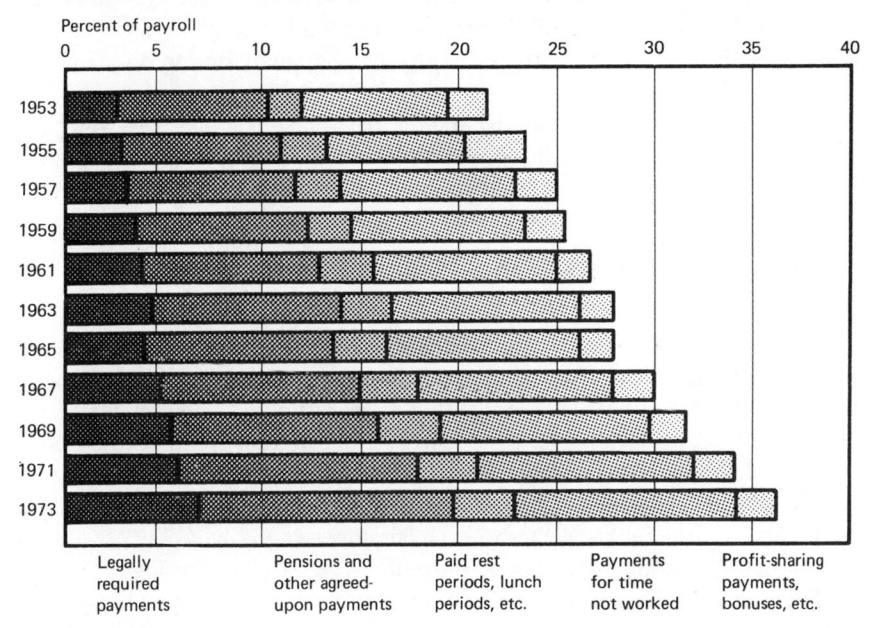

Percent of payroll, years 1953, 1955, 1957, 1959, 1961, 1963, 1965, 1967, 1969, 1971, 1973.

Categories: Legally required payments | Pensions and other agreed-upon payments | Paid rest periods, lunch periods, etc. | Payments for time not worked | Profit-sharing payments, bonuses, etc.

Source: *Employee Benefits 1973* (Washington, D.C.: Chamber of Commerce of the United States, 1974), p. 28.

Social Security

Old-age, Survivors, and Disability Insurance (OASDI) and Hospital Insurance (HI) benefits are popularly called Social Security and "Medicare." They are financed jointly by the employee and employer through payroll taxes imposed under the Federal Insurance Contributions Act and are often called FICA taxes. Amendments to the law in 1966 made the most drastic changes in the original Social Security Act since its enactment in 1935. Not only were OASDI benefits and taxes increased, but two new benefits were made available for persons aged 65 and over. Hospital Insurance and Supplementary Medical Insurance (SMI) together make up what is commonly called the "Medicare" program. As of 1976, OASDI and HI were financed by a tax of 5.85 percent of the first $15,300 of the employee's annual earnings, withheld by the employer and matched by an equal percentage paid by the firm. (11) The receipts from this tax are paid to the government and go into federal OASDI and HI trust funds. The federal government pays the OASDI benefits directly to eligible individuals, and HI payments are made directly to the hospital or handled through a private insurance company. SMI is a voluntary program, and those who sign up for it pay $6.70 a month and the federal government pays an equal amount. This program helps to pay doctor bills and provides numerous other health benefits and services.

Under this program, retired persons who are covered can start receiving retirement checks as early as age 62. Workers who become "severely disabled" before age 65 can receive disability income. If a worker dies, certain members of the family can receive either a lump-sum payment or monthly income checks.

Under Medicare, people over 65 and disabled persons under 65—who have been entitled to Social Security disability benefits for 24 or more consecutive months—receive help in paying their hospital and insurance payments.

Unemployment compensation

Unemployment benefits are paid by each state to unemployed individuals who are willing and able to work and whose former employment terminated under certain specified conditions. The amount and duration of benefits vary with each state and with each individual case, although amendments to the law in 1966 set up some federal standards. The program is financed by taxes which only the employer pays. The amount of tax *varies according to the individual firm's experience rating,* but in 1976 the maximum was 3.2 percent of the first $4,200 paid in wages to each employee annually. (12) This experience-rating factor encourages a firm to minimize its labor turnover.

The amount of compensation received by eligible workers, which varies among states, is determined by their previous wage rates and periods of employment. Usually the benefits are received for 26 weeks, but this is sometimes raised by Congress during periods of emergency. There is currently an effort to set federal standards requiring minimum benefit levels at 50 percent of a worker's weekly wage.

Research studies conducted by Ronald G. Ehrenberg of Cornell University and Ronald Oazaca of the University of Massachusetts indicate that an increase in unemployment benefits appears to increase the length of unemployment for younger males and females but induces older males and middle-age females to do even more productive job searches. (13)

Workers' compensation

All states have provisions whereby firms must make provisions for paying medical and hospital bills and partially pay for wages lost by the employee because of industrial illness or accidents. The entire cost is paid by the employer— either through approved insurance companies, special funds set up by the firm, or in state funds (considerable effort is being made by some states to make state funds mandatory).

For the employee who is the head of the household, workers' compensation is probably the most important of all benefits received, as it guarantees a continuation of income if one is disabled or dies. Also, the expenses for medical care and rehabilitation to return the employee to a productive life are paid by the insurance.

A secondary benefit of the system is the promotion of occupational safety

FIGURE 19-3
Major gains since 1972: Workers compensation benefits as a percentage of take-home pay

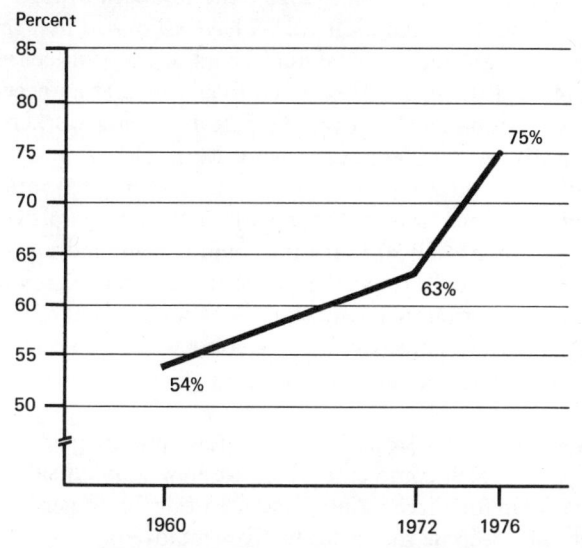

Source: "Modern Workers' Compensation," *Journal of American Insurance*, vol. 51, no. 2 (Winter 1975–76), p. 16.

through the economic incentives forced upon the employer. If the incidence of work injuries is low, the improvement is reflected in a reduction of the insurance cost. Thus, efforts by personnel executives to create safer work environments can reduce the total personnel costs of their organization.

As shown in Figure 19–3, workers' compensation benefits currently replace about 75 percent of the typical worker's spendable earnings, on the average.

VOLUNTARY PROGRAMS

The voluntary programs will be covered under the following headings: supplemental pay, including pay for leisure, overtime, and similar provisions, and unemployment protection; health protection and insurance provisions, including hospital and medical bills, sick leave, and life insurance; and retirement and others, including thrift plans such as stock purchases and bonuses and perquisites and job amenities.

Supplemental pay

Supplemental pay is provided for three types of activity, namely, increasing pay for time not worked, pay for working overtime or on special occasions, and unemployed pay.

Pay for time not worked. One of the main problems facing personnel administrators today is the increasing emphasis upon time away from the job—at the firm's expense. This practice takes several forms, namely, vacations, holidays, and time off for other reasons such as sick leave, jury duty, and compassionate leave. The long-range trend has been toward reducing the total number of hours worked each year. I have estimated that the work year has decreased from around 3,700 annual hours in the 19th century to about 1,800 now, (14) and the trend is expected to continue at an accelerated rate. It has also been estimated that over the past 100 years workers have made a lifetime gain of over 50,000 hours free of work. (15)

Paid vacations; bonuses in lieu of vacations. The original rationale behind granting paid vacations was to permit employees to improve themselves through rest and relaxation so that they could become more productive employees. Also, they could improve their material position by growing their own food, building or repairing their physical possessions, and in other ways. Now, however, vacations are considered as deferred wages. Payment for unused vacation time is, therefore, paid to employees when they terminate their employment.

Five-week periods away from the job are now commonplace. Also, in some industries, such as steel, some employees are now granted sabbatical leaves. These vacations are for three months and are designed to permit the workers to relax, rest, and become more productive employees.

It is felt that here is an area where the managers, unions, government, and individual employees can cooperate to help solve some of the problems caused by automation. If the workers were encouraged to take refresher courses, training programs, or otherwise develop themselves to satisfy the increasing needs of automation, they would become more productive.

Payment for holidays not worked or bonuses in lieu of such holidays. Most managers feel that workers will be more productive if they are permitted time off to celebrate holidays. This practice gives employees time to rest, relax, and get away from the routine of the job without fear of financial loss. Therefore, they should be better workers because of the improved morale and job satisfaction generated.

Pay for time spent on the job, but not working, such as for rest, lunch, washup, travel, clothes change, and get ready. The rationale for these payments is that employees need a break in the monotony of the job and provision for getting away from the routine of the work. Also, it is felt that they should be paid for work interruptions or delays beyond their control.

Pay for overtime and other special times. Today management has a new problem—workers no longer want to work overtime. The added compensation that overtime represents is not enough of an incentive to cause people to give up their leisure time. However, some organizations require overtime. Apparently women and young people are less willing to work overtime than other demographic groups. (16) There are several ways that management can overcome this difficulty. Using temporary help is one possible solution. Using workers from other parts of the organization might be another solution. Finally, compensatory time off might be used where legal.

Although the five-day week is still dominant, (17) variations are significant. In the first national survey of workweeks, the Labor Department found that, in May 1974, 82 percent of full-time workers put in five days; 1.1 million were on 3-to-4½-day schedules, including 653,000 working an even four-day week; and 16 percent of local government workers, 4½ days or less. (18) Even longer workweeks—up to seven days—involve 9.4 million workers. Mining and retail trade employees most often work more than five days.

Low pay influences many long workweeks. It was found that while five-day workers average $4.17 an hour those working six or seven days earn a little more than $3.60 an hour. Yet, workers on four-day schedules "were about as likely as five-day workers to be absent," the survey indicates.

Contributions to privately financed employment benefit funds. These payments are sometimes called by the misnomers "guaranteed annual wages," or "guaranteed annual employment." In reality, the payments to the employees are additions to their unemployment compensation payments and are designed to stabilize employment.

Research has consistently shown that workers prefer security and stability of earnings more than the opportunity of earning exceptional amounts of payment. During recent years, as workers have become more security conscious, the issue of stabilizing employment has become an increasingly important aspect of compensation.

There are two methods for assuring employees of regular incomes. The first is to guarantee them work, regardless of the amount of income. The second is to guarantee a certain amount of income, regardless of whether they work or not. One of the outstanding examples of the former is Procter and Gamble's plan; Ford Motor Company's supplemental unemployment benefit plan is an example of the second.

Guaranteed employment. The Procter and Gamble plan guarantees employees with two years of service 48 weeks of work at the standard workweek until the time of their retirement. Each employee is assured of 1,920 hours of work a year minus vacation time, paid holidays, and time off for floods, strikes, and other purposes. The company also reserves the right to reduce the standard workweek to 30 hours if necessary. The company reserves the right to transfer employees but only within rigid seniority provisions maintained in the employee's contract.

There have also been problems associated with stabilizing employment. Particularly because of the seniority provisions when a worker is transferred, there is the inevitable "bumping." This has considerably increased training costs. It is felt that in the long run this gives the firm a flexible work force, which is desirable. As the company has a policy of not changing methods until it is able to absorb the people, there has been a slowdown in the introduction of improved manufacturing methods.

"Guaranteed income." The *supplemental unemployment benefit* (SUB) plan is based upon the concept of employees working and drawing wages as long as they can; when they can no longer work, they receive unemployment

compensation from the state and other benefits from the company. In other words, the plan incorporates the philosophy of coordinating public and private plans for easing the problems of unemployment. (19)

The program is based upon the principles of limited liability, whereby the amount the company must pay is fixed, and of predictable minimum costs, whereby the company pays a fixed amount into the fund each year.

The plan, which was initiated in 1955 through agreement between the Ford Motor Company and the United Auto Workers, attempts to guarantee a certain level of income.

These benefits, added to the state unemployment compensation, will provide the unemployed workers with a given percentage of their straight-time pay after taxes for a 40–hour week for the first four weeks of layoff. After that they are assured of a slightly lower percentage of their straight-time pay. While it does not guarantee employment at a given wage, it does provide a means of economic security for a period of time.

As the more affluent plans provide the worker with up to 95 percent of usual "take home pay," they have led to a peculiar situation for the unions. As employees with the least seniority are the ones first laid off and as they usually do not have much vested interest in the SUBs, current proposals are now being made that where such a plan is in effect the workers with the greatest seniority be the first ones laid off.

Health protection

Another aspect of security is the desire to be taken care of during periods of illness, both for yourself and your family. The second large group of fringe payments deals with providing for medical and hospital attention, as well as providing pay while the employee is sick. Also, provisions are made for providing benefits in case of the death of the employee.

Life, sickness, accident, medical, and hospitalization insurance premiums, and death benefits. The potential inducement value of insurance arrangements resides in their ability partially to satisfy the workers' desire for security. For example, hospitalization and medical insurance benefits tend to put their minds at ease concerning the cost of medical care, even though the necessity for that care is not removed. Life insurance policies and death benefits tend to set their minds at ease concerning the loss of earning power suffered by their dependents in the event of their death.

Regardless of how effective such a medical program is, it rarely, if ever, covers all necessary costs.

Paid sick leave. These benefits are granted to employees as a basis for relieving them of the worry of financial loss resulting from conditions beyond their control. However, this arrangement can be easily abused and often is. The feeling that the employees have that much time coming to them seems to be prevalent. Therefore, frequently employees will take the time off, even if it is not entirely necessary. As a consequence, many organizations require a doctor's certificate as a proof of illness or will not pay the first day or two of illness. Some organizations even pay a bonus to workers for not taking their sick leave time.

At present, there is much controversy over whether pregnancy is a disability, resulting in paid sick leave. In one case, *Newman* v. *Delta Air Lines,* the court cited the 1973 EEOC guidelines dealing with pregnancy as not legally binding on the courts. Therefore, pregnancy was not considered a disability or sickness. In another case, *Wetzel* v. *Liberty Mutual Insurance,* it was determined that pregnancy was a long-term disability and was covered, as many ailments limited to men were, in the insurance plan. Therefore, the requirement that the employee return to work within three months after childbirth was in violation of Title VII. In December 1976, the Supreme Court decided, in the *General Electric Case,* that this is not so.

> Xerox Corporation began covering pregnancy in 1972 as if it were similar to any other injury or illness, namely, as a temporary disability. A study of 178 salaried employees whose pregnancies terminated in 1973 showed benefit costs averaging $1,544 per claim. Of the group, 82 returned to work, while 96 quit after receiving their disability pay. While time off ranged from 7 to 226 days, the average was 75. (20)

Retirement

For the last two decades, government, unions, and managers have cooperated to create new jobs for younger employees by encouraging and providing for early retirement of the older workers. As there was an excess of workers, it was deemed socially desirable to create jobs for the younger individuals by making early retirement attractive for the senior employees.

Rationale for retirement. Early retirement is nothing new. Miners have been able to retire at age 55 for some years now; auto workers, regardless of age, can collect $625 a month for life after spending 30 years in the shop; and military personnel can retire after 20 years service to pursue a second career. Federal Civil Service permits workers with 30 years of service to retire on full pension at age 55.

Many workers are tired of working and seek early retirement as a release; others are urged by management to retire early so the organization can reduce its employment in older employees. Regardless of which is the predominant reason, if either, the number of workers on early retirement tripled between 1964 and 1974, while the proportion of all retired persons doubled.

Feasibility of early retirement. Early retirement has become feasible by combining private pension plans with government retirement programs, such as social security. The result has been that the years workers spend outside the labor force have increased from 16.1 in 1900 to 25.2 in 1960. (21)

As shown in earlier chapters, there is now developing an acute shortage of skilled personnel. Governmental and industrial leaders are beginning to question the early retirement policy. It is felt that the current prosperity is creating labor shortages that are likely to become worse, and no longer is any social purpose served by hastening the retirement of experienced workers possessing productive skills that the economy requires. The present need is to find ways of increasing the supply of skilled personnel rather than trying to limit it.

Managerial approaches to retirement. It is generally accepted that a planned program of retirement to be successful must start 20 to 25 years before actual retirement. That time is required to build up enough financial resources in order to have sufficient income to enjoy the new life. Yet, employees are not doing an adequate job of self-preparation. Consequently, it becomes a function of personnel executives to see that this is done properly. For example, a study of those aged 35–64 found 97 percent believing in early planning but only 28 percent actually doing anything about it. (22)

A study was conducted in 28 firms to determine what business is doing about early retirement for executives. (23) The research found that approximately 75 percent of executive retirements, during the five years preceding the study, took place before 65.

Helping employees prepare for retirement. Research has shown that despite the same chronological age of workers, there are vast differences in their psychological ages. (24) It is felt that now is the time for management to return to the policy of using selectivity in retiring individuals just as it does in hiring them in order to conserve needed skilled personnel. Also, research has shown that *how* management handles the retirement of older workers has a great influence upon their perception of it as reward or punishment. (25) As they get older they tend to resent retirement for they perceive of it as an indication that they have become "social and economic castoffs." (26) The general profile of workers about to retire shows them to be in good health with their life centered around job and family. The research also indicates that the two primary problems of the retiree is how to spend the extra 172 hours per month and how to live on reduced income.

Personnel executives are now helping potential retirees adjust to these and their other problems. For example, a survey of 800 companies by the Conference Board showed that 88 percent of the companies gave preretirement assistance to their employees. This is up from 65 percent ten years earlier. Over 96 percent of the companies provided some form of postretirement assistance, even if it was only sending a list of publications with the pension check. As shown in Table 19–1, most of the preretirement assistance takes the form of providing financial information. Yet, other information is also provided.

Another problem personnel executives face is knowing what kind of assistance to give retiring employees. For example, an outstanding study of 200 retired employees showed a variation between the information sought by employees before retirement, the problems faced after retirement, and the information they then sought from the organization. Health was seventh on the list of preretirement information sought; it became the most serious problem of the retirees after retirement (27) (see Table 19–2); and it was the number one bit of information sought after retirement.

Retiree Problems
 also
Pre-Retirement Assistance

TABLE 19-1
Preretirement assistance given by 800 companies

Employees are offered	Percent of companies offering
No preretirement assistance.	12
Financial information only.	46
Financial and health information only.	21
Financial information, plus written counseling in other areas	8
Financial information, plus personal counseling in other areas	13

Source: J. Roger O'Meara, "Retirement—The Eighth Age of Man," *Conference Board Record,* vol. 11, no. 10 (October 1974), pp. 59-64.

Providing and protecting retirement benefits. During the last two decades, there have been dramatic improvements in retirement benefits for working Americans. According to the Bureau of Labor Statistics, 65 percent of private, nonfarm workers were employed in establishments offering pension plans. (28)

However, these dramatic improvements will probably not continue. Retirement experts say that workers and their representatives will find managers of pension plans struggling to find ways of providing the benefits already promised. Several things have happened to cause this, including the effort to protect and guarantee retirement benefits for employees. It has been estimated that the *Pension Reform Act* alone has added 5 to 7 percent to the average firm's annual pension bill. (29) The law was passed to protect and guarantee retirement benefits for over 30 million workers and to encourage the creation of new plans for 40 million other workers not covered. Indications are that it may be working in the opposite direction. In 1975, the last year when plans

TABLE 19-2
Seriousness of retiree problems

Problems	Rank of seriousness
Health.	1
Money and financial matters	2
Too much free time.	3
Lack of personal and social contacts	4
Food and nutrition.	5
Transportation.	6
Housing	7

Source: William H. Holley, Jr., and Hubert S. Field, Jr., "The Design of a Retirement Preparation Program: A Case History," *Personnel Journal,* vol. 53, no. 7 (July 1974), p. 529. Reprinted with permission of *Personnel Journal,* copyright July 1974.

could be dropped, almost 6,000—more than 4 times the expected number and 5½ times the normal number—were dropped, primarily by smaller firms. (30)

The Pension Reform Act provides considerable protection to present employees covered by a pension plan. Some of the benefits are:

1. Anyone is eligible for the plan, regardless of age;
2. Employees must be given a nonforfeitable right to the pension within 5 to 15 years, depending upon conditions;
3. Employers are responsible for keeping the fund solvent;
4. The surviving spouse must receive 50 percent of the employee's retirement benefits;
5. A federal agency insures the rights of employees and retirees in the fund regardless of bankruptcy of the firm;
6. Employees not covered by a pension program can set up an individual retirement account (IRA) or a Keogh Plan; and
7. The employees must be provided information and details about the program in language "the average employee can understand." (31)

Employers have several alternatives under the law. These vary from having no plan at all up to and including having a fixed benefit pension plan with a general benefit level providing predictable benefits to employees.

Others

Some other employee benefits which can be used by an organization are employee discounts, stock purchase plans, tuition refunds, educational benefits trusts, and others.

IMPLICATIONS AND APPLICATIONS FOR PERSONNEL EXECUTIVES

It is now generally accepted that organizations have a responsibility for maintaining steady employment or for assisting workers to overcome the ill effects of unemployment. In cooperation with governments, institutions have tried to fulfill this responsibility. Also, efforts have been made to permit the workers to retire sufficiently early to enjoy the benefits of their working life.

It is becoming increasingly obvious that these benefits are costly and that the employees should be apprised of this fact. Alert management will use research, analysis, and various control devices to maintain a competitive position relative to these benefits.

What choices do personnel executives have? An obvious—but not very feasible—alternative is to discontinue, or curtail, such benefit plans. However, in addition to the practical problems of making the conversion, the absence of benefits would negatively repel prospective employees, even though their presence does not attract new employees.

A second possible solution is to publicize company benefits through reports,

Co. Report to Employees on TOTAL Earnings

FIGURE 19–4
Company report to employees on total earnings

Your paychecks are the main measure of what your job at ════ is worth to you and your family. But since they are not the full measure of your **total** compensation, ════ has prepared for you . . .

a summary of what you really earned last year

1. YOUR CASH COMPENSATION for 1968 including base salary, overtime, bonus, commissions, etc.   **$ 22,958**

2. YOUR BENEFITS under the ════ Security Program as of Jan. 1, 1969

☒ Denotes **benefits** paid for entirely by ════
☒ Denotes benefits for which you contribute

AT YOUR DEATH before retirement

☒ Basic Group Life Insurance $ 48,720 •

☒ Voluntary Group Life Insurance $ 48,720 •

☐ Retirement Plan contributions made to Dec. 1959, plus compound interest to 1/1/69 $

Total payable at death from any cause $ 87,440

☒ Additional Accidental Death Benefits (voluntary) $ 80,000

•These benefits are normally payable in a lump sum, although you or your beneficiary may elect to have any or all of them held at interest or paid either in installments or as a life income.

DURING DISABILITY your benefits include

☒ Sick Leave, including disability benefits: based on your service, full salary of $ 2,030 a month continues for up to 4 months. If salary is continued for a period of less than 6 months, you can receive 65% of salary up to a maximum benefit of $100 a week for the balance of the 6-month period

☒ Long-term Disability Income Insurance (voluntary): $ 1,014 a month starting the 7th month and continuing while disabled until age 65, including any primary Social Security and Retirement Plan benefits that may be payable

☒ Basic Group Life Insurance of $ 48,720 continues to 65 if you are totally and permanently disabled

☒ Voluntary Group Life Insurance of $ 48,720 also continues to 65 if you are totally and permanently disabled and you maintain your contributions

☒ Additional Accidental Dismemberment or Total and Permanent Disability Benefits (voluntary)—up to $ 80,000

MEDICAL EXPENSE BENEFITS for you and each eligible dependent

☒ Hospital care: semi-private room and board plus other hospital expenses paid in full for up to *365* days, or up to *730* days if you have 10 or more years' service (120-day maximum for mental illness or TB)

☒ Surgical, anesthesia and obstetrical expenses up to reasonable and customary limits are paid in full if you are earning less than $7500 a year; or if you earn $7500 or more, these expenses are paid at the same level as for employees earning under $7500 a year

☒ Benefits for radiation therapy, diagnostic x-ray and laboratory examination, blood transfusions and doctors' hospital visits are also payable per schedules

☒ Extended Medical Expense coverage pays up to $20,000 in benefits per person (voluntary)

WHEN YOU RETIRE—income and insurance

☒ Income from the ════ Retirement Plan starting at age 65, approximately $ 762 a mo.
(for illustrative purposes, benefits are based on your 1968 earnings, excluding overtime . . . actual benefits will depend on average earnings in 5 highest consecutive years during last 15 years before retirement)

☒ Income from your Social Security starting at age 65, approximately $ 200 a mo.
(based on benefits payable under current law)
Total estimated income $ 962 a mo.

☒ Basic Group Life Insurance—minimum $ 12,180
☒ Voluntary Group Life Insurance—minimum $ 12,180

☒ Medical benefits are provided through Medicare (at age 65) and/or through Company Plans

3. YOUR "HIDDEN PAYCHECK"

For 1968, ════ contributed about $ 13,135,000 to provide the benefits outlined above for you and other salaried people.
Based on your earnings, your share of that was about $ 3,420 —including the Company's cost for Social Security, but not Workmen's Compensation and Unemployment Compensation.

Added to your cash compensation, your actual earnings for the year 1968 were thus: . . . .   **$ 26,378**

Source: Reprinted from "Turning Pay into Compensation," *Industry Week*, vol. 166, no. 15 (April 13, 1970), p. 33.

bulletin boards, house organs, and others. See Figure 19-4 for how one firm does this.

> Thiokol Chemical Corporation has attacked this problem by making its employees more aware of the extent of the company's—and their—contribution to the benefit program. It provides them with a report of both parties' contribution entitled "Your Annual Benefit Report." (32)

A modification of this publicity aspect is to provide an increased awareness of benefits by making employees choose which ones they want. These flexible benefits, or the "cafeteria" approach to benefits, has the advantage of forcing the employees to become aware of their benefits and to choose how they would like to receive these benefits.

> Around 11,000 employees at TRW's Redondo Beach operations have been given the opportunity to choose their own group insurance package, tailored to meet their personal needs. After information was sent to employees by mail, 80 percent of the employees requested some change in their hospital, medical, life, and dismemberment insurance. (33)

Finally, some form of control can be exercised over the expansion of these benefits. This is the approach most companies are now taking.

Regardless of management's perception of employee benefits, they are here to stay. In order *to attract and hold competent employees,* an organization must offer benefits that compare favorably with those offered by competitors. The great need is to balance the cost with the returns received in improved job satisfaction and productivity. This requires a different approach to benefit planning and decision making than has been followed by most companies in the past.

For employee benefits to be most effective, they must be geared to the preferences of employees. Recent research provides some general guides for the personnel executive's use. In general, as employees' income, age, and length of service increase, their attitude toward the fringes becomes more favorable. (34) Also, workers with favorable job attitudes favor sick leave, vacations, and pensions, while those with unfavorable attitudes prefer pay raises. Finally, clerical workers prefer vacations more than physical workers. (35)

DISCUSSION QUESTIONS

1. (*a*) What are employee benefits? (*b*) Why and how did they come into use in industry?
2. What are the major objectives of employee benefits and to what extent have these objectives been reached?
3. (*a*) Why is stabilized employment desirable from points of view of the individual and management? (*b*) What employee benefits would you apply to achieve that purpose?

4. What are the primary intentions of the legally required as opposed to the voluntarily arranged employee benefit programs?
5. Would you advocate letting all employees determine their own "compensation package"? Explain.
6. If employee benefits are not effective in motivating employees, then why do employers continue to use them?
7. Why would you, as a personnel manager, favor early retirement for the employees of your institution? Why not?
8. How would you go about preparing them for retirement?

REFERENCES AND SUGGESTIONS FOR FURTHER STUDY

1. R. C. S. Trahair, "The Worker's Judgment of Pay and Additional Benefits: An Empirical Study," *Human Relations*, vol. 23, no. 3 (June 1970), pp. 201–23.
2. Michael Reagan, "Fringe Benefits," *New Republic* (June 15, 1963), p. 7.
   Considerably more research needs to be done to determine the causes of this reduced labor turnover. It is not known to what extent fringe benefits have *caused* less turnover or if it *results* from other variables.
3. Irwin Weinstock and Arthur A. Thompson, "Administrative Sensitivity to Economic Needs of Employees: Some Distorting Mechanisms," *Academy of Management Journal*, vol. 10, no. 1 (March 1967), pp. 17–25.
4. Jay R. Shuster, "The Trouble with Employee Benefit Programs," *Business Management*, vol. 39, no. 6 (March 1971), pp. 34–37.
5. M. Scott Myers, "Who Are Your Motivated Workers?" *Harvard Business Review*, vol. 42, no. 1 (January–February 1964), pp. 85–86; Frederick Herzberg et al., *The Motivation to Work*, 2d ed. (New York: John Wiley & Sons, Inc., 1959), pp. 59–83.
6. David A. Harrington, "How to Improve the Return from Your Fringe Benefit Program," *Personnel Journal*, vol. 49, no. 7 (July 1970), pp. 604–5.
7. William B. Werther, Jr., "A New Direction in Rethinking Fringe Benefits," *MSU Business Topics*, vol. 22, no. 1 (Winter 1974), pp. 35–40.
8. Vernon, "Extra Benefits: A Two-Way Street," *Nation's Business*, vol. 62, no. 9 (September 1974), pp. 55–56.
9. T. J. Gordon and R. E. LeBleu, "Employee Benefits, 1970–1985," *Harvard Business Review*, vol. 48, no. 1 (January–February 1970), pp. 93–107.
10. Economic Analysis and Study Group, Chamber of Commerce of the United States, *Employee Benefits 1975* (Washington, D.C., 1976). This series of studies is probably the most comprehensive pertaining to this topic. Much of the information in this chapter is influenced by this study.
11. The rate is already scheduled to increase to 6.05 percent for each of them in 1978; 6.30 in 1981; and 6.45 in 1986.

    For self-employed persons, the figure is 7.9 percent, and they pay the total amount themselves. The rates are to increase to: 8.10 percent in 1978; 8.35 in 1981; and 8.50 in 1986.

    The base is expected to rise automatically to $16,500 in 1977 and to $21,600 by 1980.

The tax rate and the base upon which it is levied is subject to regular modification by Congress, so call the local Social Security office for the latest figures.
12. This 3.2 percent is divided into 0.5 to the federal government—to cover administrative costs—and 2.7 to the state where it is collected. The benefits to unemployed persons come from this latter fund.
13. Reported in the *Wall Street Journal* (October 6, 1975), p. 10.
14. Leon C. Megginson and Kae H. Chung, "Human Ecology in the Twenty-First Century," *Personnel Administration*, vol. 33, no. 2 (May–June 1970), p. 52.
15. Lillian Harris, "Work and Leisure: Putting It All Together," *Manpower*, vol. 7, no. 1 (January 1975), pp. 23–26.
16. W. N. Penzer, "When They Don't Want Any Overtime," *Supervisory Management*, vol. 18, no. 11 (November 1973), pp. 2–7.
17. Partially because of the large number of unemployed resulting from the recent recession and partly as a long-term goal, labor unions are now trying to reduce the workweek to 32–35 hours without any reduction in pay. Regardless of what happens in the bargaining, though, workers already are putting in fewer hours. Since 1947, the average hours worked per week in nonfarm businesses fell from 40.3 to 36.1, or a decline of 10.4 percent, regardless of recessions or economic booms.

    The UAW obtained seven extra days off, with pay, from Ford Motor Company in 1976, for a total of 40 paid days off.
18. "How Many Days Make a Workweek?" *Wall Street Journal* (June 24, 1975), p. 1.
19. See "Three Studies of Employee Benefit Plans," *Monthly Labor Review*, vol. 89, no. 4 (April 1966), pp. 381–95, for a study of supplemental unemployment benefits, which are a form of guaranteed income.
20. *U.S. News & World Report* (May 13, 1974), p. 59.
21. Stuart H. Garfinkle, "The Length of Working Life for Males, 1900–1960," Manpower Report No. 8 (Washington, D.C.: U.S. Department of Labor, Office of Manpower, Automation, and Training, July 1963), p. 7.
22. Patricia L. Kasschaw, "Reevaluating the Need for Retirement Preparation Programs," *Industrial Gerontology*, vol. 1, no. 1 (Winter 1974), pp. 42–59.
23. James Walker, "The New Appeal of Early Retirement," *Business Horizons*, vol. 18, no. 3 (June 1975), pp. 43–48.
24. Allen R. Salem, "A Study of Reactions to Retirement," *Personnel Administration*, vol. 26, no. 3 (May–June 1963), pp. 8–16.
25. Gerald Gallop, "Retirement—Reward or Punishment," *Personnel Journal*, vol. 49, no. 4 (April 1970), pp. 338–40.
26. " 'Senior Power'—A Growing Force in Politics," *U.S. News & World Report*, vol. 70, no. 21 (May 24, 1971), p. 66. This article is an excellent analysis of problems facing today's older people.
27. See William H. Holley, Jr., and Hubert S. Field, Jr., "The Design of a Retirement Preparation Program: A Case History," *Personnel Journal*, vol. 53, no. 7 (July 1974), pp. 527–30 and 535, for an excellent presentation of a retirement program which reflects the needs of employees and yet meets company objectives.

28. These plans were distributed as follows: manufacturing, 79 percent; nonmanufacturing, 55 percent, with trade and services having only 48 percent and mining having 89 percent; unionized firms, 91 percent; nonunionized firms, 52 percent; office personnel, 72 percent; nonoffice, 58 percent; establishments with over 500 employees, 93 percent; 100–499 employees, 76 percent; and less than 100 employees, 38 percent. See Donald R. Bell, "Prevalence of Private Retirement Plans," *Monthly Labor Review,* vol. 98, no. 10 (October 1975), pp. 17–20.

29. See "Why Bigger Pensions Will Be Harder to Come By," *U.S. News & World Report* (March 15, 1976), p. 77–79, for further details.

30. A.S.P.A., *Washington Newsletter* (March 10, 1976).

31. See Donald G. Carlson, "Responding to the Pension Reform Law," *Harvard Business Review,* vol. 52, no. 6 (November–December 1974), pp. 133–45, for an excellent analysis and timetable for the law.

32. L. W. Littig, "Personalizing Company Benefits," *Personnel Journal,* vol. 45, no. 7 (July–August 1966), pp. 417–18.

33. "Flexible Benefits: How One Company Does It," *Personnel Administrator,* vol. 19, no. 8 (November 1974), p. 51.

34. Mark R. Greene, "Fringe Benefits or Salary?" *Journal of Marketing,* vol. 27, no. 4 (October 1963), pp. 63–68.

35. Stanley M. Nealey, "Pay and Benefit Preference," *Industrial Relations,* vol. 3, no. 1 (October 1963), pp. 17–28.

Chapter 20

Using discipline as a penalty system

Current concepts of discipline
  Positive and negative discipline
  Practical definitions

How discipline is achieved under the judicial due process
  Major disciplinary problems
  Establishing rules for conduct
  Penalties for violating rules
  Disciplinary procedure to be followed

Authority for administering discipline
  The role of the supervisor
  The role of unions

Discipline in nonbusiness organizations

Implications and applications

20
Using discipline as a penalty system

"No man is free who cannot command himself."
PYTHAGORAS

"Good order is the foundation of all good things."
BURKE

George Meany, head of the AFL-CIO, called the Massachusetts chiefs of that organization to Washington and ordered them to rescind an antibusing resolution they had passed at their state convention. If they did not, they would be suspended.

That *Wall Street Journal* news item illustrates the use of discipline by nonbusiness organizations. The use of discipline as a penalty—or negative reward—system is found in all types of institutions.

Implicit in the discussion of reward systems in previous chapters has been the need for discipline to achieve personnel effectiveness, for effective performance requires the maintenance of discipline (internally and externally imposed) by both managerial and nonmanagerial personnel.

The material in this chapter is based upon the assumption that employees prefer to work with a well-organized, well-trained, and well-disciplined group rather than with one that is not. It has been shown that employees want to be supervised on "an adequate scale," "not too much—but also not too little." (1) While individuals do not want to be personally disciplined, they do want to work in a disciplined group, for they benefit from discipline and suffer from disorder. Successful supervisors know how to find this middle road that allows their subordinates to know exactly what they can and cannot do.

Empirical research has shown that the traditional approaches to discipline have been, and still are, effective motivational factors in cases where the individual is to be informed of a single mistake. (2) However, in recurring cases it is of little value. In fact, even the newer methods do not always provide solutions to all cases of deviant behavior.

The purpose of this chapter is to determine what discipline is, how it is achieved under the judicial due process method, the authority for administering discipline, and discipline in nonbusiness organizations.

CURRENT CONCEPTS OF DISCIPLINE

When asked the meaning of the word "discipline," even learned persons will at first associate it with the act of punishment. This is no coincidence, for discipline, in its narrowest sense, is used to refer to the act of imposing penalties for "wrong" behavior. But this is only part of the meaning of the word. There is also a positive element in discipline. As the word "discipline" is derived from the word "disciple" meaning "a follower," the implication is that good discipline presupposes good leadership.

Positive and negative discipline

As can be seen from these three practical definitions, discipline can be positive and activating, or it may be negative and restraining. In either case, it is the force which prompts an individual or group to observe policies, rules, regulations, and procedures that are deemed necessary to the attainment of objectives.

Positive discipline. The positive type provides workers with greater freedom of self-expression. It promotes emotional satisfaction instead of emotional conflict and results in coordination and cooperation with a minimum need for formal authority. It can be achieved best when group objectives and procedures are well known and are a basis for individual behavior.

One form of positive discipline is the *preventive method*. The best way to deal with problem workers is not to hire them in the first place. Know the details of the job to be filled, try to spot nonwork-related factors in the individual's background which might cause problems. For workers already on the payroll, learn as much as you can about what is really wrong with them. Is the employee lacking in skill? Are there psychological problems—on the job or off the job? The personnel manager might find that the supervisor is part of the disciplinary problem. (3)

Positive discipline, as exemplified by the previous illustration, is based upon the principles of "respondent conditioning" and "operant conditioning." *Respondent conditioning* says that anything which is consistently paired with something else will eventually produce the same response as the first thing. *Operant conditioning* says that you can increase the frequency of an action by following it up as quickly as feasible with a positive reward.

A classic example of discipline without punishment has been in effect several years at a plywood mill in Canada. (4) (See Appendix A for how the plan works.)

Negative discipline. Negative discipline involves force or an outward influence. This type of discipline need not be extreme and it is used best in organizations *only* when the positive type fails. Force will often cause a person to change outwardly but not mentally and emotionally.

As the choice as to which type of discipline to use resides with each manager, no generalizations can be made at this time. Suffice to say, effective personnel managers will vary the type of discipline used to suit the situation and their subordinates. (5) Yet, they need to beware, for threats create a state of anxiety in workers and tend to lead to poor performance. (6)

Practical definitions

The term "discipline" has three meanings in this book. They are:
1. Self-discipline;
2. The necessary condition for orderly behavior; and
3. The act of training and punishing.

Discipline as self-control. The first meaning of the word maintains that discipline is training that corrects, molds, strengthens, or perfects. Discipline, in this sense, refers to the development of an individual, i.e., one's efforts at self-control for the purpose of adjusting oneself to certain needs and demands. This may be called self-discipline.

It is self-evident that self-discipline is extremely important in administrators, managers, and supervisors. If they do not have control, how can they instill it in their subordinates? Even if they do have it, there is still a potential danger, for research indicates that attempts by managers to indicate improvement needs to employees are likely to be perceived by the subordinates as threats to their self-esteem. (7) This, in turn, leads to defensive behavior.

This form of discipline is based upon two psychological principles. First, *punishment seldom produces desired results and often produces undesired results.* Second, *a self-respecting person tends to be a better worker than one who is not.* (8)

Discipline as conditions of orderly behavior. The second concept considers discipline as the condition necessary to obtain orderly behavior in an organization. This implies keeping order and individual employee control among a group of workers by using methods that build morale and *esprit de corps*.

An experimental study has shown the validity of this statement, for it showed that obedience is one of the most basic elements in the structure of social life. (9) It was shown that the subjects of the experiment acted against their own value system and often expressed bitter disapproval of the orders but, nevertheless, obeyed the orders given to them. When the above conditions prevailed, there was considerable tension generated between the subjects and the order given.

The existence of these standards of behavior is but one of the necessary elements; the members of the organization have to accept them and adhere to them for effectiveness. This acceptance is often difficult because of the contradictory behavior of management. For example, a study of 100 large- and medium-sized firms found that while less than 50 percent of them had written policies concerning discipline of clerical and white-collar workers 70 percent of them did penalize employees for excessive absenteeism. (10)

Discipline as the judicial due process. The third concept considers discipline as a judicial due process based upon training and punishing. Thus, discipline is a form of punishment which a person incurs as a result of an undesirable act. Its function is not to change past behavior but to prevent a recurrence of the act in the future. (11)

As applied to modern personnel management, judicial due process involves establishing "laws," or rules which cannot be violated with impunity; setting specific penalties for infringements upon these rules, with progressive degrees in the severity of penalties; and imposing the penalties upon infractors only after determining the extent of guilt, and taking any mitigating circumstances into consideration. (12)

The due-process concept is based upon four assumptions which are usually upheld by arbitrators. These are: *(a)* the rules must be "reasonable"; *(b)* employees must have a clear idea of what is expected of them; *(c)* the employer has a right to have a well-disciplined, cooperative work force; and *(d)* managers have the authority to administer discipline when rules are violated.

HOW DISCIPLINE IS ACHIEVED UNDER THE JUDICIAL DUE PROCESS

In reality, the act of punishing or applying disciplinary action cannot be studied by itself. It is necessary to study it through the grounds for disciplinary action, the procedure followed, and the penalties imposed. (13) These will now be discussed.

Major disciplinary problems

One of the best studies of the extent of disciplinary problems was done by the Bureau of National Affairs Personnel Policies Forum in 1973–74. (14) It found that the most serious disciplinary problems in the firms studied—from the point of view of frequency and occurrence—included absenteeism and/or tardiness, 79 percent; productivity, poor work habits and/or attitudes, 11 percent; and others, 16 percent. (See Table 20–1.)

Another way of classifying these problems is by the severity of the consequences of the actions. One such system, which has proven to be applicable to the world of work, is:

1. *Minor infractions* which do little harm or result in few serious consequences when viewed in isolation, but may be serious when they accumulate;
2. *Major violations* that substantially interfere with orderly operations; and
3. *Intolerable offenses* of such drastic—or illegal—nature that they severely strain or endanger employment relationships. (15)

Minor infractions. Absenteeism and tardiness are the most prevalent types of minor infraction. (16) The problems seem to center around a failure to be

TABLE 20-1
Seriousness of employee discipline problems (percent of companies)

	Type of industry			Size		All companies
	Manu-facturing	Nonmanu-facturing	Non-business	Small	Large	
Most serious disciplinary problem today*						
Absenteeism and/or tardiness	84	73	77	84	75	79
Productivity, poor work habits and/or attitudes	10	11	15	8	14	11
Other (see discussion)	13	22	17	20	14	16

* Percentages add to more than 100 because responses fell in more than one category.
Source: *Employee Conduct and Discipline* (Washington, D.C.: Bureau of National Affairs, Personnel Policies Forum, Survey No. 102, August 1973), p. 2.

present when needed, without apparent regard or consideration for others. Some variations of this problem are taking too long for breaks, leaving early, and being "missing in action."

How to handle unscheduled absences is a growing problem for personnel executives. During the last decade, the problem grew in intensity and severity—but seems to be leveling off now. (17) The level of short-term unscheduled absences is about three-fourths greater than long-term absences. However, the rate of absences for a period is a function of the industry, occupation, sex, and age. Railroads and other transportation, mining, and medical and hospitals have the highest absence rates. Wholesale trade; other professionals; and finance, insurance, and real estate have the lowest rate.

Managerial and professional and technical employees have the lowest rate; while operatives, laborers, and service personnel have the highest rate.

Some other minor infractions are negligence, "horseplay," minor violation of a rule, wage garnishment, and carelessness.

Major violations. The most frequent major violations center around failure to carry out orders, lying, cheating, stealing, and violating safety rules. A typical example is refusing to carry out instructions.

Intolerable offenses. There are some offenses so grave, and whose consequences are so serious, that they are decreed to result in immediate discharge. Some examples are possession of, and threat to use, weapons; the use of "hard drugs" and narcotics on the job; fighting resulting in serious harm to others; serious theft; falsifying employment documents; willful destruction to property; and smoking in an area of inflammables—if it is posted.

The nature of the organization's operations determines what is an intolerable offense, as what is acceptable in one type industry might not be in another. A head nurse in a large hospital explained such a situation.

I am responsible for staffing units for best coverage on the 3 to 11 shift. Saturday, when staffing was short, we had an unusual amount of admissions because of an explosion about 10 miles away. The house was very busy, especially on medical units. There were four employees on each unit, except one unit had five people—three nurses and two nurses aides. The intensive care unit desperately needed another nurse. Joe Blo, my only male nurse on duty, was versatile and able to care for male patients.

I asked Mr. Blo to work on the busy unit. He became very angry and stated that if he were not needed on his assigned unit he would go home and come back when he was needed. I gave him every opportunity to work, explaining that he was my choice because he was flexible, knowledgeable, and could help with the male patients. He became hostile and said I was unfair, that I always asked him to do extra work because he was the only male in the house. This may have been true, as male nurses are in the minority.

He was so upset I could not reason with him. I told him it was his decision if he left and not mine, but I felt as if he would be making a mistake. I also informed him that it would mean termination if he left a nursing unit understaffed.

Mr. Blo clocked out and left. He was terminated at that time.

Safety. Partly for humanitarian reasons and partly as a result of the Occupational Safety and Health Act, safety violations are now being considered as a major, or even intolerable, offense, depending upon the severity of the infraction. Some of the most severe penalties are being imposed for the more flagrant and repeated violations. (18) (This law will be discussed in detail in Chapter 24.)

Establishing rules for conduct

As with any other judicial due process, rules of behavior should be predetermined and announced. If employees are expected to adhere to the rules and regulations, then they must know what they are and what their leeway is in adhering to them. (19) In most organizations, there is some form of statement of expected conduct. Such formal rules were found in 85 percent of the companies participating in the PPF study. As expected, the larger organizations followed this practice more frequently than the smaller ones.

Even in those organizations without formal rules, there are instructions as to expected behavior and employees know that they will be formally or informally appraised of their conduct in performing their job.

In unionized organizations and in many public organizations, there will be stated penalties for infraction of the rules (See Appendix B for an example from a large unionized manufacturing plant).

Penalties for violating rules

This indiscriminate use of dismissal, as well as management's carelessness in selecting penalties, has been a major flaw in administering discipline and has led to the unionization of many organizations. The type and variety of penalties to be used, as well as the manner in which they are employed, are usually limited by contract, by the fear of entry of a union, and/or by governmental action. (20)

Types of penalties. The main types of penalties are the following. First, there is the simple *oral warning* which is not placed on the employee's record but can be recalled as evidence later on. Actually, it is inadmissible as a basis of proof and is usually only intended to be instructional.

Next, the *oral warning which goes on the employee's record* helps avoid the charge of gathering evidence after the fact.

The *written reprimand,* which usually comes from a source higher than the immediate supervisor, is more official and may be challenged by the employee.

Suspension, which usually consists of a layoff lasting from a short period of days to a number of months, is an even more serious penalty.

The ultimate penalty is the *discharge,* which constitutes a break in service and wipes out the worker's seniority. Most arbitrators are reluctant to sustain a discharge because it is the economic equivalent of capital punishment, especially since it affects a person's family, as well as the individual. Justification must be strictly established, as discharge is almost always subject to the grievance procedure and arbitration. Most arbitrators tend to be influenced by whether the facts upon which the discharge was based were accurate, whether the penalty was excessive in light of the offense, and by the individual's past record.

Some other penalties used are *demotions, transfers,* and *withholding benefits* such as promotions, raises, or bonuses. Demotion or transfer is generally used only if the employee is still of value to the organization but is involved in a personality clash, or is on a job which is above the individual's ability.

It should be remembered when imposing penalties that employees want to know that their treatment will be equal under equal conditions and that *it is the offensive action which is being punished and not the workers themselves.*

Using graduated code of penalties. Unions and most personnel executives favor some type of graduated code of penalties which become increasingly severe after the first violation. One of the main advantages of this arrangement is that it tends to be standardized and consistent.

In a graduated plan, the first time a *serious offense* (theft, for example) is committed, the person may be discharged. For other less serious acts, punishment will become more severe with each offense. For example, there may be *(a)* an initial oral warning, *(b)* a written warning, *(c)* a suspension, and *(d)* discharge.

Disciplinary procedure to be followed

Adherence to established orderly procedures is the essence of the due process concept of discipline. As injustice thrives on privacy, the best guarantee of truth is the free exchange of views in an open forum between the accused,

FIGURE 20–1
An example of disciplinary procedure using graduated penalties

Offenses	Enforcement			
	First Action step	Second action step	Third action step	Fourth action step
Minor Minor infractions which do not do great damage or have serious consequence when viewed individually but may be considered serious when accumulated.	Education and informal warning or warnings by first-line supervisor.	Warning in presence of union representative by first-line supervisor.	Warning or written reprimand by higher supervision in presence of union representative; and/or suspension up to 2 days.	Becomes a major offense and is handled accordingly. (Does not necessarily involve immediate suspension.)
		Second offense	*Third offense*	
Major Violations that substantially interfere with production or damage morale; or when seriousness of offense is apparent to a reasonable mind; or an accumulation of minor offenses.	*First offense* *Step 1:* Immediately remove employee from job and have report to higher supervision. *Step 2:* Suspension up to 5 days, plus a written reprimand or written final warning, if necessary.	*Step 1:* Immediately remove employee from job and have report to higher supervision. *Step 2:* Written final warning. Suspension up to 10 days, or discharge if final warning was given for first offense.	*Step 1:* Immediately remove employee from job and have report to higher supervision. *Step 2:* Discharge.	
Intolerable Offenses of a criminal or drastic nature which strain employment relationship or would be outrageous to most people.	*First offense* *Step 1:* Immediately remove employee from job and have report to industrial-relations department. *Step 2:* Discharge.			

Pointers

1. Economic penalties (such as suspensions, transfers, discharges) should be imposed only by higher supervision after consultation with industrial-relations department.
2. Written final warnings should always be accompanied by an economic penalty.
3. To be considered a *second* offense, violations should occur within a year of the first offense.

Source: Walter Collins and Herman Harrow, "Does the Penalty Match the Offense?" *Supervisory Management*, vol. 3, no. 9 (September 1958), p. 20. Reprinted by permission of the publisher. © 1958 by American Management Assn., Inc.

the accuser, and their representatives. No method assures this exchange as well as an orderly disciplinary procedure.

Adhere to previously established rules and penalties. In order to meet the test of judicial due process, discipline must be properly administered by the superior in accord with the previously published rules. Penalties should be based upon specific charges with notices given to the employee—and union, if there is one—usually in advance of management's attempt to take corrective action. The charges, and their underlying reasons, should be definite and provable, and there should be provisions for a prompt hearing, protests, and appeals.

One of the best procedures to assure achieving this goal is to follow a simple procedure using the following steps: (21)

1. Investigate the facts.
    a. Interview witnesses, including the charged employee, and obtain signed statements.
    b. Review the documentary evidence.
    c. Visit the site of the incident.
2. Ascertain guilt.
3. Determine the appropriate penalty.
    a. Examine the applicable company policy and collective bargaining agreement.
    b. Investigate how other similar cases have been handled.
    c. Review the employee's file.
4. Apply the penalty as judiciously as feasible.

Example of a disciplinary procedure. In summary, the main provisions in the proper formal procedure are to have definite charges, to notify the employee and union in writing of the offense, to have some provision for the employee to answer charges either by protest or appeal, and to establish a definite scale of remedies.

While every organization will have its own system of rules and punishments—according to the behavior desired of its personnel—it is essential that everyone concerned know of the existence of the system and that supervisors use good judgment when applying it. Figure 20–1 is an example of a typical program, although it is by no means the only pattern possible.

AUTHORITY FOR ADMINISTERING DISCIPLINE

Usually the policies, rules, and regulations for employee behavior are established by top and middle management with the assistance and guidance of the personnel manager. Yet, those tend to be policed and enforced by the first-line supervisor. This strong delegation of authority to supervisors is supported by organizational theory and is psychologically sound.

An overgeneralization is, at lower levels of discipline involving warnings, the first-line supervisor usually has final authority; at the middle level, involving suspensions, line supervisors and managers have the final authority; while at the top levels, involving discharges, the authority is about evenly split between line managers and personnel executives. Therefore, as the severity increases, the role of the first-line supervisor decreases and the role of the personnel executive increases. The personnel executive's role is greater in small companies than in large, in nonbusiness organizations than in business firms.

The role of the supervisor

While line supervisors have traditionally been the key figures in disciplinary processes, that role has been diminishing. In the 1920s, personnel departments began to encroach upon the supervisor's prerogative, and, in the 1930s, unions began to undermine it. Management began to change from the authoritarian to the participative approach, which emphasizes positive rather than negative discipline and assumes that the majority of employees want to conform to rules. Since only a minority will require disciplinary action, punishment will be given in such a way that the employees will realize that they need to change and will do it themselves.

The effective supervisors are usually considerate of their subordinates and rely heavily upon favorable personal relationships to accomplish the job of maintaining a high level of performance. Thus, because of fear of destroying these personal relationships, the effective supervisors are the very ones who are least inclined to carry out the kind of disciplinary action that is established at the top. In other words, supervisors are likely to avoid administering severe disciplinary action because of the likelihood of generating undesirable effects. (22)

Unfortunately, some top managers become so isolated from the workers —and supervisors—that they lose touch with reality and may even place the blame for poor discipline on the supervisor.

> Increasing absenteeism, turnover, and grievances among blue-collar workers at a large paper plant prompted the plant manager to send its foremen to an intensive, one-week Fundamentals of Supervision course. The training had no effect.
>
> Formal grievances in the plant indicated that the workers were bitter about traditional "bread-and-butter" issues such as rates of pay, fringe benefits, and work standards. However, top management was not able to recognize the problem. Management felt that the grievances must be due to a "lack of understanding," which was the foremen's job to correct. Even after a subsequent opinion survey determined the true reason for the dissatisfaction of the workers, the plant manager refused to accept the findings at face value.

The personnel officer needs to train and counsel supervisors that in order to be more effective they must remember that: Every job should carry with it a certain margin for error; overconcentration upon avoiding errors stifles accomplishment and can encourage subordinates to postpone decisions or avoid them altogether; and a different way should not be mistaken for a wrong way.

The role of unions

The role of unions in applying discipline cannot be ignored. Management's right to discipline employees has been modified to the extent that these employee organizations have grown. Not only do they serve as catalysts for the adoption of new ideas concerning the disciplinary process, but they have also contributed significantly to the development of that process through negotiating the labor agreement and using its grievance procedure.

Some of the major "principles" that unions and arbitrators insist upon are: (*a*) a discharge can occur only for just cause; (*b*) the burden of proof has been shifted from the individual to the employer; (c) more formal procedures are used; and (d) management actions must meet the due process clause. These changes have substantially added to the burdens of the first-line supervisor.

In enforcing these fundamentals, arbitrators look to see if the policies established and penalties assessed meet the following criteria: (a) Is the requirement a reasonable one? (b) Has it been clearly communicated? (c) Has it been consistently enforced? and (d) Is it met by a penalty appropriate to the act?

A periodic survey of 400 representative contracts by the Bureau of National Affairs (BNA) found that 97 percent had discipline and discharge provisions—99 percent in manufacturing and 92 percent in other industries. (23) Four out of five had provision for discharge for "cause" or "just cause"; two out of three provided for discharge for specific charges.

DISCIPLINE IN NONBUSINESS ORGANIZATIONS (24)

Not only is discipline a problem in business firms, but also in government, (25) unions, sports, and voluntary organizations.

Federal agencies were required by Executive Order 10988 to set up a formal appeals system regarding adverse actions against employees. The agencies are thus responsible not only for disciplining employees, but also for receiving and adjudicating appeals. As an added protection, the appeals have to be decided at an administrative level higher than the level that took the adverse action. It was felt that this added appellate responsibility should cause agencies to reevaluate their disciplinary policies and practices, thus improving all stages in the process of dealing with employees in trouble.

Employees were given three options, namely, to appeal first to their own agency, to appeal to the Civil Service Commission, or to go to their agency first and then appeal to the commission. Experience shows that an increasing number are using the third alternative, with their appeals going through local, regional, and national appeals offices up to, and terminating in, the Board of Appeals and Review.

Unions can punish their members for many activities, including actions during a strike. The members can also file grievances against their local leaders all the way to the national convention.

In *professional sports,* players and managers can be disciplined by outside authorities.

IMPLICATIONS AND APPLICATIONS

It can be concluded from the information available that discipline is necessary for the successful performance of the personnel function.

Employee discipline is a process of internal and external control. Yet, discipline is not merely punishment; it is also training which corrects and strengthens.

The personnel manager's view of this control function has switched from the traditional one of discipline as punishment to the modern approach of attempting to make rules more reasonable, understanding, and considerate. Efforts are being made to encourage self-discipline and voluntary compliance with rules. When punishment is called for, a careful study is made to see that the punishment "fits the crime" and reasons are given for all rules and their enforcement.

The supervisor is still the individual most frequently held responsible for discipline, especially at the lower level involving warnings and even suspensions. At the higher levels of severity, especially discharges, the other line managers and personnel executives become more involved.

Unions have played a major role in bringing about this change in philosophy. Their impact shows up not only in company policy but also in the supervisor's role, regardless of whether the firm is unionized or not. But no matter how much influence unions have had on the disciplinary process, the right to discipline is still a prerogative of management; the main change is that personnel managers must be sure they follow the due-process procedures.

Yet, in spite of this progress, discipline is still largely negative, operating through penalties for wrong behavior rather than rewards for right action. Therefore, to be effective, it must be enforced. The manner of enforcement in turn acts upon the morale of the organization. One of the most difficult tasks of personnel management is to strike an acceptable balance between severity and leniency in administering discipline.

DISCUSSION QUESTIONS

1. What is discipline? Why is discipline important to organizations?
2. To what extent is the concept of self-control important as a means of discipline?
3. What are the necessary conditions to obtain orderly behavior in organizations?
4. Why is the judicial due process necessary as a means of discipline?
5. What are the major disciplinary problems—from a numerical point of view?
6. What is the union's role in the disciplinary process?
7. To what extent can a supervisor play a role as a disciplinary instrument in a unionized firm?
8. Who should administer discipline? Explain.

APPENDIX A: HOW A PLAN OF DISCIPLINING WITHOUT PUNISHING OPERATES IN PRACTICE

A plan of disciplining without punishing operates as follows:

1. When an employee does something meriting punishment, there are casual, private reminders from the departmental supervisor in a friendly but factual manner.

2. If a second transgression occurs within four to six weeks, the reminders are repeated.
3. A third occurrence within a "reasonable time" (usually four to six weeks) leads to another discussion, this time with a shift supervisor involved. At this point, an attempt is made to determine the roots of the employee's problem. For example,
    a. Does the worker like the job?
    b. Is the worker unable to tolerate the work routine?
    c. Are there personal or domestic problems?
    d. Is the worker able and willing to abide by the rules in the future?
4. If a fourth incident occurs within six to eight weeks, the worker's supervisor and the plant superintendent have a "final" discussion with the individual.
    a. The worker is informed that another incident will result in termination.
    b. A record of this discussion is sent to the worker's home.
5. Continued "good performance" over a period of several months leads to a clearing of the record.
    a. One step at a time.
    b. In reverse order.
6. Applying Skinner's "reinforcement" principle, when there is *any* improvement the supervisor lets the worker know it is appreciated.

APPENDIX B: SHOP RULES TYPICAL IN UNIONIZED PLANTS
Actual rules in a large nationwide manufacturing company

Rules	1st offense	2nd offense	3rd offense
1. Stealing private or company property	Discharge		
2. Material falsification of any company record	Discharge		
3. Gambling on company property	Discharge		
4. Fighting on company property	Discharge		
5. Refusal to obey orders of supervisor	Discharge		
6. Deliberate destruction or abuse of company property	Discharge		
7. Reporting to work or working while under the influence of intoxicating beverages and/or narcotics or other drugs or having possession of same on company property	Discharge		
8. Possession of weapons on company premises	Discharge		
9. Immoral conduct on company property	Discharge		
10. Sleeping during working hours	Discharge		
11. Absent three consecutive days without notification	Voluntary termination		
12. Willfully punching somebody else's timecard	Discharge		
13. Leaving premises during working hours without permission	Discharge		
14. Personal work on company time	Written warning	2 Days layoff	Discharge
15. Personal conduct at work dangerous to others	Written warning	2 Days layoff	Discharge
16. Solicitation for any cause during working time without permission	Written warning	2 Days layoff	Discharge
17. Distribution of literature during working hours or in areas of work without permission	Written warning	2 Days layoff	Discharge
18. Repeated failure to punch time card	Written warning	2 Days layoff	Discharge
19. Visiting other departments during working hours without permission	Written warning	2 Days layoff	Discharge
20. Stopping work before break time, lunch time, or quitting time or not performing assigned work	Written warning	2 Days layoff	Discharge
21. Posting, removal or tampering with bulletin board notices without authority	Written warning	2 Days layoff	Discharge
22. Threatening, intimidating, coercing or interfering with employees or supervision at any time	Written warning	2 Days layoff	Discharge
23. Poor or careless workmanship	Written warning	2 Days layoff	Discharge
24. Leaving early and/or failure to be at assigned work area at the start or end of shifts, breaks and/or meal periods	Written warning	2 Days layoff	Discharge
25. Using abusive language or making false or malicious statements concerning any employee, the company or its products	Written warning	2 Days layoff	Discharge
26. Distracting the attention of others or causing confusion by unnecessary shouting, catcalls or demonstrations in plant	Written warning	2 Days layoff	Discharge
27. Littering or contributing to poor housekeeping, unsanitary or unsafe conditions on plant premises	Written warning	2 Days layoff	Discharge
28. Negligence of safety rules of common safety practices	Written warning	2 Days layoff	Discharge
29. Restricting output or intentional slowdown	Written warning	5 Days layoff	Discharge
30. Unexcused absence	Written warning		
31. Unexcused tardiness	Written warning		

Receipt of any combination of five (5) of the above offenses within a one (1) year period will result in the employee's automatic discharge.

Written notices or warning or other disciplinary action shall not be used as a basis for further discipline after the employee has maintained a clear record of conduct for one year.

Source: *Employee Conduct and Discipline* (Washington, D.C.: Bureau of National Affairs, Personnel Policies Forum, Survey no. 102, August 1973), p. 30.

REFERENCES AND SUGGESTIONS FOR FURTHER STUDY

1. Irvin H. McMaster found that the supervisor's training is a key to success, as is timing, or knowing when to discipline. "Unusual Aspects of Discipline," *Supervision,* vol. 36, no. 4 (April 1974), p. 19.
2. Gene S. Booker, "Behavioral Aspects of Disciplinary Action," *Personnel Journal,* vol. 48, no. 7 (July 1969), pp. 525–29.
3. See David Sirota and Alan Wolfson, "Pragmatic Approach to People Problems," *Harvard Business Review,* vol. 51, no. 1 (January–Feburary 1973), pp. 120–28, for a good example of preventive problem solving.
4. See John Huberman, "Discipline without Punishment Lives," *Harvard Business Review,* vol. 53, no. 4 (July–August 1975), pp. 6–8, for more details.
5. According to the new field of organizational behavior modification, punishment is still sometimes used to modify behavior. See Fred Luthans and Robert Kreitner, "The Role of Punishment in Organizational Behavior Modification," *Public Personnel Management,* vol. 2, no. 3 (May–June 1973), p. 159, for a discussion of this and a practical example.
6. See Dick Prather, "Managing Human Resources," *Journal of Systems Management,* vol. 22, no. 12 (December 1971), pp. 22–25, for further details. He also presents some methods of controlling employee behavior which have operated successfully and unsuccessfully.
7. Emanuel Kay, Herbert H. Meyer, and John R. P. French, Jr., "Effect of Threat in a Performance Appraisal Interview," *Journal of Applied Psychology,* vol. 49, no. 5 (October 1965), pp. 311–17.
8. John Huberman, "Discipline without Punishment," *Harvard Business Review,* vol. 42, no. 4 (July–August 1964), pp. 62–68.
9. Stanley Milgram, "Behavioral Study of Obedience," *Journal of Abnormal and Social Psychology,* vol. 67, no. 4 (October 1963), pp. 371–78.
10. "The Nagging Problem of Absenteeism and Tardiness," *Business Management* vol. 33, no. 1 (October 1967), pp. 12–16.
11. Bess Ritter poses the thought that disciplinary problems may be caused by unexplainable friction between the supervisor and the subordinate. Usually these can be handled through training, rotation, or counseling. "What to Do about the Problem Worker," *Supervision,* vol. 36, no. 9 (September 1974), pp. 23–24.
12. J. B. P. Lindha and Robert J. Wherry, "Determinants of Norm Violating Behavior in a Simulated Industrial Setting," *Personnel Psychology,* vol. 18, no. 4 (Winter 1965), pp. 403–12.
13. For a more concise explanation, especially of the "due process of law" concept, see William G. Scott, "An Issue in Administrative Justice: Managerial Appeal Systems," *Management International,* 1966, pp. 37–53.
14. The Personnel Policies Forum of the Bureau of National Affairs surveyed 200 of its member companies concerning their problems and policies with discipline. The 185 organizations responding included large and small ones, ranging in size from 29 to 150,000 employees; manufacturing and nonmanufacturing firms; and public and nonprofit health and educational institutions. *Employee Conduct and Discipline* (Washington, D.C.: Bureau of National Affairs, Personnel Policies Forum, Survey No. 102, August 1973), p. 1.

482 Personnel and human resources administration

15. See Walter Collins and Herman Harrow, "Does the Penalty Match the Offense?" *Supervisory Management,* vol. 3, no. 9 (September 1958), p. 18 ff, for a discussion of these type offenses and suggested penalties. See Figure 20–1 for a summary of their findings.

16. See Charles C. Denova, "Controlling Absenteeism," *Supervision,* vol. 36, no. 4 (April 1974), p. 20 ff, for some good suggestions on how to reduce absenteeism.

17. Janice Neipert Hedges, "Unscheduled Absence from Work—An Update," *Monthly Labor Review,* vol. 98, no. 8 (August 1975), pp. 38, for further details.

18. In a study of five electric utility firms, seven levels of managers were asked to rate cases involving violations of rules by hourly workers on a disciplinary action scale. *Cases involving safety violations were judged more severely by all levels of management.* Philip Shaak and Milton Schwartz, "Uniformity of Policy Interpretation among Managers in the Utility Industry," *Academy of Management Journal,* vol. 16, no. 1 (March 1973), pp. 77–83.

19. Preventing rule violations and imposing penalties pose tough problems for the manager. Many rules cannot be applied stringently. Many personnel managers, fortunately, do have some leeway in their application. The amount of leeway depends on such factors as position, number of subordinates, union contract, and relationships with management. See Robert L. Mathis and William M. Jenkins, Jr., in "Rules for Rule-Makers," *Supervisory Management,* vol. 19, no. 1 (January 1974), pp. 19–24, for some guidelines to making and applying rules, including: (*a*) *a rule must be necessary,*(*b*) *rules must be widely applicable,* (*c*) *rules should be consistent with organizational policies and objectives,* (*d*) *rules should be communicated to everyone* (*e*) *rules should be clear and understandable,* (*f*) *rules should be reasonable,* (*g*) *rules should be enforceable,* and (*h*) *the penalty should fit the rule violation.*

20. A growing problem area is the discipline of minority members, who have additional appeals options open to them. One arbitrator has ruled that employers should "give a black employee an additional chance for redemption, while denying this chance to white employees under similar circumstances." See Kenneth Jennings, "Arbitrators, Blacks, and Discipline," *Personnel Journal,* vol. 54, no. 1 (January 1975), pp. 32–37, for further details.

21. This procedure is based upon the recommendations of Dennis M. Sullivan, a labor relations specialist, in "Employee Discipline: Beware the 'Company Position,' " *Personnel Journal,* vol. 53, no. 9 (September 1974), pp. 692–95.

22. Persons in higher levels of management take a stronger, perhaps more punitive, position on matters of discipline than those at the lower levels. One explanation is that first-line supervisors are inclined to give stronger consideration to individual circumstances and behavior than is top management. Also, supervisors are somewhat reluctant to follow rules in a strict fashion for fear they will lose the cooperation of subordinates if they are too severe. Shaak and Schwartz, "Uniformity of Policy Interpretation," *Academy of Management Journal,* pp. 77–83.

23. "Basic Patterns in Union Contracts: Discipline and Discharge," *Datagraph, Bulletin to Management* (Washington, D.C.: Bureau of National Affairs, May 15, 1975).

24. The disciplinary procedures described in this chapter have primarily been "hierar-

chical," or that administered by the organizational hierarchy. Yet, there are other systems. For example, William G. Scott has found nonhierarchical systems in the government, the military, unions, and nonwork situations. See "Organization Government: The Prospects for a Truly Participative System," *Public Administration Review,* vol. 29, no. 1 (January–February 1969), pp. 43–53.

George Odiorne advocated a positive approach to discipline, or discipline by objectives, whereby: (*a*) discipline tends to be voluntarily accepted; (*b*) discipline is a behavior modifier; (*c*) meeting organizational objectives may require breaking rules and regulations; (*d*) rules and regulations should be reviewed periodically to see if they do help achieve organizational objectives; and (*e*) each individual is responsible for one's own output, and these differences can be explained in terms of individual results. See *Personnel Administration by Objectives* (Homewood, Ill.: Richard D. Irwin, Inc., 1971), Chapter 18.

25. The state of New York recently changed its disciplinary procedure. People were rarely disciplined under the old procedure, or there was so much "red tape" involved the case would go to court and be dragged out over extended periods and at considerable cost.

The new procedure, which resulted from the 1972–73 negotiations for a new contract for 95 percent of the workers, is prompt, flexible, and the managers can handle it without the need for attorneys.

More actions have been taken under the new procedure than the old.

See Robert J. Donahue (chief of the employee relations and services section in the personnel office of the State Department of Social Services), "Disciplinary Actions in New York State Service—A Radical Change," *Public Personnel Management,* vol. 4, no. 2 (March–April 1975), pp. 110–12, for details.

CASES FOR FURTHER STUDY

V-1. What Determines Wages?

The following letter was received from the vice president of personnel of a medium-sized insurance company in answer to the question: "How do you actually determine your rates of pay?"

Dear Professor:

Regardless of the type of wage plan to be adopted, whether based upon a time-basis of payment or one related to output, certain parameters can be established. Minimum wage rates have been established by governmental regulations through such acts as the Fair Labor Standards Act, the Walsh-Healey Act, and the Davis-Bacon Act. At the opposite end of the spectrum, it can be said that maximum wage rates are largely determined by management's philosophy toward the sharing of gains or its largesse.

In situations where labor is a direct cost, as in some service organizations, the extent of competition is a primary factor influencing the wage rate employed by the firm. An item not often considered directly is the efficiency of management itself. An inefficient management might find the resulting low profits sufficient cause to maintain a low wage rate.

The cost of living within contiguous areas is another force exerting an influence on the level of wages. Within a given community, the wage paid for a given type of work will, like water, seek its own level. In order to attract workers, the organization must, therefore, meet the local competition for the type of labor it seeks. If the firm is to maintain competition within its industry, and market its product outside its local community, the wage level paid within the firm's industry will influence the wage rate decision.

Benefits other than the basic wage are as much a part of the cost of labor as the basic wage rate itself. If the firm's situation is such that there is only a given amount available from the sale of its product to pay wages, then the extent to which benefits are paid must be a determining factor in the establishment of the basic wage rate. Management's philosophy toward workers will include a desire to reward past service, efficiency, or cooperation in some cases. From this desire there might arise individual differences in wage rates within given job descriptions.

Finally, the labor contract in force between the firm and the union is an additional component in the wage rate decision. It is true, however, that competition within the community for workers will force the nonunion company to approximate the unionized competitor in wage rate. In addition, a nonunion firm may, in its desire to remain nonunion, approximate the going union rate.

These items have been found to play a dominant part, in the past few years, in shaping any wage plan which we put into effect.

Sincerely yours,
Mary Walker
Vice President, Personnel

Questions

1. (*a*) Whose right is it to set wages? (*b*) Explain.
2. (*a*) Assuming (1) a natural human dignity and (2) a competitive market with labor mobility, what influence should labor unions exert in the shaping of wage rates? (*b*) Explain.
3. (*a*) Differentiate between (1) internal and (2) external pressures which determine the wage rate in this firm. (*b*) What are some pressures the vice president did not mention?
4. What influence does the employee's wage rate have on job performance?

V-2. Ward Chemical Company

The Ward Chemical Company operated in several southern and southwestern states and employed 1,250 employees throughout the region. The company, which was engaged in the manufacturing and merchandising of chemical products, recently found it necessary to increase its labor force to handle an increased volume of business.

The personnel policies and practices of the organization were governed by a personnel policy manual which had been prepared 15 years earlier and had been revised from time to time.

The personnel director of the company, faced with numerous complex problems, felt that some of the provisions of the manual should be revised in order to assure greater flexibility.

Part A

Joe Blank, whose employment became effective on June 10, was terminated on September 20, on the basis that he had not developed into a "satisfactory employee." New employees were rated at the end of 30 and 90 days, and their permanent status was based upon the results. Also, existing personnel were rated at the end of a 30-day period after moving from one job classification to another. The rating points ranged between 16 and 40 points. In both cases, the employee's earnings were also determined by the ratings.

Joe's first rating, dated July 12, showed a rating of 22 points. His second rating, September 12, remained at 22 points. The fact that this employee's merit rating did not increase during the period concerned management. In viewing his case, it was found that Joe had been absent from work from August

21 through August 30, during which time he was in a clinic under the care of a psychiatrist who had diagnosed his case as "anxiety reaction."

The union contract stated that new employees remained temporary and could be terminated at the discretion of management at any time until they had "completed 90 days' service." Management did not consider this type of absence from work to be "service" and terminated the employee without consulting the union representatives.

The union did not agree with this interpretation of the contract and contended that this employee had completed 90 days' service 90 days after employment date. A grievance was filed asking that Joe Blank be reinstated in his job with no loss of pay.

Questions

1. Why do you think the personnel director thought the manual should be revised?
2. Was this a valid use of personnel ratings? Explain your answer.
3. Should wages be based upon merit ratings? Give the "pros" and "cons."
4. Should Joe have been terminated when he was? Explain.
5. If you were the manager who had to answer the grievance, what would you say?

Part B

The junior "technicians" and "chemists" were paid a monthly salary, based on a 40-hour workweek. Also, they were paid overtime at the rate of "time-and-one-half" based on their normal monthly salary converted to an hourly rate. They normally worked 45 hours per week, for which they received their regular salary plus the overtime payment for the extra 5 hours.

This system, however, posed a problem whenever an official holiday occurred within a normal workweek. As they then only worked 37 hours, they lost their premium pay for overtime. The company official directly responsible for the laboratory operations had consistently refused the request of the laboratory manager that these men be allowed an eight-hour credit for the official holiday. Although the laboratory manager had pointed out that the men were being penalized because a holiday fell within the workweek, the request was consistently denied.

As employees continued to complain about the uncredited time, the personnel director called a special conference of the company's officials to resolve the problem. It was learned in this conference that there had been no uniform practices on this matter of overtime pay for holidays for this type of personnel. In fact, some of the other divisions had been crediting time for official holidays.

Questions

1. Should there be a uniform policy for these and other employees? Explain.
2. What should the policy be for overtime for these employees? Explain.

Part C

Frank Franklin had been with the firm for about 15 years, which was practically as long as the firm had been in existence. He had been promoted to department head and had remained in that position for 12 years.

Recently management felt that new blood was needed in the department to increase the efficiency and quality of the work performed. An increasing amount of difficulty had been occurring in the design work performed by this department which had resulted in complaints from clients and loss of repeat work. Management evaluated one cause of the problem as the general lack of technical skill and thoroughness on the part of the department head, as well as his apparent lack of ability to keep up with more recent developments in his field.

Mr. Franklin was given a new position in the business promotion area of the firm. His work was considered "very good," but it seemed to lack the enthusiasm really necessary for effective promotional activities.

Recently Mr. Franklin, then in his fifties, developed a heart problem which would permanently preclude his use in any field that required extensive travel or demanding work. Management was faced with the problem of what to do with this man, since an early retirement plan had not been established.

Faced with the problem, the company decided to study a medical retirement plan through the personnel policies committee. The committee suggested a proposal under which an employee would be permitted to retire if he were declared to be physically incapable of performing the job for which he was qualified. The employee would qualify for these benefits after 15 years service and, of course, after being declared unfit to perform his position. If a position other than that normally performed could be satisfactorily filled by the employee without further impairment to his health, he would be offered it as an alternative to disability retirement. However, jobs were not to be created to take care of specific situations.

Questions

1. Evaluate the handling of this case by the firm.
2. Appraise the disability retirement program pointing out its strong and weak points.
3. What alternative policy could you come up with? Explain.
4. What should be the interaction between ability, performance, health, and retirement, if any?

V–3. Mid-Western Printing, Incorporated*

Bob Scott, personnel manager of Mid-Western Printing, Incorporated, sat despondently reviewing Paul Carter's personnel file. Carter, a high school

---

* Prepared by Dr. William J. Bigoness of the Graduate School of Business Administration, University of North Carolina.

graduate, married, and the father of two teenage children, began his employment with Mid-Western six years ago as a binder machine operator. During his six years of employment, Carter had advanced slowly to his current position of skilled printer.

Carter completed his initial three-month probationary period with a satisfactory evaluation. He then became a permanent employee and member of the local printers' union. Subsequent annual performance appraisals, although not exceptional, were satisfactory. During the past year, however, Carter's performance had seriously deteriorated, thereby necessitating the current decision confronting Scott.

In November 1973, following several violations of company personnel policies, Carter was given a two-day suspension without pay for failure to call in sick. Carter's 1973 performance appraisal, submitted to the personnel department in early January 1974 by Hal Biddle, foreman of Carter's section, evaluated Carter's performance as "inadequate" and "below average." Specific areas of criticisms included tardiness, failure to call in sick, a high rate of absenteeism, poor body hygiene resulting in complaints from fellow workers, and an inability to reach acceptable performance standards. When queried regarding a possible explanation for these deficiencies, Carter responded, "It's just a rough time. The kids are running around and a few other personal things like that."

Three weeks following his performance appraisal, Carter committed a serious printing and collating error while filling a routine order. This error cost Mid-Western in excess of $700 to rectify. Carter was sent a formal written reprimand following this incident.

In March 1974, Biddle met with Scott and informed him that Carter's performance had continued to decline and that he now appeared incapable of performing the job responsibilities of a skilled printer. Biddle maintained that placing Carter on temporary probation was the only reasonable course of action. After consulting with Rod Gardner, the union steward, who admitted having observed Carter's declining effectiveness, it was decided to place Carter on eight weeks' probationary status.

Later that day Scott met with Carter, reiterated the accumulated incidents of unsatisfactory performance and explained the reasons which necessitated the disciplinary action. Scott assured Carter of his hope that he would be able to resolve successfully his current difficulties and to continue his employment at Mid-Western. Scott emphasized the company's willingness to assist Carter in any way it could. Carter remained silent throughout most of the conversation. Upon leaving, he commented, "I guess I'll just have to try to do a little better."

On May 25, 1974, Scott, Biddle, and Gardner all agreed that Carter had shown improvement during his probationary period. Although his body hygiene remained a problem and he was still not a "top notch" employee, his overall improvement warranted reinstatement as a permanent employee. Carter was notified immediately of his renewed permanent status.

Three days later, Carter reported at his scheduled time for work. Shortly thereafter, he realized that he had forgotten his glasses, without which he was unable to operate the printing press. He obtained permission to return promptly. Carter was neither seen nor heard from for the remainder of the day. When confronted the next morning by the shop foreman regarding his unexplained disappearance, Carter responded he had been unable to locate his glasses until 5:20 p.m. by which time his work shift had ended.

Questions

1. Evaluate the disciplinary system used by the firm.
2. How do you explain Carter's behavior?
3. How do you explain the union's behavior?
4. What would you do if you were the personnel manager? Explain.

part six

Effects of industrial relations on personnel administration

21. How industrial relations affect personnel administration
22. Improving industrial relations in the individual organization

Cases:
    VI–1. *The Union Blow*
    VI–2. *The Discharge of Sleeping Beauty*

Introduction

As has been indicated throughout this text, labor unions are one of the most powerful groups in the United States, and they influence all aspects of personnel and human resources administration, whether an organization is unionized or not. Directly or indirectly, the decisions of personnel managers are made with the unconscious realization that those decisions will be subject to scrutiny by union officers or recruiters. Consequently, the scope of the personnel executive's discretion has been considerably narrowed.

As shown in Figure VI–1, industrial relations forms part of the environmental constraint upon the performance of the personnel function.

Chapter 21 deals with the overall effects of unions on the personnel function, while Chapter 22 shows how the personnel function in an individual organization is affected by the entry of a union.

It is seen in Chapter 21 that a consequence of unionization is a widening of the gap between management and the individual employee, management's rights have been restricted, and employees tend to obtain a greater degree of satisfaction from union membership than from organizational affiliation.

Chapter 22 shows what happens when the union enters. The administration of the agreement is also covered in the chapter.

FIGURE VI-1
How industrial relations fits into the overall personnel system

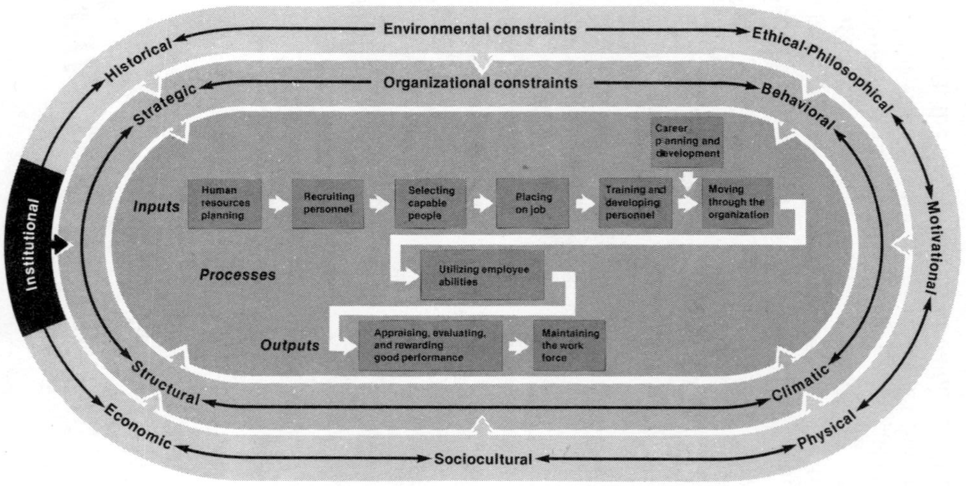

Chapter 21

How industrial relations affect personnel administration

Laws providing the industrial-relations framework
  The National Labor Relations Act, 1935
  The Labor-Management Relations Act, 1947
  Labor-Management Reporting and Disclosure Act of 1959

What are union objectives?

How do unions achieve their objectives?
  Organization
  Recognition as exclusive bargaining agent
  Collective bargaining
  Union security
  Grievance procedure and arbitration
  The strike

Some changing union tactics
  *Some **causes** of the changes*
  Changes are causing unions to use newer methods

Membership in unions and employee associations

Implications and applications for personnel executives

21
How industrial relations affect personnel administration

In union there is strength
AESOP, *The Bundle of Sticks*

In *Coppage* v. *Kansas* and *Adair* v. *U.S.,* Charles Evans Hughes, said, "The right to join labor unions is undisputed and has been the subject of frequent affirmation in judicial opinions. . . . The right to join them, as against coercive action to the contrary, may be the legitimate subject of protection in the exercise of the police authority of the states."

This statement illustrates the importance of labor unions and employee associations and the considerable influence they have on personnel administration. They influence almost every aspect of the personnel function in almost every institution, in every industry, and in every sector—private and public.

Although these organizations have existed since the beginning of the republic, it was only during the last four decades that they began to have such a powerful influence upon personnel administration. Labor's "Magna Carta" was the *Clayton Act of 1914,* which declared that labor unions were not to be considered illegal combinations or conspiracies in restraint of trade under the *Sherman Antitrust Act of 1890*—which is still binding upon management. (1) While the effectiveness of the law was hampered between then and 1932 by court decisions and the "yellow dog" contract (which required a worker not to participate in union activities as a condition of employment), it has provided labor unions with the unique position of strength they now enjoy.

When World War I ended, organized labor was in a prominent position in government. This position has continuously improved since then—with slight interruptions. Labor has also increased its hold over economic affairs pertaining to the activities of organizations *and* individuals.

This chapter will explore the rate(s) played by unions and other employee associations and how they affect the performance of the personnel functions by personnel executives. The most pertinent laws will be discussed, union objectives and the ways of achieving them will be discussed, and their relevance to personnel executives will be explained.

LAWS PROVIDING THE INDUSTRIAL-RELATIONS FRAMEWORK

During the 1930s, there was a decline in the power of unions, at least on a national scale. Inadequate leadership, division within the ranks, public reaction to some of the excesses of union leaders during World War I, and improved personnel management leadership caused the prestige and membership of national unions to decline. Consequently, employees turned from national unions to a system of employee representation plans that were company-sponsored—and often controlled by management. The results of this movement were reflected in declining national union membership and less union activity.

The prevailing opinion was that the government should remain a neutral observer in the labor relations field—at least as far as management was concerned. A break in this philosophy occurred in 1932 with the passage of the *Norris-La Guardia (Anti-Injunction) Act*, which prohibited the enforcement of "yellow dog" contracts which required employees to agree to refrain from union activities as a condition of employment. It also restricted the use of injunctions against unions by the courts—except in unusual cases where severe violence or damage occurred.

The National Labor Relations Act, 1935

As shown in Chapter 4, the beginning of the present period of union preeminence began in 1935 with the passage of the *National Labor Relations Act* (commonly called the *Wagner Act*). With this law, the government ceased its position of neutrality and became "pro-labor." Using the rationale of eliminating "the causes of certain substantial obstructions to the free flow of commerce and to mitigate and eliminate these obstructions," Congress took an active role to advance the fortunes of unions and to restrict the activities of management.

Rights of employees. Employees have essentially five rights under *section 7* of this act, namely the right to:

1. Self-organization;
2. Form, join, or assist labor organizations of their own choosing;
3. Bargain collectively through those representatives;
4. Engage in concerted activities needed for mutual aid or protection; and
5. Refrain from, as well as engage in, such concerted activities, except where there is a valid union shop agreement.

Both management and unions were granted rights and privileges, as well as duties and responsibilities. In essence, management can not prevent, or interfere with, employees from participating in industrial-relations activities, and unions can not force management to discriminate against them.

Administration of the act. The judicial powers of the act are vested in a five-person National Labor Relations Board (NLRB), while its administrative duties are handled by the General Counsel. The primary responsibilities of the NLRB are to determine if a majority of the employees want a union to represent them; set up the procedures for elections to determine their choice of a bargaining agent; and investigate and prosecute complaints of unfair labor practices under the law.

The representation elections and investigation of unfair labor practices are conducted by the General Counsel—on a regional basis, while the judicial decisions involving unfair labor practices are made by the board in Washington.

The Labor-Management Relations Act, 1947

As the Wagner Act constricted the activities of management while encouraging the development of unions—without restrictions—many abuses arose on both sides, but particularly on labor's. In 1946, following World War II with its evidences of union power, a concerned public elected a Congress committed to correcting the pro-labor nature of the law. By 1947, public opinion was so great that Congress passed—over President Truman's veto—the *Labor-Management Relations Act, 1947* (commonly called the *Taft-Hartley Act.*)

In essence, the act *substantially* amended the *Wagner Act* by making it more "even-handed," as now both management and unions could commit unfair labor practices.

Another effect was to prohibit the closed shop agreement—except in some specific instances—and limit the union shop agreement in states that prohibited it—under *section 14(b)*.* The net effect of this was quite significant, for under the *closed shop agreement* workers had to join the union before getting a job, so employers could not choose their own employees but had to accept those chosen by the unions; under the *union shop agreement,* employers have the right to choose the people of their choice, and only then do the employees have to join the union. Other benefits to the company were: the right to sue unions in court for breach of contract where unlawful strikes and boycotts are engaged in; the right to call an NLRB election if it does not believe the union represents its employees; and to receive a 60-day vote notice, with provisions for mediation and conciliation by the Federal Mediation and Conciliation Service, which was established under the law.

Labor-Management Reporting and Disclosure Act of 1959

Because of allegations of corruption and abuse of employees by some unions, Congress passed the *Labor-Management Reporting and Disclosure Act*

---

* This section gave states the right to pass laws prohibiting the union shop. These "right-to-work" laws take priority over the federal law. They are now found in 20 states but are a favorite target of unions.

of *1959 (commonly called the Landrum-Griffin Act)*. While the primary purpose of the law was to regulate the internal activities of unions, particularly their relationship with their members, there were a few provisons which pertained to management. In general, management was prevented from making illegal payments to a union to influence its negotiations for an agreement for its members. Also, it speeded up the election process by using regional organizations rather than the centralized NLRB. In the building and construction industry, a prehire union contract was permitted whereby union membership could be required after seven days, rather than the usual 30-day waiting period.

The main provision of the act was to protect union members from possible coercive and abusive actions by a few unscrupulous labor leaders.

WHAT ARE UNION OBJECTIVES?

One of the best presentations of the reason for the existence of unions was the statement that our society creates "a disordered dust of individuals," (2) so that an individual worker is helpless in the face of the economic and social power of groups of individuals and institutions. Thus, workers must advance, not as individuals, but as Longfellow said in the *Song of Hiawatha;*

> All your strength is in your union,
> All your danger is in your discord;
> Therefore be at peace henceforward,
> And as brothers live together.

The practical objectives of employee associations are almost always:

1. Higher pay;
2. Shorter hours of work (daily, weekly, and annually);
3. Improved working conditions, both physical and sociopsychological; and
4. Improved security, both of the person and the job.

Another way of stating this is to say that there are three cardinal principles upon which unionism is based, and, if any one of them is threatened, the union and its members will fight back. They are: (*a*) in unity there is strength, (*b*) equal pay for the same job, and (*c*) employment practices based upon seniority. (As will be seen in the next chapter, this last principle is now being challenged by equal employment opportunities.)

HOW DO UNIONS ACHIEVE THEIR OBJECTIVES?

How do unions accomplish their goals? The methods used traditionally have been organization, recognition, collective bargaining, union security, processing grievances, arbitration, strikes and the threat of strike, boycotts, union labels, checkoff of union dues, and many others.

After discussing the most important of these methods, some of the newer techniques now being emphasized will be discussed.

Organization

As one of the basic tenets of unionism is that "in union there is strength," the first thing that must be done is to organize the individuals in the target organization into a union or employee association.

Types of union organizations. There are three types of unions classified according to their membership. The *craft union* has only members with a particular skill needed to do a particular job, e.g., electricians. An *industrial union* accepts members from an entire industry, regardless of their skill or job, e.g., automobile workers. A *general union* (earlier called a *labor union*), such as the United Mine Workers of America accepts any type of worker from almost any industry. In addition, there are *professional employee associations* which negotiate for their members, such as the National Education Association.

The workers in a given geographic region are organized into a *local*. The local may include workers from a single plant or from a given geographic area.

If the union is *independent,* it operates on its own and is not *affiliated* with a larger *national or international* union. The *independent union,* which may represent only the employees of one firm, is not bound by the jurisdiction of any other group. Approximately 3 million workers belong to independent unions, and they seem to have the same geographic distribution as that of national unions. Apparently there is also the same industrial pattern among independent unions as among national unions.

New organizational efforts. The organizational and recruiting efforts of unions have tended to vary with changes in the economic, social, and political environments. This axiom is also true at the present time. Union strategists are planning that the labor movement, like government, will strive for a new relevance to American life and a broader commitment to social changes in the coming period. (3) Thus, its size, power, militancy, and economic demands will increase, and a new "union mix" with new leadership will develop to include the new workers entering the labor force, in spite of the distrust they have for unions. (4)

The new organizational drives will probably occur in the public sector—including FBI clerks, military personnel, (5) police, and firefighters; professionals—including teachers, medical personnel, athletes, dentists, and lawyers; persons in service industries; and agricultural workers.

Public employees. The primary thrust of union organizing activities is now toward organizing public employees. As a result of government recognition, especially the issuance of Executive Order 10988 in 1962, public employee unions have become the fastest growing labor organizations in the country. (6) This order was amended by Executive Order 11491 in 1969 and Executive Order 11616 in 1971, which set up a form of collective bargaining for employees of the federal government. (7) These orders effectively amended the Wagner Act and the Taft-Hartley Act which specifically exempted government employees from coverage under those laws.

Foreign service officers of the U.S. State Department are now represented by the American Foreign Service Association. Efforts are under way to organize members of the U.S. Armed Forces, as has been done in Germany.

Guests at the NLRB's gala 40th anniversary dinner in Washington in 1975 were handed leaflets by representatives of the NLRB employees' union charging the agency with "unfair labor practices," "bad-faith negotiations," and inadequate pay rates.

Many states have followed the federal example by passing laws permitting state, local, and municipal workers to engage in union activities. (8) The results of these organizing efforts are shown in Figure 21–1.

Professionals. Traditionally professors and teachers, doctors and nurses, athletes, lawyers, and other professionals have thought of themselves as just that—professionals—who were "above" union activities. Yet, when these groups found themselves falling far behind union members in rewards and benefits during the 1960s, they adopted union methods.

An organization of interns and resident physicians, the Physicians National Housestaff Association, with some 18,000 members in American hospitals voted in 1975 to become a bargaining union.

In September 1975, the players of five National Football League teams voted to strike if their demands were not met. While one game was struck, strikes against the others were averted.

FIGURE 21–1
In past decade . . . A doubling of government workers in unions

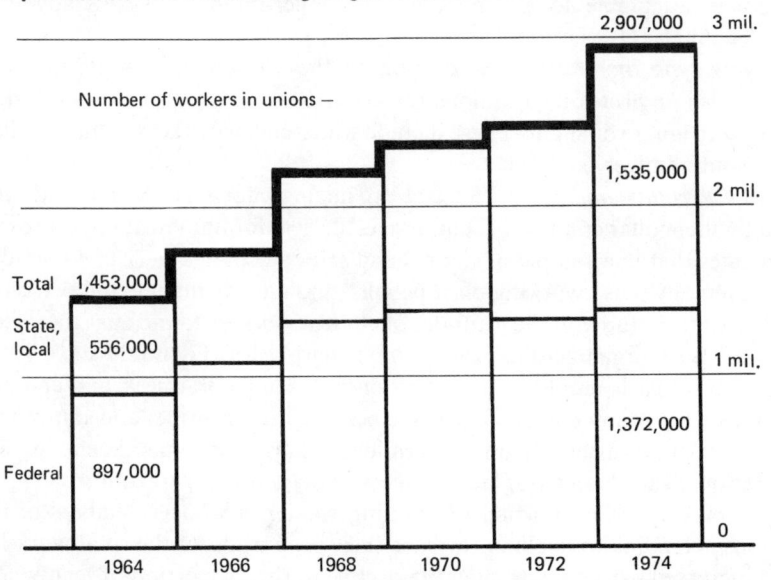

	1964	1974
Total	1,453,000	2,907,000
State, local	556,000	1,535,000
Federal	897,000	1,372,000

Source: Reprinted from *U.S. News & World Report* (September 1, 1975), p. 22. Copyright 1975 U.S. News & World Report, Inc.

College and university faculty members are finding certain trade union concepts—such as bargaining over salaries and job security—to their liking. (9) Three organizations—the American Association of University Professors (AAUP), American Federation of Teachers (AFT), and National Educational Association (NEA)—are currently competing to represent this level of academic personnel. Regardless of which one predominates, university administrators can expect greater efforts on the part of all three to represent their faculties as bargaining agents.

> Stanford University reports that more than one-fifth of all full-time college teachers are now represented by unions.

Employees of service industries. A third of organizational activities is in the service industries which are rapidly expanding. This is particularly true in retailing, including the food service industry—especially restaurants.

Agricultural employees. A fourth area of union effort is in agriculture, especially in the vast grape, lettuce, citrus, and cotton-growing industries of California. The state's Agricultural Labor Relations Act, which was passed in 1975 to "establish an orderly legal framework for organizing and bargaining" in those fields, is expected to serve as a model for other states where millions of field laborers present a tempting target for union organizers. While there are vast differences between agriculture and industrial and construction union activities, the Agricultural Labor Relations Board (ALRB) must follow precedents of the NLRB in enforcing the law—where applicable.

These new organizing activities will apparently be an irresistible force for several reasons. There will also be increased militancy, for unionism has become acceptable to the middle- and upper-middle-class employees and professionals. (10)

New type members. In addition to these organizing activities in new industries or professions, unions are concentrating on groups they formerly tended to ignore or slight. These include white-collar workers, females, minorities, and younger employees.

White-collar employees. Special organizing efforts are being made to recruit white-collar employees. This is a fertile field for unionization, for research indicates that in a sample of clerical and sales personnel, over one-half identified themselves as "working-class people" and not as "managerial personnel." (11) Another study on the attitudes of clerical workers found that their feeling toward their organizations had become sharply less favorable since 1966 in the areas of basic employment conditions, personnel practices, and communications. (12) Many clerical jobs have become dull, routine, and unrewarding —almost like assembly-line operations—and there has been increased depersonalization and fragmentation of many work organizations.

Women. The proportion of working women who are members of labor unions is tending to decline—even as their proportion of the total work force has increased—even faster than the decline in the proportion of men who are union members. (13) However, the number of female union members is increasing. The significance of this fact is that many union-management agreements—as well as federal and state laws—are in disagreement with Title VII of the Civil Rights Act of 1964. Thus, management—and union leaders—face the dilemma of which takes precedence.

At the 1975 AFL-CIO national convention, the female delegation organized the Coalition of Labor Union Women (CLUW). (14)

Black employees. Black employees constitute another fast-growing target of union organizers. In 1970, there were approximately 2 million black trade unionists, and the number was growing because of education and training. Yet there appears to be considerable racial discrimination which is forcing blacks to consider organizing along racial lines or rejecting the collective bargaining process altogether. (15) However, an appellate court has directed one union to take affirmative action through apprenticeship and membership programs to meet a 1977 racial goal. (16)

Young workers. Young employees are posing problems for union-management relations. As they tend to be more educated than their older colleagues and have different values, they seek different settlements from collective bargaining, which will lead to more rejections of agreements. (17) These workers will probably be more individualistic and seek more variations in benefits. The results will be quite significant for unions, as the average seniority among skilled tradesmen in 1973 was 10–12 years.

Recognition as exclusive bargaining agent

The second way unions achieve their goals is by becoming recognized as the employees' exclusive bargaining agent with management. It then has the *sole* right to be the advocate of *all* employees—union members *and* nonunion members—in their dealing with management.

Management may *voluntarily* recognize the union because of its philosophical beliefs or *be forced to* through the union's superior economic strength. Yet, the usual way is through a *secret ballot election* conducted by the (NLRB). If a majority of the employees voting vote for the union, it is designated by the board as the exclusive representative for all employees for purposes of bargaining over wages, hours, and other terms and conditions of employment.

During recent years, the union success rate has slipped. Unions won 51 percent of the NLRB-conducted elections in fiscal 1974, down from 56 percent in 1970. (18) This figure does not convey a true picture, for many organizing efforts never get to the election stage. Conventional "wisdom" is that unions can expect to secure only one new bargaining unit for every six organizational drives initiated.

Collective bargaining

The third method of achieving their objectives is through collective bargaining. Once the union is recognized as the employees' exclusive bargaining agent, it begins negotiating an agreement* with management. In general, this procedure can be defined as agreeing to a rate of exchange between effort and dignity of the employees (labor's viewpoint) and productivity (management's view). There is considerable opposition to this concept, though most authorities view collective bargaining as an economic power struggle between two powerful opponents.

What is collective bargaining? The Taft-Hartley Act defined collective bargaining as:

> The performance of the mutual obligation of the employer and the representative of the employees to meet at reasonable times and confer in good faith with respect to wages, hours, and other terms and conditions or employment, or the negotiation of an agreement, . . . and the execution of a written contract incorporating any agreement reached if requested by either party, but such obligation does not compel either party to agree to a proposal or require the making of a concession.

If the parties agree on terms, a contract is signed; if not, outside *mediation* or *conciliation* is used. If this does not work, the union will strike,† or, in some unusual circumstances, the parties will agree to *arbitrate* the points of disagreement. Although the law does not require that an agreement be signed, a precedent-breaking NLRB decision, which was upheld by the 4th U.S. Circuit Court, forced the H. K. Porter Company to grant the checkoff of union dues, although the union was unable to get the firm to grant it during negotiations. (19) There is now much pressure for compulsory arbitration to protect the public from losses resulting from strikes, especially in public institutions.

Some current trends in bargaining demands. This discussion would not be realistic if it were not said that unions are continuing to seek higher wages, shorter annual hours, and improved personal and job security—as well as agreements providing for increased compulsory union membership, although in modified forms.

Specifically current bargaining demands center around *eliminating interregional, intercity, and interjob pay differentials between allegedly comparable jobs* and *obtaining increased employee benefits.* Unions continue to insist upon a system of single job rates rather than continuing to accept bilaterally negotiated, differentiated job wages with the individual's specific merit rate being determined by management—through the use of performance appraisals. Also, pressure is building up to have everyone paid a fixed salary, rather than on the hourly or piece rate basis.

Efforts are being made to *restore greater differentials between job classifica-*

---

* Although the word "contract" is often used in this context, the proper one is "agreement," for section 502 of the Taft-Hartley Act prohibits the requiring of "an *individual* employee to render labor or service without his consent." However, the two terms will be used interchangeably in this text.

† Although the term "strike" has been used here, the correct terminology should be "strikes and/or lockouts." The lockout is where the company effectively closes its premises to the employees in order to achieve its demands.

tions, especially for the higher skilled jobs. Also, "catch-up" in wage adjustments, especially in contracts with "cost of living adjustments" (COLA), is sought. Agreements are calling for the removal of ceilings ("caps") on how much can be obtained through COLA.

Union demands for *employee benefits* now center around emphasis upon payment for time not worked, especially longer vacations and more holidays. Demand is also growing for a shorter workweek (35 hours, with two and one-half times base rate for overtime).

Paid *psychiatric assistance* for union members and their families is being asked for on the grounds that job pressures tend to cause mental health problems. More *convenience in personal shopping,* such as barber and beauty shops near the work area, are being requested so that workers can take time off from work (with pay) to obtain these "necessities."

Isolation pay for employees who must work by themselves because of dislocations and disruptions to the organization's social system caused by automation is being demanded by unions.

Emphasis is being placed upon *retirement benefits*—especially earlier retirement based on years of service alone, not age plus service—and *better pensions.* Portability of private pensions will also be a cardinal demand.

Finally, management is "trading off" *lifetime guarantees* of jobs for union members in exchange for the right to automate operations—or otherwise increase effectiveness. (20)

Union security

From the union's point of view, one of the most preferable methods of achieving its objectives is through some type of security for itself. This usually takes the form of contract clauses granting a closed shop, a union shop, an agency shop, or some other arrangement that will give the union control over hiring, supervising, and discharging workers.

The *closed shop,* which is largely illegal, required workers to be members of the union before they can be hired. It is found in the construction and maritime industries, where employees are obtained from union hiring halls.

When a *union shop* clause is agreed upon, all present employees and all new employees who are subsequently hired must join the union in 30 days or be discharged.

Under the *agency shop* agreement, workers must pay the union for serving as their bargaining agent, even if they don't join the union.

> Six tenured professors at Ferris State College in Big Rapids, Michigan, were sent dismissal notices after they refused to pay an "agency fee" required by the university's contract with its faculty union, an affiliate of the National Education Association.

The union shop is illegal in the 20 states that have "right-to-work" laws authorized under section 14(b) of the Taft-Hartley Act. This section of the federal law permits state laws prohibiting compulsory union membership to take precedence over the federal law.

In addition to these union security provisions, around 86 percent of all agreements provide for the *checkoff,* (21) whereby the employer withholds the union dues from the pay check of each union member who signs an affidavit agreeing to such deduction. While this provision does require the employer to serve as a collection agent for the union, it also eliminates the need for union officers to come onto the employer's premises to collect dues from delinquent members. In addition, it prevents the employer from having to discharge a capable employee who might be expelled from the union for nonpayment of dues.

Grievance procedure and arbitration

The next way unions achieve their goals is interpreting the provisions of the agreement, once it is signed. Being a legal document, the contract must be subject to legal, as well as practical, interpretation and implementation, and this involves the grievance procedure. When employees feel they have been unfairly treated, they ask the union steward (or union stewardess) to file a grievence against management. This complaint may be either oral or in writing. The supervisor must answer the grievance by correcting the situation or channeling it "up the line." When the unresolved grievance gets to the chief executive officer of the union and firm, it must be resolved or sent to an outsider for settlement. Most grievances are resolved before that time.

In every labor-management disagreement, a point is reached past which further discussion between the two parties becomes wasteful to the organization as a whole. It is at this point, then, that the two sides should submit the case in point to some form of outside arbitration. Thus, the ultimate step in handling a grievance between an employee and an employer is the arbitration procedure, whereby an outsider interprets the meaning of the contract and makes a binding decision. In essence, the contract is the "law"; when a worker, the union, or management breaks the law, the arbitrator serves as jury and judge to determine guilt and impose sentence or penalty.

The strike

The ultimate strategy used by the unions to achieve their objectives is the strike, while the corresponding management device is the lockout. In general, most union leaders do not like to use this device because it is costly, carries a certain amount of social stigma to the ones walking the picket line, and is potentially dangerous to the union because of the loss of membership and loss of power if the strike fails. (22) In fact, only about 4 percent of the 12,000 contracts terminating annually result in strikes. (23) Yet research has shown that strikes have a direct and positive effect on the size of settlements. (24)

Although the strike itself is the ultimate device in collective bargaining and is the technique resorted to when all other methods of resolving differences fail, the *threat of a strike* is a continuing factor in almost all negotiations.

SOME CHANGING UNION TACTICS

Traditional unions are declining in relative importance as *economic entities*. They now tend to achieve their goals through devices other than economic and moral persuasion. U.S. unions are in the throes of two contradictory developments. There is a new surge of social and economic inventiveness in adapting collective bargaining to the requirements of rapid technological change. Concurrently, there are severe, adverse challenges to the traditional structure of labor unions. There are several compelling reasons for the trend away from traditional unions, but only the most dramatic and powerful of these will be discussed.

Some *causes* of the changes

Declining favor with "liberals" and intellectuals. First, unions are tending to lose favor with the "liberals" and intellectuals. This trend, which began in the 1950s, reversed the previous favorable trend begun in the 1920s. (25)

Unions are losing public support. Second, the public—which is beginning to be concerned with the growing concentration of political and economic power in the hands of union leaders—is not as committed to the concept of unionism. The growth of large unions with tremendous memberships and resources, with one union (and union leader) controlling an entire industry and negotiating industrywide, has raised questions in the minds of many people. (26)

Opinion Research Corporation found that public opposition to the continued growth of unions in membership and power has risen, with 71 percent of the public polled feeling that unions were "either too big or big enough." Union efforts are construed as being against the public interest, with 59 percent of those surveyed blaming union demands and steadily rising labor costs for "causing the United States to price itself out of world markets." (27) Many also blame labor for contributing to inflation, which affects everyone who buys the products labor produces, including the vast majority who do not share in the wage increases gained by union members, but are the victims of the vicious circle of "wage-price" increases.

Managers becoming better negotiators. Third, employer representatives are becoming more adroit in engaging in the "game" of collective bargaining. They are continuing to acquire expertise in the *quid pro quo,* or "higgling," approach to bargaining. The loss of numerous management privileges has caused managers to become aware that their relations with unions must be based more upon a "good offensive," rather than upon the defensive approach. If this is not done, they will lose even more prerogatives.

Thus, instead of merely assenting to, or dissenting from, the multitudinous demands presented by the union representatives, they now present a similar list of their own proposals to give them bargaining power to counteract the demands of the union leaders. Consequently, the unions are less able to achieve major concessions without giving up something in return.

Technological development hampers unionism. Finally, automation and technological development are diminishing the effectiveness of traditional unionism. Although most union leaders recognize the inevitability of automation, they continue to oppose its application, for it has adversely affected unions in several ways. This trend is based upon the following factors: The nature of work and jobs is changing so that a higher-level personnel is required, and this group does not favor traditional unionism; group solidarity is reduced by the complexities and physical dispersion caused by the technological revolution; as the number of jobs outside the bargaining units, e.g., scientific, technical, professional, clerical sales, and service jobs, increase, union power is being eroded; and automated facilities are reducing the effectiveness of strikes, since supervisory personnel can operate the machines, at least until they need maintenance or replacement.

Changes are causing unions to use newer methods

For these and other reasons, unions have shifted their *primary emphasis from economic tactics to political pressures.* Union leaders have turned increasingly to governmental action as a means of achieving their objectives, in addition to using the more traditional actions. Consequently, it is believed that union activities now revolve around the exercise of political pressures as the organizations attempt to achieve their objectives through sanctions—other than economic.

Federal and state legislation. Labor organizations attempt to obtain concessions through the passage of federal and state legislation. Examples of the objectives which unions hope to achieve in this manner are: the repeal of Section 14(b); increased wages and reduced hours; and the passage of other types of social legislation, including government jobs—if private ones are not available.

Executive orders. Orders issued by the President are being used increasingly to achieve union objectives. Examples of these are Executive Orders 10988, 11491, and 11616, which required governmental administrators to permit their subordinates to join unions and then to recognize these organizations as the employees' exclusive bargaining agents—even though the Taft-Hartley Act *prohibited* this practice.

Interpretations by governmental agencies this practice. Interpretations and decisions by agencies such as the U.S. Employment Service, the Wage and Hour Division of the Department of Labor, and the NLRB are achieving for the unions what they have been unable to achieve through collective bargaining. The General Counsel of the board said, "The most significant recent development in collective bargaining is the increasing concern of the federal

MEMBERSHIP IN UNIONS AND EMPLOYEE ASSOCIATIONS

All the factors discussed in this chapter have an effect on the number of employees joining unions. The most spectacular gains in union membership occurred from 1935, with the passage of the Wagner Act, to 1947, with the passage of the Taft-Hartley Act. A second growth period was from 1950 to 1956. The third growth period was from the mid-1960s to the 1970s. (See Figure 21–2.)

In 1935, there were 3.5 million union members, accounting for around 7 percent of the total labor force, and 13 percent of employees in nonagricultural establishments. The number of union members continued to grow until 1956; declined until 1963; and then started climbing until it reached 19.4 million in 1972, which was 22 percent of the total labor force and 27 percent of nonagricultural employment. However, as a percentage of the nation's work force, union membership has declined for the last two decades. (See Figure 21–3.)

The Bureau of Labor Statistics started gathering data on membership in employee associations—other than unions—during 1967–68. Membership in unions and these associations increased from 20.7 million in 1968 to 21.7 million in 1972 (See Table 21–1).

FIGURE 21–2
Membership of national unions and associations, 1930–72*

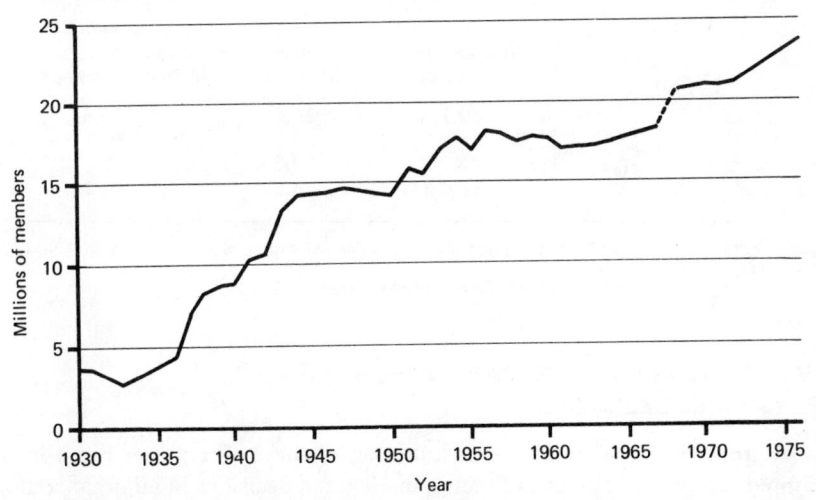

* (Exclusive of Canadian membership.) The dashed lines beginning in 1967–68 indicate that employee associations that bargain collectively were first reported then.
Source: U.S. Department of Labor, Bureau of Labor Statistics.

FIGURE 21-3
Membership of national unions and associations as a percent of total labor force and of employees in nonagricultural establishments, 1930-72*

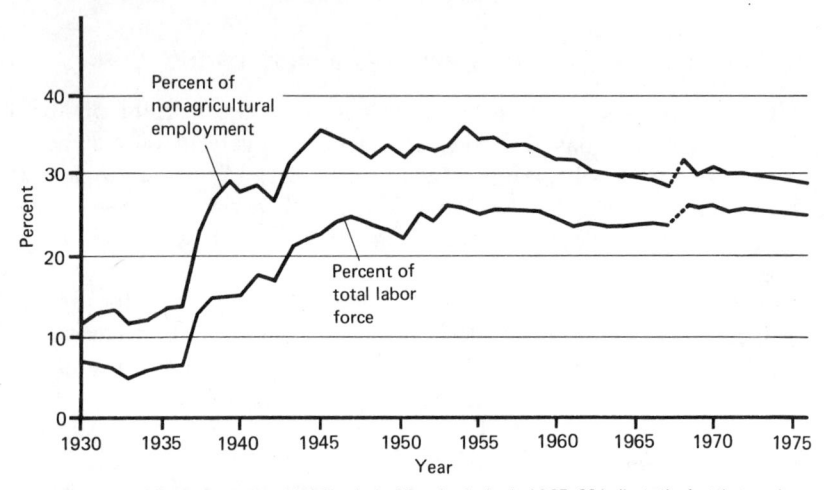

*(Exclusive of Canadian membership.) The dashed lines beginning in 1967-68 indicate the fact that employee associations that bargain collectively were first reported then.
Source: U.S. Department of Labor, Bureau of Labor Statistics.

It is interesting to see which industries are the most heavily unionized. As can be seen from Table 21-2, there is a wide dispersion in the extent of unionization.

TABLE 21-1
Membership in national unions and employee associations*

	Number in millions	Percent of total labor force	Percent in nonagricultural establishments
1968	20.7	25.2	30.5
1970	21.2	24.7	30.1
1972	21.7	24.3	29.8
1976	22.8	24.5	29.1

* Includes total reported membership, excluding Canadian, but including other areas outside the United States.
Source: U.S. Department of Labor, Bureau of Labor Statistics.

IMPLICATIONS AND APPLICATIONS FOR PERSONNEL EXECUTIVES

At present, labor unions constitute one of the major power blocs in the United States. Directly or indirectly, managerial decisions in all organizations are greatly influenced by the effect of the growing strength of unions. Consequently, the scope of managerial discretion has been considerably narrowed.

TABLE 21-2
Industries ranked by the degree of union organization

75 percent and over
1. Transportation
2. Contract construction
3. Ordnance
4. Paper
5. Electrical machinery
6. Transportation equipment

50 percent to less than 75 percent
7. Primary metals
8. Food and kindred products
9. Mining
10. Apparel
11. Tobacco manufactures
12. Petroleum
13. Manufacturing
14. Fabricated metals
15. Telephone and telegraph
16. Stone, clay, and glass products
17. Federal government
18. Rubber

25 percent to less than 50 percent
19. Printing, publishing
20. Leather
21. Furniture
22. Electric, gas utilities
23. Machinery
24. Chemicals
25. Lumber

Less than 25 percent
26. Nonmanufacturing
27. Textile mill products
28. Government
29. Instruments
30. Service
31. Local government
32. State government
33. Trade
34. Agriculture and fishing
35. Finance

Now, instead of management acting unilaterally to reward or punish employees, it must operate bilaterally through the union. Decisions affecting employees are now made collectively at the bargaining (and arbitration) tables, instead of individually by the supervisor when and where the need arises. Wages, hours, and other terms and conditions of employment are largely decided outside of management's sphere of discretion.

It is felt that the basic objectives of collective bargaining in this country have been met, with a tendency toward the following consequences: The gap between management and the individual employee has widened; there has been a broadening of the scope of collective bargaining with a consequent impingement upon (and narrowing of) managerial rights; unilateral action has given way to collective bargaining; rank-and-file employees have tended to obtain a greater degree of satisfaction from union membership than they have obtained from organizational affiliation; and there has been a shifting of loyalty from organizations—and their managers, to unions—and their leaders.

Now, there is a need for changing the philosophies, precepts, strategies, and tactics of industrial relations. The function of unions should now be to maintain the advantages already achieved and, at the same time, to accept joint responsibility and leadership in striving to solve some of the problems currently facing the country.

Since a growing number of white-collar and professional employees are becoming union members, personnel executives should focus clearly on the specific needs and concerns of their own work force rather than "doing what others are doing." Second, as career dissatisfaction is a factor that contributes to militancy, management should provide a different professional hierarchy similar to the "dual-promotion ladder" available to many scientists and engineers in most industrial organizations employing professionals.

Finally, personnel managers need to realize that militancy is increasing among white-collar, young, and professional employees and constantly need to search for methods of combating it.

DISCUSSION QUESTIONS

1. What are the new organizational goals of unions today as far as organizing employees is concerned? (*a*) From an industry point of view? (*b*) From a demographic or occupational point of view?
2. What are the most important laws pertaining to the collective bargaining context, and what does each attempt to do?
3. (*a*) Briefly describe the stages of union development from 1930 to 1960. (*b*) What major changes occurred in union development during that period?
4. What has been happening, and is happening, in industrial relations, or union activities, since 1960?
5. (*a*) What are the purposes and goals of unions? (*b*) Discuss the changing concepts of union goals.
6. (*a*) What are the traditional means of achieving union goals? (*b*) Discuss each of them in detail. (*c*) What are the new methods? (*d*) Describe each of them.
7. (*a*) Is the strike the most powerful means of achieving union goals? (*b*) Discuss the significance of the strike to management, the union, the workers, and the nation's economy.

REFERENCES AND SUGGESTIONS FOR FURTHER STUDY

1. The rationale for amending the Sherman Act to preclude labor organizations was the belief that a person's labor is a human right, not a commodity. It is interesting to note that this concept is diametrically opposed to that of Karl Marx who emphasized that the value of a product was equal to the value of the labor embodied in it. Therefore, the value of labor tended to equal the value of the goods produced.
2. Solomon Barkin, "A Trade Unionist Appraises Management Personnel Philosophy," *Harvard Business Review*, vol. 28, no. 5 (September 1950), pp. 59–64.
3. See Elton T. Reeves, "Which Way, Labor Relations," *Personnel Administrator*, vol. 19, no. 6 (September 1974), pp. 15–16, for a discussion of changes in the work force which will require changing labor-management relations.
4. For verification of this suggestion, see "Labor: When the Old Guard Leaves," *Business Week* (September 15, 1975), p. 69. It is believed that the new labor leaders will be more militant but largely nonideological.

5. See "Military Maneuver: Union Plans '76 Drive to Represent Servicemen; Legalities Are Explored, and Pentagon Shudders," *Wall Street Journal* (June 27, 1975), p. 24, for details of this movement.
6. See Louis V. Imundo, Jr., "Why Federal Government Employees Join Unions: A Study of AFGE Local 916," *Public Personnel Management*, vol. 2, no. 1, (January–February 1973), pp. 23–28, for an explanation of the attraction of unions for such employees. The reasons are primarily psychological (protection of their "rights") and economic (wage and benefit increases).

    In 1975, more than half of the nation's state and local government employees belonged to labor unions, reported the Census Bureau. Of the 9.2 million full-time nonfederal workers, 4.7 million, or 51 percent, were union members. That compared with a 41-percent union membership rate in 1972. Seventy-four percent of the firemen and 72 percent of the teachers were organized, the newest study shows. The U.S. Civil Service Commission reported that the number of federal workers covered by labor agreements topped the 1 million mark for the first time in 1975. See *U.S. News and World Report* (March 22, 1976), p. 68.
7. While the union shop and agency shop are *not* permitted, there is provision for exclusive representation by a single union, approved by a majority of those voting. Eligibility for voting and the bargaining units are decided by the Assistant Secretary of Labor for Management Relations with provision for appeal to a federal Labor Relations Council, composed of the Chairman of the Civil Service Commission, the Secretary of Labor, and members of the Executive Office. Bargaining is restricted to issues not determined by legislation; so compensation rates and fringe benefits are outside of the relationship. If there is an impasse in negotiations, arbitration is provided from a Federal Services Impasse Panel, which may impose a settlement. Strikes are illegal.
8. There may be a counter trend in progress. A Gallup poll found that 52 percent of the respondents did not think policemen should be permitted to strike; 55 percent opposed the right of firefighters to strike; while 47 percent thought sanitation people should be permitted to strike, 46 percent were opposed. See "Public Employees versus the Cities," *Business Week* (July 21, 1975), pp. 50–57; and "Public Employees Lose Leverage," *Business Week* (December 22, 1975), p. 15, for other examples of a negative reaction to public unions.

    The following incident tends to verify this trend. After the San Francisco police walked off the job demanding a 13-percent increase in pay in August 1975, the city's population voted 5 to 2 for a proposition forbidding strikes by police and firefighters. See "Voters Speak Up on Local Issues," *U.S. News & World Report* (November 17, 1975), p. 30
9. See Joseph W. Garbarino, "Faculty Unionism: From Theory to Practice," *Industrial Relations*, vol. 11, no. 1 (February 1972), pp. 1–10, for an analysis of the bargaining experience of five four-year institutions of higher learning. See also "Faculty Unionism in Institutions of Higher Education," *Monthly Labor Review*, vol. 97, no. 4, (April 1974), pp. 48–50.
10. See Joseph A. Alutto and James A. Belasco, "Determinants of Attitudinal Militancy among Nurses and Teachers," *Industrial and Labor Relations Review*, vol. 27, no. 2 (January 1974), pp. 216–27, for a study of attitudes of about 900 teachers and nurses toward collective bargaining by professional workers. It was found that the groups defined "militancy" differently. The teachers thought of it as

accepting collective bargaining through a professional association; for nurses, it entailed reliance on unions and strikes.

Teachers in rural areas were more militant than those in urban areas.

While sex and marital status had little effect on such attitudes, age did. Older professionals favored professional associations and collective bargaining over unions and strikes.

For another explanation of—and examples of—these attitudinal changes, see "Labor: Doctors, Nurses, Teachers—Why More Are Joining Unions," *U.S. News & World Report* (November 10, 1975), pp. 61–62.

11. John Shea, "Would Foremen Unionize?" *Personnel Journal,* vol. 49, no. 11 (November 1970), pp. 926–31.

12. Alfred Vogel, "Your Clerical Workers Are Ripe for Unionism," *Harvard Business Review,* vol. 49, no. 2 (March–April 1971), pp. 48–54.

   See also Erwin S. Stanton, "White Collar Unionization: New Challenge to Management," *Personnel Journal,* vol. 51, no. 2 (February 1972), pp. 118–24, for some ideas on preparing for the entry of the union and what you can do about it.

13. Edna E. Raphael, "Working Women and Their Membership in Labor Unions," *Monthly Labor Review,* vol. 97, no. 5 (May 1974), p. 27.

14. *Wall Street Journal* (October 21, 1975), p. 1.

15. See Leonard A. Rapping, "Unions-Induced Racial Entry Barrier," *Journal of Human Resources,* vol. 5, no. 4 (Fall 1970), pp. 447–74, for an estimate of the impact of collective bargaining on the occupational and industrial position of blacks, relative to whites. Interest is centered on measuring the union's effect on market *exclusion, not discrimination.* Union barriers may be tending to force the excluded groups to concentrate in low-paying jobs and thereby contribute to market discrimination.

16. "Significant Decisions in Labor Cases: *Rios* v. *Steamfitters Local 638; United States* v. *Steamfitters Local 638,"* *Monthly Labor Review,* vol. 97, no. 11 (November 1974), pp. 59–60.

17. Matthew A. Kelly, "The Contract Rejection Problem: A Positive Labor Management Approach," *Labor Law Journal,* vol. 20, no. 7 (July 1969), pp. 404–15.

18. See *Wall Street Journal* (October 8, 1974), p. 1, for other details.

19. Wallace B. Nelson, "Coercion on Collective Bargaining," *Labor Law Review,* vol. 21, no. 1 (January 1970), p. 45 ff.

20. For example, New York's major commercial printing firms signed a 10-year contract allowing them to introduce automated composing-room techniques in exchange for lifetime guarantees of jobs for all regular full-time printers. See "Printers, New York City Printing Firms Tentatively Agree on 10-Year Labor Pact," *Wall Street Journal* (October 28, 1975), p. 4, for details of this and an earlier similar agreement.

21. *Collective Bargaining: Negotiations and Contracts,* vol. 2 (Washington, D.C.: Bureau of National Affairs, 1971) p. 87.3.

22. See John Chamberlain, "Should the Unions Agree to Give Up Strikes?" *National Review,* (May 11, 1973), pp. 516–18, for some novel suggestions—some made by union intellectuals for union leaders—on alternatives to the strike.

23. According to Secretary of Labor, W. J. Usery, the average employee lost less than two hours of a full-year of normal work in 1974 due to strikes. See "The Outlook for Labor-Management Peace in Today's America," *Labor Law Journal,* vol. 25, no. 4 (April 1974), p. 195 ff.
24. D. Q. Mills, "Wage Determination in Contract Construction," *Industrial Relations,* vol. 10, no. 1 (February 1971), pp. 72–85.
25. Maurice F. Newfeld, "The Historical Relationship of Liberals and Intellectuals to Organized Labor in the United States," *Annals of the American Academy of Political and Social Science,* vol. 350 (November 1963), pp. 115–28.
26. "The Use and Abuse of Power," *Saturday Review,* vol. 45, no. 2 (January 13, 1962), pp. 32–34.
27. "Trouble Plagues the House of Labor," *Business Week* (October 28, 1972), pp. 66–76.
28. Stuart Rothman, "Collective Bargaining and the Public Interest," *Business Horizons,* vol. 5, no. 2 (Summer 1962), p. 69.

Chapter 22

Improving industrial relations in the individual organization

A model for predicting the degree of conflict
    The conflict-cooperation continuum
    Factors affecting degree of cooperation

Recognizing the union
    Effects of political, economic, and organizational climates
    Effects of employee attitudes
    How a union becomes recognized as the bargaining agent

Negotiating the agreement
    Theoretical base
    Developing a bargaining strategy
    The bargaining procedure
    The impasse
    The agreement is reached

Living with the agreement
    Handling grievances
    Arbitration

Implications and applications
    Changed employee attitudes
    Management's right to manage has been restricted
    The supervisor's right to supervise has been limited

Improving industrial relations in the individual organization 22

People don't ask for facts in making up their minds. They would rather have one good, soul-satisfying emotion than a dozen facts.
ROBERT KEITH LEAVITT

In 1937, in an effort to organize the employees of Ford Motor Company, Walter Reuther and a group of unionists did battle with the firm's guards at an overpass between buildings at the Ford River Rouge Plant. That bloody struggle, in which 16 union leaders (including six women) were badly beaten, eventually led to the unionization of Ford. (1)

This incident is an extreme example of conflict between union and management representatives, but by no means has it been an isolated one. The drive to unionize an organization is socially and psychologically unsettling, for it disrupts a going set of relationships, it undermines long-established customs, it activates conscious hostilities and brings unconscious ones to the surface, and from beginning to end it appeals to the emotions. (2)

Conventional wisdom states that the entry of a union is evidence of mismanagement; if this mismanagement is removed, then the union will not enter. Unfortunately this is not true! In certain industries and in some areas, unions tend to be very strong, regardless of the actions of management. However, there tends to be almost a universal resistance to unionization, even among unions themselves. (3)

Although sweeping generalizations are dangerous—inasmuch as they necessarily are somewhat inaccurate in specific cases—an attempt is made in this chapter to outline some of the factors which contribute to improving industrial relations in a given organization. Special emphasis will be given to a model for predicting the degree of conflict or cooperation, what to expect when the union enters to organize employees, how management recognizes the union as the exclusive bargaining agent for its employees, what is involved in negotiating the agreement, and how to live with it.

A MODEL FOR PREDICTING THE DEGREE OF CONFLICT

Some years ago, a colleague and I attempted to identify and isolate selected variables which influence the degree of union-management conflict. (4) The results included a model which could be used to predict the extent of conflict or cooperation under modifying assumptions and given factors. Figure 22–1 is a graphical summation of the significant forces found to affect the level of conflict between union and management.

The conflict-cooperation continuum

As the union-management relationship is a system in which each of the factors is interrelated and interacting, (5) the two-directional arrows between each of the conflictual "variables" is intended to show the interrelatedness of, and interaction between, each of them.

The model also shows that the resulting level of conflict "feeds back" upon the conflictual variables and further influences the two groups toward a greater or lesser degree of conflict in future relationships.

Modern organization theory accepts unions as seekers of power and relationships among power holders and power centers. Therefore, coalitions involving unions and other power holders—including governments—is perceived as legitimate. Finally, unions are seen as a means by which members exert control over day-to-day working conditions, as well as their long-term personal destinies. (6)

FIGURE 22–1
A suggested model for predicting the degree of conflict or cooperation between management and union leaders

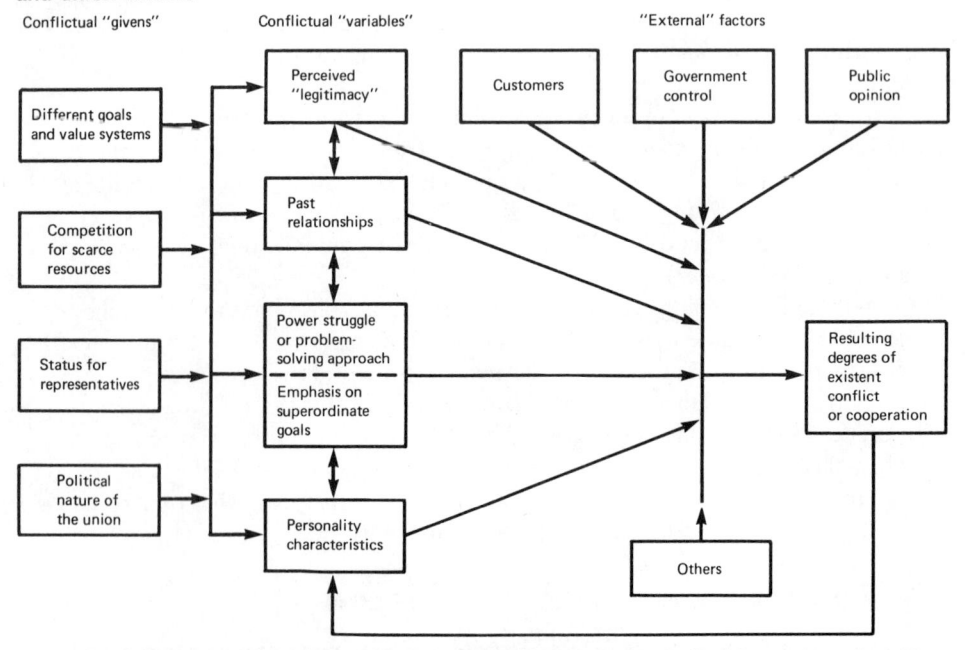

Source: L. C. Megginson and C. Ray Gullett, "A Predictive Model of Union-Management Conflict," *Personnel Journal*, vol. 49, no. 6 (June 1970), p. 502. Reprinted with permission, *Personnel Journal*, copyright June 1970.

Ordinarily managerial resistance to the union declines once the contract is signed. Then both parties usually try to find some way to live reasonably amicably with each other and, indeed, often find there are many areas where mutual cooperation helps everyone concerned. For example, a study of the attitudes of managers in 37 business establishments found that about 29 percent of those interviewed felt that the union was "no problem" in terms of the scope and depth of union participation in management matters; 45 percent felt that union interference was "not serious." Only 26 percent were "seriously concerned" about union interference. (7)

Factors affecting degree of cooperation

There are many factors affecting the degree of cooperation between management and union leaders. They include the quasi-political nature of union and personality factors.

The quasi-political nature of the union. This aspect of unions was discussed in the previous chapter. They are not economic entities in the same sense as business organizations; instead, they must promote solidarity with their ranks in order to be effective. Psychologists and sociologists have found through research that one way of generating unanimity within the ranks of unions is to focus attention on the "unfair" and "unjust" behavior of some outside force toward the members—usually provided by management. A research project found increased solidarity and cooperativeness within the group at the very time when intergroup hostility was at its peak, that is, during the period when unions and management were agreeing that they could not live with each other. (8) In order to maintain in-group solidarity, union leadership may find it necessary to create a degree of worker dissatisfaction with current managerial actions. (9)

Personality factors. These are also intervening variables. Research has shown that employee relations managers tend primarily to be concerned with vertical relationships with their superiors, while union officials tend to be more horizontally-oriented toward their peers; the former were presumed to have identified successfully with their fathers, while the latter tended to be more democratic or liberal and oriented toward their brothers. (10) Also, the cultural backgrounds are different, for most union leaders rise from the ranks of employees, come from a working-class heritage, have little education beyond high school, and do not have a professional background, as opposed to management personnel who do. (11)

Research also shows that the participants "take on the coloring" of the organization to which they belong. Newly elected union stewards tend to become more pro union than before, while supervisors who are newly promoted tend to become more pro management. (12) However, it has been found that the relationships between management and union leaders tend to become less conflictual as time passes and they become more experienced in dealing with one another. (13)

RECOGNIZING THE UNION

Before the union can negotiate an agreement with the employer, it first must be recognized as the exclusive bargaining agent for the employees. This, in turn, requires that at least some of the employees join the union as a result of an organizing drive. Therefore, we need to see why workers join unions, as well as the influence of organizational climate on the organizing drive.

Effects of political, economic, and organizational climates

American attitudes have changed toward unions as the latter have grown and modified their goals and policies. Unions are now perceived as satisfying a variety of employee needs, from subsistence to self-actualization. Regardless of how they are viewed, unions change their strategy with variations in the economic and political climates, (14) as well as organizational climate—as shown above. It has been shown that organizations with a favorable climate have less difficulty with the union than those with a negative, antagonistic attitude.

When a union wishes to be recognized, the initiative may come from the employees themselves or from the union. Sometimes the workers are already unionized, and the drive for membership comes from a rival union. In general, it has been shown that where there is interunion rivalry with more than one union attempting to sway the allegiance of the workers there will be a greater degree of conflict generated between management and the union. (15)

Effects of employee attitudes

There are no simple explanations of why workers join or reject unions. A primary reason for the complexity of the problem is that human motivation is exceedingly complex: A wide range of motivations exist in varying degree at any one time. Second, environmental pressures are constantly shifting; these pressures influence workers in first one direction and then another. A third reason why it is impossible to isolate the specific reason for a given worker's decision is the previously mentioned emotionalism associated with the organizing drive. Rational, logical arguments for joining the union are given to the workers by the organizer who attempts to get them to join the union, but these are a minor part of the recruiter's technique. There is a concentration upon emotional appeals to powerful human drives: "(*a*) the desire for economic improvement, (*b*) the craving to belong to the group, and (*c*) the impulse toward aggression and hostility." (16)

Another reason it is so difficult to isolate reasons for union membership is because of conflicting research findings. In 1951, it was found that not one worker said one joined the union primarily to obtain higher wages but that they were important (17); in 1965, the reasons were to insure job security, build employee self-confidence, and release job-oriented frustrations (18); in 1967, union membership was found to be an expression of dissatisfaction with some aspect of their job (19); and, in 1969, employees joined unions for better job conditions, improved supervision, better communication with management, more democracy in the work place, higher morale, and increased employee unity. (20)

In spite of these limitations upon our knowledge, however, some generalizations can be made. These should help personnel executives be better prepared to cope with the union when it enters.

Reasons why workers join unions. The foremost reasons for joining unions can be summarized as the workers' search for: steady employment with adequate income; the rationalization of personnel policies; a voice in decisions affecting their welfare; protection from economic hazards beyond their control; recognition and participation; and compulsion.

Steady employment with adequate income. Abundant research is available to prove that probably the most basic desire of employees in our culture—yesterday, today, and tomorrow—is for security, especially economic security. In fact, job security takes priority over the amount of wages paid to employees as a determinant of job satisfaction. Therefore, to the extent the union can convince workers that it (better than management or anyone else) can assure them steady jobs at a satisfactory wage, they probably will join the union.

Rationalization of personnel policies. Some workers may join unions to redress supposed grievances against their supervisor or the organization. If management is viewed as acting irrationally, illogically, discriminatorily, or prejudicially toward them, workers will be inclined toward unionization. As employee security is also based upon management's personnel policies, workers prefer assignment to jobs, transfers and promotions, discipline, layoffs and rehires, and other rewards and punishments to be governed by predetermined rules. They also want a voice in the determining and enforcing of these rules in person or through their representatives. In other words, they may feel that with the union there will be less favoritism and discrimination.

A voice in decisions affecting their welfare. Being part of a union allows workers to have a voice in affairs that affect them. Workers may be motivated to join unions because they want to be able to communicate their frustrations, aims, feelings, and ideas to their superiors, or to seek an outlet when advancement in the organization is blocked. Workers may improve their position through the union, perhaps because of an improved bargaining position or by being elected to a union office.

Protection from economic hazards beyond their control. Workers are subjected to many hazards beyond their control, such as sickness, accidents, and death, and many of them cannot plan and provide for coping with these personal tragedies. Rightly or wrongly, the workers feel that their employers are partially or wholly responsible for helping them to overcome such adversities.

Recognition and participation. Fellow workers may strongly influence an employee either to join or reject the union. As one of our basic needs is the urge to be accepted by the group, to belong, and to get along with others, becoming a union member may cause workers to gain respect in the eyes of their peers. Cultural factors may also lead the worker either way, for if a worker's parents and neighbors have always belonged to unions, there will be a strong tendency for the worker to join the union. Research also shows that recreational and social activities associated with unions provide an added incentive for some workers. (21)

Compulsion. It would be unrealistic not to accept the fact that some workers are compelled to join the union in order to get a particular job or in order not to be treated like a social outcast. (22) For example, certain union security provisions, such as the union shop, maintenance of membership, and checkoff, require union membership. Also, the labor laws, executive orders, and administrative decisions in government organizations are designed to force union membership in the 30 states not having right-to-work laws.

There is no clear answer as to the desirability of right-to-work laws. From an economic point of view, their proponents say they result in faster rates of growth in wages and personal income; their opponents say they depress wages and retard economic growth. However, the evidence seems to be that they have had little effect on economic development, one way or the other. From a political point of view, their opponents say that the laws prevent the signing of union-shop agreements with employers, which strikes at the core of union security, union strength, and tends to destroy unionism. The proponents of the laws say that unions do not need further strengthening because they are adequately protected under present law. From a moral point of view, the proponents of the laws say individuals have the inherent "freedom of voluntary association," while opponents say that the majority should rule and there should be no "free riders."

A survey by the Opinion Research Corporation showed that 60 percent of the American public believe in voluntary unionism in the form of the open shop; 66 percent believe that workers should be free to join or to refuse to join unions; 70 percent feel that workers should not be fired for refusing to join; while 61 percent believe that the right-to-work laws should be retained. (23)

Reasons why workers do not join unions. Since about 75 percent of employees in nonfarm establishments do not belong to unions, there must be some compelling reasons—or forces—why they resist joining. In addition to these forces, the lack of aggressive organizing efforts on the part of some unions also explains why workers do not join unions. As shown in Chapter 21, this is now changing!

The lack of a compelling reason. Part of the reason for this phenomenon lies in the fact that some employees simply lack reasons for joining unions, as they consider their wages adequate, their working conditions satisfactory, and their other needs reasonably well met. In essence, they are content; and *discontent* is associated with union membership. (24) Also, they feel they can progress on their own abilities, which they consider superior to those of the group.

They identify with management. Some employees tend to identify themselves more closely with management and, therefore, shun unions. White-collar, scientific, technical, and professional employees identify with management and thus hope for promotion into supervisory and executive levels. This does not result from "snob appeal," as a study of such workers found that while 67 percent saw themselves as being more educated than plant workers, and 53 percent thought they were more ambitious, only 35 percent felt they were in a higher social group. (25)

They distrust unions. Many employees distrust unions and what they stand for: They may feel that the union stands for "collectivism," "socialism," and the "welfare state," and against individual freedom and initiative. Also, workers see that the public suffers when strikes occur in some companies or industries.

They fear corruption in unions. Another rationale for not joining is the evidence of corruption unearthed by Senator McClellan's Senate Select Committee on Improper Activities in the Labor and Management Field. (26) It was shown that a significant minority of corrupt labor leaders were extorting bribes from companies for not striking against them, stealing from employee health and welfare funds, and accepting bribes from management for "sweetheart contracts," whereby concessions were made to employers at the expense of the employees. These malpractices scare some workers so that they do not want to be affiliated with the union movement, even if most unions are free of these taints.

Reasons for members' lack of participation. It is an observable fact that many union members are apathetic and do not actively participate in union activities. Some of this apathy is explained by compulsory membership, fear, and distrust, as shown above. But there are other more basic issues. For example, a study of white-collar unions in Australia revealed that the variables which influenced the behavior of union members were: class identification; members' occupations; promotional opportunities; physical isolation; perceptions of confronting industrial problems; satisfaction received from union effort; and attitudes of union leadership. (27)

Earlier studies in the United States showed that members ultimately participate in their union if they accept the work, workplace, fellow workers, and the "working class" as being a very meaningful part of their life (28); if not, they remain passive. Surveys of union-member expectations find that while union members do emphasize economic, work-related issues (commonly called "bread-and-butter" issues), those who are most active also believe in much broader objectives. Apparently those who take membership lightly tend to think in terms of bread-and-butter issues; those who support the union enthusiastically tend to expect more from it.

How a union becomes recognized as the bargaining agent

As shown in Chapter 21, there are three ways a union can become the bargaining agent for employees. But, the usual procedure is for a union, the employer, or a group of employees to file a petition for an election with the regional director of the NLRB. An examiner holds a hearing to see if the board has jurisdiction and if there is sufficient interest to warrant holding an election. At this time, the order in which the choices will appear on the ballot is determined, with one space always being provided for "no union." The *bargaining unit* is also defined at that time. This unit is a group of employees recognized by the employer—or the appropriate agency—as the appropriate unit to be represented by the union for bargaining purposes. The determination of the appropriate bargaining unit by the examiner is usually based upon the preference of the employees; the historic practice in the organization; similarities in working conditions, jobs, and skills; and common practice in the industry. Usually the unit is comprised of those workers—usually 30 percent of the work force—who petitioned for the election. This is one of the more important aspects of collective bargaining, as the unit chosen largely determines whether the union will win the election or not.

One of the important questions includes who is to be excluded from the bargaining unit. The general rule is to *include those with a commonality of interest* with their fellow employees and to exclude those whose interests more nearly approach those of management.*

The NLRB then proceeds to hold the election within 30 to 60 days, during which time both sides try to influence the employees' decision.

The NLRB not only supervises the election, but provides ballots, boxes, watchers at the poll, a count of the votes, and the certification of the one who wins the election. If there are two unions and neither of them obtains a majority vote, then either the two unions or the one union and no union are on a ballot in a runoff. To win an election, the union must obtain over 50 percent of the votes of those voting. If it does, then it is certified as being the exclusive bargaining agent for *all* the employees in the bargaining unit.

Management has the right to try to dissuade workers from voting in favor of the union until 24 hours before the election. But they cannot promise a reward or threaten reprisal. (See Appendix A for things you can do when the union tries to organize your company, and Appendix B for what you cannot do.)

In general, management's efforts to obtain a "no union" vote tend to follow a predictable pattern. (29) Large employers emphasize emotional issues, while smaller employers stress the effect of the union upon job security. The more unemployed in the area, the more the managers stress danger of job loss. Employers in smaller cities emphasize personal contact, while big-city managers mention management rights.

A study of union attempts to organize white-collar groups found the union

---

* Usually the union would like to get a bargaining unit which it thinks will vote for it, while management just as strongly tries to structure the bargaining unit to vote against the union. However, by law, guards, supervisors, and managerial and professional personnel are excluded from the unit.

winning 67 percent of them. They were more successful where the workers asked the union in, where workers kept union activities from management, where the firm's blue-collar workers were already represented by the union, where the work groups were small, and where communications were poor. (30)

It was found that the unions won 22 of 26 elections where there was no personal contact between the employer and employees, and 21 of 41 where there was personal contact, but only 24 of 73 where the firm used both written and personal communications.

It has been estimated that the average employer loses $124 per worker during an NLRB certification election. For larger plants with over 1,000 workers, the cost decreases to $102. (31)

NEGOTIATING THE AGREEMENT

Collective bargaining is the "heart" of industrial relations, for it is through that procedure that the terms and conditions under which the two parties will live together are determined. Collective bargaining is the *mutual obligation* of *representatives* of the employer and employees to meet at *reasonable times* and *confer in good faith* over *wages, hours, and other terms and conditions of employment.*

Theoretical base

However, regardless of its legal definition, collective bargaining is a social, as well as a legal and economic, process. Therefore, the same behavioral theories apply to it as apply to other aspects of human behavior. It involves the emotions of people that seek expression in the annual round of ceremonial activities. (32) These activities are important in mobilizing emotions—of management *and* the workers—and forming attitudes to support appropriate behavior in both the union and the organization. Management must allow these emotions to be expressed in the "ritual" of the bargaining process, or they may break out in other damaging ways such as strikes or decreased production. (33)

Developing a bargaining strategy

While each bargaining session is different, depending upon the negotiators and the situation, there are some useful generalizations that can be made at this time. Management should never "give" any concessions to the union but should allow itself to be persuaded, for labor negotiators will perceive themselves as being inferior if concessions are given to them rather than won from management. Gifts are not made to equals except when the receiver is in a position to make gifts in return.

Other suggestions are:

1. Prepare continually for negotiations;
2. Prepare a list of demands comparable to that which the union usually presents, then bargain on each issue on a *quid pro quo* basis;
3. *Don't plead inability to pay* for a requested benefit unless you are prepared to open your books to the union;
4. Determine in advance which are your *cardinal demands,* i.e., those for which you are willing to take a strike rather than yield; and
5. Don't belittle your employees, for you must "live with them" when the negotiating stops. (34)

The bargaining procedure

Bargaining can take place between a single employer and the union, between multiple employers in a given area, a sector of an industry, or for a whole industry. By a wide margin, most agreements are negotiated between one employer and its union. In case of more than one union, the employer negotiates with each one of them individually. This sometimes leads to the "whiplash," whereby as each union settles with the employer, the next union asks for the same settlement, plus a little more. By the time it comes to the last union, it is in a strategic position for it can stop the entire operation by calling its members out on a strike.

Single or multiple employer bargaining. There is a rationale to the choice of company against which a union will focus its bargaining strategy. Research has shown that unions choose one of the large firms with which to do battle over the terms of a contract that will set precedence not only for the single industry but often for other important segments of the business community as well. (35) It can be seen that the large firm is in a strategic place in the collective bargaining pattern setting which makes it susceptible to industrial conflict with the unions with which it deals. Conversely, the very small firms are highly dependent upon the patterns set by the larger firms as they are in a relatively weak bargaining position and usually can do little to resist the demands of a large and powerful union.

The bargaining teams. Managerial bargaining teams usually consist of three or four members. The personnel director is almost always not only on the team but the chief spokesman. Other members will include the plant manager, the operating superintendent, and occasionally a lawyer or other technical advisor.

The union team is usually larger, including some five to seven representatives, with seven being the usual number—usually the shop stewards or committeemen, the officers of the local, and representatives of the regional or national organization.

As organizations tend to be hierarchical, it is relatively easy to have a designated spokesman and for the other members to speak only when called upon or when in caucus. This gives a more united front than is presented by the union, which is more democratic and which frequently has "splits" among the members, often on an occupational basis.

When and where to bargain. The law only requires bargaining during "normal work periods," but, if negotiations are reaching a crisis, then management may wish to bargain for longer periods of time. However, as one of the tactics of the union is to wear management down, it has been found that this is not desirable except on special occasions.

While it is legal to bargain on the organization's premises, experience shows that the union will make management "pay" for exercising this prerogative. Instead, it is much more desirable and feasible to meet at some neutral place, usually a motel or hotel.

How to bargain. The law requires bargaining "in good faith," which means that while the employer does not have to accept the union's demands it does require that these demands be listened to and valid counter offers be made. (36) This is one of the "stickiest" areas of industrial relations, along with determining the bargaining unit.

The impasse

Collective bargaining is a "give and take" process, with the union usually offering a large number of proposals in the form of demands. These are countered with counter offers or proposals by management, also usually in the form of demands. During the early history of collective bargaining, management did not submit demands but merely answered the union's. It was found that management was giving up everything and receiving nothing in return. Now, there is the *quid pro quo* bargaining with each side giving and receiving.

However, a point may have been reached where neither side is willing to yield on a point, particularly if it is one of the cardinal demands of either the union or management. This point is called the "impasse." An example of negotiating over wages will best illustrate this point.

How the impasse occurs. The bargaining theory of wages (see Chapter 16 for further details) states that the wage level depends upon the interplay between management and labor through the collective bargaining procedure. Thus, wages will be determined by the relative bargaining power of the labor union and the company. The theory was modified by Pigou to include the range theory of bargaining, whereby there would be in one instance a range of practical bargaining and in the other area there would not be such a range. (37) (See Figure 22–2.) In the first instance, the union would have an upper limit on its demands and a lower limit that was its "sticking point." The firm would have a lower limit on its offer and an upper limit which was its sticking point. As long as the union's sticking point was lower than the firm's, there was an area of practical bargaining, and the specific rate was determined within that area. When the union's sticking point was higher than the firm's, an impasse was reached; there was no area for practical bargaining, and either a strike or lockout occurred.

FIGURE 22-2
The collective bargaining process under conditions of practical bargaining and impasse

First condition: Range of practical bargaining

Union demands:		Company offer:
Upper limit on demands ---------- $3.50/hr.		
	---------- $3.35	Sticking point
	{ Range of practical bargaining }	
Sticking point ---------- $3.20		
	$3.05	Lower limit on company offer

Second condition: Impasse; no area for practical bargaining

Union demands:		Company offer:
Upper limit on demands ---------- $3.50/hr.		
Sticking point ---------- $3.35 ----------		
	No area for practical bargaining	
	---------- $3.30 ----------	Sticking point
	$3.05 ----------	Lower limit on offer

The bargaining theory offers the most pragmatic explanation of how the negotiating process works.

What to do when the impasse occurs. There are three alternatives when impasse occurs, namely, mediation or conciliation, arbitration, or a strike or lockout.

Mediation or conciliation. The Taft-Hartley Act provided for the Federal Mediation and Conciliation Service (FMCS) to offer its services when a major strike is going to occur. During the preliminaries and negotiations, the FMCS is available to try to keep the two parties negotiating. If a strike or lockout occurs, the mediator will meet with both parties to try to find out what they really want and what they are willing to concede. Usually a face-saving solution is found which brings the parties together and ends the strike.

Mediation has been found to be more effective in rural areas and smaller communities, when both parties invite the mediator in and pay for the service and when the parties are aware of the consequences of the failure of mediation —either a strike or binding arbitration. (38)

There are indications that there is a growing desire to settle labor disputes without work stoppages. While public employees are generally not permitted to strike, private-sector unions appear to recognize the fact that there is little long-term advantage, economic or otherwise, to strikes. Agreements reached by the United Steelworkers of Americia and the aluminum industry employees are examples of what seems to be a growing trend in American labor organizations to use mediation and conciliation as an alternative to strikes. (39)

Arbitration. Arbitration is used infrequently to settle disputes at this level in the private sector. Instead, it is usually reserved for administering the contract. However, it is used extensively in the public sector.

Compulsory arbitration, with an outside arbitrator rendering a binding decision on both parties, is now being resorted to as an alternative to strikes, especially in the public sector.

Strike or lockout. If all else fails, the union has the right to strike the company, and the company has the right to lockout the employees in order to gain their objectives. They are the ultimate *weapons* in collective bargaining but are used infrequently. According to the *1975 Manpower Report of the President,* there were only 5,900 work stoppages, involving 2.7 million workers who were idle 48 million worker days, which was 0.24 percent of the estimated total working time, and the strike lasted an average of 18 days per person. The vast majority of strikes are over general wage changes, with plant administration and union organization and security running second and third. The Bureau of Labor Statistics has estimated that fewer than 4 percent of contract negotiations result in strikes.

An overgeneralization is that union leaders prefer not to use the strike, just as management prefers not to use the lockout.

The agreement is reached

Ultimately the agreement is reached. While there is no legal requirement for signing a document, almost always there is a memorandum of agreement prepared and signed by both parties. However, it does not become official until the workers and top management sign it.

Content of agreement. While there is no standard format, as each union and organization has its own set of agreements upon which the contract is based, the typical format would include the following subjects: (*a*) purpose and intent of the parties; (*b*) scope of the agreement; (*c*) management rights; (*d*) *union security and dues checkoff;* (*e*) other responsibilities; (*f*) adjustment of grievances; (*g*) provisions for arbitration; (*h*) disciplinary procedures; (*i*) rates of pay; (*j*) hours of work, including overtime and special time; (*k*) work rules; (*l*) benefits, including vacations, holidays, insurance, and pensions; (*m*) health and safety provisions; (*n*) employee security and seniority provisions, including promotions, layoffs-recalls, and transfers; and (*o*) duration and reopening date.

Approval or rejection of agreement. After it is signed, the union representatives must "sell" the agreement to the members for their ratification. While this step was taken for granted for many years, there is now a trend toward rejecting the agreement. According to the FMCS, it closed 7,975 joint-meeting cases. (40) Of those, 988 involved contract rejections. However, rejections were found to prevail in a relatively few unions; 11 international unions were found to be responsible for 55 percent of all rejections. The primary cause of rejections was lack of recommendation by the union negotiators.

LIVING WITH THE AGREEMENT

The process is not over when negotiations terminate in the signing of an agreement. It must be communicated to those affected by its provisions, people must be prepared for living with it, and the machinery must be set up to interpret and implement the settlement of grievances arising from the understanding.

Research has shown the important role played by the supervisor and the shop steward. Selekman called these individuals the "pivots of the whole structure of relationships" upon which the effective administration of the agreement ultimately rests. (41) They live in close association with each other and provide the machinery of adjustment of complaints requiring enforcement under the contract. To the extent that these individuals are trained in administering the contract, the organization—and union—will benefit.

Supervisors' consideration for subordinates is also important in reducing grievances. For example, a study showed that supervisors who had high consideration for subordinates had low grievance rates; those with low scores on consideration had high grievance rates; but those with medium scores on consideration had grievance rates that varied with the degree of structure in attempting to achieve organizational goals. (42)

Later research showed that a training program for both supervisors and union stewards in a large organization handling around 3,000 grievances per year resulted in a decline in the number of grievances per 100 employees from 17 to 7, and the percentage settled at the first step increased from 33 to 54 percent. (43)

The importance of supervisors and stewards working together was demonstrated in another study which showed that supervisors who process grievances faster have fewer to process. (44)

Handling grievances

It is human nature to complain about things which displease us. Some employees become dissatsified with personal problems and bring those frustrations to the job where they will complain to management about them. Other complaints originate because employees are dissatisfied with various aspects of their job. Employees placed on a job which does not meet their talents, or for which they are inadequately prepared, will complain about it. Yet, research has indicated that grievances do not appear to be more prevalent in one job or occupation than in others. (45) Workers also complain about supervisory practices, including attitudes, behavior, and decisions. A common cause of complaints is a supervisor who plays favorites, does not keep promises, or is too demanding of subordinates.

FIGURE 22–3
A typical grievance procedure

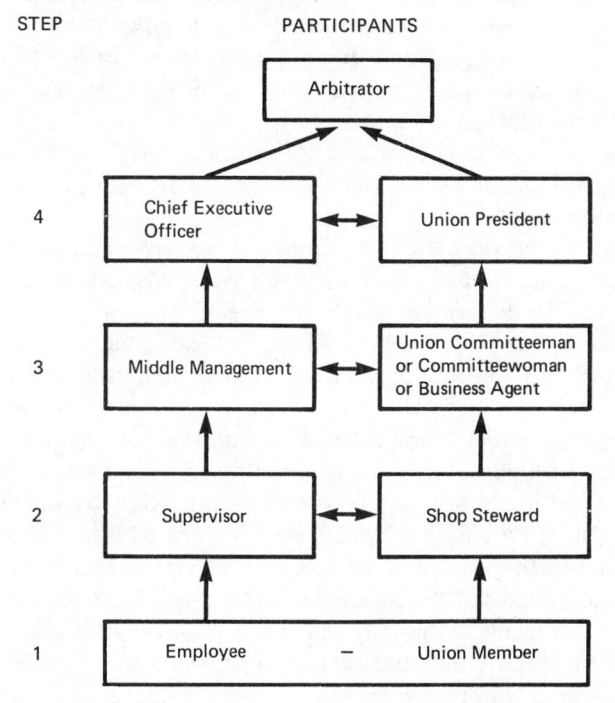

STEP	PARTICIPANTS
4	Chief Executive Officer ↔ Union President (both → Arbitrator)
3	Middle Management ↔ Union Committeeman or Committeewoman or Business Agent
2	Supervisor ↔ Shop Steward
1	Employee — Union Member

For purposes of this discussion, we will look at grievances resulting from the labor agreement. It has been shown that most grievances involve disputes related to employee discipline rather than interpretation of the provisions of the agreement. (46)

The grievance procedure in unionized organizations. The form and substance of the grievance procedure depends on the size of the industry and the size and structure of the organization and union.* A typical grievance procedure is shown in Figure 22–3. This one would be found in a manufacturing organization with a union which has a local president.

The *first step* in a formal grievance procedure originates with the employee complaining to the supervisor over a presumed wrong. It may be a violation of the contract or something the supervisor has done which dissatisfies the employee. If satisfaction is given, that may be the end of it. However, usually the employee, who is also a union member, goes to the shop steward and presents the grievance. The shop steward then goes to the supervisor to try to obtain satisfaction. The vast majority of grievances are settled at this point. For example, 77 percent of written grievances under the GM-UAW agreement are settled at this point. (47)

---

* The procedure will conform to the company and union organization with a step at each of the hierarchical levels, from the supervisor to the chief executive officer.

If satisfaction is not obtained, *step two* finds the steward going to the committeeman or committeewoman, or the local business agent. This official then goes to the superior of the supervisor who handled the grievance in the first place. Another large proportion of grievances is settled at this point.

Third, the union president and the chief executive officer try to resolve the difference. If so, that ends the procedure.

Finally, if the two chief executive officers cannot resolve the grievance, it is submitted to outside arbitration, with a mutually agreed-upon arbitrator making the decision.

Very often supervisors can help improve employee-employer relationships if they understand the characteristics of employees who are more prone to file grievances. One study showed that the more sensitive people are the more they file (48); younger employees who are better educated but lower paid tend to file more (49); and white employees, with less service, who are also veterans file more. (50)

Handling complaints in nonunion organizations. The majority of nonunion organizations do not have specific provisions for handling employee complaints. (51) Yet many organizations with no collective bargaining or recognized union have established formal grievance procedures that are in many ways comparable to formal union grievance procedures. Many of these permit complaints to go beyond the immediate supervisor to committees composed of higher-level executives, usually under the responsibility of the personnel officer, and to review committees consisting of the top executives. However, arbitration is usually not provided for. The primary purpose of these unilaterally created arrangements is to assure fairness in employee relations and to improve employee attitudes, rather than interpretation of personnel policies and practices.

These arrangements are frequently found in the public sector. (52)

Some organizations now have an *ombudsman*—either male or female—to help resolve complaints and grievances and to improve the communications between management and subordinates.

Arbitration

If satisfaction cannot be obtained from the internal administration of the grievance procedure, the question goes outside to arbitration, where a neutral party hears the evidence, evaluates the findings, and renders a decision, including implementation.

Almost all agreements have provision for grievance procedures, and around 95 percent of them contain requirements for arbitration as the last step in the procedure. (53)

There are a number of problems associated with the use of this procedure. Part of the difficulty results from the fact that arbitration has, to a degree, departed from its initial "advantages." In its beginning, arbitration was supported because it provided a relatively quick, cheap method of settling industrial disputes. It is no longer cheap or quick, as there is a shortage of new, acceptable arbitrators; there are delays in selecting panels and presenting the findings; and the proceedings are becoming increasingly formal. Much of the delay and lack of new talent stems from the fact that both management and labor prefer experienced arbitrators. Consequently, the experienced ones are overworked and the new ones are unable to gain experience.

IMPLICATIONS AND APPLICATIONS

Some degree of conflict is always present in every union-management relationship. As the union is the *advocate* of its members, who are employees of management, it automatically becomes the *adversary* of the organization and management.

On the whole, the trend in labor relations has moved away from a posture of conflict toward a more accommodating and cooperative relationship. Yet, the union-management relationship is still not one of enthusiastic acceptance by each side, but is one which can be termed as "antagonistic cooperation."

"The union's up to something."

Courtesy of Publishers, Hall Syndicate

Changed employee attitudes

The unions' impact upon personnel administration has been great, particularly in the area of employee attitudes and loyalties. The increased influence of unions has reduced management's chances of molding workers into the "ideal form" it would like, for managerial techniques must be modified to be in harmony with collective bargaining and government policy. Some changes have been so profound as to require a new philosophy of personnel administration, namely, the partnership concept and the due process approach. Yet, unionization does not necessarily imply disloyalty to the company on the part of employees. In a study of packinghouse workers, 73 percent expressed favorable sentiments toward the company, as well as the union. (54)

Management's right to manage has been restricted

Although there is no unanimity as to the impact of unions on the personnel function, it can be stated in general that there are three primary effects. First, the *content* of personnel policies and practices has improved. Second, the *decision-making process* has been altered, directly or indirectly. Some decisions may now be made only after consultation with the employees' representatives, while others require mutual consent. Third, the *execution of policies and practices* is now subject to organized scrutiny and criticism.

The Supreme Court's theory is that a company's legal right to manage its operations is open to question whenever the parties have agreed in the contract to arbitrate differences concerning the construction and interpretation of the agreement. (55) It is also questioned whenever the union contends that an act by management is inconsistent with implied understanding of the parties, or alleges intentions never expressed in the agreement at all, or is inconsistent with matters entirely outside the contract.

The supervisors' right to supervise has been limited

Regardless of the philosophies, activities, and policies of the top managers, and regardless of the effectiveness of the negotiators in the collective bargaining procedure, *successful labor relations are achieved only through the efforts of the first-line supervisors.* During World War II, the position of the supervisors deteriorated until many of them considered themselves as only rank-and-file employees and joined their subordinates' unions. Two factors contributed to this trend. First, the emergence of the power of the union shop steward exerted pressure by removing the supervisor's right to reward and punish subordinates. Second, other managers, including personnel managers, did not give enough consideration to the supervisor as a "member of the management team."

However, if supervisors are to fulfill their role in labor-management relations crises, they must be supplied with all pertinent communications pertaining to policies and procedures and be permitted to participate in the collective bargaining procedure. While it is not necessary that they be at the bargaining table, per se, they should be included in preparing the set of demands that are presented to the union, be apprised of negotiating progress, and be instructed and trained in interpreting the agreement. Also, higher management should provide them with loyal support in their relationships with employees and the union shop steward, especially in grievance handling.

These changes are reflected in these comments by a practicing personnel manager.

> The requirements of personnel management are somewhat different in unionized operations than they are in a nonunionized organization. Unionization leaves little flexibility for the personnel managers, for the agreement covers practically all aspects of the employee-employer relationship. In nonunion plants, a greater load is placed on line supervision to manage people, as well as production. While line supervision carries the larger load of personnel management in those operations, the results are in most cases gratifying, but there is a need to police their actions to insure that there is reasonable consistency in administering company policies and rules—or a union will enter!

DISCUSSION QUESTIONS

1. One of the objectives of the LMRA, as specified by Congress, is that it is intended to reduce interferences to interstate commerce arising out of labor disputes. If that is so, how do you explain the large number of strikes that grew out of the organization of employees and collective bargaining?
2. (*a*) Why do workers join a union? (*b*) Why do they reject the union?
3. (*a*) Do you believe union power will increase more in the future? (*b*) Why or why not?
4. How are supervisory relationships with employees affected in a unionized organization?
5. What are some characteristics of an effective grievance procedure?
6. How can a personnel manager prepare to handle grievances more effectively?
7. Describe the preparations you would make for bargaining with labor unions.
8. Why are many small business managers "antiunion"?

APPENDIX A: TWENTY-SEVEN THINGS YOU CAN DO WHEN A UNION TRIES TO ORGANIZE YOUR COMPANY

1. Keep outside organizers off premises.
2. Inform employees from time to time on the benefits they presently enjoy. (Avoid veiled promises or threats.)

Source: Curtis Tate, L. C. Megginson, Charles R. Scott, Jr., and Lyle Trueblood, *Successful Small Business Management* (Dallas, Tex.: Business Publications, Inc., 1975), pp. 382–84.

3. Inform employees that signing a union authorization card does not mean they must vote for the union if there is an election.
4. Inform employees of the disadvantages of belonging to the union, such as the possibility of strikes, serving in a picket line, dues, fines, assessments, and one-man or clique rule.
5. Inform employees that you prefer to deal with them rather than have the union or any other outsider settle grievances.
6. Tell employees what you think about unions and about union policies.
7. Inform employees about any prior experience you have had with unions and whatever you know about the union officials trying to organize them.
8. Inform employees that the law permits you to hire a new employee to replace any employee who goes on strike for economic reasons.
9. Inform employees that no union can obtain more than you as an employer are able to give.
10. Inform employees how their wages and benefits compare with unionized or nonunionized concerns, where wages are lower and benefits less desirable.
11. Inform employees that the local union probably will be dominated by the international union, and that they, the members, will have little to say in its operations.
12. Inform employees of any untrue or misleading statements made by the organizer. You may give employees the correct facts.
13. Inform employees of known racketeering, Communist, or other undesirable elements which may be active in the union.
14. Give opinions on unions and union leaders, even in derogatory terms.
15. Distribute information about unions such as disclosures of the McClellan Committee.
16. Reply to union attacks on company policies or practices.
17. Give legal position on labor-management matters.
18. Advise employees of their legal rights, provided you do not engage or finance an employee suit or proceeding.
19. Declare a fixed policy in opposition to compulsory union membership contracts.
20. Campaign against union seeking to represent the employees.
21. Tell employees you do not like to deal with unions.
22. Insist that any solicitation of membership or discussion of union affairs be conducted outside of working time.
23. Administer discipline, layoff, grievance, and the like without regard to union membership or nonmembership of the employees involved.
24. Treat both union and nonunion employees alike in making assignments of preferred work, desired overtime, and so on.
25. Enforce plant rules impartially, regardless of the employee's membership activity in a union.
26. Tell employees, if they ask, that they are free to join or not to join any organization, so far as their status with the company is concerned.

27. Tell employees that their *personal* and *job* security will be determined by the economic prosperity of the company. Profits are an important essential in this picture.

APPENDIX B: TWENTY-TWO THINGS YOU CANNOT DO WHEN THEY TRY TO ORGANIZE

1. Engage in surveillance of employees to determine who is or is not participating in the union program, attend union meetings or engage in any undercover activities for this purpose.
2. Threaten, intimidate or punish employees who engage in union activity.
3. Request information from employees about union matters, meetings, and so on. Employees may of their own volition give such information without prompting. You may listen but not ask questions.
4. Prevent employee union representatives from soliciting memberships during nonworking time.
5. Grant wage increases, special concessions or promises of any kind to keep the union out.
6. Question a prospective employee about an affiliation with a labor organization.
7. Threaten to close up or move the plant, curtail operations, or reduce employee benefits.
8. Engage in any discriminatory practices, such as work assignments, overtime, layoffs, promotions, wage increases, or any other practices which could be regarded as preferential treatment for certain employees.
9. Discriminate against union people when disciplining employees for a specific action, and permit nonunion employees to go unpunished for the same action.
10. Transfer workers on the basis of teaming up nonunion employees to separate them from union employees.
11. Deviate in any way from known company policies for the primary purpose of eliminating a union employee.
12. Intimate, advise, or indicate, in any way, that unionization will force the company to layoff employees, take away company benefits or privileges enjoyed, or any other changes that could be regarded as a curtailment of privileges.
13. Make statements to the effect that you will not deal with a union.
14. Give any financial support or other assistance to employees who support or oppose the union.
15. Visit the homes of employees to urge them to oppose or reject the union in its campaign.
16. Be a party to a petition or circular against the union, or encourage employees to circulate such a petition.

Source: Curtis Tate, L. C. Megginson, Charles R. Scott, Jr., and Lyle Trueblood, *Successful Small Business Management* (Dallas, Tex.: Business Publications, Inc., 1975), pp. 384–85.

17. Make any promises of promotions, benefits, wage increases, or any other item that would induce employees to oppose the union.
18. Engage in discussions or arguments that may lead to physical encounters with employees over the union question.
19. Use a third party to threaten or coerce a union member, or attempt to influence their vote through this medium.
20. Question employees on whether or not they have or have not affiliated or signed with the union.
21. Use the word "never" in any predictions or attitudes about the union or its promises or demands.
22. Talk about tomorrow. You can talk about yesterday or today, when you give examples or reasons, instead of tomorrow, to avoid making a prediction or conviction which may be interpreted as a threat or promise by the union or the NLRB.

REFERENCES AND SUGGESTIONS FOR FURTHER STUDY

1. See Roger Rapoport, "The Battle of the Overpass," *Wall Street Journal* (May 25, 1967), p. 12, for further details of this unfortunate incident.
2. This conclusion is based upon Benjamin M. Selekman, *Labor Relations and Human Relations* (New York: McGraw-Hill Book Co., 1947), chap. 2. As this book—and a lecture by its author—were one of my first introductions to unions—aside from previous membership in three unions—it has had a great influence upon the material in this chapter. You are encouraged to read it, as it is a "classic" in the field.
3. For example, AFL-CIO union organizers formed a union called the "Field Representatives Federation" and sought recognition for it. Recognition was denied on the grounds that the organizers were "representatives of management." It subsequently won recognition after the NLRB stepped in. See *Business Week* (January 14, 1961), p. 99, for further details.
4. L. C. Megginson and C. Ray Gullett, "A Predictive Model of Union-Management Conflict," *Personnel Journal,* vol. 49, no. 6 (June 1970), pp. 495–503.
5. See E. Wight Bakke, Clark Kerr, and Charles W. Anrod, eds., *Union, Management, and the Public,* 3d ed. (New York: Harcourt, Brace and World, 1967), pp. 1–15, for an excellent discussion of the role of industrial relations systems.
6. See Robert B. McKersie and Richard E. Walton, "The Theory of Bargaining," *Industrial and Labor Relations Review,* vol. 19, no. 2 (April 1966), pp. 414–24; and Ross Stagner and Hjalmar Rosen, *Psychology of Union-Management Relations* (Belmont, Calif.: Wadsworth Publishing Co. Inc., 1965), for variations of this theory.
7. See M. Derber, W. E. Chalmers, and T. Edelman, "Union Participation in Plant Decision-Making," *Industrial and Labor Relations Review,* vol. 15, no. 5 (October 1961), p. 92 ff., for further results of the study.
8. Muzafer Sherif *et. al.,* eds., *Intergroup Conflict and Cooperation* (Norman, Okla.: University Book Exchange, 1961), p. 202.
9. Selekman, *Labor Relations and Human Relations,* Chap. 2.

10. Ross Stagner, *Psychology of Industrial Conflict* (New York: John Wiley & Sons, 1956).
11. Derek Bok and John Dunlop, *Labor and the American Community* (New York: Simon & Schuster, 1970).
12. See Seymour Lieberman, "The Relationship between Attitudes and Roles: A Natural Field Experiment," *American Psychologist,* vol. 9, no. 8 (August 1954), pp. 418–19, for other results.
13. See Arthur A. Sloane and Fred Witney, *Labor Relations* (Englewood Cliffs, N.J.: Prentice-Hall, Inc., 1967), p. 170, for an explanation of how this is true of many such relationships.
14. See Mark Perlman, *Labor Union Theories in America* (Evanston, Ill.: Row, Peterson & Company, 1958), for an explanation of how the political and economic environments affect union strategy.
15. A. W. Kornhauser, R. Dublin, and A. M. Ross, eds., *Industrial Conflict* (New York: McGraw-Hill Book Co., 1954), p. 508.
16. Selekman, *Labor Relations and Human Relations,* p. 15.
17. J. Seidman, J. London, and B. Karsh, "Why Workers Join Unions," *The Annals of the American Academy of Political and Social Science,* vol. 274 (March 1951), p. 84 ff.
18. Stagner and Rosen, *Psychology of Industrial Conflict.*
19. Irving Brotslaw, "Attitude of Retail Workers toward Union Organization," *Labor Law Journal,* vol. 18, no. 5 (March 1967), p. 164 ff.
20. V. C. Sherman, "Unionism and the Nonunion Company," *Personnel Journal,* vol. 48, no. 6 (June 1969), pp. 413–22.
21. See Seymour M. Lipset, "Trade Unions and Social Structure," *Industrial Relations: A Journal of Economy and Society,* vol. 1, no. 1 (October–November 1961), pp. 75–89, especially the section dealing with "Social Structure: Source of American Unionism."
22. R. W. Rideout, "Trade Unions: Some Social and Legal Problems I," *Human Relations,* vol. 17, no. 1 (February 1964), pp. 73–95.
23. Gerald J. Skibbins and Caroline S. Weymar, "The 'Right-to-Work' Controversy," *Harvard Business Review,* vol. 44, no. 4 (July–August 1966), pp. 6–19, 162–66.
24. For example, research has shown that organizers find it easier to organize white-collar employees working on machines (such as key-punch or comptometer machines) than to attract those doing more creative and less mechanized duties. See Everet M. Kassalow, "Occupational Functions of Trade Unionism in the United States," *White Collar Report* (January 9, 1961), p. 7, for further findings.
25. See *Can Management Hold White-Collar Employee Loyalty?* (Princeton, N.J.: Opinion Research Corporation, 1957), p. 10 ff., for these and other results.
26. This committee was established to investigate malpractices in union-management relations. Its findings resulted in the passage of the *Labor-Management Reporting and Disclosure Act of 1959.*
27. R. M. Martin, "Class Identification and Trade Union Behavior," *Journal of Industrial Relations,* vol. 7, no. 2 (July 1965), pp. 131–49.
28. William Spinrod, "Correlates of Trade Union Participation: A Summary of the Literature," *American Sociological Review,* vol. 25, no. 2 (April 1960), pp. 237–44.

29. See John E. Drotning, "The Union Representation Election: A Study in Persuasion," *Monthly Labor Review,* vol. 88, no. 8 (August 1964), pp. 938–43, for these and other results of the study.
30. Edward Curtin, *White-Collar Unionization* (New York: National Industrial Conference Board, Studies in Personnel Policy, No. 220, 1970).
31. Woodruff Imherman, as quoted in *Wall Street Journal* (September 9, 1975), p. 1.
32. See Harry Levinson, "Stress at the Bargaining Table," *Personnel,* vol. 42, no. 2 (March–April 1965), pp. 17–23, for a discussion of the psychological forces at play during the collective bargaining procedure.
33. See Albert A. Blum, "Collective Bargaining—Ritual or Reality?" *Harvard Business Review,* vol. 39, no. 6 (November–December 1961), p. 64, for a description of the ritualistic nature of those negotiations.
34. See Walter Wingo, "How to Win at the Bargaining Table," *Nation's Business,* vol. 58, no. 2 (February 1970), pp. 38–42, for suggestions for management bargaining strategy.
35. Clark Kerr, *Labor and Management in Industrial Society* (Garden City, N.Y.: Doubleday and Co., Inc., 1964), pp. 150–51.

    For an interesting discussion of the structure of collective bargaining as it applies to coordinated bargaining, see Abraham Cohen, "Coordinated Bargaining and Structure of Collective Bargaining," *Labor Law Journal,* vol. 26, no. 6 (June 1975), pp. 375–86.
36. See Archibald Cox, "The Duty to Bargain in Good Faith," *Harvard Law Review,* vol. 71 (June 1958), pp. 1401–52, for an analysis of the NLRB and judicial history of the "good faith" clause.
37. A. C. Pigou, *The Economics of Welfare,* 4th ed. (London: Macmillan & Co., Ltd., 1933), pp. 450–61.
38. See Jean McKelvey, "Fact Finding in Public Employment Disputes: Promise or Illusion," *Industrial and Labor Relations Review,* vol. 22, no. 4 (July 1969), pp. 528–43.
39. George Bennett, "New Horizons for Mediation," *Personnel,* vol. 51, no. 1 (January–February 1974), pp. 43–52, for other examples of using mediation in public institutions.
40. See D. R. Burke and L. Rubin, "Is Contract Rejection a Major Collective Bargaining Problem?" *Industrial and Labor Relations Review,* vol. 26, no. 1 (January 1973), pp. 820–33, for more information on the extent and causes of rejections.

    See also John S. Breenebaum, "New Influences at the Bargaining Table: The Rebellious Rank and File," *Personnel,* vol. 49, no. 2 (March–April 1972), pp. 20–23.
41. Selekman, *Labor Relations and Human Relations,* p. 50.
42. E. A. Fleishman and E. F. Harris, "Patterns of Leadership Behavior Related to Employee Grievances and Turnover," *Personnel Psychology,* vol. 15, no. 1 (Spring 1962), pp. 45–53.
43. J. C. Pettefer, "Effective Grievance Administration," *California Management Review,* vol. 12, no. 1 (Winter 1970), pp. 12–18.
44. Phillip Ash, "The Parties to the Grievance," *Personnel Psychology,* vol. 23, no. 1 (Spring 1970), pp. 13–37.

45. Ibid.
46. J. H. McGuckin, "Grist for the Arbitrators' Mill: What GM and the UAW Argue about," *Labor Law Journal,* vol. 22, no. 3 (March 1971), pp. 165–72.
47. Quoted in H. J. Chruden and A. W. Sherman, *Personnel Management,* 5th ed. (Cincinnati, O.: South-Western Publishing Co., 1976), p. 416.
48. Stagner, *Psychology of Industrial Conflict.*
49. Howard A. Sulkin and Robert W. Pranis, "Comparison of Grievants with Nongrievants in a Heavy Machinery Company," *Personnel Psychology,* vol. 20, no. 2 (Summer 1967), pp. 111–19.
50. Ash, "The Parties to the Grievance," *Personnel Psychology,* pp. 13–37.
51. W. G. Scott, *The Management of Conflict* (New York: Holt, Rinehart & Winston, Inc., 1963).
52. See Julius N. Draznin, "A New Approach to Grievance Handling in the Federal Sector," *Personnel Journal,* vol. 53, no. 11 (November 1974), pp. 822–24.
53. W. J. Usery, Jr., "Some Attempts to Reduce Arbitration Costs and Delays," *Monthly Labor Review,* vol. 95, no. 11 (November 1972).
54. Theodore V. Purcell, "Dual Allegiance to Company and Union Packinghouse Workers," *Personnel Psychology,* vol. 7, no. 2 (Spring 1954), pp. 48–58.
55. Franklin B. Snyder, "What Has the Supreme Court Done to Arbitration?" *Labor Law Journal,* vol. 12, no. 2 (February 1961), pp. 93–93.

CASES FOR FURTHER STUDY

VI-1. The Union Blow*

The union first tried to organize the employees of Southern Offshore Fabricators (SOF) in 1963. After a national union organizer had persuaded enough employees to sign cards in support of the union, an election was held in 1964. The vote was seven to one against the union.

In February 1975, the union again petitioned for an election to certify it as the exclusive bargaining agent in three of the seven divisions of SOF, and that each division should be a bargaining unit. The company took the stand that there should be only one bargaining unit, and it should include all seven of its divisions because of the close relationship between what happened in one division and its effects on the others. In March, the company appealed to the National Labor Relations Board (NLRB), which ruled in its favor.

The NLRB gave the union 30 days in which to gain support from 30 percent of the employees in all seven divisions. If the union failed to gain such support, it would have to wait at least six months before repetitioning.

The union began its campaign to gain support by inducing workers in different areas from which all the employees came to visit employees at their homes with and without the union representatives. The union also encouraged union sympathizers to "talk union" during breaks on the job.

To combat union influence, the company planned meetings with 20 to 30 employees at a time. Prior to these meetings, the personnel manager met with the specialist in charge of employee benefits. To determine what was to be said at the meetings, these two people went over every written page in the company files describing employee benefits and discussed those things unwritten but understood.

During the meetings with employees—each of which lasted two to three hours over a period of seven weeks—three representatives of management sat down and "talked Southern Offshore Fabricators" to the employees. Although taking personnel away from the job lowered production, management felt the cost was necessary to preserve the continued effective functioning of the company.

From these meetings, management learned things that had never reached the front office before.

To learn and exchange information, supervisors were meeting every month

---

* Prepared by Laura Badeau of Louisiana State University.

with the employees, but only about half of them had been relaying what they had learned to their superiors. For example, the handling of pay raises was found to be unsatisfactory to employees out in the field. People were being bypassed for raises and then not being told why. Raises were not based on seniority at SOF but on initiative, ability to learn fast, and performance. Promotions, too, were not based on seniority. Instead, management reviewed a prospective manager's ability, job performance, and popularity with the other men.

In these meetings, management explained that the union could not dictate how things were going to be run at SOF. All present employee benefits would be put aside, and management and the union would negotiate what future benefits would be. According to the employees, the union was talking about raising the present pay rate of $6.65 up to $7.75 to $8.50 per hour. Management showed the workers copies of union contracts with other steel fabricating and offshore companies in the area. These unionized employees were being paid at the same wage rate as SOF's employees. Management asked how could the union do better at SOF.

After about two weeks of these meetings, attitudes and questions started to change as the grapevine relayed what management was saying. Employees began to realize that what was being told them by the union organizers, and how the union was going to provide such extras, were two different matters.

Management continued explaining in further meetings that SOF was a service company to the oil industry and had to operate 24 hours per day, seven days per week. Jobs were awarded in this industry through competitive bidding. Working under union conditions would mean uncertainties about meeting deadlines and being caught by a contract's penalty clause. When bidding on jobs, the company would have to stipulate that it could meet deadlines, "providing there would be no union interference." According to management, SOF had to be available to oil companies as needed, and the union would keep management from making firm commitments.

SOF had a history of few layoffs. In 1969–70, when the Secretary of the Interior discontinued offshore federal leases in the Gulf of Mexico, the situation was so critical that the company could have laid off 500 workers. Instead, it made work for all except 125 people. Also, management reminded the workers that it usually found chores for its employees to do when work was slow.

To paint a clearer picture, management explained that a competitor, McDuff & Company, had been one of the better steel fabrication and offshore companies in the southern area. Ten years earlier, the company employees had unionized, with the result that the firm was no longer considered a competitor in the field. Because of strikes and walkouts, McDuff had been unable to serve the industry. Before McDuff unionized, employees were not laid off when work was slow; after unionization, layoffs became common. Management felt it had no control over its employees. Thus, when there was no work, why should management keep these people on the payroll? Consequently, the better skilled workers migrated to other companies where there was year-round employment.

The efforts of management were successful. When the union had to petition all seven divisions of SOF, the union did not have the 30 percent support necessary for an election. On September 15, 1975, the union was notified by the board that there would be no election. Management never knew if the union would have been able to gain the support in the three divisions first petitioned. Management was aware, however, that the union probably had difficulty in effectively reaching employees in all seven divisions because employee homes were spread over a relatively large geographical area. It was also felt that many who signed cards in support of the union had probably left the company by the time the board requested the payroll of those eligible to vote. Turnover, especially of younger employees in the fabricators division, has been relatively high in the last few years. Management also inferred that many who signed union cards were new employees who were not yet concerned with the long-term welfare of the company.

As a result of the meetings held, several changes were brought about. Before the meetings, pay raises had been initiated by superintendents in the divisions, and there was no set time period for evaluation. The superintendents could evaluate employees whenever they wanted to, and favoritism played a part in such decisions. Afterwards, pay raises were initiated by leadermen (pushers). Every three months, a superintendent and the leadermen evaluated a worker. If one was not given a merit raise, the employee was told why.

Although meetings were no longer held with employees, a suggestion box system for grievances and constructive ideas was put into effect.

Management still waited, however, wondering when a sign of unionism on the scene would next appear.

Questions

1. Evaluate management's approach to the union's efforts.
2. What would you have done differently in view of the law?
3. How do you explain the change in employee attitude?

VI-2. The Discharge of Sleeping Beauty*

Company: Reynolds Metals Company, Corpus Christi, Texas.
Union: Aluminum Workers International Union, AFL–CIO.

On August 6, 1974, Allen Walston was discharged for sleeping while on duty. He filed a grievance two days later, protesting his discharge and request-

---

* Prepared by I. B. Helburn of the University of Texas at Austin and Darold T. Barnum, Associate Professor of Labor Relations, Division of Business, Indiana University Northwest, Gary.

ing full reinstatement with back pay. The grievance was not resolved, and the case went to arbitration in accordance with Article VI of the union-management contract. The parties agreed that the grievance was properly before the arbitrator and jointly identified the issue as: Was the discharge of Allen Walston for proper and just cause? If not, what is the appropriate remedy?

BACKGROUND

Walston began working at the Reynolds plant in April 1969. Five years later at the time of his discharge, he was a trainee under area foreman, Ben Chavez. He had received no written warnings in the three months preceding his termination.

On August 4, two days before his discharge, Walston was working the "graveyard" (midnight–8:00 A.M.) shift. Chavez needed to see him and thus paged Walston twice using the public address system. Walston did not respond. Sometime later he did appear and said that noise had kept him from hearing the call. Chavez tore up the written reprimand he had intended to give Walston for sleeping on the job. He did, however, counsel Walston about failure to appear when paged. He also discussed Walston's generally poor work record with him, as he had already done on several previous occasions.

On August 6, 1974, Walston was again working the graveyard (midnight–8:00 A.M.) shift. He had been taking aspirin and Dristan for several days, as he had been bothered by sinus trouble. Chavez saw Walston at 5:45 A.M. when the employee came to the office for a piece of equipment. Then about 30 minutes later, Chavez and general foreman Clarke (in the hospital at the time of the hearing) found Walston in a prone position on top of a tool locker, his head on an makeshift "pillow."

The locker was located on the third and highest floor of a filter building across the street from Walston's work area. No other employees were in the locker area because no work was being done there on this particular night. There was a snack bar used for coffee breaks on the same floor, about 50 to 75 yards from the tool locker. Coffee breaks were generally taken about 6 A.M., with employees allowed to be away from their worksites for approximately 10 minutes.

After finding Walston on the locker, Chavez called plant security and had Walston escorted to the office. There Chavez asked for an explanation of the incident, but Walston gave him none. Chavez then told the employee that he was being discharged for sleeping on the job and that he could pick up his formal termination notice from personnel when that office opened in the morning. The security guard escorted Walston directly to his locker to collect his belongings, and from there, off the plant grounds. Walston was the first employee Chavez had fired in his 18 years as a foreman at Reynolds Metals.

On August 8, Walston filed a grievance through his Union, but it was denied by the company. The case was arbitrated on December 19, 1974.

COMPANY POSITION

The company claimed the right to discharge under Article XXIII of the Agreement because Walston's sleeping was deliberate. It maintained that premeditation was shown by the resting place, the pillow, and the deep sleep in which Walston was found.

Chavez testified that upon finding Walston he first called Walston's name several times while standing next to him. Walston did not respond until after Chavez had shaken him four times. Then Walston sat up and said, "I'm sick." At that point the foreman called plant security.

Chavez further testified that Walston was resting his head on an army field jacket stuffed with rags. Chavez said that he had never seen the jacket before, that with the warm August weather there was no need for a jacket, and that there had been no rags in the building or work area. Chavez also noted that Walston had what appeared to be a jacket with him when he finally left the plant grounds, and that the "pillow" was gone the next day when Chavez checked the area.

The foreman knew that Walston had been taking medicine for his sinus trouble, but noted that he had not asked to go to First Aid. Had he done so, permission would have been granted.

Regarding the incident two nights earlier, Chavez said that when Walston did appear he looked as though he had been sleeping. The warning was torn up because the foreman hoped that talking to Walston and giving him the benefit of the doubt would encourage him to do better. The Company attorney claimed that another employee, whom the Company would not name nor call to testify, later reported that Walston had indeed been sleeping in a pickup truck.

Chavez also testified that Walston was "irresponsible, lackadaisical, and lazy" and that he needed much more supervision than other "problem" employees. The Company attorney said that Walston was disliked by fellow employees because of his poor performance.

The Company agreed that employees did doze on coffee breaks when they were in the snack bar or the operations shack, and that such employees were simply awakened and sent back to work without being disciplined. It was argued, nevertheless, that such dozing was different from Walston's deliberate and premeditated sleeping, and that Walston's behavior was serious enough to warrant discharge. The Company cited an arbitration decision in another company, in which the arbitrator upheld the discharge of an employee found sleeping in a tractor he was supposed to be operating.

UNION POSITION

The union responded that Walston had not preplanned his pillow, hid himself, or purposely fallen asleep.

Walston said he left his work area about 6 A.M. He took five to seven minutes to walk from his worksite to the locker area, stopping to tell other employees he was going to rest rather than to have coffee, and to call him if he was needed. He wanted the rest rather than the coffee because of his sinus condition, which was bothering him considerably, particularly since earlier in the evening he had had to use a pistol-grip compressed air hammer.

Walston admitted to resting on the tool locker, but would only say that it was possible he was sleeping, although he did not think so. He said he did hear his name being called but did not feel Chavez shake him.

Walston denied having a jacket as a pillow, saying that his head was resting on a piece of cloth and some rags that he found on the locker. This piece of cloth had neither buttons nor sleeves. He further testified that he could not have recovered a jacket from the tool locker since he was escorted by plant security from the time Chavez found him until he left the grounds.

Also, the Union argued that since Chavez had not seen Walston lie down, he could not say the bed had been deliberately made. And, no Company employee had ever been terminated for sleeping on the job.

Walston claimed that on the August 4 shift, he had not heard Chavez call him because of the noise of some nearby pumps, which obscured the public address system. When he was told by Henry Cooper, a fellow employee, that Chavez wanted to see him, he went directly to the office. Cooper's testimony supported Walston's story.

Finally, the Union pointed out that in the arbitration decision cited by the Company, the discharged employee had not been taking medicine and had been given one written warning and two short suspensions in the two weeks prior to dismissal. Thus, the circumstances did not apply to the Walston case. Although the union did not dispute the Company's right to discharge under Article XXIII, they argued that proper and just cause was lacking and that full back pay and allowances were due.

SELECTED AGREEMENT PROVISIONS

The following provisions of the Agreement are pertinent to the Walston case:

Article V, Section 1: In the event an employee in the opinion of the company has acted in such a manner as to deserve discharge he may be immediately suspended and the chairman of the Grievance Committee, or his designated representative, shall be informed of the reason for the Company action. Such notice will be given on the same day as notice is transmitted to the employee involved.

Article V, Section 2: Should the employee, within five (5) working days of the suspension, believe that he should not be discharged, he and/or his Union Representative may present his complaint in writing to the Company Personnel representative (third step of the grievance procedure), who will give the matter prompt and thorough consideration.

Article V, Section 3: Should it be found upon investigation as provided in Article VI hereof that an employee has been unjustly treated, such employees [sic] shall be immediately reinstated in his former position without loss of seniority and shall be compensated for all time lost in an amount based on his average straight time hourly rate of pay for the pay period next preceding such suspension, or other such adjustment as may be mutually agreed to by the Company and the Union, or determined to be proper by an arbitrator.

Article VI, Section 1: Failing satisfactory adjustment by the Director of Labor Relations, the grievance may be submitted to arbitration by either party. The decision of the arbitrator shall be final and binding on all affected parties.

Article X: The following understandings shall apply to plant working rules number 9 to 17, inclusive: When an employee receives a warning under one of the aforementioned working rules, he may have this warning removed from his record if he does not receive another warning under any of the aforementioned rules within three months after the date of this warning.

Article XXIII: It is recognized that, subject to the provisions of this Agreement, the operations of the plant and the direction of the working force including the rights to hire, lay off, suspend and discharge any employee for proper and just cause are vested exclusively with the Company.

Plant Working Rules (part of contract): For those persons who fail to properly conduct themselves, the following penalties have been established and will be enforced. Violations of rules 1–8 will result in discharge for the first offense. Violations of rules 9–17 will draw a written warning for the first offense, and discharge for the second. Violations of rules 18 and 19 will draw written warnings for the first and second offenses, and discharge for the third.

1. Fighting.
2. Refusal to obey orders.
3. Possession of a lethal weapon.
4. Possession or use of drugs or alcoholic beverages in the plant.
5. Theft.
6. Moral offenses.
7. Willful destruction of company property.
8. Deliberately tampering with or punching another employee's time card.
9. Violation of a safety regulation which could result in injury.
10. Failure to wear prescribed safety equipment.
11. Loafing.
12. Poor work.
13. Leaving work area without permission of foreman.
14. Leaving operating post without proper relief or without permission of employee's foreman.
15. Horseplay.
16. Failure to have badge in possession.
17. Soliciting funds without consent of Company.
18. Unexcused tardiness.
19. Absence without leave.

Questions

1. What must the company prove to have the discharge upheld?
2. What must the union show if Walston is to gain full reinstatement with back pay?
3. Evaluate the arguments of each side.
4. As arbitrator, how would you rule? Why?
5. As management, how would you attempt to prevent a similar arbitration case in the future?
6. What are the strengths and weaknesses of the discipline system found in plant rules 1 through 17 in this case?

part seven

Maintaining the work force

23. Handling difficult people problems
24. Maintaining health and safety
25. Coping with the future

Cases:
    VII–1.   *The Recalcitrant Orderly*
    VII–2.   *Jack Moran*
    VII–3.   *The Case of Sam Sawyer*

Introduction

We are now coming to the end of this study of personnel administration. The employees have been selected, trained and developed, compensated for their performance, and have either joined—or refused to join—a union. The personnel executive must now see that these employees are taken care of and that their needs are satisfied so that they will be productive employees and receive satisfaction from performing their job.

While all sections of this book have dealt with maintaining employees, this part will specifically look at handling difficult people problems, maintaining health and safety, and coping with the future. Figure VII–1 shows how this activity fits into the overall personnel system.

Chapter 23 looks at some of the problems involved in dealing with some difficult people problems. Specific attention is given to counseling employees with their job-related problems, as well as their personal problems. The job-related problems tend to deal with performance appraisal and discipline, including absenteeism, safety, and retirement.

Some of the personal problems requiring counseling and guidance are physical illness, mental and emotional problems, and chemical dependency—including alcoholism and drug addiction.

Some problems involved with maintaining occupational health and safety are discussed in Chapter 24. After looking at some of the problems associated with maintaining mental health and some of the causes of safety problems, the *Occupational Safety and Health Act* is studied in considerable detail.

FIGURE VII-1
How maintaining the work force fits into the overall personnel system

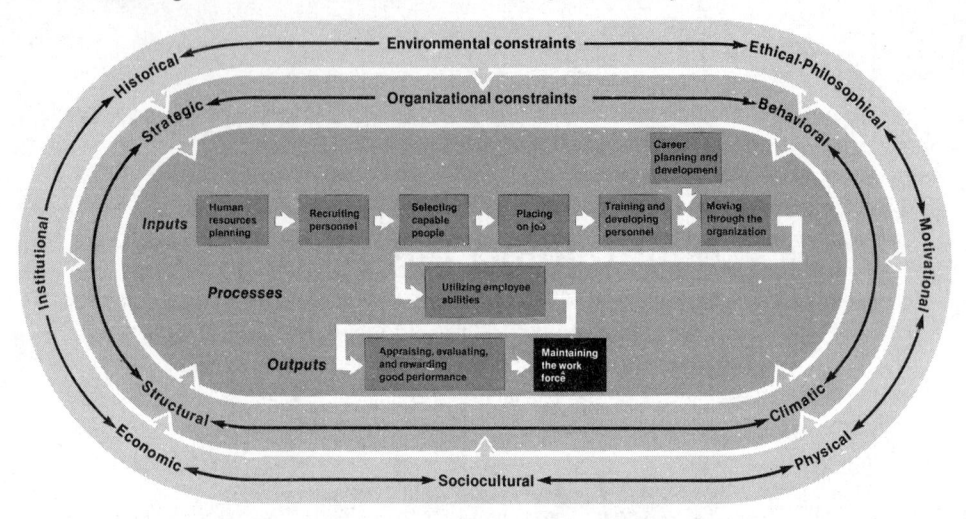

In Chapter 25, you are presented with some of the expected changes which will affect the performance of the personnel function during the next decade. Then some of the characteristics and preparation for personnel are looked at. Finally, the need for personnel research and a philosophy of management is discussed.

Chapter 23

Handling difficult people problems

Role of counseling
    What the counseling process involves
    Benefits of counseling
    Some problems involved in counseling and guidance

Areas requiring counseling
    Job-related activities
    Personal problems

Implications and applications for personnel executives

23
Handling difficult people problems

Advice is seldom welcome; and those who want it the most always like it the least.

LORD CHESTERFIELD

An "in-plant" counseling program at Norton Company uses employees who are "faithful and trustworthy" and who understand the business to be available at any time during the day to help their fellow employees solve their problems. The aim is to take the burden off management's shoulders and to increase the workers' efficiency by settling worries quickly and in a private and confidential manner. (1)

This unique example illustrates another function of personnel executives, providing counseling and guidance for employees. The effective personnel manager is the one who knows when to become involved in this often unpleasant function. As most managers are not adequately trained to perform the function, it is often preferable to bring in a professional therapist; however, personnel managers must know when they should do the counseling and when someone else should. Therefore, the purpose of this chapter is to give some guidelines concerning the role of counseling, to discuss some areas where counseling is required, and to make suggestions for improving the counseling and guidance procedure.

ROLE OF COUNSELING

Managerial counseling is designed to help employees do a better job and provide them with an understanding of their relationships with their superiors, fellow workers, and subordinates. Although there are many factors involved in making an employee a more productive and cooperative individual within the group, counseling has come to be accepted as an important part of the managerial procedure, for it operates at all levels and with all subordinates and is not restricted to any one level of supervision.

While counseling is not new, it has been improved as our knowledge of human behavior has expanded. For example, it is now known that aggressive behavior is a function of both anger and learned habits, usually operating together. Aggression usually has a certain pattern which can be anticipated and predicted. (2) Effective personnel managers can be on the lookout for the cues to such aggressive behavior and can apply counseling, or discipline, whichever is needed, when they see it coming.

What the counseling process involves

How does counseling operate? In the first place, it operates in a conversational setting between two people. When a third party comes into the picture, it is no longer counseling, but a conference. One can talk with another person and can draw that individual out; one can "set the other one straight" and pointed in the right direction. But if there are three people involved, it is not counseling, for counseling is always a bilateral relationship.

Providing counseling and guidance is also a matter of communication, but it is a two-way communicative process. While it is desirable to convery meaning to subordinates, it is likewise important to learn from them what the manager needs to know in order to be of assistance.

Benefits of counseling

There are many benefits received from *effective* counseling, both to those being counseled and those doing the counseling.

As counseling reduces anxiety, fear, and distrust, it tends to develop good working relationships, fortify them, and strengthen them so that areas of misunderstanding and apprehension can be cleared up. It tends to get disturbed relationships back on a two-way, working together, cooperative basis. This benefit is significant as it is estimated that about one-half of the employees who come to industrial medical departments for treatment have emotional problems. (3)

As there can be no organization without systematic interpersonal relationships, counseling may improve these relationships and make the interactions more pleasant. It is a way of at least being able to sit down and talk to other persons and tell them quite frankly where they stand.

Some problems involved in counseling and guidance

As with any other managerial activity, there are many problems involved in providing counsel and guidance. To the extent these problems are recognized and judiciously overcome, the process should be most effective.

One of the first problems involved in counseling is *fear on the part of the counselor.* (4) One aspect of this type of fear is our reluctance to tell others of their weaknesses and shortcomings—and our fear and reluctance to see our own. Basically these fears are the result of people distrusting one another. People dread what they do not understand. They fear that they will make a mess of things, or worse than that, cause the subordinate "not to like them anymore." Ironically enough, this rarely happens if the proper relationship is established. In fact, most of the difficulties in counseling arise from emotional problems within the one doing the counseling. They result from emotions that are overdone, overexaggerated; and rarely is there a basis for anyone to be afraid.

Another problem is that counseling may involve a *conflict of human values,* and most interpersonal problems revolve around differences in people's values. (5) People have a value system which is composed of their ideology, or way of thinking about individuals or ideas; their beliefs, convictions, and conceptions of truth or right; and their values, or the quality of excellence, usefulness, desirability, or worth. This value system provides them with a shock absorber to cushion them against the ugly realities of life. When counseling threatens the subordinate's value system, it threatens the foundations of the subordinate's life. Employees' cultural background has much to do with their attitudes toward life, their superiors and colleagues, and the roles they assume as members of the work team. As these individuals have various prejudices, such as color, ethnic, sectional, monetary, union-management relations, language, age, and even sex, these factors, which tend to form fixed attitudes, become part of the context of counseling.

Finally, there is the problem of *complementarity of symptoms.* If a subordinate has an alcohol problem and is counseled in overcoming it, there may then be periods of depression. In other words, when counseling is successfully provided, it does not necessarily mean the employee is cured; there may only be an escape into other problem areas.

AREAS REQUIRING COUNSELING

Counseling involves all aspects of personnel relations. It begins with the employment procedure and does not terminate until the worker leaves the company—if then. Yet, there are certain areas where counseling is practiced more frequently than in others. These areas include job-related activities and personal problems.

Job-related activities

While all aspects of job performance are subject to counseling, the most prevalent ones are performance appraisal, discipline—including absenteeism, safety, and retirement.

Performance appraisal. Management is responsible for informing employees of their progress, for knowing their status is one of the greatest desires of today's workers. Motivation is based upon setting goals, stimulating employees to achieve them, appraising them of their progress. The key factor is the follow-up appraisal interview, as discussed in Chapter 14.

According to the theory of appraisal interviews, the line manager, after appraising the performance of a subordinate, should discuss the results with him to help him see his strengths and weaknesses more clearly. This procedure

THE WALL STREET JOURNAL

"I've noticed, Jenkins, that you've been driving yourself of late—nice going!"

© 1976. Reprinted by permission of the *Wall Street Journal* and Bo Brown.

should motivate the subordinate to build on his strengths and eliminate his weaknesses.

In institutions where people are judged on the basis of the results of their work and where an attempt is made to orient the appraisal discussion to the job, rarely is a healthy superior-subordinate relationship destroyed. It has been shown that where rating forms focus on personality traits, appraisal interviews usually are carried out halfheartedly and with little success. (6)

Disciplinary cases. As was shown in Chapter 20, there are times when counseling does not suffice and disciplinary action becomes needed. It is unnecessary to go into this subject any further at this time, except to indicate that one important part of discipline is counseling the involved workers. Personnel managers must decide the borderline between these two aspects of their job if it is necessary to make a distinction.

The most frequent disciplinary problem is absenteeism, which has always been a problem, but is apparently being accentuated at present. Some of this loss of work is unavoidable for numerous reasons. Yet, the avoidable part is substantial and needs controlling. (7) It is now known that much of this loss is caused by illness brought on by the worker's reaction to stress in the work situation. (8) Psychiatrists are aware that many adults revert to childlike behavior when faced by difficult and complex situations. If this loss of work is the result of negligence or lack of responsibility, the personnel manager may correct it through counseling; if it is caused by illness, it may be referred to the medical staff; if it is caused by mental illness, it may require outside professional treatment.

Safety. As will be shown in Chapter 24, the entire area of safety requires considerable counseling and guidance, as it is largely a matter of attitudes. The role of the personnel executive is primarily one of assisting operating managers to perform this function.

Retirement. As shown in Chapter 19, employees need considerable preparation for retirement, especially of benefits coming to them. The personnel executive is primarily responsible for this type of counseling.

Personal problems

Some of the personal problems requiring counsel and guidance are illness, mental and emotional problems, and chemical dependency.

Physical illness. One area of employees' lives which is of concern to personnel executives and is an area for counseling is their physical health. Only to the extent that employees are physically well are they capable of performing their assigned tasks. This type of counseling involves ascertaining that employees are well when they come to work and continue to stay so while on the job. Also, if off-the-job activities are impairing the performance of any individuals, then management should advise them how to improve their work performance.

One particularly difficult area of counseling is knowing when a physical impairment reaches the stage at which an individual is no longer employable or at which time one must take sick leave. As human organs do diminish in quality and strength and as the deterioration may be gradual, judgment is needed to decide when reduced efficiency can no longer be tolerated but corrective action must be taken. This type of decision requires value judgments that are not easily made and counseling that is difficult to do.

Mental and emotional illness. This discussion starts from the assumption that all of us are emotionally upset at one time or another. Yet, the fact that we are mildly disturbed does not mean we need hospitalization or psychiatric treatment. However, when the work situation develops stress in the weak spot, we will have difficulty. Thus, one outstanding authority estimates that "the incidence of mental illness, then, is not one out of twenty or some other proportionate statistic, rather it is one out of one." (9) Obviously it is only the more erratic and emotionally disturbed persons who require counseling, but one research study of personnel managers performing their role of counseling shows that maladjusted employees cost industry between $3 and $12 billion annually. (10) The American Medical Association recognizes mental illness, which is one of the top four diseases, as one of the most complex and pressing health problems in the nation, as the mentally ill occupy one-half of all hospital beds in the country. (11)

Emotional problems are caused by many intangible, complex, and interrelated factors. Some are rooted in our basic personality structure and become manifest as we pass through the stages of growth toward our occupational goals. Others seem to be associated with physical disorder or some handicapping disability. Another group of emotional reactions result directly from external environmental factors or interpersonal conflicts, which in the work situation are referred to as *occupational stress.* (12)

Regardless of the sources of these problems, to the extent they interfere with job performance they are subject to personnel counseling. Where feasible, managers may counsel employees as to possible improvements in their behavior or toward seeking professional advice, depending upon the severity of the behavioral deviations.

It is truly ironic that our culture, which spawns the pressures, tensions, and stresses which result in strains upon the human mind, cannot tolerate the individual who succumbs to those strains. This generalization is particularly true of the organizational environment with its pressures for conformity and for striving to "succeed," in terms of financial, ego, and social gratification. Also the pace of events and multiplicity of problems in modern business adds stress to the employee's mind, which is already burdened with the pressures of family, social, religious, and governmental problems.

Even then, we are hypocritically discriminating, for we will accept employees who suffer physical impairment from this strain—heart attacks, for example—but we tend to be intolerant of those who suffer the outward manifestations resulting from mental strains. The former are socially acceptable; the latter are not. One possible explanation of this human inconsistency may be the fact that all of us are victims of mental and emotional illness in some degree and at some time. Also, previous notions about mental illness related it to witchcraft and sorcery, as witness the former use of the term "lunacy" for the disease. Thus, we are a little queasy around someone who manifests the disease of which we are so fearful.

An indication of the severity of these external pressures is shown by the fact that of the four primary causes of illness—heart trouble, mental illness, cancer, and alcoholism—*three are directly attributable to stress and strain and even the fourth one—cancer—may be indirectly caused by these factors.*

One research study has shown that counseling is an effective method of aiding the emotionally disturbed person. It has resulted in reduced absenteeism and tardiness, while increasing morale and productivity. (13) While few firms train their managers to detect stress and strain symptoms, (14) most personnel managers are in favor of counseling to overcome this problem.

Chemical dependency. The most prominent health problems are alcoholism and drug addiction, called *chemical dependency* in hospitals. They have received such wide attention because of the noticeable and negative effect on job performance and because they are so widespread and growing in severity.

Alcoholism. An increasingly costly problem facing personnel executives —in terms of economic and human factors—is alcoholism. The National Council on Alcoholism estimates that in any large company 5 to 10 percent of the employees have a drinking problem. (15) According to the National Institute on Alcohol Abuse and Alcoholism, of the 9 million alcoholics, 45 percent are professional or managerial, 30 percent are blue-collar, and 25 percent are white-collar. (16)

It has been estimated that alcoholic employees cost industry an estimated annual loss of over $2 billion, resulting from accident, absenteeism, sickness, and lowered productivity. (17) This cost results from the fact that these problem workers have about three times as many accidents, are absent around three times as frequently, and require almost three times as much in sickness payments as average workers. Other inestimable losses occur from inefficiencies and slowdowns, interpersonal problems, and the necessity to discharge highly trained and skilled employees.

In addition to the alcoholics, "four other persons are direct victims of the erratic behavior characteristics of the victims of the disease." (18) This disease, long viewed as essentially a moral issue calling for social censure and punishment, is now being approached as a medical-social problem requiring the combined skills of medicine, psychiatry, and sociology. It is the fourth greatest cause of serious illness in the country.

> The employees of a private clinic consisted of an office manager—who performed the personnel function—a receptionist, two nurses, a lab technician, and a typist. The receptionist, who was married and had three children, was "quite capable" in her work and got along with everyone including the patients and was doing an outstanding job.
>
> About six months ago, she began to receive many phone calls during the day from her husband, who was an alcoholic. At times, he kept her on the phone for long periods, and she would call one of the other employees and ask her to answer the other lines. When it reached the point where she could not handle appointments for patients or handle the incoming calls as she should, the doctors called the employees into one of their meetings and asked what they thought about the situation. It was decided that due to the receptionist's inability to carry out her duties, which was affecting the clinic in various ways, she should be discharged.

In spite of the above facts, one recent survey shows that almost 20 percent of the executives interviewed felt their company had no alcoholics on the payroll. (19) This survey showed that supervisors go to great lengths to protect alcoholic employees, even refusing to give performance records during "bad times," failing to record symptoms until they become chronic, and considering such employees "to have a bit of a drinking problem."

As the basic hypothesis of this book is that if one understands human behavior, one can predict it, and if one can predict it, one can control it—managers need to understand the causes of alcoholism if they are going to be able to counsel employees so afflicted. Although there is no definitive answer to why a social drinker becomes a problem drinker, recent scientific literature indicates there are many roots of the disease. These include the following gratifications a person hopes to derive from excessive drinking: a decrease in anxieties and tensions; an excuse for failures; relief from pain; a solution to conflicts; a means of retaliation against persecutions; a means to slow but sure self-destruction; a social lubricant; a sexual stimulant; a way to make behavior appear more feminine or masculine; a condition where underlying motives can be unconsciously released; and a substitute for affection and other gratifying interpersonal relationships that have been denied in other areas. (20)

Experience has shown that where an enlightened and consistent policy toward alcoholic employees has been worked out, the problem has been minimized. Such a policy usually recognizes that alcoholism is a disease; managers attempt to identify the symptoms by which the alcoholic can be recognized early, to set up steps to assist such employees, and to set limits of tolerance—including immediate discharge if the employee doesn't take treatment. The better company programs have two advantages; they can detect alcoholism early, and they can force workers to take treatment or lose their jobs. They have been amazingly successful. (21)

Drugs. While it is still less prevalent than alcoholism, drug addiction is increasingly posing a problem for personnel managers. A study of 80 firms by the Research Institute of America found 90 percent of them had "some incident" of drug abuse on their premises; another one found 53 percent of 222 firms were aware of a "drug problem in their organization, but only 18 percent had a formal drug policy. (22) Another survey of 50 New York companies published by the New York Chamber of Commerce revealed 45 organizations with evidence of drug abuse. (23) One company attributed a 20-percent fall-off in performance to drugs; another spent $75,000 during 1969 just to replace drug-addicted employees.

Drugs are also more difficult for industry to contain, for when the dope addict gets into an organization, the "pusher" is often not too far behind trying to make converts with the zeal of a missionary—or the drug users may sell it to other workers to provide their own drugs. Of 95 addicts in various rehabilitation centers in New York City, 91 admitted using drugs during working hours; 68 confessed to criminal behavior at work, including stealing from the employer and fellow employees; and 48 had sold drugs to other employees. (24)

Representatives from 130 companies gathered for an American Management Association seminar on drug abuse in industry and were told that the drug problem is found all the way from the last hard-core employee brought in on the personnel program up to and including senior vice presidents who have been with the firm for a long time. (25) Companies are increasing their security departments, doing medical tests for drugs on applicants, instituting companywide education programs, helping those who are discovered to be on drugs prove themselves, and hiring or rehiring employees certified to be ex-addicts. Yet many of these procedures are not proving very effective.

These are several models personnel executives can use in tackling the problem. (26) First, using an approach similar to the JOBS programs, a given firm would be paid by the government to hire an addict already in a rehabilitation program. Second, a group of companies would set up a treatment center for their employees, who would be given a leave of absence. This approach has proven successful at the Downtown Drug Center in New York. Third, groups of business and labor leaders would serve as liasion between companies and programs combating drug abuse. This approach, as exemplified by PACT (Provide Addict Care Today), proved successful in New York. Fourth, collaboration of institutions with specialized capabilities to supplement each other.

IMPLICATIONS AND APPLICATIONS FOR PERSONNEL EXECUTIVES

A certain number of employees in all organizations will be found to have personality difficulties that result in strain. Sometimes these stresses are connected with the job, but equally often they are based upon home problems, relations with fellow employees, the general makeup of the individual, or the pressures caused by the complexities of present-day living. To meet the needs of such people, personnel executives need to become familiar with counseling needs and techniques. Some companies, recognizing the inextricable relationship between family problems and work problems, have set up in-plant counseling services with outside professional counselors. (27) The personnel manager of a chemical firm writes:

> The use of industrial psychologists as counselors is becoming quite prevalent and has much merit. Properly arranged, the employee has the opportunity to discuss problems, personal or otherwise, in confidence with an individual representing management—yet not a part of the management team on a regularly scheduled basis. Problems of like nature relative to company affairs are brought to the attention of the proper management official by the psychologist, and steps are taken to make the necessary correction.
>
> The use of a temperament scale of each employee by the employee's immediate supervisor assists in an understanding of the employee's strengths and weaknesses and provides the supervisor with the basic information needed to counsel subordinates properly. The availability of a professional medical person on site is a comforting adjunct to the needs of counseling and is a counseling tool often overlooked.

Employee counseling must not detract from normal grievance procedures and the regular channels of authority and responsibility. Also, it is essential that adequate machinery exist for adjustment of differences arising from work conditions, as contrasted with individual personality problems. Some firms have had success in achieving positive results through broad educational programs, often undertaken jointly with the union.

Although counseling is exceedingly important (probably because it is), it is extremely difficult. Thus, either specially trained counselors should be used, or personnel managers should have special training in order to know not only how to counsel, but, more importantly, when to do it and when not to.

To be most effective, certain boundaries and parameters need to be established for the areas we have considered. Although the practice of management encompasses many areas of knowledge, including human relationships, it is generally considered to be most desirable to: *Steer clear of personal problems except to the extent that they influence the employee's or other's work relationships; restrict counseling to the employee's job performance; and have the counseling and guidance* as specific as feasible. Instead of telling workers their job performance "is poor," tell them they only reached 75 percent of their work goal or they have been tardy and absent a given number of times. Thus, each employee has something concrete to work on in improving job performance.

Complicating this problem is the fact that when employees get into trouble away from work, it could have something to do with their feelings for the job or their supervisor. Consequently, one of management's toughest jobs is to know when, and how deeply, to become involved in an employee's personal life.

In general, employee counseling has proven most effective when it was concerned principally with the person's work relationships, performance, reliability, dependability, thoroughness, efficiency, interpersonal relationships with others, and related activities. It can be seen that all these aspects of counseling are concerned with the factors that either add to or detract from job performance rather than just the width of the individual's total environment.

The hypothesis is proposed that the *unfavorable attitudes of managerial and nonmanagerial personnel toward employees with mental or emotional illness or its behavioral manifestations tend to hasten the resignations or dismissals of those employees.* (28) These attitudes tend to be illogical, fallacious, intolerant, and unwarranted, and they are usually based upon prejudices and biases. Yet their effect is to call into play the self-fulfilling prophecy so that those with the problem are driven by the attitudes of their fellow workers to act the way they are expected to act. These actions then become the basis of the resignation or discharge.

DISCUSSION QUESTIONS

1. (*a*) What is the role of counseling in personnel and human resources administration? (*b*) Why is it so important?
2. "When a third party comes into the picture, it is no longer counseling, but a conference." Comment.
3. (*a*) What benefits can you expect from effective counseling? (*b*) Explain how and why the benefits arise.
4. "Counseling should avoid personal problems." (*a*) What is the reason behind this statement? (*b*) What is the limitation of the statement from the manager's point of view? (*c*) What is the reasonable boundary in dealing with an employee's personal life in counseling?

5. Discuss the different role and areas of counseling, if any, provided by the immediate supervisor and a professional counselor.
6. Do you agree that drugs are as great as problem in industry as shown in this chapter? Explain.

REFERENCES AND SUGGESTIONS FOR FURTHER STUDY

1. See "Norton Delegates Personnel Affairs to the Workers," *International Management,* vol. 30, no. 6 (June 1975), pp. 48–50, for further details. Although the "counselors" do not have authority to settle problems themselves, they can make recommendations. Also, they are trained to see that problems get to the people who can settle them.
2. Leonard Berkowitz, "Aggressive Cues in Aggressive Behavior and Hostility Catharsis," *Psychological Review,* vol. 71, no. 2 (March 1964), pp. 104–22.
3. Leonard E. Himler M.D., "Emotional Problems in Industry: Recognition and Preventive Measures," *Industrial Medicine and Surgery,* vol. 30, no. 4 (April 1961), pp. 131–34.
4. It has been shown experimentally that such fear adversely affects not only the performance of productive tasks but also the person's verbal behavior. See James H. Geer, "Effect of Fear Arousal upon Task Performance and Verbal Behavior," *Journal of Abnormal Psychology,* vol. 71, no. 2 (April 1966), pp. 119–23.
5. Robert N. McMurry, "Conflicts in Human Values," *Harvard Business Review,* vol. 41, no. 3 (May–June 1963), pp. 130–45.
6. Robert K. Stolz, "Can Appraisal Interviews Be Made More Effective?" *Personnel,* vol. 38, no. 2 (March–April 1961), pp. 32–37.
7. See R. Oliver Gibson, "Toward a Conceptualization of Absence Behavior of Personnel in Organizations," *Administrative Science Quarterly,* vol. 11, no. 1 (June 1966), pp. 107–33, for some propositions to help management understand employee absences.
8. E. F. Buyniski, "Stress-Sickness-Supervision," *Personnel Administration,* vol. 25, no. 4 (July–August 1962), pp. 38–43.
9. Harry Levinson, "What Killed Bob Lyons?" *Harvard Business Review,* vol. 41, no. 1 (January–February 1963), p. 142.
10. Gerald H. Graham, "Recognizing Emotional Disturbance Symptoms," *Personnel Administrator,* vol. 15, no. 4 (July–August 1970), pp. 3–7.
11. Frederick L. Patry, M.D., "Mental Health," *Journal of Rehabilitation,* vol. 29, no. 4 (July–August 1963), p. 19.
12. For example, Dr. Frank Hartman has found that middle-level executives have more psychiatric problems than others, for they have ambiguous assignments and expectations. These problems are created by the individuals, not by the company situations. See "Why Executives Need Psychiatrists," *Dunn's Business Review,* vol. 102, no. 11 (November 1973), p. 12 ff., for further details.

   Harry Levinson, a noted psychologist, finds the character of the executive likely to be vulnerable to suicide. They are intelligent, ambitious, and capable men and women with high aspirations and capability for uncomprehending guilt. Consequently, no matter what their achievement, they view themselves as inadequate and subject to guilt. See "On Executive Suicide," *Harvard Business Review,*

vol. 53, no. 4 (July–August 1975), pp. 118–23, for suggestions on how to recognize the depression symptoms.
13. Graham, "Recognizing Emotional Disturbance Symptoms," *Personnel Administrator*, pp. 3–7.
14. Dean J. Mark Miller of West Georgia College reported in an unpublished document entitled, "Emotional First-Aid in Georgia," that while 183 firms studied look to the first-line supervisor to report workers with emotional stress, 87 percent did not have supervisors who were trained to identify or detect emotional stress problems in workers and 80 percent did not have supervisors who were trained in helping such workers.
15. See "Alcoholism: Everybody's Business," *Bell Telephone Magazine*, vol. 54, no. 1 (January–February 1975), pp. 7–9, for further details.
16. As reported in David W. Hacker, "Did His Job Make Him Drink?" *National Observer*, (November 1975), pp. 1 and 20.

    It is also estimated that one out of every 12 managers is an alcoholic. See Thomas J. Murray, "The Fight to Save Alcoholic Executives," *Management Review*, vol. 62, no. 9 (September 1973), pp. 41–43.
17. "Alcoholism: A Growing Medical-Social Problem," *Statistical Bulletin*, Metropolitan Life Insurance Co., vol. 48 (April 1967), pp. 7–10.
18. Frances I. Colonna, M.D., "Management and the Problem Drinker," *Management Review*, vol. 48, no. 9 (September 1959), pp. 22–29.
19. Lewis F. Presnall, "What's Wrong with Alcoholism Control Programs?" *Personnel*, vol. 47, no. 2 (March–April 1970), pp. 38–43.
20. Robert Turfboer, M.D., "Alcoholism: Management's Problem?" *Advanced Management*, vol. 25, no. 8 (September 1960), pp. 14–15 and 24.
21. See Roger Ricklefs, "Drinkers at Work: Firms Act to Uncover the Secret Alcoholics, Make Them Get Help," *Wall Street Journal* (December 1, 1975), pp. 1 and 12, for details about these programs and the experience of firms using them.
22. See Jerome Siegel and Eric H. Schoof, "Corporate Responsiveness to the Drug Abuse Problems," *Personnel*, vol. 50, no. 6 (November–December 1973), pp. 8–14, for this and other research findings on the impact of the drug abuse problem and some options employers have for coping with it.
23. Linda Gutstein, "Drug Addicts Worry Industry," *Parade* (February 14, 1971), pp. 4–5.
24. Siegel and Schoof, "Corporate Responsiveness," *Personnel*, pp. 8–14.
25. Gutstein, "Drug Addicts Worry Industry," *Parade*, pp. 4–5.
26. However, these programs must be specifically designed around the needs of the employee and the cost effectiveness to the organization. See Rolf Rogers and John Colbert, "Drug Abuse and Organizational Response: A Review and Evaluation," *Personnel Journal*, vol. 54, no. 5 (May 1975), pp. 266–71, for further details.
27. See Cavin P. Leeman, "Contracting for an Employee Counseling Service," *Harvard Business Review*, vol. 52, no. 2 (March–April 1974), p. 20 ff., for an evaluation of the effectiveness of this method.
28. This hypothesis is based upon the thoughts expressed in Charles D. Whatley, Jr., "Employer Attitudes, Discharged Patients, and Job Durability," *Mental Hygiene*, vol. 48, no. 1 (January 1964), pp. 121–31.

Chapter 24

Maintaining health and safety

Why occupational health and safety are so important
    What are we talking about?
    The need for health and safety programs
    Requirements for effective health and safety programs

Maintaining occupational health

Maintaining safety
    Factors affecting safety
    Causes of accidents

What can be done to improve safety
    Measure the extent of the problem
    Take corrective action

Occupational Safety and Health Act
    Purpose
    Coverage
    Rights and responsibilities
    Enforcement
    Evaluating its effectiveness

Implications and applications for personnel executives

24
Maintaining health and safety

No man is an island, entire of itself; . . . any man's death diminishes me, because I am involved in Mankinde; and therefore never send to know for whom the bell tolls; it tolls for thee.

JOHN DONNE

Statistics show that during the average workday one worker is injured in the U.S. every *14 seconds* and one worker is killed every *37 minutes*. Each year, over 14,000 workers are killed in job-related activities, and 2.4 million workers are seriously injured at a cost of $11.5 billion in lost wages, reduced output (from over 50 million employee days lost to disabling injuries), and others. (1) Approximately 20,000 occupational health nurses are now at work in industry, business, and commerce. These nurses are "human ecologists" whose purpose is to safeguard the health and well-being of the nation's most important natural resource—its work force. (2)

These figures provide a rough approximation of the significance of occupational health and safety to today's personnel executives. Employers have now realized that the health and safety of their employees is a matter of good economics—as well as being humanitarian. Unconcerned employers suffer decreased performance and increased medical and insurance costs as a direct result of their apathetic attitude toward health and safety policies.

This chapter will explore the background of health and safety problems, look at some occupational health problems, study the safety problem in industry, and look at how the Occupational Safety and Health Act of 1970 (OSHA) is affecting occupational health and safety in this country.

WHY OCCUPATIONAL HEALTH AND SAFETY ARE SO IMPORTANT

The problem involved in providing health and safety in the work setting is one of degree, that is, how much safety should be provided, what should be done to protect health, who should pay for the protection, and what will be the effectiveness of providing health and safety. In his research on OSHA, Fred Foulkes did not find anyone who disagreed with its purpose of providing a safe and healthful work place. (3)

Providing and improving healthy working conditions is nothing new, for it has been done for at least the last 65 years. Management has provided air conditioning and ventilation systems in plants and offices, greater control of toxic materials, improved sound-proofing, better illumination, and clean washrooms and cafeterias. Pace-setting companies have usually included certain health and safety standards with manufacturing standards. Many industrial diseases such as anthrax, silicosis, and phossy-jaw have almost disappeared, although science has brought new ones such as radiation hazards in uranium processing plants. (4) As accident prevention is regarded as cheaper and more socially responsible than compulsory accident insurance, the new emphasis on safety has led to changing concepts in engineering and the establishment of personnel safety programs. (5) However, problems in industrial health and safety have not gone away despite technological progress but have become magnified.

What are we talking about?

While safety professionals insist that the term *safety* is all-encompassing and includes *health,* a distinction will be made between them in this chapter.

Safety hazards. Safety hazards are those aspects of the work environment which can cause burns, electrical shock, cuts, bruises, sprains, broken bones, and the loss of limbs, eyesight, or hearing. Generally, the harm is immediate and sometimes violent, is often associated with industrial equipment or the physical environment, and often involves an employment task that requires care and training. Such injuries increased nearly 29 percent from 1961 to 1970.

Health hazards. Typical health hazards include physical and biological agents and toxic and carcinogenic chemicals and dusts, often in combination with noise, heat, and other forms of stress. The interaction of health hazards and the human organism can occur either through the senses by absorption through the skin, by ingestion, or by inhalation. The results of these interactions can be respiratory disease, heart disease, cancer, neurological disorders, systemic poisonings, or a shortening of life expectancy due to general physiological deterioration. The disease or sickness can be acute or chronic, can require a long latency period to appear even if the original exposure occurs briefly, and can be difficult or impossible to diagnose early or with certainty. (It should also be noted that disease can give rise to accidents.) The Public Health Service estimates that there are 390,000 *new* cases of occupational disease each year. Other analyses suggest that as many as 100,000 deaths occur each year as a result of occupational disease. (6)

The effects of health hazards—unlike safety hazards—may be slow, cumulative, irreversible, and complicated by nonoccupational factors. While an unguarded blade in a circular saw may present a severe and immediate or "imminent" danger, it is often difficult to perceive the severity or imminent danger contained in a brief exposure to a potential carcinogen that can take years to cause a tumor or death. However, the probability of dying from cancer may be just as high as being injured by the saw.

The need for health and safety programs

The need for health and safety programs has been recognized for a long time. As indicated in Chapter 19, worker's compensation laws have been in effect since around the turn of the century; many safety-type organizations were organized about the same time, including the National Fire Protection Association (1895), the National Safety Council (1912), and the American Society of Safety Engineers (1925).

The cost factor. The cost of occupational hazards (in terms of lost wages, medical expenses, insurance claims, production delays, lost time of co-workers and equipment damage) was estimated by the National Safety Council at $15 billion during 1974. This figure, approximately 1 percent of the gross national product, is likely to be a gross understatement of even the direct costs to the GNP of both occupational injuries and illness. (7) An estimated 28 million workdays were lost through absenteeism and restricted activity during 1973, according to the Bureau of Labor Statistics. This reported figure is equivalent to a loss of 112,000 worker-years of work. (8) The estimate includes not only actual days lost from work but also days in which employees were restricted from performing all the duties of their permanent job.

Affected occupations. The incidence of occupational illness is not the same for all members of the labor force. Miners, construction and transportation workers, and blue-collar and lower-level supervisory personnel in manufacturing industries experience the greatest incidence of both occupational disease and injury.

Occupational health problems are not limited to industrial or agricultural workers, for they affect white-collar workers and corporate executives as well. *Dentists* are being studied for the possible effects of x-radiation, mercury, and anesthetics on them, having the highest rate of suicide of any professional group, and a higher incidence of diseases of the nervous system, leukemia, and lymphatic malignancies. *Operating room nursing* personnel suffer several times the miscarriage rates of other nurses and give birth to a larger proportion of children with congenital deformities. *Cosmetologists* (beauticians) display excess cancer and respiratory and cardiac disease. *Administrators* are far more likely to develop coronary disease than are scientists and engineers.

Some specific areas of need. The health and safety issue is not very much a bargaining issue. For example, the 1973 strike between the Oil, Chemical, and Atomic Workers Union and Shell Oil in Houston, Texas, was billed as America's first environmental strike. The union demanded the health and safety provisions previously agreed to by other large industries, including (*a*) periodic surveys of the work place by qualified industrial health consultants who would provide workers with the survey's results—and include measurements of exposures to hazardous materials, (*b*) periodic relevant physical examinations, and (*c*) medical tests at the company's expense. (9)

Noise. The UAW union calls the problem of noise the single greatest health hazard of the work place. Exposure to constant high noise levels can damage workers' hearing, make them irritable and inefficient, and drown out warning cries of impending danger. (10)

Another area where "noise" is a problem is work places when loud music is played for considerable periods of time. (11)

Heart disease. Only 25 percent of heart disease, the leading cause of death in the United States, is "explained" by known physiological and environmental factors, such as overweight, hypertension, serum cholesterol, and cigarette smoking. (12) Quite possibly, a substantial proportion of the 75 percent of heart disease risk which is presently unaccounted for could be related to work and its attendant hazards, particularly *stress.*

Cancer. Another growing area is cancer. Cancer is the second leading cause of death in the United States today, and its incidence has risen rapidly with industrialization. In 1900, 4 percent of deaths was attributable to cancer, but by 1968 the proportion was 16 percent.

> In coke-oven plants, for example, studies show that because of coal tar pitch emissions, workers are ten times more likely to get lung cancer than other workers. (13)

It is not presently known how much is occupationally related, but there seems to be a general consensus among cancer researchers and environmentalists that probably one-half of this figure is complicated by occupational factors. The experience of chemists, asbestos workers, underground uranium miners, and rubber workers, as well as other occupational groups, amply documents the case that "excess" cancer of various types is indeed occupationally related.

Respiratory diseases. Chronic diseases of the respiratory system are becoming major causes of death and disability. Chronic bronchitis and emphysema are the fastest growing diseases in the United States, doubling every five years. This doubling rate equals that of the increases in the petrochemical industries. (14) Much of the respiratory disease which plagues the worker is also known to be job-related.

Requirements for effective health and safety programs

The problems in the work environment are complex and demand both long- and short-term interdisciplinary approaches for their solution. Consequently, in order to reduce occupational injuries and diseases, either research and medicine, the law and the regulatory process, or market incentives, or a combination of all will have to be used.

Use of preventive medicine. Occupational health problems can be most effectively dealt with through the practice of preventive medicine, and it is exceedingly underdeveloped in the United States. Also, preventive medicine is not tied sufficiently to the treatment establishments for effective reduction of occupational diseases. Preventive medicine needs a different kind of approach—one which emphasizes the reduction of exposure to potentially harmful substances.

The personnel executive's role. The responsibility for health care and accident prevention ultimately rests with management in private businesses. They need to take whatever steps are necessary by way of engineering or employee education and control to guard against injuries and to keep the company's accident experience at least as low as the average for the industry.

There is a documented trend toward shifting responsibility for safety matters—as is true of other personnel activities—upwards within a company to the personnel executive who is increasingly tending to be a vice president. Also, the more progressive companies are centralizing the safety function at the corporate level—apparently in an effort to achieve more uniformity in safety and health standards throughout the organization.

MAINTAINING OCCUPATIONAL HEALTH

In addition to providing more efficient performance, health services serve as an effective employee benefit for the workers and helps in recruiting. Yet, it does have drawbacks, including rising costs and the search for qualified medical personnel.

The essential principles upon which health care planning is based are accessibility and distribution of the services, continuity of care, complete care, coordination, and a broad base of inputs. While the companies are providing the financial wherewithal to employees, the government has decreed through the *Health Maintenance Organization Act of 1973* (*HMP*) that medical health and guidance be made available, along with environmental health, including relief from air and water pollution.

While many organizations have enlarged their health care programs in the past ten years, few are truly involved in improving the system. In fact, research has shown that top executives do not give a high priority to health care.

There are two basic components required for valid safety and health standards. First, the hazards must be identified, and, second, there must be special procedures to prevent their occurrence. But herein is one of the problems and obstacles involving health care: How do you measure fatalities from disease? Also, how do you get adequate data about the rates of death from occupational causes unless there are ways of measurement? For example, the Bureau of Labor Statistics figures of work-related deaths for 1972 was 11,000, but the estimates of the National Safety Council were about 14,100, or a difference of up to 28 percent. (15) A related problem involves the diagnosis of occupational diseases. The latter point is particularly pertinent when an employee contracts a disease with one employer, and it becomes evident after he is employed with another one.

MAINTAINING SAFETY

Occupational safety is a condition involving *relative* freedom from danger or injury. Although totally safe conditions are theoretically possible, they are rarely found in the organizational world. Therefore, what I am referring to in this discussion is for the organization to maintain a condition whereby the employees will *feel* safe and secure. Although employees often cause accidents, not all accidents are caused by employees, for there are many other causes.*

Factors affecting safety

There are several factors affecting the safety of an organization. The ones that will be discussed in this section are organizational size, type of industry, and attitudinal factors.

Organizational size. It is a paradox that the smallest and largest organizations tend to be the safest places to work. Companies with under 20 employees or over 1,000 are considerably safer than those in between. Apparently the most dangerous organizations are those with between 50 and 1,000 employees. (16) Apparently the reason for this phenomenon is that owners and managers of small businesses are usually not as safety conscious—or are not able from a resource point of view to take the measures to prevent accidents—as are other organizations.

Type of industry. As seen in Figure 24-1, the type of industry has a great deal to do with the accident frequency and severity rates. There are two generalizations which can be made from these figures. First, the lowest frequency rates seem to be among the heavy industries which could be expected to be more dangerous, whereas some of the supposedly safe industries have higher rates. The second generalization is the lack of correlation between the frequency and severity rates. For example, while the automobile industry is the safest, as far as frequency, it is fourth as far as severity is concerned.

As can be seen from Figure 24-2, the severity rate has declined over the decades and has stabilized around 650. However, the frequency rate declined to a low of 6.26 between 1962 and 1964 and then climbed to 10.5 in 1974. Part of this change was in improved reporting methodology and industry representation.

In order for personnel executives to understand and be able to improve their accident ratings, the ratings should be compared with the average for the industry in which they are operating.

Attitudinal factors. Many human variables, both personal and organizational, influence safety. However, only management attitudes and style, job satisfaction, and personal characteristics will be discussed.

Management attitudes and style. Several studies have indicated that management attitudes and style may be an important determinant of the way the organizational members think about safety. Some such attitudes and style encourage subordinates to take individual responsibility for safety, while others may encourage a belief that safety is a management responsibility.

> A study of 14 essentially identical coal mines in England showed that before nationalization they had essentially a random accident rate ranging from 90 to

---

* I still vividly remember how incensed we pilots were in World War II when an accident was caused by a malfunction in the plane, but the report would come back reading "pilot error" because we had not detected the malfunction in time to prevent the accident.

FIGURE 24-1
Frequency and severity rates for firms reporting to the national safety council, 1974

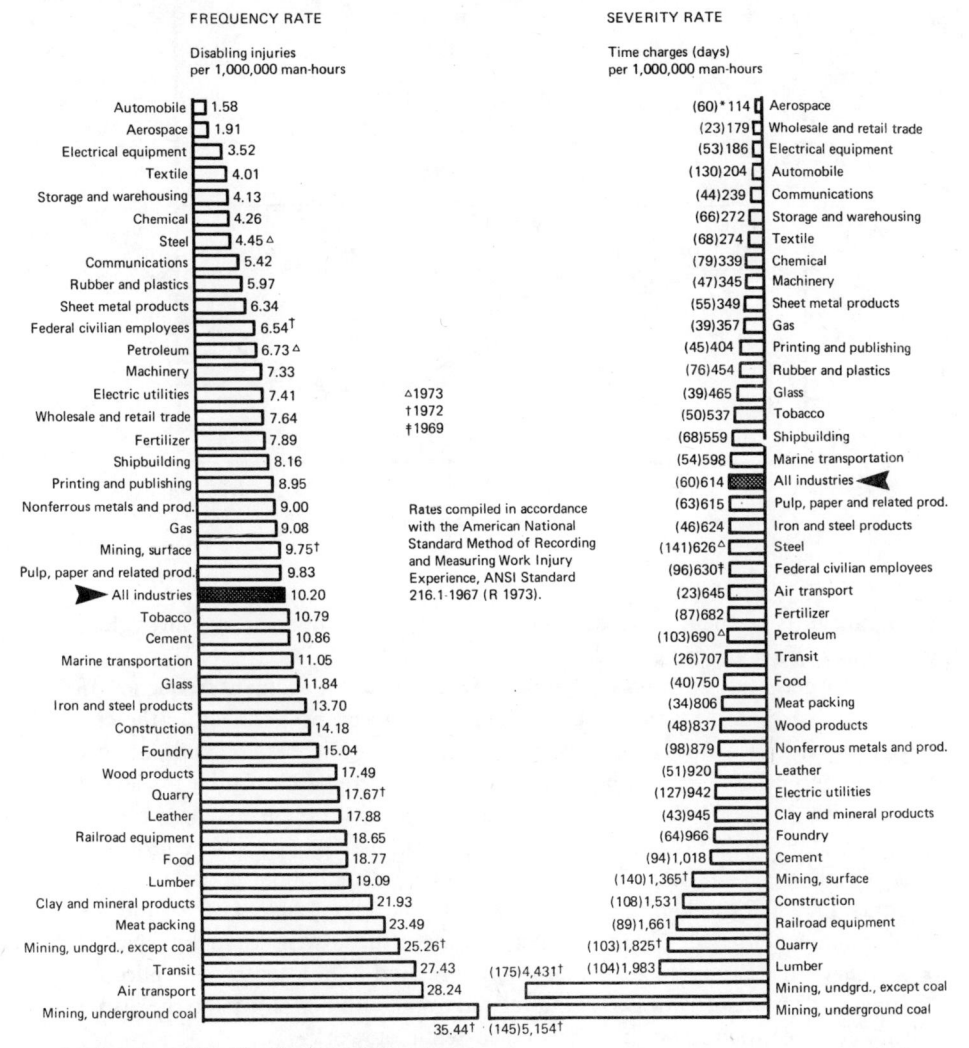

	FREQUENCY RATE Disabling injuries per 1,000,000 man-hours		SEVERITY RATE Time charges (days) per 1,000,000 man-hours	
Automobile	1.58	(60)* 114	Aerospace
Aerospace	1.91	(23) 179	Wholesale and retail trade
Electrical equipment	3.52	(53) 186	Electrical equipment
Textile	4.01	(130) 204	Automobile
Storage and warehousing	4.13	(44) 239	Communications
Chemical	4.26	(66) 272	Storage and warehousing
Steel	4.45 △	(68) 274	Textile
Communications	5.42	(79) 339	Chemical
Rubber and plastics	5.97	(47) 345	Machinery
Sheet metal products	6.34	(55) 349	Sheet metal products
Federal civilian employees	6.54 †	(39) 357	Gas
Petroleum	6.73 △	(45) 404	Printing and publishing
Machinery	7.33	(76) 454	Rubber and plastics
Electric utilities	7.41	(39) 465	Glass
Wholesale and retail trade	7.64	(50) 537	Tobacco
Fertilizer	7.89	(68) 559	Shipbuilding
Shipbuilding	8.16	(54) 598	Marine transportation
Printing and publishing	8.95	(60) 614	All industries ◄
Nonferrous metals and prod.	9.00	(63) 615	Pulp, paper and related prod.
Gas	9.08	(46) 624	Iron and steel products
Mining, surface	9.75 †	(141) 626 △	Steel
Pulp, paper and related prod.	9.83	(96) 630 †	Federal civilian employees
► All industries	10.20	(23) 645	Air transport
Tobacco	10.79	(87) 682	Fertilizer
Cement	10.86	(103) 690 △	Petroleum
Marine transportation	11.05	(26) 707	Transit
Glass	11.84	(40) 750	Food
Iron and steel products	13.70	(34) 806	Meat packing
Construction	14.18	(48) 837	Wood products
Foundry	15.04	(98) 879	Nonferrous metals and prod.
Wood products	17.49	(51) 920	Leather
Quarry	17.67 †	(127) 942	Electric utilities
Leather	17.88	(43) 945	Clay and mineral products
Railroad equipment	18.65	(64) 966	Foundry
Food	18.77	(94) 1,018	Cement
Lumber	19.09	(140) 1,365 †	Mining, surface
Clay and mineral products	21.93	(108) 1,531	Construction
Meat packing	23.49	(89) 1,661	Railroad equipment
Mining, undgrd., except coal	25.26 †	(103) 1,825 †	Quarry
Transit	27.43	(104) 1,983	Lumber
Air transport	28.24	(175) 4,431 †	Mining, undgrd., except coal
Mining, underground coal	35.44 †	(145) 5,154 †	Mining, underground coal

△ 1973
† 1972
‡ 1969

Rates compiled in accordance with the American National Standard Method of Recording and Measuring Work Injury Experience, ANSI Standard 216.1-1967 (R 1973).

Source: National Safety Council, Accident Facts, 1975 ed., p. 26.
* Figures in parentheses show average days charged per case.

220 accidents per 100,000 worker shifts worked. After nationalization, accident rates seemed to be related to the groupings of the mines for administrative purposes. One group of mines had a rate of around 110 and the second group had rates around 180. (17)

Another study of two groups of fork lift truck operators, working under different managers within the same warehouse, found that the manager may

FIGURE 24-2
Trends in frequency and severity rates, for "all industries," 1926-74

Source: National Safety Council, Accident Facts, 1975 ed., p. 28.

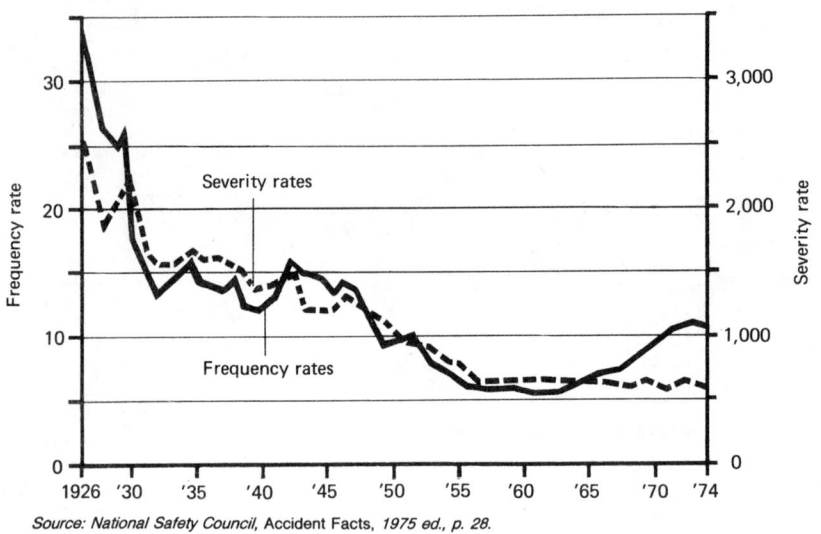

significantly influence the way subordinates think about safety through the support the manager provides. (18)

Another study showed that in firms with low work accident frequency and severity rates, top management is highly interested and involved in the company's overall safety programs and actually participates in, and supports, safety activities. The finding was strongly supported to a significant level of .05, with probably the most important reason for the effectiveness of these activities being that they show other members of management—and ultimately all employees—that the "boss" is strongly concerned about controlling accidents. (19) The study also showed that first-line supervisors with a wide span of management had a higher injury rate than those with a narrow span.

An earlier study of leadership styles related subordinate perceptions of supervisory consideration as being related to the number of trips to the dispensary for treatment of injuries sustained while at work. (20)

Job satisfaction. There is also a relationship between job satisfaction and safety. Indications are that job enrichment programs may not only make employees happier, but also they have a positive effect on safety. A study at one plant showed a close link between job satisfaction and a low injury rate. (21)

Personal characteristics. There is a growing conviction among safety engineers that accident liability is as much a product of individual characteristics as it is of improper working conditions or the employee's physical condition. Patterns of accident frequency have been studied, and it has been concluded that there are accident-prone personalities and that there is sufficient correlation between that type of personality and recognizable syndromes peculiar to it so that such personalities can be isolated during the selection procedure. Yet, it is not always feasible to be this selective.

No less than seven syndromes have been found to be peculiar to the "injury-repeaters," as they are usually called. (22) In an effort to draw a composite picture of injury-repeaters in lay terms, it can be said that they are the blunt, abrupt, and impatient type of personality who are quick to translate enthusiasms—or irritations—into physical reaction; they are instinctive mavericks, compelled to cultivate a feeling of superiority over the people and institutions around them, as shown by a contempt for most of the prohibitions and warnings the employees encounter, including counseling concerning safety; they generally are given high scores on tests intended to measure degrees of "introversial and extroversial distractibility"; and they react to pain in a different manner from those workers whose records are relatively accident-free. While is cannot be said that accident-prone employees enjoy pain, it can be stated that they do not fear it, nor does it bother them nearly as much as it does other workers.

Another study found that accidents are caused by individuals who show tendencies toward emotional insecurity, low motivation, and egocentric aggressiveness. (23) This study corroborated an earlier one which concluded that accident-prone individuals showed hostility toward themselves. (24)

A further dimension is added with the finding that most industrial injuries occur in persons between the ages of 20 and 24. Above that age, the injury rate becomes progressively lower. (25)

A previously mentioned study found that in firms where a high percentage of the employees were married, the accident rate was lower. (26)

It appears from the progress made thus far that a short test which will determine accident-proneness is possible, and further studies are being conducted with this objective in view.

Causes of accidents

Accidents are caused; they do not *just happen*. Among the many causes are human factors—as just mentioned—environmental causes, and technical causes.

Human causes. Resistance to safety rules is bound to occur and personnel executives should be prepared for it. Unsafe personal acts, such as removing safety devices or making them inoperable, horseplay, fighting, and improper attitudes, lead to accidents.

Environmental causes. Some of the environmental causes of accidents are climatic variables, such as disorderly housekeeping, poor ventilation, improper or inadequate lighting, and job-related stress or tension.

Technical causes. Technical causes of accidents involve such things as unsafe chemical, mechanical, or physical conditions such as defective conditions of tools and equipment, unsafe mechanical construction or design, lack

OUT OUR WAY — By J. R. Williams

January 31, 1969.

of—or improper—personal protective equipment, and inadequate mechanical guards for machines or work areas.

Research shows that the majority of accidents are due to a combination of causes, not just human, environmental, or technical acting alone. (27)

WHAT CAN BE DONE TO IMPROVE SAFETY

There are essentially two things personnel executives can do to improve safety in their organizations, First, they can recognize and measure the extent of the problem. Second, they can take corrective action.

Measure the extent of the problem

If personnel executives are really to understand the magnitude of the safety question, they must be able to measure its frequency and severity. This has been standardized so that organizations can compare their rates with national and industry figures. Although several statistics are computed, the most frequently used ones are the accident frequency rate and the accident severity rate. These rates were established by the National Safety Council and are today almost universally recognized and accepted in all business and nonbusiness organizations.

The *accident frequency rate* is computed as follows:

$$\text{Accident frequency rate} = \frac{\text{Number of lost-time accidents} \times 1{,}000{,}000}{\text{Number of employee hours in the period}}$$

The *accident severity rate* is computed as follows:

$$\text{Accident severity rate} = \frac{\text{Number of work days lost} \times 1{,}000{,}000}{\text{Number of employee hours in the period}}$$

There is considerable controversy as to which of these two rates is the more accurate measure of overall organizational safety. Most personnel and safety experts tend to accept the frequency rate as the more significant and sensitive indicator of overall safety performance, as the severity of a given accident is largely a matter of chance. To reiterate, the main advantage of using these rates is that personnel executives can not only properly evaluate their own internal safety conditions currently—and historically—but they can also compare their safety records with those of other firms in the same industry and other organizations in the same community.

It has been suggested by OSHA that accidents be reported as number of injuries per 100 full-time employees per year, which would be a much simpler and easier understood method.

Take corrective action

The following cases will illustrate what three firms have done to reduce accidents and improve health and safety.

> Questor, a firm with plants in 18 states and 8 foreign countries, has waged an all-out war on safety and health hazards for the past three years. The results include improvements in Ohio alone, where the firm insures itself, of savings of $375,000, including a drop in the cost of workers' compensation from 6½ cents per employee hour in 1972 to 4½ cents in 1973. (28)

> The Palmetto Stevedoring Company in Charlestown, South Carolina, had a 198-percent debit on its workers' compensation payment when the owner's daughter went to work part-time doing things like signing checks. She noticed that large checks for workers' compensation insurance were related to the accident rate experienced by the company. Through her efforts to get a safety program started, the accident rate was lowered considerably, and the firm soon had a 28-percent credit in its workers' compensation payments. (29)

> Dow Chemical Company found about 30 off-the-job disabling injuries for every one employee injured at work. Management went to work persuading employees and their families to think about safety constantly. The main thrust was to create a family and community awareness of safety through the use of a slogan, "Life is Fragile—Handle with Care," including the attached logo. Within a year, employee disabling injuries were found to be drastically reduced, which meant savings to the company. (30)

OCCUPATIONAL SAFETY AND HEALTH ACT

OSHA was passed December 29, 1970, and went into effect April 28, 1971. During the four years prior to its passage, more Americans had been killed on the job than in the Vietnam War, and, despite existing state and federal regulations, the situation was worsening with industrial injuries and occupational disease on the rise. The act was drawn up because of the failure of state governments, labor, and management to provide safe and healthy working conditions. The original act involved a lot of red tape and was generally unworkable. However, Congress revised it, and it now promises a significant improvement in health and safety on the job.

Purpose

The purpose of the law is "to assure so far as possible every working man and woman in the nation safe and healthful working conditions and to preserve our human resources." The Occupational Safety and Health Administration is to implement this mandate by:

1. Encouraging employers and employees to reduce hazards in the workplace, and start—or improve—existing safety and health programs;
2. Establishing employer and employee responsibilities;
3. Setting mandatory job safety and health standards;

4. Providing an effective enforcement program;
5. Encouraging the states to assume the fullest responsibility for administering and enforcing their own occupational safety and health programs that are to be at least as effective as the federal program; and
6. Providing for reporting procedures on job injuries, illnesses, and fatalities.

Coverage

The act covers every employer in a business affecting interstate commerce. The only exclusions from the law's coverage are government agencies and employers covered by other federal safety and health laws, such as the Coal Mine Health and Safety Act and the Atomic Energy Act. By official Labor Department interpretation, the phrase, "businesses affecting interstate commerce," as used in the OSHA statute, can mean every person, corporation, partnership, proprietorship, or other entity which hire one or more employees anywhere in the United States, or on the outer continental shelf, or in the nation's territories, possessions, and protectorates. (31) At least 13.5 million employers fall into this broad category.

Rights and responsibilities

The *responsibilities of employers* are to provide a workplace free from safety and health hazards; safe tools with which to work; equal standards for all employees without regard to race, sex, religion, or national origin; and compliance with established standards.

The act *requires employees* to comply with occupational safety and health standards, as well as all rules, regulations, and orders issued under the law that apply to their own actions and conduct.

Some of the *employers' rights* are to:

1. Request and receive proper identification of OSHA personnel prior to inspection of their workplace;
2. Be advised by OSHA personnel of the reason for the inspection;
3. Participate in the walkaround inspection of the workplace with the compliance officers and in the opening and closing conferences with them; and
4. Borrow money from the Small Business Administration to comply with OSHA standards.

Some of the *employees' rights* are to:

1. Obtain a copy of the OSHA standards and other rules from their employer, the OSHA office, or the Government Printing Office;
2. Request information from their employer on safety and health hazards in their work area, on precautions they need to take, and on what they must do if they are involved in an accident or exposed to toxic substances;

3. Request the OSHA area director, in writing, to conduct an inspection if they believe a hazardous condition exists in their workplace; and
4. File a complaint to OSHA within 30 days if they believe they have been discriminated against because of asserting their right under the act.

Enforcement

The law is enforced by the Occupational Safety and Health Administration, located in the Department of Labor, and the Occupational Safety and Health Review Commission.

Agencies. The function of the Occupational Safety and Health Administration is to develop standards, to conduct inspections, to see that the standards are followed, and to enforce actions through citations and penalties where the standards are not met.

The Occupational Safety and Health Review Commission has only one function, namely, to settle contested enforcement actions between the Department of Labor and the employers, employees, and/or unions.

Procedures. In enforcing the law, the inspectors have two important powers. First, they have the right to enter a workplace without advance warning to the employer and to inspect for compliance with the act. (32) Second, the inspectors have the authority to propose penalties for violations of the standards. It would be very difficult to enforce correction of violations without this right. The penalties OSHA can impose may be a fine as high as $20,000 and/or a year in prison for serious, willful violations resulting in death. A penalty fine as high as $1,000 per day may be imposed without going to court.

Priorities. It would be unrealistic to assume that all businesses can be inspected with any degree of frequency. Consequently, a system of "worst-first" has been devised. Under this system, federal compliance officers are empowered to investigate firms selected for inspection according to the following priorities:

1. Whenever catastrophies and/or fatalities are reported;
2. Whenever employee complaints of unsafe or unhealthful conditions are submitted to OSHA; and
3. Whenever it is apparent that an injury rate for an industry is higher than the national average.

While the overall accident rate is 15.1 million worker-hours worked, the rate for targeted industries is: longshoring, 70; meat and meat products, 43; roofing and sheet metal, 43; lumber and wood products, 34; and miscellaneous transport, 33. If you are in one of these industries, you can expect a visit from the OSHA inspector.

Evaluating its effectiveness

In evaluating the effectiveness of the law, we need to look at some of the criticisms of it first and then look at some of the benefits received. Only the criticisms of management will be presented, although employees and unions also have complaints.

Some criticisms. Management views regarding enforcement of OSHA range from general satisfaction to calls for outright repeal of the act as an unnecessary infringement on employer rights. Some specific criticisms are: (*a*) the standards are complex and vague and often hard to understand; (*b*) the matter of jurisdiction, or who has control over what; (*c*) the volume and detail of statistics and recordkeeping; and (*d*) cost.

Vague and complex standards. Managers state that the "standards are too complex and too vague. They are difficult to interpret and hard to comply with." (33) It is claimed that some sections are too general to explain completely how precautions should be taken. The standards that were adopted were industry standards, which were often drafted by representatives from selected industries. Consequently, standards were issued to apply to all businesses that should only be applied to representative industries. There is now an effort being made to change from equipment and specifications standards to performance standards.

Jurisdiction. Another problem of major concern is over jurisdiction, or who has control over what actions. The act allows certain federal agencies which exercise statutory authority to continue to prescribe or enforce standards and regulations affecting occupational safety and health. Some jurisdictional disputes have arisen between the Departments of Labor, Transportation, and Interior. (34) In addition, some 26 states have now complied with the requirements of the law and are beginning to assume responsibility for enforcing it. Some of these state laws are more stringent than the federal ones.

Statistics and recordkeeping. Many managers contend that this aspect of the law is the most onerous one and requires the most time, effort, and money. (35)

Cost. Cost is an important factor, and the economic impact is now being considered by the Review Commission. It ruled that Continental Can did not have to spend $32 million for engineering controls to reduce noise when protective equipment would protect the employees' hearing. (36)

It has been estimated that the law will increase construction costs between 10 to 20 percent and add over $10 billion to the price of construction. (37)

OSHA's attempt to set new noise standards for all work sites effective January 1, 1978, illustrates the cost problem. OSHA is seeking a 90-decibel noise level, but the Environmental Protection Agency is seeking a 75-decibel level. The cost would be $13.5 billion for 90 decibels, but $31 billion for 75 decibels. While labor unions are in favor of the tougher standards, management, being cost-conscious, is in favor of the more lenient 90 decibels. (38)

An outstanding specialist in labor and personnel relations asserts that the expense of meeting the new standards is a one-time cost which will produce safer and more healthful working environments which should result in decreased costs for insurance and medical expenses, lost time, and yet result in higher productivity. (39)

Some achievements. Safety experts have long complained about the apathy of employees and management toward safety. OSHA has now changed all that. In a survey of 116 companies, the Conference Board found that 67 had issued stronger safety policies and had more numerous policy statements concerning safety. When asked whether conformity to OSHA required an increase in spending on safety-related equipment, 83 percent said yes. (40) The general consensus of the companies was that OSHA had succeeded in fostering an increased awareness of safety and health on the part of both employees and management.

In a study of major union agreements referring to health and safety before and after 1971, it was found that 10 percent of them had increased their general statements concerning safety. The percentage of companies pledging compliance with public safety codes increased from 41 to 51. (41)

A study of 800 companies with over 500 employees each was conducted to see how their health care programs had been effected. A marked increase was noted, as preemployment physical examinations increased from 63 to 71 percent, while the percentage of work-related periodic medical exams increased from 40 percent to 53 percent. (42) These statistics are most encouraging, especially as this is preventive medicine rather than curative, and this type saves lives.

From April 28, 1971, through August 1974, OSHA made 172,000 inspections, issued 115,000 citations alleging 592,000 violations. (43) But the real question is how effective were those inspections. In a study of union officials—as representatives of the workers and their views—19 percent felt the state agencies were doing the better job of enforcing and inspecting standards; 25 percent favored local inspection; while 56 percent felt that the federal inspections and enforcement procedures were the most effective. (44)

IMPLICATIONS AND APPLICATIONS FOR PERSONNEL EXECUTIVES

Today top management—including personnel executives—is paying more attention to safety than ever before. As companies have become aware of their responsibilities under OSHA, they have tended to organize to get the job done. Management seems to be giving added force to its commitment to health and safety, both from humanitarian and cost points of view. (45)

OSHA is a much needed piece of legislation. But, just as with any law, its success lies in how vigorously it is enforced, and, with this law in particular, it is essential that there be cooperation from both management and labor. It seems that this is now being done. Hopefully, lives will be saved, our human resources will be enhanced, and our economic well-being will be improved.

DISCUSSION QUESTIONS

1. Differentiate between health hazards and safety hazards.
2. What are the major occupational diseases in the United States?

3. What are the provisions of the Health Maintenance Organization Act of 1973?
4. How are accidents measured?
5. What are the objectives of OSHA? Whom does it cover?
6. Evaluate the effectiveness of OSHA.

REFERENCES AND SUGGESTIONS FOR FURTHER STUDY

1. "Surprisingly Higher Cost of a Safer Environment," *Business Week* (September 14, 1974), pp. 102–103.
2. Patricia E. O'Brien, "Health, Safety, and the Corporate Balance Sheet," *Personnel Journal*, vol. 52, no. 9 (August 1973), pp. 725–29.
3. See Fred K. Foulkes, "Learning to Live with OSHA," *Harvard Business Review*, vol. 51, no. 6 (November–December 1973), pp. 57–67. This is one of the best articles about OSHA. It should be read!
4. Ibid.
5. *Steel Facts*, vol. 3, no. 230 (1975), p. 11.
6. See *The President's Report on Occupational Safety and Health* (U.S. Department of Labor, Health, Education and Welfare, 1975); and Occupational Safety and Health Review Commission, 1972, p. 111.
7. It has been estimated that a reduction of one day per year in the annual rate of absenteeism among the U.S. labor force would add $10 billion to the GNP. See *Protecting the Health of Eighty Million Americans* (U.S. Department of Health, Education, and Welfare, Public Health Service, 1965), for further details.

    Much disease resulting in absenteeism is probably occupationally related, although it is not reported or recognized as such. Many of the other costs of chronic occupational illness—early death or retirement, reduced efficiency, family and community problems—are also not reflected in the National Safety Council's estimates.
8. The definitions and distinctions are based upon Nicholas A. Ashford, "Worker Health and Safety: An Area of Conflict," *Monthly Labor Review*, vol. 98, no. 9 (September 1975), pp. 3–11.
9. "Settling for Less on Health and Safety," *Business Week* (May 1973), p. 63.
10. T. B. Copeland, "Clamoring for Action," *Newsweek* (July 7, 1975), p. 52.
11. For an example of this, see the case problem on p. 602.
12. *Work in America: Report of a Special Task Force to the Secretary of Health, Education, and Welfare* (Cambridge, Mass.: MIT Press, 1973), p. 79.
13. Walter Perlick and Raymond V. Lesikar, *Introduction to Business*, rev. ed. (Dallas, Tex.: Business Publications, Inc., 1975), p. 220.
14. Ashford, "Worker Health and Safety," *Monthly Labor Review*, pp. 3–11.
15. Peter S. Barth, "Health and Safety Programs: Industrial Relations Perspectives, OSHA, and Workers' Compensation: Some Insights into Fatalities," *Labor Law Journal*, vol. 26, no. 8 (August 1975), pp. 486–91.
16. *Injury Rates in Factories, New York State* (New York State Department of Labor, Division of Research and Statistics, 1966).
17. R. W. Revans, *The Theory and Practice of Management* (London: Macdonald,

1966), as quoted in R. L. M. Dunbar, "Manager's Influence on Subordinates' Thinking about Safety," *Academy of Management Journal,* vol. 18, no. 2 (June 1975), pp. 364–69.
18. Ibid.
19. Rollin H. Simonds, "OSHA Compliance: Safety Is Good Business," *Personnel,* vol. 50, no. 4 (July–August 1973), pp. 30–39.
20. E. A. Fleishman, E. F. Harris, and H. E. Burtt, *Leadership and Supervision in Industry* (Columbus, O.: Ohio State University, Bureau of Educational Research, No. 33), p. 63 ff.
21. George Clack, "Safety after the Revolution," *Job Safety and Health,* vol. 3, no. 5 (May 1975), pp. 5–8.
22. Thomas N. Jenkins, "The Accident-Prone Personality: A Preliminary Study," *Personnel,* vol. 33, no. 1 (July 1956), pp. 29–32.
23. J. R. Block and William J. Campbell, "Physical Disability and Industrial Safety," *Personnel Journal,* vol. 42, no. 3 (March 1963), pp. 117–20.
24. Earl J. Kronenberger, "Interpersonal Aspects of Industrial Accident and Nonaccident Employees," *Engineering and Industrial Psychology,* vol. 2, no. 2 (Summer 1960), pp. 57–61.
25. L. F. Senger, "Workman's Compensation Costs," *Best's Insurance News,* fire and casualty ed., vol. 63, no. 10 (February 1963), p. 89.
26. Simonds, "OSHA Compliance," *Personnel,* pp. 30–39.
27. W. N. McBain, "Arousal, Monotony, and Accidents in Line Driving," *Journal of Applied Psychology,* vol. 54, no. 8 (August 1970), pp. 509–19.
28. "Safety = Profits = Jobs," *Job Safety and Health,* vol. 3, no. 5 (May 1975), p. 10 ff.
29. "A Safety Lady on the Dock," *Job Safety and Health,* vol. 3, no. 6 (June 1975), p. 17 ff.
30. "Life Is Fragile—Handle with Care," *Job Safety and Health,* vol. 3, no. 8 (August 1975), p. 4 ff.
31. Since January 1973, businesses with fewer than eight employees are no longer required to maintain injury and illness records. Still, these firms must report fatalities and accidents that hospitalize five or more persons, and small business accident and illness rates will still be reflected in BLS statistics.
32. This right has been restricted in at least one instance. For example, the U.S. District Court in Sherman, Texas, said, "The federal government cannot enter a workplace without the owner's consent unless it first obtains a search warrant." See *Business Week* (April 12, 1976), p. 95, for further details. This decision is being appealed by OSHA.
33. Alexander J. Reis, "Three Years of OSHA: The View from within," *Monthly Labor Review,* vol. 98, no. 3 (March 1975), pp. 35–36.
34. Frank R. Barnako, "Enforcing Job Safety: A Managerial View," *Monthly Labor Review,* vol. 98, no. 3 (March 1975), pp. 36–39.
35. Ibid.
36. Ibid.
37. "Where the Safety Law Goes Haywire," *Nation's Business,* vol. 60, no. 6 (June 1972), pp. 40–47.

38. "A Rising Clamor over Noise Levels," *Business Week* (June 30, 1975), p. 34.
39. Foulkes, "Learning to Live with OSHA," *Harvard Business Review*, pp. 57–67.
40. Donald J. Petersen, "The Impact of OSHA on Management—A First Look," *Conference Board Record*, vol. 10, no. 10 (October 1973), pp. 22–25.
41. Winston Tillery, "Safety and Health Provisions before and after OSHA," *Monthly Labor Review*, vol. 98, no. 8 (September 1975), pp. 40–42.
42. Seymour Lusterman, "Industry's Role in Health Care," *Personnel Administrator*, vol. 19, no. 2 (March–April 1974), p. 39.
43. Reis, "Three Years of OSHA," *Monthly Labor Review*, pp. 35–36.
44. John Zalussky, "The Worker Views the Enforcement of Safety Laws," *Labor Law Journal*, vol. 26, no. 4 (April 1975), pp. 224–35.
45. A poll in upstate New York showed that while many businessmen still resent OSHA, those who have been inspected by it support it more than those who have not. While only 45 percent of businesses which have not been inspected think the agency protects the workers' safety, 78 percent of those who have been inspected believe that it does. Also, only 5 percent of those who had not been inspected thought the OSHA rules were clear, compared to 40 percent of those who were inspected. It was also found that while four-fifths of the surveyed companies were cited for violations during inspections, only 6 percent appealed the citations. See *Wall Street Journal* (April 27, 1976), p. 1, for further details.

Chapter 25

Coping with the future

Expected modifications of the environment
　　Changing work environment
　　Changing organizational environment

Expected changes in personnel functions
　　Recruiting, selecting, and developing employees
　　Rewarding the work force
　　More complicated industrial relations
　　Maintaining the work force

Qualifications needed in future personnel executives
　　How personnel directors view their jobs
　　Specifications for personnel candidates

What is needed to perform the personnel function successfully
　　The need for personnel research
　　Developing a positive managerial philosophy

Quo vadis, Personnel Executive?

25
Coping with the future

I learned the most amazing new truth yesterday. I can scarcely wait for tomorrow.
ALBERT EINSTEIN

The future enters into us, in order to transform itself in us, long before it happens.
RAINER MARIA RILKE

Many people are highly skeptical of present administrative and organizational concepts and practices. In addition, there is substantial—and often justifiable—disillusionment with managerial theory and practice as a means for achieving social, economic, and political goals. Professionalism in management and elsewhere is increasingly mistrusted and under attack. It appears that these political, social, and economic systems are open to change, and much innovation is occurring. To meet changing needs, new organizational forms are appearing and new management precepts are evolving. (1)

These thoughts by Dalton McFarland tend to corroborate the conclusion reached in the Preface that performing the personnel and human resource function in the future will be exceedingly more difficult and complex—but more challenging and rewarding.

That's what this chapter is all about! First, we will explore some of the changes expected in the organizational and work environment, predict some modifications of the personnel functions to be performed, view what type executives will be needed to perform those functions, and then see what will be required of them to carry out successfully their duties and responsibilities, including the development of a philosophy and the use of personnel research.

EXPECTED MODIFICATIONS OF THE ENVIRONMENT

The analytical processes and logical evaluations that resulted in the conclusions reached in this book were based upon five basic premises. First, *as personnel and human resources administration is inherent in all aspects of administration, it is the primary function and responsibility of all managers,* regardless of the nature of their activities or their place in the institution's hierarchy.

Second, *the specific technical personnel functions are no longer assigned to lower levels of managerial activites;* they must also be viewed as part of the higher administrative activities to be performed by *personnel executives at the highest organizational levels.*

Third, *the performance of these functions must embrace the concept of the whole person,* for managers deal with employees as they actually exist in the work environment, not in the idealistic state in which management would like them to exist.

Fourth, as organizations exist in a given culture, *personnel administration cannot be understood outside of the context of the total economic, technological, political, and social environment in which it is performed.*

Fifth, the participants in these functions have changed. *The functions are performed by more capable and more professional administrators;* the same generalization is true of those being administered to.

The basic hypothesis of this text has been: *If one understands human behavior, one can predict that behavior; if one can predict behavior, one can direct and control it.* As management's objective is to direct employee activities, it logically follows that there is a need to predict them. Yet, in order to predict, it is necessary to understand the cause and effect relationships leading to employee behavior. Therefore, the purpose of the material in this book has been to help you understand employee behavior so that you can better perform the personnel administration function.

Based upon these premises and hypotheses, the previous chapters have attempted to develop a philosophical, theoretical, and technical presentation of the latest thoughts in the field. Little effort was made to present the techniques and practices required to implement those findings. Instead, the objective has been to evolve certain generalizations which you can then apply in the context and environment in which you find yourself as a manager.

It should be helpful to you to have some idea of the organizational world in which you will work. This final chapter is devoted to *estimating* the changes that will probably occur in your work environment in the next decade. These estimates *are not necessarily what I favor or advocate, but what I expect will occur,* based upon what has happened in the past—and is currently happening.

Changing work environment

The performance of the personnel management function will change drastically during the next decade because of the changing work environment. The "agricultural society" lasted around 250 years and was replaced by the "industrial society" which has become the victim of its own success. In its place has risen the services sector—education, professions, government, and nonprofit institutions. This "postindustrial society" will exist in a work environment which is the result of several unrestrainable and inexorable, although sometimes imperceptible, trends. The most important of these are: Employees are achieving a position of economic independence, but are more dependent philosophically and psychologically; the government is becoming increasingly involved in the employer-employee relationship; unions are shifting from economic to quasi-political positions; an overwhelmingly rapid technological revolution is occurring; organizational life is becoming increasingly complex; managerial frontiers are shifting from the realm of increasing physical production to that of improving interpersonal relationships and social responsibility; and the knowledge of human behavior is increasing at a rapid rate.

While these trends have already been discussed in detail, suffice it to say here that they constitute the environment in which personnel executives perform their job. The truly effective managers will not only be influenced by this environment, but, if Mary Parker Follett was right, (2) they will modify it to enhance their own positions.

There are two observations to be added to the earlier material, as they have not been adequately covered. The newer technologies will change the very process of management as it has changed the production and distribution of goods and commodities. (3) Basically this means that the expansion of computer technology and its related systems will extend management's range of capabilities. The personnel role will be that of developing people who are willing and able to cope with change. As the next decade promises to accelerate the momentum of change begun in the 1960s, personnel executives must become change agents and begin to act creatively and voluntarily, rather than reluctantly reacting to outside change agents. In addition to economic and technological forecasting, you must plan ahead for social and political changes. Attitudinal changes will call for more emphasis on quality of product, modification of the work ethic—with greater acceptance of leisure as a valid activity, a rejection of authoritarianism, a growing belief in the values of participating and involvement, and a heightened respect for individual dignity. The emphasis must be based upon greater consideration for the *rights and needs of the individual.* Blanket arrangements and uniform plans will no longer meet the needs of people in organizations.

Changing public attitudes will demand that managers of private business become more involved in problems of social responsibility. Personnel work will take on a new community relations dimension, for in the next ten years managers will find that they must deal with activist groups in much the same manner that they dealt with unions in the past. The major point that personnel managers must keep constantly in mind and remind those groups about is that *only a thriving profitable company can provide new jobs and meet social responsibilities,* for "the smaller the profit a company makes, the smaller must be the effort it can make toward meeting public goals"—including equal employment opportunities, health and safety, and ecology. Even public institutions *must* become more cost effective—if they are to be accepted by the public.

Changing organizational environment

Organizational relationships will also undergo drastic changes. Not only will *organizational planning and development* (OD) be emphasized instead of the older methods, but greater consideration will be given to the human resource, the role of the personnel specialist, and the first-line supervisor.

Increasing importance of human resources. As organizations are in reality human organisms, the financial and physical resources are relatively unproductive until combined with the human resources. Therefore, future performance of the personnel function will not be based upon the "factor of production" or the "human relations" philosophy, but upon the "human resource" concept, whereby employees are treated with human dignity and worth, but their output will be judged by the economic criteria of efficiency and effectiveness. Management will no longer assume that the cause and effect relationship is:

Employee participation → Job satisfaction → Increased performance.

Instead, it will assume that:

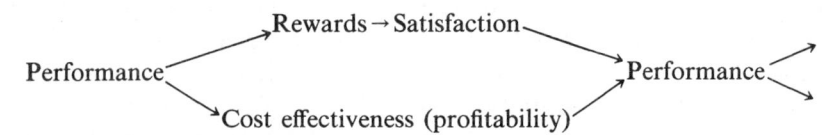

$$\text{Performance} \begin{cases} \text{Rewards} \to \text{Satisfaction} \\ \text{Cost effectiveness (profitability)} \end{cases} \text{Performance}$$

New authority for personnel executives. Organizations will become larger, more interrelated and complex, and will assume different shapes. The organizational relationships will tend to approximate the wheel shape rather than the pyramid. The latter is to be found where employees have a sense of security; the former is used where there is a sense of threatened danger and insecurity. As this sense of threatened security will probably prevail, the organizational shapes will change. The matrix, or project, organizational relationships will probably be used as they are so adaptable to complex and changing situations.

The increasing complexity of the legal environment, integration of business and nonbusiness activities, and rapid industrialization and urbanization will lead to an increase in organizational size and complexity. Consequently, organizations will tend to become more impersonal; conformity will tend further to replace individualism; and a growing isolation of top executives from other members of the organization and a separation of the employees themselves from one another will result. Social groupings will be minimized because of mechanization; employee isolation will increase as a result. A sense of alienation, isolation, loneliness, frustration, and impotence will result.

As work has become more complex, as employees have tended to become more specialized, and as the geographical location of work and decision making have become more centralized, there has occurred a change in the type of authority relationship.

As the personnel function becomes more important, functional authority will tend to replace staff authority as the dominant authority-responsibility relationship. This limited form of line authority over the specialized functions for which the personnel manager is responsible is necessary for several reasons, including the growing number of specialized employees; line management's inability to evaluate and control its performance; the growing responsibility of these specialists for profitable productivity; geographic decentralization of operations; closer contact between the supervisors and their subordinates; an increase in the number of higher intellectual jobs with the consequent decrease in manual work; and interdependence between jobs.

New status for personnel administration. A basic tenet of this book is that the mobilization and allocation of human resources is of greater concern and import to organizations than the management of financial and physical resources. With nonhuman resources, it is people who determine their fate. Yet, too few institutions are presently planning for human resources in any but a very short-term way. Therefore, the role of personnel executives will expand and their image will change during the next decade. The staff position of personnel directors as advisors of line personnel will be minimized, and, in its place, there should be directors of personnel and human resources who guard the people investment through centralized control and inspection. These directors will probably report directly to the chief executive officer and be a party to planning all activities affecting personnel—directly or indirectly—from the beginning. These people will not be personnel managers with a new title, but executives with training in information systems programming, budgeting, and organizational theory, as well as being expert in the use of the behavioral and management sciences.

EXPECTED CHANGES IN PERSONNEL FUNCTIONS

In addition to these modifications of the work and organizational environments, the performance of the personnel functions will also change drastically. While it is impossible to discuss all expected changes in the limited space available, some of the more significant ones will be discussed.

Recruiting, selecting, and developing employees

Personnel executives will deal with a changed work force. All aspects of building and developing the work team will change. Possibly the greatest change will occur in *validating recruitment, selection, and development criteria* which will provide more objective bases upon which to make better and more defensible decisions.

Changes in the labor force. Many factors, including the previously mentioned ones, will result in drastic changes in the size and composition of the nation's labor force. These changes will greatly influence the performance of the personnel function in each organization.

This labor force will be composed of a declining proportion of younger and older workers, and an increasing proportion in the "prime working age" group, the 35–44 year olds; an increasing number and percentage of females, especially of working wives and mothers—and they will be found in all job categories; and about the same proportion of blacks—but they will be in higher level positions. The same will be true of other minorities.

The demand for this labor force will continue to shift toward service-producing industries and away from goods-producing industries. The greatest increase in demand will come from the service industries—except household service—with government following; declines will occur fastest in agriculture and mining. There will also be occupational shifts away from blue-collar and farm jobs and toward white-collar and service ones—especially the professional and technical, and clerical positions.

As there is a direct and positive correlation between a nation's educational level and its productivity, the increasing educational attainment of members of the work force is significant. As this relationship is delayed by around ten years, the current enhancement of educational levels and abilities—especially of blacks—should be reflected in increased performance by the end of the next decade.

Recruiting and selecting employees. For legal and economic reasons, human resource planning will become increasingly important and sophisticated. Organizations must have affirmative action programs—based upon defensible planning—for recruiting minorities, women, disabled, and older workers. More objective and analytical methods will be used, including the computer.

New supply sources for personnel will be utilized; temporary personnel—including retired personnel, even blue-collar workers—will be used extensively in technical and professional, clerical, janitorial, and maintenance activities. This will avoid the "fixed" expenses of hiring full-time people. Finally, selection will be handled increasingly through the employment agencies, especially for recruiting clerical and professional personnel.

Public policy will prevent subjective selection. Instead, more valid selection criteria based upon extensive research will result in improved selection.

Electronic data processing will increasingly be used in selection, particularly in obtaining, analyzing, and evaluating data hitherto unattainable. Biographical information, including the weighted application blank and biographical information blank, will substitute for testing, which will decline in use. Instead, it will be used to determine if a potential employee is trainable, but, even then, "cultural bias" must be removed from the test, and it must be validated to job performance.

The group approach to interviewing potential recruits on company visits will be used in order to save officials' time and effort and to provide for more red-carpet treatment of prospects.

Providing management succession. The supply of managers relative to the demand will improve during the decade. However, there will be three pressure points. First, the job itself will become so much more demanding that those who aspire to progress in management will need to develop themselves continually to keep from becoming obsolete. Second, the new entrants into the management ranks have different value systems, aspirations, life-styles, and perceptions of their function. They will tend to question, challenge, and modify existing patterns of authority-responsibility relationships and behavior. Third, the large number of plateaued executives who entered the managerial ranks during the 1960s will find themselves increasingly under pressure to leave the organizations to make room for younger persons. There is nowhere for these individuals to go, except out. This problem will probably not be corrected during the coming decade.

Maximizing employee potential. Education, training, and development will be modified, becoming more dynamic and continuous. Potential employees will remain outside the work force for longer periods of time while receiving additional formal education. Yet, even after they are hired, they will need longer, more complex, and more specialized and individualized development and career guidance. Nonmanagerial—as well as managerial—personnel must spend from 10 to 20 percent of their time on the job in personal development. (4) Employee training and development will become so highly specialized that it cannot be accomplished by individual organizations but must be done on a cooperative basis by public and/or private institutions. Government programs will become increasingly important. The use of educational television and programmed learning will continue to expand.

Rewarding the work force

Although less emphasis will be given *to money per se* as an incentive to improve performance, financial gain will continue to be a motivational factor. However, as a stimulus to perform better, its value will be in satisfying the social, ego, and achievement needs rather than as an economic medium; greater use will be made of companywide group bonus plans, rather than individual ones. Less use will be made of incentive wage plans because of the difficulty of administering them, especially in terms of relating productivity to individual effort.

Hourly paid employees will tend to receive one rate of pay per job, instead of having their rate unilaterally set within predetermined wage ranges by management using merit ratings. Essentially, anyone with the minimum requirements to perform the job will receive the going rate. The pressure to use salary rather than an hourly rate for covered personnel will grow. The use of job evaluation and merit rating will decline in significance, except for the middle- and upper-level management jobs. At those levels, security, autonomy, esteem, achievement, and other factors mean more than economic compensation.

The Fair Labor Standards Act will be extended to most of the remaining uncovered organizations regardless of whether they are engaged in business or not. Wage differentials between white and nonwhite and male and female employees will decline.

Employee benefits will continue to expand in number and cost—especially toward lifetime employment and early retirement. However, there will probably be more emphasis upon individualized "packages" rather than granting the same benefits to everyone.

The annual hours of work will decline, and probably the four-day week will become a viable alternative for those who choose it. Almost certainly, the 40-hour, five-day workweek will be reduced.

More complicated industrial relations

As organizations have become larger and more complex, as employees have received less satisfaction from their jobs, and as the prevailing philosophy has turned from individualism to shared activities, employee orientation has shifted from the organization and management to outside employee associations, of which the union is the typical example.

The following trends are expected: Union power will increase, but emphasis will be placed upon quasi-political activities such as legislation, executive orders, and administrative decisions, rather than the more traditional economic approaches of collective bargaining and striking. Compulsory arbitration will be used in public organizations. Organizational and recruiting efforts will be directed at public, professional, and agricultural employees, especially white-collar and black workers. Bargaining demands will concentrate on reducing hours worked, "isolation" pay, and additional personal benefits provided during working hours and at institutional expense. Union membership will continue to decline as a percentage of the work force.

The changing composition of the work force will cause nonunionized personnel to seek affiliation with professional and learned societies, which will serve as their agents for establishing terms and conditions of employment.

Maintaining the work force

The two prevailing concepts of *work* will be the leisure and pleasure concept and the human-needs concept. The former, which will be accepted by the mass of employees, views work as a way of providing funds to buy leisure time in which to have pleasure. Emphasis upon this concept leads to pressure for shorter hours of work. The latter concept, which will tend to be accepted by the scientific, technical, professional, managerial, clerical, and sales personnel, is based upon the concept that work satisfies the basic human needs. *Job enrichment* programs will increase in importance as a motivational and developmental technique.

Although *motivation* will continue to be important, the higher-level personnel would have a greater degree of "self-motivation" from the expanded job content and higher educational levels. Consequently, emphasis will be placed upon using incentives which will stimulate the employees through appealing to their self-fulfillment needs, particularly their desire for achievement, accomplishment, and pride of workmanship. The use of *management by objectives* as a motivational device will become increasingly popular.

Counseling will require an increasing proportion of the personnel executive's time. It will take two forms, that which is job-related, including career development activities, and personal problems, including absenteeism, illness, and chemical dependency.

Internally imposed *discipline* will continue to be sought in subordinates but will prove to be just as elusive as previously. Externally imposed discipline will be based even more upon the due-process concept.

Although the need for individualism will continue to be felt, and nonconforming individualists will be sought—and rewarded—for their excellence and creativity, the pressure for conformity will be even greater.

QUALIFICATIONS NEEDED IN FUTURE PERSONNEL EXECUTIVES

There are no definite and generally acceptable specifications available to guide you in preparing for a professional career in personnel and human resources administration. Instead, many myths and generalizations have evolved concerning the education, experience, and personal characteristics needed in order to perform the personnel function. However, several studies do offer you some assistance in making this important decision.

How personnel directors view their jobs

In one study, a questionnaire was sent to 200 directors of personnel at the corporate, divisional, and plant levels in various business organizations throughout the United States. (5) It sought information about the executives' qualifications, characteristics, interests, and background in order to test the validity of the following generalizations:

1. Most personnel administrators view their jobs as only temporary assignments. Some superior has put them into personnel without giving them much choice, and they try to get out of personnel work as soon as they find good escape routes;
2. Personnel administrators vary greatly according to the background experience which they had prior to their entry into personnel work;
3. Personnel administrators have widely differing formal educational backgrounds; and
4. Personnel administrators receive little specific training in performing the personnel function from the companies in which they work. People who work in personnel are pretty much self-trained in their specialized field of work.

The findings of the study suggested the following generalizations concerning the characteristics of these personnel professionals:

1. Most directors of personnel view their work with some degree of permanence and tend to have a strong desire to remain in it. (6) The directors

follow through with their desires by actually staying in personnel administration for many years;
2. Approximately one-third of today's personnel directors have spent their entire business careers in personnel administration work; the others entered the personnel field from widely differing business positions. There are only minor differences, however, in the total average years which have been spent in personnel work by those entering from other fields and those who have made personnel their complete business careers;
3. Most of them hold at least a bachelor's degree from a college or university, and some hold additional advanced degrees. The major fields of study in which they have earned their college degrees are widely varied. Regardless of their collegiate majors, a majority of those with college degrees have taken at least a few basic personnel-oriented courses; and
4. The training received by most personnel administrators from their companies before they are given responsibilities for the performance of personnel administration tasks is limited. Apparently training is received after the acceptance of responsibility or is gained through self-training.

Specifications for personnel candidates

The usual specifications for personnel candidates are extremely varied, as is also true for their educational requirements. Some organizations look for candidates that have degrees in personnel or business administration; others want social scientists; while others lean toward candidates with legal or technical degrees. A bachelor's degree may be enough in some companies, but other organizations are looking for M.B.A.'s and Ph.D.'s.

Fred Foulkes has concluded that a vice president for personnel should: be problem-oriented and involved with present *and* future problems of the firm; have initiative and an aggressive stance, rather than being passive or reactive; and be willing to assume an "advocacy or conscience-of-the corporation" role. (7)

It can be generalized from these and other studies, (8) that personnel executives of the future will need to be highly educated, interested in people-type activities, have a background in organizational activities, and have "outward going personalities." They will be in a high position in the firm's hierarchy and enjoy increasing prestige and status.

> The Monsanto Chemical Company found that the most successful technique was to *interview continuously* for personnel candidates in order to find the exceptional candidates before an opening developed. (9) This approach required that the firm anticipate need for personnel candidates a year in advance and that it interview in advance of specific openings. This method resulted in the specifications of the job being raised.
>
> As far as education is concerned, the firm prefers persons with a master's degree in personnel administration, industrial relations, psychology, business

administration, economics, liberal arts, English, history, sociology, or social science.

As the personnel function requires the ability to think, to handle abstract facts, to analyze problems, and to develop solutions, interviews are used to select candidates with high intellectual ability. Scholastic achievements are important but are not the sole determining factor. The interview is also relied upon to judge personality, as the company looks for a person who "can work with all kinds of people." Along with personality, and closely related to it, is the interest of the candidate both in people and in personal work.

WHAT IS NEEDED TO PERFORM THE PERSONNEL FUNCTION SUCCESSFULLY

Leonardo da Vinci said: "Those who are enamoured of practice without science are like a pilot who goes into a ship without a rudder or compass and never has any certainty where he is going. Practice should always be based upon a sound knowledge of theory." This statement illustrates the truth that performing the personnel function requires more than mere techniques and tools for working with people. An effective on-going personnel program is based upon a living, practical philosophy, dependent upon theoretical knowledge for its effective application. This knowledge is constantly being expanded by the researchers in the behavioral science and managerial fields. In turn, this managerial philosophy and theoretical knowledge must be applied effectively by capable people.

The need for personnel research (10)

Current personnel research is quite varied in scope, methods, and techniques used. However, the common thread found in all the organizations doing it is that they attempt to study human behavior by using scientific procedures. There are some who believe that a science of human behavior is unattainable and that the same scientific procedures used to gain knowledge of the natural sciences cannot be adapted to the study of humans in an organizational setting. While not becoming involved in that argument, I will *assume* that they are applicable to personnel management and behavioral studies.

Characteristics of the scientific approach. The scientific approach has much to offer personnel executives in the study of human behavior in their organizations. While most writers agree that there is no single scientific method, but rather several methods that can be and are used, it is thus better to say that *there is a scientific approach*. It tends to have the following characteristics:

1. *The procedures are public,* which means that a scientific report contains a complete description of what was done. This enables other researchers in the field to follow each step of the investigation as if they were actually present.

2. *The definitions are precise,* and the procedures used, the variables measured, and how they were measured are clearly stated.
3. *The collecting of data is objective,* so there should be no bias in collecting data and interpreting results.
4. *The findings must be replicable,* so that any researcher in the field can test the findings or results of a study by attempting to reproduce them.
5. *The approach is systematic and cumulative,* so that a unified body of knowledge can be developed. Thus, a major purpose of the behavioral science approach to personnel is to develop an organized system of verified hypotheses about people.
6. *The purposes are explanation, understanding, and prediction,* so that if one determines "why" and "how" and is able to provide proof, one can then predict the particular conditions under which specific events will occur. *Prediction is the ultimate objective of personnel research!*

These characteristics constitute the basic nature of the scientific approach, that is, its objective, systematic, and controlled nature, which enables others to have confidence in the outcome of the research.

Characteristics of personnel research. In addition to understanding the characteristics of the scientific approach to doing research in human behavior, personnel executives should also understand the characteristics of personnel research. There are three dimensions which determine the level of, validity of, and usefulness of this type research. They are the degree of control exercised by the researcher, the level of its outcome, and the breadth of its application.

Degree of control. One way of classifying personnel research is by the degree of control exercised by researchers. When a study is described as a laboratory investigation, it is implied that the researchers make their observations and record their data in a highly controlled situation. When a researcher conducts an experiment using an experimental group and a control group, this is usually a *laboratory study.* (11) In a *field study,* the only control involves selecting time, place, and subjects for making observations, recording data, and analyzing it. When *library research* is used to solve a problem, it is implied that the researcher seeks a solution by gathering and synthesizing observations made by others.

Level of outcome. A second way to classify a personnel research study is in terms of its level of outcome. A study concerned only with what something is like is called *descriptive.* When the outcome is used to anticipate the future, it is called *predictive.* If it seeks an answer to the question of "why"—that is, looking for a cause and effect relationship—the study is described as *diagnostic.* You can see that description is usually the first step to both prediction and diagnosis.

Breadth of application. Probably the most widely used dimension for distinguishing among types of personnel research is the use to be made of the findings. The first distinction to be made is between *pure* and *applied research.*

In *pure research* the motive is mainly one of curiosity, as the research is interested in finding out about a given phenomenon, but has little or no thought of the immediate use or application to which the results may be put. Yet, much pure research often ends up being widely applied, even through its original purpose was intellectual curiosity. *Applied research* is concerned with solving practical problems.

Service research is usually done for some administrator who wants a study done to solve a particular problem.

Action research may be done to gain interest and attention of some group or to bring about some organizational or personal improvement. This type usually turns out to be strictly practical and limited to a particular situation.

Who does personnel research? Personnel research is not too prevalent at present and is not anticipated to be so in the near future. An exhaustive survey done several years ago found that private, nonresearch firms conducted about 39 percent of such research; universities conducted 34 percent; the federal government, 22 percent; and private business, only 5 percent. (12) Firms performing their own personnel research are almost invariably large ones, (13) such as American Telephone & Telegraph, General Electric, General Motors, IBM, Sears, and Texas Instruments. (14)

A study, primarily of large manufacturing firms, found 89 percent of them had assigned primary responsibility for personnel research to the personnel department. (15)

Personnel research tends to be dominated by industrial psychologists, most of whom have their doctorates, although research is increasingly being done by personnel graduates. One study found that 90 percent of those conducting personnel research for private firms were psychologists. (16) Another study found the best departments were staffed by Ph.D.'s in psychology or personnel. (17)

Extent of personnel research. Personnel departments have been found to spend around 3 percent of their total expenditures for personnel research. For example, one survey found that a group of manufacturing firms having a total personnel department employee ratio of 0.77 only allocated 0.02 to research activities. (18) Yet, almost all research studies show that while the figures are small, they are increasing with each survey. Another study found only about 100 firms employing one or more people who worked at least half time on personnel research. (19) The average number of researchers per firm has been found to be three or four, with very few companies employing over ten. (20)

Areas of research. One of the earliest studies of the areas being researched found the four most dominant subjects being surveyed by 50 companies were: selection, training and development, attitudes and leadership, and measurement devices. (21) A second survey of 44 companies found 98 percent were doing research on selection; 75 percent, opinion measurement; 30 percent, training and development; 20 percent, appraisal; 18 percent, motivation; 16 percent, organizational effectiveness; and 10 percent on others, including counseling. (22)

While these are the areas actually being researched, what are the fields needing more research? A later study of personnel administrators found that 60 percent of them sought research in employee motivation; 59 percent, in managerial selection and training. (23) Another study of personnel executives found their estimates of research needs were: selection of minority groups, placing and training the disadvantaged, turnover, evaluation of training and development, management appraisal, and opinion surveys. (24)

Methods used. As indicated earlier, there are many methods used. First, the method actually selected will depend upon the degree of *realism* sought. If this is the desire, then some form of "field" research such as surveys, field experiments, or case studies will be used because of their natural and regular conditions and realistic setting.

Second, the *scope* of the research will determine the method used. The field research mentioned is broader in scope for it permits researchers to measure many factors that might be missing in a laboratory setting.

The degree of *precision* required would also influence the choice of methods. Laboratory research ordinarily is more precise in measurement than is typically possible in the field. The use of multiple observations and repeated measures allow the researcher to obtain more accurate information about the variables being studied.

The degree of *control* also influences the method used. In the laboratory, researchers have much greater control over what happens, whereas in the field there are many disruptive factors.

Evaluation of personnel research. Very little research has been done on evaluating personnel research. However, what has been done indicates that personnel research, so far, has very little significant impact on top management. Also, it is estimated that as few as 15 corporations actually use their research facilities as fully as they could. (25)

A mid-Victorian educator expressed the need for meaningful research when he said, "He who learns from one occupied in learning drinks of a running stream. He who learns from one who has learned all he has to teach drinks 'the green mantle of the stagnant pool.' " (26)

Developing a positive managerial philosophy

In addition to an understanding of the codified body of knowledge that we call the fundamentals of management, derived from research, personnel administrators need to have a personal philosophy of management. In applying these fundamental concepts to given situations, managers will modify them to conform to, or at least be compatible with, their own philosophical principles and to know how to adapt them to the culture, social system, and technological complex within which the managers operate.

This observation should remind us of the inability to apply a given solution to all situations. Rather, we need to recognize the importance of developing for ourselves some general concepts to be applied to a particular situation involving a specific person or group of persons at a given period of time and under a given set of circumstances. Our set of principles would then serve as the boundaries, or parameters, within which we attempt to solve (or resolve) the problems involved.

It is hoped, then, that you will develop such a philosophy and apply it to the solution of personnel problems, rather than try to find a formula to be applied to all situations. Such a philosophy would tend to be long-lived and universally applicable, whereas techniques tend to be short-lived and have only limited applicability.

QUO VADIS, PERSONNEL EXECUTIVE?

Some of the trends and problems facing the personnel executives of the future have been presented in this chapter. (27) It has been shown that performing the personnel function will be exceedingly more difficult and complex—but more challenging and rewarding. It will demand more capable managerial personnel because more highly educated, skilled, and developed employees will be supervised. Thus, personnel executives will need more scientific and technical knowledge themselves in order to operate more effectively. Finally, new horizons for performing service to the organization, employees, and society will become available.

How these factors will be, or should be, handled is the question now facing us. Perhaps we'll become efficient enough that the "necessary" productive work individuals must perform will occupy such a small percentage of their time that finding fulfillment and satisfaction through economically rewarding work will dwindle in importance and leisure time satisfaction will become the main objective. Until such a time arrives, personnel executives must continue to harmonize individual needs with organizational needs. This has never been a historically easy task nor does it appear that it will be in the future. *Herein lies the challenge of personnel and human resources administrators, namely, to deliberately shape and enhance management knowledge so that it will prove most useful in the modern, postindustrial society.*

DISCUSSION QUESTIONS

1. What is your estimate of the future of personnel administration? Try to show where you differ with the author in his projections.
2. To the best of your knowledge, have any of his predictions proven to be erroneous? Explain.
3. Has the need for personnel research been overestimated? Explain.
4. Is a philosophy of personnel administration really as important as stated? Explain.
5. What kind of academic and background preparation should a personnel executive have?

REFERENCES AND SUGGESTIONS FOR FURTHER STUDY

1. Dalton E. McFarland, "From the Corporate State to the Managed Pluralism," *The Conference Board Record*, vol. 12, no. 7 (July 1975), pp. 14–20.
2. See H. C. Metcalf and L. Urwick, eds., *Dynamic Administration: The Collected Papers of Mary Parker Follett* (Bath: Management Publications Trust, Ltd., 1941), especially "Constructive Conflict," and "Business as an Integrative Unity."
3. John Diebold, "The 1970s: Decade of Entrepreneurs," *Business Today*, vol. 5, no. 2 (Summer 1970), pp. 49–56.
4. It has been predicted that personnel administrators may eventually spend around 40 percent of their working time in training—just to keep up with the rapid changes being brought about by science and technology. As the educational system does not change as quickly as an organization's technological development, new and different training programs must be created for developing employees for future needs, including how to cope with change itself. Finally, education will be a continual, lifetime, integrative process. See James M. Mitchell and Rolfe Schroeder, "Future Shock for Personnel Administration," *Public Personnel Management*, vol. 3, no. 4 (July–August 1974), pp. 265–69, for other aspects of change as they affect personnel administrators.
5. O. Jeff Harris, "Personnel Administrators—The Truth about Their Backgrounds," *MSU Business Topics*, vol. 17, no. 3 (Summer 1969), pp. 22–29.
6. This finding was corroborated in another study which indicated that 70 percent of personnel managers wish to remain in the personnel field and only a small minority view it as a ladder of achievement to line management. See Julius Rezler, "Role of Industrial Relations Centers in the Education of Personnel Managers," *Personnel Journal*, vol. 50, no. 1 (January 1971), pp. 64–68.

    These findings were found to be true to a considerable extent in the 1973 American Society of Personnel Administration (ASPA) membership profile survey. The composite ASPA member was a white male, 41 years old, with at least a college degree. Over 50 percent had either worked on, or completed, one advance degree and had been in the field ten years or less. They *like it and intend to stay*. For further information, see "Who's Who in ASPA?" *Personnel Administrator*, vol. 20, no. 1A (February 1975), pp. 27–28.
7. See Fred K. Foulkes, "The Expanding Role of the Personnel Function," *Harvard Business Review*, vol. 53, no. 2 (March–April 1975), pp. 71–84, for the results of these studies.
8. Arthur J. D. Cook, "Personnel Practices in a Developing Area," *Personnel Journal*, vol. 46, no. 5 (May 1967), pp. 302–6; Carlie Spencer and Carmella Singer, "The Personnel Function in Medium and Small Firms," *Personnel Practice Bulletin*, vol. 26, no. 1 (March 1970), pp. 42–47; D. R. Fredericks, "Position of the Personnel Manager," *Management International Review*, no. 4 (1966), pp. 88–90; and Sigvard Rubenowitz, "Personnel Management Organization in Some European Societies," *Management International Review*, vol. 8, nos. 4–5 (1968), pp. 74–92.
9. Howard M. Mitchell, "Selecting and Developing Personnel Professionals," *Personnel Journal*, vol. 49, no. 7 (July 1970), pp. 583–89.
10. The material in this section has been heavily influenced by Bernard Berelson and Gary Steiner, *Human Behavior: An Inventory of Scientific Findings* (New York:

Harcourt, Brace & World, 1964), Chap. 1 and 2. This is one of the better discussions of research methodology—as well as findings in the field of human behavior. It is strongly urged that you read it!

11. Researchers, government officials, and others are becoming concerned about the ethical dilemmas involved in doing big, complex social experiments with humans. They are asking questions like these: Must the subject be told the purpose of an experiment, even if it biases the results? Can researchers keep information about a person confidential from governmental agencies that might use it to the person's detriment? What obligation is there to make sure that subjects don't suffer when the experiment ends? See Alan L. Otten, "Ethical Quandaries," *Wall Street Journal* (September 18, 1975), p. 20.

12. Cecil Goode, *Personnel Research Frontiers* (Chicago: Public Personnel Assn., 1958).

13. Harold Flanders, "The AT&T Company Manpower Laboratory, Circa 1971," *1971 Proceedings of the Academy of Management,* pp. 203–06.

14. Thomas A. Patten, Jr., "Personnel Research: Status Key," *Management of Personnel Quarterly,* vol. 4, no. 4 (Fall 1965), pp. 15–23.

15. National Industrial Conference Board, *Personnel Administration: Changing Scope and Organization* (Studies in Personnel Policy, no. 203, 1966), p. 26.

16. W. C. Byham, *The Uses of Personnel Research* (New York: American Management Assn., Research Study No. 91, 1968).

17. J. R. Hinrichs, "Characteristics of the Personnel Research Function," *Personnel Journal,* vol. 48, no. 9 (August 1969), pp. 597–604.

18. Roberta J. Nelson, *et.al.,* "Personnel Ratios, 1960: An Analytical Look," *Personnel,* vol. 37, no. 6 (November–December 1960), pp. 18–28.

19. Hinrichs, "Characteristics of the Personnel Research Function," *Personnel Journal,* pp. 597–604.

20. Dean Berry, *The Politics of Personnel Research* (Ann Arbor, Mich.: University of Michigan, Bureau of Industrial Relations, 1967).

21. Ibid.

22. Byham, *The Uses of Personnel Research.*

23. G. C. Thornton, III, "Image of Industrial Psychology among Personnel Administrators," *Journal of Applies Psychology,* vol. 53, no. 5 (October 1969), pp. 437 ff.

24. Berry, *The Politics of Personnel Research.*

25. Byham, *The Uses of Personnel Research.*

26. Quoted by Mary E. Murphy in "The Teaching of Social Accounting: A Research Planning Paper," *Accounting Review,* vol. 32, no. 4 (October 1957), p. 637.

27. See Leon C. Megginson and Kae H. Chung, "Human Ecology in the Twenty-First Century," *Personnel Administration,* vol. 33, no. 2 (May–June 1970), pp. 46–55, for further details.

CASES FOR FURTHER STUDY

VII–1. The Recalcitrant Orderly

The head nurse in a large nursing home reported a problem to Mary Powell, the assistant administrator, who was responsible for the personnel function.

> Jim has a very bad attitude about his job and fellow employees. He was hired as a male orderly but acts as though he were doing us a favor by working for us. He gripes about everything: He gripes about the pay and the working hours, and he talks about his fellow employees behind their backs. He tries to give the impression that he is too good to do certain things and that certain jobs are "beneath his dignity." When you ask him to do something, he comes back with, "Why don't you do it yourself?"
>
> We tried to talk with him about the different job descriptions of an orderly and a nurse and explain to him that when I ask him to do something, it's usually because I'm busy doing something he's not allowed to do—such as giving medications.
>
> He has had several years of college, and this may be why he feels he's better than an orderly, but still no one made him take the job, and we are giving him an opportunity to earn some money while going to college.

Questions

1. What does the case show about the meaning of work to various types of employees?
2. What does it show about the effects of the general environment upon employee relations?
3. What would you advise the head nurse to do now? Explain!

VII–2. Jack Moran

Jack Moran, a long-time employee of the Practical Public Utility Company, had achieved his position (normally one held by a technical graduate) through the ranks, was recognized as quite competent in his field of activity, and was respected by his associates.

After 15 years of service, although his performance was not noticeably affected, there were indications that Jack's domestic life was unhappy. It was company policy not to let these matters be of concern unless they interfered with a man's efficiency or unless they were of such nature as to blemish the reputation of the company.

However, in addition to the evidences of domestic troubles, it began to appear that Jack was drinking too much. Besides some obvious physical evidences, frequent one-day absences from the job, particularly following a weekend, pointed to the possibility of abnormal drinking.

Jack and his wife obtained a divorce, and he remarried shortly thereafter. Jack was then transferred to an area where the company had recently opened a new office.

During the next year, a number of instances occurred which indicated that he was continuing to drink to excess and that his new marriage was not working out satisfactorily. In one of these cases, he actually assaulted his wife during a brawl in public. Due to the circumstances (both the place and those present), the scene caused some concern to the company; such a display by one of its employees certainly would not help its public image. As a result, the company felt that Jack should be removed from this assignment, so he was returned to the home office.

Before being given another assignment, Jack was given a warning by Frank Moore, the head of the department. This warning was the strongest that could be given short of dismissal, and Jack's attitude was that of very sincere appreciation for having been given another chance. Although the new assignment constituted a lowering of his position and status, no change was made in his rate of compensation.

For a period of nearly a year, Jack's conduct and job performance improved. His reputation in his new assignment was growing more favorable, and outwardly it appeared that the problem no longer existed; it was known, however, that it did exist. Jack's drinking began to get out of hand. He and his second wife were estranged, divorce action was in progress, and she was making quite a nuisance of herself, both in pestering Jack and Jack's supervisor, Henry Blane. It appeared to the latter that in her conversations with him her only aim was to belittle Jack in the eyes of the company. Henry was not particularly disturbed by the telephone calls and had said nothing about them to Jack.

Jack, too, was apparently taking things in stride until suddenly, without warning, he failed to appear for work one morning. He was presumed to be sick, although no formal notification had been made. The next afternoon, Henry was notified by the police in a city some 200 miles away that Jack had been picked up in a condition which indicated that he was suffering from acute alcoholism.

After several weeks of hospitalization and rest at home and on the advice of company medical authorities and Jack's personal physician, Jack returned to work. His wife agreed to a reconciliation if Jack would do something about his drinking problem. Continued employment was, at this time, made conditional on Jack's total abstinence from alcoholic beverages and his promise to seek help if he needed it from an agency such as Alcoholics Anonymous or the state alcoholic treatment center.

Jack joined a local A.A. group, and, for approximately a year now, the company has had no more loyal employee. Even though an assignment of lesser responsibility had to be given, there was no complaint from Jack, and his performance has been excellent. Inasmuch as Jack has been performing a job much less demanding than his former position, Frank Moore and the personnel manager decided his salary would have to be reduced to a level more comparable with the job he has been doing.

Questions

1. (*a*) When should the company have been concerned with Jack's drinking? (*b*) Should it have become concerned? (*c*) Evaluate the company policy, or lack of policy, concerning alcoholic employees.
2. (*a*) Should Frank Moore have done more than warn Jack? (*b*) Explain your answer.
3. (*a*) Would you recommend Jack for promotion again? (*b*) Why or why not?
4. (*a*) What does this case illustrate about alcoholism as a progressive illness? (*b*) What does it show about discipline as a judicial process? (*c*) Explain how the due-process concept was or was not followed in this case. (Refer to Chapter 20, if needed.)
5. (*a*) Was the firm ethically "right" in making his continued employment conditional upon the two circumstances? (*b*) Explain.
6. Would you treat this type illness differently from physical illness? Mental illness? Explain why.

VII-3. The Case of Sam Sawyer*

Sam Sawyer was a top-rated operator in a building devoted to a five-stage batch process involving material with a high percentage of caustic soda. The five stages in the process were located on five separate floors. In addition to controlling temperatures carefully on various pieces of equipment and making sure that the time cycles were closely controlled, the operators moved the material in open buggies from one stage to the proper chute located in the floor and dumped the material through the chute to equipment on the floor below, where the next stage took place.

Because of the corrosive nature of the material, eye protection in the form of close-fitting goggles had been provided for a number of years. Up until a year ago, the safety rules only required that goggles be worn when removing material from equipment, since it was during the unloading operations that the greatest possibility of injury existed. The wearing of goggles at other times was up to the discretion of the operator.

At two stages in the process, the material was light and fluffy, and there were occasional backdrafts through the chutes causing it to fly. There had been three cases of minor eye irritations from this cause. Consequently, the safety

---

* Prepared by Bruce Gunn, Florida State University.

rule was changed about a year ago, and operators had been required to wear goggles whenever they were near exposed material.

David Watts, who had been the foreman for two years, had come to the plant three years ago directly from engineering school. Prior to becoming foreman, he had worked on all five stages of the operation and had gotten along well with all the men. He felt "very kindly toward them" because they had taught him the "tricks of the trade" so that by the time he became foreman he had a thorough knowledge of the operations.

Watt's shift supervisor was very safety-minded, believing that "all personal injuries can be prevented." He was quite insistent that safety rules "be followed to the letter."

Sam Sawyer, the oldest operator in point of service, had been working on this particular operation for 20 years and was an outstanding operator on all five stages. Because of his years of experience and his excellence as an operator, he was looked up to by the rest of the men. He had an outstanding safety record, which was one of the best in the plant, as he had had only one minor injury in all his years of service.

When the new safety rule went into effect about a year ago, Dave Watts was bothered because everyone went along with it except Sam, who resisted the change in the rule. This caused some difficulty in selling the rule to the other men because they respected his opinions. His main contention was that it was unnecessary to wear goggles except when unloading equipment. However, after much discussion he agreed to go along with the rule.

During the past six months, Dave caught Sam without his goggles on on four occasions. He had a strong feeling that Sam was not complying with the safety rule fully and that his opinions were unchanged. Dave suspected that Sam was complying with the rule only while he was around. On half a dozen occasions he had had the feeling that Sam had put the goggles over his eyes just as the foreman came on the floor. Prior to the rule change, Sam had worn his goggles around his neck when they were not needed, but he started wearing them pushed up on his forehead. The foreman's suspicions were confirmed three days ago when he came upon Sam unexpectedly and saw him bob his head to shift the goggles from his forehead to his eyes.

Question

1. What would you do if you were the supervisor?

part eight

Integrating cases

Cases:
VIII–1. The Move
VIII–2. Affirmative Action in Theory and in Practice
VIII–3. A Challenging Job

INTEGRATING CASES

VIII-1. The Move *

Burnett's Department Store, a retail establishment located in a modern two-story company-owned building in the downtown area of a highly industrialized and unionized city, was known for fine service and merchandise.

The building contained the main offices, 50 selling departments, and the staff departments, as well as a restaurant, which was leased to a local independent food service. There were "around 450 employees." Also, it "was very profitable."

To face the challenge of the car-oriented shopper, and in the spirit of servicing the customer to the best of its ability, Burnett's decided to establish a branch in a new shopping center located near the more heavily populated suburban communities. The owners planned to occupy the new branch store in about 15 months.

As the result of the planned expansion, the major challenges to Burnett's were: (*a*) to set up organizational relationships between the main store and the new branch store, while still attempting to maintain the unique management philosophy that proved successful for over 70 years; and (*b*) to establish procedures for recruiting, hiring, and training and developing personnel for the new branch without depleting the main store operations.

Burnett's had been established by Joe Burnett in the early 1900s as a family country general store. From a modest beginning, the business had grown steadily, doubling in space every five years, but remained a family-held corporation over the years. In 1975, the founder's sons, Arthur and James, operated the store.

Arthur Burnett, president of the company, and James, operations manager, were vastly different in temperament but functioned well as a team, for the abilities of one complimented the abilities of the other. By spending most of their time on the buying floor, they personally directed the major operations of the store. In addition, the owners and the employees had the opportunity to develop a "warm, personal relationship with customers and to know their personal preferences."

The *personnel division* performed the following functions: recruitment, selection, and placement of full-time and part-time employees to meet departmental needs—as specified by the "buyers"; generalized sales training; em-

---

* Prepared by Loretta L. Mazzaroppi, Fairleigh Dickinson University, Madison.

ployee recordkeeping and payroll; and publication and distribution of a weekly newsletter. Joan Wadsworth, the personnel director, together with a small staff, handled the personnel functions, as well as servicing the cashiering function.

There was no evidence that the company utilized personnel budgets and/or employee predictions at the main store as a basis of recruiting and selecting personnel and for training and development activities. Neither did the company have formalized job specifications prepared as a basis for recruiting and selecting personnel.

An outside consulting agency had been engaged to establish job descriptions for nonexempt employees, as well as a wage and salary guide.

Company policies and procedures

The owners' main objective, which gave purpose and direction to the firm's personnel, was "to provide courtesy and service to our customers." The store had no established written policies, although some general practices had developed over the years. These were passed along from the managers to the employees by word of mouth on a "need-to-know" basis.

There was rarely any interaction between planning activities at the general management, personnel, department heads, and/or the individual employee levels. Instead, each problem was dealt with separately, and the decision was based on the particular incident. The key factor was that one of the owners was readily available to handle the situation. There was little, if any, participation of nonmanagerial personnel in the decision-making process.

Buyers (managers) were provided with manuals which outlined buying procedures.

The guidelines for employees who were responsible for the day-to-day activities of the business were presented in an *employee handbook* distributed to all new personnel (full-time and part-time). This *handbook* described employee benefits, policies and procedures covering various job responsibilities, and methods of handling various types of transactions—as well as "sales tips."

The *Newsletter,* prepared by a member of the personnel division, was distributed weekly and provided employees with current news items of particular interest to them "as members of the Burnett team."

Burnett's operated under the "open door" policy whereby an employee with the knowledge (but not necessarily with the approval) of her supervisor or department head was free to discuss problems directly with one of the owners.

The store offered its employees many benefits, including profit-sharing-thrift plans, liberal discounts on personal purchases, hospitalization and life insurance, annual paid vacations, and paid sick leave. The company had also encouraged employees to further their education through an employee tuition reimbursement program. In addition, the company occasionally sponsored in-training programs for supervisory and managerial personnel.

Multiunit operation

It was planned that Burnett's branch store would be organized according to the equal-stores concept, while concentrating major management functions —including buying—at the main store headequarters. There would be centralization of major responsibilities in the main store headquarters, with the exception of selling which would be decentralized.

The decisions made by the functional divisions (merchandising, store operations and sales promotion, personnel, and finance and control) would be transmitted to both the main store and the branch store through the general sales manager, a position that had been created prior to the branch store opening. The general merchandise manager had the responsibility of directing and coordinating merchandising and selling for the main store and the branch store.

The major objective of this central organizational concept was to achieve the efficiencies and the economies of a chain store organization, as well as to avoid the friction and overlapping of responsibilities between the branch store and the parent store. Within this planning framework, Burnett's management had to adopt a system for appraising the degree to which it and its components would achieve the goals that had been set.

With the decision to expand to a multiunit operation, a major consideration for both Arthur and James Burnett was how they would maintain the unique philosophy that had been their trademark over the years as owner-managers or whether they would move toward professional management.

The owners recognized that "the expansion to a multiunit operation would require accounting for human resources."

The hiring and development of personnel would result in a major outlay of cash. Therefore, by the identification of personnel needs through effective personnel planning and using the results for personnel decisions, extensive cost avoidance could take place within the personnel function.

An effective planning program would enable the firm to ensure that properly qualified managerial personnel would be available when needed. This plan would be a basic requirement for the effective administration and direction of such functions as recruiting and training and would, in fact, aid in the reduction—if not the elimination of—recruiting on a "crisis basis."

Burnett's had no formal personnel forecasts as to how many people would be required to fulfill expansion plans. Although a branch store manager had been hired from the outside, he had no formal job description, specified assigned responsibilities, or delegated authority. The assumption was that the branch store manager would function as a sales manager and work with the general merchandise manager and the buyers to advise them on merchandise needs in order to maintain a basic stock of staple items. Sales performance and merchandising profits of the branch would be the responsibility of the branch store manager. In addition, he would represent the store to the community and deal with the management of the shopping center in which it would be located.

Since the main store employees would have the option of transferring to the new branch location, a decision that faced Mrs. Wadsworth of personnel was how to develop a method of evaluating employees in order to determine at which store the present employees would be placed so they could operate most productively. This provision would be a way of reducing turnover and increasing morale and productivity.

In addition, efforts had to be expended to study the labor market in an effort to attract employees with the appropriate skills and qualifications to fill the jobs that would be vacant at the main store because of transfers and new positions available at the branch store.

In order to develop the individuals into efficient and effective employees, the personnel director had to plan for their training and development, while accounting for the costs and quality of training programs. Burnett's realized the need to develop subordinates in a systematic manner, thus "creating the basic condition for their own regeneration." This required continuous educational, training, and developmental programs for nonmanagerial, as well as managerial personnel.

Questions

1. Evaluate the personnel program of this organization.
2. Assume that you are the personnel director, and prepare a personnel planning program for the firm.

VIII-2. Affirmative Action in Theory and in Practice *

The Apex plant, an operating facility of Petrochem Corporation, was one of many plants operating as part of the petrochemical complex of the Gulf coastal region. Much of the industrial growth in this region was relatively recent so Apex, like many other plants in this area, was a modern growth-oriented facility.

The firm's affirmative action plan: Background

During recent years, Petrochem Corporation had taken a firm stand as an "equal opportunity employer," and Apex was working under an affirmative action plan (AAP) with the goal of achieving within five years a work force mixture which matched that of the recruiting area in both ethnic background and sex.

To achieve this work force distribution at both the exempt and nonexempt

---

* Prepared by Linda Calvert, University of Houston, Clear Lake.

levels while maintaining its basic entry standards, Apex recruited extensively at black universities and vocational schools. The plant also maintained close contact with other state universities, private employment agencies, the state employment agency, local high schools, and various civic and community groups. However, the prime source of both minority and female applicants had been, and continued to be, referrals by the Apex plant employees themselves.

Although the plant had considered offering training courses for applicants who fell below minimum standards, this approach had been avoided since previous experience had shown that job applicants tended to view acceptance into the training courses as tantamount to a job offer. However, the plant had worked through the local school board in providing various cooperative and adult education courses. The plant also maintained an active summer hire program which was used to identify potential minority group employees.

Apex's in-house program for minority groups consisted of compiling a work history for each minority group member and then assessing promotional potential. Additional training needed, as well as potential openings, were identified. Any time openings actually did develop, the affirmative action list was reviewed for potential candidates.

All AAPs were reviewed and updated on a quarterly basis. First-line supervisors were responsible for individual training and development while upper-level management scrutinized departmental compliance with the goals set.

The affirmative action plan: Application

When Charles Gunn, age 22, was hired, he was the third black technician to be employed in the Alpha unit. Carl Myers, the first black hired was then supervisor of "D" shift; the second black hired, Henry Sherman, was a technician on "C" shift. Exhibit 1 gives a partial organizational structure for the Alpha unit.

Prior to joining Petrochem, Charles had completed three years in the U.S.

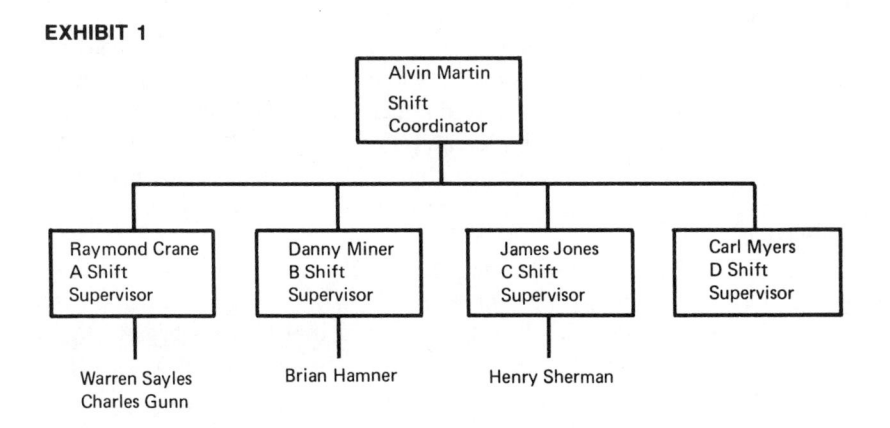

EXHIBIT 1

```
                    Alvin Martin
                    Shift
                    Coordinator
        ┌──────────────┬──────────────┬──────────────┐
  Raymond Crane   Danny Miner    James Jones    Carl Myers
  A Shift         B Shift        C Shift        D Shift
  Supervisor      Supervisor     Supervisor     Supervisor
        │              │              │
  Warren Sayles   Brian Hamner   Henry Sherman
  Charles Gunn
```

Army as a radio operator. He had entered the military immediately after high school because he figured his low "C" average in high school would not be sufficient to see him through college.

The personnel manager placed Charles on the "A" shift of the Alpha unit with Raymond Crane as his supervisor and Warren Sayles, another technician, as his "trainer." Raymond had been hired three years earlier as a technician immediately after he finished college. With his strong technical background, he had "done extremely well" and two years later was promoted to supervisor—six months before Charles was hired.

Warren, the trainer for "A" shift, had had about three years of college and was unquestionably the best technician on that particular shift. When Warren found out that he would be training Charles, he expressed some "apprehensions about training a black," since he had never worked side by side with a black before. However, he had trained several other technicians and said he would do his best.

When Charles reported to Alpha unit, Raymond introduced him to the other technicians, showed him his locker, gave him some study guides, and turned him over to Warren. (The study guides were basically a list of questions which the trainees should be able to answer once they had learned the unit operations from the trainer.)

Since Charles Gunn, the new technician, was told to spend this training period "in his trainer's back pocket," Warren and Charles were almost inseparable for the next five months. Charles asked questions; Warren answered. They went over the extractive and recovery systems, schematics of the process, start-up and shut-down procedures, reading and sampling methods, and procedures for logging information.

About once a month Warren and Charles sat down to evaluate the progress Charles was making. In the first of these sessions, Warren noted that Charles was not making any progress at all. After two or three months, Warren noted slight—but not satisfactory—progress.

After five months, Charles was still only taking samples, a procedure normally picked up in the first few weeks of training. Warren felt that Charles was not putting forth the effort needed to learn the job. Charles agreed that he needed to improve but did not agree that he was not putting forth satisfactory effort. The reports passed along to Raymond during this period reflected Warren's evaluation of Charles but did not contain any of Charles's reactions.

About six months after Charles had started to work, Warren went on vacation. Although supervisors normally assign a trainee to someone else if their trainer goes on vacation, Raymond neglected to make such a reassignment for Charles.

Meanwhile Henry Sherman, the other black technician, had been placed on temporary duty with "A" shift, and, thus, "Charles gravitated rather naturally to Henry." It was during this period that Charles began to grasp just how far behind the other technicians he really was. However, with Henry using simplified examples and then applying them to the unit processes, Charles began to grasp things that had completely escaped him before. By the end of a week, Charles understood the extractive process of the unit—the most difficult part of the unit to learn.

Within a couple of days after Warren returned from vacation, Warren and Charles again sat down for an evaluation session and again Warren reiterated Charles's lack of progress. But Charles was not satisfied this time. For the next few days he thought things over and asked questions of the other technicians to make sure that he really did understand the extractive process. Finally, he went back to Warren, and, at the end of Warren's first week back from vacation, they held their first meeting with Raymond.

Charles felt that he understood the extractive process of the unit, but Warren did not agree. The session boiled down to bickering and was finally brought to a close with Raymond's nonchalant, "You guys will just have to work this thing out yourselves."

Things simmered along for the next three or four days with Charles still dissatisfied but uncertain about what to do next. Things came to a head the next Monday morning when Alvin Martin, the shift coordinator, ran into Charles. Since Alvin rarely saw the technicians, he tried to use any chance meeting with them to get a quick reading on "the mood of the troops."

Alvin's question, "How are things going?" was all Charles needed to pour out his frustrations.

Alvin reacted by immediately setting up a meeting with Raymond and Charles. In this meeting Raymond stated that Charles was at best "a marginal performer" or perhaps even "a slow learner." Charles countered with charges of discrimination in his training. Raymond came back with the fact that if Charles had, indeed, learned the extractive process of the unit, then he must have been getting proper training. Not willing to back down, Charles explained that Henry had taught him this particular part of the unit while Warren was on vacation.

Charles left the meeting with the understanding that his performance was, in fact, deficient in several areas, and he would need to work on these things. Alvin and Raymond then continued "hot and heavy" for the next several hours.

Charles had told a story "heavily steeped in racial overtones." Though he admitted that Warren had answered all his questions without irritation, Charles felt that Warren had not volunteered as much information as he had to the other technicians. (Later talks with the other technicians tended to confirm this statement.)

At that point, though, the hostilities were pretty firmly entrenched, and Alvin felt that a change had to be made—but what? Since Henry had proven that Charles could learn, and since Charles worked well with Henry, a move to "C" shift was pretty tempting. Or, there was "D" shift, run by Carl Myers, the only black supervisor.

Alvin finally decided that moving Charles to "C" or to "D" shift was simply an easy way out and represented, at best, a temporary solution. Charles was transferred to "B" shift.

Charles's new supervisor was Danny Miner, who had a two-year technical degree and had taught mathematics and drawing at a vocational-technical college. Danny had worked around blacks on a "give-and-take" basis nearly all of his life and had no real apprehensions about Charles joining his shift. On Charles's first day, Danny sat down and explained what he expected of Charles, and what Charles could expect from him.

During that week, he and Charles did what is known as a "walk through" of the unit. Starting at the front door and going to the back door, Danny and Charles went through the unit with Charles explaining everything that he could about the unit. Danny could see Charles had a lot of problems but that he did understand the extractive process—again the most difficult part of the unit's work.

Danny continued to ask questions and listen. He used Carl as a sounding board—trying to find out more about Charles, trying to find the best way to work with him. In his conversations with the new employee, Danny soon found out that he had only taken General Math and Algebra I in high school, had made a "D" in chemistry, and had avoided physics.

In the military service, Charles had had problems when he started in the school for radio operators, but he eventually caught up and did well. Danny concluded that Charles could learn but simply had to be brought along more slowly than the other technicians.

After the first week, Danny decided to turn Charles over to Brian Hamner for training. Brian was not "the best technician in the unit," according to the personnel manager. In fact, he was average in just about every sense of the word. He was methodical—neither too fast nor too slow. He was dependable, somewhat of a stickler for detail, and had plenty of patience.

Although this assignment worked out well, there was some subsequent talk of rotating Charles to other technicians to improve his technical skills. However, the decision was made to work with both Brian and Charles on technical skills rather than singling Charles out for special training.

After four years, Charles was "not considered supervisory material," according to the personnel manager, but he was an "average" to "above average" performer and was taking some correspondence courses to upgrade his technical skills.

Questions
1. Evaluate Apex's affirmative action plan.
2. Was Charles properly placed? Explain.
3. What does this case illustrate about the problems of developing minority employees?

4. (*a*) Evaluate the training program set up for Charles. (*b*) How could it have been improved?
5. How do you explain Raymond's attitude?
6. Why work with both Brian and Charles instead of "singling" Charles out for special training?
7. Evaluate the way Danny handled Charles.
8. What would you suggest doing now, if you were the personnel manager?

VIII–3. A Challenging Job *

Data Systems Management, Incorporated (DSM), was formed 12 years ago in a major U.S. city. The company grew slowly for two years, but then revenues doubled each year for the next six years. DSM was principally engaged in designing complete electronic data processing systems for corporate customers and then installing and operating the systems. The firm effectively became the customer's data processing department under long-term contracts of five to eight years. At the time of this case, the company employed over 1,000 people, with approximately 70 percent of them being systems engineers.

Recruiting and interviewing

The firm's recruiting policy was to bring in either fully qualified systems engineers—who also possessed management and leadership capabilities—or to hire individuals who had these qualities and the aptitude to become competent systems engineers.

Lee Williams was attracted to the company by its reputation for high-caliber personnel, by the glamour of the computer field, and an ad in the largest daily newspaper in the firm's home city. (See Exhibit 1.) Williams was a veteran of seven years in the U.S. Air Force and had an MBA from a large midwestern university.

After completing and mailing a detailed application form and biographical questionnaire, Williams was visited by a recruiter from the firm's personnel office, who, although having been with DSM only two weeks, was very adept at answering William's questions about the firm. After a two-hour interview and the completion of a 30-minute computer programming aptitude test, Williams was told that he had passed the first hurdle and would be flown to company headquarters for a "team interview."

That interview was conducted by three systems engineers and the personnel manager who questioned Williams for approximately three hours about virtually all facets of his background or personality that might bear on his success with the company, including his aspirations, successes, failures, and self-

---
* Prepared by James Donald Powell, University of Nevada, Las Vegas.

EXHIBIT 1
DSM's employment advertisement

DSM is a young, growing, successful computer company that can offer you an outstanding business opportunity NOW. DSM is interested in individuals that are skilled in *or meet the qualifications to be trained in:*

1. Commercial systems design and programming.
2. Computer operations.
3. Recruiting.

DSM needs men and women who are willing to do whatever it takes, as long as it is fair and honest, to get the job done. *You must be flexible in your working hours and be willing to travel and relocate.*

DSM is a great environment for men and women with leadership experience and maturity who are trustworthy, unselfish, results-oriented, self-reliant, and have a record of success. Your future at DSM is limited only by your ability.

---

doubts. At the conclusion of this interview, Williams was introduced to Morton Benson, head of DSM's systems engineer trainee program, who questioned him briefly and then made a job offer.

After Williams quickly accepted, he was told that it was company policy for each hiree to take a fairly detailed aptitude and personality test. This test was designed to be a final check on the suitability of the job applicant. Williams was told that in about two weeks, when the test results were back, he would be sent a formal contract.

At the end of two weeks, Benson called Williams. The following conversation occurred.

Test results

Benson: Lee, the results of your test are back and we have a problem. Some of your answers indicate that you would probably have trouble functioning effectively in our environment.

Williams: What specifically were the problem areas, Mr. Benson?

Benson: Well, according to the results (see the Appendix for the test results), you rate low in "social dominance," which indicates that you might be hesitant to make decisions that might be unpopular, though correct. The other area of concern is that the test indicates that you prefer "structured situations," and we just don't have many of those in DSM.

Williams: On that last point, Mr. Benson, I think the test reflected more the military environment in which I have been during the last seven years rather than my real preferences.

Benson: What about the "social dominance" problem?

Williams: I think the test question that related to that area was, "Would you take the initiative in bringing life into a dull party?" I had difficulty answering that one for there wasn't an answer on the test for what I would actually do at a dull party. I wouldn't attempt to bring it to life, I would *just leave*. Another question asked, "Would you mind returning merchandise to a department store?" I admit that

I don't like to return things that I've bought, but I don't feel that the dislike can be generalized to include business situations.

Benson: Let me ask you a specific question along that line. Today I have to tell two new employees, who haven't even gotten their families settled here in town, that they leave tomorrow for an extended stay at one of our west coast projects. Would it bother you to tell someone that sort of news?

Williams: Not if there were no other way to handle the situation.

Benson: Well, let me tell you this. That personality test was administered to the top people in our company. Their personality profiles serve as the basis for judging all the new people who take the test. We feel that a person who scores low on particular aspects of the test will be at a competitive disadvantage in the company. I hired one man, who is in the training program now, in spite of his test results, and that guy is in my office every other day for something.

Williams: All I can tell you is that I feel that I can compete against the company people I met in the team interview. I just don't think I'll be at a disadvantage.

Benson: O.K., Lee, I'll get a contract in the mail to you and will see you when you get here.

First assignment

William's first month with DSM was spent in self-study, as he had much to learn about computers and the health insurance field, in which he was to concentrate. Then he was assigned to a customer account in a midwestern city. The assignment came as a mild shock, as he had assumed that he would initially be staying at company headquarters. He had leased a home and settled his family in a town near DSM's home office.

Following company policy, Williams took his wife and child with him (at company expense).

Williams was part of a five-man systems group responsible for installing a data processing system in a health insurance firm. Although the actual computer programming and processing were done back at company headquarters, Williams and the others were responsible for learning the customer's business and acting as an interface between the system designers and the customer.

The work was challenging and Williams felt that he was gaining valuable experience. But after several months, the pace began to have its effects on Williams's family. He often worked 75 to 90 hours each week and typically worked seven days a week for weeks on end. His wife, new in unfamiliar surroundings and left virtually alone in caring for their small child, began to question Williams about the real value of such a job. Williams wondered if the company's rising profits were the result of accomplishing "twelve-man jobs with five-man teams."

Toward the end of the project, after Williams had been with the company about eight months, he received his first appraisal interview. He was told that he had "done excellent work on the project." As evidence of management's appreciation, he was given an $800 bonus. He was then told to take a couple of weeks off to get his family settled at his new assignment.

Programming school

Williams's next assignment was to go back to the home office for schooling in computer programming. As with the previous project, the pace was set so that the men were forced to work extremely hard just to keep up. Williams was trying very hard to learn how to program, but he made some concessions to his family's desire for attention. Although he knew he was falling behind in his classwork, he would occasionally spend Sunday with his family, rather than at the office.

Although Williams knew that he needed help, he hesitated to ask, since the instructor was Morton Benson, the man who had hired him—reluctantly. Williams remembered Benson's comment about the man who "was in my office every other day" and was determined to succeed without Benson's help. When at last he had to admit failure, Williams was asked to see the personnel manager.

Resolution

Williams was told that inability to program was an insurmountable handicap to advancement in the company, and, for that reason, it would be a disservice to him for the firm to retain him as an employee. He was temporarily assigned to another part of the company and was asked to work out a program of work/job hunting for approximately six weeks, after which he would be terminated with two-weeks' severance pay.

Questions

1. Evaluate the firm's recruiting and selection procedure.
2. Would you suggest any changes? Explain.
3. Should Williams have been hired? Defend your answer.
4. From the test results, how would you describe Williams?
5. Evaluate the placement policies of this firm.
6. Was the decision to terminate Williams the right one? Explain.
7. What would you have done in this case if you had been in Williams's place?

APPENDIX: LEE WILLIAMS'S APTITUDES AND PERSONALITY TEST RESULTS

Mr. Lee H. Williams   Systems engineer trainee

I. Motivation and job interest:

The incentives or motivations of this man certainly point him toward the business world, for he has a very tough-minded, highly economic, and investigative attitude. He is interested in communications and here we look at the persuasive interest. Computational and scientific job interests are not particularly strong. But the detail and the literary interests seem well developed. He is interested in words as is noted by the very high literary interest.

II. Capacity for work:

Mr. Williams's aptitudes are quite high. He had seven problems correct on the math test, which is a "fair" performance, but he did very well on all of the other capacity tests. Speed of thinking is first rate, the judgment factor is well developed, and persuasiveness looks good. This man's insight into people is quite well developed.

III. Personality and temperament:

We look at the lines at the top of the personality and temperament chart, and we see indications of a self-sufficient temperament but not a very tough one. Social independence is low, as he is eager to please, and he may be

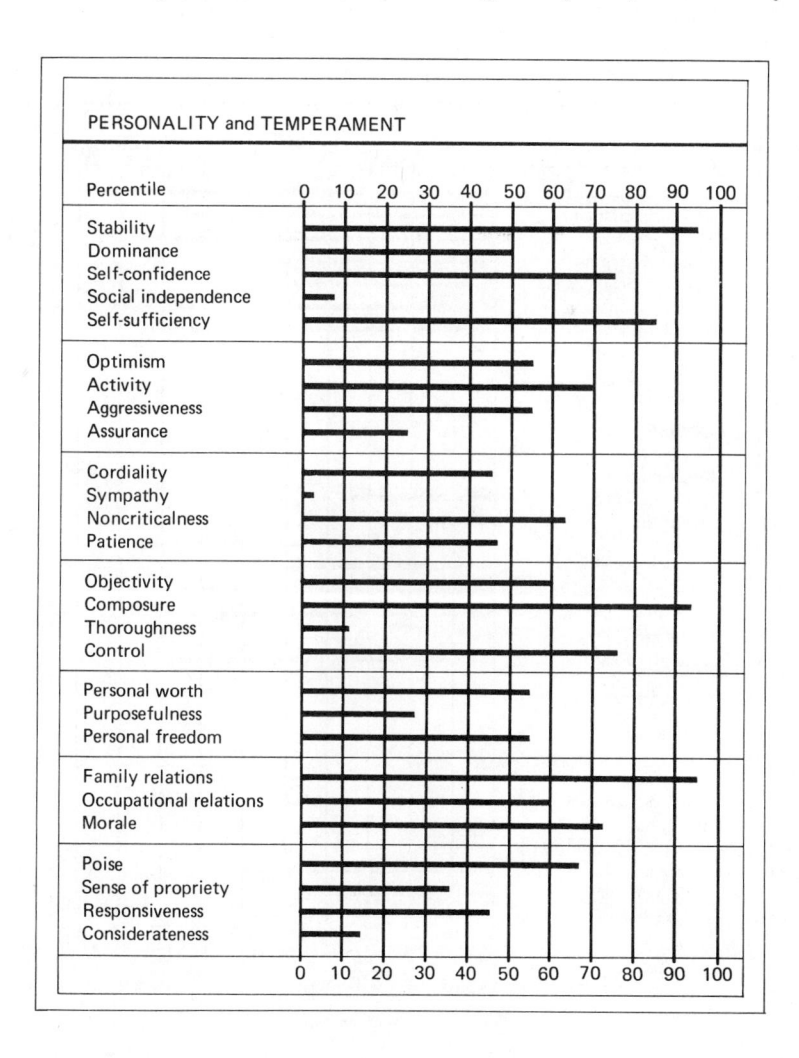

PERSONALITY and TEMPERAMENT

Percentile	0 10 20 30 40 50 60 70 80 90 100
Stability	
Dominance	
Self-confidence	
Social independence	
Self-sufficiency	
Optimism	
Activity	
Aggressiveness	
Assurance	
Cordiality	
Sympathy	
Noncriticalness	
Patience	
Objectivity	
Composure	
Thoroughness	
Control	
Personal worth	
Purposefulness	
Personal freedom	
Family relations	
Occupational relations	
Morale	
Poise	
Sense of propriety	
Responsiveness	
Considerateness	

somewhat hesitant in his decisions simply because of this desire to please. There is quite a "dip" in dominance between stability and self-confidence. In our estimate, he tends to be overly cautious with people. We do not pick up indications of strong aggressiveness or of strong self-assurance. He comes across as composed and controlled; he is not jumpy, edgy, or impulsive. While not highly rated as far as thoroughness is concerned, we do note his detail interest. He may not love the routine of the job, but he will cope with it.

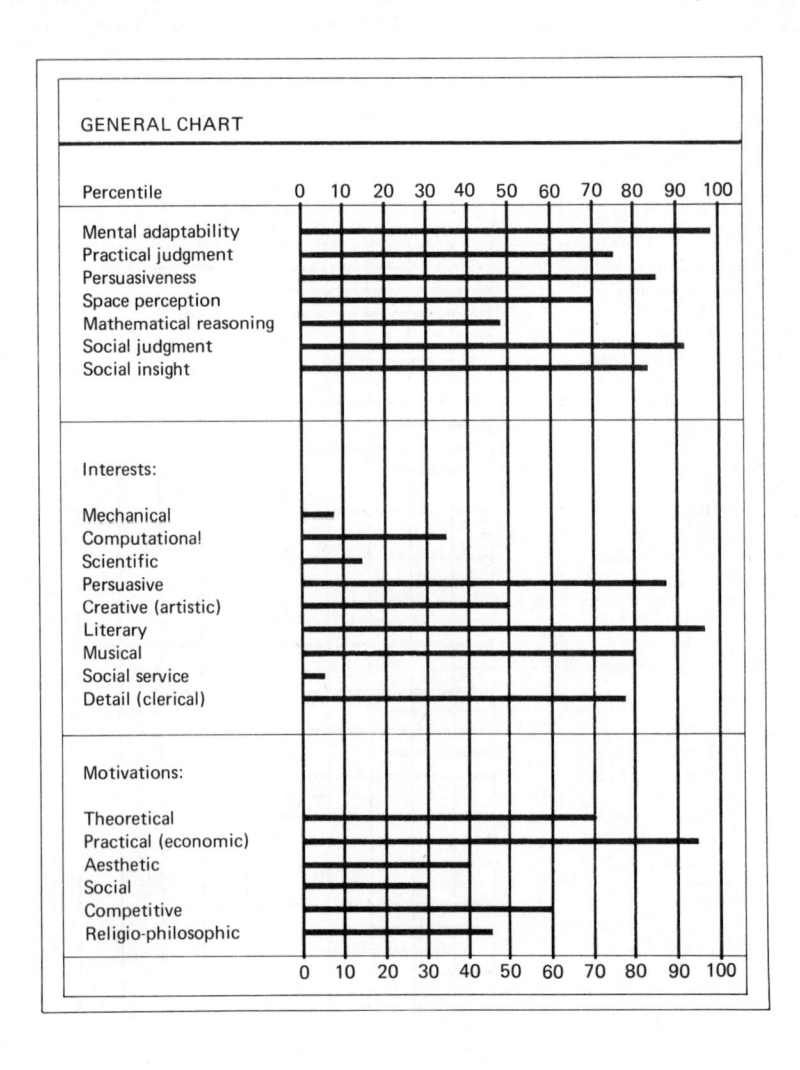

The estimate of personal worth is neither high nor low but seems about right considering his education and experience. Low sympathy (1 percent) means he tends to be cautious with people. He is perhaps a bit reserved with them. While not withdrawing from them necessarily, he is the kind of person who seems to have been hurt somewhere, and he will tend not always to extend himself in an emotional way. As compensation for low sympathy, he does have very high scores in social judgment and social insight.

IV. Conclusions:

This is a very bright man with a strong motivation for business. He is a well-composed type of person, very self-sufficient in manner.

We think a problem may show up in two areas. First, the personality pattern where there is an underdevelopment of dominance, and a relatively low social independence factor. A person may appear pleasant and well poised in a face-to-face relationship, but this can conceal a tendency to be somewhat edgy about decisions, about exerting force in face-to-face situations, and can conceal the tendency to be somewhat more concerned with what other people think than is necessary.

The other problem area is the aggressiveness-assurance one. We think he will tend to want a situation where he has a well-structured program in front of him and will tend to feel somewhat less easy in a situation or job climate less well-structured where he is expected to reach out and set the tempo and to establish the dimensions of the job. He is apt to be more concerned than he should be about the interpersonal relationships and less concerned with the objectives of accomplishing a given objective or target.

We do not, therefore, feel this individual measures up to the standards that have been set for your systems engineer trainee program.

indexes

Case index

A

Affirmative Action in Theory and Practice (VIII–2), 610–15
Average Company, Inc. (II–1), 140–41

C

The Case of Tom Sawyer (VII–3), 602–3
A Challenging Job (VIII–3), 615–21
Companywide Seniority (III–1), 265

D–J

The Discharge of Sleeping Beauty (VI–2), 542–46
Division of Labor (II–2), 141–42
Jack Moran (VII–2), 600–602

L–M

Louis Kemp (IV–1), 369–70
Mid-Western Printing, Incorporated (V–3), 487–89
The Move (VIII–1), 607–10

N–O

The New Work Force (II–3), 142–43
OK! Who's Passing the Buck? (I–2), 40–44
Outside Help (III–2), 266

P–R

The Pepper Bush (I–1), 39–40
The Recalcitrant Orderly (VII–1), 600

S

Selection: In Theory and in Practice (III–3), 266–67
Sinclaire University (IV–2), 370–72

T

Technical Obsolescence (IV–3), 372–74
To Do or Not to Do? (III–4), 267–70

U–W

The Union Blow (VI–1), 540–42
Ward Chemical Company (V–2), 485–87
What Determines Wages (V–1), 484–85

Name index

A

Adams, J. S., 443
Addleman, R., 190
Alderfer, C. P., 190
Aldis, O., 440
Alexander, K. O., 394
Allen, B. V., 216
Allen, L. A., 366
Alpander, G. G., 322
Alutto, J. A., 38, 511
Anderson, L., 367
Anderson, P. E., 190
Andler, E. C., 320
Andrews, I. R., 243, 415, 418
Anrod, C. W., 536
Appley, L. A., 28, 38
Argyris, C., 322
Arnold, B. C., 216
Ash, P., 538, 539
Ashenfelter, O., 416
Asher, J. J., 240
Ashford, N. A., 579
Asinof, P., 244
Athan, P. W., 14

B

Babbage, C., 141
Bachs, M. E., 241
Badeau, L., 540
Bakke, E. W., 366, 536
Barkin, S., 510
Barnako, F. R., 580
Barnard, C., 10, 15
Barnett, R. S., 242
Barnum, D. T., 542
Barth, P. S., 579
Bartlett, J. B., 168
Bartol, K., 139
Beach, D. N., 346
Beason, G. M., 217
Beatty, R. W., 322
Beer, M., 416, 417
Behrend, H., 393
Belasco, J. A., 38, 511
Belcher, D. W., 393, 442

Bell, D. R., 465
Belt, J. A., 217
Bemis, S., 139
Bendix, R., 109
Bennett, G., 538
Bennett, W. E., 322
Bennis, W. G., 367
Benson, C. A., 346
Berelson, B., 294, 393, 598
Berkowitz, L., 560
Berkshire, J. R., 345
Berry, D., 599
Berzon, B., 368
Bevan, R. V., 400, 415
Bigoness, W. J., 487
Blake, R. R., 320
Blansfield, M. G., 320
Blaug, M., 170
Blitz, R. C., 139
Block, J. R., 580
Blum, A. A., 538
Bok, D., 537
Bolon, D. S., 370
Booker, G., 480
Bottenberg, R. A., 215
Bowen, C. P., Jr., 319
Bowlby, R. L., 294
Bradshaw, T. F., 402
Bray, D. W., 244
Breenebaum, J. S., 538
Brennan, M. J., 13
Brenner, M. H., 417
Briggs, G. E., 294
Brooks, T. R., 439
Brotslaw, I., 437
Brown, W., 111
Brynildsen, R. D., 345
Buchanan, P. C., 321
Bucher, G. C., 295
Buckley, J. W., 295
Buel, W. D., 241
Burack, E. H., 170, 293
Burke, D. R., 538
Burkholder, R. C., 40
Burns, J. E., 415, 416
Burtt, H. E., 580

Name Index

Butkus, A. A., 322
Buton, G. E., 239
Buyniski, E. F., 560
Buzenberg, M. E., 322
Byham, W. C., 241, 599

C

Calhoon, R., 322
Calme, B. E., 84
Calvert, L., 610
Cameron, C. G., 394
Campbell, J. P., 321
Campbell, W. J., 580
Cannedy, R. C., 243
Carlson, D. G., 465
Carp, F. M., 368
Carrigan, S. B., 321
Carrington, J. H., 64
Carroll, S. J., Jr., 217, 244, 320
Carter, C. F., 215
Cass, E. L., 111, 367
Cassell, F. H., 168, 418
Cassels, L., 320
Cattell, J. M., 10
Chalmers, W. E., 536
Chalupsky, A. A., 442
Chamberlain, J., 512
Cheek, L. M., 37, 170
Chemers, M. M., 367
Cherry, R., 346
Chesterfield, L., 550
Chiu, J. S. Y., 417
Christensen, C. R., 263, 443
Chruden, H. J., 539
Chung, K. H., 366, 464, 599
Clack, G., 580
Clark, B., 415
Cohen, A., 538
Cohen, B. M., 333
Colbert, J., 561
Colby, J. D., 335, 345
Coleman, B. P., 170
Collins, W., 474, 481
Colonna, F. I., 561
Colvin, C. O., 416
Conant, E. H., 345
Cook, A. J. D., 598
Copeland, T. B., 579
Corson, J. J., 366
Costello, T. W., 216, 294, 320
Cox, A., 538
Cox, I. H., 415, 440
Craig, P. G., 138
Crandall, R. E., 439
Crane, D. P., 293
Crawford, T., 394
Cummings, L. L., 351, 366, 367
Curra, W. S., 345
Curtin, E., 538
Czarnecki, E. R., 442

D

Dale, J. D., 440
Dallas, S. F., 190
Dalson, G. W., 346
Darsey, N. S., 188
Davey, H. W., 63
Davis, C. S., 322
Davis, D. P., 368
Dawis, R. V., 240
Deckard, N. S., 170
Dempsey, F. K., Jr., 189
DeNisi, A. S., 239
Dennis, T. L., 188, 189
Denova, C., 64, 481
Denzler, R. D., 113, 366, 393
Derber, M., 536
Dick, W. G., 440
Dickinson, C., 393
Dickson, P., 113
Dickson, W. J., 14, 440
Donahue, R. J., 483
Dooher, M. J., 345
Doty, R. A., 263, 264
Douglas, W. A., 188
Downes, C. W., 243
Draznin, J. N., 539
Driscoll, J. B., 244
Drotning, J. E., 538
Drucker, P. F., 110, 297, 338, 346
Dubin, R., 110, 112
Dublin, R., 537
Duerr, E. C., 440
Dufty, N. F., 393
Dukes, C. W., 189
Dunbar, R. L. M., 580
Dunlop, J., 375, 537
Dunnett, M. D., 240, 242, 416

E

Edelman, T., 536
Edens, F. N., 241
Edge, A. G., 189
Ehrenberg, R. G., 452
Einstein, A., 3, 246, 583
Elbing, A. O., 417
Endicott, F. S., 189
England, G. W., 240
Evans, W. A., 417
Ewing, D. W., 263

F

Fay, P. P., 346
Fayol, H., 10, 14, 431, 441
Fels, L. G., 216, 244
Fenn, D. H., Jr., 82
Ferber, R. C., 295
Ference, T. P., 343, 346
Ferrari, M. R., 109
Ferrell, O., 190

Fiedler, F. E., 7, 14, 320, 367
Field, H. S., Jr., 459, 464
Fiman, B. G., 366
Fine, S. A., 160, 170
Flamholtz, E. G., 168
Flanders, D. P., 190
Flanders, H., 599
Fleishman, E. A., 264, 538, 580
Flowers, V. S., 109
Fogel, W. A., 417
Follett, M. P., 10, 14, 367
Foreman, W. J., 320
Fossum, J. A., 242
Foster, H. G., 295
Foster, K. E., 418
Foulkes, F. K., 37, 113, 324, 345, 563, 579, 581, 598
Fraedrich, R., 440
France, R. R., 395
Fredia, A. J., 264
French, J. R. P., 417, 481
Friedlander, F., 112, 366
Frost, C. F., 442
Frost, P., 297
Fryer, D. H., 215
Fryer, M. A., 111
Fuller, S. H., 17
Fulmer, R. M., 188, 321
Fulmer, W. E., 188

G

Gailbraith, G. S., 397
Gale, H. F., 110
Gannon, M. J., 319
Garbarino, J. W., 511
Gardiner, G., 17
Garfinkle, S. H., 464
Gavett, T. W., 138, 394
Geer, J. H., 560
Geisler, E., 171
Gellerman, S. W., 420
Gery, G. J., 416, 417
Ghiselli, E. E., 229, 243, 244, 263, 264
Gibson, R. O., 560
Gilbray, C. L., 139
Gilbreth, F., 9
Gilbreth, L., 9, 10, 14
Gilmer, B. v. H., 217
Ginzberg, E., 13, 100, 112
Glueck, W. F., 346
Golden, L. L. L., 64
Goldstein, A., 321
Goldstein, I. L., 240
Gomersall, E. R., 290
Goode, C., 599
Gooding, J., 138, 416
Gordon, O., 241
Gordon, R., 321
Gordon, T. J., 463
Gottier, R. F., 243

Graham, G. H., 560, 561
Grant, D. L., 244
Green, C., 393
Greene, M. R., 465
Greenwood, R., 189
Griffin, C. E., 82
Grix, J. J., 113
Groothuis, A. P., 442
Gruenfeld, L. W., 320
Gruiner, L. E., 321
Grusky, O., 368
Guion, R. M., 217, 243
Gullett, C. R., 38, 516, 536
Gunn, B., 602
Gurin, P., 190
Gustafson, D. P., 188, 189
Guthrie, R. R., 38, 170
Gutstein, L., 561

H

Hacker, D. W., 561
Hailstones, T. J., 13
Haire, M., 393, 421
Hand, H., 322
Harding, F. O., 215
Harman, J. R., Jr., 263
Harper, S. F., 345
Harrell, T. W., 241, 264
Harrington, D. A., 463
Harris, E. F., 538, 580
Harris, L., 464
Harris, O. J., Jr., 294, 598
Harrow, H., 474, 481
Hart, L. D., 415
Hartman, F., 560
Hayden, R. J., 327
Haynes, U., Jr., 295
Healey, J., 168, 171
Hedges, J. N., 139, 481
Heinen, J. S., 322
Helburn, I. B., 442, 542
Henderson, C., 82
Henderson, R. I., 442
Heneman, H. G., III, 244
Henneberger, H. E., 110
Henry, E. R., 215
Henry, M. M., 415, 418
Herman, S. M., 36
Hershey, R., 241
Herzberg, F., 338–39, 346, 360–61, 367, 368, 463
Hess, H. R., 244
Hess, L. R., 239
Hicks, J. A., 263
Hicks, J. R., 394
Hickson, D. J., 415
Highland, R. W., 345
Himler, L. E., 560
Hinrichs, J. R., 241, 320, 599
Hodgetts, R. M., 263, 264

Hodgson, R., 242
Hoffman, C., 393
Hoffman, L. R., 440
Hofstede, G. H., 36
Hogue, J. P., 241
Holdsworth, R., 217
Holland, C. W., 216
Holley, W. H., Jr., 459, 464
Holt, H., 295
Holzman, R. S., 346
House, R. J., 320, 321, 322, 416
Howell, J., 321
Howell, W. J., 441
Howton, F. L., 109
Hubbell, R., 442
Huberman, J., 480, 481
Hueber, D. F., 242
Huegli, J. M., 244
Hughes, C. E., 494
Hulme, R. D., 400, 415
Hundady, R. J., 442
Huneryager, S. G., 320
Huntsman, B., 417
Huttner, L., 263, 264
Hyatt, J. C., 84

I

Imherman, W., 538
Imundo, L. V., Jr., 511
Inkeles, A., 112
Inskeep, G. C., 241

J

Jacoby, N. H., 63
Jain, H. C., 215
Janger, A. R., 38
Janis, I. L., 216
Jeffcry, T. E., 440
Jenkins, T. N., 580
Jenkins, W. M., Jr., 482
Jennings, E. E., 346
Jennings, K., 482
Johnson, E. A., 108
Johnson, R. W., 240
Johnson, T. W., 370
Johnston, J., 244
Jones, L. V., 440
Jordan, S., 215

K

Kagerer, R., 85
Kapell, H., 368
Kappel, F. R., 264
Karn, H. W., 217
Karsh, B., 537
Kassalow, E. M., 537
Kasschaw, P. L., 464
Kassum, M. S., 416
Katz, B. J., 139
Kaun, D. E., 364

Kay, E., 417, 481
Kegan, D. L., 322
Kelleher, E. J., 216
Kelly, M. A., 512
Kerr, C., 536, 538
Kerr, W. A., 216
Kert, R. L., 14
Keyser, M., 216
Kilbridge, M., 295
Kindall, A. F., 346
King, A. G., 108
Kinnane, J. F., 108
Kleinschord, W., 346
Kornhauser, A. W., 537
Kovacs, S., 244
Kraut, A. I., 264
Kreitner, R., 480
Kronenberger, E. J., 580
Kulhovy, R. W., 243

L

Lancaster, H., 217
Lane, I. M., 215, 216, 239, 242, 243, 264, 321, 345
Langsdale, J. A., 243
Lanser, H. P., 417
Laurence, S., 322
Lawler, E. E., III, 351, 363–64, 366, 368, 416, 417, 418
Lawrence, P. R., 96, 111, 112, 366
Lean, W., 138
Leavitt, H. J., 13
Leavitt, R. K., 515
Le Bleu, R. E., 463
Lee, H. C., 113
Lee, S. M., 190
Leeman, C. P., 561
Lefkowitz, J., 295
Lerner, M. J., 393
Lesieur, F., 442
Lesikar, R. V., 579
Levine, J., 190
Levinson, H., 22, 38, 320, 538, 560
Levy, S., 263
Lewellan, W. G., 417
Lewis, L. E., 424, 440
Lieberman, S., 537
Likert, R., 393
Lindenauer, G., 190
Lindha, J. B. P., 481
Ling, C. C., 62
Lippitt, G. L., 294
Lipset, S. M., 537
Lipsett, L., 242
Lissey, K. W., 170
Littig, L. W., 465
Litton, R., 393
Livingston, J. S., 320
Lockwood, H. C., 241, 417
Lofquist, L. H., 240

Name Index

London, J., 537
Longest, B. B., Jr., 264
Lorge, I., 366
Lorsch, J. W., 321, 367
Luk, H., 190
Lusterman, S., 581
Luthans, F., 263, 264, 480

Mc

McBain, W. N., 580
McClaughty, J., 442
McClelland, D. C., 5, 14, 339, 360–61, 394
McClelland, W. K., 64, 368
McCord, C. G., 190
McCormick, E. J., 239
McFarland, D., 583, 598
McGlashan, R., 39
McGregor, D., 313, 338, 350, 355, 360, 366, 367
McGuckin, J. H., 539
McGuire, J. W., 417
McIntosh, S. S., 15
McKelvey, J., 538
McKersie, R. B., 536
McLanathan, F. L., 368
McLaughlin, D., 36
McManus, D. L., 440
McMaster, I. H., 480
McMurry, R. N., 560
McNamar, R., 260, 261
McNamara, W. J., 294

M

Machiavelli, 7, 14
Maetzold, J., 240
Mahoney, T. A., 417
Maier, N. R. F., 367, 440
Maloney, P. W., 320
Mandell, M. M., 243
Margulies, N., 321
Marion, B. W., 294
Marquis, V., 345
Marshall, A., 62, 383, 441
Martin, R. A., 215
Martin, R. M., 537
Maslow, A. H., 338, 360, 368
Matarazzo, J. D., 216
Mathis, R. L., 482
Matthews, A. T., 263
Maurer, J. K., 100, 112
Mausner, B., 346, 367
Mayfield, E. C., 244
Mayfield, H., 109
Mayo, E., 10
Mead, M., 14, 294
Meany, G., 467
Mee, J. F., 13
Megginson, L. C., 464
Meiklejohn, R. P., 417
Melville, N. T., 216

Metzger, B. L., 441, 442
Meyer, H. D., 263, 264
Meyer, H. E., 345
Meyer, H. H., 345, 417, 481
Meyer, P., 241
Miles, R. E., 321, 366
Milgram, S., 481
Miller, J. M., 561
Miller, P., 215
Mills, D. Q., 513
Miner, J. B., 241
Miner, M. G., 415
Mitchell, H. M., 598
Mitchell, J. M., 598
Moffie, D. J., 322
Monday, R. W., 241
Morse, J. J., 321
Morse, N., 111, 368
Morse, R. J., 215
Mouton, J. S., 320
Mruk, E. S., 417
Murray, T. J., 561
Murthy, K. R. S., 417
Myers, C. A., 15
Myers, M. S., 290, 362, 463

N

Nagle, B. F., 215
Nash, A. N., 217, 320
Nath, M., 170
Navas, A. N., 170
Naylor, J. G., 294
Nealey, S. M., 465
Nelson, R. J., 599
Nelson, W. B., 512
Newcomer, M., 109
Newfield, M. F., 513
Noe, W. R., Jr., 346
Novack, S. R., 225
Nutter, J. W., 440

O

Oazaca, R., 452
O'Brien, J. K., 322
O'Brien, P. E., 579
Odiorne, G., 482
O'Donnel, L. W., 295
O'Meara, J. R., 459
O'Neil, T. J., 170
Oriel, A. E., 295
Otis, J. L., 241
Otten, A. L., 242, 599

P

Pable, M. W., 108
Paine, F. T., 321
Parsons, S. E., 241
Patchen, M., 368
Patry, F. L., 560
Patten, T., Jr., 82, 599

632 Name Index

Pattenaude, R. L., 36
Patton, A., 417
Paukert, F., 170
Paul, R. J., 345
Penzer, W. N., 464
Pepys, S., 397
Perley, J. D., 17
Perlick, W., 579
Perlman, M., 537
Peters, D. R., 264
Petersen, D. J., 581
Peterson, D. J., 217
Peterson, R. B., 190
Pettefer, J. C., 538
Phelan, J. G., 242
Pickens, W., 244
Pierson, F., 321
Polding, M. E., 170
Polin, A., 215
Porter, L. W., 321, 351, 366, 368, 417
Powell, J. D., 615
Powell, R. M., 263, 319, 322
Pranis, R. W., 539
Prather, D., 481
Prenting, T. O., 216
Presnall, L. F., 561
Pressel, G. L., 263
Preston, M., 170
Prien, E. P., 216, 241
Prieve, E. A., 294
Pronsky, J., 415
Puckett, E., 442
Purcell, T. V., 539
Pyle, W. C., 14
Pyron, H. C., 217

R

Rabourn, O. N., 216
Raia, A., 321
Randall, R. L., 320
Raphael, E. E., 512
Raphael, M. A., 243
Rapoport, R., 109, 536
Rapping, L. A., 512
Rawls, D. J., 263, 264
Rawls, J. R., 263, 264
Reagan, M., 463
Reed, D. H., 263
Reeves, E. T., 510
Reif, W. E., 383
Reis, A. J., 580, 581
Revans, R. W., 579
Rezler, J., 111, 394, 598
Rice, W. V., 39
Ricklefs, R., 561
Rideout, R. W., 537
Rilke, R. M., 583
Ritter, B., 481
Ritzer, G., 37
Roberts, T. S., 303

Robertson, D. E., 243, 346
Roethlisberger, F. J., 10, 14, 263, 440, 443
Rogers, R., 561
Romnes, H. I., 169
Ronan, W. W., 216
Rosen, E., 263
Rosen, H., 536
Rosen, S., 394
Rosenbaum, B. L., 242
Rosensteel, D., 442
Ross, A. M., 537
Rothe, H. F., 439
Rothman, S., 513
Rowl, A. R., 321
Rubenowitz, S., 598
Rubin, L., 538
Ruh, R. A., 442

S

Sadler, P., 367
Saikowski, C., 393
Salem, A. R., 464
Salter, M. S., 417
Sanborn, H., 415
Sanders, R., 244
Sanford, A. C., 367
Sashkin, M., 367
Saslow, G., 216
Sayles, L. R., 415
Schaffer, B. K., 190
Schaffer, R. H., 367
Scheible, P. L., 393
Schein, E. H., 320
Schilz, J. H., 216
Schimmin, S., 393, 440
Schlachter, J. L., 264
Schmidt, W. H., 295, 354, 355, 367
Schneider, E. V., 62
Schneier, C. E., 169
Schoof, E. H., 561
Schrieber, D. E., 393
Schriver, W. R., 294
Schroeder, R., 598
Schuh, A. J., 240, 241
Schuster, F. E., 346
Schuster, J. R., 415, 417
Schwab, D. P., 244, 351, 366, 393, 428, 440
Schwartz, M., 481, 482
Scott, C. R., Jr., 533, 535
Scott, L. C., 293
Scott, R. D., 240
Scott, W. D., 10
Scott, W. G., 481, 482, 539
Segal, M., 394
Seidman, J., 531
Selekman, B. M., 536, 537, 538
Sellie, C., 169
Senger, L. F., 580
Sforza, C., 14
Shaak, P., 481, 482

Name Index

Shapiro, H. J., 442
Sharma, J. M., 215
Shea, J., 512
Sheldon, O., 10, 14
Sheppard, H. L., 139
Sherif, M., 536
Sherman, A. W., 539
Sherman, J. M., 440
Sherman, V. C., 537
Shuster, J. R., 463
Shuster, L. J., 393
Sidowski, J., 394
Siegel, J., 561
Siegel, L., 215, 216, 239, 242, 243, 264, 321, 345
Simonds, R. H., 580
Singer, C., 598
Sirota, D., 480
Skahill, F. J., 190
Skeels, J. W., 188
Skibbins, G. J., 537
Skinner, B. F., 363, 368
Skole, R., 113
Sloan, S., 393
Sloane, A. A., 537
Slocum, J. W., Jr., 322, 367
Smith, A., 14, 48, 62
Smith, R. D., 217
Smithers, D., 348, 365
Smyth, R. L., 442
Snyder, F. B., 539
Snyderman, B. B., 346, 367
Soloman, L. N., 368
Somerville, J. D., 319
Sonnabend, R. P., 320
Sorcher, M., 321
Sorensen, P. F., Jr., 293
Sorensen, T. C., 112, 113
Souerwine, A. H., 241
Spencer, C., 598
Spencer, H., 170
Spinrod, W., 537
Stagner, R., 536, 537, 539
Stanton, E. S., 512
Steinberg, H., 217
Steiner, G. A., 294, 393, 598
Stelluto, G. L., 424
Stinson, J. F., 402
Stolz, R. K., 560
Stone, J. B., 263
Stoner, J. A. F., 343, 346
Stopel, M., 263
Strauss, G., 415
Sulkin, H. A., 539
Sullivan, D. M., 482
Sweet, D., 170
Sydiaha, D., 243

T

Tannenbaum, R., 354, 355, 367
Tarneja, R. S., 441

Tate, C., 533, 535
Tatge, W., 264
Taylor, F. W., 5, 9, 14, 31, 50, 62, 115, 360, 442
Tead, O., 10, 14
Tello, A., 393
Tharp, M., 139
This, L. E., 294
Thobley, S., 322
Thompson, A. A., 463
Thompson, J., 263
Thompson, P. H., 346, 415
Thornton, G. C., III, 599
Tillery, W., 581
Toren, P., 368
Tosi, H. L., 416
Towl, A. R., 321
Trahair, R. C. S., 463
Trice, H., 37
Trieb, S. E., 294
Trueblood, L., 533, 535
Tschirgi, H., 244
Tuckman, J., 366
Turfboer, R., 561

U

Ullman, J. C., 189
Underwood, W. J., 321
Urwich, L., 14, 598

V

Valenzi, E., 243
Vardhan, H., 215
Varney, G. H., 442
Venning, M., 138
Vitola, B. M., 368
Vogel, A., 511
Vroom, V. H., 363, 368

W

Wagner, E. E., 241, 264
Wahba, M. A., 442
Wald, R. M., 263, 264
Walker, J. W., 168, 169, 170, 263, 264, 346, 464
Walker, W. B., 345
Wallace, R. L., 335, 345, 442
Walsh, D. J., 170
Walsh, E., 111
Walsh, E. B., 82, 190
Walsh, R. J., 239
Walton, R. E., 536
Warren, E. K., 343, 346
Wayne, R., 241
Weale, W. B., 190
Webster, E. C., 244
Weinstock, I., 463
Weintraub, J., 111
Weintraub, S., 394
Weiss, D. J., 240
Weiss, R. S., 111

Weitz, J., 243
Wellford, R. C., 320
Wentorf, D. A., 294
Werniment, P. F., 368
Werther, W. B., Jr., 463
Wessman, F., 320
Wexley, K., 244
Weymar, C. S., 537
Whatley, C. D., Jr., 561
Wherry, R. J., 215, 581
Whisler, T. L., 345
White, B. L., 440
Whitlock, G. H., 345
Wiener, D. N., 320
Wiens, A. N., 216
Wild, R., 112
Williams, G. B., 241
Wilson, J. E., 264, 320
Wingo, W., 538
Winter, R. E., 111
Witney, F., 537
Wolfe, J., 295
Wolfson, A., 480

Worthy, J. C., 367
Wortman, M. S., Jr., 188
Wren, D., 14
Wundt, W., 10

Y

Yamamura, K., 394
Yoder, D., 243
Young, A., 443
Yukl, G., 244

Z

Zaleznik, A., 263, 443
Zalkind, S. S., 216, 294, 320
Zalussky, J., 581
Zechar, Dale, 241
Zeitlein, L. R., 346
Zenger, J. H., 215, 322
Ziderman, A., 170
Zieden-Weber, M., 215
Zimmer, F. C., 111, 367
Zimmer, T. W., 111
Zola, J., 241

Index

A

Abilities, mathematical, 305
Absenteeism, 552–53
Academy of Management, 383
Accidents
 causes of, 571–72
 frequency and severity rates, 568–70, 573
Achievement tests; *see* Test(s) and testing
Adair v. *U.S.,* 494
Adaptability, 281, 305
Administrative skills, 305–6; *see also* Executive development
 developing, 309–11
  case analysis, 309
  job rotation, 310–11
  management internships, 311
  multiple management, 309
  planned progression, 310
  simulation, 309–10
Advertising, 179
Affirmative action programs (AAPs), 37–38, 75, 159–60, 185; *see also* Personnel and human resources planning
AFL-CIO, 501
Age Discrimination in Employment Act of 1967, 70, 75, 136, 185
Agencies; *see* Employment agencies
Agency shop, 503
Agents, change, 311
Agricultural Labor Relations Act, 500
Agriculture Department, 75
Alcoholism, 555–57
Alienation, employee, 93–94
American Association of University Professors (AAUP), 500
American Federation of Labor (AFL), 50
American Federation of Teachers (AFT), 500
American Society of Personnel Administration (ASPA), 208
American Society of Safety Engineers, 565
American Telephone & Telegraph Company (AT&T), 22, 70, 185, 196, 224, 259, 319
Anticipatory assignments; *see* Administrative skills
Application blank, 205; *see also* Weighted application blank

Appraisals; *see also* Career planning and development
 employee, 326
 management, 301
 performance, 326; *see also* Performance appraisal(s)
 purposes of, 326–27
 selection, 326
Apprenticeship training, 286; *see also* Development, personnel
Aptitude tests; *see* Test(s) and testing
Arbitration, 527, 530–31; *see also* Union(s) and employee associations
Asia, 134
Assessment centers, 259–60, 301
Atomic Energy Act of 1954, 77
Attitude(s), 305
 modifying, 306–7, 311–14
Australia, 130, 134, 382
Austria, 134
Authority
 functional, 31–33
 line, 31
 staff, 31
Authorization to hire, 203
Automation, 95, 97

B

"Baby boom" generation, 117
"Baby bust" generation, 117
Background information, verifying, 208–10
 methods used, 210
 reference checks, validity of, 210
 sources used
  credit check, 209
  references, 209
  transcripts, 209
Balancing-Agriculture with Industry (BAWI), 81
Bargaining agent; *see* Union(s) and employee associations
Behavior, organizational, 310
Behavioral science, 11; *see also* Employee, behavior
Belgium, 134
Bell System, 153, 185

635

Bennett Test of Mechanical Comprehension, 229
Bias, 237
Biographical data, 205-6
Biographical information blank (BIB), 205, 238
  validity as a predictor, 225-26
Biographical inventory, 205-6, 237-38; *see also* Selection
Blacks, 100, 134-36, 185; *see also* Minorities
Blue-collar workers, 115, 125-26
  sources of, 176-78
Bona fide occupational qualifications (BFOQ), 75, 185
Bonus plans; *see* Compensation, employee benefits
Bulgaria, 134
Bureau of Apprenticeship & Training; *see* Labor Department
Bureau of National Affairs (BNA), 22-23, 399, 470, 477
Business games, 309-10

C

Canada, 5, 130, 134, 163
Canadian National Railways, 250
Candidate Identification System (CIS), 260
Career
  development workshops, 324
  education, 277
  guidance, 324
  management, 324
  weekend, 183
Career planning and development, 323-46
  counseling, 336
  groups needing special attention, 341-44
    managers with special problems, 342-43
    new entrants into management ranks, 341-42
Case analysis; *see* Administrative skills
Change agents, 311
Checklist, 332-34; *see also* Performance appraisal(s)
Checkoff, 504
China, 381-82
Civil rights; *see* Equal employment opportunities
Civil Rights Act of 1964, 57, 68, 70, 73, 140, 185, 501; *see also* Title VII
Civil Rights Division; *see* Justice Department, Civil Rights Division
Civil Service Commission, 73
Classroom instruction; *see* Development, personnel
Clayton Act of 1914, 50, 494
Clean Air Act of 1970, 80
Clinical approach, 223
Closed circuit television, 183
Closed shop, 503
Coaching, 302, 308-9

Coalition of Labor Union Women (CLUW), 501
Code of Federal Regulations (CFR), 71
Collective bargaining; *see also* Compensation *and* Union(s) and employment associations
  agreement reached, 527-28
  current trends in demands, 502-3
  definition of, 502
  impasse in, 525-27
  living with agreement, 528
  negotiating the agreement, 523-28
  procedure, 524-25
College recruiting; *see* Personnel, recruiting
Columbia's Graduate School of Business, 183
Committee on Classification of Personnel, 51
Communications, 305
Compensation, 76; *see also* Fair Labor Standards Act of 1938 *and* Wage and salary administration
  determining overall policies, 380-95
    effects of collective bargaining, 388-89
    effects of comparable wages, 390-91
    effects of governmental factors, 387-88; *see also* Wage and hour laws
    effects of standard and cost of living, 389
  employee benefits; *see* Employee, benefits
  factors affecting, 384-91
    what organization is able to pay, 385-86
    what organization is willing to pay, 384-85
    what organization must pay, 386-91
  functions of, 380-84
    equity, 380-81
    motivational, 381-83
  job rate differentials
    based on race, 403
    based on sex, 402-3
    determining, 404-8
    efforts to reduce, 403
    and job evaluation, 404-8
    steps in procedure, 405-8
  policies, 397-400
    pay for time or performance, 398
    salaries for everyone, 399
    secret or open policies, 399-400
    types of wage rates, 397-400
    using "fixed" or "variable" package, 398
  rates of pay
    converting employee appraisals into pay rates, 409
    determining individual, 408-10
    merit rating, 409-10; *see also* Performance appraisal(s)
  remuneration, managerial, 410-13
  using to provide equity, 396-418
  using to reward performance, 419-43
    bonus plans, 434
    companywide productivity sharing systems, 435-36

Subject Index 637

Compensation, 76—*Cont.*
  using to reward performance—*Cont.*
    incentive wages, 421–29
    merit wages, 433–34
    profit-sharing plans, 429–32
    underlying theory, 420–21
    wage and salary compression, 403–4
Compliance experience; *see* Personnel, recruiting
Compliance reviews, 67
Comprehensive Employment & Training Act of 1973 (CETA), 76, 277–78
Computer, electronic, 54
Concept Mastery Test, 257
Conciliation, 502, 526
Concurrent validity; *see* Validity
Congress of Industrial Organizations (CIO), 50
Consumer Price Index (CPI), 62
Contingency theory of leadership, 7
Contingency theory of management, 7
Contrast effect, 237
Cooperative work programs, 183, 311
COPE, 81
Cornell, 182
Correspondence
  courses; *see* Development, personnel
  schools, 178
Cost-effectiveness approach; *see* Personnel development
Cost of living adjustments (COLA), 503
Counseling, 336, 591
  areas requiring, 552
    absenteeism, 552–53
    discipline, 466–83, 552–54
    performance appraisals, 552–53; *see also* Performance appraisal(s)
    personal problems, 554–58
    retirement, 552, 554
    safety, 552, 554
  benefits of, 551
  problems involved in, 551–52
  role of, 550–52
Craftsmen, foremen, and kindred workers, 126
Credit check; *see* Background information, verifying
Criteria, 198–201, 219–22, 254–56
Critical incidents, 301
Cross-cultural movement, 91
Culture
  American, 62
  Anglo-Saxon, 62
  Hallstatt, 62
Cultural anthropology, 11
Cultural environment, 107
Czechoslovakia, 134

D

Davis-Bacon Act; *see* Public Construction Act of 1931
Death benefits, 456

Denmark, 134
Depth interview, 235
Detroit Edison case, 185
Development
  objectives of, 281
  organizational (OD); *see* Training
  programs
    designing; *see* Personnel development
    predictors of success in, 305
    special groups needing, 302–4
    strategies used in selecting participants for, 304–5
  systems approach to, 283
Development, executive; *see* Executive development
Development, personnel (employee)
  off-the-job techniques, 286–88
    classroom instruction, 287
    correspondence courses, 288
    educational television, 288
    extension courses, 288
    programmed instruction, 287–88
    teaching machines, 287–88
    vestibule training, 287
  on-the-job techniques, 285–86
    apprenticeship training, 286
    internship training, 286
    on-the-job training, 286
Diagnostic Interviewer's Guide (DIG), 235
Dictionary of Occupational Titles, 96, 160
Disabled workers, 186
Discipline, 466–83
  authority for administering, 475–77
  concepts of, 468–70
  definition of, 469–70
  examples of rules and penalties, 473–75, 478–80
  how achieved, 470–75
  in nonbusiness organizations, 477
  supervisors and, 475–76
  unions and, 476–77
Discrimination
  in compensation, 76, 402–3
  in employment, 73–76, 159–60, 184–86
Drugs; *see* Employee, personal problems
Duke Power; *see* Griggs v. *Duke Power Company*

E

East Germany, 134
Economic Council of Canada, 163
Economics, 3
  goods-producing, 116
  service-type, 116
Education; *see also* Personnel and human resources
  career, 277
  changing pattern, 132
  definition, 275
  and earnings, 109–10

638 Subject Index

Educational television, 295, *see also* Development, personnel
EEO-1, 71
Efficiency rating, 325; *see also* Performance appraisal(s)
Electronic assistance, 180
Empathy, 305–6
Employee
  alienation, 93–94
  appraisals; *see* Compensation *and* Performance appraisal(s)
  associations; *see* Union(s) and employee associations
  behavior
    contributions of behavioral scientists, 11
    early contributors to knowledge of, 7–10
    Hawthorne experiments, 10, 336
    increasing knowledge of, 7–11
    toward a more rational approach to, 9–10
  economic independence of, 58–60
  initial contact with, 203
  learning curves, 279–80
  personal problems, 554–58
    alcoholism, 555–57
    chemical dependency, 555–58
    drugs, 557–58
    physical illness, 554
    mental and emotional illnesses, 554–55
  potential, maximizing, 271–368
  public; *see* Union(s) and employee associations
  qualities sought in, 200
  rating, 325–26; *see also* Performance appraisal(s)
  referral programs, 178–79
  turnover, 93
Employee benefits, 444–65
  classification of, 449–50
  cost of, 450
  definition of, 448–49
  extent of, 450
  health protection, 456–57
  legally required, 450–53
    Social Security, 450–52
    unemployment insurance, 450, 452
    worker's compensation, 450, 452–53
  supplemental pay, 453–56
  union demands for, 503
  voluntary programs, 453–60
Employee Retirement Income Security Act of 1974, 77
Employee Stock Option Plans (ESOP), 432
Employment Act of 1946, 55, 118
Employment agencies
  private, 177
  public, 177
  specialized, 178
Employment Standards Division; *see* Labor Department
Endicott Report, 182

England, 14, 134, 381–82
Environment, 274; *see also* Future, coping with
Equal employment opportunities, 56–57, 68
Equal Employment Opportunities Act of 1972, 70, 73; *see also* Civil Rights Act of 1964 *and* Title VII
Equal Employment Opportunities Commission (EEOC), 62, 66, 70, 73, 83, 167, 176, 185, 204, 206, 221, 238
Equal Pay Act of 1963, 76, 403
Equity, 105
Escalator clauses, 390
Europe, 134
Examination, medical, 210
Executive development, 296–321; *see also* Managers, education of
  appraising and evaluating, 315–16
    evaluating, difficulty of, 315
    methodology, 315–16
    relating evaluations to objectives, 316–17
  content of activities, 306
  determining needs, 301–7
    who needs it, criteria for determining, 302–4
    who should be developed, criteria for determining, 305–7
  establishing parameters to, 299–301
    role of executives in, 299–301
    role of self-development in, 300–301
  groups needing special attention, 317–18
  methods used in developing, 307–15
    administrative skills, 309–11
    attitudes, 311–14
    general knowledge, 314–15
    philosophies, 311–14
    policy decisions, 307–8
    technological knowledge and skills, 308–9
  model for, 298
  objectives of, 298–99
    individual growth, 299
    organizational goals, 298
  university programs, 314
Executive orders, 70–71
  8802, 84
  10925, 57, 84
  10988, 71, 498
  11246, 70, 74, 403
  11375, 70, 74, 403
  11616, 498
Executives; *see also* Managerial, personnel
  plateaued, 343–44
  supermobile, 343
Exempt personnel, 387
Expectancy models, 105
Expectations, 352
Experiential learning, 310, 312
Extension courses; *see* Development, personnel
Exxon, 149, 319

F

Face validity; *see* Validity
Factor-of-production approach, 350
Fair Credit Reporting Act, 209
Fair Labor Standards Act of 1938, 53, 76, 589
Farm workers, 126
Faulty predictors, 258
Federal Coal Mine Health and Safety Act, 77
Federal Communications Commission (FCC), 185
Federal Mediation and Conciliation Service (FMCS), 526–27
Federal Register, 71
Feedback, 316
Females; *see* Minorities *and* Women
Ferris State College, 503
Financial rewards as motivators, 381–83, 419–43
Finland, 134
First-line supervisors, 29–30
Florida State University, 183
Forced choice rating scale, 331–32; *see also* Performance appraisal(s)
Forced distribution, 330; *see also* Performance appraisal(s)
Ford Motor Company, 352, 382, 455, 464, 515
Fortune, 246
Fortune 500, 341
France, 130, 134, 163
Free-enterprise system, 48
Fringe benefits, 54; *see also* Compensation, employee benefits
Functional authority, 31–33
Functional job analysis (FJA), 160–63
and EEOC and OFCCP guidelines, 162–63
what it does, 162
Future, coping with, 582–99
expected changes in personnel function, 587–91
expected modifications of environment, 583–87
organizational environment, 585–87
work environment, 584–85
new status for personnel administration, 587
personnel executive, quo vadis? 597
qualifications needed in future personnel executives, 591–93
successful performance of personnel function, what is needed, 593–97

G

Gallup polls, 113
General Electric Company, 149, 248, 409
General Motors, 17, 74, 84, 113, 133, 389–90
Germany, 130
Goal theory, 105
Goods-producing economies, 116

Governmental involvement; *see* Personnel and human resource administration, institutional context of
Graphic rating scale, 330–31; *see also* Performance appraisal(s)
Great Britain, 128, 130, 134
Grievance procedure; *see* Industrial relations *and* Union(s) and employee associations
Grievances, handling, 528–30; *see also* Collective bargaining *and* Union(s) and employee associations
Griggs v. *Duke Power Company*, 71, 206, 208, 221
Guaranteed employment, 455
Guaranteed income, 455–56
Guidance; *see* Counseling
Guild system, 47

H

Halo effect, 237, 328
Harvard Business School, 366
"Hawthorne experiments," 350, 423
50th Anniversary Symposium, 96
Health and safety, 76; *see also* Occupational health and safety
Health Maintenance Organization Act of 1973 (HMO), 567
Heredity, 274
Historical perspective, 45–64
Holidays, 76
Horn effect, 237, 328
Hours of work, 76
Human relations
approach, 350–51
movement, 52
Human resources
approach, 351
definition of, 4
importance of, 4–7, 586
in direct production of goods, 6
need for creative environment, 6
need for flexibility and creativity, 6–7
need for interaction of resources, 6
limitations to development of, 7
problems involved in utilization, 4–5
role in economic and organizational development, 5–7
in economic development, 5
in organizational development, 5–6
Hungary, 134

I

IBM, 149, 227, 276, 319
Illinois Institute of Technology, 275
Illness; *see* Employee, personal problems
In-basket technique, 309–10
Incentive wages; *see also* Compensation
advantages of, 422
definition of, 421
disadvantages of, 422

640 Subject Index

Incentive wages—*Cont.*
  effects of using, 423–26
    upon employee earnings, 426
    upon productivity, 425–26
    other, 426
  evaluating motivational effect of, 428–29
  objectives of plans, 421–22
  prevalence of, 422–23
  requirements
    for installing system, 427
    for successful use of, 427–28
  and unions, 426–27
  what plan to use, 428
Incidents, critical, 301
In-depth interview, 208
Indians, 276
Individual retirement account (IRA), 460
Individual, role of, 278–79
Industrial psychology, 11; *see also* Employee, behavior
Industrial relations; *see also* Union(s) and employee associations
  conflict in, 515–17
    conflict-cooperation continuum, 516–17
    cooperation factors affecting degree of, 517
  improving in individual organization, 514–39
  laws providing framework, 495–97
  more complicated, 590
  unions and employee associations, 497–505
Industrial Relations Association of Chicago, 98
Industrial Revolution, 8, 47–48, 95, 101
Information, gathering and evaluating; *see* Selection
Injury repeaters, 571
Insurance, 456
Intelligence, 305
  of managers; *see* Managers
  tests; *see* Test(s) and testing
Interests; *see* Test(s) and testing
International Telephone & Telegraph Corporation, 248
Internship training; *see* Development, personnel
Interpersonal skills, 305
Interstate commerce, 53, 69
Interviews; *see also* Selection
  perceptual constraints, 236–37
    bias, 237
    contrast effect, 237
    halo effect, 237
    horn effect, 237
  procedural constraints, 235–36
    reliability problems, 235–36
    validity problems, 236
  types of
    in-depth, 208
    preliminary, 203

Interviews—*Cont.*
  types of—*Cont.*
    stress, 235
    structured, 233–36
    unstructured, 233, 236
  using, 238–39
Inventory
  biographical, 205–6; *see also* Selection
  of existing personnel, 153
  of skills, 302
Ireland, 134
Isolation pay, 503
Italy, 130, 134

J

Japan, 130, 134, 386
Job(s), 102–3
  bank, 276
  brief and qualifications, 152, 168
  definition of, 99
  design, 151
  dissatisfaction, 103–6
    education and, 104
    efforts to overcome, 104–6
    extent of, 104
    race and, 104
    sex and, 104
  enlargement and enrichment programs, 104, 590
  grading, 405–6
  managerial, 250–53
    changed content of, 248–49
  pricing, 407
  redesign, 104
  requirements, 151–53
    qualitative aspects, 151–52
    quantitative requirements, 152–53
  rotation, 310–11
  systems, 104
  satisfaction, 107
  and safety, 570–71
  specification, 151–52, 405
  success
    criteria of, 254–56
    valid predictors of, 256–58
  what workers want from, 102–3
    blue-collar workers, 103
    college students, 102
    supervisors, 103
Job analysis, 151, 301, 405
Job description, 151–52, 405
Job enrichment, 104, 590
Job evaluation; *see* Compensation
Job Opportunities in the Business Sector (JOBS), 76, 557
Job specifications, 151–52, 405
Jones & Laughlin Steel Company, 427
Justice Department, Civil Rights Division, 73

Subject Index   641

K

Kaiser Steel Long-Range Sharing Plan, 435–36
Keogh Plan, 460
Knight case, 79
Knights of Labor, 50
Knowledge
  acquiring general, 314–15
  effects on performance, 92
  technical, 305
Kuder Preference Record, 229

L

Labor Department, 66, 77–78, 185
  Bureau of Apprenticeship & Training, 75
  Employment Standards Division, 73, 75
  Office of Federal Contract Compliance Programs (OFCCP), 73–74
Labor force; *see also* Employees *and* Work force
  changes in, 587–88
  classification of
    blue-collar, 115, 125–26
    disabled, 186
    minorities, 134–37, 185
      blacks, 134–36
      Spanish-speaking, 135
    nonwhite, 115, 131–34
    older workers, 136–37, 185–86
    primary, 118
    secondary, 118
    Vietnam era veterans, 136
    white-collar, 115, 124–25
    women, 115, 185
    young people, 130–31
  demand for, 119–28
    by industries, 119–23
    by occupations, 124, 127
    trends in other countries, 128
  factors affecting changes in, 115–19
    in economic environment, 116–19
    in general environment, 116
  supply of, 128–30
    in other countries, 130
    in United States, 128–30
  trends in, 115–39
    other countries, 134
Labor-Management Relations Act of 1947 (LMRA), 63, 71, 78–79; *see also* Taft-Hartley Act
Labor-Management Reporting and Disclosure Act of 1959, 78, 496–97
Labor organizations; *see* Industrial relations *and* Union(s) and employee associations
Labor turnover
  layoff rate, 59
  quit rate, 59
Laboratory training; *see* Training
Landrum-Griffin Act; *see* Labor-Management Reporting and Disclosure Act of 1959
Law of effect, 282–83

Law of supply and demand, 391
Law of wage share, 385–86
Leadership style; *see also* Personnel, maximizing growth
  causes of effective, 353
  determining style to use, 356–57
  effects on employee growth, 353–57
  factors affecting, 353
  types of, 354–57
    authoritarian approach, 354–56
    free-rein approach, 356
    participative approach, 356
Learning
  curves, employee, 279–80
  experiential, 310
Leased manpower; *see* Temporary help
Lifetime employment, 503
Line authority, 31
Line management; *see* Personnel function
Lockout(s), 502, 527
Lordstown strike, 104
Luxembourg, 134

M

McGill University, 237
McMurray Patterned Interview Form, 233–34
Magna Carta, 494
Management
  development; *see* Executive development
  job
    changed content of, 248–49
    different levels of, 250–52
    requirements of, 252–53
  multiple, 309
  personnel, 246–64; *see also* Managerial, personnel
Management by objectives (MBO), 363, 590
  in career development, 338–41
  evaluating effectiveness of, 340–41
  requirements for successful use, 339–40
    advantages, 340
    disadvantages, 340
    elements of, 339–40
  underlying concepts, 338–39
Managerial
  elite, 90
  grid, 314
  personnel, 246–64
    determining need for, 249
    determining supply of, 249–50
    distinction between supervisory and executive, 251
    selecting, 245–64
    shortage of, 247–49
  philosophy, 596–97
  planning, 249–53
  talent
    criteria of job success, 254–56
    how to identify, 253–58
    valid predictors of, 256–58

Managers
education of, 257
intelligence of, 256–57
interests of, 257
personality of, 257–58
of small businesses, 317
Manpower, 149
development; see Executive development and Personnel and human resources development
planning, 149
Manpower Development & Training Act of 1962, 76, 277; see also Comprehensive Employment and Training Act of 1973
Manufacturer's training schools, 178
Marginal productivity theory, 386
Marshall Plan, 55
Mathematical abilities, 305
Maturity, 305
MBAs, Cornell, 182–83
Mediation, 502, 506; see also Federal Mediation and Conciliation Service
Medical examinations, 210–11
Medicare, 451–52
Merit rating, 325; see also Performance appraisal(s)
Merit wages; see also Compensation
evaluating motivational effect of increases, 433–34
logic of increases, 433
using as stimulants to productivity, 433–34
Methods-time-measurement (MTM), 169
Minimum wages; 76, 387–88
Minnesota Clerical Tests, 229
Minorities, 73–76, 134–36, 185, 317, 342; see also Blacks; Indians; and Women
Money as a motivator, 399
Moody v. Albermarle Paper Company, 221
Motion studies, 151
Motivation, 326, 357–64, 590
effects on employee growth, 357–64
to learn, 305
multidimensional, 359
need for positive, 282–83
role of, 358–59
theories of, 359–64
content models, 360–61
prescriptive models, 359–60
process models, 360, 361–64
theory of wages, 381–84, 419–43
Multiple appraisals, 334–35; see also Performance appraisal(s)
Multiple management, 309
Multiple predictors, 258
Murray Thematic Appercetion Test (TAT), 230
Myart v. Motorola, 221

N
National Apprenticeship Act of 1937, 76, 277
National Center for Productivity and Quality of Working Life, 13
National Commission on Productivity, 117
National Council on Alcoholism, 555
National Education Association (NEA), 498, 500, 503
National Fire Protection Association, 565
National Home Study Council, 288
National Industrial Conference Board (NICB), 22–23, 177, 197, 206, 209, 211, 213, 284, 293, 431, 458
National Institute on Alcohol Abuse, 556
National Labor Relations Act of 1935 (NLRA), 53, 70, 78–79, 81, 495–96; see also Industrial relations and Wagner Act
administration of, 495–96
rights of employees, 495
Section 7, 495
National Labor Relations Board (NLRB), 79, 495–96, 499–500, 502, 506, 522–23
NLRB v. Jones and Laughlin Steel Corporation, 53, 69, 80
National Safety Council, 565, 567, 573
Need for achievement (Nach), 339, 360–61
Needs hierarchy, 360
Netherlands, 134, 163
Newman v. Delta Air Lines, 457
Nonfarm laborers, 126
Nonwhite employees, 115; see also Blacks and Minorities
Norris-La Guardia (Anti-Injunction) Act, 495
Norway, 134
Nunn-Bush Shoe Company Plan, 435–36

O
Occupation, definition of, 99
Occupational health and safety, 562–81
health hazards, 564
importance of, 563–67
maintaining health, 567
maintaining safety, 567–72
factors affecting, 568–71
improvement of, 572–74
need for programs, 564–66
requirements of programs, 566–67
preventive medicine, 566
safety hazards, 564
specific areas of need, 565–66
cancer, 566
heart disease, 565–66
noise, 565
respiratory diseases, 566
stress, 566
Occupational patterns, changing, 132–33
Occupational Safety & Health Act (OSHA), 70, 77, 547, 563, 573–78
coverage, 575
enforcement of, 576

Occupational Safety & Health Act—*Cont.*
  evaluating effectiveness of, 576–78
    achievements, 578
    criticisms of, 577
  purpose of, 574–75
  rights and responsibilities, 575
    employees, 575–76
    employers, 575
Occupational Safety & Health Review Commission, 77, 576–77
Office of Federal Contract Compliance Programs (OFCCP), 162, 167, 176, 204, 206, 238
Ohio State University, 285
Old-age pensions, 53
Old-age, Survivors, and Disability Insurance (OASDI), 451
Older workers, 136–37, 185–86
On-the-job training, 285–86, 308
Operant-reinforcement analysis, 105
Operators and skilled workers, 125–26
Organization for Economic Cooperation and Development (OECD), 118
Organizational behavior, 310
Organizational behavior modification (OBM), 105
Organizational development (OD); *see* Training
Orientation, 285
Otis Quick-Scoring Mental Ability Tests, 229
Overtime, 454
Owens-Corning Fiberglass, 166

P

Paired comparison ratings, 330
Peer ratings, 329–30
Penalty system; *see* Discipline
Pension Reform Act, 460; *see also* Employee Retirement Income Security Act of 1974
People problems, handling, 549–61
Perception
  managerial, 352
  role of, 300–301
Performance
  criteria for successful, 192
  identifying criteria of successful, 198–99
  predictors of successful, 192
Performance appraisal(s); *see also* Compensation *and* Counseling
  making more effective, 334–35
  methods of, 329–34
    checklist, 329, 331–34
    essay, 329, 331
    ranking, 329–30
    rating, 329–31
  multiple appraisals, 334–35
  performance review, 334
    problems of validity and reliability, 328–29

Performance appraisal(s)—*Cont.*
  performance review—*Cont.*
    purposes of, 326–27
    theory underlying, 327–28
Performance rating, 326; *see also* Performance appraisal
Personal data sheet; *see* Application blank
Personality; *see* Managers *and* Test(s) and testing
Personnel; *see* Personnel and human resources
Personnel administration; *see* Personnel and human resources administration
Personnel administrator; *see* Personnel and human resources administrator
Personnel department, 212
Personnel development; *see* Personnel and human resources development
Personnel executive(s); *see* Personnel and human resources administrator(s)
Personnel function; *see* Personnel and human resources administration
Personnel and human resources; *see also* Employee; Labor force; *and* Workers
  importance of, 4–7
  managerial, 246–64
  maximizing potential of, 271–368
    role of individual's self-perception, 348–53
    role of motivation, 357–64
    role of superior's leadership, 349–57
  problems involved in using, 4–5
  role in organizations, 2–15
  sources of, 173–79
    external, 176–79
    internal, 175–76
    theoretical, 173–75
Personnel and human resources administration
  changes in, 587–91
  context of, 43–44
  definition of, 18
  effects of industrial relations on, 491–534
  environment in which occurs, 86–113
    educational, 92–95
    sociocultural, 88–92
    technological, 95–98
    work, 98–106
  governmental involvement in, 66–85
    areas of involvement, 69–71
    functions involved in, 71
    how to cope with, 80–81
  historical context of, 45–64
  importance of, 17–38
  improving role of, 18–23
    high status, 20–23
    low status, 18–20
  need for successful, 593–95
  responsibility for performing, 28–30
    first-line supervision, 29–30
    middle management, 29
    personnel specialists, 30
    top management, 29

Subject Index

Personnel and human resources administrator(s), 317
  authority of, 586–87
  functions performed by, 23–28
  improving status of, 18–23
  qualities needed of, 591–93
  responsibility of, 30
Personnel and human resources development, 271–368; *see also* Executive development
  definition of, 275
  evaluating effectiveness of, 288–91
    methods used in determining, 279–80
  methods of, 285–88
    off-the-job techniques, 286–88
    on-the-job techniques, 285–86
  needs, 279–81
  objectives, 275–76
  principles of learning, 282–83
  programs, 281–88
    how conducted, 285–88
    what taught, 284
    who conducts them, 284
  responsibility for, 277–79
    individual's, 278–79
    organization's, 278
    society's, 277–78
    union's, 278
  strategies, 273–95
Personnel and human resources planning, 147–71, 192
  definition of, 148
  evaluating effectiveness of, 163–64
    cost effectiveness approach, 164
  functions involved in, 150–53
    designing and redesigning jobs, 151
    determining job requirements, 151–53
  importance of, 149–50
  new approach to, 160–63
  objectives of, 150
  in other economies, 163
  place in selection system, 149
  stages of, 153–54
  steps in, 154–60
Personnel and human resources recruiting, 145–46, 173–90, 192, 587–88
  college recruiting, 181–84
    evaluating effectiveness of, 184
  definition of, 145–46, 173
  effects of public policy on, 184–86
  evaluating effectiveness of, 186
  methods used in, 179–84
    advertising, 179
    consultants, 180
    electronic assistance, 180–81
    employee referrals, 179
    scouting, 180
Personnel and human resources selection, 146, 191–264
  criteria, 198–201
    identifying, 198–99
    predictors of success, 198–201
  policies, 193–98
    fitting people to jobs or fitting jobs to people, 196–97
    screening out or screening in, 194–96
    using same or differentiated procedure, 197–98
  procedure, 191–217
    authorization to hire, 203
    communicating decision
    evaluating information about applicants, 146, 211, 219–44
    gathering information about applicants, 202–11, 222
    making decision to accept or reject, 212–13
    stages in, 193–244
  purposes of, 194
  stages in; *see* Procedures, model
  of supervisory and executive talent, 246–64
    criteria, 254–56
    determining requirements, 252–53
    predictors of success, 256–58
    techniques of, 258–61
  techniques, or selection instruments, 219–22
    accuracy of, 222
    validity of, 219–22
Personnel planning replacement chart, 157–58
Personnel progress report, 279
Personnel research
  areas of, 595–96
  characteristics of, 594–95
  evaluating, 596
  extent of, 595
  methods used, 596
  need for, 593–96
  who does, 595
Personnel system, 30
Philosophies, modifying, 306–7, 311–14
Physiological motives, 102
Planned progression; *see* Administrative skills
Planning; *see also* Career planning and development
  managerial, 249–53
  organizational, 249–50
  personnel; *see* Personnel and human resources planning
Poland, 134
Polygraph, 208
Porter-Lawler model, 363–64
Portugal, 134
Predictive validity; *see* Validity
Predictors, 192–93, 198–201, 225–26
  faulty, 258
  multiple, 258
Pregnancy benefits, 457

Subject Index

Preliminary interview, 203
Primary workers, 118
Principles of learning, 282
Privacy, invasion of, 227
Problem analysis, 279
Procedures, model, 193
Procter and Gamble Plan, 455
Productivity, changes in, 116–18
Productivity sharing systems, companywide
    Kaiser Steel Long-Range Sharing Plan, 435–36
    Lincoln Incentive Compensation Plan, 435
    Nunn-Bush Shoe Company Plan, 435–36
    Rucker Share-of-Production Plan, 435–36
    Scanlon Plan, 435
Proficiency; *see* Tests
Profit sharing, 429–32; *see also* Compensation
    definition of, 430
    effects of using, 431–32
    evaluating effect of, 432
    extent of usage, 430–31
    objectives of, 429–30
    types of, 430
Profit-Sharing Research Foundation (PSRF), 431
Programmed instruction, 287–88
Progress report, personnel, 279
Progression within organization, 336–38
Promotions, 153, 175, 337
    merit, 337
    seniority, 337
Psychological testing; *see* Test(s) and testing
Public Construction Act of 1931, 76
Public Contracts Act of 1936, 76
Punishment, 363
Puritanic theory of work, 101

R

Rates of pay; *see* Compensation
Rating, peer or buddy, 329–30; *see also* Performance appraisal(s)
Ratio, selection, 199
Recruiting and selecting personnel, 145–264, 587–88
Recruitment; *see* Personnel and human resources recruiting
Reference checks, validity of, 210
References, 209
Referrals, employee, 178–79
Rehabilitation Act of 1973, 75
Reinforcement, 284, 363
Reliability, 198, 221, 222; *see also* Performance appraisal(s)
    problems in interviewing, 235–36
        interrater, 236
        intrarater, 235–36
        validity, 236
    problems in performance appraisals, 328
Remuneration; *see* Compensation
Research; *see* Personnel research

Research Institute of America, 557
Résumé, 205
    validity as predictor, 226
Retirement, 457–60; *see also* Counseling
    benefits, 503
    early, 457–58
    helping employees prepare for, 458
    managerial approaches to, 458
    rationale for, 457–58
Retraining, 281
Reward and penalty systems, 375–78
    effects on personnel effectiveness, 375–483
Right-to-work laws, 81, 503
Risks, willingness to take, 305
Role perception, 300–301
Role playing, 309–10, 312
Romania, 134
Rorschach Test, 230
Rotation, job, 310–11
Rucker Share-of-Production Plan, 435–36
Rules of conduct; *see* Discipline
Russia, 134

S

Sabbaticals, 314–15
Safety; *see* Counseling; Discipline; *and* Health and safety
Salaries; *see* Compensation *and* Wage and salary administration
Scanlon Plan, 435
Scientific management, 5–6, 9–10, 50, 115, 350, 360, 593–94
Scientists, sources of, 178–79
Scouting, 180
Screening in, 194
Screening out, 194
Secondary workers, 118
Secret ballot elections, 501
Secretary of Labor, 85
Section 14(b), 78, 496, 503
Section 7, 78
Selection; *see also* Personnel and human resources selection
    appraisal, 326
    criteria, 198–201
    ratio, 199
Self-appraisal, 334; *see also* Performance appraisal(s)
Self-control; *see* Discipline
Self-development; *see* Executive development
Self-perception
    enhancing individual's, 348–53
    importance of, 307
Senate Select Committee on Improper Activities, 521
Seniority, 337
Sensitivity training; *see* Training
Serfdom, 47

646   Subject Index

Service
  economy, 116
  industries, 120
  rating, 325
  workers, 126
Service Contract Act of 1965, 76
Servicemen's Readjustment Act of 1944, 55, 277
Sex differentials, 402–3
Sex stereotyping, 188; *see also* Women
Sherman Antitrust Act of 1890, 50, 494, 510
Ship Destination Test, 257
Short Employment Tests (SET), 229
Sick leave, 456–57
Simon-Benet tests of mental abilities, 10
Simulation, 309–10
Skills
  administrative, 305–6
  interpersonal, 305
  inventory, 302
  technical, 305
Slavery, 47
Small business managers, 317
Social responsibility, 57
Social security; *see* Employee, benefits
Social Security Act, 53, 77
Sociology, 11
Spanish-surnamed people, 135–36, 185; *see also* Minorities
Sputnik I, 55, 56
Staffing; *see* Recruiting and selecting personnel *and* Selection
Standard Oil of California case, 185–86
Standard Oil of New Jersey, 256, 258
Stanford Research Institute, 96
Stanford University, 500
Statistical analysis, 223
Stereotyping, sex, 188
Stress interviews, 235
Strike, 504–5, 527; *see also* Union(s) and employee associations
Structured interview, 233
Success, predictors of, 192, 198–201, 305
Succession, providing management, 588–89
Summer internships, 183
Supervisory and executive talent; *see* Personnel and human resources selection
Supplemental unemployment benefit (SUB), 455–56
Sweden, 130, 134
Synthetic validity; *see* Validity

T

Taft-Hartley Act, 498, 502, 503, 506, 507, 526; *see also* Labor-Management Relations Act of 1947
Teaching machines, 287–88
Team
  building, 310
  concept, developing, 307

Technical knowledge and skills, improving, 308–9
Technological development, 107
Technological environment; *see* Personnel and human resources administration
Temporary assignments, 311
Temporary help, 177–78
Test(s) and testing, 195, 201–2, 206–8, 226–31
  achievement or proficiency, 230
  aptitudes, 229
  arguments in favor of, 227–28
  battery of, 231, 258
  criticisms of, 226–27
  intelligence, 228–29
  interests, 229
  personality, 229–30
  types of
    by characteristics measured, 228–30
    by format, 228
  using, 238
  validation of, 231
T-group training; *see* Training
Thematic Evaluation of Managerial Potential (TEMP), 230
Theory X, 350–51
Theory Y, 313, 338, 350–51, 360
Thurstone Primary Mental Ability Test, 257
Thurstone Test of Mental Alertness, 229, 257
Title VII, 70–71, 74, 76, 82–83, 221, 403; *see also* Civil Rights Act of 1964
Top management; *see* Personnel function
Training; *see also* Executive development *and* Personnel and human resources development
  definition of, 274–75
  evaluating research findings, 312
  laboratory, 311–13
    goals of, 311
    methodology, 312
    sensitivity, 311
    T-group, 311
  needs survey, 279
Transcripts, 209
Transfers, 153, 338
Turnover, employee, 93, 153

U

Underemployed, 277
Unemployment insurance; *see* Employee, benefits
Unemployment rate, changes in, 118–19
Union(s) and employee associations, 499–500; *see also* Industrial relations
  arbitration, 504, 527
    bargaining agent, 501, 521–23
  blacks and, 501
  collective bargaining, 501–3
  corruption in, 521
  grievance procedure, 504
  lack of participation by members, 521

Union(s) and employee associations—*Cont.*
  management's right to manage and supervisor's right to supervise, 532-33
  membership, 507-9
    new type, 500-501
  objectives, 497
    how objectives are achieved, 497-505
  organizing, 498-501
    new efforts, 498-500
  professionals, 499-500
  public employees, 498-99
  quasi-political nature of, 517
  reasons for joining, 519-20
  reasons for not joining, 520-21
  recognizing, 518-23
  service industry employees, 500
  security, 503-4
  strike, 504-5, 527
    tactics, 505-7
  types of, 498
    craft, 498
    general, 498
    independent, 498
    industrial, 498
    labor, 498
    professional employee associations, 498
  white-collar and, 500
  women and, 500-501
  young workers and, 501
Union shop, 63, 78, 503
United Auto Workers (UAW), 389-90, 464
United Kingdom, 163
United Mine Workers of America, 498
United States, 5
United States Employment Service (USES), 75, 276, 293, 506; *see also* Job(s) bank
United States Supreme Court, 46, 53, 71, 79, 206, 221, 531
United Steel Workers Union, 427
Universality of management, 91
University executive development programs, 314
University of Massachusetts, 452
University of Minnesota, 317
University of Texas, 89
Unknown factors, importance of, 301
Unstructured interview; *see* Interview
Unwarranted expectations; *see* Work
Upgrading, 175, 336-37
U.S.S.R., 382

V

Vacations, paid, 454
Validity, 198, 220-21, 236, 328-29; *see also* Performance appraisal *and* Selection
  effects of public policy on, 221
  in interviewing, 236
  types of, 220-21
    concurrent, 220
    face, 220

Validity—*Cont.*
  types of—*Cont.*
    predictive, 220
    synthetic, 220-21
  what is, 220
Values, 306-7
Vestibule training, 287
Vietnam era veterans, 136; *see also* Minorities
Vietnam Era Veterans' Readjustment Assistance Act of 1972, 75
Vocational interest blank, 229
Vocational-technical schools, 178

W

Wage(s), 375; *see also* Compensation
  bargaining theory of, 526-27
  comparable, 390-91
    area rates, 391
    industry rates, 390-91
  differentials, 401-3
    job, 401
    occupational, 401
    race, 403
    sex, 402-3
    skill, 401
  going, 307
  minimum, 76, 387-88
  motivational theory of, 436-37
  prevailing, 387
  rates; *see* Compensation
Wage and hour laws, 387-88; *see also* Equal Pay Act of 1963; Davis-Bacon Act; Fair Labor Standards Act of 1938; *and* Public Contracts Act of 1936
Wage and salary administration, 375-465; *see also* Compensation
Wage and salary compression, 403-4
Wagner Act, 54, 495, 496, 498, 501; *see also* National Labor Relations Act of 1935
Walsh-Healey Act; *see* Public Cont Act of 1936
Wayne State University, 66
Weighted application blank (WAB), 205
  validity as predictor, 223-25
West Germany, 134
Western Electric Hawthorne plant, 10
Wharton School, 183
Wheaton Glass Company, 403
White-collar workers, 115, 124-25; *see also* Personnel and human resources
  sources of, 178-79
Whole person concept, 197
Women, 115, 131-34, 317, 342; *see also* Minorities
Women's liberation movement, 57
Wonderlic Personnel Test, 229
Work
  balancing work and leisure, 101-2
  changing perceptions of, 101-2
  changing nature of, 98-106, 584-85
  definition of, 99

Work—*Cont.*
  intrinsic value of, 101, 107
  moral value of, 101
  necessary to satisfy human needs, 102
  Puritanic theory of, 101
  roles played by, 99–101
  unwarranted expectations of 106
Work in America, 98
Work data analysis, 279
Work ethic, 101
Work force, maintaining, 547–48; *see also* Labor force; Personnel and human resources; *and* Workers
Work improvement suggestion systems, 104
Worker Alienation Research and Technical Assistance Act of 1972, 99
Workers
  demand for, by industries, 119–23
    in goods-producing industries, 121–23
    in service-producing industries, 119–21

Workers—*Cont.*
  demand for, by occupation, 124–27
    blue-collar, 125–26
    farm workers, 126
    service workers, 126
    white-collar, 124–25
  growth needs, 127
  replacement needs, 126–27
Workers' compensation, 77; *see also* Employee benefits
Working hours, flexible, 104
Worklife patterns, changing, 131–32
Workmen's compensation laws, 77
Workweek, shorter, 104

Y

Yellow dog contract, 494–95
Young people, 130–31, 341–42; *see also* Union(s) and employee associations

This book has been set in 10 and 9 point Times Roman, leaded 2 points. Part numbers are 18 point Helvetica and part titles are 18 point Helvetica medium. Chapter numbers are 28 point Helvetica and chapter titles are 18 point Helvetica. The size of the type page is 27 by 46½ picas.